The Relations of Nations

HERE,
there
&
everywhere

Jay Nordlinger

Here, There & Everywhere:

Collected Writings of

Jay Nordlinger

HERE, THERE & EVERYWHERE
Collected Writings of Jay Nordlinger

To obtain more information, or to order bulk copies for educational or business uses, please contact:

National Review Books
215 Lexington Avenue, 11th Floor
New York, NY 10016

www.nationalreview.com

ISBN: 0-9758998-2-1

Jacket Design by Luba Kolomytseva

PRINTED IN THE UNITED STATES OF AMERICA

TO WILLIAM F. BUCKLEY JR.

Table of Contents

Preface xv

SOCIETY

Is There a Dr. in the House?: What's in an honorific 3
A Snowy City: And a flaky mayor 8
'Gutter' Politics: Playing the name game 10
Take Your Boxes and . . . A nation of race rebels? 14
People's Romances: A special Valentine's Day issue says something
    ugly about us 18
Anxiety in Steel Country: A mill town trembles and waits 23
Most Hated U: A visit to Bob Jones 29
'Soli Deo Gloria': Not your average music camp 36
'Bang': Guns, rap, and silence 41
Hand It to Them: Rediscovering American Scripture 46
Bassackwards: Construction Spanish and other signs of the times 51
Little Suppressors: Dealing with the bookstore clerk who hates you 55
Button It: Wearing your political heart on your sleeve—or your lapel,
    wherever 59
December's C-Word: Who would have thought that 'Christmas' would
    become verboten? (Don't answer that) 62

POLITICS

Weathering the Storm: The final days of a Bush campaignsman 69
The Race Ace: Clinton at his most shameful 77
Clinton's Rosenberg Case: Before we 'move on' 81
The GOP's Burden: The color of the convention 86
Going Timeless: Who dares give up the 'newspaper of record'? 90
Dems on the Hot Seat: If only! 94
The Joy of Tokenism: Or if not joy, something 96

PEOPLE

A Voice for Our Time: Those who think that Bush can't talk should think again 103
Conquest's Conquest: A man and his admirers 109
Being Sharansky: On Russia, Israel, 'Reaganite readings' 114
Reagan in Full: An array of pre-presidential writings 120
Our Splendid Cuss: The likable Phil Gramm 126
Arab Scribe: Naguib Mahfouz, a personal appreciation 131
Star-in-Waiting: Meet George W.'s foreign-policy czarina 136
Albright Then, Albright Now: From Democratic campaigns to the Kosovo campaign, a long way 143
Power Dem: The strange rise of a hatemonger 151
The Political Garrison Keillor: Writer, poet-philosopher, hater 160
Shrill Waters: The life and career of 'Big Bad Max' 167
The Attack Man: Bob Shrum and the Democratic style 172
Rosie O'Donnell, Political Activist: A celebrity and her platform 180
Air Rummy: A conversation with the secretary of defense—and the missus 187
Ashcroft with Horns: This is dedicated to the one they hate 193
Cap, a Life: Weinberger's journey from the Golden Gate onward 200
Yes, He Has Lived: The invaluable Richard Pipes 204
Rodney Rules: Dangerfield at 80 208
Brief Encounter: Ring Lardner Jr., at home 211

THE WORLD

Change and Determination: After 9/11, a shaking up 215
European Communities: A report from Greece and Albania 222
A Case of Liberation: Think, for a moment, about Iraq's Marsh Arabs 227
Thanks for the MEMRI (.org): An institute, and its website, bring the Arab world to light 231
Terror on Trial: Thinking about Shining Path, and those like them 237
Doses of Davos: Chronicles from on high 242
Davos-in-the-Desert: Chronicles from the Middle East 266
About Sudan: What has been done? What can be done? 278
Albania Votes: An emerging democracy, emerges 285
Solzhenitsyn at Harvard: His words are 'more relevant than ever' 289

CUBA AND CHINA

Who Cares About Cuba?: Ninety miles away, far from our minds 297
Che Chic: It's *très* disgusting 305

'I Can't Just Do Nothing': A heroine out of Cuba 310
Youth with Unfathomable Courage: An independent news agency in
    Cuba 314
Meet the Diaz-Balarts: A couple of Castro's 'nephews'—in
    Congress 319
In Castro's Corner: A story of red and black 325
An Eye on China: Remarks at an award ceremony 331
Bearing Witness: With Anne Frank and Aleksandr Solzhenitsyn at her
    back, Youqin Wang chronicles the Cultural Revolution 336
Look and See: Confronting the Chinese Gulag 340
Prisoner of the PRC: The experience of a Falun Gong practitioner 343

GOLF
My Country, Ryder Wrong: Patriotism, nationalism, and glory 349
Tiger Time: The wonder of an American hero 351
Hunting Tiger: Everyone wants a piece of him 357
Hootie vs. Hootie: The morality play surrounding Augusta
    National 364
The Immortal Hogan: One man's greatness 368
Dream Beat: Reporting from a PGA Tour tournament 372
Golf at the Movies: Lamenting *Tin Cup*, etc. 374

MUSIC
Farewell, Fat Man: Luciano Pavarotti bows out 381
The Comeback Kid: Leon Fleisher with two hands 384
Jackie, Oh!: A 'pops recital' from Marilyn Horne 387
The Underwear Festival 390
Mozart & Co. 394
Mozart Minus One 397
The Big One 401
Mere Excellence: Farewell to Maestro Kurt Masur 405
Yankee Doodle Discs: Classical music from American pens 409
One Vote for Willson: On the creator of *The Music Man* 414
The Color of Music: Racial politics spreads its poison
    everywhere 418
The *Shine* Man: Critics are wrongly enraged at the David Helfgott
    'circus' 425
Singing His Own Song: The nonconforming, and wonderful,
    Lee Hoiby 429
Wild About Earl: A virtuoso pianist at 90 433
Daughter of the Vikings: Birgit Nilsson, 1918–2000 436

American Sounds: The music of our presidential campaigns 439
Stagedoor Jay: The confessions of a Price-head 443

PERSONAL
Love on the Arno: Studying abroad, becoming an American 449
A Name of My Own: Me and Reagan 452
A Man and His Primer: On (not) learning Greek 455
Brother of the Bride: Weddings, receptions, and glory 457
Miracle of the Mundane: A change of tire, a change of self 459
'Travel Is Broadening': An extraordinary seatmate 461
Showdown on WEIR-AM: Rockin' and rollin' on West Virginia
    radio 463
The Conservative on Campus: Some memories, some points 465
Alexandria the Great: Egypt's 'second,' fabulous city 475

Index   481

Preface

*H*ere, *There & Everywhere* is a grab bag of a book, as its title may suggest. It contains pieces from many locales, and about many subjects. The book is organized into eight chapters, beginning with "Society."

In this chapter, there are pieces on the honorific "Dr.," the pronunciation of place-names, the behavior of bookstore clerks—that sort of thing. The second chapter is "Politics." And the first piece here is on Election Night 2000—a very strange evening (and early morning), as you may recall.

"People" gives you 19 of them—people, that is. Among them are two presidents and two comedians (and, yes, there is a difference). In "The World," I have a speech in Greece, reports from Davos, reports from the Middle East, a speech at Harvard. And then comes a chapter called "Cuba and China."

People sometimes say, "Why do you write so often about human rights in Cuba and China?" And one answer is, "Because so few others do. The fields are rather open." Cubans, in particular, suffer from the neglect of the world press, or, worse, misrepresentation. I've offered a few crumbs; Cubans act as though these were big fat loaves.

Next comes a brief chapter on golf—and then one on music. In this latter chapter, I have no criticism, really, but rather feature pieces: mainly essays on personalities. The book closes with a chapter called "Personal."

Some of the decisions about where to put these pieces were pretty arbitrary—maybe even a little capricious! For example, I have put a piece on the *New York Times* in "Politics." Speaking of the *Times*, what do you do with a piece on their campaign against the Augusta National Golf Club? You could put it in "Society"; I put it in "Golf."

I have written some introductory notes, where I thought them necessary, or helpful. Otherwise, you should be able to jump right in.

And I have resisted the temptation to make myself look better—or smarter or more prescient or less dumb—by after-the-fact editing. I have left the pieces almost exactly as they were originally published. When I re-read them, I winced a few times. But I did no tampering, bowdlerizing, or covering up. I will live with my words.

Besides which, a number of these babies are snapshots in time.

Believe it or not, I had no idea that "Here, There, and Everywhere" was a Beatles song until I'd titled this book. (The Beatles aren't necessarily my bag, although I like "Penny Lane" as much as the next guy—probably more than the next guy.) Hearing the title, a few people have said, "Oh, like the Beatles song?" Er, no—like the English expression. Which is where the Beatles got *their* title, too.

And not three weeks ago I was sitting on a plane, next to someone reading a book on the Fab Four: *Here, There, and Everywhere*. Ah, well.

I owe a lot to *National Review*, my professional home for almost ten years now. Its editor, Rich Lowry, has afforded me a great many opportunities. (And those opportunities are indicated in this book.) Jack Fowler, *NR*'s publisher, is top-of-the-line, as was Ed Capano before him. Jack was the indispensable shepherd of this book.

Chris McEvoy, Luba Kolomytseva, Nathan Goulding, John Virtes, Elena Koly, Amy Tyler, and others made valuable contributions. I am grateful to all my *NR* colleagues. And I'm grateful to Bill Kristol, crack and starry editor of *The Weekly Standard*—a magazine from which many of these pieces are drawn.

Bill Buckley has been the dedicatee of innumerable books, and he is the natural and right dedicatee of this one. I said to him, "As the dedicatee, at least you won't have to write the foreword!" (WFB has probably written more forewords than anyone else in history.) What can I say about him? That he is my favorite writer? That he has had incalculable influences on me? That he is perpetually kind, and interesting, and lovable, and thrilling?

I could say those things, and a million more. But I'll zip it, for now. Bill Buckley is not responsible for the contents of these pages, heaven knows. But I can't imagine doing what I do without him—without his example.

—*JAY NORDLINGER*

SOCIETY

Is There a Dr. in the House?

What's in an honorific

It was amazing, how much interest this topic generated. To be called "Dr." or not to be called "Dr."—that is an extremely serious, extremely touchy question in America, as my mail proved. This fairly whimsical piece provoked as much mail as anything I have ever written. Perhaps you are not surprised (and I'm not either, really).

What's in an honorific? Not Shakespearean, I realize, but it is our topic for today. The question came up—not for the first time—when the *New York Times* ran its several articles on the Cornel West controversy at Harvard. (West, a star professor in the Afro-American Studies department, was tiffing with the university's new president, Lawrence Summers. It seems that Summers wanted West to straighten up his scholarly and professorial act. West, quite naturally, got upset.) Some of us suspicious types noticed that the *Times* referred to West and other Afro-Am profs as "Dr."—"Dr. West," "Dr. Gates," "Dr. Wilson"—while referring to Summers as plain ol' "Mr." (The *Times* did the same with the school's former president, Neil Rudenstine. All these people have Ph.D.'s, of course.) This was passing strange—the kind of thing that "made you go, 'Hmmm,'" in the words of the old rap song.

How's that? First, the *Times* seldom refers to *any* Ph.D. as "Dr." The head of Mt. Sinai Hospital, yes; the Nobel Prize winner in physics, perhaps. But an English prof or a sociologist or a drama teacher or something? Unusual. Second, all of the men referred to as "Dr." were black, while the palefaces were "Mr." Was this an act of racial condescension, the attempt of a great liberal newspaper to puff these aggrieved black academics—whose seriousness and academic legitimacy are repeatedly and rightly questioned—up? It seemed to many of us that this was likely. Issues of this kind were addressed by Roger Kimball in the last *National Review*, in his piece on the West controversy, titled, pointedly enough, "Dr. West and Mr. Summers."

The *Times* weren't the only white liberals in the game. Al Hunt, in his column for the *Wall Street Journal*, referred to West as "Dr.," "Professor," and "Mr.," covering all bases (and that was a lot of titles for a short column); Summers got "Mr." and "President."

These questions may seem trivial—and they *are* trivial, in the context of a war against terrorism and all—but they include in them enduring cultural and national questions. Cornel West and his like (not that there are many of his like, West being a pretty singular character) are very big on pride, self-esteem, and what Aretha Franklin called "R-E-S-P-E-C-T." He's exactly the type to insist on, and elicit, "Dr." (though he's also been known to refer to himself—with great frequency, as a matter of fact—as "Brother West").

It turns out that West did indeed insist on "Dr." It is the policy of the *New York Times* to leave it up to the individual—to the individual Ph.D.-holder, that is—how he is to be referred to in the paper (though "Dr." can't be used for an honorary degree, thank goodness). (Physicians and dentists get "Dr." as a matter of course.) A senior news editor at the *Times* confirmed to me that West has informed the paper that he wants "Dr.," while Summers—the youngest man ever tenured in the Harvard economics department, by the way—wants "Mr." (Arthur Schlesinger Jr.—by the way, again—has fought all his life against being called "Dr." He never earned a Ph.D., having been made a Harvard professor without one. Come to think of it, this may speak well for a Ph.D.)

Another official at the *Times*—in the public-relations department—told me that the paper's reporters make it a habit to ask subjects who hold Ph.D.'s how they'd like to be referred to. This, however, would be news to many people.

I know several people—Ph.D.-holders—who've been quoted regularly in the *Times* for many years who tell me they've never been asked such a question. (They're called "Mr." or "Ms.") These include big-time, true-blue, super-serious academics. When I mentioned this to the senior news editor, he replied that these people need only give the word, and they'll be "Dr." (You know who you are; be it on your conscience.)

In the West controversy, the *Times* wasn't quite consistent. In late December—right off the bat—West was "Dr." But in a January 13 article, he was "Mr." (No word yet on whether he's planning a lawsuit.) (For that matter, "Dr. Gates"—Henry Louis "Skip" Gates Jr.—was merely "Mr.," too.) On December 29, Charles Ogletree—a (black) law professor at Harvard and a key ally of West—was "Mr." Later, on January 4, he was bumped to "Dr." It would appear that he requested "Dr." (although the particular reporter could have bestowed it on her own). It would also appear that Ogletree is the first law prof in history, or at least recent history, to be called "Dr." in the *Times*, or most anywhere else. ("Dr. Bork," anyone?)

As for the *Wall Street Journal*, the stylebook says that a Ph.D. is called "Dr." "if appropriate in context and if the individual desires it." The editorial page, however—always independent and (gloriously) contrarian—won't give you "Dr." unless you wear a white coat and stethoscope. The paper at large also requires that Martin Luther King, though dead, be called "Dr. King," always. And this, the editorial page follows. King is virtually the only non-physician in this society always to be called "Dr." (and virtually the only dead person as well).

In fact, "Dr. King" is one of the great linguistic sacred cows in America. The *Times* does "Dr. King," too, though many great and eminent persons who are dead are referred to in those pages by their last names only (e.g., Einstein). (Odd that Martin Luther King should be more a doctor than Einstein, don't you think?) It was one of Bill Bennett's masterstrokes, while he was secretary of education, to refer to King as "Rev. King." One year, he was the Reagan cabinet member selected to go down to Atlanta to represent the administration on Martin Luther King Day. He made a point of referring to the great man as "Rev. King," which was both startling and soothing to the ear. Bennett was reminding his audience of the religious nature of this figure, at a time when conservatives in general were trying to restore the place of religion in public affairs.

Why, indeed, should King be "Dr."? It is true that ours is a country in which black men, not long ago, were routinely called "boy" (or worse); we are properly conscious of dignity and redress. But what is more significant about MLK? That he repeatedly put his life on the line so that black Americans could, at long last, become fully Americans—eventually losing his life because of it—or that, early in his life, he managed to plagiarize his way to a Ph.D.? Anyone, practically, can get a Ph.D.; very few can be a Martin Luther King Jr.

Back to the *Times* for a moment: It still burns many old-timers that the paper once referred to Fidel Castro as "Dr. Castro." (The dictator took a law degree from the University of Havana.) The queer practice of "Dr. Castro" lives on among certain leftists, and in many British newspapers, not only the *Guardian*, which loves Communist dictators, but the *Daily Telegraph*, which doesn't. Of course, absolute rulers are always lavishing titles on themselves (including "General," although, as many have noted, it's strange that Col. Qaddafi never moved himself up). Elena Ceausescu, the late (and bullet-riddled) First Lady of Romania, gave herself a Ph.D. in chemistry. She also had chemists write books in her name and arranged to have many prizes awarded to her in that discipline.

In 1986, the *Times* achieved something of a stylistic breakthrough, assenting to "Ms." This allowed Gloria Steinem to utter what must be the best line of her career: "Now I don't have to be 'Miss Steinem from *Ms.* magazine.'" Put it in *Bartlett's*, maybe. The *Times* is pro-choice on a woman's honorific, as on abortion: One can select "Miss," "Mrs.," or "Ms." Hillary Clinton must have chosen "Mrs." somewhere along the line. Imagine the thought process—the machinations, the considerations, the strategic ins and outs—that went into her decision!

Besides Martin Luther King, the most famous non-stethoscope-wearing "Dr." in America is Kissinger—though HK long ago asked the *Times* to call him "Mr." (which it does). (I've always thought "Dr. Kissinger" rather natural for the man, given his background in Germany: *Herr Doktor* and all that.) Another former secretary of state, Madeleine Albright, had a curious transformation. At first in the *Times*, she was "Mrs."; then "Ms."; then, finally, she was "Dr."—at her request ("Doctor's Orders," as a title in the *Times* put it!). (Must be the funniest *Times* headline ever, which, admittedly, isn't saying much.) As the paper reported in that story, Albright asked for "Dr." because "I worked hard for it" (meaning, her Ph.D.). The *Times* recorded that "she wondered whether the change might make her appear insecure," but she went ahead and asked for it anyway. Her teacher at Columbia, Zbigniew Brzezinski, national security adviser in the Carter administration, is "Mr." in the *Times*.

Condoleezza Rice, the current national security adviser, is "Ms. Rice"— her choice. Yet White House spokesmen routinely refer to her as "Dr. Rice." This is somewhat strange, because the president's chief economic adviser, Lawrence Lindsey, is very much a "Dr."—Ph.D. in economics from Harvard—but is never, as far as I can tell, called "Dr." He's "Mr." (or just "Larry"). Why should this be? Is this a sneaking bit of racial condescension or puffery? Is it a bit of gender-related condescension or puffery? Is it a harkening back to an earlier national security adviser, Dr. K? Or it is because there are a lot of Texans and southerners around the White House?

There is very much a North/South split in this country about "Dr.," as about so many other things. It is common practice for professors in the

South to be called "Dr." At the universities I attended—northern—you would sooner have struck a professor than called him "Dr." In fact, it was something if the sullen and self-absorbed students grunted their acknowledgement of the prof at all.

Feelings about "Dr." are bound up in that bitch-goddess, Status. (Yes, I know: James said Success. But Status is a sister.) The best line in either Austin Powers movie belongs to Dr. Evil, who, when addressed as "Mr.," says, "I didn't spend six years in evil medical school to be called 'Mr.,' thank you very much!" Our senior editor Jeffrey Hart, professor emeritus of English at Dartmouth, remembers serving as a campaign adviser to Nixon (not that this is necessarily a segue from evil). To Jeff's amusement, Nixon called him "Dr. Hart." This accords with the Nixon we know: class-conscious, status-nervous, chip-on-the-shouldery, the boy from Whittier who received a tuition scholarship to Harvard but couldn't go, because the family didn't have the money to transport him to and from Massachusetts. Nixon, according to Jeff, would also say, "I'm no Ph.D., but . . .," before launching into a disquisition on some arcane topic.

For some, to be called "Dr." is a way of saying, "I am some*body*," in the words of the Rev. Jesse Jackson. (Ah, "the Rev. Mr. Jackson" and "the Rev. Al Sharpton"—that's "a whole 'nother" article, as we say in my family.) Many years ago, another *NR* senior editor, Rick Brookhiser, surveying all the mail sent to Bill Buckley, adjudged that the most interesting letters were those from prison. And the least interesting? The ones from people who signed themselves "Ph.D." I know someone who's a lawyer in West Virginia who has found that the surest way to rattle his opposition's expert Ph.D. witness is to refer to him as "Mr."

But then, I have another acquaintance who earned a Ph.D. in biochem—and he pleads for his "Dr." because, "There aren't many perks in this line of work, and I'd like my little payoff from polite society." Well, at least he's not a drama teacher. The bulk of the Ph.D.'s I know balk at being called anything but "Mr." (or maybe "Professor," in the case of academics), believing that "Dr." has come to mean Marcus Welby, and that's about it. As for those who feel slighted when they are "Dr."-less, all we can say is, "Ph.D., heal thyself."

—January 25, 2002
National Review Online

A Snowy City

And a flaky mayor

A blizzard is a rare thing in Washington, D.C., and when one hits—the city is almost comically unprepared. Especially when it is governed by Marion Barry. Remember him? He was mayor of our nation's capital, four times elected.

The thaw has begun here in Washington, D.C., and it looks like we can resume lollygagging through life. We had another snowstorm a couple of weeks back. Well, not a storm exactly—more like seven inches of pretty, powdery snow, barely enough to keep a third-grader in Duluth from skateboarding to school. But it was a big deal in the nation's capital, leading to semi-paralysis.

It was not as big a deal, however, as the Blizzard of Our Times, which struck in mid-January. This was the genuine article, the most severe snowstorm since 1922, when President Harding was endeavoring to give the nation "not nostrums but normalcy," and a teapot of scandal was brewing. Snow, in any amount, affects the District more harshly than it does other places. Washingtonians are amusingly skittish at the slightest drop of precipitation. And the city government! Joke about it if you like, but you can't really know it until you've lived under it—particularly with two feet of snow on the ground.

At first, it was kind of fun. Everyone likes a break from the routine. And there's something satisfying about a tiny dose of hardship. ("Gee, I'd really like to report to work or visit my aunt in Gaithersburg, but I'm forced to sit in my recliner wrapped in a blanket, watching *Sally Jessy*.") Adventure was in the air. Out for a walk on Day One, I encountered a Grizzly Adams–like man with a television camera and a microphone, freelancing for the local news. "What the heck are you doing out here?" he asked. Being naturally shy, I delivered a five-minute monologue into the camera: "This is nothing compared with my boyhood in Michigan"; "I refuse to permit Nature's furies to confine me to my room"; "Isn't the city tranquil and lovely?"

Neighbor was helping neighbor, and it seemed that civil society was in bloom. I took pleasure in pushing one car after another out of its predicament. Provisions were being purchased for the elderly, and pregnant women were being rushed to hospitals in the Jeeps of strangers. "It brings out the best in us," or so the anchormen told us, repeatedly.

In time, the novelty faded. Patience wore thin and tempers grew short. I began to resent those stuck cars, squealing and smoking. They should never have been taken out in the first place. Their owners were being greedy and selfish, imposing unnecessary burdens on passersby. We are of course happy to help the distressed; but we also expect people not to be so thoughtless and witless as to place themselves in positions demanding the heroism of a weary cavalry.

The fault, truth to tell, lay with the city's government. It was almost malicious in its incompetence. Streets were unplowed, and subway service was drastically curtailed. Unable to drive, people took to the underground—Calcutta-like masses of them—glaring and shoving, snarling and cursing. The social situation was chaotic and tense; for a few days, it seemed on the verge of dangerous.

And Mayor Marion S. Barry: He was on television, speechifying, pacifying, lying. He could boast that, despite everything, the city was still handing out parking tickets left and right. Those who habitually reelect the mayor might have realized that we pay a price for awarding the top job to a convicted cocaine user and self-professed sex addict. Everyone likes a little flair in the mayor's office, sure; but there comes a time when you appreciate a little Robert Taft to go with your Earl Long. (Cracked a colleague of mine, "If anyone should know about 'snow,' it's Marion Barry.") ("Cracked"?)

My street was never plowed. By the city, that is. The exasperated Dutch embassy down the block finally hired a private contractor to do it. (Hey, there's something: I'm bailed out by a foreign socialist government in the face of inaction by my local socialist government.) The mail wasn't delivered for a week, either, giving the lie to that fabled old creed. You needn't have had a portrait of Milton Friedman on your wall to cry out for some privatization.

Can we live in a civil society presided over by a government demonstrably uncivil? As I neared maybe the fifth stuck car of one morning's walk, I thought briefly of turning away, in reproachful disgust. ("Kill the lights and draw the shades, Ma! Dumb Charlie's got his rig stuck in the mud again.") But conscience pricked, and a good thing. The driver was a young, bewildered foreign woman, fearful of my approach. When she saw that

I meant to assist, she was touchingly grateful, and the power of Good Samaritanism was affirmed again.

A truism reasserts itself and is relearned: Government in a liberal republic should fulfill its elementary responsibilities: protect citizens from crime; pick up the trash; put out the fires; shovel the snow. A city that will not perform these functions soon returns its inhabitants to that state of nature from which, Hobbes tells us, the race escaped only through the agency of civil society in the first place.

—February 26, 1996
The Weekly Standard

'Gutter' Politics

Playing the name game

When the War on Terror began, and the Arab world became extremely important, Qatar was in the news, more than it had been. And that brought some awkward pronunciation—and led to the romping below.

I'm not going to say "gutter." That's what we're supposed to say now, instead of Qatar—instead of "Qa-TAHR." It's the latest thing. From time immemorial—defined as the moment of my birth on—we've said "Qa-TAHR." All red-blooded Amurricans say "Qa-TAHR." But the other day, I even heard Condi Rice—the otherwise unimpeachable Condi Rice—say "gutter." I almost busted a gut.

I'm not going to say "cobble" either. That's the new Kabul, as you know—the new "Ka-BUHL." In the highest administration councils, there was a contretemps—a reported contretemps, I should say—on this very subject. Donald Rumsfeld complained, "I think the top diplomat of this country ought to know how to pronounce the name of the Afghan capital." He was talking about Colin Powell. Rumsfeld, apparently, is a "cobble" man, and Powell is a "Ka-BUHL" man. Powell responded—again, reportedly—"Well, where I come from, it's Ka-BUHL."

I'm a shameless Rummy booster, but I'm strongly with Powell on this one.

If you start to go native on the pronunciation of foreign capitals and other places, there's no end to it. None. I called up the Qatari embassy in Washington. The receptionist answered, "Good morning, Embassy of Qa-TAHR." I smiled. I then asked—this was a native—how Qataris ("gut-terees"?) pronounced the name of their country. She said "gutter," or some-thing close. But one gets the feeling that she wouldn't say "gutter" when speaking in English. Neither would an American say "United States" instead of "Etats-Unis" when speaking French.

And then there's the matter of the sheer ugliness—aural ugliness —of both "gutter" and "cobble." (Is that ethnocentric—sound-o-centric?) When I discussed this issue on the Web, a reader wrote in, "Afghanistan's capital city certainly appears to be a hellhole, but at least the name Kabul—Ka-BUHL—lent it a certain Eastern allure. 'Cobble,' on the other hand, fails entirely to inspire the right vision. Where's the romance in 'cobble'? And 'gutter'! Ugh!"

Yes, ugh. For a while—when the bombs started falling over there—some news dorks were saying "Afghanis" instead of the proper "Afghans," in an effort, it seems, to sound in-the-know. Fortunately, they have stopped now, for the most part.

But the general problem persists. Last winter, I was thinking of starting a "Torino Watch." Why? Katie Couric was broadcasting from the Salt Lake City Olympics, and she was looking forward to the next Winter Olympics, to be held in . . . "Torino," she said. Why she said "Torino," instead of good ol' Turin, is shrouded in mystery. Would-be sophisticates are always saying "Torino" instead of Turin and "Milano" instead of Milan. But, oddly, they don't say Roma—except "when in Rome," presumably—and they don't say "Venezia" (Venice), "Firenze" (Florence), or "Napoli" (Naples).

Even I, though, draw the line at "Leghorn": I say Livorno. But this puts me at odds with Winston Churchill, who wrote to his foreign secretary in 1941, "If you approve I should like Livorno to be called in the English—Leghorn." Though "if at any time you are conversing agreeably with Mussolini in Italian, Livorno would be correct." This is the same Churchill who would write, four years later, "I do not consider that names that have been familiar for generations in England should be altered to study the whims of foreigners living in those parts." Without a firm stand, "the B.B.C. will be pronouncing Paris 'Paree.' Foreign names were made for Englishmen, not Englishmen for foreign names."

Harrumph. But there is a point—or several—and one of them is consistency. Katie Couric may swing with "Torino," but she'd never say "Köln" instead of Cologne, and she probably wouldn't refer back to the (horrendous) "München" Olympics. Nor would she pretend that the 2004 Summer Games will be held in "Athena."

In some cases, you just can't take the politics out of the pronunciation. You recall the great controversy over "Nicaragua," in the 1980s: When Peter Jennings rolled that "r," you just knew he hated the contras. Same with the broadcasters of NPR (nicknamed by right-wingers and other realists "Radio Managua"). Charles Krauthammer wrote a semi-famous column on this topic, admonishing, "Give foreign words their most mundane English rendering": no umlauts or other curlicues.

And yet the sandal-friendly Left just can't give up their Spanish (or faux-Spanish) pronunciations, thinking it makes them extra-cool and sympathetic. One Hispanic gentleman wrote me, "I've even heard 'Cooba' when a liberal really wants to feel my pain." Another man wrote of a college friend whose parents are Spanish, though she herself grew up in Virginia. "Freshman year, she always said 'Barcelona,' normally. Over the summer, she must have discovered her 'roots,' because by sophomore year she was dressing in all black and saying 'Bar-thay-lona.'" Sure.

And I especially liked this: "I am a student in southern California, and am constantly angered by the insistence of so many that one use a Spanish accent when pronouncing Spanish names. I have on occasion asked professors who do this to pronounce my last name with a southern drawl (as I'm from the South). And I once asked a fellow student to pronounce my last name without an American accent, 'as it was intended to be pronounced back in England.'" This sort of cheek is good for the soul.

And do you ever say Peking? Only when ordering duck, huh? There's something vaguely right-wing about saying Peking instead of Beijing, isn't there? I always feel a little frisson of rebellion when I do so. If you wanted to be a real weirdo, you could say Peiping.

I heard from a man who said, "I have six (mostly grown) children, and I've done my best with them, but I can't fight the tyranny of PC pronunciation. Of particular annoyance is 'Beijing' for 'Peking,' which I believe to be a perfectly acceptable anglicization. Of course, my daughter named my granddaughter 'Sionnain' (read: 'Shannon')." You could hear his sighs over the Internet.

I know puffed-up people who say "Côte d'Ivoire" (which they always pronounce in poor French) instead of "Ivory Coast." What's wrong with

"Ivory Coast," if you got it? Besides which, are we to use the language of the colonizing oppressor? Surely there must be a suitable African name, maybe even with a click or two.

I suppose that countries—like people—should be called what they want to be called, but I have a hard time swallowing "Myanmar" instead of Burma, and I'm very cross about "Burkina Faso" instead of the Upper Volta. I'm especially attached to the Upper Volta, because its capital has the best name of any capital: Ouagadougou. Luckily, they have not yet changed that. India—or someone—changed Bombay to "Mumbai," but I'm happy to report that that's not yet catching on. Or is it? (Churchill wrote—back in 1945—"Bad luck always pursues peoples who change the names of their cities.") I don't have any inclination to say "Siam" instead of "Thailand" or "Formosa" instead of "Taiwan." I'm not that retrograde. It could be that we want pronunciations—and many other things—to stay just as they were when we ourselves came of age.

When it comes to enunciating things foreign, my view is, "In for a penny, in for a pound." (Is that too English—I mean, British?) If you're going to go part of the way, you should really go all of the way. I had a Dutch friend in college who was amused at his art-history teacher. The teacher tried to be all fancy, saying "Gogh" the Dutch way—with all that throat-scraping—instead of good ol' "go." But he left the "van" as it was, in English: like the vehicle you tote the family around in. That made his attempt at authenticity laughable, or at least incomplete.

We have our pretenders in music, too. For example, there's a perfectly acceptable English way of saying Debussy—"DEB-you-see." But when striving Americans try to say it the French way, they screw it all up, never getting the "u" correct, and usually—wrongly—accenting the second syllable. Also, you may enjoy knowing that the Wagner Society in New York City is run by a couple named: Wagner (pronounced as in Mayor Robert Wagner, not as in Richard—and the composer's first name, in turn, is not pronounced as in "Little").

One law I stick to is that everyone has the right to have his name —his personal name—pronounced however he wants. No ifs, ands, or buts. Midway through his career, Tony Dorsett switched his name from "DORsit" to "Dor-SETT." According to the newspapers, his mother wasn't too thrilled about this. I once knew a guy who refused to pronounce Leonard Bernstein's name the way the conductor liked it: "Bernstine," to rhyme with "vine." (Lenny used to say, "You wouldn't say 'Gertrude Steen,' would you?") The guy I knew thought he was putting Bernstein down when he said "steen," or not letting the old performer get away with anything.

And do you know the cherished story about Ira Gershwin? A woman walks in to audition for him. She starts to sing, "You say eether and I say eether, / You say neether and I say neether . . . ," and Ira breaks in, "Thank you, Mrs. Leveen!" The woman, affronted, huffs, "It's Le-vine!"

My model in these matters is the late general, diplomat, and linguist Vernon Walters. He spoke nine languages, and was renowned for his mastery. He anglicized absolutely everything. When referring to the head German SOB in World War I, for instance, he'd say "William the Second." And if it was good enough for Walters . . .

I'll leave you with one more foreign capital. The story's complicated, but Bangkok, to Thais, is not merely "Bangkok." In fact, it's not "Bangkok" at all. The capital has a long, long formal name, and, to make matters even more interesting, the Thai language acknowledges no spaces between words (within a sentence or concept). So, I give you "Krungthepmahanakhonamonrattanakosinmahintharaayuthayama-hadilokphopnoppharatratchathaniburiromudomratchaniwetmahasathana-monpimanawatansathitsakkathattiyawitsanukamprasit."

—November 11, 2002
National Review

Take Your
Boxes and . . .

A nation of race rebels?

W hen the *Michigan* decisions were handed down—the ones that upheld affirmative action—many Americans underwent a bout of race-pondering. Of course, race is never far from our eyes: It's on our forms, for one thing. When applying to college, for a marriage license, for a loan: There are those boxes, demanding that we check White, African-American, Aleut, what have you.

A lot of Americans don't like this very much—and not all of them are lily-white. Ward Connerly, remember, is the force behind the Racial Privacy Initiative in California. This is the measure that would prevent governmental bodies from classifying individuals by race (with some prudent exceptions). Connerly wrote a piece for *National Review* on this subject titled "Don't Box Me In"—a phrase that captured the restless desire of many people to get free of color, to the extent possible. The magazine ran a cartoon with the piece that had a woman filling out a form and asking, "Can't I just check 'American'?" (The answer, madam, is no.) The ACLU has attacked Connerly's initiative as—natch—"racist." Thus is black white and white black (so to speak).

Shortly after the *Michigan* decisions, we at *National Review* ran a piece on our website decrying the Court's action and wondering what to do about it. Was a little rebellion in order? Should we meekly comply with these racial checkboxes? When facing the little devils, white people tend to think they're about to get the shaft. And those from approved minorities may feel a related anxiety: "Sure, I want to get in, or get the job, or get the loan—but this way? How can I know?"

Letters poured in from readers of the site, each with a story, or a fear, or a grievance—or some clever suggestion. Together, they showed a nation (or a slice of a nation) mightily sick of the race game, and the steady South Africanization of American life, where blood and shade hold stubborn sway.

One man said, "What would happen to affirmative-action programs if a significant portion of college applicants intentionally misreported their races? Even if most applications were marked correctly, a little civil disobedience could introduce a large enough margin of error to bring out the pure intellectual chaos and moral repugnance of affirmative action. Think about it: Schools would be forced to confirm, visually, the race of every applicant who claimed to be a minority. The explicit process of racial classification, the naked barbarity of the data collection: This would render affirmative action politically indefensible. What dean of admissions wouldn't be uncomfortable in front of Fox News cameras turning away a previously accepted student on the first day of class because he or she had the incorrect pigmentation?"

An intriguing question, more broadly: To what lengths would admissions offices go to verify the race or ethnicity of an applicant? How anthropological would they get? Would there be a medical unit at the ready, prepared to examine blood and assess DNA?

The letters we received clearly show that many white students feel themselves kept out of universities because of their damning skin—in other words, their "privilege" makes them unprivileged. They say, "I had these glittering credentials, including an A average, top test scores, and a trunkful of prizes. And my counselor said, 'Don't tell anyone, but if you could mark another race box, you could get in anywhere.'" Of course, this may be nonsense: but, again, how does one know? This is one of the effects of the system, raising suspicions in people of all colors. It creates martyrs and victims even when they should not exist. Whether this is good for societal harmony is easily answered.

Some people simply "decide to become a minority," by hook or crook. Everyone has a favorite tale to tell. I knew a girl in college—a pretty white girl from Minnesota who played golf—who received a scholarship for being an Indian. If she was an Indian, so is Annika Sorenstam, let me tell you. One young writer to NR was also planning on claiming a misty Indian ancestry: "If there has to be a bias, I want it in my favor." Other palefaces are discovering an African American on some limb of the family tree. This may confer a whole new meaning on "passing."

A great many people answer "human" when asked about their race. Said a reader, "A pollster phoned me, and after we waded through sex, age, and income, she asked me about race. When I answered 'human,' she said, quick as a flash, 'Thank you, we already have enough data on that group.'" Another reader urged a national campaign to induce Americans to enter "human" on all the various forms: "We can have a website—www.OnlyHuman.org. This could be huge, man. Huge!"

Evolution-minded readers suggested that everyone record "African-American" on grounds that we all originate at Olduvai Gorge, or wherever. In other words, each of us is a descendant of Lucy (the famous skeleton, not the flame-haired comedic actress). Other people have their own dodges: "I always answer 'Black Irish.'" Some Jews are especially flummoxed. One man informed us, "My father, of blessed memory, was not enough of a white European to get into Cornell. My son may be too much of a white European to get into Cornell." Another man wrote—responding to a point about who qualifies as a minority—"When I found out that Jews were no longer a minority, I had my first good night's sleep in 2,000 years!"

Many correspondents wished to say that, although they could benefit from a convenient check in a winning box—having a pleasingly Spanish name, for example—they have refused, finding such favoritism distasteful, contrary to their view of America, and a little dishonest. ("There is nothing 'Hispanic' about us! We don't even like beans!")

What about getting hitched? Do race and marriage go together like a horse and carriage? "Jay, I found myself thinking of you and Ward Connerly while my fiancé and I were filling out a marriage-license application at the Milwaukee County Courthouse." (Who doesn't think of Ward Connerly and me when applying for a marriage license?) "Down at the bottom of the form were boxes to indicate the race or races of the intendeds. I looked at my fiancé and said, 'Hey, shall we leave this blank?' 'Yeah,' he responded, 'it's none of their business anyway.' So, with a tingle of excitement at our rebellion, we turned in our form."

But The Man stood in the way: "Upon being asked why the boxes were blank, we responded that we preferred not to answer that question. Of course, we were promptly informed that the State of Wisconsin will not issue a marriage license without recording the race(s) of the two people to be married. Not being in a position to move out of state, we abjectly complied, as people usually do when they are up against robotic bureaucrats. So, that was that. But we tried!"

Many readers brought up the problem of their mixed-race children: how to declare them (or whether to declare them, racially). "Do we make the system work for us, feeling like hypocrites and cheats, or do we stick to our principles, asserting ourselves as Americans?"

A man from Hawaii said, "Upon the birth of our daughter last year, the state sent the forms necessary to acquire a birth certificate. When I, as the father, was asked for my race, I did what I always do: check the box that says Other and write 'human.' A week later, a very serious-looking letter arrived, informing me that 'human' was not a race recognized by the State of Hawaii. I was warned that, unless the form were completed properly, my daughter's birth certificate would list the father's race as 'unknown.' So it reads, forever more. I am pleased with my little act of civil disobedience, and look forward to explaining it to my daughter when she is old enough to ask. (My wife, however, is not so pleased with the implication . . .)"

Of particular poignancy was this: "What about those of us who are adopted and don't know our race? Without boring you with the details, I was born to an unmarried woman in Germany and it's clear I am not exclusively of one race. Yet since I am adopted and the birth certificate doesn't name a father (and I have never searched for either biological parent), I will never know what race I am. Surely there must be some legislation before

Congress enabling me to identify myself properly and thereby regain my self-esteem. If the government is going to continue to make race an issue, then there must be a commission formed to study the suffering of folks like me who were racially neutered. I am a man without racial identity and I need a telethon or something."

Finally, I would like to introduce you to a mortgage broker you may appreciate knowing. He works at home, taking clients' applications by phone. He has the habit of checking Other and filling in "American" when race is demanded (as it always is, on the standard form). "I have fought many a battle with dimwitted yet determined underwriters who insist that I must check something more 'accurate.' When I point out to them that I take applications over the phone and can't possibly know the races of my borrowers, I am repeatedly told that I should make guesses, based on the sound of my clients' voices. If this weren't true, it would be hilarious."

There is much hilarity in these letters (and, gathered together, they would make an instructive compendium). But the subject is depressingly serious. Our governmental institutions may get *more* race-crazy, not less. But perhaps we are building a nation of race rebels, refusing to play along. One letter we received had a signature and then, in parentheses—simply as a statement—"Race Withheld."

—August 11, 2003
National Review

People's Romances

A special Valentine's Day issue
says something ugly about us

I s it worth remarking, at this late date, on the near-total acceptance of adultery in contemporary society? Or is it like noting that it is dark at night, or that the car has replaced the horse-drawn carriage? It seemed to happen so fast, really. One day, adultery was an acknowledged evil, a grave sin against God, outlawed by the Ten Commandments. Then seemingly overnight, it was as ordinary as laughter, or gardening, and anyone who raised an objection to it was a prude, a mental dinosaur, a zealot.

These thoughts are occasioned by a bible for today, *People* magazine, which devoted a special Valentine's Day issue to "The Greatest Love Stories of the Century." Predictably, it was fun to read, offering as it did short biographies of 30 dream couples, adorned with sigh-inducing photographs. There were Bogie and Bacall, Liz and Dick, Gable and Lombard—even Sid and Nancy, of punk-rock notoriety. But as the stories unfolded, an unwitting theme persisted: These unions, many of them, were founded on adultery. They were made possible by the betrayal of some husband or wife. And *People* scarcely bothered to notice, hardly pausing to acknowledge the injured ones to whom vows had been made. Yet there they were, hovering in the background like ghosts. They were the victims of these "greatest love stories," and normally it is victims who receive the lion's share of attention in *People*. But these discarded spouses were unwelcome guests at this party. They were mentioned briefly, with annoyance, if at all, then set aside, as in life, so that the action could proceed.

Of *People*'s 30 romances, 14 involved adultery (that is, began with it). Oh, there were the token square couples among the 30, like the Rev. Billy Graham and his wife Ruth, and even a cartoon pairing (Popeye and Olive Oyl). Also, there were instances like that of Charlie Chaplin, who was an Olympic-caliber adulterer but happened to be between marriages to teenagers when he met Eugene O'Neill's daughter. In three of the 14 cases, both parties were married; in 10 of them, the man alone was, and in one, only the woman was. Eight of the 14 couples never wed; five of the 30 later divorced, and others may yet.

The celebration kicks off with Richard Burton and Elizabeth Taylor. Both were married when they combusted on the set of *Cleopatra*. *People* records that, "despite numerous flings," Burton was "still joined to his first wife, Sybil, the mother of his two young daughters." Taylor was married to her fourth husband, Eddie Fisher (who had left Debbie Reynolds to marry her). Alarmed by press rumblings, Fisher flew to the set "to stand guard." But "it was too late." At some point, Burton apparently was tempted to return to his wife, but he overcame it. The Vatican, for its part, denounced Taylor with a phrase that deserves common currency: "erotic vagrancy." When Burton died, his fourth wife prevented Taylor (who had married him twice) from attending the funeral, which *People* makes out to be unsporting. And, in a way, it was, considering how casual these arrangements were.

Did you know that Mrs. Simpson had a husband when she met the prince, later King Edward VIII? That there was, in fact, a Mr. Simpson? Yes, and his name was Ernest. *People* paints him as a cooperative sort, for he "soon slipped into the background, and the Prince began squiring Wallis alone." Later, the love-respecting Windsor "orchestrated their divorce," and the rest is abdication and other history.

The account of Frank Sinatra and Ava Gardner is particularly instructive. He was married, with three children, when "he and Ava started partying in 1948"—"started partying" being a new euphemism for a sin that now dares not speak its name. (The word "adultery" does not darken the pages of the special issue.) The MGM studio, which employed Sinatra and Gardner, was none too pleased with its stars. Explains *People*, "It was, after all, the age of morals clauses in contracts and puritanical public opinion," and here we have true colors, as vivid as they can be: opposition to adultery and to the destruction of family as "puritanical."

Ably representing the Communist view are Diego Rivera and Frida Kahlo, who, though not among the Adulterous 14, were anything but opposed to adultery and, with raised consciousnesses, practiced it enthusiastically. Of her husband's prolific philandering, Kahlo remarked, "Diego is not anybody's husband and never will be, but he is a great comrade"—a neat summation of a point of view that used to be identified almost exclusively with the Left. Marital fidelity was a shackle of the old, oppressive order, bourgeois and religious, which the new utopia would smash.

Dashiell Hammett and Lillian Hellman, another Stalinist couple, were both married when they met, but "they eventually got rid of their respective spouses" (who go unnamed). Hammett and Hellman never wed, but "stood by each other, most courageously during the communist witch-hunts of the '50s."

"Courageously"? Let us not suppose that *People* shrinks from judgment. Its language fairly abounds in judgmentalism, steering the reader in ways both subtle and not. Clark Gable "was tiring of his second wife," who "had no interest in duck shooting or fishing, his chief passions." When his affair with Carole Lombard was reported, "the exposure hastened Gable's divorce from the reluctant [Mrs. Gable]," who, it is implied, need not be wept over, because "she walked off with a sizable settlement." (Her name was Ria.) *People*'s evident position is that the union of two such beauties as Gable and Lombard was so urgent, so desirable—practically demanded by the heavens—that only a selfish and myopic wretch could stand in the way.

So too with Spencer Tracy and Katharine Hepburn. *People* describes

Tracy as "a guilt-ridden Catholic, old-fashioned enough to be scandalized by the brusque actress in rumpled trousers"—but not so guilt-ridden and old-fashioned as to refrain from committing adultery with her for decades. After Tracy's death, Hepburn telephoned his wife, Louise, who gave her, "I thought you were a rumor." "The rebuff stung," says *People*, "but Hepburn's love had given her thick skin." The depth of Louise Tracy's skin is not considered. She is merely resented for refusing to grant her husband a divorce, thus cheating a love more glamorous.

Humphrey Bogart may have been married when he met the sizzling Lauren Bacall, but *People* hastens to assure that it was "a deteriorating marriage (his third)," and besides, the woman drank. Bogie and Bacall were thoughtful adulterers: For a full year, "the two held clandestine trysts wherever they could—always careful not to further enrage" Mayo Bogart.

Mrs. William Randolph Hearst is rapped for not releasing her husband to the showgirl Marion Davies. Hearst's sons "thought Marion an interloper" and, after the old man's death, "banished her from the empire." Boris Pasternak had his real-life Lara, a mistress, but about Mrs. Pasternak the magazine is silent. Not even her name is given.

Seldom is *People* shy about imposing a moral view on what it reports. Here, for example, is what it says about Chaplin's inclinations toward Stalinism: "His outspoken support for Russia's plight against the Nazis contradicted the nation's growing anti-Communist sentiment." It takes a champion manipulation of words to cast totalitarian politics in such a light.

And not to judge adultery is, in fact, to pass judgment—on its victims. The liberal, broad-minded soul who declines to judge adultery says to those betrayed, "I do not respect your suffering enough to criticize or scorn those who caused it." This same soul would not hesitate, of course, to condemn a Klansman, not merely because of the repugnance of Klan ideology but also because he would not wish to break faith with the Klan's many victims.

Historically, America has had a point of view about adultery. It has been against. And certain American elites have always considered this a sign of national immaturity: The Europeans are so much better, so much more *adult*, about this kind of thing, unbeholden to the Pilgrims' silly pieties and superstitions. But in recent decades, America has, sadly, grown up, and its stance against adultery and for faithfulness has significantly weakened.

After all, if you wanted to appall a right-thinking person in 1992, you might have tried saying, "I'm not sure that a blatant adulterer should be president." Public discussion of adultery in that campaign year was largely hushed. Candidate Clinton announced on *60 Minutes* that it was none of our business, and that, pretty much, was that. When he was elected with 43 percent of the vote, there was relief in some quarters that, at long last, known adultery was no longer disqualifying for higher offce. Americans were starting to loosen up, starting to behave more like their European betters—were becoming less "puritanical," *People* might say.

Further proof of progress came when Henry Cisneros was installed in the Clinton cabinet. He had been forced from his job as mayor of San Antonio, but, in this new day, he would not be barred from a place of honor, no matter that he had paid off his mistress, then lied about it. What did marital fidelity have to do with running the government, anyway?

So, Hester Prynne could breathe easier on this side of the Atlantic. Joyless Americans were measurably less apt to plaster A's onto the waywardly adventurous.

Many social observers predict another "awakening" here, or contend that even now one is underway. Still, it seems unlikely that adultery will regain the infamy it merits anytime soon. The few who bring it up are still regarded as freaks by respectable society. Suggest that Martin Luther King's faithlesshess to his wife diminishes his heroism, despite his accomplishments in the public realm, and you will be treated, if not with indignant disbelief, with pity, as one would respond to a retarded child. The same is true of FDR, Eisenhower, JFK, LBJ—and of the exalted lovers of *People* magazine. Who, after all, has heard of Sybil Burton? Of Louise Tracy? Of the first Mrs. Sinatra? Of the "reluctant" Mrs. Gable? But there they are, or were: silent accusers, tear-stained witnesses, rebuking those who forsook them and sobering those who would pause to remember.

—April 29, 1996
The Weekly Standard

Anxiety in Steel Country

A mill town trembles and waits

I'm not sure I've ever been so moved by a reporting trip as I was by this one—by the one that resulted in the below piece. (The year was 1999.) Like you, perhaps, I couldn't be clearer about free trade—its efficacy, the blessings it bestows. But not everyone wins (even if most do).

Weirton, West Virginia

P oliticians like to come here to make a point. They go to the Millsop Community Center, between the library and the Presbyterian church. John Kennedy spoke there in 1960, having discovered that not every American summers on Cape Cod. Bill Clinton spoke there in 1992, on the first stop of his now-legendary bus tour. And Pat Buchanan spoke there on March 1, in effect launching his 2000 presidential campaign. To each candidate, townspeople—most of them steelworkers and their families—gave a tumultuous ovation.

Few here, though, are cheering for Clinton now. This solidly Democratic town is ripe for the Republican Buchanan and his "economic nationalism," as the steel industry is reeling from a recent surge in "dumped" imports. At Weirton Steel, the town's dominant employer, nearly 1,000 workers have been laid off since November, and the company has lost millions of dollars. Buchanan thinks he knows whom to blame, and so do most Weirtonians: foreign countries that "dump" steel into the U.S. market, and the administration that refuses to stand up to them, in the name of the "global economy."

In Buchanan's distinctive rhetoric, "the people of Weirton are looking down the barrel of a gun." Yet "the global economy's apologists in Washington don't like to talk about the Weirtons of America," preferring to believe that "all Americans are floating on a wave of Wall Street prosperity." The local union leader, Mark Glyptis, in a similar vein, never tires of saying that "Wall Street"—particularly as represented by Treasury secretary Robert Rubin—"is forgetting about Main Street." If Clinton or his heir apparent, Al Gore, ever tries to return to Weirton, he says, "I'll run him out of town."

When Clinton did his JFK act in 1992, he told Weirton that, as president, he would "strictly enforce" laws that forbid the "dumping" of "unfair, subsidized steel." If foreign governments "are doing things for their steel that we're not doing for ours," he said, "they shouldn't have access to our market." His remarks, captured on videotape, are very familiar in the Ohio Valley, played again and again on television. Gore can be seen nodding solemnly. At a recent meeting, Weirton Steel president Richard Riederer handed Clinton a copy of the infamous tape—just as a reminder.

Weirton, a town of 22,000, is aflame with anger, resentment, and bewilderment. Mainly, people are afraid. You can sense fear in the eyes and conversation of almost everyone you meet. "I hear they're laying off another 500," says one man to another. "They're saying something about 25 years" (referring to a worker's seniority). Weirtonians whisper such rumors as though talking about some dread disease, which could sooner or later consume the entire population. They hope they will be able to ride out yet another downturn in a notoriously cyclical business, but, deep down, they worry that the end is really coming for them.

Their fury at Clinton—for whom practically everyone voted, twice—is startling. The more rattled ones say that betrayal must run in his blood. Laid-off workers—many of whom are Vietnam veterans—are quick to remind you that Clinton dodged the draft, failing his country then, failing it now. "Tell those idiots in Washington," says one, "that America is going to be a Third World country, with no industrial base. There's going to be no middle class—just the rich and the poor. They say they're 'free traders,' but they're really 'free traitors': T-R-A-I-T-O-R-S."

Not only are people here incensed at Clinton, they are dismayed at their fellow Americans, whom they consider unpatriotic for ignoring their plight. "What's really killing us," says union official Dave Gossett, "is that the American people are tolerating this. They are apparently willing to let the industry just go and die." The mayor, Dean Harris (who is also a mill worker), says that nothing less than "the American Dream is being taken from us. We thought that if we worked hard, we'd attain that dream, and now we're losing it. The strange thing is, everyone else is flourishing."

In Weirton, the company and the people are one. Nestled in the northern panhandle of the state, 35 miles from Pittsburgh, this has been a steel town since the early part of the century, when E. T. Weir founded his mill. Generations of Weirtonians—chiefly of Italian and East European ancestry—have committed their sweat to the company, establishing a way of life that once seemed as permanent as the Ohio River. A young person may have desired to escape the mill, but it was there for him if he needed it, and it provided a dignified living.

By the early 1980s, however, the company had become bloated and inefficient, unable to compete in a more aggressive market. It then "went E.S.O.P.," adopting an Employee Stock Ownership Plan that allowed it to survive, if in "leaner and meaner" form. The workforce dropped from a high of 13,000 to about 4,600 today (including those laid off). The reduction took place "gentle-like," as one worker explains, primarily through retirement, with little further hiring. Ten years ago—here is the measure of efficiency in the industry—it took 6.5 "man-hours" to produce a ton of steel. Now, it takes a mere 1.2.

Even so, the company was knocked on its back last November when Russia, Brazil, and Japan flooded the U.S. market with below-cost steel, rendering Weirton's product hopelessly overpriced. The community, in mortal danger, rallied to "Stand Up for Steel," as every sign in the Valley proclaims. On January 20, in the dead of night, 75 buses pulled out of Weirton, carrying what seemed like the whole town to Washington for a march. The new militants strode from the Capitol to the White House, where Rep. Bob Ney—who represents the neighboring Ohio district—stormed the gates, guerrilla-like.

"We're not leaving until someone comes out and listens to us!" he shouted at the guards. Eventually, an aide from the legislative-affairs office emerged, and the demonstrators rode back to Weirton, exhausted but satisfied that they had delivered a message.

Indeed, they had. In February, the Commerce Department imposed or negotiated restrictions on a sizable portion of foreign steel. The administration had already offered U.S. companies a tax break and other "trade adjustment" relief. Still, the industry and its advocates are unappeased. Mark Glyptis charges that the administration is planning for the "death" of domestic steel, not its recovery. "The Ohio Valley," he promises, "will not be turned into a hospice." Ney, too, insists that "we're not going to be bought off." He is white-hot about the issue, like every other pol in Steel Country. Several bills, proposing varying degrees of protection, are now circulating in Congress.

The dilemma, according to the steel caucus, is not the classic one of free trade versus protectionism. Oh no. Rather, it is a matter of enforcing "anti-dumping" laws that now rust on the books. "We can compete with anybody in the world," goes the refrain, "but only if we have a fair shot. We ask for no favors." Dean Harris says that even if Weirton Steel had no pay-roll at all—if the company paid its workers zero—it would *still* be helpless against "illegal foreign steel." As Dick Riederer puts it, "They can't put us out of business legally. But they can do it *illegally*."

Not long ago, Riederer plunked down in front of Gore a picture from a newspaper, showing a Russian steelworker on the job. "Do you see that, Mr. Vice President?" he said. "We haven't made steel by that method in years. That's how our grandfathers used to do it. It is laughably inefficient and expensive and uncompetitive. Yet they're destroying us, through dumping."

Most strikingly, there is a pervasive sense here that "our fate is out of our hands." It is a phrase you hear from everyone, from Riederer to the humblest wage earner. "We did everything we were asked to do," people say. "We downsized, we modernized, we made sacrifices. But none of that matters. It's still not good enough. What do we do now? Who can tell us?"

Harris knows that further change is coming, and he is urging his fellow citizens to prepare for it. In his State of the City address before the local Rotary chapter, he says, "We can't afford any longer to be a one-horse town. We have to find some other horses to ride, if we're going to stay in the race." Dave Gossett says that he cannot in good conscience encourage teenagers to follow their parents and grandparents into the mill. Riederer, like everyone else, stresses education, saying that "we have to take the young ones and show them more of life."

And yet, many in Weirton view the mill as something close to their birthright, the place of their destiny, for good or ill. Gossett sighs that "this is a family company in a family-oriented town." One woman remembers sitting in her grandfather's yard as a girl, looking at the mill, watching as the cranes bent and rose, and the furnaces belched and spewed. "It was all so reassuring," she says. "The mill was the center of our world. It meant everything. Nothing could disturb it." Riederer notes that it is an abiding sense of entitlement—the mill as mother's milk—that Weirton, step by step, will have to overcome.

Speaking for many, Gossett laments that there is no "solidarity" any-more in the country, certainly not among unions. Steelworkers remember the "Buy American" campaign in the auto industry, when laid-off assemblymen took sledgehammers to Hondas. Now, the United Auto Workers—who build cars profitably with "dumped" steel—seem indifferent to their steelworking brethren. When Weirton steelworkers asked UAW members at a nearby GM plant to join them in a rally, they were met with an embarrassed silence.

Gossett, like others, is especially concerned for middle-aged workers, who (in a local expression) only "know mill." The current situation is "terrifying" for them, he says. "I've worked with these people for years, and I have no idea what to say to them. I look at them, and they're scared. I want to do something for them—have them mow my lawn for ten dollars, whatever—but I have a wife and children of my own." Harris and Riederer, too, have trouble knowing what to say. They can hardly bear to walk down the street or into a store anymore, besieged as they are by shaken workers.

The specter of social breakdown hangs in the air. Judy Raveaux, in typical Weirton fashion, remembers the precise date on which her husband was laid off in the early '80s. (He is laid off once more.) She and their children moved in with her parents. He went to North Carolina, where he found a job in a cookie factory. She cleaned bars in the middle of the night, often taking her sleeping children with her. After two and a half years, the mill beckoned her husband back to work. Of all the couples they knew in that period, they are the only pair who managed to stay married. Alcoholism, debauchery, and despair—those unlovely attendants on joblessness—took their toll. "I feel sorry for the Russians," she says, along with everyone else, "but . . ."

As mayor, Harris does his best to cheer the troops. As an hourly laborer, he too frets for his family. He has so far retained his mill job—the mayor's position pays a pittance—but he has been laid off four times in the past. He is able to tell audiences, "The president [Bill Clinton] says he can feel your pain, but I have *actually felt it*." When he reflects on the prospects for those tossed out in middle age, his eyes fill with tears, and he is forced to turn away. Some will land on their feet, sure, but others are ill equipped to "roll with the punches" and "start over from scratch." Weirton is not like a traveling circus, which, facing lean times, can fold its tent and move in a caravan to the next town. There are . . . complications.

Obviously, the siren song of Buchananism is deafening here. Die-hard Democrats are ready to pull the lever for a populist Republican who will pin their woes on a foreign menace and the callous neglect of Big Money. The question—quite legitimate—for the rest of the country is, Should Americans in general care whether the steel industry lives or dies? There are only about 160,000 steelworkers left in the country, a relatively tiny number. (They could all fit into one and a half Rose Bowls.) The national economy is climbing through the roof, thanks to the global economy so hated in Weirton. Free traders can only shake their heads at the wildly disproportionate political clout the steel industry wields. James K. Glassman, the writer and analyst, points out that there is a certain romanticism about steel, a feeling that, somehow, the production of that metal makes a country "serious."

Brink Lindsey of the Cato Institute observes that the steelworkers are like the farmers, another dwindling band. They reside in the popular imagination as the salt of the earth, connecting America to its glorious, nation-building past. While the forces of both groups have become meager, their political lobbies remain strong, skewing the proper order of things. The domestic oil industry is hurting too, notes Lindsey, but nobody—least of all factions in Congress—is squawking about slapping tariffs on foreign oil. The availability of cheaper commodities has indisputably been a boon to the overall economy. Adam Smith, cars-killed-horse-buggies, et cetera, et cetera.

And yet and yet. The logic of the market is wise to hold its tongue in Weirton, where the question nags, "But what about the people?" Bob Rubin is demonized here because he makes (perfectly truthful) statements like, "We have larger concerns than the steel industry." In Weirton, however, as Dean Harris emphasizes, there is no larger concern than how to hold body and soul together. Dick Riederer, who is utterly without illusions, gets down to brass tacks when he says, "We're going to have to decide as a society whether we want a domestic steel industry." (Steel people resort to a national-security argument, which the free traders easily puncture.)

If the answer is no—as it may well be—someone will have to think for a moment about what to do with the few—the very few, relatively—who have been wrecked by a phenomenon that has made the many fantastically rich.

Meanwhile, Weirton is trembling. And in Buchanan's pocket.

—March 22, 1999
National Review

Most Hated U.

A visit to Bob Jones

In the year 2000, Bob Jones University was a fairly hot topic. This piece recalls why, and explores that peculiar campus itself.

Greenville, South Carolina

F unny, but they don't look like beasts. They don't have horns and tails. Neither are they wearing white sheets. On the contrary, these students at Bob Jones University seem astoundingly kind, sensitive, bright, and sincere. They attend what must be the most hated university in the country. Their school has become a symbol of much that is repugnant in American life. And they have had no real chance to defend themselves in the long, trying months since "February."

That's what they call it: "February." All over campus, this word is shorthand for the controversy that occurred at the time of the South Carolina primary. Having lost to John McCain in New Hampshire, George W. Bush arrived in this state needing a victory. He hightailed it to Bob Jones, obviously trying to appeal to bedrock conservatives. It seemed nothing out of the ordinary: The school had long been a stop on the Republican trail. Ronald Reagan had been here; the first George Bush had been here; Bob Dole had been here. But when George W. Bush addressed these students— giving his usual, milquetoast speech—a storm broke out. Its reverberations are being felt still.

The school was held to be a) racist and b) anti-Catholic. Bush, unlike the pols who had preceded him, was tainted. McCain and the national press played the governor's visit for all it was worth. Bush won the South Carolina primary, but stumbled again in Michigan. McCain's camp placed calls to Catholic households—these were the notorious "Catholic Voter Alerts"—warning that Bush was in league with the worst element. Liberal journalists who had never before had a friendly word to say about religion suddenly had an opportunity to pose as Defenders of the Faith. Sen. Bob Torricelli, Democrat of New Jersey, introduced a resolution condemning the university. Bush went on to secure the nomination, but Democrats—gleeful—vowed to hang Bob Jones around the candidate's neck all the way to November.

These same Democrats have labeled Bush's recent travels the "Bob Jones Redemption Tour." The Democratic National Committee even had T-shirts printed up to this effect. The committee has advised candidates around the country to "play the Bob Jones card" against the GOP this fall. So damaging is Bush's Bob Jones appearance thought to be, many believe that he must name a Catholic running mate, as though in repentance. (Of course, they also think that such a move would be wise politics even if "February" had never taken place.) BJU—a Christian-fundamentalist institution founded in 1927—is now not only the most despised school in America; it is also one of the best known.

All of this leaves people on campus shaking their heads in amazement. "It's crazy," says the school's president, Bob Jones III. "Just crazy." Students report that, before the controversy, some of their friends thought BJU was a golf school—as in Bobby Jones. Still others thought of Kool-Aid—as in Jim Jones, who led a mass suicide in the 1970s. Says one sophomore, Adam Lee, "The coverage has been unreal. I mean, why are we so important? Of course, we believe we are very special, but this is kind of ridiculous." People here agree that the controversy has strengthened them: renewed their commitment to their faith, their campus, and one another. A senior, Eva Motter, points out that Christians are enjoined to "rejoice in adversity" and to "confound the wise." She and others view "February" as God's way, however unexpected, of lifting the university up.

Naturally, not everyone here is totally at ease with the school's wide-spread notoriety. When fundamentalists brush up against the larger world, they tend to get burned. Members of this community are distrustful of journalists, who make little effort to understand them or their doctrine. They are happy to stand apart from the world—it is a matter of honor, and Biblical injunction—but they would also like to be understood, listened to, rather than dismissed as bigots, boobs, and worse. A university spokesman, Jonathan Pait, notes that most outsiders assume "we're a bunch of kooks in high-water pants—polyester, of course." Complains Eva Motter: "People don't bother to find out who we are. Our accusers haven't been here. They're influenced by the media, and they take what the media says at face value."

BLACK AND WHITE

The indictment against Bob Jones contains the two aforementioned counts: racism and anti-Catholicism. The charge of racism stems mainly from the school's most infamous rule—a ban on interracial dating. In fact, this is the issue over which Bob Jones lost its tax exemption in 1983. The policy was rescinded in March of this year, following the Bush–McCain fiasco. (Said McCain, speaking rhetorically to the campus, "Thank goodness: Now you're into the 18th century. Try the 21st century.")

One of the problems with the rule, BJU-ers plead, is that it was next to impossible to explain to outsiders. However you sliced it, it looked baldly and obnoxiously racist. The ban, they say, had nothing to do with true racism—the belief that some races are inferior to others. Rather, it related to doctrinal notions involving one-world government, the Antichrist, and ecumenism generally. To an ear not attuned to fundamentalism, it has something to do with the U.N. In any case, says President Jones, "the policy was never talked about, never preached about, never taught about—was no big deal. But to the media, it was everything. They made it the defining fact about BJU. And it's just not us. We are not racists. And I was tired of seeing them do that to us. Our mission here—our God-called mission—is so much greater, so much more important. So I said, 'If this thing is standing between us and that mission, let's leave it aside, so we can get on with life.'"

The student body, unsurprisingly, is largely white, although not without some color—a stroll through the dining hall is proof enough of that. Kids come here from all 50 states and over 40 different countries. Ask about racial numbers, though, and school officials bristle. They argue a case that, years ago, would have been regarded as nobly liberal. "We don't concern ourselves with racial statistics," says Jonathan Pait, "because we treat our students as individuals, as sons and daughters of God, as members of our family. We don't have any quotas here or anything like that. We're just people." He makes the point that it is other, secular schools that are obsessed with race—not Bob Jones. These other institutions think according to race, admit by race, organize by race. "And here it means nothing. Yet we're the ones who are supposed to be racist! It makes me mad."

The students, too, are stung by the image of racism. "That's what hurts the most," says David Schwingle, a senior. "You know you're not a racist, but people may assume you are." To be a BJU student is, in a sense, to be presumed guilty. Indeed, these kids bear a burden that is probably unique in all the land: They are required to defend their school, and to justify their presence at it. Adam Lee had a particularly troubling experience. "I was undergoing some medical treatment, and was taking some stress tests. In the middle of them, the doctor asked me where I was from, where I went to school—the normal questions. And when I told him, he blew up at me. He totally ignored the tests." Talk about stress.

Another senior, Catherine McQuaid, emphasizes that about 40 percent of the students here do volunteer work in Greenville—out among the poorest, who are predominantly black and Hispanic. She says, not a little peeved, "I grew up in Chicago, and my best friends were black or other minorities. I have had two minority roommates since I came here. It's just not something we think about. I work with black kids, help them with their homework before their parents get home so they don't have to be latchkey kids. Really, I don't think I've ever run into someone here at Bob Jones who's manifested any sort of racist attitude at all."

Some find it particularly painful that black high-school students—fundamentalist ones—may shrink from attending BJU because of what they hear about it. "So," says Adam Lee, "there's a joy in my heart when I see a black freshman on campus. I go out of my way to get to know him. In my church back home"—this is in Jamesburg, N.J.—"there are all kinds of people: from Africa, from the islands, and so on. I like that sort of environment."

All of us have been conditioned to scoff at defenses of the some-of-my-best-friends-are-black variety. But, when utterly earnest—even importunate—they have a certain power.

CHURCH VS. CHURCH

Then there is the matter of anti-Catholicism. When George W. Bush had piqued interest in the school, it was noticed that BJU had on its website some harshly anti-Catholic material. This was found in the (electronic) archives of a magazine called *Faith for the Family*, published at Bob Jones from 1973 to 1986. Articles from this periodical include language that shocks the modern sensibility. "Satanic," for example, is not the fare of everyday conversation in most places. But to contend that these writings are especially anti-Catholic is somewhat curious. They oppose (to put it mildly) any religion at all that differs from Bob Jones-style fundamentalism. They give hell—literally—to Mormons, Christian Scientists, Jehovah's Witnesses, "liberal Protestants," and other Christian sects, to say nothing of Muslims, Hindus, and so on. One piece is entitled "Seventh-Day Adventism: Christian or Cult?" (In the world of BJU, this is not exactly a stumper.)

Yet, in the midst of all this equal-opportunity vituperating, it was the anti-Catholicism that hogged most of the attention. All of it, really. Exhibit

A in the case against the university was "Romanism and the Charismatic Movement" by Bob Jones Jr., late father of the current president (and son of the school's founder). The article's subhead? "Because they ignore the Word of God, both papists and charismatics are doing the work of the devil." Rough stuff. But John McCain did not issue "Charismatic Voter Alerts" in Michigan. And there is no clamor for Bush to anoint a charismatic running mate (though a little charisma never hurt a candidate).

As with the interracial-dating question, BJU-ers find it hard to explain to others that, despite their extraordinary language, they are not anti-Catholic or anti-anyone else. The problem, they say, is that society at large does not take religion seriously and is "theologically illiterate." Many here stress that they have better relations with serious Catholics—orthodox, true-believing ones—than they do with those who are merely social, or casual, Catholics. In other words, Bob Jones III would be more comfortable with a traditional priest or nun than with a Massachusetts political hand. People who are adamant about religion, one way or another, tend to understand one another, to know what is at stake. And they are also apt to be, like the BJU community, defiantly anti-ecumenical.

As Jonathan Pait puts it, "We don't seek dialogue, we don't seek common ground, we don't make concessions. We stand firm on what we believe. But we accept people where they are. And the Bible commands us to love." In modern America, says President Jones, "if you don't say the politically correct thing, or if you stand strong on what you believe—in our case, salvation by grace through faith in the shed blood of Jesus Christ; if you're not promoting the ecumenical agenda, where everybody's beliefs have to be on parity and equally right—this whole postmodern idea that two opposing views can both be right; if you don't do that, why, you're a bigot or you're intolerant. And that is nonsensical."

Kristel Pender, an education major from Kansas City, gets to the nub of it: "We're trying to serve the Lord here, as best we can. That doesn't mean we hate other people. Just the opposite." Adds Catherine McQuaid, "I come from a Catholic background. I was raised a Catholic, and my father is a Catholic. It was hard for him at first, but after years of contact with Bob Jones, he has come to trust the people here and know that they do not hate Catholics, that they have a love for all people, and that he can trust them with the education of his children."

Jeremy McMorris, a recent graduate from Mio, Mich., is forthright, in typical BJU fashion: "If what we say is true, then what Catholics say cannot be true; and if what they say is true, then what we say cannot be true.

It's not that we hate them. It's just that, when you have 100 percent gusto about something, you are often required to say no and refuse to accept something else. The world may see that as hatred, and if we're coming across in a hateful manner, then shame on us and we need to change. But our message is one of love, and that was Christ's message."

'STRANGERS AND PILGRIMS'

This is a far, far cry from your standard American university: outwardly, inwardly. The people—young and old—are almost freakishly polite. They talk openly about God and their Savior, as others might talk about politics, sports, or sex. They say grace before meals. Their campus is dotted with Biblical quotations. They don't have to lock up their belongings. There is no litter, no graffiti, no blaring rock music, no cursing, no drinking, no smoking, no shouting. In other words, it is hell for most college students. But for these, it is very heaven. The rules and atmosphere, they insist, are liberating, enabling them to concentrate on what matters: becoming "soldiers for Christ."

BJU kids know full well that they are different; they have no illusions about what others think of them. They can't help wondering, though, why, in a country chock-full of differences—one that prides itself, increasingly, on differences—they are singled out for calumny. They pounce on the fact that Al Gore, also during the primary season, spoke at an Orthodox synagogue in New York. Only men and boys were allowed to hear him; women and girls stood outside. Yet no one tagged him with sexism. The vice president had merely met Americans where they were. No political rival and no journalist pretended that Gore had endorsed the views or practices of his audience.

One of the things that "February" has done is fire up school spirit. An embattled platoon is likely to be a feistier, gutsier one. A high moment occurred on March 3, when President Jones appeared on Larry King's CNN program to explain himself and his campus. People here have tremendous respect for King, and an almost pathetic gratitude to him, for what they see as his fairness. On the big night, the students watched on wide-screen TVs. There were cheers, tears, high-fives. Says Jeremy McMorris, "It was kind of like watching your team win the Super Bowl." David Schwingle allows that "I was so excited, I went out and bought a new [Bob Jones] T-shirt."

If BJU is a mystery to the rest of the world, the rest of the world is, to a degree, a mystery to BJU. Says Adam Lee, "Yes, we dress differently, we act differently. When people come here, they see people who are clean-cut, who have morals and standards, who stand up for something they believe in, who just want to help others and love and spread the Word of the Lord . . . and they balk. Why?" And yet the students don't spend too long fretting over general opinion. "We know that the world will frown on us," says Jeremy McMorris. "We expect that. The time to be worried is when the world smiles on us. We are supposed to be strangers and pilgrims," journeying toward a "strait gate."

No one here seems weary of the fight, or oppressed by societal ridicule, or tempted to draw back. Adam Lee puts it with a fervency rarely witnessed: "Christians are supposed to have a joy when they suffer for Christ. Christ suffered for us. I don't necessarily relish it, but it's just another way of saying, 'Lord, I love you, I want to serve you, I want to stand up for you.' In the early church, people were *really* persecuted. We face nothing by comparison. People were imprisoned, forced into catacombs, set on fire, fed to lions. They would *die* for their faith. They *believed* in something *We* believe in something. We know we're different from the world, sure—but because of Christ. Because of our love for him."

Damn strange kids, these. They appear, like the Biblical Nathanael, wholly without guile. They are unfazed by materialism. They can lift their gazes above their own groins. They think, evidently, on high things. Is there room for them in this allegedly diversity-mad country of ours? Can we spare them a tile in our "gorgeous mosaic"? Are they so leprous that they are unfit even to be spoken to by presidential candidates? The weird thing is this: For people who are supposed to be such haters, they are very loving, gentle. And because they stand with their chins up against the majority's scorn, they are brave.

You could say—and hardly anyone would contradict you—that Bob Jones students are the uncoolest kids in America. But that, of course, would depend on what you mean by cool.

—July 17, 2000
National Review

'Soli Deo Gloria'

Not your average music camp

I n America, of course, there's a summer camp for everything, and everyone. Vegan canoeing and computing? No problem. There's a great variety of music camps, too, from swanky ones like Tanglewood and Aspen to Bob's Bugle Bash, down by the creek. Unique among these is The MasterWorks Festival, in Winona Lake, Ind. It is a music camp for Christians, featuring Bible study and "Christian fellowship," along with normal musical activities. This is a peculiar slice of American musical life, and of American religious life, and of America itself.

You might think that this camp would be rather rinky-dink, musically— more Jim and Tammy Faye than Tanglewood. You would be wrong. Don't be embarrassed, however, because even some of the students shared this belief. David Bridges, a brass player from the Cincinnati Conservatory, says, "When I first heard about this Christian music festival, I was very skeptical. I figured it would be a bunch of nice, sweet people, singing hymns and having praise and worship." But he found, to his wonder and delight, that the place is top-notch. So do others.

MasterWorks attracts both top students and top faculty (and the two usually go together, the world over). Some of the most notable performers and teachers in the world participate in the camp, "outing" themselves as earnest Christians, in a way, and giving young people examples to follow. Letting them know that they're not alone. Midori, the violinist (just one name, please), has been there. Christopher Parkening, the guitarist, is a favorite. And then you have John Nelson, the conductor, Philip Smith, principal trumpet for the New York Philharmonic, and Lawrence Dutton, violist for the Emerson String Quartet. The conductor Jahja Ling has visited there, testifying about the Christian experience in China (as well as leading the orchestra). Stephen Clapp, dean of the Juilliard School—a mighty secular position—teaches there. Other faculty come from most of the major orchestras and conservatories in the country, and also from such institutions as the American Ballet Theater (MasterWorks branches beyond music, into dance and drama).

All involved seem to have a sense of being at home, of completeness. As Delta David Gier, assistant conductor for the New York Philharmonic, puts it, "The fusion of our two great concerns, music and faith, finds full expression [at the camp]." More than one camper speaks of not being "on the fringe," but in a central place, among the like-minded. Rebekah Bayles, a theater student from Virginia, says, "The people around me are so open and free—I don't feel like I have to be anything other than what I am. No one is looking at me with judgmental eyes." Over and over, campers give some variation of, "I wasn't quite sure that real musicians could be real Christians, or that real Christians could be true musicians. But now I see it all around me."

Patrick Kavanaugh is the camp's director, and well familiar with this phenomenon. "Imagine," he says, "that you're a high-school violinist [of the religious, churchy sort]. You have two lives. You have your church friends—who don't know a thing about music, couldn't care less about it, and may look with suspicion on it—and you have your youth-orchestra friends, who couldn't care less about your religion, unless they think it's kooky or weird. But here, the two sides come together, mingling, integrated." Besides which, our violinist may share a stand in the orchestra with a member of, say, the Boston Symphony—and that violinist leaves the camp newly fortified about the future.

A MUSICAL MINISTRY

The MasterWorks Festival is an offshoot of the Christian Performing Artists' Fellowship, or CPAF. If that sounds like the Fellowship of Christian Athletes, it is. Kavanaugh—who is also head of CPAF—says, "We're very similar, and good friends. We follow an amazingly similar strategy." Kavanaugh, his wife Barbara (a cellist), and some of their friends founded CPAF in 1984, intending it as a "ministry" to the performing-arts world, which they thought was sorely in need of it. They started small, finding members and helpers through word-of-mouth, and have grown considerably. CPAF now has over 1,000 members, with chapters in about 50 music schools, 30 orchestras, and various opera companies and other outfits. Members belong to some 50 different denominations. "Recruiting" consists essentially of tacking a sheet on a bulletin board—if the relevant institution will permit it—saying, "Christian fellowship, Tuesday at 4. Y'all come."

And, in perhaps surprising numbers, they do. People seeking this kind of activity and company come out of the woodwork. CPAF may not be well known to the world at large, but, as Kavanaugh says—not boastfully—"If you're a classical musician and you're a Christian, you know about us."

Christians of the CPAF sort are far from a majority in the performing arts—that's part of why they want to join. But they wouldn't fit into a phone booth either. In fact, they could get up a pretty good orchestra, opera company, dance troupe, camp—and they do.

The presiding spirit of The MasterWorks Festival is Kavanaugh himself, an amazing piece of work. Nashville-born, and a composer, conductor, and musicologist, he's part good ol' boy, part musical intellectual, and part impresario. He studied composition with, among others, John Cage, "in the Village" (that would be Greenwich). Often, he composes in microtones, a practice not typically associated with the evangelical-Christian world, somehow. ("There are countless microtones within conventional tones." But how can the average person possibly hear them? "Ah, come on, we are fearfully and wonderfully made!") Much of the world would identify him with the dreaded Religious Right—and yet he is an audaciously radical composer. In fact, he has the usual gripes of the contemporary composer: that the concert world is too conservative, that it ignores difficult and pioneering music, etc. He catches some flak from the "Christian music" crowd, too. Once, he penned an article for a magazine entitled, "Does Godliness Equal Tonality?"

Confronted with the idea that he's a rather unusual Joe, he says, "Yeah, but you know, I feel like Ozzie Nelson. I don't feel interesting at all. Don't watch porno, don't cheat on my wife. I like to stay at home, write wacky music." True, though, "we don't just sit around and pop popcorn and go to church socials." Kavanaugh himself has two sets of friends, who have little to do with each other: "Got my church friends, and then these nutty Village people who come to hear my music. 'What in the world?' they say. 'Is that guy still readin' the Bible?'"

Kavanaugh is the author of seven books, including a best-seller, *The Spiritual Lives of the Great Composers*. He explains that most musical biographies "don't even mention the very strong and consequential faith that a lot of these guys had. I mean, there was one biography of Bach that never mentioned his faith. I mean, Bach? Some are more obvious than others, but that's absurd."

IN SUNDAY COUNTRY

The MasterWorks Festival began just five years ago, in 1997. From '97 through '01, it was in central New York, at Houghton College. This year, it moved to Indiana, to Winona Lake, on the campus of Grace College. The town is best known as the home of Billy Sunday, the old ballplayer-turned-evangelist. It's about an hour from Fort Wayne, an hour from South Bend, and about an hour and a half from Chicago, "the town that Billy Sunday could not shut down" (as the song says).

MasterWorks is, in many respects, an ordinary music camp, with concerto competitions, arduous practice, and general musical inundation. It also has elements of a "normal" camp—a camp camp—such as bonfires on the beach, s'mores, and even a Gong Show (an occasion of high hilarity). But it is clearly apart. You see a license plate that says "SELAH." You see students in clusters, with Bibles open. And you see a lot of prayer—hear it, too. MasterWorkers pray before each concert, and before each rehearsal, and before each audition (when it is most appreciated, according to the campers). They'll pray at the drop of a hat. "Sometimes when we're frazzled in rehearsal," says Kavanaugh, "we'll just stop everything and pray, till we get it back together." And when they're not praying, they're "fellowshipping," which is a verb at MasterWorks: "Y'all, if you're going to fellowship, fellowship outside, please, because we're trying to rehearse here!"

Students obviously appreciate the bonds that form. Pat Kavanaugh likes to relate that, in only five years, two marriages have come out of the camp. (Students range from age 14 to about 26; most are in college.) Throughout the year, campers chatter back and forth on e-mail lists. They have come from 49 states—there's yet to be a Hawaiian—and from about 25 countries. As in most musical settings, there is a multiplicity of colors, ethnicities, and accents. Kavanaugh mentions something touching, a little startling, about those from the former Soviet bloc: They're especially eager to eat—even the (unspectacular) cafeteria food.

These kids—and faculty—come from a variety of "faith traditions," too. There are Methodists, Lutherans, Presbyterians, Episcopalians, Baptists, Catholics, Russian Orthodox. Kavanaugh says, merrily, "We got wild charismatics, we got guys from Bible church who think that the charismatics are crazy—it's fun, it's a blast." In addition, "kids meet people from all over Christendom, and they find out that those from other churches aren't ogres after all. That's one of the best byproducts of the whole thing." There are no prescribed prayers, either. "When we come together to pray, it's amazing. You got stately Methodist prayers, with 'thee's and 'thou's, and you got charismatics, calling down fire on the place, then some other guy from a Bible church will start prophesying." The director is very strict about one thing: no sectarian bickering. "I don't care whether you were sprinkled or dunked. I don't have time for such nonsense. There's tremendous work to be done—people are hurting out there."

To teach at MasterWorks, there is a single criterion (beyond the musical): that one be "a believer." (There's no such requirement for students—only the audition.) Otherwise, matters both artistic and religious are left to individual conscience. Says Kavanaugh, "We got one guy [in the theater department] who won't kiss anyone but his wife, and we got another guy, who loves the Lord—not to mention his wife—just as much, who will." No work—no opera, for example—is Bowdlerized. The wicked stage is still the wicked stage. There are limits, of course. The English National Opera recently put on a *Don Giovanni* that was described by one critic as a "coke-fueled fellatio fest." That, you won't see in Winona Lake (or most anywhere else). But sensibilities aren't dainty.

Many campers say that they're working against two tugs: from their church, saying, "This world is not for you"; and from the arts world, saying . . . well, "This world is not for the likes of you." Amadeus Gois, a baritone from Brazil, says—about opera in particular—"It's good to know that so many Christians are involved. And they're normal opera singers! We have people from the Metropolitan Opera and other big houses. It's reassuring."

A JOYFUL NOISE

A staple of the camp is the daily Bible study, from a program devised by Kavanaugh and a colleague. As their syllabus says, "This is not a typical Bible study" to be found at the local church. "As Paul strove to be 'Jew to the Jew, and Greek to the Greek,' the MasterClass [as the Bible program is called] strives to address issues high in the minds of our students." The study program patterns the sonata form: exposition, development, and recapitulation. Topics include "Being faithful with your talent," "Nervousness in performing," "Egomania vs. humility," "Handling criticism and critics," "Competitiveness," and "Is your art your god?"

And the students seem to eat it up. They appear to be not only happy at the camp, but relieved. Aeja Killworth, a violist from the Peabody Conservatory, says, "We're all taking pleasure in each other's talent. To take joy in someone else's ability—that helps you to be less jealous, less focused on yourself. You serve God, and you serve others. And our world, usually, is so dog-eat-dog." Chris Frankie, a violinist about to enter the Cleveland Institute, says, "With this kind of atmosphere, everything's ultimately more fun. You're not feeling put down, you're feeling lifted up. We're here to make music, not to dust someone else."

And yet, of course, some element of competition is ever present, this being music, and life. Standards at MasterWorks rise every year. Some campers who attended in previous summers, are not accepted now. And of performers and teachers, many more want to take part than there is room for. Kavanaugh can afford to be picky.

Funds, naturally, are a constant worry. Most of the campers are on scholarship. The foreign students couldn't afford to get out of their home airports. MasterWorks, like its parent, CPAF, survives on individual donations and the support of a handful of foundations. Kavanaugh is in a precarious position: "Government won't touch us, of course, and the arts won't touch us, because we're Christians." But fellow Christians are wary, too. They might ask, "Why aren't you in India or something? Why mess around with the performing arts?" But this, insists Kavanaugh, is "a huge mission field."

Before he's through, he hopes to have established a total of seven MasterWorks Festivals, all over the world. The next one—for which the planning is nearly complete—will be in England. MasterWorks takes for its motto, "Soli Deo Gloria," or, "To God alone be the glory." Bach used to mark his manuscripts this way (using the initials S.D.G.); he carved the saying into his organ at Leipzig. Christopher Parkening relates that he keeps a note on his music stand. It says, "Chris, what are you here for?" For what purpose do you make music? This is the question they ask in Winona Lake, and elsewhere, and, by all evidence, they rejoice in the answer.

—September 2, 2002
National Review

'Bang'

Guns, rap, and silence

A lot of people were interested in the Sean "Puffy" Combs trial: fans of rap music; celebrity-watchers; connoisseurs of popular culture. But one group of people showed no interest whatsoever: gun-control activists. This was rather strange—a dog that didn't bark. The Combs case was awash in guns; so is Combs's world—that of rap, or "hip-hop." But the gun-controllers prefer to ignore this dark corner. Their indifference, or passivity, may be taken to represent a broader failure of liberalism to confront ghetto culture—to look it in the eye and cry, "No!"

Combs—known as "Puff Daddy"—is a major figure in rap, the boss of a record label called "Bad Boy." (Another label is called "Murder, Inc."—one refreshing thing about the rappers is their lack of pretense.) The Combs case dominated New York at the beginning of this year, the trial of a century that is still very young. What happened is this: In December 1999, Combs visited a nightclub with his girlfriend (the pop star Jennifer Lopez), a few "associates," and several of his guns. Someone insulted Combs. Shooting broke out. Three people were injured, two of them badly. Then Combs and his group fled the scene. When the police finally caught up with the getaway car—or rather, the getaway Lincoln Navigator SUV—they found two guns. Combs was subsequently charged with illegal weapons possession and bribery (he had tried to get his driver to accept responsibility for the guns). The rapper's guilt seemed clear, but he denied everything.

In a now–de rigueur move, Combs hired Johnnie Cochran, the O.J. lawyer, who composed a few new rhymes and flashed his smile at the jury. Combs got off. One of those "associates," however, was not so lucky: Jamal "Shyne" Barrow—a rapper described as Combs's protégé—was found guilty of first-degree assault. He now faces 25 years in prison.

So, another day, another rap case—this time, no one died. It's easy to look away from rap and its nature. But it should not be so, and it certainly shouldn't be so for gun-controllers. Thug rappers should be their worst nightmare (and a lot of other people's). Yet the anti-gun activists would rather go after Charlton Heston, rednecks, and other soft targets. It's far more comfortable to torment the NRA, which advocates not only gun rights but gun safety, than to get in the faces of "gangsta" rappers, who glory in guns and gun violence in song after song after song. Most people, by now, are familiar with rap's hideous and constant degradation of women (where are the feminists, incidentally?). They are less familiar with rap's celebration of the gun. Back in 1992, there was a brief furor over a rap called "Cop Killer." The idea of gunning down policemen is certainly an attention-getter. But if rappers are enthusing only about killing one another, that seems to be another matter, something to be swept under the rug.

Liberals have occasionally been interested in this subject. Tipper and Al Gore were, before Hollywood bit their heads off. Usually, though, when you try to interest liberals in the horrors of today's worst music, they roll their eyes and recall how their parents railed against "Elvis's pelvis." Ah, the two magic words: "Elvis's pelvis." Say them, and you shut down any discussion about, for example, rap's effects on the young. And doesn't every generation murmur, with a sigh and a shake of the head, "Kids today . . ."? But any sensate being can see that "gangsta" rap—with its sanction, even urging, of rape, murder, and other abuse—has nothing at all in common with Elvis Presley's swaying hips. It must be, in part, a fear of uncoolness—of fogeydom—that keeps many people from coming to grips with rap. They are perfectly happy to claim that the sight of Joe Camel causes millions of young'uns to smoke cigarettes; but they are reluctant to consider what rap—poured constantly into young ears—might do.

THE OBJECT OF THEIR AFFECTIONS

Rappers sing of guns with almost lascivious glee. They express close to an erotic feeling about their "pieces": "glocks" (for the Austrian manufacturer), "gats" (short for Gatlings), "nines" or "ninas" (for 9-mm pistols), and so on in a long and chilling lexicon. Bullets and clips are lingered over as eyes and lips might be in love songs. Here's a sample from "Trigga Gots No Heart" by the rapper Spice 1: "Caps [bullets] peel from gangsters in my 'hood. You better use that nina 'cause that deuce-deuce [.22-caliber weapon] ain't no good, and I'm taking up a hobby, maniac murderin', doin' massacre robbery." There is no end of material like this. The rapper Notorious B.I.G., slain by gun in 1997, sang, "Somebody's gotta die. Let the gunshots blow. Somebody's gotta die. Nobody gotta know that I killed yo' a** in the midst, kid." And, "Don't fill them clips too high. Give them bullets room to breathe. Damn, where was I?" Dr. Dre had a hit called "Rat-Tat-Tat-Tat," whose refrain went, "Never hesitate to put a nigga on his back. Rat-tat-tat-tat to the tat like that, and I never hesitate to put a nigga on his back."

During the Combs trial, some thought that Shyne Barrow's lyrics would do the young man no good. They are horrible, but since millions of kids drink them in, their parents might as well know them, too. In "Bad Boyz," Barrow raps, "Now tell me, who wanna f*** with us? Ashes to ashes, dust to dust. I bang—and let your f***in' brains hang . . . My point is double-fours [a .44 magnum] at your f***in' jaws, pointed hollow point sh** [this is bullet terminology], four point six [?], need I say more? Or do you get the point, b**ch?" In another track—"Bang"—he says, "Niggas wanna bang. We could bang out till the clip's done, or your vital arteries hang out." And: "Got my mind right, like Al Pacino and Nino. I head to Capitol Hill to kidnap Janet Reno. Words droppin' and shockin', guns cockin' and poppin', somebody call Cochran" (that would be the lawyer Johnnie—life imitating art, or is it the other way around?). Barrow continues, "No time to waste, nine in my waist, ready for war, any time, any place. F*** it, just another case."

Are these words meant to be taken seriously, or are they just play—disturbing, maybe, but basically harmless? Shyne Barrow did, indeed, have a "nine in his waist" at that nightclub, and it appears to have been luck that he didn't kill the people he hit. Moral relativism, however, is rife in discussion about rap (such as it is). Barrow's lawyer, Murray Richman, made the following, delicious comment to the *New York Post* last December: "Dostoyevsky wrote about murder—does that implicate him as a murderer?" Or "when Eartha Kitt salaciously sings 'Santa, Baby,' does that mean she really wants to sleep with Santa Claus?" This sort of statement is meant to be a conversation-stopper, like "Elvis's pelvis." You know: Dostoyevsky, Eartha Kitt, Shyne Barrow—artists all, and liable to be misunderstood by the conservative and hung-up. "Kids today . . ."—ha ha.

Now, gun-control groups are concerned—and why shouldn't they be?—with laws and loopholes and gun shows and accidents in homes and Charlton Heston and, of course, school shootings, out of which they make hay. They say nothing about hip-hop culture, and next to nothing about popular culture generally. The groups put out a steady stream of press releases: praising states' "safety initiatives," trying to shame manufacturers, worrying about "children's health." In fact, they seem to burrow into every nook and cranny of American life—but keep mum about the ghetto and its anthems.

Nancy Hwa is spokesman for Handgun Control, Inc. (the Jim and Sarah Brady group). She says that her organization has "called on people in the creative industry not to glamorize guns," but has not dealt with hip-hop in particular. "Other targets have a more direct relationship with getting your hands on guns," she says—for example, "sales at gun shows." And no one group, she sensibly points out, can cover everything. Plus, "when it comes right down to it, you can listen to rap or Marilyn Manson or country music, and, in the end, as long as the young person can't get their hands on a gun, all they're guilty of is questionable taste in music." For Handgun Control, Inc., the issue is "access," plain and simple.

Ted Pascoe speaks for Do It for the Kids!, a gun-control group in Colorado. "We don't address it," he says of the rap issue. "We have enough trouble with the Second Amendment without attacking the First as well." Meaning? "Well, there is a perception in this country that individuals enjoy the protections conferred by the Second Amendment. But that amendment only confers on states the right to maintain militias. So the individual has no standing in court to make Second Amendment claims. However, Americans tend to believe they do have the right to bear arms. So, it's troublesome, because whenever you start talking about passing stronger gun laws, a lot of folks—even if they're not involved in the issue, or vested in it—can invoke the Second Amendment and sometimes effectively take the wind out of your sails." A stance against rap, says Pascoe, would only bring trouble: "The large number of gun-control groups don't want to be seen as attacking every element in the Constitution, or more than one. I think that the First Amendment contains rights that we *do* enjoy—that individuals have First Amendment rights."

The confusion of rights and responsibilities—of "what you got a right to do and what is right to do," as the supreme fogey Bill Bennett puts it—is an old one.

Andy Pelosi, who represents New Yorkers Against Gun Violence, says that his group "really focuses on legislative issues—we've done a little bit of violence in the media, but not rap. " He makes the point that "it would be unfair to look at one genre without looking at the others. You could make a case about heavy metal, alternative rock—you wouldn't want to single out just rap." This would, indeed, be a painful step for most liberals. It would involve a clash of their pieties: gun control—outright demonization of the gun—and a taboo against taking issue with black culture in any of its aspects. The old "No enemies to the left" might mingle with a new slogan: "No enemies among blacks" (with Clarence Thomas and the other Toms excepted, of course).

'SILENCE KILLS'
The country is engaged in a great debate over gun control; but there should be no disagreement about the awfulness—why not go all the way? the evil—of the most violent, dehumanizing, and desensitizing rap. The inner city is bleeding from gun crime. White America should probably think harder about the perpetual Columbines taking place in ghettos. Of course, many excuse rap on grounds that it merely reflects life on the mean streets. And whether this stuff has bloody consequences is an open question. In 1993, a rapper called Masta Ace, talking to the *St. Petersburg Times*, said, "It's like a Schwarzenegger movie—you don't come out wanting to shoot anybody." But he quickly had a second thought: "I think it does shape mentalities and helps develop a callousness to where you could really shoot somebody and not think twice about it."

Sure: There's only so much a gun-control group or conservative alarm-raisers or anyone else can do about (what might be termed) hate rap. But activists, who love to talk—it is their principal activity—might at least talk.

A group called the Campus Alliance to End Gun Violence proclaims as its number-one position, "Gun violence disproportionately preys on the young. Silence kills. We must speak." Well, all right: Minus a right-wing militia or two, there is only one class of people—an extremely wealthy and popular class of people—that actually *exalts* gun violence. So . . . ?

—April 16, 2001
National Review

Hand It to Them

Rediscovering American Scripture

This piece caused many requests to borrow my copy of the National Education Association's citizen handbook (granted), and many inquiries into publishing the book again. To my knowledge, it was never republished. Still a good idea, however.

L ooking idly at my bookcase the other day, I fixed on a volume I had never noticed before: *The American Citizens Handbook*. It had come to me, I realized, from an old friend who was moving and unloading some books. It had sat on my shelf, ignored, for years. As I fingered this book, it seemed a relic from a distant, and glowing, past. What's more, it was the product of—could this be true?—the National Education Association. Coming to know this book made me practically weep for a liberalism that has been lost, and an Americanism, too.

I did some poking around, and soon learned that I was not the first "conservative" (as descendants of Jefferson are now forced to call themselves) to take an interest in the *Handbook*. Michael Farris, the home-schooling leader in Virginia, discovered it in the mid-1980s. Then the education secretary, William Bennett, used it in a speech. He challenged the NEA to reissue the book, or, if it would not, to permit others to do so. The association responded flummoxed and embarrassed. One spokesman explained, "The world has changed a lot" (ah, and so has the NEA). Another sniffed, "We've got lots of other books if [Bennett] wants to pay for them."

Some years later, Lamar Alexander, running for president, mentioned the *Handbook* as a "virtual user's guide to America." Mike Farris tells me that he once met the man hired by the NEA to destroy the final 10,000 copies of the book. Had he been asked to burn them? asked Farris. That would be too good to be true—and it was. The man had buried them.

The NEA should hardly be embarrassed by this volume; it may be the highest service it has ever performed. The book first appeared in 1941, to coincide with National Citizenship Day (September 17). It went through six editions, of which I have the last, published in 1968.

The book was the project of Joy Elmer Morgan, a Nebraska-born educator and writer who lived from 1889 to 1974. For several decades, he was editor of the NEA's *Journal*. (I should affirm here that Joy Elmer Morgan was, indeed, a man. When I was quite young, I knew an old man named Shirley, who one day confided to me, "Everything was fine in my life till that darn Shirley Temple came along.") Morgan's name is seldom mentioned today, although he is reviled in certain right-wing publications as a proponent of world government and all-around threat. If Morgan could stand as the "Left," however, conservatives would dance in the streets.

The *Handbook* is a great treasury. It was originally intended to prepare young citizens for their responsibilities as voters, and as adults generally. It is a compilation of just about everything that is significant and outstanding about the United States. The work is serious, earnest, heartfelt. It is, as the NEA noted in the 1968 edition, both "inspirational and informative." It is, of course, patriotic, but in the most thoughtful way. There is nothing blinkered or rah-rah about it. The book might appear to the contemporary reader quaint—something on the order of a girl's memory album, circa 1909—but, as I absorbed its pages, I was startled by the power it carried. It puts forth an American creed, although this creed is a big and generous one, waiting to be embraced by anyone, or rejected by anyone—including the NEA.

At the end of his introduction, Morgan exhorts: "Read this book carefully; study the documents on which your rights as a citizen are based; memorize its songs and poetry." A body could do worse.

The opening essay, as well, belongs to Morgan: "Your Citizenship in the Making." Its most striking quality, along with wisdom, is gratitude: "It is a high privilege to be a citizen of the United States. There are those in less fortunate circumstances who would gladly give all they possess for the mere chance to come here to live." That is a bracing statement, and an obviously true one. Try out a couple more of Morgan's bracing, obviously true statements:

> Democracy can find its fullest expression in the roots of religion,
> which has ever emphasized the Fatherhood of God and the
> Brotherhood of Man. For democracy to reach its highest fruition,
> our society must include that larger liberty and justice preached so
> eloquently by the Hebrew Prophets and by Jesus.

> No one would contend that the Constitution is a perfect docu-
> ment. The very men who framed it were conscious of its short-
> comings. . . . We have our difficulties agreeing among ourselves
> as to what we want the Constitution to be and how we want it to
> be interpreted or administered. But these are small matters as
> compared with the great fact of the Constitution itself, standing
> between us and chaos, between us and a return to the brutalities
> and confusion of earlier centuries.

Talk like that can, today, get you laughed out of school—quite literally.

The next section of the *Handbook* lays out the "Characteristics of the
Good Democratic Citizen." (A lot of these titles cannot help provoking
present-day giggles, which is part of our problem.) In 1949, a branch of the
Defense Department asked a branch of the NEA to come up with a description of the "good democratic citizen." A committee was duly formed, and a
document resulted, listing 24 characteristics, with subsets for each. What is
most remarkable about them is the balance they achieve. They are a beautiful melding of the "liberal" and the "conservative." For example, under
"Respects and upholds the law and its agencies," we have, "[The good
democratic citizen] respects and supports officers who enforce the law, but
does not permit his zeal for law enforcement to encourage officials to
infringe upon guaranteed civil rights." (We also read, "understands what perjury means and testifies honestly"—ahem.) On the international front, we
have, "Knows about, critically evaluates, and supports promising efforts to
prevent war, but stands ready to defend his country against tyranny and
aggression."

Several of these characteristics, the NEA would choke to enunciate
today. "Since the people are intelligent enough to govern themselves, they
do not need protection by censorship"—this would appear to preclude campus speech codes. Furthermore, that good democratic citizen "rejects all
group claims to special privilege"—bad news for affirmative action. And get
a load of this one: Under "Puts the general welfare above his own whenever a choice between them is necessary," we read, "avoids the abuse of pub-

lic benefits (e.g., the misuse of unemployment compensation by a process of malingering)." This is truly a foreign language.

This section, like the *Handbook* itself, is hardly naïve or unrealistic. The effect of the whole is not at all treacly or goody-goody. Yet it is a strong antidote to cynicism and the suffocating cloak of irony: Our good democratic citizen "is critically aware of differences between democratic ideals and accomplishments, but works to improve accomplishments and refuses to become cynical about the differences."

An essay by Henry Steele Commager comes as a hell of a jolt. If anyone represents the old liberalism—the liberalism of this volume—it is Commager. The gulf between him and, say, Eric Foner today is enormous. Of course, Professor Foner is no liberal; we simply have to call him that, in accordance with a foolish and misleading political taxonomy. (Angela Davis, the Communist Party official, is often described in the press as a liberal, as we Right-types have long liked to note.) In "Our Schools Have Kept Us Free" (another of those titles), Commager makes a stirring case for common education, and in particular for its assimilative power. "How, after all, [are] millions of newcomers to become 'Americans'—in language, in ways of life and thought, in citizenship?" The common school, he writes, has served "the cause of American democracy." The truth is,

> this most heterogeneous of modern societies—profoundly varied in racial background, religious faith, social and economic interest—has ever seemed the most easy prey to forces of riotous privilege and ruinous division. These forces have not prevailed; they have been routed, above all, in the schoolrooms and on the playgrounds of America.

Commager wrote these words in 1950. And how are the "forces of riotous privilege and ruinous division" faring now? Pretty well, huh? This is what compels us "conservatives" to retreat to school choice and let-a-thousand-flowers-bloom, the common school, which bound the country together, having crumbled, not least because of the illiberal urgings and practices of the NEA.

The *Handbook* is stocked with key documents (the Magna Carta, the Gettysburg Address), portraits, mini-bios, aphorisms, telling facts, assorted tidbits. Its second half is dominated by the "Golden Treasury" (sigh, snort), which is an anthology of literary and other items with which civilized people should be acquainted. It begins with the Bible, moves on to Buddha,

Confucius, Mohammed, et al., and continues in a glorious potpourri, a store-house of pluralism and diversity (a good word stolen and perverted by a race-obsessed New Left). We have in this book the evidence of a nation, and a civilization. Here, the bond holds firm; the salt retains its savour.

But who will taste? America is a young country, as everyone says, but we seem to have lost so quickly our . . . our nationhood. Our cultural and spiritual nationhood. This handbook was last published in 1968, but it might as well be an archeological find, a dusty curiosity. An NEA statement produced in the book—"Education for All American Youth"—seems almost reactionary today. Why? How did what was liberal become "conservative" (or worse) so fast? How did it happen that "liberals," in the late 1990s, rallied around—with pulsing passion—a president who had a) used a 21-year-old intern for sex, b) perjured himself in court proceedings, c) abused his office, d) tampered with witnesses, e) cheated, lied, defamed, f)—but that is another rant (though a clearly related one). The good liberal fashioners of *The American Citizens Handbook* could never have been Clintonites.

This little book—or not so little: over 600 pages—undeniably did something to me, and for me: It stirred what some guy once called "mystic chords of memory." It would do the same for others. And if that memory were totally absent, the book would install it.

I tell you, I will never give up my copy—I would fear not finding another. I would like to share it with children. While reading it, I refrained even from making notes in it, unwilling to deface it. It is sick, though—positively sick—that I should feel this way. That I should feel that I possess something rare and talismanic, something quasi-forbidden, almost underground. This stuff should be as common as water—and it was. It should be again. It could be again, if people wanted it, demanded it. All those volumes that lie a-molderin' in their grave: We should dig 'em up.

—May 14, 2001
National Review

Bassackwards

Construction Spanish and
other signs of the times

America, of course, has always been a place of many languages, along with our common tongue, English. German, its cousin Yiddish, Chinese, Italian, Polish—they have all been spoken here, especially in homes and community centers. But Spanish in today's America is something else: a language coddled, bowed to, enshrined.

We could talk about "bilingual education," which too often turns out to be monolingual education, and in the wrong tongue. We could talk about Spanish-language election ballots. We could talk about "For English, press 1. *Para español, oprima el dos*." But let's talk, instead, about Construction Spanish.

Classes in—shall we call it "Con. Span."?—have sprouted up all over America. These are classes designed to teach contractors, supervisors, and other bosses in the construction business how to speak to their Hispanic workers. The bosses aren't learning Spanish, exactly; they will not be reading *Don Quixote*. This is a specialized language: *casco* for hard hat; *montacarga* for forklift; *pistola de clavos* for nail gun.

But wouldn't it be better, for all concerned, if the workers learned "hard hat," "forklift," and "nail gun"? We must put off such foolish questions, for the moment.

Construction Spanish is an example of what has been called "Survival Spanish," or "Command Spanish"—bits of Spanish acquired for a specific purpose. You can get trained in Restaurant Spanish, Fireman Spanish, or Health Care Spanish. And this last Spanish has sub-branches, such as Dental Spanish and Physical Therapy Spanish. Also, you can buy books and tapes that tell you how to converse with your gardener or maid, if that is your need.

But Construction Spanish has loomed especially large lately, for an obvious reason: the predominance of Hispanics in that field. Go into a Lowe's or Home Depot—stores that sell building materials—and you will see signs in Spanish (quite naturally). And you can buy any number of glossaries or handbooks. My favorite is *Spanish on the Job*, for its ad copy:

> No previous knowledge of Spanish is necessary. All words are phonetically spelled out to assure correct pronunciation. Trust me, yelling in English isn't going to help.

Let me yell, just a little bit. The old deal was, you came to America and you assimilated into the culture. You presumably wanted to, otherwise you wouldn't have immigrated. You retained your mother tongue, of course, and you figured your children would know it, and you hoped your grandchildren would be interested (although that was no guarantee). But you were in America, and America included English. Hooray!

And what of now? Forgetting an immigrant mindset, what is the general American mindset? An article published in the *Washington Post* a few years ago shed some light. It concerned a Northern Virginia county, Fairfax, which had trained 450 of its employees in Spanish. A Fairfax official explained, "As we saw the changing demographics of the county, we said, 'How are we responding to the needs of new residents of the county?'" Not by encouraging their assimilation, that's for sure.

Hispanic immigrants had joined the sanitation department, so an assistant superintendent there took Spanish for Garbage Workers. (Really.) He said, "In our type of business, it's something we're gonna have to learn." It was not too long ago that immigrants thought English was something *they* had to learn. They did not expect their employers or supervisors to take Survival Polish or Survival Serbian; they saw to it that they acquired some Survival English.

The *Post*'s reporter found one person, a middle-aged "supervisor on building projects in downtown Washington," who was not too happy about the new order. He acknowledged to the reporter that he wished his workers would simply learn English. But they were not—so he enrolled in Construction Spanish. "I'm not saying I like what's happening," he said. "But I figure I can't fight it."

Which is a near-perfect expression of cultural defeatism.

There is always a tug between the pragmatic and the idealistic, or the short term and the long term. You want assimilation and acculturation; but you also want to do business in the here and now, in whatever language. You want to be considerate of the immigrant, who has enough challenges, without a new language; but you are not pleased to see him trapped in a linguistic ghetto—barrio-ization, some people have called it.

I consider myself a veteran of the Spanish wars, although I participated in the most minor of ways. Years ago, I was working at a firm in Washington, D.C. We were told that, when we wanted boxes thrown away, we had to mark them "BASURA." *Basura* is the Spanish word for trash. And all of our janitors were Hispanic.

Everything in my traditional-American soul rebelled at writing "BASURA," thinking it a gross act of separatism, and probably an insult to the workers. "Why don't we write 'TRASH'?" I asked. "We're in America, and we don't want anyone walled off. We want them to join the American family. How will they ever rise in our society if they don't learn English? In Guatemala, we would write 'BASURA.' But here we write 'TRASH.'"

That didn't go over terribly well, and I made no headway. But I took to writing "BASURA/TRASH" on my boxes to be thrown out. That was my pathetic little stand: a word, a slash, and another word. But I liked it.

A while back, I wrote about this experience in a *National Review Online* column, and the subject provoked a ton of mail. I seemed to have touched some national nerve. Many Hispanics wrote of their frustration and resentment at having been shunted into Spanish-only classes, or "bilingual" classes that were the usual Spanish-preservation rackets. And a former manager of custodial crews in Phoenix wrote the following:

> I once spent a few months trying to convince people in the corporate offices of a major insurance company that my employees didn't need orders in Spanish. They may have been willing to do menial labor, but that didn't mean that they were stupid, and it was condescending to think they couldn't learn a simple five-letter word in the English language.

Namely, "trash."

Another correspondent added a twist, saying, "Here in Chicago, the big offices distribute stickers to be placed on garbage items. They read, 'GARBAGE/BASURA/SMIECI,'" laying it out in English, Spanish, and Polish.

Still another reader contributed this:

> An acquaintance once told me that, years ago, when he was preparing for a job that involved supervising an office cleaning crew, the guy he was replacing suggested that he come in a half-hour early each day of the fol-

lowing week so he could learn enough Spanish to deal with the crew. The new guy replied: "I've got a better idea: Why don't you have them come in a half-hour early each day to learn enough English to deal with me?"

A stirring protest against the backasswardness of contemporary American life.

At that Washington firm, a young janitor and I became friends, and I learned that he had no dictionary: no English-Spanish, Spanish-English dictionary. I got him one. That night, he left me a note that contained one word: "Grasias." Mainly because of the misspelling, I'm sure, it was one of the most touching notes I have ever received.

Yet I am under no illusion that everyone who comes to America is dying to melt into the pot. Is aching to bear out the national motto, *E pluribus unum*. Years before I worked at the Washington firm, I worked at a public golf course in Michigan, and we had many leagues, one of which was the "Korean League." I was appalled at this, mortified for those good Americans of Korean origin who played every Wednesday afternoon.

So, brimming with idealism, I said to the leader of the group, "We should call it the Korean-American League or something else, right? Because you are fellow Americans, and it's not right to call it the Korean League." He looked at me blankly and said, "No, we're Koreans." Oh.

In any case, I tried—and so should all Americans, I dare say (native and immigrant alike). Of course, when you talk as I have, in this piece, someone always accuses you of being a jingo, boob, or xenophobe. People who can't find their way to the toilet in any European capital will paint you as a foe of languages. Will say that you're "afraid of the Other."

This even happened to S. I. Hayakawa, the famed linguist and politician. He was the fellow who founded U.S. English, the lobbying group. Hayakawa liked to say, "Bilingualism for the individual is fine, but not for a country." I imagine he spoke more languages than most people have toes. Yet that did not spare him the usual accusations.

I assure the reader that I like Spanish as much as the next guy—actually, considerably more. And Con. Span., Dental Span., and all the rest of the Spans. are hardly the worst threat we face. Moreover, I trust that Americanization will sometime kick in, for the masses of newly arrived Hispanics. But if it doesn't, we will lose a lot—all of us will.

—January 29, 2007
National Review

Little Suppressors

Dealing with the bookstore clerk who hates you

This piece was written amid the controversies of the '04 presidential election campaign. But its theme, I'm afraid, is eternal . . .

Conservatives like to tell war stories—and refute them, à la the Swift Boat Vets—and some of those stories concern bookstores. And the people who work in them. Who tend to be . . . well, not exactly the most conservative-friendly people in the world. The bookstore leftist is more standard than the bookstore cat. And conservatives have often found these stores to be hostile territory.

In recent weeks, reports have circulated that customers—or would-be customers—are having a hard time finding *Unfit for Command*, John O'Neill's anti-Kerry book. Conservatives have suspected that stores are keeping it from them, or that clerks are deep-sixing them, or that something untoward is happening. Paranoia is in the air.

But sometimes paranoids can be on to something. I don't scoff at these suspicions, mainly because of my own experience—most of it in Ann Arbor, Mich., my hometown. (Ann Arbor is a bookseller's paradise, and, in some ways, a conservative's hell.) I worked at a store called "The Little Professor." The manager there—a nice guy, actually—wouldn't put out conservative magazines and gun magazines. He flat refused to bring them to the floor, acting as censor. My brilliant (and conservative) friend Eddie Krause came up with a new name for the store: "The Little Suppressor."

It may be hard to believe, but it took something like an act of courage to buy a conservative magazine in an Ann Arbor bookstore. I used to dread it—the clerk was almost invariably cold, and he often bristled, and sometimes you got snotty remarks. It was a relief just to get through a purchase without incident. And I know many who could give the same testimony.

In truth, it could be dicey to ask for a bag—yes, a bag. That made you a despoiler of the environment, you see.

I know a journalist who lived in the Ann Arbor of the West, Berkeley. Purchasing his *National Review*s and *American Spectator*s at Moe's, he would say to the clerk, "Well, just keeping an eye on what the enemy is doing"—anything to get by. These tactics may not be brave, but, gosh, are they human.

As the Swift controversy heated up, the two bookselling giants, Borders and Barnes & Noble, were besieged by callers angry that they could not find *Unfit for Command*. Conservatives hollered, "J'accuse!" Both companies pleaded that it was the fault of the publisher, our beloved Regnery— the supplier had not printed enough copies to meet demand. Liberals, for their part, also besieged the companies, demanding that they pull the book from their shelves.

Come with me, now, to BordersUnion.org, "The Borders Books Employee Union Web Site." Herein lie some revelations—or confirmations. In notes to one another, Borders clerks have been griping about having to sell *Unfit for Command*, to the troglodytes who seek it. Although not every seeker is a trog: According to one clerk, "We did have a college professor come in looking for [the book]. She teaches a writing class and wanted to use it as an example of a 'false book.'" Or maybe she just wanted to read it and wished to avoid grief from the clerk?

But let's get to the nitty-gritty. Writes a Borders Books beauty,

> We're "finding" [note those quotation marks] that most of the few copies we're getting are damaged and need to be sent back. So sad. Too bad, Bushies! Regnery needs to be more careful. I'm hearing from people at two other stores that this seems to be common.
>
> Why should we help destroy what's left of our country?

Back for a second crack, our man exhorts,

> You guys don't actually HAVE to sell the thing! Just "carelessly" hide the boxes, "accidentally" drop them off pallets, "forget" to stock the ones you have, and then suggest a nice Al Franken or Michael Moore book as a substitute. Borders wants those recommends [sic], remember?
>
> I don't care if these Neanderthals in fancy suits get mad at me [fancy suits?]. They aren't regular customers anyway. Other

than "Left Behind" books, they don't read. Anything you can do
to make them feel unwelcome is only fair.

Another Borders beauty writes, "I wish [conservative customers] really knew how little respect I have for them." Oh, we know, babe—we know.

Not long ago, readers of *National Review Online* sent in to me their experiences of trying to buy *Unfit*, and of dealing with bookstore clerks in general. Care for a (very) small sampling of their observations?

In Littleton, Colo., a Borders clerk told a customer that the store manager had decided not to stock *Unfit for Command*—it was "not in the best interests of the store." (The manager was a Kerry supporter, the clerk allowed.) At a Barnes & Noble in Cherry Hill, N.J., a clerk told a customer that the publisher had "recalled" the book, owing to "errors." The customer doubted it and said so. The woman merely shrugged. Elsewhere, a clerk refused to give a customer the advertised discount. Why? "That book is full of lies."

NRO readers from all over the country report that *Unfit for Command* and other conservative books tend to be in some bookstore Siberia, while bouquets of anti-Bush books are front and center. (Some clerks at BordersUnion.org have gloated about this.) As for the rude treatment—that's par for the course.

"After 9/11, my wife went to a Borders to get the Barbara Olson book *The Final Days*, and was told by the clerk what a 'disgusting book' it was. This was just before the clerk admitted that she hadn't actually read the book." Reports another reader, "My sister went to buy *The Anti-Chomsky Reader* for my birthday, and the clerk went on and on about how great Chomsky was. My sister stopped him by saying, 'Please: I get enough of his views from my teacher.'" Everyone's got a tale, or eight.

How low will they go, our friends the clerks? Well, one conservative was surprised that his mom got him a copy of *Rush Limbaugh Is a Big Fat Idiot* for Christmas. (That is an Al Franken book.) It turned out that Mom had gone to the store looking for the latest Limbaugh book, as her son adores him. And the clerk had explained to her that the Franken book was infinitely better, and would be more appreciated than the Limbaugh book—which was really bad. "So my mom, who was in her late 70s at the time and has never paid much attention to politics, got me Franken's book instead." Asks our reader, at the end of his letter, "Who would be so horrible as to take advantage of a little old lady buying a Christmas present for her son?"

I think we know.

With the rise of the Internet, and Internet ordering, all of this unpleas-
antness could be a thing of the past. We can merely click, rather than brave
little suppressors. (Actually, it's not their suppression that's so bad—it's
their commentary.) But should we have to deal with them again, may we
summon the spirit of this guy:

> A while back, I paid a visit to our local bookstore (I live in south-
> ern New Jersey) with the intent of perusing the new release
> *Michael Moore Is a Big Fat Stupid White Man* [these titles are
> getting out of hand]. I looked on the new-release, bestseller, and
> new non-fiction racks—nothing. I wandered around for a while
> and then headed up to the information desk. The clerk, [unflat-
> tering description of looks goes here], smiles at me. Here's a fair-
> ly accurate transcript:
>
> CLERK. How may I help you?
> ME. I'm looking for *Michael Moore Is a Big Fat Stupid White
> Man*.
> CLERK (still smiling). You mean *Stupid White Men* by Michael
> Moore . . .
> ME. No. *Michael Moore Is a Big Fat Stupid White Man*. It's a
> new release.
> CLERK. We don't have it.
> ME. Are you sure? It's very popular.
> CLERK (tight-lipped). Never heard of it. (Looks past me.) Can I
> help the next person, please?
> ME. Excuse me, but can you check on your computer?
> CLERK (very annoyed). Fine. (Bangs away at the keyboard. Scrolls
> down the screen at warp speed.) No. Doesn't exist.
> ME (spying it on the screen). Wait—there it is.
> CLERK (extremely annoyed). Oh . . . um . . . yesss. We only received
> one copy. It's in the back.
> ME. Where in the back?
> CLERK (loudly). In the political science section!
> ME. Thanks!
>
> I searched this section. The book was nowhere to be found.
> I walk back to the desk.
>
> ME. Pardon me, but I couldn't find it.

(Clerk curses under her breath and slams her pen on the counter. Slams swinging door. Marches to the back of the store.)

I could not believe what she did next. She grabs a step ladder and climbs up. The book was lying flat on the top row of books—with the spine toward the back so you couldn't see the title. She grabs the book, climbs down, and slams it into my chest. Her face beet red, she screams, "HERE!!! ARE YOU HAPPY NOW, YOU FRIGGIN' FASCIST?!?!"

I was shocked—but I figured it was time for some Brooklyn diplomacy. I walk up to the counter again.

ME. Excuse me: Do you have *Treason* by Ann Coulter? In the bestseller section? I couldn't find it . . .

—September 27, 2004
National Review

Button It

Wearing your political heart on your sleeve—or your lapel, wherever

Another piece that bloomed in the '04 presidential campaign.

Wednesday morning brought an unusual sight: the sight of no Kerry-Edwards buttons. I'm talking about Manhattan, and I'm talking about the day after the election. For the previous weeks, the city had been a sea of Kerry-Edwards buttons, buttons everywhere, including in concert halls and opera houses (where I spend many evenings, as a critic).

At first, the buttons were sort of a trickle; then they gushed. Night after night, I'd be surrounded by Kerry-Edwards buttons, in Carnegie Hall, in the Metropolitan Opera House—wherever. And not once did I spot a Bush-

Cheney button (except on a marvelously brave friend, defying the masses
around her). Initially, I was sort of amused by the buttons, but, later, sort of
annoyed. Why were these people wearing them, anyway? Didn't they realize that everyone else was voting for Kerry and Edwards too? (Ahem—
almost everyone else.) Surely they didn't have to persuade anybody; their
fellows were already persuaded.

Maybe they wanted to tout their own virtue. Wearing a Kerry-Edwards
button, in that atmosphere, was the equivalent of saying, "I'm a good person," or, "I hate all things bad." Maybe they were seeking comfort in the
herd—having a big group hug, saying, "Aren't we all grand?" I think that's
what I disliked most about the button-wearing: It was so easy, so safe.
Wearing a Bush-Cheney button in one of those halls (as my exceptional
friend did)—that would have been daring, admirable at some level. But this
other was just joining up with the mob.

I mean, I doubt I would have worn a Bush-Cheney button in Waco, or
Provo. It would have been a little embarrassing.

Sort of like joining the Democratic club at Harvard Law School. I met
with Harvard Law Republicans recently, and asked whether there was a
Democratic club. They said, "Yes, but not many people join it. You might
as well join a club called the Harvard Law School Human Beings. Where's
the distinction?"

As the days ticked off to Nov. 2 [Election Day], I found myself increasingly . . . well, ticked off, by the button-wearing around me. I sought
psychoanalysis from a wiser head, our Richard Brookhiser. I said, "Why
should I be so bothered, Rick?" The doctor replied, "First, you're not for
Kerry and Edwards—you have to take that into consideration. Second, you
object to the imposition of others' political views on you."

He told about walking down the street in New Paltz, N.Y. And this
sunny afternoon, there was a bad traffic jam. A woman who happened by
said to him, "They'd better get out of their cars and stop bombing Iraq for
oil, d'you know what I mean?" Huh? What? Do I know you? And, no, I
don't really know what you mean!

Third, continued Rick—answering my query—who the hell wears
political buttons in concert halls and opera houses? Or in court or at church?
It's simply inappropriate.

Ah, about court. I heard from a reader of *National Review Online*—
after we'd opened a discussion about buttons—who is an administrative
law judge for a federal agency. He wrote, "Our office has six judges, four
of whom are conservative Republicans, two of whom are unknown, politi-

cally. We actually had an attorney show up to represent a client wearing a Kerry button. It struck me as the height of ignorance and arrogance." Yes, ignorance and arrogance, a bad combo.

I also heard from many Manhattanites who were brave enough to wear Bush-Cheney buttons on the street. (I never saw any—except on *National Review* colleagues, and you know how we are.) These Republican buttoneers were subjected to a variety of jeers and snubs and threats. The saddest note came from a Vietnamese American, whose relatives had experienced "reeducation" camps and other horrors. He sported a "Vietnamese Americans Against Kerry" button—"until someone stopped me and delivered a lecture on the Bush police state. When I brought up the *real* police state my family had lived in, he brushed that off" and kept on about Bush. "I decided to stop wearing the button because I couldn't take the blind idiocy."

More amusing was a letter from a fellow journalist: "There's a man who walks his dog mornings in Central Park who wears a T-shirt reading 'Another Dalton Parent for Bush-Cheney.'" Dalton is a tony prep school on the Upper East Side. "My first instinct was to congratulate him—and then I found myself in full New York mode, edging away from him, thinking, 'What if something's wrong with the poor guy?' Now I look the other way." That is classic.

Some correspondents were so rude as to suggest that, if you wore an American-flag lapel pin, you were in effect wearing a Bush-Cheney button. How McCarthyite (the suggestion, that is)! And yet, I have a friend who is an expat in "Old Europe," and he wears such a pin—expecting and knowing that people will take it to be pro-administration. On the flip side, I heard from someone who dined next to an American tourist wearing a Kerry-Edwards button in a French village. In all likelihood, the button-wearer wanted to assure the natives that he wasn't one of *those* Americans. Or was he just buying protection? Sort of like generations of American students who have slapped the Canadian maple leaf on their backpacks?

Speaking of McCarthyism, a young man from Virginia had just moved to Boulder. He had license plates that said "Fight Terrorism." (He had witnessed the 9/11 attack on the Pentagon.) A woman pulled up next to him and started berating him for being a Republican. Now, how did she know? And if a conservative had made that assumption—McCarthy City, baby!

But this has got to take the cake: On Election Day—before the results were known—a Harvard graduate student yelled joyously in a hallway, "I love America! I love democracy!" Someone shushed him, saying, "Enough of your homophobic views"!

Me, I've never liked political buttons or bumper stickers, maintaining that innocent others should be free from our commentary. You could argue that I have a forum, e.g., this magazine. But a) I didn't always, and b) no one has to read the magazine. (We're going to try to get Ashcroft to do something about that before he leaves the Justice Department.) And life is tense enough without, say, making half the people hate you as you drive down the road.

One of our readers has it in for one bumper sticker in particular—the one that says, "Another Family for Peace." *Ugh*. He thought of fashioning a sticker that said, "Another Family for War," or—a different tack— "Another Family for Freedom." His son came up with something really sly: "Another Family for Peace in Our Time."

Sometime in the wee hours of Nov. 3, the Kerry-Edwards paraphernalia vanished from Manhattan, like species gone suddenly extinct. I suppose that, if the Democrats had won, I would have seen the buttons in concert halls and opera houses for, oh, about a week longer—as people celebrated, congratulating themselves, and giving one another high fives in button form.

But, no, they're not wearing those little devils. They look naked without them. Better, too.

—November 29, 2004
National Review

December's C-Word

Who would have thought that 'Christmas' would become verboten? (Don't answer that)

When you go to Capitol Hill, you'd better not call the Christmas tree the Christmas tree: It's the "Capitol Holiday Tree," and that's official. (Hang on, aren't the Republicans in charge?) The White House is still holding firm, however: The tree over which it presides remains the National Christmas Tree.

I don't know about y'all in the more Neanderthal parts of America, but in the less Neanderthal, "Christmas" is pretty gauche. When you say "Merry Christmas," you might better have belched. On a recent Sunday, I attended a Christmas concert at Lincoln Center (New York)—the soprano Deborah Voigt was singing with the New York Philharmonic. The program said "holiday concert," of course. But a poster outside said "Christmas Concert." Apparently, someone had not quite gotten with the program (so to speak)—hope he wasn't fired!

A lot of us have been irked by "Happy Holidays," in place of "Merry Christmas," for a long time. Many years ago, I was working at a large firm in Washington, and it was "Happy Holidays," "Happy Holidays," "Happy Holidays," until you wanted to scream. One afternoon, just before Christmas, I said to a friend there, "Merry Christmas." I said it in a soft, gentle, but kind of mischievous way. He just grinned at me, understandingly. You would have thought we were engaging in something subversive, which was just plain weird.

Incidentally, Thanksgiving may be in trouble—I mean, the word. A couple of years ago, as I was touching down in my home state, the stewardess (oops, there I go again) said, "And a happy holiday to everyone." She meant Thanksgiving. But the word seemed a little risky, somehow. More and more, I hear, after that long weekend, "Did you have a good holiday?" Et tu, Thanksgiving?

It's astonishing how many people have internalized the "holiday" business. At that Debbie Voigt concert, I was with a friend who said, at intermission, "I just love the holiday." I had to say, "You mean Christmas?" And she said, "Yes! That's what I mean! How did I get out of the habit of saying that?" One does. It's even possible to be proud. When I was in college, a kid came back to the dorm and announced, beaming, "Today, I said the president and his *spouse*"—meaning Ronald and Nancy Reagan—"and I didn't even have to think about it. It came naturally." He was in no danger of saying *wife*.

Every December, I write about holidayitis, and so do loads of others. In fact, there's a vast literature on this subject, if "literature" is not too grand a word for Internet kvetching and other popular expressions of protest. A website called GrinchList.com is fairly typical—it was created "in response to" a "growing censorship" and to "revisionist policies and practices concerning Christmas," evident in stores, schools, offices, and media. Yes, there's fed-uppery in the land. And *National Review* readers are among the feddest up. How do I know? Because on our website recently—NationalReview.com—I invited readers to give examples of holiday/Christmas outrages, or annoyances, and they responded with a thunderous yawp.

As several readers tell it, even ushers in church, reflexively, wish people a "happy holiday." They have to be reminded, "We're in our own church! It's okay to say 'Merry Christmas'!" One man pointed out that the Salvation Army's mission is, in its words, "to preach the gospel of Jesus Christ and to meet human needs in His name." Yet while our reader was bell-ringing, he was admonished by a co-worker not to say "Merry Christmas."

And how about those Christmas trees? Everywhere, they're called "holiday trees," but in some places they're called "unity trees," "culture trees," or even "seasonal conifers." A high-school activities director wrote to me, "Every year we have a program once known as The Giving Tree." (This has to do with helping needy families.) "But a tree is apparently a potent religious symbol, capable of inducing alienation, or even conversion." So The Giving Tree became The Giving Snowman—which became The Giving Snowperson. No, really.

In the workplace, "Christmas" is a faux pas, at best. One company lists its holidays thus: "New Year's Day, Presidents' Day, Memorial Day, Independence Day, Labor Day, Thanksgiving Day [yes], and December 25th." *December 25th.* These people could not bring themselves to utter the C-word. Christmas parties are out, and in are, of course, holiday parties, seasonal gatherings, and end-of-year celebrations. A man writes, "My law firm does a 'Christmas in April' charity event. But it's 'holiday' at Christmas! I'd like them to do a 'Christmas in April' in December for a change." One company decided to avoid naming holidays altogether: Now they just have "scheduled down days."

Schools? Gimme a break. Christmas may not be mentioned in the properly modern American school. A Christmas party is apt to be a "snowflake social." And the Christmas concert has gone the way of the McGuffey Reader, or slate: These are winter concerts, with nothing too Jesusy, please, or maybe "nights of seasonal entertainment" (a new one on me).

Well, surely you're left with a Secret Santa, aren't you? Nice, secular Santa? No way. Mr. Claus is entirely too Christmas-specific. At a Harvard dorm, they were going to have a Secret Santa, but orthodoxy asserted itself, and the name was changed to Secret Winter Snow Friend. My correspondent says, "I made a plea on behalf of all anagram lovers that we compromise and use the name 'Secret Satan.'" Elsewhere, Secret Santas have become Winter Wizards.

For years, the City of Pittsburgh had "Sparkle Season," complete with a mascot, Sparkle, who, it was widely observed, looked rather like a flamboyant Klansman. Now they have, simply, "Downtown Pittsburgh: A Holiday Tradition with a New Twist." (Sparkle was twist enough for me.) In San Diego, "Christmas on the Prado" has become "December Nights." Other localities hold a "Frost Time Festival." The euphemisms are almost invariably gag-making.

Business is playing ball, too—oh, is it. Roughly a million readers wrote me to protest a TV ad from a pet-product company. A husband is teasing his wife about all the presents she's bought for their dog. "But it's his first holiday!" she pleads. Really? Wasn't he around for Veterans Day? Starbucks sells both "Christmas Blend" and "Holiday Blend," depending. Depending on what, I'm not quite sure. And in card sections of supermarkets, you may see "Birthday," "Graduation," "Hanukkah," etc., and then—once more—"December 25th." The naming of all other holidays seems kosher. Even Easter.

Among our readers, a great many Jews said, essentially, "If you're saying 'holiday' on my account, please stop! It grates!" In my experience, the more religious, or even culturally serious, a person is, the more he's apt to dislike "Happy Holidays." The blandly generic has no taste. And I salute the reader who wrote, "Have you ever attended someone else's party—someone's birthday, anniversary, graduation? It wasn't your event, but didn't you share the joy? That's how I feel. I'm not Christian, but I look forward to Christmas every year. Especially the music."

Ah, the music, and what's happened to it: That's a whole 'nother volume of complaint.

Many traditionalists seize on the fact that "holidays" derives from "holy days," so, really, the joke's on those who think that they're skirting something with "holidays." True: and "decimate" used to mean one of every ten, blah, blah, blah. There is no great etymological comfort.

But if it's comfort you want, you may look to the White House, and its current occupant. A peppy lady in Connecticut says, "Before the lighting of the National Christmas Tree, the TV commentators were going on and on about a 'festival of lights' and the 'holiday tree' and all that. And then the president comes on, and he says 'Christmas' about a jillion times, and even worse stuff, like 'star in the East' and 'God's purpose.' It was thrilling!"

Forgive me for ending on a political note—even in a political magazine—but I must ask: Do you have the feeling that George W. Bush is the last un-PC—even anti-PC—president we'll ever have? He calls terrorists

terrorists, when he's not calling them evildoers. He says "Merry Christmas" with abandon (I happen to know). Put it this way: If, sometime before 2009, the National Christmas Tree has switched to National Holiday Tree, Bush did not win the 2004 election.

—December 31, 2003
National Review

POLITICS

Weathering the Storm

The final days of a Bush campaignsman

I wrote this piece in a very odd period: the period following Election Night 2000, when the outcome was undetermined. I said in this piece—quoting my father-in-law, actually—that I feared the "post-election" would end only when Vice President Gore won. That turned out to be . . . not right, and I'm still sort of amazed by that fact.

E lection Day in Austin dawned dark and stormy.
Well, it did. The previous day, Monday, had been beautiful—a touch of Texas fall. But this was a gloomy, ominous day.

I went in to work around noon—no sense coming in earlier, I'd been told. Election Morning is always a funny, jittery period—there are little rumors, little anecdotes ("My Aunt Bess said turnout was big in Rochester"), but nothing solid. Nothing even remotely solid.

I'd been in Austin since mid-September, having taken a leave from *National Review*. Had come to write speeches. And I was hopeful we were going to win. In fact, I *thought* we were going to win, and pretty comfortably.

Besides which: Bush was going to make a fine president—maybe even an extraordinary one. If for Social Security reform alone, it was important that he win. Then there was respect for the rule of law and all that.

When I got to the office, people were in a state of nervous anticipation. At about one o'clock, we got some preliminary figures: Neck and neck in Florida. ("That's good! The Panhandle votes late—and they're our people.") Three down in Pennsylvania. ("That's good too!" I wasn't sure why, but I trusted it was.) Badly down in Michigan. That, we'd expected. We'd been going south there for the last few days.

Stupid Michigan (my home state).

By late afternoon, it was clear we wouldn't have a blowout—maybe a nice, solid win, but not a blowout. Nothing of (senior) Bush 1988 proportions, which I'd anticipated—though quietly.

Of course, I'd been worried about the Zogby poll. On Election Eve, he showed Gore up, by two points. Some of us were thinking that Zogby'd be embarrassed, tarnished, on Election Day—"the *Chicago Daily Tribune* of 2000"! (That paper, of course, had been the one that blared "DEWEY DEFEATS TRUMAN.") Boy, would he have egg on his face! And wasn't he polling in the daytime, when people—our people, working people, people busy doing useful things—weren't home?

Yeah, but he wasn't an idiot, Zogby. I mean, he could adjust for that. And he might be right.

Before long, we could see that the election was very, very . . . "tight." That was our word for it, the word of the night: tight. Michigan was still bad; Pennsylvania didn't look so hot; but Florida was okay, and that was the ball game. We'd have preferred a triumphant march through the states, but, hey: As I'd heard Jack Germond say many times on *The McLaughlin Group*, when you win, you win—mandate, schmandate. No one remembers the margin. There's a winner and there's a loser—and the winner governs.

WAITING AND WONDERING

We had a couple of things on our schedule that evening: a reception for staff and friends, at the Stephen F. Austin Hotel, a few blocks from the (beautiful, majestic, red-granite) capitol; then the outdoor celebration in front of the capitol, where Governor Bush—no, President-elect Bush!—would give his victory speech (a model of humility and graciousness). We—certainly I—expected the speech to come shortly after ten o'clock, our time, after the polls had closed on the West Coast.

Decency would at last return to Washington. The Clinton-Gore poison would finally be flushed out.

Not wanting to hang around the office—just being nervous with colleagues and glancing at television—I headed for the reception at the hotel—to be nervous with colleagues and glance at television. The place was packed with celebrants, or would-be celebrants; a dozen TVs were spaced around two rooms, tuned to various channels.

As the returns came in, I began to wonder what had gone . . . you know: wrong. Well, not exactly wrong, but not exactly swimmingly. Someone said that the "late-breakers"—those voters who made up their minds at the last minute—had gone heavily to Gore. A substantial portion of them cited as their reason: DUI.

That stupid drunk-driving thing. This was the Democrats' ultimate dirty trick (if you don't count stealing the election, but more on that later). The report was true, of course: Bush had been pulled over in 1976. But it was still a dirty trick, as every sensitive mind realizes. A friend of mine put it this way: On the Thursday before the election, you spring on the public that your opponent, 24 years ago—*a quarter of a century ago*, is the other way to put it—saw a psychiatrist. (Shades of Eagleton.) He is perfectly well now. Moreover, he has spoken repeatedly of his past troubles, though in a fairly general way, and of his gratitude at overcoming them.

Your report is true. But is it also a dirty trick? Sure.

We also heard that there had been an immense black turnout, making the difference in several states. When, I wondered, would Republicans learn to talk to black voters? And what should they say? Same thing they say to everyone else, I should think. I would fall over dead—of joy—if some candidate, somewhere, spoke to a black audience about . . . missile defense. Why not? They're Americans, too, and they're presumably interested in being protected from nuclear attack.

Of course, we had faced the most hideous tactics the Democrats could scare up. Their ads all but accused Bush of lynching a black man in Texas. Gore went around campaigning with the dead man's sister. (Our vice president knows that subtle politics is for fools.) He suggested that our judicial philosophy was a throwback to slavery. Janet Reno—in a reprise of her 1998 trick—pretended that Republicans were about to suppress the black vote. You know: We were just sitting there at the polling places, waiting to demand of black voters that they guess the number of beans in a jar.

Again, hideous stuff: but entirely predictable. Democratic race-baiting, especially in late October, early November, is as given as the sunrise. And Gore's people—Bob Shrum, Donna Brazile, Gore himself—are hardly amateurs; indeed, they wrote the book.

Speaking of Brazile: I had long worried about her "ground game." She was always boasting of it. What did it mean, exactly? I mean, I understood, vaguely, that it had to do with turnout. But what did it involve, specifically? Simple, innocuous phone calls and knocks on doors—or cheating? We knew one thing: Gore volunteers from New York were enticing the homeless to the polls with cigarette packs.

Great. Didn't Gore sort of oppose tobacco? Something about a dead sister?

Yet another sinking feeling: Social Security. When Bush had proposed his reform, back in May, I thought it magnificent and laudable—but, of course, politically risky; perhaps even suicidal. Why give the Democrats a chance to accuse you of rounding on old people? But then, they'd do it anyway—and if you're going to get clobbered, you might as well get some reform out of it, on the chance you get in.

Bush had been fantastically responsible—even heroic—on Social Security. And now the Democrats were making him pay for it. Just as they'd promised.

And then there was our old friend liberal media bias. Oh, goodness: Don't get me started. When I joined the campaign, I was a firm believer in media bias, and all its terrible effects. Halfway through, I concluded I'd been a little naïve—it's worse than even I had thought.

In the office, we Bushies were surrounded by television sets, going day and night. Sometimes I listened to music through headphones, so as not to hear what our friends were saying. I played a little game: When Katie Couric was interviewing someone, I could tell—I swear—whether she was interviewing a Republican or a Democrat *by the look on her face.* Amazing.

Conservatives, I find, usually make too much or too little of media bias. The more common error, I now believe, is to make too little of it. As Kate O'Beirne says, it's amazing that a Republican *ever* wins.

One of the worst things, of course, about a rough Election Night is having to hear the television people report it. They can't help looking pleased as punch. For instance, I thought some of the newscasters would wet themselves when announcing that Hillary Clinton had won in New York.

I was reminded of a story about Reagan (as we junkies so often are): It's November '82, and he's watching the midterm results, in the White House residence. The Republicans have had a lousy day; a lady correspondent is saying so. Reagan says—to himself, under his breath—"Wipe the glee off your face, sister."

I've always loved that: "Wipe the glee off your face, sister." Exactly.

UP AND DOWN

At the Stephen F. Austin, it was hard to follow the results. As you were milling about—getting a drink, chatting idly—what you relied on was crowd reaction: There'd be a cheer. Then you'd rush to a TV to see what the fuss was about.

Bush carries Ohio! Yes, but that had been expected. Nothing to go nuts over. Bush carries Tennessee! That's satisfying—for obvious reasons—but, again, expected. Bush carries Arkansas! Ditto. (Speaking of which, Rush had vowed to turn out every one of his listeners. Had they showed? And don't they constitute something like half the country? If only.)

At some point in the night, there was a roar that shook the rafters. It was a deafening, sustained, almost animalistic roar: The networks had reversed themselves and given Florida to Bush! After sprinting and stumbling to the TVs, we thrust our three-fingered "W" signs at the glowing "electoral maps," in quasi-Nuremberg style (which embarrassed me, slightly, at the time).

Hang on: It proved not to be so good as all that. The networks had merely taken Florida out of the Gore column and placed it back among the undetermineds. But still, it was a reprieve—a new lease on life. (The clichés came thick and fast that night.)

In the Electoral College, the vote was eerily close. The popular vote? Even more so. Ever since I was a child, in Ann Arbor, I had measured people, crowds, by the Michigan football stadium—which seats about 100,000. And in this great big continental nation—stretching from the Atlantic Ocean to the Pacific, encompassing 270 million people—it was coming down to a couple of Michigan football stadiums. In some states—Wisconsin, Iowa, New Mexico, Oregon, Florida—it was coming down to a couple of rows. Unreal.

The hours wore on. State after state we were hoping to win . . . fell. The room got somewhat woozy. People were a little unsteady, a little strange—confused. Me, not least. It appeared we wouldn't know the final results until dawn. I didn't want to turn away, go to bed. We had come this far, and this, after all, was history. Couldn't one sleep later?

But at one o'clock, I gave way. It was my feet, frankly. I had been standing since about 6:30, and couldn't bear it any longer. So I said my goodbyes—made my apologies—and headed back to the office, to pick up my briefcase. Then I'd go home.

As I trudged down Congress Avenue—the hotel is at Congress and Seventh; the office is at Congress and Third; the capitol is at about Congress and Eleventh—I placed one last call to Rich Lowry. He was in a cab, returning from a TV studio to *National Review*'s offices in New York. As we talked, he had another call. Would I hold?

In a flash, he was back: A friend of his had relayed big news: Bush had won! *We* had won! They had given us Florida.

With a lighter step, I ducked into the office, to fetch that briefcase. About twenty other staffers were there—hugging, high-fiving, and basically acting like something wonderful and necessary had happened, which it had.

We piled out of the office, to join the throng at the capitol—to hear and hail our Chief. It was a thrilling, probably unforgettable walk, those eight blocks up the street. Jubilation filled the air, as people cheered and wept and shouted and honked their horns. I called my wife back in New York, and held my cellphone aloft, so she could take in the sounds and the atmosphere.

Once at the capitol, we went through the metal detectors—can't be too cautious for the President-elect!—and huddled in front of the stage. It was cold, windy, and raining hard. But, in our orange "W. 2000" hats, we waved our little American flags and waited happily for Gore to concede, and our man to come on.

On either side of the stage were large TV screens, so we could follow everything on the networks. It was getting colder, windier, rainier. My feet were screaming. Where was Gore?

In due course, his motorcade pulled up to the site in Nashville where he was to bow out. That was good. But he wasn't appearing . . . and wasn't appearing. We kept staring at those large screens: What gives?

Eventually, we learned that something unusual was taking place in Florida. Gore had placed a second call to the Governor to retract his concession. It seemed there would be a recount.

Uh-oh. A super-close race. Ample room for Democratic mischief. Thoughts of 1960.

And then, who should appear, on those giant screens, but "Billy" Daley, the mayor's son. Great. He was vowing that the "campaign" would continue. It always does, doesn't it? The Clinton-Gore folks gave us the "permanent campaign." It continues in victory; it continues in defeat; it just goes on and on, without end.

We were somewhat frozen, bewildered. This was, we kept saying, "surreal." Now, I've never been sure of the precise meaning of "surreal." I suspect that it is as misused as "ironic," which people say whenever they mean interesting, or odd, or coincidental, or remarkable. I should, once and for all, get a handle on "surreal." But not now: "Surreal" must stand.

So there, surreally, was Daley. He acted like a man who knew something—something we *didn't* know. How could he be so confident? They had lost the election, and this was merely a pro forma recount. What were they going to do—cheat?

Bush, like Gore, wasn't going to come out. Instead we heard from our own campaign chairman, Don Evans, who said, essentially . . . thanks, and stay tuned.

By now, it was 4 A.M. Having tried to leave three hours before, I now walked back to my room. The wind whipped like something out of the Apocalypse. My umbrella turned inside out, practically shredding—had to throw it away. You might think of Lear on the heath, if you were the dramatic type.

At 5, I went to bed, full of fear.

THE MIND REELS

The next day, Wednesday, we were supposed to enjoy a program of festivities—a lunch, a party. But those were canceled—or "postponed," we were all saying.

So I had plenty of time—way too much time—for my special brand of foreboding. I thought of a hundred things, none of them comforting, which included:

Back in Cold War days, we used to hear criticism—particularly from liberals—that the Soviets weren't "ten feet tall." As in, "Oh, come on: The Soviets aren't ten feet tall!" This comment would usually be directed at a conservative who feared that the American team was going to get its clock cleaned by Moscow.

Well, I confess to fearing that, when it comes to politics—the lowdown kind—the Democrats are ten feet tall. They're simply better at politics than we are. They are certainly better at fraud. For them, politics is war (or, at a minimum, a "blood sport"). On Election Night, Donna Brazile "messaged" to Gore: "Don't surrender!"

That's war language. It is not election—certainly *post-election*—language.

Okay, more thoughts: You can't cheat Reagan out of a 49-state victory over Mondale. But with the vote this close? Piece o' cake.

I thought of what Clinton said to Dick Morris on the night the Lewinsky scandal broke. Morris had done a quickie poll for the president, reporting that the public wouldn't forgive a tryst with an intern if accompanied by perjury. "Well," said Clinton, "we'll just have to win."

I could hear the Gore camp: "Well, we'll just have to win."

I thought of the Bork battle, one of our worst failures. The Democrats pummeled him and pummeled him. Ted Kennedy, the ACLU, Norman Lear, Gregory Peck—all of them: They called him a Nazi (in a word). And we, the good guys, stood by, not wanting to "politicize" the matter, staying above the fray, appearing statesmanlike, being true to the process, trusting in the right.

And we got screwed—"Borked," we would later call it.

By midday Wednesday, we were approaching urban-myth time. Someone said that ballot boxes had materialized—just like that—in a couple of black churches. You're kidding? Voting in church? Where was the wall-of-separation crowd now?

Then I thought of the players: Jeb was governor, yeah. But he would recuse himself and be sweet. Meantime, the attorney general was a Democrat—Gore's state chairman. And that reminds me: What about the *federal* attorney general? The snatcher of Elián? What can she do, with her unlovely Justice Department? And what can *Clinton* do? He's not just going to sit around, revering the Constitution, is he?

All of a sudden, Jesse Jackson's down there, yelling, shaking his fist. The scene has turned racial. But then, it always does in America—the Democrats see to it that it does.

I felt myself pulled down into the fever swamps. We had always maintained they'd "say or do anything" for power. Well, would they? The mind spun with awful scenarios—scenarios of Democratic swindle. A half-delirium crept in—but a half-delirium based on reason and experience. Probably the worst kind.

I was to depart Austin on Thursday—an awkward juncture, I know, but New York, and this magazine, awaited me. On Wednesday night, I went to Earl Campbell's barbecue place, on Sixth Street, for a final, enormous bowl of chili. As a special treat, Earl himself was there—for the first time of my month-and-a-half stay. The former NFL (and University of Texas) great looked like he could still run through a brick wall, smiling that gentle smile of his.

Into the small hours, I talked, and worried, with another campaignsman. As we were wrapping up, his cellphone rang. He blanched, slightly. Hanging up, he remarked, "Some ugliness in Florida."

Indeed.

LIMBO CITY

The next morning, I packed, and took a long, solemn listen to the Beethoven C-sharp-minor quartet. Then—with the most disquieting feeling of incompletion—I boarded a plane.

When I got home, I could barely stand to hear the television. My wife wanted to listen to the news; I retreated to the other room. I *did* catch a glimpse of (Gore campaign spokesman) Chris Lehane, in dark glasses, overseeing the nonsense in Palm Beach. Somehow he no longer seemed twerpy or dorky. Instead he was . . . menacing, as though out of a night-mare—as though engaged in a colossal theft.

My father-in-law called. And he put in a single sentence everything I was thinking, fearing: "The only way for this to end is for Gore to win." Yes: They'll press and press, and bully and bully, and maneuver and maneuver until they get the numbers they desire. Then they'll say, "Game over." And the Republicans will withdraw graciously—as we always do—muttering about the good of the country.

Right this moment, it is Monday, November 13. Our magazine has to go to press. We don't yet know who will take the oath on January 20. And—to borrow a recent phrase from Governor Bush: a splendid man who would make a superb U.S. president—here we sit.

—December 4, 2000
National Review

The Race Ace

Clinton at his most shameful

You may not remember the Lewinsky period, or remember it only dimly. And you may remember even more dimly the role that race—believe it or not—played in this unseemly drama. The below piece brings it all back (I'm afraid). Some of the names, and the parts these people played, have grown obscure, but you may find yourself saying—as I did, on re-reading—"Oh, yeah."

Did you know the House managers were white? Yes, they were. Lily. And if you were tempted to forget, you were reminded every two seconds by the Democrats and their cheerleaders in the media. As the ever-dependable Eleanor Clift put it, "All they were missing was white sheets." They were like "night riders." (Clift, mind you, is one of the whitest women who ever lived.)

So you hadn't realized the Clinton scandal was about race? You weren't paying attention. From the beginning, this affair was soaked in race, like everything else in America, no matter how far afield it would seem to the tranquil mind. Black political leaders made it that way. So, to an extent, did white demagogues on the Democratic left. But Bill Clinton, more than anyone else, is responsible. He plays race as shrewdly as any other southern governor. He's not a boob, like his predecessor in Arkansas, Orval Faubus. But at least as much as Faubus, he knows the nasty magic of black and white, and, healer though he likes to imagine himself, he has used his presidency to aggravate the country's racial sores.

Whenever Clinton gets into trouble, he reaches for black people, as if for a shield. On the very first weekend of the Monica mess, he called Jesse Jackson, his old rival, to invite him to watch the Super Bowl. The two of them, Jackson said, "had prayer." Then Jackson "had prayer" with Chelsea Clinton. Before you knew it, he had become part of the family. Jackson also got a hold of Betty Currie, who was feared to be wavering, not yet committed to the cover-up. He urged her to choose "prayer over panic." White House aides were sure to inform the media just how grateful the Clintons were to their handy rev.

Day by day, color wormed its way into the drama. Reporters noted the special enthusiasm of black congressmen at the State of the Union address. Vernon Jordan, the presidential fixer, reminded everyone of his civil-rights struggles. Black lawyers were everywhere: Jordan himself, of course; Frank Carter, to whom he had driven Miss Monica; and several others. (This was a year before Cheryl Mills pulled her Selma act on the Senate floor.) Clinton aides, off the record, crowed about the blackness of the federal grand jury.

In March, there was the famous Africa trip, on which Clinton lugged his so-critical secretary, Currie, along with virtually every other prominent black person in the country. (One of them was Tom Joyner, the black-radio star, who had placed Clinton in his "Adulterers Hall of Fame.") In South Africa, Clinton wrapped himself around Nelson Mandela, literally and otherwise, to deliver an unmistakable message: Our struggle is one; the hating Right has always sought to persecute the loving Left; we shall—one day, preferably before the dress is discovered and tested—overcome.

Soon, Clinton took on the status of martyr in black America, a position he did nothing to discourage. Joyner's and other black talk shows began to portray him as another O. J. Simpson (and this was meant flatteringly). Charlie Rangel and many others compared him to Martin Luther King, who had been hounded by J. Edgar Hoover with sex tapes—just like Linda Tripp's. Black politicians and writers spoke incessantly of a "lynch mob." Toni Morrison pronounced Clinton "our first black president." Joseph Lowery offered, "It's the saxophone: The man has soul." It was left to the

Harvard psychiatrist Alvin Poussaint to explain that black people "circulate rumors that Clinton has black ancestry," so powerful is his bond with them.

Clinton obviously reveled in this, as, for a liberal of his type, there is no higher validation of goodness than the approval of black people. It washes away every complaint. In myriad ways, Clinton linked the cause of his political survival to the cause of black progress, warning of the social night that would fall if his enemies triumphed over him. After his semi-confession speech in August, he traveled to a black church to praise his "God of second chances." Everybody sang "We Shall Overcome."

When the Starr report hit Congress, the Black Caucus sprang into action. Maxine Waters said that she was "here in the name of my slave ancestors," to halt the railroading of a race hero. Jesse Jackson Jr. claimed that the Republicans wanted to impeach, not Clinton, but, among other things, "affirmative action" and "equal protection." John Lewis, invoking the authority of his genuinely heroic past, begged, "Let us act in the spirit of the Great Teacher, in the spirit of Gandhi, in the spirit of King." Thus was the moral capital of a beloved movement spent on Clinton.

As November approached, Clinton couldn't resist a little electoral mischief. His Justice Department—without a wisp of evidence—charged that Republicans were planning to "intimidate" black voters at the polls. Clinton, the Civil Rights President, huffed that "to scare people off from voting is totally abhorrent" and "un-American." In Missouri, Democrats ran an ad on black radio that went, "When you don't vote, you let another church explode. When you don't vote, you allow another cross to burn." And so on. Similar tactics were employed in other states.

Most important, Clinton granted an Election Eve interview to Tavis Smiley of Black Entertainment Television, after months of ducking the press at large. (In this, he stole a page from Simpson, who went to BET after his acquittal in Los Angeles.) Asked how his party would fare the next day, Clinton answered, "I feel good about it, but it depends upon who votes" (wink, wink). And was the impeachment drive against him fueled by conservative resentment of his closeness to black people? "It may be," Clinton reflected—just may be—"that that's a source of anger and animosity toward me." Later, Smiley remarked that Clinton had shown himself to be "an honorary brother": "He's certainly been treated like a Negro."

At last came the trial, when the managers—white, you know—went to work. Bob Herbert of the *New York Times* promptly declared that the process was rendered illegitimate by the presence of Strom Thurmond and William Rehnquist, both veterans of "the campaigns to keep the heavy boot of segregation firmly planted on the throats of black people." It was also revealed—oh, Christmas morning!—that Trent Lott and Bob Barr had addressed a Klan-like group in the South. Didn't that cinch it? How could they possibly sit in judgment of the civil-rights-loving Clinton? At a Jackson-organized rally, a Hispanic congressman, Jose Serrano, muscled into the act: "They don't want *him*," he shouted. "They want *us*!" They all sang "We Shall Overcome."

Clinton's legal team, everyone noticed, was a nicely diverse bunch. There was Mills, of course, the trump card. But also the paralyzed Charles Ruff, who in the Sixties—the Sixties, that humane decade—had contracted a disease in Africa. Africa. Where black people live. Not, say, Finland. Then Clinton (you could have seen this coming a hundred miles away) placed Rosa Parks in his State of the Union gallery. Shortly after, he flew to Atlanta to honor another member of the pantheon, Henry Aaron, who, Clinton recalled, battled "a dark, deep undercurrent" of racism as he neared Babe Ruth's record—not unlike, lay the implication, a certain stoic president.

The coup de grâce, however, was Mills, an "African American," she stated, in case anyone had missed it. The managers, she scolded, were "not playing fair by Mrs. Currie" (whom the Senate quailed from calling as a witness). How dare they invoke the holy name of civil rights for some big-haired trailer-park tramp! Why, Clinton's grandfather once owned a store that "catered primarily to African Americans," and who were these crackers to convict him? "I'm not worried about civil rights," Mills said, "because this president's record on civil rights is unimpeachable." Case closed. End of discussion. Race—King Race—had won the day, as seemingly it must.

It is often said that Clinton is lucky in his enemies. Less often is it said that he is lucky in his friends. As Roger Wilkins has observed, he uses black people as props, and they, in turn, oblige him (although in one memorable instance, Tiger Woods, who despises racialism, would not). Clinton is an undisputed master of racial manipulation. He succeeded in framing his impeachment ordeal as a conflict between liberal humanity and conservative evil. He got to be what is best about his region: Atticus Finch. Who but a racist could oppose a president on whom black people were so keen?

Disgracefully, at the close of the century, race talk clogs the air. It shouldn't be so. After everything the country had endured, and gained, it hardly needed a manufactured race storm. Clinton exploited an intern for sex, arranged a cover-up, lied under oath, and obstructed justice. It had nothing—not one thing—to do with race. Race injures enough in American life without being dragged into an unrelated arena. But Clinton and his allies insisted on doing exactly that. Clinton stoked the fires of racial division for the sake of his own pasty-white skin. And that—no matter how liberal he thinks he is—is far more damnable than any depraved hijinks with an asinine girl.

—March 8, 1999
National Review

Clinton's Rosenberg Case

Before we 'move on' . . .

Do you remember President Clinton's last hours in office? They were filled with pardons and sentence commutations. The pardon of Marc Rich, a criminal financier who had fled the country, grabbed the headlines. And the curious case of Susan Rosenberg was almost completely ignored. It is that case that the below piece addresses.

Bill Clinton's last days in office were busy ones; and the stomach still revolts from them. Hours before his successor was sworn in, Clinton granted clemency to a pair of longtime terrorists from the Weather Underground, Susan Rosenberg and Linda Sue Evans. These women are less well known than the glam figures Bernadine Dohrn and Kathy Boudin, but they are deadly enough. For the last decade and a half, they have been on the roll call of the darlings of the violent Left, along with Mumia Abu-Jamal, Leonard Peltier, and other "political" killers. Their world is unforgettably described in Peter Collier and David Horowitz's 1989 book, *Destructive Generation*.

Rosenberg and Evans were the kind the authors dub "radical airheads." These were white women, brought up in privilege, who placed themselves in the service of more unflinching killers, usually black. They were support players in the Underground: drivers of getaway cars, haulers of weapons, securers of safehouses. They let others pull the trigger, but were always faithful abettors. In the 1970s and '80s, Rosenberg and Evans participated in a string of armed robberies and other crimes, leaving corpses, mayhem, and fear in their wake.

The two belonged primarily to the Weather group, but all such outfits worked together, in an alliance of terror: the May 19th Communist Organization, the Black Liberation Army, the Red Guerrilla Resistance, the Republic of New Afrika, and so on. Collectively, they were known, in positively bourgeois fashion, as "The Family."

Rosenberg—on whom we will focus—was born in 1956 and grew up on the Upper West Side of Manhattan. Her father was a dentist, her mother involved with the theater. The girl attended the "progressive" Walden School and, at 17, traveled to Cuba as a member of a "youth work brigade." In time, she left such activities for the harder action of The Family.

The Family's most notorious crime occurred on October 20, 1981, in Nanuet, N.Y. This was the operation code-named "Big Dance." (Details of the crime are given in John Castellucci's 1986 book, *Big Dance*. Castellucci, a reporter with the *Providence Journal*, remains a leading authority on the case and its many actors.) The gang held up a Brink's truck, killing a guard named Peter Paige. In flight, they killed two police officers, Waverly Brown and Edward O'Grady. Brown had been the first black man admitted to the local force—a real pioneer. This fact should be remembered in light of the contention of Rosenberg et al. that they were dedicated to black people and black progress everywhere.

Rosenberg's role in the crime was that of getaway driver and general accomplice. Four of her partners were immediately caught. At least eight others escaped, including Rosenberg herself.

Their ranks somewhat thinned, The Family continued with their robberies, bombings, and other assaults. In 1983 came their attack on the U.S. Capitol. Their bombs killed no one, but caused considerable damage and spooked the nation. A statement sent to a radio station read: "We purposely aimed our attack at the institutions of imperialist rule rather than at individual members of the ruling class. We did not choose to kill any of them this time. But their lives are not sacred." Rosenberg, Linda Sue Evans, and five of their cohorts were indicted for the Capitol bombing. Their numerous other targets included the Naval War College, an Israeli-owned company, and a patrolmen's benevolent association.

Relatively little is known of Rosenberg's years as a fugitive; she has not told. We know, however, that she lived for a period in New Haven, Conn., with a fellow terrorist, Marilyn Jean Buck. Buck was known as the "quartermaster" of The Family, responsible for abundant matériel.

Law enforcement caught a break on November 29, 1984, when Rosenberg was spotted at a storage facility in Cherry Hill, N.J.: She was loading over 700 pounds of explosives into a rented bin. She also had with her an arsenal of guns, and the accouterments of her trade: *The Anarchist Cookbook, Guerrilla Warfare*, counterfeit police IDs. In addition, she had plans for future attacks. The explosives Rosenberg was handling were enough to destroy the entire area; she was charged with transporting them "with intent to kill and injure." Yelled Rosenberg, as she was led away, "We're caught, but we're not defeated. Long live the armed struggle."

In a tense trial, with helicopters whirring overhead and the courthouse thick with guards, Rosenberg pleaded innocent. "We are not criminals," she said. "We are revolutionary guerrillas. We are from an armed clandestine movement within the United States." She wore an Arafat-style headdress and lectured the court about the Middle East, Central America, and other subjects. Her claque in the courtroom cheered and whooped. When Rosenberg was convicted, she raised her fist in defiance and delivered yet more "revolutionary" speeches. It was not she who had lost, she said, but the U.S. government, which had been exposed as an enemy of the people. She asked the court to give her the maximum sentence—the better for revolutionary ferment—and got it: 58 years, for weapons possession and conspiracy. No punishment had ever been so severe in such a case. Satisifed, prosecutors declined to pursue charges relating to the Brink's murders and the other crimes.

A couple of months later, police got another break: Marilyn Jean Buck and Linda Sue Evans, operating together, were detected and nabbed outside a diner in Dobbs Ferry, N.Y. At their trial, they, too, preached revolution and waved fists. One of Evans's slogans was "Free the land."

These are some of the bare facts; the enormity of them is not to be missed. In June 1986, when Rosenberg and the others were safely in prison, another huge cache of explosives was discovered in New Haven, abandoned by them. It had been a close call. The explosives were leaking and dangerous when police, after evacuating the neighborhood, removed them. The Family had not intended this material for a Fourth of July display.

In prison, Rosenberg managed to keep her name before a devoted leftist public. She complained of ill treatment, and a documentary was made about her and her fellow inmates, who included other Family members (and one member of a related family: the Manson Family's Lynette "Squeaky" Fromme, who tried to kill President Ford). Rosenberg signed her letters "Venceremos, Susan." The usual lot—William Kunstler, Noam Chomsky, Daniel Berrigan—signed petitions demanding her release. She wrote "A

Poem for Mumia [Abu-Jamal]," which featured the lines: "Their message is so clear / Do not be Black / Do not be radical / Do not be a political prisoner / There is still time to / SHAKE IT LOOSE."

In a 1990 interview, she said, "I don't consider myself an extraordinary person at all, but I do believe that my comrades and I made extraordinary decisions." She utterly rejected the sweet, poetic label "prisoner of conscience": "I am *not* a prisoner of conscience. For all of us here, it is our political beliefs that have led us to take action that put us into antagonistic conflict with the government. My ideas led to certain actions that led to this ongoing conflict with the government."

All the while, she was what wardens term a "model prisoner." She got a master's degree, developed an "AIDS curriculum," and caused few problems. Sometimes she claimed to have renounced violence, and at other times she affirmed the "right of oppressed peoples to armed struggle." It is possible she saw, and sees, no contradiction. Her statements have been, to say the least, confused. In the mid-'90s, she came up for parole. She expressed a kind of regret for the explosives at Cherry Hill—the crime for which she was convicted—but denied involvement in the Brink's robbery and her other acts of terror. Wrote U.S. attorney Mary Jo White to the parole commission, "Even if Susan Rosenberg now professes a change of heart about her pursuit of violence as a means to achieve her political objectives, the wreckage she has left in her wake is too enormous to overlook."

But Rosenberg and her allies mounted a smooth campaign. Last December, *60 Minutes* did a segment on her that was extraordinary for its softness, and soft-headedness. It left the impression that Rosenberg was basically a political leafleteer, perhaps caught up with the wrong crowd. To read a transcript of the segment, in light of the totality of the information on Rosenberg, is jaw-dropping.

Remarkable, too, was the spectacle of Susan Rosenberg mouthing legal arguments—a form of the old "popular frontism." It was unfair, she said, that her crimes as a whole weighed on the parole commission, when she had been tried only for the particular explosives. Officials were failing their duty, she said, were being untrue to the legal system. Of course, this was the system of the very government she had given her life to destroying. She had always forsworn use of the American process as "counterrevolutionary." Prosecutors respond, in part, that Rosenberg chose to flee rather than stand trial for—to give one example—the Brink's robbery. And the weapons sentence was supposed to put Rosenberg away, pretty much for good.

Yet her release was a cause of the Left, and Rosenberg petitioned for presidential clemency. She must have been heartened by Clinton's August 1999 springing of Puerto Rican terrorists in New York, Weather-like criminals she proudly acknowledged as her comrades. And the Puerto Ricans had not even asked for clemency; Clinton had simply bestowed it on them, as his wife ran for the Senate. One of those who went to bat for Rosenberg was Congressman Jerrold Nadler, who represents the Rosenberg family on the Upper West Side. As a member of the Judiciary Committee, Nadler had been a key defender of Clinton's at the time of the president's impeachment.

On the morning of George W. Bush's inauguration, Clinton gave Rosenberg what she wanted. He did the same for Linda Sue Evans. They walked.

When the news hit, the cries of the victims' families were almost unbearable to hear. Their incomprehension at what the president had done was heartbreaking. They were not unforgiving people, they said; rather, Rosenberg—to stick with the chief figure—had not shown any remorse for what had happened to them. She had never said she was sorry, never owned up to any responsibility. One victim's widow said, "I never believed in my heart Clinton would do this. After Oklahoma City, how could you pardon anybody who was caught in this country with weapons of mass destruction?"

New York mayor Rudolph Giuliani, who, as a U.S. attorney, had prosecuted the Brink's case, said, "I'm shocked." The city's police commissioner, Bernard Kerik, who had also dealt with Rosenberg, said, "It sickens me." Even Hillary Clinton's fellow senator from New York, Democrat Charles Schumer, denounced Clinton's action.

Rosenberg, for her part, returned to her parents' apartment on West 90th Street. She rode out to Coney Island to see the ocean. In a radio interview, she said—blandly, passively, self-absolvingly—"It was an extreme time." No, it was not. She was extreme in it. And she knew exactly what she was doing, embraced a choice, on a kind of principle. David Horowitz put it neatly the other day: "That's radicals for you: They declare war on you, arm themselves, make bombs, and kill people, but when you catch them, they're just idealists, and they feel persecuted. I'm sure that's Rosenberg's mentality today."

A passage from his and Peter Collier's book applies here. It has a Weatherman, after years of crime, rejoining society and marveling, "Guilty as hell, free as a bird—America is a great country."

—March 19, 2001
National Review

The GOP's Burden

The color of the convention

A long time ago, Henry Kissinger had an enduring insight: that liberals "preempt the categories." By that he meant that liberals decide what we may and may not discuss; if we rumble, it is on their turf.

Seldom has this been truer than during the Republican convention in Philadelphia. The media, so heavy with liberals (crude as it may be to point out), were pleased to talk about abortion; they were also inclined to talk a little about gay rights; but mainly they wanted to talk about race. And so the coverage of the convention was almost entirely painted in black and white.

The Republicans, of course, did their part—they always do. They desperately, pathetically, wanted to be seen as a party of "inclusion." Their slogan was "Renewing America's Purpose—Together" (as opposed, apparently, to man by man). They peppered the stage with black and Hispanic speakers; they have done so for the last several conventions, but the media treated it as new. The convention's co-chairmen were Rep. J. C. Watts, Rep. Jennifer Dunn, and Rep. Henry Bonilla. In other words, the Republicans offered—for those of you keeping score at home, and recent weeks have been about nothing if not score-keeping—a black, a woman, and a Hispanic. We are deep into the territory of Secretary James Watt, who once announced that liberals ought to be satisfied with a commission he had appointed, composed as it was of "a black, a woman, two Jews, and a cripple."

But it hardly mattered what the Republicans did onstage, because the big media were most interested—almost exclusively interested—in the color of the delegates on the floor. What liberals saw was not a gathering of Americans with certain views and political commitments, but a sea of damning white. And, as usual, the Republicans were inept in defending themselves. They prove in a thousand different ways that they have accepted—have internalized—the Democratic critique of them. They act guilty;

they go around cringing. They quake to affirm their principles and ideals, which are admirably liberal (old-liberal) ones. Now, more than ever, race is the GOP's burden.

Republicans respond, wearily, that they're damned if they do, damned if they don't. Stage a convention without regard to race, and you are attacked as a racist. Stage one that is color-conscious, and you are attacked as a fraud. The liberals' criticism is rich: They spend day and night demonizing the Republicans as a party antagonistic to blacks; then, having succeeded, they look on their handiwork—a party from which blacks shrink—and profess shock.

In Philadelphia, race fever began on Opening Night, when Colin Powell stepped up to the microphone. To the delight of the GOP's harshest critics, the general decided to spank the Republicans on race. He chastised those who "miss no opportunity to roundly and loudly condemn affirmative action that helped a few thousand black kids get an education," but who emit "hardly a whimper" about "affirmative action for lobbyists who load our federal tax code with preferences for special interests."

Rarely do politicians get cheaper than Powell was here. His was an equation that defies logic, that affronts common sense. Leaving that aside, however, whom does he think he was scolding? The Republicans are the party of the flat tax (to the extent that there is any movement at all toward such a system). They are the party of reforming the IRS, of equality of opportunity, of equality under the law. You might have thought that the die-hard Republicans assembled in the hall would take offense; instead, they just smiled and applauded, determined to hold their peace.

In the course of his speech, Powell uttered . . . well, "hardly a whim-per" of criticism of the Democratic party. He preferred to lecture his fellow Republicans. He insisted—as all the Bushies do—that they "reach out to minority communities, and particularly the African-American community." What's more, "it must be a sustained effort. It must be every day. It must be for real."

This sounded like, more than anything else, a call for Democratic-style posturing and pandering. It insulted, or should have insulted, sincere Republicans of long standing, including President [George H. W.] Bush, who was sitting right in front of Powell. A few Republicans were reminded of Nancy Reagan's reaction to Vice President Bush's 1988 call for "a kinder, gentler nation." Turning to Maureen Reagan, who was sitting next to her, she said, "Kinder and gentler than who?"

What, we may ask, does Powell think the Republican party has been doing since at least the rise of his old boss, Ronald Reagan? The general might have applauded the Republicans for being the party of all Americans—eschewing tribalism, Balkanization, the poisonous identity politics. When you face down the Soviet Union, liberalize the economy, push for school reform, break welfare dependency, try to return constitutional order to the judiciary, make war against crime—for whom do you do it? For Americans, presumably; all of them; "every day"; "for real." Powell, like so many others in his party, did not sound like a Republican entirely secure in his own (philosophical and spiritual) skin.

Next, the general declared that Republicans "must listen to and speak with all leaders of the black community, regardless of political affiliation or philosophy." Consider the ramifications of this demand. Powell must mean that Republicans should—no, "must"—sit down with Al Sharpton and Louis Farrakhan. How about Khalid Muhammad? He is certainly a leader; he has followers. And Powell did say "regardless." So . . .

On Night Two, Condoleezza Rice took the stage. It fell to this foreign-policy adviser, a Russianist, to touch the golden core of her party's thinking. Explaining why she became a Republican, she said, "I found a party that sees me as an individual, not as part of a group. I found a party . . ."—but the remainder of her statement could scarcely be heard. The applause for that first sentence was too great, too insistent, too ecstatic. Her words were possibly the most thrilling of the whole convention.

Surveying the Republican show, the press was almost fascinating in its monomania. All over the elite media, they were lined up like Rockettes. Liberals were obsessed with numbers—counting up blacks, counting up Hispanics, counting up women. Never have so many been so demographic. CNN announced that the convention was merely 4.1—point-one, mind you!—percent black. Others offered their own statistics, snorting at "country-club golfers on the convention floor," "well-fed white guys," "a bunch of rich old white guys," and so on.

Bob Herbert, columnist for the *New York Times*, did not disappoint. He is one of the country's chief purveyors of the GOP-as-Klan worldview. Wrote Herbert, "It was disheartening to see Colin Powell up there doing his bit to help mask the reality of the G.O.P., a party that since the 1960s has been relentlessly hostile to the interests of black Americans." The Harvard sociologist Orlando Patterson, also writing in the *Times*, said that "the GOP platform calls for cultural and ethnic policies favored by the party's fringes, belying Mr. Bush's eloquent pleas for racial equality." Another *Times* columnist, Maureen Dowd, even noted that, "in 1962, W.'s uncle Jonathan made the front page of *Variety* when he considered reviving a black-face minstrel show Off Broadway."

But the cake was taken by Bruce Morton of CNN. He told his viewers that "inclusion is not universal here," because "the GOP platform says, 'We will attain equal opportunity without quotas or other forms of preferential treatment.'" You may need to read that bit twice in order to grasp its import.

Everywhere, it was remarked that the Republican nominees were "two white oil men." This became the trope *du jour*, or *de la saison*. Curiously, Al Gore and other Democrats are never called "white" or "white men." They get to be white men without being labeled as such. In the three months until Election Day, will Gore and Joe Lieberman ever, once, be described as "a pair of white men"? George W. Bush and Dick Cheney, though, seem forever tagged: "two white men"; "two white oil men."

It would be refreshing—world-shaking—if some Republican, some-where, answered, "So what? So what if our candidates are white, if most of our convention delegates are white? What matters is what we think, what we wish to do, the kind of people we are, and not materially." A more self-confident party would plunk down its agenda—missile defense, school choice, tax cuts, Social Security reform, opposition to abortion—and say, "Here it is: not a white or a black agenda, but an American one. How about it?" In addition, a party that quit the racialist game might find itself reward-ed; it might, for example, progress beyond a lousy 10 or 12 percent of black votes.

Conservatives like to recall an incident that took place in late 1992, dur-ing the presidential transition. A Clinton factotum stopped by the National Endowment for the Humanities with a clipboard, checking off names. What the factotum was doing was taking a hard look at the agency's women with Hispanic names, to ensure that they themselves were Hispanic, and not (say) merely married to Hispanic men. This stands as the epitome of Democratic racialism. And the Republican party, if it were true to itself, would tell the Democrats exactly what they can do with that clipboard.

—August 28, 2000
National Review

Going *Timesless*

Who dares give up the 'newspaper of record'?

L ast fall, President Bush caused something of a scandal when he made an admission to Fox News's Brit Hume: He is not much of a newspaper-reader or TV-watcher; he prefers to get his news from his staff, with no opinion mixed in. For many people, this revelation was further proof that our president is a dolt, too abnormal to serve in that job.

I have an even more shocking revelation: Many people in this country don't read the *New York Times*, and by "people," I don't mean Ma and Pa, I mean major writers and journalists, plenty of whom live in Manhattan.

Mark Helprin, the novelist and essayist, does not live in Manhattan—he lives in Virginia—but he might still be expected to read the *Times*. He does not, however. And when certain people find this out, "They look at me as if I had just slaughtered Mary's little lamb." They are incredulous, and perhaps a little frightened. How can someone—especially on so high a level—function without the *New York Times*? Helprin manages, reading many newspapers and magazines—just not the "paper of record." He stresses that one should never read anything out of habit; if reading becomes habitual rather than helpful, give it up.

Our colleague David Frum tells about the time he was working out on the treadmill, reading *The Economist*, as he had weekly for years. And "suddenly it hit me: I hate this magazine. I have hated it for a very long time." He tossed that issue aside and never looked back. (Needless to say, he is still made aware of certain articles in *The Economist*: such as hostile reviews of his books.)

William F. Buckley Jr. once remarked—as a prelude to some complaint about the *Times*—that doing without that paper would be "like going about without arms and legs." The *Times* is still the essential news habit of much of elite America (pardon the term). And, of course, this paper affects all of America's media, whether individual Americans know it or not. "No one here in Duluth reads the *New York Times*," I sometimes hear, "so why should I pay attention? Aren't some of you guys obsessed?" But what our

Minnesotan fails to appreciate is that everyone who supplies him his news—whether in print or over the air—does read the *Times*. And is profoundly influenced by it. The paper is in the bloodstream of this nation's media.

Nevertheless, more and more public-affairs types are going without it, and they don't feel ignorant. Moreover, they feel liberated. I have a friend who, many years ago, gave up reading anything about race. Anything at all. That was just a personal policy, formulated and stuck to. And he said that he found himself happier. So it is with many people who have gone *Times*less. We are talking mainly about conservatives, of course, but their beef is not so much with the *Times*'s bias as with its partisanship (if you will accept the distinction). Oh, yes, and with its pretentiousness.

Many of these ex-*Times* readers can give you the exact year, or even the exact day, of their withdrawal. "Four years ago." "Nine years ago." "Last June." Quite a few seem to have quit the paper in recent years, since 9/11, and since the Jayson Blair scandal (he was the con artist who was a rising star at the *Times*), and since former editor Howell Raines's bizarre crusade against Augusta National Golf Club.

Michael Barone, the all-knowing Washington political journalist, stopped reading the *Times* in August 2002. (Like many ex-*Times* readers, however, he still sees the occasional article on the web, or checks in with a preferred columnist.) Barone finds that he is saving a lot of time. He also finds that he is on a surer news footing: Too many of the *Times*'s stories were questionable, "and I thought, 'I have to go on television, I have to be accurate, and this isn't helping.'"

Another writer reports that he read the *Times* regularly "from 1965 until July 26, 2001," when a last-straw item appeared. "I do get pertinent articles on the Internet and see the occasional copy in a hotel, but the *Times* is out of my life after 36 years, and I find I have more time in the day without sacrificing important knowledge of the world." This writer does miss the computer section, however—called "Circuits." And the obituaries (those pages being the very last ones some of us would do without).

A number of writers and editors feel they need to look at the *Times* just to know what the Gray Lady is up to. Says one major New York editor, "I read it for the same reason you had to look at intelligence reports on Germany in World War II." A noted Washington-based political journalist says, "I consider reading it an odious professional duty." He complains not just about the news and editorial pages. (The radical journalist George Seldes, in one of his books, had a chapter called "How to Read the Editorial

Pages." It consisted of one word: "Don't.") No, "it's the arts pages and the food pages and the headlines and the captions—it's every nook and cranny of that paper."

It will probably not surprise his critics that Rush Limbaugh doesn't read the *Times*; he hasn't "for a couple of years." First, "there is no longer enough difference between the editorial pages and the news pages, particularly the front page." Second, "I found myself questioning the accuracy of the paper based on my own knowledge. I too often wondered, 'Hmmm—is that true?'" Third, "the *New York Times* is just one of many nearly identical components of the mainstream media. The point is, I know what I'm going to see or hear anywhere in the mainstream media. They are all a giant cliché now. I know them like I know my whole naked body, not just the back of my hand."

What about the fear that, if you don't read the *Times*, you'll miss out on some "national conversation"? Among the scoffers is Peter Kirsanow, a Bush-appointed member of the U.S. Civil Rights Commission: "I've gone long, blissful stretches without reading the *Times* and have found that during such periods I remain as well informed as when I read it regularly—but without the residual anger, anxiety, and irritability. Since reading the *Times* is not mandatory where I live—in the mid-Atlantic states—even among the elites—I'm not viewed as illiterate simply because my conversation for the day hasn't been directed by R. W. Apple or Maureen Dowd."

Speaking of the sticks: Sometime in the mid-1990s, the *Times* wrote a blistering editorial about Jesse Helms. The senator's new, eager press secretary quickly drafted a letter to the editor, and took it in to the senator. Helms, of course, had not seen the editorial. He glanced at the letter and said, "That's nice, son. Do whatever you want with it. But understand something: I don't care what the *New York Times* says about me, and no one I care about cares what the *New York Times* says about me." Therein lay some of the senator's power.

Aside from bias, partisanship, pomposity, or other defects, some just find the paper dull. The southern (and decidedly un-dull) writer Dave Shiflett says, "I still read the *Times*, but not like I used to. It's simply a bore most days, despite its evangelical political mission, which should at least liven up its prose. No such luck. A dull evangelist is easy to ignore, especially when there are so many vibrant news sources available. There's simply nothing special about the *Times*, or at least special enough to warrant a wade through what is, on a daily basis, the flattest selection of prose published anywhere outside the State Department."

Hilton Kramer, editor of *The New Criterion*—and for 17 years a top critic at the *Times*—once made a quip about Max Frankel, editor of the *Times* from 1986 to 1994: "He gave New Yorkers their Sundays back"—so dull (in this view) had that behemoth become.

The proliferation of media has lessened the importance of the *Times*; so have the newspaper's mistakes (which include too great a kinship with the Democratic National Committee). To be sure, there are some unmissable individuals in the paper, such as John F. Burns in Iraq. But, seemingly every day, journalists and others are discovering that they don't have to consume the whole deal.

A final story. Michael Ledeen, the foreign-policy analyst, hasn't read the *Times* in years—but when young, he did read a columnist named John Crosby in the *New York Herald Tribune*. Crosby did not like radio. He wrote that one of his great pleasures in life was to look at the radio schedule every morning and then realize, throughout the day, what he was missing. For example, he'd be in the park with his granddaughter and say, "Becky, guess what we're not listening to on the radio now! Isn't that great!" Says Ledeen, "I feel the same way about the *New York Times*. When someone says, 'Did you see such and such in the *Times* today?' I can always smile and say no."

And yet some of us can't wean ourselves away, and may never. Lou Cannon, the veteran journalist associated with the *Washington Post*, says, "My view of the *Times* is that it is what it is, and there's nothing I can do about it." So true of this great paper, and of much of life.

—March 22, 2004
National Review

Dems on the Hot Seat

If only!

I sort of blush to read this op-ed piece, written long ago—it's a bit of a diatribe. But I confess to liking it!

P rominent in every conservative's repertoire is an anecdote concerning Pauline Kael, the venerable former film critic of *The New Yorker*. After Election Day 1972, it seems, she professed shock at Richard Nixon's 49-state landslide over George McGovern, because, you see, she didn't know anyone who had voted for Nixon.

While this may be firmly part of conservative lore, does it have anything to do with the present, when the country abounds in right-leaning institutions and Congress itself is led by Newt Gingrich and Trent Lott? Consider a conversation I had not long ago with a cousin of mine, a bright and friendly woman whom I have come to know only recently. When politics came up, she fixed me with an earnest gaze and said, "I have to tell you something: I have never met a decent person who was a Republican. I don't mean to give offense, but I'm curious: Why are you a Republican?"

And the thought came to me that I am frequently on the defensive about my affiliation, which is odd, given the low esteem in which I hold the Democratic party. Somehow the burden seems always to be on the Republican; rarely is the Democrat called on to explain himself. It is simply assumed, in many quarters, that the Democratic party is the natural home of the reasonable and good. And that the Republican party is home to the shallow and venal, or to those who have had so warping a life experience that they, against their better inclinations, wind up in the wrong camp.

As Republicanism is the departure—the quirk, the apostasy—it falls to the Republican to provide justification. Sometimes, the Democrat, trying to be helpful, will suggest that the Republican is perhaps a bit cranky about taxation: He thinks there's too much of it (i.e., he's stingy with his earnings). Tip O'Neill spent much of the 1980s claiming that Ronald Reagan became a Republican when he landed in Hollywood and started pulling down those big studio paychecks. More than one Democrat has snorted, "Maybe someday I'll be rich enough to join the Republicans."

It would probably startle many Democrats to be asked, "Why do you belong to that party?" They may admit to certain flaws, but they appear not to doubt that their hearts, with their votes, are in the right place. And they tend to imagine that Republican criticism is relatively benign. "Republicans," they'll say, "think of us as a little naive, a little too idealistic, a little too trusting in the virtue and efficacy of government." George McGovern himself is wont to say (with perfect condescension) that the country "needs both liberals and conservatives"—liberals to ascend from barbarism, conservatives to "keep the books" and "manage the pace and scope of change."

It would amaze cloistered Democrats to learn of the depth of Republican disagreement with them. Some Republicans think of their party as not merely misguided or incorrect but, in many respects, abhorrent.

Democrats may view themselves as the party of enlightenment and humanity. But Republicans are apt to view them as the party of abortion on demand; the party of welfare dependency; the party of generational poverty (for the first time in American history); the party that turned its back on equal opportunity; the party of race-based policy and color-as-destiny; the party of what (Democrat) Arthur Schlesinger Jr. calls "the disuniting of America"; the party that, in the latter stage of the Cold War, succumbed to appeasement and apologetics; the party long tolerant of drugs; the party that undermined sexual norms that had proven useful for generations; the party of a popular culture that has laid waste to sound convictions about God, man, and community; the party of union coerciveness; the party discouraging of entrepreneurship and punishing of success; the party of greed and envy; the party of taxation that would be so confiscatory as to border on thievery; the party of intolerance of religion and religious people; the party that has turned the universities into ideological prisons, stifling free inquiry and debate; the party that has so perverted criminal law that citizens openly scoff at their own judicial system; the party that has made public schooling the plaything of education-association militants; the party that has abandoned sensible conservation for a kind of neo-pantheistic Earth-worship; the party that is grudging about military preparedness; the party that is maniacally hostile to even the notion of anti-missile defenses; the party that demands public subsidy of execrable, hateful "art"; the party that anathe-matizes smoking, of all things, while ignoring a thousand worse patholo-gies; the party that labors day and night to control the lives of ordinary men and women, whom it at turns patronizes and despises.

Well. How's that for an icebreaker? The point is, Democrats aren't used to being talked to this way. They are accustomed to being congratulated and praised. They were the ones, after all, who looked after the begrimed, tuber-cular miners of Harlan County. They were the ones "in the forefront of the civil rights movement" (forgetting George Wallace, Orval Faubus, Lester Maddox, et al.). They are the ones who talk the language of compassion and love. And they believe that all this should give them a free pass in perpetu-ity. Republicans should simply accept their essential goodness—if not their outright superiority—and confine their criticisms to the periphery: Maybe Medicare costs are rising a little too quickly, and maybe AmeriCorps is kind of a goofy idea, because, true, they aren't really volunteers.

The dirty little secret is, some Republicans hold a severer view. And they look forward to the day when Democrats are made to state —by cousins and others—just what they're doing in a party like that.

—September 12, 1996
Washington Times

The Joy of Tokenism

Or if not joy, something . . .

Years ago, Henry Kissinger invited Bill Buckley to speak to his students at Harvard, in order, said Bill, to exhibit to them one of the more "exotic specimens in the American political zoo." We conservatives are more familiar now than we were then, but we still give off a whiff of exoticism—in certain quarters.

Recently, I was invited to attend a Renaissance Weekend. These are the famous conclaves associated with Bill and Hillary Clinton. Founded 25 years ago by another couple, Phil and Linda Lader, the weekends include people from many walks of life, talking about a variety of subjects on a slew of panels. In response to the Renaissance phenomenon, some conservatives set up a weekend of their own, the Dark Ages Weekend, ha, ha. (This type of humor is indispensable to our psyche—the conservative psyche.)

The Laders don't want Renaissance Weekend to be an exclusively left-leaning and Democratic affair, and they go out of their way to welcome and even protect their right-leaning guests. They are, in fact, the soul of kindness, hospitality, and ecumenism. This is our kind of Democrat, *National Review* readers. He is a policy expert, a business whiz, and a former ambassador to the U.K. (in the second term of Clinton); she is a dynamo whose résumé includes the National Prayer Breakfast.

One of their guests plunked herself next to me and said, "You're here because of affirmative action, you know." I said that I favored philosophical and political affirmative action—even tokenism. I favor it, for example, on university faculties, where it's often missing. In my day—I doubt much has changed—"diversity" meant a black Marxist, a white Marxist, a Hispanic Marxist, a lesbian Marxist . . .

If you're a conservative, involved in public questions, you're used to being a kind of token. You have a special role to play. The late Jerry Nachman produced Bill Maher's *Politically Incorrect*, and he would tell me, "Now, Jay, your job is to sit in the Hitler chair. Somebody's gotta do it."

Truth is, we should probably not pass up such opportunities, because you never know what good you might do, or whom you might reach. Never up, never in, as we say in golf.

Sometimes I worry that we—we professional righties—spend too much time around the likeminded (despite our sideline in tokenism). This is surely true of lefties as well. At Renaissance, I noticed that, when they talked to me, they sort of assumed that I would agree that Bush is a moron—even if I, for whatever weird reasons, supported his policies. They were incredulous when I said that I found the president smart as a whip, in addition to right (i.e., correct).

It was a trying few days for the conservatives—some of them closeted—in attendance. One woman spoke of a perpetual knot in her stomach, and her tongue bitten in half (although we were all encouraged to speak, by the magnificent Laders). I will give you a lowlight: One attendee said that she worried about the status of women in Iraq—for women had been respected under the prior regime (Saddam's), and this new, U.S.-imposed government might just turn back the clock. This remark was greeted by a burst of applause.

Speaking of audience reaction: Have you ever noticed that the Left hisses? Yes, they hiss. This was certainly true in my hometown of Ann Arbor, Mich., where, when they objected to something in a movie, they hissed. I have always thought it a most unattractive practice, carrying with it some menace, a hint of violence. At Renaissance, when someone mentioned that the U.S., in fact, went into Iraq with allies, not without, there was hissing.

More benignly, I observed a lot of shaking of heads—when I spoke, I mean! This reminded me, if I needed reminding: When a speaker is saying something with which you disagree, don't shake your head (unless absolutely necessary).

And here's a peril you may not have thought of: If you're a journalist—especially an opinion journalist—you're liable to run into someone about whom you have written negatively. This puts another kind of knot in the stomach. I knew a journalist in Washington who said that, after several years' work there, he simply couldn't go out anymore. I know the feeling. As a music critic, I am scared to death to meet a musician—and have often had to get myself out of a situation where it was likely. As a political critic, it is hardly any better.

I lack entirely the brass of Hilton Kramer, the eminent art critic and co-founder of *The New Criterion*. At a dinner once, he and Woody Allen were seated next to each other. The actor said, "So, Mr. Kramer, do you find it embarrassing when you encounter people whose work you have slammed?" "No," replied Hilton: "I think they should be embarrassed for having made such lousy art." Later on, Hilton realized that he had once criticized a movie that Allen was in (*The Front*).

I had no such encounter—this time.

What one did have, in abundance, was Bush-hatred. You may have heard about it. It's real. This is a hatred that can be febrile, unhinged. For example, you hear a lot of talk about fascism—yes, fascism. One man, exasperated, got up and said, "Come on, guys, fascism is not coming tomorrow." Someone piped up, "It's already here." In his introduction to the book he has just edited, *Understanding Anti-Americanism*, the sociologist Paul Hollander cites many recent charges of fascism, from people generally regarded as serious.

And, of course, there is a great deal of concern about what the Europeans think. What good is a president, or an administration, of whom the French—those arbiters—disapprove?

It so happened that, during this weekend, I was reading a biography of Lincoln, and noted that many of the denunciations of the 16th president sounded familiar. After a Lincoln speech, the editor of the (Democratic) *Chicago Times* wrote, "The cheek of every American must tingle with shame as he reads the silly, flat and dishwatery utterances of the man who has to be pointed out to intelligent foreigners as the President of the United States."

The speech to which the editor was referring was the Gettysburg Address.

I hope that some of today's hysterics will be embarrassed, later, by what they said about George W. Bush, as many of Lincoln's critics must have been embarrassed. (They called him "gorilla," "ape," "baboon"—primatological putdowns seemed to rule the day.) But who knows?

Reaching out across partisan lines is wonderful—and necessary—but there are some people you simply cannot reach. What do you say to a lady who says that, through Tom DeLay et al., "theocracy" has come, and that one must rise in the middle of the night to listen to the BBC, in order to have the truth, because the American media are covering up for Bush? If you're me, you can say nothing, except to mutter something about habitation on different planets.

Sometimes, even muttering is hard. Put yourself in my shoes, dear reader. You're at an Upper East Side dinner party. The conversation turns political (uh-oh) and to 9/11. Someone mentions that the Pennsylvania plane was possibly destined for the White House. Your hostess says, "It's a shame President Bush wasn't killed that day."

Do you a) leave, b) make a joke, c) rebuke, d) try to employ sweet argument—what?

Please realize that there was nothing hypothetical about this situation. (I did a mixture of the above—ineptly.)

At Renaissance Weekend, there were some strident left-wingers, sure, but there were also many earnest and good liberals. One of my favorites commented on the regret of a woman who said that young teenagers were using cellphones to "hook up" for sex. "I don't just think that teenagers shouldn't use cellphones for sex," said this man; "I don't think teenagers should be allowed to have cellphones!"

And a good many liberals were awfully warm to this conservative.

Most of the compliments were sincere, I'd say. Others were of the "For a fat girl, you don't sweat much" variety. I noted something else in that Lincoln biography. He said, "I have endured a great deal of ridicule without much malice, and have received a great deal of kindness not quite free from ridicule. I am used to it." I'm no Lincoln, believe me, but I know what he is saying.

In any event, animals in the political zoo ought to emit their roars, and they ought to be heard of all other animals. Conservatives ought to lift up their voices and sing, even—or especially—in habitats that seem uncongenial.

And it's important that we listen to the liberals too, right? Well . . . we can always turn on NPR, or PBS, or open the *New York Times*, or watch Peter Jennings. But then, the other side can tune in to Rush, can't they? (Though he, we always add, is not a government entity.)

We hear that there are Two Americas—and not just economically—and that we operate in different spheres. Liberals have their media, and we, increasingly, have ours; liberals have their conclaves, and we have ours. Phil and Linda Lader seek to mix it up a little. Life cannot be a *National Review* cruise (alas).

Or a *Nation* cruise!

—August 9, 2004
National Review

PEOPLE

A Voice for Our Time

Those who think that Bush can't talk should think again

This essay served as the introduction to a collection of speeches and remarks by President George W. Bush, published by National Review *in 2003. The essay was also published in* National Review *magazine.*

For a man reputed to be "verbally challenged," George W. Bush has given some important speeches—some impressive ones, too. Words matter a great deal to this president. In fact, when all is said and done, his presidency may be known for its rhetoric (among other things). Then George W. Bush, the tongue-tied embarrassment, will have the last laugh—yet another last laugh. "Misunderestimated" once more.

Of course, it makes a difference that we are at war. September 11 "changed everything," we're told, and it certainly changed the Bush presidency. A president must find his voice in wartime, as in no other time. Woodrow Wilson gave many excellent speeches, on a wide range of subjects. But it is his war oratory we remember. Franklin Roosevelt had the Great Depression, but then he became "Dr. Win the War," rising from a date of infamy to put paid to Tojoism and Hitlerism alike. Abraham Lincoln? He was sharp and eloquent on agricultural policy, as on everything else. But . . .

George W. Bush is an interesting mixture: He is a Texan and an Easterner; he is Establishment and counter-Establishment; he is fancy and folksy; he is forceful and jocular; he is presidential and everyday. His formal speeches tend to be elegant, polished affairs, composed by top-notch speechwriters (about whom, more later). But he does well enough on his own: whether winging it before an audience or responding to reporters. When he is most purely himself, he is blunt, unfussy, a little salty—Trumanesque.

In July 2002, he was asked about the status of Osama bin Laden. "He may be alive," the president said. "If he is, we'll get him. If he's not, we got him." Speechwriters could labor for weeks and not come up with anything better.

This is also a quick and funny president. We all have our favorite examples, and I will cite one of mine, impressed on me by David Frum (a former Bush speechwriter himself, and the author of the superb memoir *The Right Man: The Surprise Presidency of George W. Bush*). Ozzy Osbourne was a guest at a big, noisy Washington dinner. Pointing out his funky tresses, the famous rocker-druggie said, "Mr. President, you should wear your hair like mine!" Bush responded, "Second term, Ozzy, second term."

WORDS TO GO WITH DEEDS

National Review has put together an interesting book. It's called *"We Will Prevail": President George W. Bush on War, Terrorism, and Freedom*. The book is a compilation of speeches and statements issuing from Bush since September 11. It contains very big speeches, like State of the Union addresses, and smaller—though equally resonant—statements: like the president's message through a bullhorn to rescue workers at Ground Zero. It features the defining speech at West Point, but also what Bush said while lighting the national Christmas tree. We see him, and hear him, before a variety of audiences, in a variety of settings. He talks to military personnel, world leaders, the employees of the Dixie Printing Company (Glen Burnie, Md.). We get not only a sense of the time, but a sense of the job of president—and a sense, I dare say, of America itself.

To peruse this volume is to be forced to live through September 11 and its aftermath—once again. It's surprising how much can be forgotten, in such a short space. (The Taliban, anyone?) The president himself recognized this tendency early on. Here he is on October 4, 2001: "I fully understand . . . there will be times when people feel a sense of normalcy—and I hope that happens sooner rather than later —and that September 11th may be a distant memory to some. But not to me, and not to this nation." Some 13 months later, he said, "One of my jobs is to make sure nobody gets complacent. One of my jobs is to remind people of the stark realities that we face. See, every morning I go into that great Oval Office and read threats to our country—every morning. . . . Some of them are blowhards [!], but we take every one of them seriously. It's the new reality."

Indeed.

As has often been noted, the president, on September 11, 2001, was reading to schoolchildren—a common event in that more luxurious age. Then we suffered that shock. Quick as a flash—that very day —Bush said, "We will make no distinction between the terrorists who committed these acts and those who harbor them." Many times later, he would refer to this policy as his "doctrine." He would state it and re-state it in assorted ways, giving the impression that he was ever more committed to it. He also said on September 11, "America has stood down enemies before, and we will do so this time. None of us will ever forget this day. Yet we go forward to defend freedom and all that is good and just in our world."

That may sound like the language of a comic book—but it was, to most of us, suitable language, and it reflected Bush's conviction that the current and ongoing conflict is one of good versus evil. One sees, in *"We Will Prevail,"* that he speaks frequently of "evildoers," "the evil ones," "the forces of evil," and the like. And he has been subjected to some mockery for this.

But he addressed such criticism head-on in that speech at West Point (the graduation exercises, June 1, 2002): "Some worry that it is somehow undiplomatic or impolite to speak the language of right and wrong. I disagree. Different circumstances require different methods, but not different moralities." And then he went into a flight of universalism worthy of Wilson: "Moral truth is the same in every culture, in every time, and in every place. Targeting innocent civilians for murder is always and everywhere wrong. Brutality against women is always and everywhere wrong. There can be no neutrality between justice and cruelty, between the innocent and the guilty. We are in a conflict between good and evil, and America will call evil by its name. By confronting evil and lawless regimes, we do not create a problem, we reveal a problem. And we will lead the world in opposing it."

Well, then.

A HUGE JOB, AND A DELICATE ONE

In the days and months after September 11, the president did many things: He comforted the grieving; he exalted the dead; he assuaged fears; he encouraged alertness; he pledged victory. He stepped into—and up to—any number of roles. He was mourner-in-chief, explainer-in-chief, inspirer-in-chief—and, of course, as the Constitution dictates, commander-in-chief. We see, throughout the *NR* book, that he combined what you might call the soft and the hard. He said, "I'm encouraging schoolchildren to write letters of friendship to Muslim children in different countries." He also said—just to take one example of thousands—"I'm going to talk about homeland security, but the best way to secure our homeland is to hunt the killers down one by one and bring them to justice, and that is what we're going to do."

That, too, is a constant theme from Bush: that there is no defense, traditionally understood, against our terrorist enemies. "In the face of today's new threat, the only way to pursue peace is to pursue those who threaten it." "My attitude is, the best way to secure the homeland is to unleash the mighty United States military and hunt them down and bring them to justice. And the best way to fight evil at home is to love your neighbor like you'd like to be loved yourself" (there's the soft Bush).

Over and over, Bush has explained that this is a different kind of war, without obvious precedents. "There will be times of swift, dramatic action. There will be times of steady, quiet progress." Note the following jab—a light one—at the press: "This is an unusual kind of war because it sometimes will show up on your TV screens and sometimes it won't. Sometimes there will be moments of high drama, and, of course, good reporters will be going [now there's a little audience laughter]—all kinds of hyperventilating, about this action or that action. And sometimes you won't see a thing."

The president has always understood that the world may be kindlier to an America that is down and bleeding than it is to an America that is on its feet and fighting back. To the United Nations, on November 10, 2001, he said, "After tragedy, there is time for sympathy and condolences. And my country has been grateful for both. But the time for sympathy has now passed; the time for action has arrived." In my view, this is one of the most arresting, and meaningful, lines in the entire book. On September 12, *Le Monde* had a headline, immediately to become famous: "We Are All Americans." Okay—and after?

Seldom does Bush shrink from talking straight about the nature of the enemy: "America is beginning to realize that the dreams of the terrorists and the Taliban were waking nightmares for Afghan women and their children. The Taliban murdered teenagers for laughing in the presence of soldiers. They jailed children as young as ten years old, and tortured them for the supposed crimes of their parents." And "women were banned from speaking, or laughing loudly. They were banned from riding bicycles, or attending school. They were denied basic health care," and so on.

The Beast of Baghdad? "On Saddam Hussein's orders, opponents have been decapitated, wives and mothers of political opponents have been systematically raped as a method of intimidation, and political prisoners have been forced to watch their own children being tortured." Unflinching assessments of this sort are often useful, in the eddies of debate.

A STYLE APPLAUDED AND DESPISED

As *"We Will Prevail"* unfolds, we see Bush in the full range of his moods. He is purposeful and defiant; humble and prayerful; cocky and sarcastic; angry and slashing; sentimental and weepy; playful and twitting. He has his favorite words, as we all do. One of his is "fabulous." ("What a fabulous land we have, and the reason why is because we've got such fabulous citizens." Bush says "fabulous" at least as much as any interior decorator.) He has a knack for speaking directly to people, without talking down to them: "I want to explain to you about Saddam Hussein, just quickly, if I might."

Check him out as he argues for a Department of Homeland Security: "I'm a person who believes in accountability. One reason I believe in accountability is because I understand who the American people are going to hold accountable if something happens: me. And therefore, I'm the kind of fellow who likes to pick up the phone and say, 'How we doing? How are we doing on implementing the strategy?' I don't like the idea of calling a hundred different agencies. I like to call one and say, 'Here is the strategy, and what are you doing about it? And if you're not doing something about it, I expect you to. And if you don't, I'm going to find somebody else that will do something about it.'"

Clear enough.

Sometimes Bush is archly funny. Speaking to high-school students, he said, "You've been learning this by studying your history—at least some of you by studying your history." Often he is funny-serious: "You know, when the enemy hit us, they must have not known what they were doing. I like to tell people, they must have been watching too much TV, because they didn't understand America" (thinking that we were soft, materialistic, and cringing). On another occasion, Bush said, "See, they thought we'd probably just file a lawsuit or two! . . . They don't have any idea about what makes the people here tick."

And how about the president in his full Texas-sheriff mode (as I dub it)? Before a political audience in October 2002, he said, "We still got this coalition of freedom-loving nations we're working with. And we're hunting 'em down. The other day, one of 'em popped up —popped his head up—named al-Shibh. He's no longer a problem."

This is the kind of talk that thrills Bush's fans, and exasperates his critics.

THE 'CALL OF HISTORY'

I have been thinking about this president and words for some time now. In the fall of 2000, I took a leave of absence from *National Review* to assist the speechwriting staff on the Bush campaign (ah, the flexibility of the opinion journalist). At the time, the speechwriters were Michael Gerson (the chief), John McConnell, and Matthew Scully. They are still with George W. Bush, doing an extraordinary job (a *fabulous* job). And most would agree that Bush has grown in his ability to communicate, both in his prepared, professionalized speeches and in his unscripted remarks. In fact, some of us wish that they'd unleash him more—that he would unleash himself more. Let him mangle his syntax: He still gets his point across, usually effectively.

Proof of this lies in *NR*'s collection—which begins on September 11 and concludes with the Iraq campaign. There is much repetition in the book, which cannot be helped. But Bush's utterances, taken together, are strangely compelling. As the War on Terror proceeds, he gives you new wrinkles, new information, new thrusts. When I went through the galleys, I got a shiver once or twice—reminded of something I'd forgotten. "I'm told [said Bush] that one of the pilots here, a fellow named Randy, was asked if anyone at Travis [Air Force Base] had personal connections to any of the victims of the attacks of September the 11th. And here's what he said: 'I think we all do; they're all Americans. When you strike one American, you strike us all.'"

Not long ago, I did a radio interview, whose chief purpose was to discuss this book. The interviewer began roughly as follows: "First of all, are you serious about this book? I mean, Bush and oratory? Are you doing it with some irony? Is this sort of a joke book?" He could not understand how one could view Bush as a serious and important speaker, so completely had he swallowed the caricature of Bush as a stumblebum. My suspicion, however, is that "history"—if it is fair—will recall that Bush did a splendid job rhetorically, as well as in other, more concrete respects, in a most difficult time. When it mattered a lot, his words came true. Like Ronald Reagan, he speaks as though he believes what he is saying—because he does. (You can tell, very easily, when Bush's heart isn't really in it.)

Shortly before the Iraq campaign, Bush observed that "this call of history has come to the right country." More than a few of us contend that—to borrow from David Frum's title—it came to the right man, too.

—September 29, 2003

Conquest's Conquest

A man and his admirers

W e're in something of a Robert Conquest moment—but then, we've always been in such a moment, at least since 1968, when Conquest published his book on Stalin's rule, *The Great Terror*. That was the book that shut them up. Well, many of them, anyway.

Currently, Martin Amis and Christopher Hitchens both have books out. Who are they? They're two of the jazziest British writers of their generation, and they're great friends of each other, as well as great rivals. Amis's book is called *Koba the Dread*: It's about Stalin (Koba was a nickname) and the failure of Western intellectuals to come to grips with Communism. It also touches on several personal matters. Amis addresses Hitchens directly in the book: "Comrade Hitchens!"

The latter's book is on Orwell: *Why Orwell Matters*. Part of Hitchens's project is to claim the great man for the Left, or for some sort of Left, in any case.

Other than being popular, probing, and stylish, these books have one thing in common: They're dedicated to the same man, Robert Conquest.

This is not only interesting, but also somewhat awkward, at least for the dedicatee. Amis and Hitchens have been sparring, making for a nice public show, though with a serious side. Each claims Conquest as a guiding light, and each is surely right. He has been that for many thousands, who, unlike these two authors, never met the man.

He must be one of the most important writers of the second half of the 20th century, producing a string of books that—like Solzhenitsyn's—put the lie to Communism, in particular to Soviet Communism. In the early 1990s, Richard Nixon—a fair judge of world events—said, "[Conquest's] historical courage makes him partially responsible for the death of Communism." Another high tribute came from a member of the Central Committee of the Soviet Communist Party—who denounced, and immortalized, Conquest as "Anti-Sovietchik Number One."

SITTING ON THEIR SHOULDERS

Martin Amis's father, the novelist Kingsley, was a close friend of Conquest's, although they often had rows. Kingsley liked to make up stories about Conquest (and others, of course). Perhaps the most famous is: "When asked whether he'd like to retitle a new edition of *The Great Terror*, Bob said, 'How about, *I Told You So, You F***ing Fools?*'" That sounds like Conquest, but it wasn't. Could have been. Another time, as Conquest relates—I rang him up—Kingsley published "a totally untrue story about me and a girl." When Conquest got cross with his friend, Kingsley simply transferred the tale to someone else.

At one point, exasperated, Conquest cut him off entirely: "but I gave him a general amnesty on the occasion of the collapse of the Soviet Union."

Martin Amis begins *Koba the Dread* by quoting from Conquest's 1986 book *The Harvest of Sorrow*, which documents the Soviets' terror-famine in the Ukraine. As he comments on Conquest's findings, Amis is in a kind of shocked awe. He is also gloriously, almost sputteringly, indignant, wondering how the Communists got away with it. Later in the book—taking up an old theme—Amis writes, "Everybody knows of the 6 million of the Holocaust. Nobody knows of the 6 million of the Terror-Famine" (get those capital letters).

The junior Amis seems to have come rather late to a realization of the horrors of Communism, and of the horrible Western tolerance of it, even celebration of it. This has caused some veteran anti-Communists to guffaw. But a writer of Martin Amis's skill and influence should be welcomed into this company, rather than scorned. He might be thanked for joining. A great many people in the Free West were raised on lies, or half-truths, or apologias—and when they encountered Conquest or Solzhenitsyn or somebody else, they saw.

Conquest has known Martin Amis since he was a child, and he has known Christopher Hitchens a long while too. He is sometimes tried by them—particularly by the latter—but his affection is obvious. Hitchens, for example, is always "Hitch" from Conquest's mouth.

The dedication in *Why Orwell Matters* is rather unusual. It begins, "Dedicated by permission." It's not uncommon for a writer to seek permission before dedicating, but hardly anyone has seen such permission stated. It's as though Hitchens is saying, "No, this is for real—and he doesn't mind!" The dedication continues, "To Robert Conquest—premature anti-fascist, premature anti-Stalinist, poet and mentor, and founder of the 'united front against bullshit.'"

A couple of points here, already. First, John Earl Haynes and Harvey Klehr published a peculiar, fascinating, and demolishing piece in the September 2002 *New Criterion* called "The Myth of 'Premature Anti-fascism.'" American Communists and leftists have long liked to say that the U.S. government labeled members of the Abraham Lincoln Brigade in Spain "premature anti-fascists." This is complete rubbish. The Communists, self-congratulatingly, attached the phrase to themselves. Second, Conquest was not merely an "anti-Stalinist," but an anti-Communist, period: in Russia, in Vietnam, in Europe, in the Caribbean—everywhere.

Hitchens's dedication to Conquest has amused some conservatives and irked others. Perhaps the right response is to be heartened by it. Someone remarked, "Robert Conquest is the angel sitting on Christopher Hitchens's right shoulder; Gore Vidal is the devil sitting on his left one." Indeed, the back cover of *Why Orwell Matters* contains three blurbs under the heading "Praise for Christopher Hitchens": from Vidal, Edward Said, and Susan Sontag. Those are three funny names alongside Conquest's. Vidal says, in his blurb, "I've been asked whether I wish to nominate a successor, an inheritor . . . I've decided to name Christopher Hitchens."

When I tell Conquest who the blurbists are, he laughs heartily. These guys aren't exactly members of the "united front against bullshit," are they? I inform Conquest that some fear that Hitchens is trying to co-opt him—perhaps claim him for the Left, same as he's doing with Orwell (more plausibly, to be sure). Conquest answers, "He won't get very far."

In a recent discussion on Andrew Sullivan's (great) web-site—www.AndrewSullivan.com—Hitchens said that Conquest "might not want to be identified as a full-out conservative, because he is an ex-Marxist and was a committed social democrat—and even voted for Clinton in 1992!—but he has found a sort of home on the civilized Right . . ."

On hearing this, Conquest half-chortles, half-explodes: "Ex-Marxist? Oh, come on! I was a Marxist when I was 20, and I wasn't a committed social democrat ever." As for Clinton, "I don't vote! I might have said something in Clinton's favor, knowing nothing about him in those days. I didn't think the [George H. W.] Bush administration was doing very well. I might have hoped that Clinton was a Scoop Jackson type. And, it's true, I'd like to see at least some Democrats who'd be solid, in the Jackson way." Wouldn't we all.

Well, then, how would he describe himself, politically? One writer, in *Reason*, described him as a "Burkean conservative." Conquest would allow that. He says, "I'm an anti-extremist. And I'm for a law-and-liberty culture.

Those are Orwell's words: law and liberty. I don't regard the EU as being any good for that. I am strongly against the EU. I'm against regulationism and managerialism. I'm against activism of any sort." Remember, he says, "the Nazis were keen statists, and keen on socialism: 'national socialism,' they called it." And when it comes to "conservatism"—that murky term—"I feel that, when other people and nations are veering from civilization, I would prefer to conserve. I certainly prefer Burke to Locke—but, of course, there's overlap of various sorts."

Hitchens is inarguably right to compare Conquest to Orwell, as he has. In fact, he begins his new book with a poem that Conquest wrote about Orwell in 1969. Its first lines are, "Moral and mental glaciers melting slightly / Betray the influence of his warm intent." More than a few have observed that this applies to the poet himself.

A HAPPY (COLD) WARRIOR

Conquest is now ensconced at the Hoover Institution, casting his eye on the world, writing his books as usual. We should have his memoirs before long—but first he's doing a book on the gross miseducation of the young. He's a famously amusing, fun-loving person, Conquest: full of jokes and quips and aperçus, ready to recite any number of limericks (a specialty). For someone who has spent his life immersed in the grimness of mass murder—and the reluctance of free people to face up to it—he is astoundingly merry. According to his wife, Elizabeth, as Martin Amis tells us, Conquest simply "wakes up happy."

He was born in 1917 to an American father and an English mother. Even today he holds dual citizenship. At Oxford, he was a Communist party member, but an open member, not a secret one, which somehow is typical of Conquest—more honest. It didn't take long to shake off his Communism. He would later write, "Often at the age of 18 or 20, a student meets some glittering general idea and, far from feeling any responsibility to submit it to serious questioning, henceforward follows it like a duckling imprinted with its mother." Conquest was not a duckling.

During the war, he was in the Balkans and saw exactly what the Communists were up to. He has always insisted that the facts about the Soviet Union were always available, for anyone interested in them. Trouble was, too few were interested. Everyone was in the thrall of "socialism" (though not of the "national" variety). If Idi Amin had only called himself a socialist, Conquest once said, he'd have been all right—no matter how many people he ate. Even today, they're still swooning over most any tyrant and torturer who calls himself "socialist" or "progressive." A couple of weeks ago, Steven Spielberg was held spellbound by Castro in Havana for eight hours—the "most important" in his life, said Spielberg after.

If Conquest now enjoys vindication, there's still a lot of stubborn revisionism going on in the universities, a refusal to see clear. "They're still talking absolute balls," says Conquest. "In the academy, there remains a feeling of, 'Don't let's be too rude to Stalin. He was a bad guy, yes, but the Americans were bad guys too, and so was the British Empire.'" Furthermore, "They say [disapprovingly] that we were Cold Warriors. Yes, and a bloody good show, too. A lot of people *weren't* Cold Warriors—and so much the worse for them."

The present war—that against Islamic extremism—is a different kind of war, yet with similarities. There are myths to be fought against here, too. Shortly after 9/11, Conquest wrote (for *National Review Online*), "[There is little] knowledge about the mental world of those outside the American, or Western, experience, and in particular about the mental world of the enemies of the democratic way of life. One result [is] the assumption that the enemies of Western culture can be won over by goodwill; and that the West is to blame if such approaches do not work."

Robert Conquest has never been unclear about the "mental world" of anti-democratic and murderous forces. Those who endured the Soviet Union, above all, will never forget him for it. In 1989—the super-thawing days of *glasnost*—Conquest returned to the Soviet Union for the first time since he was a student. Practically everyone in the Soviet Union had read *The Great Terror*, under the pillow, as it were. One man asked to pinch Conquest, just to reassure himself that he, Conquest, was really there, on Russian soil. And another man—a poet—came up to him on the street and, wordlessly, handed him a rose.

That, we're still doing: handing Conquest roses.

—December 9, 2002
National Review

Being Sharansky

On Russia, Israel, 'Reaganite readings' . . .

T he other day, someone asked me how old Sharansky was, and I said, "Oh, about 55." (In fact, Sharansky is 57, born in January 1948, a few months before the modern Israel.) My friend was surprised that Sharansky was so young. The ex-Soviet dissident, now a key Israeli, has been famous and important for a long time. He was only 25 when he applied for his exit visa, and not long after that he became the face of the "refuseniks."

In his astoundingly great memoir, *Fear No Evil*—published in 1988—he recounts the day of his release, when he was delivered into the hands of the American ambassador to West Germany, Richard Burt.

> All I remember from my talk with the ambassador is how astonished I was that he was only thirty-nine. "You made your career so quickly," I said.
>
> "Well," he replied, "you're also very young and made a career quickly."
>
> "Yes, but in my case the KGB helped. I trust that your achievement had nothing to do with them."

Sharansky spent nine years in the Gulag, a harrowing time in which he demonstrated what resistance is. More than 400 of those days were spent in punishment cells; more than 200 were spent on hunger strikes. His refusal to concede anything to the Soviet state was almost superhuman. This was true to the very last. When they relinquished him to the East Germans, they told him to walk straight to a waiting car—"Don't make any turns." Sharansky zig-zagged his way to that car.

Once in Israel, he might have sat back to be the hero, but the swim of events would not allow him to do so, and he entered politics. At the beginning of May, he resigned from the cabinet of Prime Minister Ariel Sharon, in protest of the prime minister's "disengagement" plan—Sharansky considers it reckless. He is now associated with Jerusalem's Shalem Center. Last fall, Sharansky came out with his second book, *The Case for Dem-*

ocracy: The Power of Freedom to Overcome Tyranny and Terror. It applies lessons gleaned from the Cold War to the current conflict—it is very, very hard on advocates of "stability." President Bush read the book while it was still in galleys. He then met with Sharansky in the Oval Office. Later, the president told the *Washington Times*, "If you want a glimpse of how I think about foreign policy, read Natan Sharansky's book."

I spoke with the author recently, while he was visiting New York. We spent about half our time on the Soviet Union—and Russia—and half on Israel. First, the Soviet Union: Did he ever think it would collapse?

"I was absolutely sure it would collapse. All of us dissidents were sure it would fall apart, because we saw how weak it was from the inside." In 1969, a friend of his, Andrei Amalrik, wrote a book called *Will the Soviet Union Survive Until 1984?* (Nineteen eighty-four was the big Orwell year, of course.) Amalrik died "in some very strange car accident," says Sharansky—this was in France, in 1980. Amalrik was therefore deprived of the chance to see how it would all turn out. In any event, when Sharansky was in prison and 1984 came around, "The KGB guys were telling me, 'It's 1984, and your friend is not here, but the Soviet Union is: It will exist forever.'" Not quite. Sharansky retains from Amalrik a compelling image: A totalitarian society is like a soldier who must point his gun at a prisoner 24 hours a day, every day. Eventually, his muscles will tire, the gun will start to sag, and the prisoner will escape.

In Sharansky's view, the three most important people in defeating the Soviet Union were Andrei Sakharov, Scoop Jackson, and Ronald Reagan. Each man shook the regime, in ways both diverse and related. What about Gorbachev?

"Of course it was good that he came to power," says Sharansky. But people inflate his role, as the former general secretary himself does. "He wanted to save the Communist system, and he gave a little bit of freedom to Soviet citizens. But he was a true Communist, and the Communists never understood that there is no such thing as a little bit of freedom: Give people a little, they will take everything." In the West, Gorbachev is seen "as this great, historic figure, who started a process of transformation"; in the Soviet Union, "we knew him to be the one trying to stop it."

And what about Solzhenitsyn? According to Sharansky, his contribution was twofold. First, "he severely undermined the regime, by exposing the truth about it to all the world." After *The Gulag Archipelago*, it was harder for the West to apologize for the Soviet Union. And in the empire itself, "he increased the number of doublethinkers." Doublethinkers? Ah, yes. Sharansky sees totalitarian societies—"fear societies," he also calls them—as containing three groups of people: the "true believers," who are committed to the regime; the dissidents, who are in open opposition; and the "doublethinkers," who may talk and act one way, but think another—they have their doubts. This third group is large and vital.

I wonder whether Sharansky ever thinks about Russia—keeps abreast of its problems, worries about its fate. He answers, "First of all, Russia is a very important part of my own history, and the history of many Jews. Second, it's a country where many Jews still live. And third, it's a country that plays a very important role in the world"—and in the current debate over democracy. There is a fourth point, too: "Some of the people who were the biggest influences on me were Russians, starting with my teacher, Sakharov." (*The Case for Democracy* is dedicated to his memory.) And who could do without the literature of Russia, especially that of the 19th century? But Israel and the Middle East present enough problems.

A CRUCIAL DEBATE

In recent months, Sharansky has squared off with a giant of Israeli history and politics, Ariel Sharon. Interestingly, Sharansky—born Anatoly Sharansky, you remember, and now Natan Sharansky—once called himself Natan Sharon. This was with his fellow Jewish activists in the Soviet Union. A generation before him, an uncle emigrated to Palestine, taking the name of Sharon.

I inquire whether Sharansky sees the prime minister as a tragic figure. "There is, in fact, something tragic about Ariel Sharon," he responds. Of course, Sharon's overall record cannot be gainsaid: He was pivotal in the Yom Kippur War, and "of the prime ministers I have worked with, he is by far the most knowledgeable, about everything connected to Israel." Moreover, "he has great respect for my past, and an interest in it, and he gave me full support in my role of coordinating the struggle against anti-Semitism. He is one of the few who think all the time about world Jewry, anti-Semitism, Jewish education—these things are important to him." But he has always been skeptical that "the other side" can liberalize and democratize, at least in time to do Israel any good.

Like others, Sharansky casts the disengagement as "an act of desperation"—even many of its supporters describe it as such. In Sharansky's telling, Sharon very much wanted to complete the peace process, but was stymied by the Palestinian leadership. So he decided to disengage, to draw a kind of line, on his own, or on Israel's own: a line that would be firm. "He sat us down and said, 'I want to stop this vicious cycle. This will do it. It will be very painful, but then Palestinian problems will be Palestinian problems. If they have unemployed, if they don't have a normal life—then it's their problem. The world will not pressure us. We'll have ten years, five years, without the pressure of the world, during which time we will strengthen our position, and hope for stability.'"

And how did Sharansky respond? "I said, 'You don't have ten years, you don't have ten *days*. To the contrary, the world will continue its pressure, and *increase* it: because you made it legitimate to dismantle settlements in exchange for nothing. They'll say that, if you gave up 20, you can give up 100. And if the Palestinians continue to fight, it's only because you didn't dismantle enough.'" Sharansky believes that "we have paid a big price, as a result of terror. We defeated them militarily, and now we're making a big concession. This is not a process—it's completely one-sided. And it has caused a terrible rift in Israeli society." Consider this, too: Hamas has already used the disengagement in its propaganda, citing it as proof positive that terrorism works.

And yes, George W. Bush is behind the plan. "You can't expect the president of the United States to be more Zionist than Ariel Sharon." But Bush shares with Sharansky the view that no real peace is possible while conditions of tyranny exist.

Sharansky met with Reagan quite a bit—some of his stories about the late president are priceless—and he has a grasp on President Bush. "Reagan called a spade a spade, and his policy was based on instinct, not on some grand strategy. But his instincts were absolutely right, and that's why he made history. He's the one who put Communism into the grave." Then this outlook—the linking of human freedom and security—"was fully abandoned by the West, including by America during President Bush's father and certainly during President Clinton." Bush 43, however, is in the Reagan mold.

"I talked to Dick Cheney, back in January 2001, before the swearing-in. I had known him when he was in Congress. I talked to him about bringing back the linkage between security and democracy, and about the mistakes of Oslo. Cheney didn't say a lot, but he was listening." I point out, "Cheney is known as a good listener." Sharansky: "Yes, but Clinton's a great listener, too—he is so understanding. But then he does nothing." Sharansky holds that Bush's call for a democratic leadership among the Palestinians is historic, hugely consequential, and overlooked. "This is a return to the ideas that Reagan was expressing: 'Our security depends on their freedom.'" This remains, however, a minority view in the world.

Speaking of the world: How does Sharansky feel when it calls his state an oppressor, and when it calls him an apologist for this oppression—a hypocrite who suffered persecution himself but now metes it out to others? Sharansky gives a quick shake of disgust, then cites an early Zionist, Ahad Ha'am, who argued that the blood libel actually worked to the advantage of the Jews. Worked to their advantage? How is that possible, given the violence and mayhem that this libel caused? "Because a Jew can know that the whole world can believe something that is nevertheless an absolute lie. I still know Russians who believe [the blood libel]! The world may say we're a Nazi-type state, that we're a big human-rights violator, that we committed atrocities at Jenin—and it's all false."

Sharansky continues, "When I moved from the Soviet Union to a free society, it reminded me—and it still reminds me—how great a democracy is, and that it has a unique record in war. I propose to friends in Europe and America that they compare the records of their own countries as democracies in war to Israel's record." Sharansky fears no such comparison.

I ask the annoying question of whether Israel will make it. "Yes, of course. I'm an optimistic person. In the Soviet Union, the KGB guys often told me, 'You will not make it out alive.' And I sometimes had doubt that I personally would survive. But I never had any doubt that our struggle would succeed." Sharansky is similarly optimistic about the survival of Israel: but it would be nice if Israelis did not have to "fight time after time for the right to have their own state. I remind you of what I said in my resignation letter: Not only are we making a tragic mistake [in the disengagement], we are also missing an opportunity of historic proportions," given the liberalizing winds now whistling through the world. Sharansky does not believe in safety absent freedom.

HIGHEST THINGS

Some people regard Sharansky as a providential figure, spared death in the Gulag to perform his work now. What does he think? "I long ago stopped asking myself whether God gives us a mission or we give ourselves a mission, in an effort to be worthy of God." He recalls the prayer that he invented for himself in prison, and mutters a little of it: "Grant me the strength, the power, the intelligence . . . and the patience to leave this jail and reach the Land of Israel in an honest and worthy way."

At the close of our conversation, I ask him about his Psalm book. Does he still have it? A pocket book of Psalms was given to him by his wife, Avital, a few days before he was arrested. He went through hell to hang on to this book. The authorities often deprived him of it. Once, he went on a "work strike," entailing several months of the punishment cell—until he got that book back. In another period, "I took my Psalm book and for days on end . . . recited all one hundred and fifty of King David's psalms, syllable by syllable." (I quote from *Fear No Evil*.) For a while, he was able to study the Bible, Old Testament and New, with a fellow prisoner, a Christian named Volodya.

> We called our sessions Reaganite readings, first, because President Reagan had declared either this year or the preceding one (it wasn't exactly clear from the Soviet press) the Year of the Bible, and second, because we realized that even the slightest improvement in our situation could be related only to a firm position on human rights by the West, especially by America, and we mentally urged Reagan to demonstrate such resolve.

One other thing about the Psalm book: It "was the only material evidence [through the nine years] of my mystical tie with Avital."

Toward the very end of his ordeal, at the airport in Moscow—Sharansky had no idea what was happening to him—he refused to board the plane before they gave him back his Psalm book. In front of photographers, he dropped to the snow, yelling for it. They gave it back to him. Once aboard—when they told him he was being released—he recited the Psalm he had always designated for his liberation day, Psalm 30: "I will extol thee, O Lord; for thou hast lifted me up, and hast not made my foes to rejoice over me."

Anyway, back in New York, sitting in a hotel dining room—I ask whether he still has the book. He grins a little, reaches inside his jacket, and produces it. There it is, this tiny book, big as life. Apparently, he has it on him always, the way one carries wallet and keys. Has he ever been in danger of losing it (I mean, lately)? "Sometimes I forget where I've put it, and it becomes more of a problem with age."

What Sharansky will not lose is his sense of purpose and right; it causes him to zig-zag through life along a very straight path.

—July 4, 2005
National Review

Reagan in Full

An array of pre-presidential writings

The below is a review of Reagan, In His Own Hand: The Writings of Ronald Reagan that Reveal His Revolutionary Vision for America.

W e were awfully excited when we first heard about it—"we" being Reaganauts (to use the original term), and "it" being a cache of documents in the former president's own hand. We had always known he was an inveterate writer, and a formidable one. And now we would be able to prove it to the world.

And that is a problem we Reagan champions have: always trying to prove that our man—undeniably a politician and leader of great skill—was an intellectual force as well. This has become an exhausting, sometimes pathetic mission. The strength of Reagan's mind has long been obvious to anyone who has given the man two seconds' thought; but, of course, many people—many influential people—are unwilling to put in a good two seconds. To them, Reagan will always be, if not quite a boob, a lightweight all the same—a lucky innocent, who stumbled onto some success as president.

About that cache of documents: Not long ago, a scholar from Carnegie Mellon, Kiron K. Skinner, was poking around Reagan's private papers for a study of the Cold War. And among those papers she found a treasure-trove of manuscripts—true manuscripts, which is to say, documents written by hand. These were radio addresses that Reagan had given between the years 1975 and 1979 (after he left the governorship of California and before he became president of the United States). There were almost 700 of them, and they showed Reagan in something close to his fullness. Together with the Hoover Institution's Martin and Annelise Anderson—veteran Reaganauts—Skinner assembled the manuscripts into this present, extraordinary volume: *Reagan, In His Own Hand*. And these writings really do, as the subtitle proclaims, "reveal" our 40th president's "revolutionary vision for America."

He was one of the great proselytizers of recent history, Reagan. He was a pamphleteer, an arguer, a persuader, a propagandist, at times an evangelist—restless and relentless. He was a shy, remote man, as we all know, but he had what must have been a compulsion to take the public by the arm and say, "See? This is the way it is. Did you hear about this? Did you ever consider that?"

And he was always writing. He seemed not only to like to write, but to need to do so. He wrote from childhood, and he always wrote well—solidly and often stylishly. Over nine decades, he wrote thousands of letters, including 276 to a pen pal who was president of a Reagan (movie) fan club. He wrote for his school newspapers, he wrote a sports column for the *Des Moines Dispatch*, he wrote speeches and statements as a union leader, he wrote as a corporate spokesman, he wrote as a political candidate, he wrote as a governor and as a president—he never stopped, at least until the day in 1994 when he wrote a stunning, heartbreaking letter to his fellow Americans, explaining why he had to withdraw from public life. In 1947, when Reagan was 36, a reporter profiling him observed, "In private life, Reagan is most interested in writing." Reagan lived a life of words. Constant, well-chosen, and, in the end, world-changing words.

The mid-'70s radio addresses were five minutes long, and they were to be delivered five days a week. Along with his newspaper column (which, unlike the radio speeches, was largely ghosted), they were Reagan's principal means of keeping in touch with the public between campaigns. The editors reproduce the manuscripts exactly as they are, with crossings-out and additions and marginal notes and misspellings and mispunctuation and instructions to the typist—everything. Now, I myself do not see the point of retaining misspellings and mispunctuation. Anyone can appreciate the drive for authenticity, but these oddities are distracting, and contribute little. Also, Reagan did not intend for the public to see his scribbles; he wrote privately and probably hurriedly, and he wrote in a kind of shorthand. The spelling and punctuation, in my view, should have been regularized, if only as a courtesy to the author.

For these addresses, Reagan wrote to a precise length, and he did so with no evident struggle—his revisions are relatively few (and they are almost invariably improvements). He took a break from the broadcasts to wage his 1976 campaign against President Ford for the Republican nomination. (In the interim, Sen. Barry Goldwater took over the radio job.) He resumed two weeks after the party's convention. And he never lost the bug to communicate by radio: As president, he instituted a weekly radio address, a practice copied by his successors.

These writings are Reagan in essence. They are profound and simple. They are folksy and informed. They are gutsy and gentle, meek and bold, indignant and relaxed. They have a little poetry, and a lot of prose (Reagan was addicted to facts and figures, and to logic; he indulges in almost no platitudes or flights of rhetoric). They are utterly natural, never contrived (professional showman though Reagan may have been). They always respect the dignity and intelligence of the audience. They show a basic sympathy for people—especially for those bent under tyranny—and they show a love of life. They show religious faith. And they show a strange, almost unbelievable patriotism.

The broadcasts bring to mind Paul Harvey, and Rush Limbaugh, and Milton Friedman's old *Free to Choose* series. One nice thing about them is that they provide a walk down Memory Lane, issues-wise: oil, the Humphrey-Hawkins bill, Namibia! Reagan would write about anything and everything, drawing from a variety of sources (and not only *Human Events*). It seems that nothing failed to engage his attention, large or small. He was endlessly curious, his mind always moving. How about this speech by Eugene Rostow, or this column by James Burnham, or this memoir from this new dissident, Bukovsky? Did you hear what happened to the refusenik Ida Nudel? Whaddya say we write the embassy? And if the Soviets could lie so flagrantly about the Katyn Forest—history matters immensely—could they be trusted on anything?

He would begin with a little enticer, such as, "If you thought the United Nations was a debating society, brace yourselves." And he liked to end with some quiet zinger. After a fairly high-minded discussion of the East–West drama, he says, "Détente: Isn't that what a farmer has with his turkey—until Thanksgiving?" Effortlessly, he mixed the high and the low. Talking about the importance of strength to deterrence, he would cite Paul Nitze, but also Will Rogers, who once quipped, "I've never seen anyone insult Jack Dempsey."

He had a clear, orderly mind, that could take an issue and wrestle it down. In October 1975, for example, he considered the Russian wheat deal, a complicated, hotly debated question. We can see the train of his thought as he considers every angle—the economic, the strategic, and the moral. Reagan winds up favoring the deal. But the larger, long-term "moral question," Reagan warns—the question of whether to do anything to sustain the Soviet economy, and thus that rule—"won't go away." For Reagan, it always came down to the moral question. We see in these radio addresses that his project, fundamentally, was moral.

Of the famed Reagan wit, there is plenty: "No wonder Gromyko describes negotiations as 'business-like & useful.' Translated from the Russian, that means, 'Uncle Sam has been skinned again.'" And there is considerable humility. Asks Reagan, "What should the United Nations' duty be to people who are subjected to vicious and inhumane torture?" (He is thinking now about that eternally vexing question: Africa.) "I must confess I don't know the answer." But Reagan dwells on the matter with utmost care, and power.

And then there is that patriotism, a patriotism that seems to make the country new again: "Every once in a while, all of us native-born Americans should make it a point to have a conversation with one who is an American by choice. They have a perspective on this country we can never have. They can do a lot to firm up our resolve to be free for another 200 yrs."

So gleaming is this volume, you could quote from almost any page. Readers may take particular delight in a robust defense of the Electoral College, made in April 1977, after Vice President Mondale proposed eliminating it. With the patience and precision of a fine civics teacher, Reagan makes the case for republican government. In a purely popular referendum, he notes, "a half-dozen rural states could show a majority for one candidate and be outvoted by one big industrial state opting for his opponent. Presidential candidates would be tempted to aim their campaigns & their promises at a cluster of metropolitan areas in a few states, and the smaller states would be without a voice." You don't say.

For me, the trait that shines most brightly through these pages is goodness—a core, manifest goodness. Here is one marginal note—or, rather, message—I especially love: It is from Reagan to his typist. At the bottom of a speech, Reagan (who often wrote while he was traveling) jots, "Sorry, the plane was bouncing around." Just a small thing, but telling. And then there is his first address after the 1976 presidential campaign. He speaks of the people he met all over the country, who stood in the rain for him, and listened to him, and solemnly weighed their choice—"the campaign trail is no place for the cynic." And with all those conscientious Americans, "only the world's worst scoundrel could intentionally let them down."

The final section of the book is given over to sundry writings, beginning with some juvenilia (which are exceptional—any mother, or teacher, would bubble over with pride) and ending with that 1994 farewell letter. The Hollywood diary, the correspondence, the slashing, expertly crafted political speeches—all are remarkable.

But if I could single out just one item, from the entire volume, it would be a 1971 letter—very long—written to the editor of a student publication at Eureka College, Reagan's alma mater. The paper has obviously denounced Reagan as a Neanderthal and foe of academic freedom, incapable of understanding the current generation. So the governor of California takes the time to explain himself and to teach these students something about philosophy, and freedom, and history. Is Reagan really a benighted rightwinger? "The first speech quoted [in the student attack] was made in 1966 before I was Gov. and while I was still making my living in Hollywood (I just slipped that latter point in, hoping you'd be reminded that Hollywood is not exactly a symbol of prudishness and sheltered living)."

Complains Reagan, "With a sureness that almost amounts to arrogance, the author of the article describes my generation of Eureka students as some kind of Rover Boys gaily playing pranks between classes in which we submitted cheerfully to being spoon-fed the customs and mores of the past. *Never* has the past been so open to question as it was in that long-ago time." For "we came to college age in the midst of a social and economic upheaval, the Great Depression, which was for real. Life was a very grim business, but somehow we managed to keep a sense of humor, which I have difficulty finding, at least on our Calif. campuses today. And we presided over the greatest econ. & social revolution the world has ever seen."

"True education," Reagan concludes, "is society's attempt to enunciate certain ultimate values upon which individuals & hence society may safely build. You have every right to ask the reason behind the mores & customs of what we refer to as civilization. Challenge, we can afford. You have no right & it makes no sense to reject the wisdom of the ages simply because it is rooted in the past. Challenge—but weigh the answers to your challenge very carefully." Ultimately, "true freedom is the freedom of self-discipline—the freedom to choose within acceptable standards. Take that framework away & you lose freedom."

This letter—which must be read in its entirety, excerpts failing to do it justice—is a small political masterpiece.

But there's more: Reagan sends a copy of his letter to the college's president, with a note saying, "I thought you might like to see this in case the editor chooses to keep it to himself." Think of it: Reagan was governor of California, a major national figure, and Eureka's most important alumnus, by far. And he not only pauses to compose this weighty letter—which must be the most significant document ever to reach that humble publication—but realizes that the punk editor may deep-six it!

So, how did this happen? How did it happen that Reagan—endowed with so great, and so obvious, a mental gift—was ever regarded as a simpleton? In a foreword to this book, George Shultz writes, "I could tell dozens of stories about specific times when Ronald Reagan displayed detailed knowledge about policy issues, and when he took decisive action based on that knowledge—without the benefit of someone whispering in his ear or sliding a note into his hand. But so ingrained is the belief that he was an amiable man—not too bright, the willing captive of his aides—that it would probably not make much difference." This may be so.

But when excerpts from the book appeared in the *The New York Times Magazine*, I got a marveling phone call from an old friend, reared in the liberal Democratic (and Reagan-hating, or at least -belittling) faith. "Can you believe it?" he said. "Can you believe how impressive these things are? They are completely at odds with the image we have of him." I could only respond, Reagan-style, "What do you mean 'we,' Kemosabe?"

Reagan-lovers will gulp down this book, and fall in love all over again; others—if they are open-minded, like my friend—will be affected. Whatever else the collection does, it proves that Reagan, in addition to the many other things he was, was a writer. As president in particular, he would have many top-flight speechwriters—Tony Dolan, Bentley Elliott, Peggy Noonan, Peter Robinson, John Podhoretz—but I think that all of them would agree that no one ever wrote for Reagan better than he wrote for himself, when he could.

I close by noting that *Reagan, In His Own Hand* carries a most unusual, and poignant, dedication: "For Ronald Reagan, who wrote the documents." For several years now, we have grown accustomed to thinking and talking about Reagan in the past tense. It cannot be helped. But we should also note that Reagan turned 90 on February 6. And after reading and rubbing my eyes at this astounding book, I can only blurt out: Hail to the Chief.

—February 19, 2001
National Review

Our Splendid Cuss

The likable Phil Gramm

A piece about the Texas senator, shortly after he announced his retirement from that august body.

A s if it weren't bad enough that Jesse Helms is leaving, Phil Gramm, too, is "moving on," to use a recently popular phrase. Thus are we right types losing our two favorite, and most stalwart, senators. Each is judged irreplaceable, indispensable, and each may be, though Gramm bristles at the suggestion: "As my grandmama used to say, 'The graveyard is full of indispensable men.'" Plus, the Founders set it up so that "it shouldn't matter who's here [in Washington]." Moreover, "Senators often say to me, 'You said, or did, exactly what I wanted to do.' But if I hadn't been here, maybe they would have."

Don't know about that one. For about 20 years, Phil Gramm has been the conservatives'—and the libertarians'—great champion and explicator. He has been almost a one-man band in defending and explaining what is sometimes called quaintly "economic freedom." He was about the only one in Washington who *really* gave a rip about property rights. In many ways, he has been the office-holding equivalent of the columnist and economist Thomas Sowell, a splendid cuss.

It is almost universally acknowledged that Gramm is brainy, principled, and fearless. It is also almost universally alleged that he is not a likable, certainly not a lovable, man, and that this hampered his effort to go further: to be president.

Some of us have long held that if America doesn't like Phil Gramm, America is nuts. What's not to like about . . . well, take a typical Gramm moment, one that has entered the lore about him, lovingly passed around by Gramm fans, or, as we have sometimes been tagged, "Gramm crackers."

He's debating education policy with some lady who represents the education establishment. The exchange goes something like this:

> GRAMM: My education proposals are premised on the fact that I care more about my children than you do.
> LADY WHO REPRESENTS THE EDUCATION ESTABLISHMENT: No, you don't.
> GRAMM: Oh? What are their names?

True, Gramm tends toward the mordant, and he doesn't mesh with an Oprah-ized, schmoozified culture of "niceness" and drippy sentiment. Many people have pointed out—and they're not entirely wrong—that Gramm is "no diplomat" and even "no politician." Yet he is certainly *some* kind of politician: He got elected, and reelected, and reelected, by whopping margins in Texas, a state of 20 million people. Gramm was an academic, an intellectual, and an individualist, yes, but he was also a canny pol, as evidenced not only by his victory margins but by his record in the House and Senate.

Announcing his retirement, he declared that he had achieved everything he had come to Washington to do: He (with the help of one or two others, maybe) had balanced the budget, cut taxes, moved power out of Washington, opened up trade, deregulated, rebuilt the military, and "rolled back the borders of Communism." He says that he never would have stood down if Al Gore had made it to the White House—he would've needed to stay as a blocker. But with Bush in, he felt the moment was right. The Republicans' loss of their Senate majority, he insists, had nothing to do with it. When Gramm talks, you tend to believe him, no matter what you think of him. It's part of his singularity.

AN AMERICAN LIFE

The Gramm story is oft told, but worth recapping. He was born at Fort Benning, Ga., to a humble military couple. Early on, his father became an invalid, leaving the family in stricken circumstances. Young Gramm was held back from several grades, and was eventually sent to military school, to straighten up and fly right. He did. He went to the University of Georgia, earning a B.A. and then staying there for a Ph.D. in economics. He never wanted to be a politician—at least at first. The great dream of his life was to become a tenured professor (an understandable goal for the ambitious product of a family that had never enjoyed much education). He got what he wanted, at Texas A&M, at the age of 30.

Before long, he was nosing about in politics. Intent on propagating his views, he wrote, as he tells it, to "150-odd civic clubs in East Texas, saying, 'If you want someone to come speak on any one of these dozen subjects, I'm your man.'" A single invitation came in: from a Lions Club in the tiny town of Wortham, "just north of Mexia." There he met the printer Dicky Flatt, who would become his emblem of the hard-working common man, whose back guvmint needed to get and stay off. Gramm's message that day was his classic: "Freedom is a great thing, America has too little of it, the government's too big, too powerful, and too expensive." ("It still is," adds the senator.)

In time—1978—he got himself elected to Congress, as a Democrat (a natural thing for a Georgian and Texan to be). When Reagan took office, Gramm realized that here was a man "who wanted to do what I had always dreamed of doing." He worked with that president to scale back the government, leading the Democratic leadership to boot him from the Budget Committee. Gramm could have switched parties on the spot—but he didn't think it was right, opting to resign and present himself as a Republican in a special election. To the people, he uttered, over and over, his semi-famous line, "I had to choose between Tip O'Neill and y'all, and I decided to stand with y'all."

Gramm says today that the Democratic party is, in fact, socialist, "if by 'socialist' you mean the redistribution of wealth, more decisions made by the central government—no question about it. My grandmother thought of the Democrats as the party of the people. What they are is the party of government." They benefit from economic ignorance, too, because the subject "is very hard to understand." Trade, in particular, is "the toughest issue I've ever dealt with, and it is also the one I feel most passionate about." The problem is, "Free trade is counterintuitive. It's like skiing. *Everyone* benefits from trade, but a *few* people benefit from protectionism, and they know who they are." They also tend to be well organized and entrenched—while the vast, trade-blessed majority remain pretty much clueless.

GRAMM CONTRA CLINTON

During Clinton's two terms, Gramm was unyielding. That president probably had no stronger foe in the Senate. Of Clinton, Gramm says, "He had an ability to communicate, like Reagan," but, unlike Reagan, "he was willing to say anything. He could do a 180 on a dime, because he was unencumbered by principles or values, as far as I could tell." Clinton could have done "real harm" if he had "tended to his business, if he had focused all his energies on his political agenda, instead of constantly throwing up roadblocks for himself. The good news is that, in eight years, Bill Clinton did America relatively little harm." His domestic program was thwarted, in large measure because a Republican House was elected in 1994. Newt Gingrich, for Gramm, is something of a tragic figure: "He was the reason the Republicans won control of the House, and, in the end, he had to leave so they could keep control of it."

As for Clinton's foreign policy, it was "weak," but "without Ivan at the gate, it didn't make any difference."

If that Clinton domestic agenda was indeed thwarted, one of the reasons was that Gramm stood—early and immovable—against nationalized health care. He said, famously, that it would pass "over my cold, dead political body." It was his adamancy that stiffened Republican spines, that kept the temporizers and defeatists from trying to split the difference. Gramm remarked that only two people in Washington had read the entire health-care bill, himself and Hillary Clinton: "She loved it, I hated it."

As a presidential candidate, Gramm seemed a good thing: a self-made man, an articulate one, certainly a driven one. He didn't go in for what was later called "compassionate conservatism," because conservatism—just plain conservatism, freedom—*was* compassionate, dammit, and why didn't more people understand that? And he was tired of being lectured to about poverty and hardship by people who had never known any.

Gramm, though, went nowhere. He raised a lot of money, but not a lot of supporters. What went wrong? "I was a poor candidate. I did a bad job. There's no one to blame but myself." What's more, "America was never going to elect me unless there was a crisis. And people didn't see a crisis in 1996. I was the wrong person at the wrong time. And there may never have been a right time for me."

Turning to the future, Gramm believes, among other things, that Social Security reform will eventually happen, because the Democrats can't demagogue it forever: "At some point, the lights go out. They run out of money," and that will be reform's hour. Gramm would like to see no income tax at all, favoring instead a consumption tax, "because the government doesn't have to know what your income is. It's a simpler system, and every-body pays." Even a flat tax won't "lead you home," because it would be strangled by exemptions. "If you get the tax away from income, you have a much better chance."

And then there's the miserable problem of race in America. Racial politics, says Gramm, is actually "dangerous" (a typically direct Gramm word). "Some people try to benefit by pitting people against one another based on race. Quotas and set-asides are *dangerous*. In America, we should judge people one at a time. When you start thinking of yourself as a group, that in itself is alien to America. Merit is the only fair way to do things. If we have a system based on merit and I don't get a promotion and someone else does, I can accept that. But if I believe the other person got it based on race, gender, or something else, it's harder to accept." The "incredible inequalities" we impose carry a steep price.

THE GUTS TO FIGHT

For all these years, Gramm has never quite been a Washington insider, though he's been an excellent player inside Washington. He never tried to be popular, and as a result he was intensely popular among those who understood and appreciated what he was doing. People like Clinton's Paul Begala used to knock him for being anti-government, and if he hated government so much, why did he spend so much time in government? Why didn't he get the hell out? Gramm is that rare, invaluable politician: a free-marketeer and anti-statist who's willing to work and succeed in politics in order to frustrate the centralizers. Someone has to. Not every Friedmanite can afford to shun government.

Can anyone replace him? Among the colleagues Gramm has been most impressed with is Mitch McConnell of Kentucky, "a great senator, who has principles and is willing to stand up for them, and to be unpopular." McConnell is, indeed, probably the most Gramm-like senator in Washington, apart from the original. Gramm also says that "if I could pick just one senator to be my own senator, it would be Don Nickles," of Oklahoma, because "he's got a good heart, and he's right on virtually everything." Finally, he suggests keeping an eye on two less familiar senators: Idaho's Mike Crapo and Alabama's Jeff Sessions.

If there's one thing Gramm is proud of, or wishes to emphasize, it's that "I've changed this town more than it has changed me. And I'm no less idealistic than I ever was." He says, "The one thing I've been committed to is freedom. Not just the freedom to say, 'I disagree with the government'"—everyone loves the First Amendment. No, "economic freedoms, which are the most important ones," and also the ones most easily encroached on. "My whole career, no matter what I've done, has been about trying to promote freedom. That's all there is."

What's not to like about that?

—October 1, 2001
National Review

Arab Scribe

Naguib Mahfouz, a personal appreciation

Naguib Mahfouz, the Egyptian writer who died on August 30, was something rare, more rare than you may suppose: He was a born writer. It's not just that Mahfouz wanted to write, but that he was compelled by nature to. In the 1980s, shortly before he won the Nobel Prize, he told an interviewer, "If the urge to write should ever leave me, I want that day to be my last." I don't know whether the urge left Mahfouz on August 30 (or before), though I doubt it. But he died, aged 94.

In his long, productive decades, he wrote some 35 novels, hundreds of short stories, screenplays, etc. People have compared him to an Englishman, Charles Dickens, and to a couple of Frenchmen: Balzac and Zola. They have also compared him to a trio of Russians: Tolstoy, Dostoevsky, and Solzhenitsyn. But like all great artists—including the writers mentioned—he was primarily himself.

He pretty much invented the novel in Arabic—that language had always favored poetry—and, in fact, he wrote classical Arabic, a very elegant tongue (according to those who know it). When he gave his Nobel Lecture in 1988, he said that the "real winner" was this language. He also said some other things, about which more in due course.

When the Nobel Committee announced its choice that year, just about none of us had heard of Mahfouz—none of us in the West, that is. But he was a household word in the Arab world, a "conscience," as has often been said, as well as a chronicler. An amusing headline appeared in *al-Ahram*, the Egyptian state newspaper: "Nobel Wins the Naguib Mahfouz Prize." The rest of us soon caught up, and Mahfouz's books made an impact, including on me.

The writer was born in 1911 in Cairo, where he would spend his entire life. As a boy, he loved European detective novels, and he would copy them over, rather as composers used to do. (Mozart, for example, copied earlier masters' scores, in order to learn.) After university, Mahfouz achieved the goal of many young Egyptian men: to land a government job. He worked in a variety of ministries, including Religious Affairs and Culture. He ended up in the State Cinema Organization, where he acted as censor—a remarkable job for a writer and artist. A number of his fellows were resentful. But you might say that someone had to do it.

Mahfouz did his civil-servant work—diligently, by all accounts—mainly in the morning, and scribbled in the afternoon. He did this until 1971, when he reached the government's retirement age of 60. Then he kept writing.

His magnum opus is *The Cairo Trilogy*, published in the mid-1950s. This trilogy—one massive book, really—is composed of three novels: *Palace Walk*, *Palace of Desire*, and *Sugar Street*. All three titles, not just the last of them, refer to Cairene streets. And Mahfouz knew those streets with extraordinary intimacy. Do you know that he left Egypt only three times in his life? He was sent on two governmental missions—to Yemen and Yugoslavia—and sought medical treatment in Britain. Mahfouz may not have been a man of the world, but he had no trouble finding the world in Cairo, and was clearly universal.

The *Trilogy* cannot be described in a couple of strokes, but suffice it to say that it is a sweeping, panoramic tale of a family across several generations, and that it stretches from World War I to the Egyptian revolution in 1952. Many critics have said that this is more a story of Egypt than of individual characters. I disagree. It is both, of course—but, for me, the personal transcends the national, historical, and political. Mahfouz is a historically informed novelist, not a literarily gifted historian. And he is at his best when he is being his least didactic.

POLITICS AND PROSE

I read the *Trilogy* in what may be considered peculiar circumstances. In November 2000—after our presidential election—I was scheduled to go to Egypt, for the first time. I wanted to prepare by reading Mahfouz, of whose books I had long been aware. (Well, since 1988, and the Nobel Prize.) And, during those weeks, I was working on the George W. Bush campaign in Austin, Texas. So I would do combat with Al Gore during the day, and return to a hotel room at night to plunge myself into Mahfouz's world.

Here's a confession that I know you'll forgive me for: I had always assumed that Mahfouz was no good, or at least not strikingly good. I assumed that Mahfouz had won the Nobel simply for being an Arab—no Arab had won the prize, and the committee is a firm respecter of affirmative action.

Indeed, many thought that, in the Mahfouz year, the prize should go to a woman, and Nadine Gordimer's name was mentioned prominently. (She would be the winner in 1991.)

Whatever the Nobel Committee's motivations, they chose a splendid novelist in Mahfouz, for those books are magical, enthralling, full of tremendous humanity and warmth. (That's a word repeatedly applied to the *Trilogy*: warmth.) I lived and died with those characters night after night, not wanting the *Trilogy* to end. After I did, in fact, finish, I resolved to read all of Mahfouz's oeuvre. I'm afraid I cannot recommend it, given limited time. In the *Trilogy*, Mahfouz seemed to touch a peak (and, in truth, the first of the novels—*Palace Walk*—is superior to the subsequent two).

After the election, I first went to Alexandria, then to Cairo. And there I wanted to walk Mahfouz's streets, just like any other *Trilogy*-besotted tourist. My friends took me to Fishawi's, the fabled café in which the writer had spent many an hour, and also to another establishment: the Naguib Mahfouz Café. Clever, alluring name!

One of the most interesting encounters I had was in Alexandria. This was with a woman who lectured at the university, and she was thoroughly modern (or at least she seemed that way): Westernized, multilingual, widely traveled. I told her of my love for the novels, and she said, "Yes, I often wish I could live in those times." I said, "Sure, sure, I know what you mean—but without the subjugation of women, of course," for they were once not allowed outside, or even to be seen through a window. She answered, "No, even with that. I'm not sure I'd mind at all."

Speaking of windows, I felt that I had been afforded a rare glimpse through one. I think what the lady meant was that she longed for the protection and comfort of hearth and home, as against the hurly-burly of the "liberated" world. I can't say for sure.

ANTENNAE AND KNIVES

Politically, Mahfouz was a mixed bag. Edward Said said that he had a "nineteenth-century liberal belief in a decent, humane society" (would that Said himself had had), and that seems plausible. Though a Muslim, Mahfouz married a Christian, and he despised Nasser. He backed Sadat and peace with Israel, which got his books banned in several Arab countries. At least one book was banned in Egypt, too: *Children of the Alley*, written in 1959. It is a religious allegory, which greatly displeased the religious authorities in Egypt. Thus was the State Cinema censor censored. But his political antennae were sharp, and he always had a sense of what was possible in Egypt, at any time.

You will recall that, in 1989, Ayatollah Khomeini issued his fatwa against Salman Rushdie, for *The Satanic Verses*. Others said, "Why not Mahfouz, too?" Egypt's "blind sheikh," Omar Abdel Rahman—whom you know as the guiding force behind the first World Trade Center attack, in 1993—was philosophical: "If this sentence had been passed on Naguib Mahfouz when he wrote *Children of the Alley*, Salman Rushdie would have realized that he had to stay within bounds."

In 1992, an Egyptian intellectual, Farag Foda, was killed by Muslim extremists. Naturally enough, police found Mahfouz's name on a list of targets. But the writer would not accept bodyguards and refused to alter his cherished routine (which included a long walk and cafés). In 1994, they got him, stabbing him through the neck. The 82-year-old Mahfouz survived, but was badly incapacitated. From his hospital room, he said, "I pray to God to make the police victorious over terrorism and to purify Egypt from this evil, in defense of people, freedom, and Islam." He also displayed a Reaganesque sangfroid and humor: When the finance minister—one of a parade of officials—came in, he quipped, "I've paid my taxes."

What about Mahfouz and Islam? In his Nobel Lecture, he tells the assembled grandees—through a proxy, for he did not travel to Stockholm—that he is "the son of two civilizations": the Pharaonic and the Islamic. Concerning the latter, he will not talk of its "conquests, which have planted thousands of minarets" all over the world; nor will he talk about "the fraternity between religions and races" that has been made possible by Islam, thanks to its "spirit of tolerance" unprecedented in all human history.

That is something we might ponder, before going on.

No, he will "introduce" this civilization to the Stockholm audience by telling a story: After Muslims defeated Byzantines in a battle, they would return Byzantine prisoners only in exchange for "a number of books of the ancient Greek heritage in philosophy, medicine, and mathematics." This, in spite of the fact that "the demander was a believer in God" while what was demanded was the "fruit of a pagan civilization."

So, by Mahfouz's testimony, this was Islam, in its essence: generous, all-embracing, and humane. Later in his lecture, he undertook to speak for the whole Third World (and, frankly, there is a lot of claptrap in this text, especially concerning black Africans and Palestinians). Mahfouz told the West, "Be not spectators to our miseries. You have to play therein a noble role befitting your status. From your position of superiority, you are responsible for any misdirection of animal, or plant, to say nothing of Man, in any of the four corners of the world."

THE BAD WITH THE GOOD

This view is taken by many people, both in the West and without. But what would Mahfouz have to say in October 2001, when President Bush—not being a "spectator"—went after the Taliban, that prime inflicter of misery? Mahfouz wrote that the "so-called war on terrorism" was "just as despicable a crime" as the 9/11 attacks. He repeated the woeful argument that counterattacks "give terrorism additional justification." But worse—worse—was to come later: when he defended, excused, and flat-out glorified the suicide bombers in Israel.

That burst my bubble, as you might imagine. And it reinforced an old lesson: not to fall in love, personally, with writers or artists you admire. To put it succinctly, divorce, if you can, *Parsifal* from the man (or celebrate the *Parsifal* in the man, while rejecting what is ugly). At the time of the Afghan war, *National Review* observed sadly that Mahfouz was "only the latest in a long line of dazzling artists who have sided with the barbarians." I tried to console myself with the thought that the writer was 90 and perhaps out of it, or that he had succumbed to some terrible pressure, or that he had been brainwashed by vile media. After all, the U.S. and its allies—including Israel—were confronting the very forces that had plunged a knife into his neck!

It could be, too, that Mahfouz did not write the offending words; that they were written under his name by government propagandists. One can only hope.

In any case, Naguib Mahfouz represented, for many, many years, an older, enlightened Arab culture—one that has been little in evidence lately. He was cultivation, not fanaticism and blood. Egypt is very proud of him—the most famous Arab writer—and well it should be: They gave him a military funeral, his coffin draped with the Egyptian flag. But Mahfouz was a writer for all the world, as the White House recognized when it lauded him on his death. (The U.S. also offered hospital treatment during Mahfouz's final illness, according to Egyptian television.)

I have no doubt that, sometime in the future, I will go back to those marvelous books—that one big book, really—forgetting, or remembering less, what was ugly in Mahfouz (or seemed to be). And I will renew my acquaintance with al-Sayyid Ahmad, Amina, Umm Hanafi, Yasin, Khadija, Fahmy, Aisha, Kamal, and all the other characters who thrilled me—with whom I lived and died—in the final weeks of the 2000 campaign.

—September 25, 2006
National Review

Star-in-Waiting

Meet George W.'s foreign-policy czarina

My first encounter with Condoleezza Rice, summer of 1999.

I t's an odd name, but one that we may all have to learn soon enough: Condoleezza. Her mother, a pianist, was thinking of the musical direction *con dolcezza*, or "with sweetness"; for her only child, she composed a variation on it.

Condoleezza Rice is known as Condi to her friends—and she may in time be known as secretary of state, or national security advisor, or ambassador to the United Nations. She is principal foreign-policy adviser to George W. Bush, and, according to those in a position to know, she is set—"locked in," says one—to assume one of the top posts in a W. administration.

Although she is relatively young—44, with the look and air of a graduate student—she is not exactly a new face. She served on the National Security Council in the administration of the first George Bush, under Brent Scowcroft, the national security adviser. There she was responsible for Soviet and East European affairs, at a time when Germany was reunifying, the Baltics were rebelling, and the Soviet Union itself was sputtering toward self-termination. She has an obvious personal affection for President Bush, as she does for his son, the governor of Texas. She has come to know George W. well in the last couple of years, and, by all accounts, the two get along famously. A Bush aide says that they vacation together; that they talk on the phone nearly every day; and that Bush trusts her completely, to manage his foreign-policy team and to provide counsel on other matters as well—including social issues. Asked the Republican question of the hour—Why W.?—Rice has an ingenuous answer: "Because I like him. And I think he ought to be president."

For the last six years, Rice has been provost of Stanford University, where she has spent her entire academic career. She stepped down in July, to take a year's leave. Provost is a powerful position at Stanford—number two, below president. Rice began the job at only 38. In fact, she has done just about everything early—the very picture of American overachievement.

She was born in Birmingham, Ala., in 1954, when Jim Crow—and that regime's local enforcer, Bull Connor—held sway. Both parents were teachers. Condi was a schoolmate of Denise McNair, one of the girls murdered in the infamous church bombing. Later the Rice family moved to Tuscaloosa, where Condi's father, John Rice, was a dean at Stillman College, a predominantly black school. Mother and father, says Rice, "felt strongly about pushing ahead in education"; their *Wunderkind*, as a result, "had lessons in everything—piano, skating, ballet, French . . ." She skipped first grade, and also the seventh.

When Condi was 13, the family moved to Colorado, so that John Rice could become a vice chancellor of the University of Denver, where he had earned an advanced degree. He was—and is—a Republican (as well as an ordained Presbyterian minister). For one thing, he abhorred the Dixiecrats who were the Democratic party in the South. For another, it was simply easier to register with the Republicans. (The Democrats, typically, had demanded that he guess the number of beans in a jar.)

Condi entered the University of Denver at 15, aiming to become a pianist. She studied one summer at the famous music camp in Aspen—"affirmative action for Colorado kids," she says. Midway through college, however, she came to the sad realization that she would not "make it" as a pianist. She did not want to become an accompanist, and she did not want "to teach 13-year-olds to murder Beethoven." So she left the music program and cast about for a different major. First she tried English literature and "hated it": It was simply too "squishy." ("That'll get me in trouble with my humanist friends.") Next she tried government, but that, too, was "not very rigorous." ("That'll get me in trouble, too.") Finally she met Josef Korbel, a former Czech diplomat, a refugee from Nazism and Communism, who headed Denver's school of international relations. "I really adored him," says Rice. "I really did. He's the reason I'm in this field. I loved his course, and I loved him. He sort of picked me out as someone who might do this well." From then on, it was "Soviet politics, Soviet everything."

Korbel, of course, was Madeleine Albright's father. ("Who would've thunk it?" admits Rice.) Rice knew the young Albright, as she, Rice, was a frequent guest in the Korbel home. The two women turned out differently in their thinking—with Rice arguably closer to Korbel's consistently tough-minded views—but America may well have the unusual experience of two successive secretaries of state who learned about the world at the same knee.

Rice was graduated at 19 and went to Notre Dame, for a master's degree. She returned to Denver for her Ph.D. and arrived at Stanford to be an assistant professor when she was 26. Eight years later, Scowcroft selected her for his NSC staff. While she was there, the new governor of California, Pete Wilson, considered appointing her to a U.S. Senate seat (which he himself had just vacated). She signaled to him, however, that she did not desire the appointment ("and I don't think I would have received it anyway"). If she *had* received and accepted it, she—not Carol Moseley-Braun, elected from Illinois in 1992—would have been the first black woman to serve in the Senate.

In the last several years, Rice has received numerous offers to become president of a university (the natural progression from provost). It is assumed that Berkeley is among the schools that sought to lure her from Palo Alto. (Invited to confirm this, she says only, "I was offered several presidencies, put it that way.") She decided, though, that she did not want "to go any further in higher ed," preferring to "get back to my roots as a Russianist." She will spend her year's leave working on a book about the end of the Cold War, serving on her various corporate boards, and "helping Governor Bush prepare" for the Oval Office—"a nice combination," she smiles.

As to those "roots," what was it, indeed, that drew her to the Soviet Union, to Russia? "I was attracted to the Byzantine nature of Soviet politics," she says, "and by power: how it operates, how it's used." She read everything she could get her hands on about World War II "and about war generally." She particularly remembers John Erickson's "great books"—*The Road to Stalingrad, The Road to Berlin*. She read Dostoevsky "rather than Tolstoy." And she encountered Solzhenitsyn: "He understood the dark side of Russia better than anyone else. Like most Russian novels, it was tragedy without redemption."

Above all, she was influenced by "people who understood the paradox of the Soviet Union—that it was essentially weak and rotting." Yet as weak and rotting as it was, "it was still exceedingly dangerous, and I think we're very fortunate to have gotten through the Cold War the way we did." Asked recently by *Time* magazine who should be named "Person of the Century," she nominated Harry Truman, who "gave the U.S. an unprecedented role in international affairs" and "fundamentally reshaped the world and planted the seeds of the Soviet Union's eventual destruction." She calls John Foster Dulles "an extraordinarily important figure," one "I would love to have met." Dulles "had it right. But philosophy and timing have to come together, and, if you think about it, what happened from 1981 to 1991 was essentially rollback [Dulles's supreme objective]. In the 1950s, though, you couldn't do that without great costs."

And Henry Kissinger, an un-Dulles? "I'm very fond of him. I think he's one of the smartest people I've ever met." So she is a Kissingerian? "I'm probably a bit of a *Realpolitiker* in that I think that power balances determine a lot. But I think that I am not in the sense that I thought that détente was probably predicated too much on the notion of the Soviet Union as a normal state, which had its interests in the international system that could somehow be accommodated. I think the Soviets simply took that as an opportunity to expand." Several days later she places a phone call, concerned about her description of herself as a *Realpolitiker*, even "probably a bit of" one. She wishes to clarify: "I am a realist. Power matters. But there can be no absence of moral content in American foreign policy, and, furthermore, the American people wouldn't accept such an absence. Europeans giggle at this and say we're naive and so on, but we're not Europeans, we're Americans—and we have different principles."

In most everything she says and writes, Rice makes clear that she is an unabashed believer in the American experiment, in the United States as a model and force for good in the world. Of Ronald Reagan, she says, "His great strength was that he had a couple of clear principles that he held to assiduously." American power was good; Soviet power was bad; the one had to be enhanced, the other diminished. "I've said to people in the press sometimes, 'Your problem with Reagan was that, he was so clear, you couldn't reinterpret him.'" Rice concedes that when Reagan delivered his electric "totalitarian evil" speech before the British Parliament in 1982, "even *I* thought, 'Oh, that's incredibly undiplomatic, and I hope it doesn't provoke an incident.' And you know what? He was absolutely right. And most important, the Soviets knew he was right—that they were going to wind up on the ash heap of history. That's what we owe him." Reagan, stresses Rice, was blessed with timing (unlike Dulles): He "mobilized the power of the United States" and "hit on a rollback strategy that challenged the Soviets" when the moment was ripe. In addition to which, "we were extraordinarily fortunate, because it's not clear to me that a leader other than Gorbachev might not have chosen to challenge back"—and that would have been a whole different ball game.

Conservatives, Rice maintains, "underestimate Gorbachev's role" in the conclusion of the Cold War: "The Soviet Union might have been weak internally, but when people say, 'Well, he had no options'—oh, he had options! He had 390,000 troops in Germany. He could have provoked a *tremendous* crisis over the Berlin Wall." Gorbachev did take repressive steps in the Baltics, but, "for some reason, he always pulled up short of using maximum force, and we should all be very grateful for that." Conservatives, Rice summarizes, underestimate the importance of Gorbachev; liberals underestimate the importance of Reagan; and "they all underestimate the importance of George [H. W.] Bush," her old boss. Is this Rice the analyst talking or Rice the loyal staffer and friend? "Well, ask yourself," she replies: "Was it inevitable that Germany unified on completely Western terms, within NATO; that Soviet troops went home, with dignity and without incident; that American troops stayed; that all of Eastern Europe was liberated and joined the Western bloc? No, it was not inevitable—and that leaves a lot of room for statecraft."

Did the Bush administration make any mistakes? "Not while I was there," she quips. Then she reflects, "It was a mistake to wait so long in Bosnia." She chalks up the administration's inaction to "fatigue": "The Gulf War was just ending, and then we got into an election season—an earlier action was probably warranted." She strongly supported this year's Kosovo war, but warned against permitting "strategic air power and especially the cruise missile" to become "national drugs." Though she is not particularly worried that the Republican party is tilting isolationist, she was dismayed at the behavior of certain Republicans in Congress, those who did "what no party should ever do: confuse the clear message that you're trying to send to an enemy when you have forces at war." Once American troops had arrived, she says, "the only thing to say to Milosevic was, 'We're going to beat you—all of us.'"

Fine, then: What about her man W., a foreign-policy neophyte? He is, notes Rice, "the governor of a border state." But come now: Isn't that a reach, a dose of spin? After all, many governors—including Jesse Ventura—are border-state governors. "No," protests Rice, "a big border state—and the last president we had who had been governor of a big border state was Ronald Reagan." At this she grins, having spun herself out. As for Bush's foreign-policy instincts, Rice reports that they are solidly internationalist: He knows that "the United States is *the* critical actor in international politics and has no choice but to be involved in the world. We're going to play a role one way or another. And we can either play it consciously and smartly, with a design, or we can sit back and pretend we're not playing a role, and play one by our absence."

On the critical issue of China, Rice favors strengthening the hand of the "liberalizers" in Beijing—those who suppose (erroneously, according to Rice) that economic liberalization can proceed without a political loosening: "I don't care if they believe that. Economic liberalization is ultimately going to lead to political liberalization—that's an iron law." She says that she would "strongly raise human-rights issues every time with the Chinese leadership," while recognizing that "you have to be careful not to cause a backlash against democratizing forces." The Chinese Communists, she is convinced, "are living on borrowed time."

When it comes to Israel, Rice professes an emotional attachment, a pull that goes beyond the bounds of the coolly analytic. Israel, she says, "is a struggling democracy in the midst of non-democratic states that would do it great harm." This was a nation that "nobody wanted to be born, that was born into a hostile environment, and that, without so strong a moral compass and so strong a people, might not have made it." For the United States, Rice contends, Israel is no less than "a moral commitment." "I've told you I'm a *Realpolitiker*, but this one is different."

Rice characterizes herself as an "all-over-the-map Republican," whose views are "hard to typecast": "very conservative" in foreign policy, "ultra-conservative" in other areas, "almost shockingly libertarian" on some issues, "moderate" on others, "liberal" on probably nothing. (She calls herself "mildly pro-choice" on abortion.)

Here is a prediction about her: If she becomes secretary of state or even something lesser, she will be big. Rock-star big. A major cultural figure, adorning the bedroom walls of innumerable kids and the covers of innumerable magazines. She is, all agree, an immensely appealing person: poised, gracious, humbly smart, still markedly southern after all these years in other parts. Her television appearances have prompted marriage proposals ("I haven't had many lately—maybe I'm getting old"). And she is very much a jock: a tennis player, an untiring follower of college and professional sports. (She knows an ex-Stanford student, Tiger Woods, slightly, and, what's more, "I strength-trained with his strength trainer—now there's a connection!") Her dream job, she has declared many times, is commissioner of the National Football League. On meeting her, the current commissioner, Paul Tagliabue, told her that he had heard she was angling for his job. "Not to worry," she answered; "but let me know when you're thinking of retiring."

Not least, she is refreshingly, strikingly, at ease on the matter of race. For years she has faced questions about her skin color and sex: Have they been advantages, responsible for her rapid rise? Disadvantages? "I don't spend too much time thinking about it," she says. "I can't go back and recreate myself as a white male" to test this proposition or that. She has enjoyed "a wonderful life, a great life," graced by ideal parents, and "I have a very, very powerful faith in God. I'm a really religious person, and I don't believe that I was put on this earth to be sour, so I'm eternally optimistic about things." She is loath "to criticize any black person for how he or she has wanted to navigate being black in America, whether it's Clarence Thomas or Maxine Waters." She does allow, however, that she wishes the "black middle class would spend less time thinking about itself and more time worrying about the witches' brew that is poverty and race. That is something that those of us who are black and privileged have a lot of responsibility for." She herself co-founded an organization in East Palo Alto for poor young people—an instance, she claims, of Bushian "compassionate conservatism."

Though power and fame now beckon her, Rice seems sincerely, almost strangely unambitious. "I have learned," she explains, "to do what works for me—and that is not to look that far ahead; to do what you're doing, do it well, and see what comes next." Years ago "I structured my life to be a concert musician. That was all I wanted to do. And it fell apart on me. I'm never going to do that again." But if her presidential horse finishes first in November 2000, she will find herself performing on a very wide stage indeed.

—August 30, 1999
National Review

Albright Then, Albright Now

From Democratic campaigns to the Kosovo campaign, a long way

This piece was written when Madeleine Albright was secretary of state. It says that, out of power, she was a dove; in power, a hawk. When Reagan and (the first) Bush were running things, she sounded like McGovern; in the Age of Clinton, she sounded more like Reagan and Bush. I might add that, when Bush's son was elected, she reverted to a McGovernite stance.

A fter the Cold War, miracles abounded, large and small. One of those—smallish but interesting—was the rebirth of Madeleine K. Albright as . . . what? A hawk? A freedom fighter? John Foster Dulles in a skirt and floppy hat? Albright's transformation has indeed been amazing. This is not the woman we knew for all those years, when, as a leading Democratic voice on foreign policy, she was assailing Ronald Reagan and his band—even George [H. W.] Bush and his—as reckless, warmongering, and dangerous. America is, to be sure, the land of self-reinvention; long may it be. Yet the secretary of state's metamorphosis—the emergence of the New Albright, as striking as any New Nixon—has gone all but unnoticed.

The Kosovo war was widely considered Albright's doing, as she had been the Clinton-administration official who pressed most insistently for it. It was also considered something of a personal project: Albright was born in Czechoslovakia and fled first the Nazis and later the Communists. Some of her relatives—the family was Jewish—were killed in the camps; others, luckier, were trapped in a Communist state. She herself was luckiest of all, brought to America, where her opportunities proved limitless. She naturally views Eastern Europe as her region and the Kosovo horror as her special responsibility. In May, *Time* magazine featured her on its cover, with the legend "Albright at War." The photo showed her at her most bellicose: in a military jacket, complete with insignia, at an air base in Germany, barking into a cellular phone. Her face was the very picture of toughness and resolve. By comparison, Margaret Thatcher during the Falklands War was a whimpering doe.

Albright now portrays herself—and is uniformly portrayed in the press—as a child of Munich; that is, a woman stamped forever by the deal struck in that city in 1938, which sacrificed Czechoslovakia to the Nazi beast and, in fact, did not prevent broader war. She takes pains to explain that she is an enemy of appeasement, a quick and uncompromising foe of any aggressor. Yet this is largely how Reagan's men, and Bush's, saw themselves, and she mocked them constantly and opposed their every significant effort. "My mindset is Munich," she now assures us; "most of my generation's is Vietnam." Her boss, President Clinton, recently praised her for "not only learning the lessons of Munich, but also of Czechoslovakia under Communism." According to *Time*, she was stalwart at a 1998 meeting of foreign ministers, held in London. The Italians and French proposed that the group use softer language toward the Serbs. Albright's aide, Jamie Rubin, whispered to her that she should probably accept. She apparently shot back, "Where do you think we are, Munich?"

With each passing day, she sounds more and more like her old bogeyman, Reagan, sometimes even mimicking his precise language. She reminds the public that America is the world's "indispensable nation." What is "at stake" in Kosovo, she says, "is the principle that aggression doesn't pay." In an eerie echo of what the Reaganauts used to insist about Nicaragua, she sniffs, "Just because you can't act everywhere doesn't mean you don't act anywhere." We almost expect her to look at her detractors, shake her head with a sad smile, and quip, "There you go again."

Just as it was considered, in some quarters, impolite in the 1940s and '50s to discuss who had done what in the world war, and just as it was considered, again in some quarters, impolite in the 1970s and '80s to discuss who had done what in the Vietnam War, it is now considered impolite to reflect on who did what—and stood for what—during the Cold War. Recriminations are bad form. Yet a little wonderment is well nigh irresistible. Ronald Reagan, in his speech to the 1992 Republican convention, one of his last addresses, said that he had heard "those speakers at that other convention," the Democratic one, "saying, 'We won the Cold War.' And I couldn't helping thinking, 'What do you mean "we"?'" Caspar Weinberger, Reagan's defense secretary, can now only chuckle bemusedly at Albright's new persona: "The kindest way of putting it is that she has seen the light and realizes the error of her ways. Who knows? Maybe she's been reading Margaret Thatcher's memoirs."

Albright's story, in every way, is a peculiarly American one: A refugee, the daughter of a diplomat, she married into a newspaper fortune, made all the right connections, became a Washington hostess, and maneuvered her way to the very top of the profession she extravagantly loves. For almost her entire career, she spoke for dovish, unassertive, accommodationist positions, not at all dissimilar to the ones she is presently deriding as weak, irresponsible—practically un-American. She was, for example, a fierce opponent of the Gulf War. In March 1991, Democratic congressmen gathered for a retreat, demoralized that the war they had sought to block had gone so well and proven so popular with the public. Albright was there to comfort them and buck them up. She observed irritably, "All problems can't be solved by bombing the bejesus out of some small country."

Three years earlier, a U.S. warship had shot down an Iranian airliner. This was a horrible, tragic mistake—not unlike, say, the bombing of a Chinese embassy, or a Swedish ambassadorial residence, or a hospital (all of which occurred in the Kosovo war). But Albright castigated the Reaganauts for "murdering innocent people." About her (now) "indispensable nation," she crabbed, "We have been brought up to believe that we are special, but we have not been behaving as if we are special."

In both words and deeds, Madeleine Albright has—no doubt—come a long way.

THE PATH TO GLORY

Albright got her start, so to speak, in the early 1970s, when her children attended an elite Washington school, called Beauvoir. She busied herself with school affairs, including fundraising, for which she showed a particular aptitude. Her talents came to the attention of a fellow parent who was working on the presidential campaign of Sen. Edmund S. Muskie of Maine. Would Albright like to organize a big-money dinner for the candidate at a local hotel? She would be delighted, and she did it well. Muskie lost the 1972 Democratic nomination to George McGovern, but Albright later landed a position on the Muskie staff, first as a fundraiser and then as a legislative assistant.

In 1976, Albright received a Ph.D. in political science from Columbia, begun in the 1960s when the family lived in New York. Among her professors had been Zbigniew Brzezinski, the canny, tough-minded Pole whom

President Carter would select as his national security adviser. When he went to the White House, Brzezinski plucked his old student from Muskie's office, making her his congressional liaison. Remembers one who worked with her then, "She was always dovish, when she was substantive at all. She was nothing like Brzezinski, as it concerned the Soviet Union. She wasn't crazy-liberal, but she was nowhere near Zbig." In 1988, Brzezinski would refuse to endorse Albright's candidate, Democratic nominee Michael Dukakis, whom he did not trust to safeguard the national interest.

After Carter's defeat at the hands of Reagan in 1980, Albright settled into life as a Georgetown hostess and networker. She was known for the dinners she staged at her home on 32nd Street, where out-of-power Democrats would go to chew over their dilemma and carp about the trigger-happy simpletons who had captured the executive branch. "These are working dinners," she once said defensively, "where people can surface their ideas to see what their validity is. People don't come for the food." She also arranged for a teaching position at Georgetown University, where she headed the Women in Foreign Service program. Her principal and abiding concern, however, was Democratic politics and the long wait for the Republicans to leave town. Asked her goal in 1991, she answered, "I would like to help elect a Democrat president."

In 1984, her horse, naturally, was Walter F. Mondale, whom she advised—even though, as it happens, he would smirk at those in thrall to, as he put it, "what I call 'the Munich analogy'" (as though he had invented the phrase). Albright was also chief foreign-policy counselor to the vice-presidential nominee, Geraldine Ferraro, who became a close friend. Recalled Ferraro later, "We hit it off right away. We tape-recorded our conversations, and I used to take the tapes with me and listen to them in the bathtub."

In this campaign, as before and after, Albright railed tirelessly against the Reagan administration for what she viewed as its undue belligerence toward the Soviet Union, its appalling adventurism around the globe, and its frightening and destabilizing defense buildup. She rarely put her positions on paper—indeed, she has written next to nothing, barely having even an op-ed piece to her name—but the press often went to her for soundbites, which she dispensed with professionalism and zest. "We have a president," she complained, "who seems to have a mindset against arms control." In 1980, Reagan had asked his famous question, "Are you better off than you were four years ago?" This time around, Albright argued, "the question should be, Do you feel safer?" The answer, she believed, should have been an obvious no.

If Albright was not an unambiguous nuclear-freezenik, she was certainly a fellow traveler of that movement. "Arms-control debates up to now have been carried on by the cognoscenti," she said, "and if you didn't understand the details of throw-weight, you couldn't participate intelligently. But one thing the freeze movement has done is strip away some of that mystique." A critical issue of the day was that of the "Euromissiles"—nuclear weapons that Reagan deployed in Western Europe in the face of tremendous pressure and even at the cost of the Soviets' quitting arms-control negotiations in a huff (they later returned, enabling Reagan to fashion his most advantageous pacts). Mondale was, to some degree, in favor of the deployment, provided it was coupled with "sustained negotiations." Ferraro flat-out opposed. As for Albright, she seems not to have declared herself unequivocally, but she did denounce "Reagan's definition of strength," which included "a destabilizing weapon like the MX, an unnecessary bomber like the B-1, and an unrealistic defense system like Star Wars."

So too was she contemptuous of the 1983 invasion of Grenada. "Of course Grenada worked," she scoffed on television. "It was the Redskins [of the National Football League] versus the Little Sisters of the Poor, and the score was 101 to nothing." Mondale allowed that he could have supported the operation if it had been truly necessary, as the Reagan administration claimed, "to save American lives"—but not for any strategic reason. Ferraro forthrightly opposed the invasion because she did not accept that Americans were, in fact, in danger. Four years later, Dukakis would state that "the only legitimate basis for our invading Grenada was to protect American lives and property," adding, "I'm not sure we'll ever know whether or not American lives and property were in jeopardy."

AGAINST REAGAN AND BUSH, UNFAILINGLY

Mondale and Ferraro, of course, went on to lose 49 states. Albright went back to her dinners, her politicking, and her television appearances. She never missed a chance to tweak Reagan and his team for their unreasonable muscularity. As one of her Republican adversaries at the time observes, "She was out of office, so whatever the Republicans were doing—it really didn't matter what—she had to support the opposite. And that demanded that she be dovish." In 1986, for instance, in one of her scores of interviews on the *MacNeil-Lehrer NewsHour*, Albright chastised the administration for its expulsion of 55 Soviets from the United States—persons who, in the classic euphemism, had "engaged in activities incompatible with their diplomatic status." "If I were a Soviet," she noted, "I would consider this kind of counterproductive if you are trying to improve the U.S.–Soviet dialogue." The expulsion had been "a little quick," and "I don't think the numbers had to be quite so large," because, for Moscow, it was "such a slap in the face." After all, she said, in one of her trademark simplifications, "Do we want an arms-control agreement or do we want to kind of have a more hostile relationship with the Soviet Union?"

By the time the 1988 campaign rolled around, Albright was itching to be principal adviser to the Democratic Number One—and she became so. She remarked to an interviewer, "I've worked very hard to get my credentials together, and I have the feeling I am able at this stage to make a contribution." In Dukakis, however, she had a shaky product. He had been a true freezenik, and there were few important Democrats to the left of him on foreign policy. Yet Albright spun for him like mad, claiming, hilariously, that he was "an active internationalist in the tradition of Harry Truman and John Kennedy." Dukakis, she said, "has a very good sense that our security problems consist of more than guns: It also consists of the threat to our economic viability, the deficit," and so on—a standard Democratic line of the period. Besides which, said Albright, Dukakis "will not be going around taking unilateral action like some lonesome cowboy." She would hit this "lonesome cowboy" theme hard, saying at another point, "The role of the U.S. is not to impose our views on our allies like some lonesome cowboy . . ."

Over and over, Albright bristled at the contention that Reagan's military refortification and his robust, anti-Communist foreign policy had enhanced the nation's position around the globe and brought about a sounder relationship with the Soviet Union, not to mention undreamed-of arms control. "Peace Through Strength" was, to her, a lie. "There is no proof," she pouted, "that the military buildup" had anything to do with a safer world. In 1989, she would say, in a typical formulation, "The irony of all this is that Ronald Reagan tells us that he won the Cold War, and, whether it's over or not, he bankrupted our budget so we do not have the funds to take advantage of the massive changes. We're absolutely hogtied to the idea we have to have a Stealth bomber and two mobile missiles." We simply "do not have enough money," she griped, "and part of that has to do with, I think, a misconstruing of how we did win the Cold War."

Throughout the campaign, she blasted the Republican nominee, George Bush, for his "Cold War rhetoric": "I don't think we need to go around rattling sabers." She objected to his "referring back to the terminology of the

Cold War" in a speech at Fulton, Mo., where Churchill named the Iron Curtain. Bush's transgression was having "basically talked about the Iron Curtain and used a lot of terminology that made us look backward." Nowhere to be found was the blunt, truth-valuing Albright of the Kosovo war.

Most extraordinary was an interview she gave in October 1988 on a television show called *American Interests*, hosted by Morton Kondracke. Antimissile defenses were a hot topic of the hour, and almost the whole of the Democratic party opposed them, although a few were willing to countenance their use as a "bargaining chip" with the Soviets. Albright lambasted Reagan's prized project as "a fantasy," and "therefore, in terms of discussing bargaining chips, what do we gain out of it, of spending trillions of dollars on a fantasy program?" But was it not true, pressed Kondracke, that, whatever its feasibility, the program had spooked and depressed the Soviets, driving them to greater concessions? "I think there's a real question about what drove them," answered Albright. "The truth is that they are in very deep economic trouble. . . . In my estimation, the Soviets are not impressed when you have billions of dollars in deficit, when you are building weapons that don't work, or when you, in effect, are putting money into some crazy astrodome plan of the sky."

Then there was the matter of Nicaragua and the Reagan Doctrine—the policy, christened by journalist Charles Krauthammer, of backing insurgency movements against Communist dictatorships. If Dukakis were elected, asked Kondracke, would that be the end of the Reagan Doctrine? "You bet," Albright replied. "Especially as far as Central America is concerned." She favored the "Arias Plan" for Nicaragua, named for the Costa Rican president who would win the Nobel Peace Prize, a plan, she said, that the Reagan administration had given "the back of its hand." The Reaganauts were at fault because "they've always held out the option that the aid to the contras would be resumed." And "the result of the Reagan Doctrine in Central America is that we have given the Ortegas an excuse to militarize their society." The United States, as imperialist meddler, had gone "swaggering around" and now Reagan was "afraid that peace might break out."

Albright did allow, on another occasion, that aid to the mujahadeen in Afghanistan was legitimate, because "the Soviets invaded Afghanistan, and nobody invaded Nicaragua." Moreover, "aid to the contras has provided the Sandinistas with an excuse for further repression." In her opinions and language, Albright in this period differed little from the leading scourges of the administration on Central America—Jim Wright, David Bonior, Christopher Dodd.

TOWARD A NEW LIFE

After Dukakis's battering at the polls, Albright became president of a liberal Democratic think tank, the Center for National Policy, among whose founders were Vernon Jordan, Cyrus Vance, and even Warren Beatty. When President Bush launched the Gulf War, Albright was aghast, arguing for a continuation of sanctions and negotiations. None of her arguments in the Balkans today came to her tongue then. When Bush rebuffed Soviet attempts at diplomatic stalling, Albright explained, "The Soviets want Saddam Hussein to save face, and the U.S. wants his head." Bush had unwisely "personalized" the conflict: the American president versus the Butcher of Baghdad. Some months after the war's conclusion, Albright, noting problems in Yugoslavia, was conspicuously crotchety and bitter at what Bush had accomplished in the Gulf: "We are so busy celebrating how we managed to institute world order in the Persian Gulf that it is interesting to see how powerless we seem to be in this situation." A year after that, when the administration was considering whether to attack Iraq again, Albright said, "If Bush has to go in and bomb Iraq now, he may only point up that he screwed up the first time." Whether Albright, at this remove—following her own experiences in Iraq, Yugoslavia, and elsewhere—has any greater sympathy for her predecessors remains unclear.

With the end of the Cold War, Albright, like the "prisonhouse of nations" itself, was liberated. She even felt free, in a 1992 *USA Today* column, to speak of "totalitarian evil." And when she joined the Clinton administration as U.N. ambassador in 1993—her shot at the big leagues at last—she was known as rather hardline, particularly in contrast to her colleagues, such as Warren Christopher, Sandy Berger, and Strobe Talbott. Her rhetoric became practically Churchillian. She had a well-publicized tussle over Bosnia with Colin Powell, then chairman of the Joint Chiefs of Staff, during which she asked, "What's the point of having this superb military you're always talking about if we can't use it?" When interrogated by reporters about the necessity of the 1994 invasion of Haiti, she snapped, "If Haiti were threatened by Communism, none of you would be raising these questions"—yet Albright, when she had her chance in the Cold War, usually shrank from what others, fortunately, were prepared to do.

Albright has led a genuinely impressive life, and there is much to admire about her, as made unmistakable by two recent biographies of her—one by *Washington Post* reporter Michael Dobbs and the other by *Time*'s Ann Blackman. She has always been privileged by material wealth, but she is acquainted with struggle, not least because of a brutal divorce in

1983—without which, she has said repeatedly, she would not have been spurred to her present success. But neither of her biographers really touches on her positions in the final stage of the Cold War or seeks to hold her to account for them. Nor does anyone else. We are surely not in the business of handing out white feathers, but we may well ask, Where were you when we needed you, and, Have you gained any appreciation of the hard, often thankless work performed by those who concluded the "long twilight struggle"? It is they, we might cluck, who made it relatively safe for Albright, Clinton, Talbott, and Berger to hold high office. Caspar Weinberger concedes that it is tempting to resent the near-total absence of self-examination and humility in this bunch: "They fought us every step of the way."

So Madeleine Albright has flexed her muscles in Kosovo. She is heralded as the conscience of the West, the benefactor of millions, the scourge of another genocidal—though this time not mustachioed—dictator. In May, turning to her, Clinton said, "Secretary Albright, thank you for being able to redeem the lessons of your life story by standing up for the freedom of the people in the Balkans." Albright is indeed a heroine to Kosovars and others staving off murder and degradation. To them, she is a positively Reagan-like figure—just another miracle of this new, decidedly better age.

—June 28, 1999
National Review

Power Dem

The strange rise of a hatemonger

If Al Sharpton was a "power Dem" in 2000, he is much more of one now.

An amazing thing has happened in New York, and in Democratic politics: Al Sharpton has become King. He is Mr. Big, The Man to See, the straw that stirs the drink. Nothing has made that clearer than the prelude to the New York primary, and the budding New York Senate race. They come in a steady parade to him, even if they show flutters of reluctance: Bill Bradley, Al Gore, Hillary Clinton. Everyone refers to this as "kissing his ring"; at times, Democrats seem willing to kiss even more. Not long ago, he was a demagogue, a race-baiter, a menace—and acknowledged as such, by all but a fringe. Day and night, he worked to make an always difficult city—New York—even more difficult, more tense. Now, however, he practically rules. He is a kind of Establishment. His record—as galling as any in our politics—is overlooked, excused, or shrugged off. It is to him that every (Democratic) knee must bow.

And another amazing thing: no penalty. Democratic bigs seem to pay no penalty whatever for their embrace of Sharpton. George W. Bush is worse off for Bob Jones University.

THE KISS OF RESPECT

Sharpton—or "The Rev," as he is known among his fans—is nothing if not mindful of his status; he must know, therefore, that his two visits to the White House last year were milestones for him. One visit was for a conference on police brutality; the other was for a ceremony honoring the New York Yankees ("I don't think Al has ever been to a Yankee game in his life," confided a friend of his to an interviewer). The more Mrs. Clinton becomes a New Yorker, and a New York politician, the friendlier the White House is to Sharpton. Last November, when the First Lady was dithering about whether to run at all, Sharpton announced that his patience was "running thin"; he wondered whether Mrs. Clinton was "too scared and too intimidated and too much of a lackey to challenge" Mayor Rudolph Giuliani, long a Sharpton foe. In due course, Mrs. Clinton declared her candidacy, and made the pilgrimage to Sharpton headquarters.

Bill Bradley needed no prodding. A self-styled Great White Father of black America, he was always eager for Sharpton's blessing, meeting with him early. He was pleased to intone Sharpton's threat-laden slogan, "No justice, no peace." He courted The Rev with breathtaking, unembarrassed ardor. After their get-together in August, Sharpton said to the press, "Mr. Bradley had a very public meeting, answered all of the questions. I think he was very impressive." Outside of Sharpton's offices, however, not everything was harmony. Bill Perkins, a black city councilman, was leaving the meeting when he was confronted by a mob, supportive chiefly of the hate-spewing Khalid Abdul Muhammad, a Sharpton ally. They hurled charges of "Uncle Tom!" and warned that (relatively) temperate politicians like Perkins should "be killed." Such is the atmosphere you enter when you consort with Sharpton, even in his present "mainstream" mode. Bradley is not known to have expressed a word of concern. Out in Iowa, he did say, "I don't agree with Al Sharpton on everything, but I think he has to be given respect." Of course.

Slowest of all to pay homage to Sharpton—but, nevertheless, in time—was Al Gore. Shortly after Mrs. Clinton's visit, Sharpton let it be known that he would not wait for the vice president indefinitely. It would be "strange," he said, if Gore declined to "show respect for the community" (in Sharpton's mind, he and "the community" are one). Within a couple of weeks, Gore did indeed huddle with Sharpton, in the Upper East Side home of Karenna Gore Schiff, his daughter. His staff initially denied that Sharpton was with the Gores, only later admitting the truth. Similarly, Gore managed not to be photographed with The Rev—an example, we may assume, of the famous Gore caution.

Then came the big debate, staged at the Apollo Theatre in Harlem. Sharpton had demanded it. When the Gore camp appeared to hesitate, he snapped, "Clearly, we need a response by the end of the week." Gore, it goes without saying, was delighted to oblige Sharpton. The Man had called, and both Democratic candidates came running. It was a high moment in Sharpton's dizzying career.

New York, you could argue, is in the midst of a broad Sharpton Moment. He is not only at the center of Democratic politics, but key to the very life of the city—orchestrating protests against the police, turning the temperature up or down on racial antagonism, as he wishes, and generally acting like the mayor of black New York. For several years now, there has been a debate over whether there is a "New Sharpton"—a more moderate, less hateful, more constructive one. He is said by his liberal defenders—and occasionally by himself—to have "grown" (a word usually applied to conservative politicians who migrate left). Bill Bradley, for one, has endorsed this view. Certainly, Sharpton gives appearances of having gone respectable. There he is with Chris Matthews on *Hardball*, talking—and not unreasonably—about "the Moynihan wing" and "the Sharpton wing" of the New York Democratic party. And there he is with Charlie Gibson on *Good Morning America*, sitting next to former mayor David Dinkins. Weird times, these: Dinkins now seems like Sharpton's mascot.

The problem with the alleged New Sharpton is that he is unsettlingly like the old one. In the tradition of Yasser Arafat, he speaks one way to his core followers on the street, and another to the public at large. If he is not yet a full-blown media darling, he is fast becoming one. Reporters get a kick out of him, finding him exciting, personable, and a joy to quote. As the liberal *New York Post* columnist Jack Newfield has pointed out, he is "dangerous because he is so likable." And only rarely is Sharpton held accountable for his offenses, both past and ongoing. The tendency to forget, or to brush aside, is close to overpowering. The time may be right, then, for a little walk down Memory Lane, as unpleasant as that may be. What manner of man have the brightest lights in the Democratic party come to accept? When they wrap their arms around Al Sharpton, what, really, are they embracing?

A RECORD OF HATE AND PAIN

No one should suppose that Sharpton is without admirable qualities. He has not attracted thousands of followers on charismatic racism alone. He has daring, tenacity, and a gift for leadership, even if repeatedly abused. He is also an American original—a self-created (and re-created) man; a go-getter; an achiever, of sorts. Born 46 years ago in Brooklyn, he was relatively middle class, until his father walked out, when he became poor. He likes to say that he agitated from the beginning: "I yelled when I was hungry. I yelled when I was wet. I yelled when all those little black bourgeois babies stayed dignified and quiet. I learned before I got out of the maternity ward that you've got to holler like hell sometimes to get what you want."

When he was four, according to the legend, he began to preach. Jesse Jackson, who became a mentor, has described him as "a child prodigy." When he was about 14, Sharpton hooked up with one of the many Jackson operations, and at 16 started the first of his own: the National Youth Movement. He was also drawn to Adam Clayton Powell, the colorful and crooked congressman from Harlem. Shortly before he died, in 1972, he had some final words for young Sharpton (in The Rev's telling): "These yellow Uncle Toms are taking over the blacks in New York. Don't you stop fighting. If you want to do something for Adam, get rid of these Uncle Toms." Later, Sharpton came under the wing of James Brown, the soul singer, who acted as a father to him ("James Brown was my father; Jesse Jackson was my teacher"). When he at last took to full-time rabble-rousing, he did so with a ferocity, lashing out at "faggots," "cocktail-sip Negroes," and even black Marxists—those who carried "that German cracker's book under their arms."

He caught a break in 1984, when Bernhard Goetz, the subway gunman and face of white backlash, shot a gang of youthful muggers. Sharpton campaigned for Goetz's head. He caught a further break two years later, when the incident known as "Howard Beach" occurred: A young black man, Michael Griffith, was chased to death by a gang of white thugs. Sharpton was developing a modus operandi: He would call victims or their families—or defendants and theirs—to offer his services, which included cash, legal counsel, and the like. Sharpton himself would serve as "adviser" and "spokesman." He quickly earned the sobriquet "Reverend 911," responding to any black-white emergency. Accused of being an ambulance chaser, he retorted: "No: I *am* the ambulance."

His greatest infamy came in 1987, with the Tawana Brawley hoax. As the journalist Nat Hentoff has put it, this is Sharpton's "Chappaquiddick." To recall the horrid affair: A girl named Tawana Brawley, after staying away from home for several days, smeared herself with dog feces, scrawled racial epithets on her body, and hopped into a garbage bag. Then she claimed that six white men, including a police officer, had raped and otherwise tormented her. All of America sat up in alarm. Bill Cosby, who was at the height of his fame and popularity, offered a large monetary award for information leading to arrests. And Al Sharpton, of course, was on the spot. Acting as the Brawley family's adviser, he urged them not to cooperate with the authorities, including the state attorney general, Robert Abrams. To cooperate with Abrams, he said, would be "to sit down with Mr. Hitler." A Sharpton sidekick, Alton Maddox, added, "Robert Abrams, you are no longer going to masturbate looking at Tawana Brawley's picture."

One of those whom Sharpton and his partners accused was an assistant district attorney, Steven Pagones, who was, needless to say, innocent (the crime never took place). After he was cleared, he held a press conference, which Sharpton, in his theatrical fashion, attempted to crash. "Your accuser has arrived!" he bellowed. Sharpton had said before, "We stated openly that Steven Pagones did it. If we're lying, sue us, so we can go into court with you and prove you did it. Sue us—sue us right now." Oddly enough, Pagones did. He spent a decade of his life pursuing a defamation case against Sharpton and his accomplices, finally winning that case one glorious, cleansing day in July of 1998. His life had been a hell—of death threats, illnesses, and assorted other agonies. He said to an interviewer in 1997, "I know that Sharpton doesn't care how I feel. [But] I will follow him and make sure he pays up as long as I live. Wherever he goes, he'll find me waiting for him." Sharpton now owes Pagones $65,000 in damages, money that the victim will probably never see. [N.B.: A group of Sharpton cronies paid off the debt for him in June 2001, to get the issue off Sharpton's back.]

At the heart of any case against Sharpton—and against the notion of a

New Sharpton—is his persecution of Steven Pagones. It has been, to use the word for which there is no substitute, evil. He has never apologized for his deeds, and nothing piques him more than to be reminded of them. "If I saved the Pope's life," he has sniped, "the media would ask me about Brawley." In soft moments, he has come close to apologizing ("I have regrets"). In harder ones, he is angrily defiant ("Never, ever!"). Liberal journalists—white—patiently explain that, for a black leader, an apology is a complicated matter: a question of politics and tactics, not of right and wrong. As Sharpton himself has said, to apologize would be "all about submission." White folk "are asking me to grovel. They want black children to say that they forced a black man coming out of the hardcore ghetto to his knees." Jesse Jackson gained nothing by apologizing for his "Hymietown" remark, so why should he? Only last year, Sharpton said of his role in the Brawley case, "If I had to do it again, I'd do it in the same way."

There was more, of course—always more. In the spring of 1989, the Central Park "wilding" occurred. That was the monstrous rape and beating of a young white woman, known to most of the world as "the jogger." The hatred heaped on her by Sharpton and his claque is almost impossible to fathom, and wrenching to review. Sharpton insisted—against all evidence—that the attackers were innocent. They were, he said, modern Scottsboro Boys, trapped in "a fit of racial hysteria." Unspeakably, he and his people charged that the victim's own boyfriend had raped and beaten her to the point of death. Outside the courthouse, they chanted, "The boyfriend did it! The boyfriend did it!" They denounced the victim as "Whore!" They screamed her name, over and over (because most publications refused to print it, though several black-owned ones did). Sharpton brought Tawana Brawley to the trial one day, to show her, he said, the difference between white justice and black justice. He arranged for her to meet the jogger's attackers, whom she greeted with comradely warmth. In another of his publicity stunts, he appealed for a psychiatrist to examine the victim. "It doesn't even have to be a black psychiatrist," he said, generously. He added: "We're not endorsing the damage to the girl—if there *was* this damage."

The horrible roll continues. August of 1991 saw "Crown Heights," the period of madness that began when a car driven by a Hasidic Jew careened out of control, killing a seven-year-old black child, Gavin Cato. Riots broke out. A rabbinical student, Yankel Rosenbaum, was lynched. Over a hundred others were injured. The city was on the verge of breaking apart. And here is what Al Sharpton had to say, in one of the most vile orations of his career, noxious with slanders familiar and novel:

The world will tell us that [Gavin Cato] was killed by accident. . . . What type of city do we have that would allow politics to rise above the blood of innocent babies? . . . Talk about how Oppenheimer in South Africa sends diamonds straight to Tel Aviv and deals with the diamond merchants right here in Crown Heights. . . . All we want to say is what Jesus said: If you offend one of these little ones, you got to pay for it. No compromise. Pay for your deeds. . . . It's no accident that we know we should not be run over. We are the royal family on the planet. We are the original man. We gazed into the stars and wrote astrology. We had a conversation and that became philosophy. . . . We will win because we are right. God is on our side.

Sharpton's rhetoric could also be rather less high-flown. "If the Jews want to get it on," he said, "tell them to pin their yarmulkes back and come over to my house."

HOW NEW?

So: When is the New Sharpton supposed to have emerged? Later in 1991, when, during a march in Brooklyn, he was stabbed in the chest, by a drunken young white. One of those who sped to his bedside was David Dinkins, then mayor, and the symbol of the black establishment that Sharpton despised and would soon replace. "I always tease Mayor Dinkins," he now likes to say, "that I looked up and thought I had died and gone to hell." In a display of magnanimity, Sharpton forgave his assailant and recommended leniency for him in court.

The supposedly sobered Sharpton quickly jumped into the electoral realm, running for the Senate in 1992 against a field he described as "recycled white trash." He finished third out of four Democrats, beating Elizabeth Holtzman, the renowned former congresswoman. Two years later, he again ran for the Senate, taking 26 percent of the vote from the incumbent, Daniel Patrick Moynihan. His most striking political showing came in 1997, when he ran for mayor. He garnered a full 32 percent of the vote in the Democratic primary, almost forcing a runoff with the winner, Ruth Messinger (who went on to be defeated by Giuliani).

All the while, Sharpton's power and influence—the sense of his legitimacy—grew. Once he had referred to Dinkins as "that nigger whore turning tricks in City Hall." By 1993, however, Dinkins could say, "I'm the mayor of New York, but Sharpton is the leader. If we didn't have an Al Sharpton, we would have to create one. Imagine if Al wasn't around. What would have happened to victims? Who would have raised our issues? Thank God for Martin [Luther King], thank God for Adam [Clayton Powell], thank God for Al." The torch had effectively been passed.

But the torching, so to speak, continued. In 1995—four years into the putative New Sharpton—there was another, fatal case in which Sharpton had a guilty hand: Freddy's Fashion Mart. In Harlem, a white store owner—no, worse: a Jewish one—was accused of driving a black store owner out of business. At one of the many rallies meant to scare the Jewish owner away, Sharpton charged that "there is a systemic and methodical strategy to eliminate our people from doing business off 125th Street. I want to make it clear . . . that we will not stand by and allow them to move this brother so that some white interloper can expand his business." Sharpton's colleague, Morris Powell, said of the Jewish owner—Sharpton's "white interloper"—"We're going to see that this cracker suffers. Reverend Sharpton is on it." Three months later, one of the protesters, Roland Smith, stormed Freddy's with a pistol, screaming, "It's on now: All blacks out!" In addition to shooting, he burned the place down. Eight people died.

Sharpton now faced a PR problem, a bump on his road to full respectability. In a manner both Sharptonian and Clintonian, he denied having even spoken at a rally at all. When tapes surfaced, he asked, "What's wrong with denouncing white interlopers?" Eventually, he decided to apologize—but only for saying "white," not "interloper."

SHAME AND HONOR

Most people, it seems—or at least most elites—have made a kind of peace with Sharpton. Two years ago, former mayor Ed Koch appeared on a cooking show with The Rev—just a pair of twinkle-eyed, cuddly New York pols, wearing aprons. But the Old Sharpton never fails to spring back. Around the time he was cooking with Koch, Sharpton was haranguing a Harlem crowd with Khalid Abdul Muhammad, the country's foremost specialist in Hitlerian rhetoric. (Free sample: "Who's pimping the world? The hairy hands of the Zionist in the world.") Pressed slightly on Muhammad, Sharpton said, "I have no problem with Khalid. My problem is Giuliani. It's not Khalid who is talking hate; it's Rudy Giuliani." As far as Sharpton was concerned, Muhammad was "an articulate and courageous brother."

And yet, much of the world is disposed to cut Sharpton miles of slack. With his charm and wit, he is seductive to many, even melting. Every reporter has a personal archive of hilarious and endearing morsels from The Rev's lips. What can they matter, though, in the face of the tremendous harm he has done? Last year, after another American delegation to Havana, Rep. Lincoln Diaz-Balart, a Florida Republican, said, "For the life of me, I just don't know how Castro can seem cute after forty years of torturing people." Sharpton, to be sure, is not Castro; but he has a lot to answer for. Eric Fettmann, an editorial writer and columnist for the *New York Post*, finds Sharpton anything but cute. He is a kind of one-man truth-and-memory squad against Sharpton. The Rev's greatest hoax, he argues, is not Tawana Brawley, but the New Sharpton. The Rev has, in fact, sued the *Post*, for damaging his reputation and inhibiting his fund-raising. The paper—delighted not least by the prospect of a legal proceeding that would open Sharpton's (dubious) books—editorialized, "Bring It On, Rev. Al."

A tragic aspect of Sharpton is that, given his talents, he could be a force for good. When the verdict in last month's Amadou Diallo trial came down, going against Sharpton and his protesters, he said, "Let not one brick be thrown." This was probably the most statesmanlike utterance of his career. But if Sharpton has shed Saul for Paul, he has provided scant evidence of it. Seldom does he resist the demagogic, the hatemongering, temptation. He is, for the most part, proudly unrepentant. And, oh, how he hates any cold-eyed look at his life and times. "They always try to scandalize you," he has complained (echoing an old spiritual). But "they," sadly, do not try to scandalize him enough. Perhaps even worse, they do nothing to scandalize those top Democrats who have bent to Sharpton's feet, raising him higher than ever.

—March 20, 2000
National Review

The Political
Garrison Keillor

Writer, poet-philosopher, hater

H e's a beloved American figure, yes, a cultural icon, the Will
Rogers—no, the Mark Twain!—of our time, a voice of reason,
enlightenment, and gentle humor, piped into our homes at least
weekly by our Good Mother, National Public Radio. He is, as his soulmate
Garry Trudeau has been reminding us lately in *Doonesbury*, a "national
treasure." But has anyone bothered to notice that he is also a horrid left-
liberal scold, dripping with contempt for nearly everything Middle American, so eaten by hatred of anything like conservatism and Republicanism
that he threatens at any moment to seek exile in Denmark? (Oh, excuse me:
He already did that, in the Reagan years.)

He, of course, is Garrison Keillor, the writer and host of *A Prairie
Home Companion* who has grown rich and famous off ridiculing his fellow
Minnesotans for the benefit of smirking elites everywhere. Weirdly enough,
he is often hailed as the voice—or at least the chronicler—of Everyman,
when instead he is a kind of anti-Everyman, a combination of H. L.
Mencken and Hillary Rodham Clinton, hammering at the "booboisie" and
flaunting what he takes to be his superior education and morals. This is a
bittersweet time for Keillor: His darling, Bill Clinton, is still standing, but
he is bloodied—almost brought down by the dark forces in American life,
the same yahoos Keillor has had to fight and suffer his entire life.

On March 18, Keillor was the headliner at a traditional Washington
event, the Radio and Television Correspondents Dinner. This is the same event
at which the radio jock Don Imus was so shocking in 1996, telling
raunchy jokes about the two Clintons, in their presence, and—worse, from
the hosts' point of view—insulting the press. The First Lady was even
grimmer than usual that night, and everyone else squirmed. Imus had
violated the rules: You're supposed to touch the president and his wife

only lightly—especially when they're fellow Children of the Sixties, for heaven's sake—and you're supposed to leave the crowd feeling pretty good about the privilege of living at the center of power.

The White House could not have been in safer hands than Keillor's. He bathed the Clintons in baby oil, massaging their most tender muscles. He began by thanking the president for his very presence, when surely the great man would have preferred "the chance to get away from Washington and its malcontents." Now he had to "sit and eat fish with a group of people who would regard your downfall as a professional opportunity." Clinton, noted Keillor, had proven "a very durable president," who had "already gone 400 days beyond when Sam Donaldson announced his resignation." F. Scott Fitzgerald had proclaimed that there are no second acts in American lives, but, oh, "he was wrong: He did not know Mr. Clinton."

And Hillary, fair Hillary! Why run for Senate from New York when you can do it in Minnesota, "a state of polite and modest people, very few of whom shave their heads on a regular basis"? (That last would be a reference to the new Minnesota governor, Jesse Ventura, Keillor's latest obsession and—come to think of it—"professional opportunity.") If the First Lady abandoned New York for Minnesota, said Keillor, her election would be "guaranteed," if only because the home folk would be so grateful for her embrace of them. "Run, Hillary, run!" was Keillor's toasty message—not the sort of thing, to be sure, that Don Imus would have offered.

What venom Keillor spilled, he spilled mainly on Ventura, about whom he seems unable to decide whether to be more furious or more pleased. He has just written a book about the governor, a mock (and mocking) autobiography that has understandably gotten under the big guy's skin. Ventura, said Keillor with typical disingenuousness, is "angry because I wrote about him." (Keillor also writes about Clinton, but, amazingly enough, the president isn't angry at him.) Ventura is "the first governor I ever came across who can sneer and swagger convincingly"—indeed, "almost as well as Patrick Buchanan." He has "a limited view of the world," of course, but "he got elected saying that he could only promise to do his best, and I would have to say that he has kept his word."

That's Keillor: clever, but surprisingly crabbed and ungenerous for someone who has been so crowned with success. He came of age in Anoka, Minn., a town apparently accursed with fundamentalist religion. According to Keillor, the people there frowned on "dancing, drinking, card playing, liberal education, and too-friendly association with non-believers." His parents subscribed to such vile fare as *Reader's Digest* and *American Home*, but at the public library, haven of higher thought, he found *The New Yorker*, and his path was set for life. "My people weren't much for literature," Keillor has written, so for him *The New Yorker* was "a fabulous sight, an immense, glittering ocean liner off the coast of Minnesota," a beacon in the black midwestern night. Keillor is a classic American type: brought up in an atmosphere he considered stifling and bent on complaining about it for the rest of his life.

In 1960, he "ran away to the University of Minnesota," where he spent "six happy years in extravagant freedom, marching against the war, shouting epithets at visiting bigwigs . . . going to theater where the actors jumped on stage naked and confronted us with their honesty and our hopeless inhibitions," etc. Keillor is to a tee a product of that decade, enthralled with JFK, mesmerized by 11/22/63, able to recite every detail of the Buddy Holly plane crash—that kind of thing. He has also spent years cultivating his resentment of the religious-minded, whom he skewers at every opportunity (which are numerous). "When Twain wrote about the religious Right of his day, 'They are good people in the worst sense of the word,'" Keillor once reflected, "we still recognize what he meant by that. Those people are still with us."

In due course, Keillor fulfilled his dream of catching on with his favorite magazine, *The New Yorker*, for which he wrote regularly until that ghastly moment in 1992 when Tina Brown took over, rescuing the moribund journal and actually making it readable and consequential again. Brown, sniffed Keillor, hadn't "changed" the magazine, but had "obliterated" it. "So long, Mr. Shawn," he sobbed, "and good night, E. B. White." He also became a star of radio, a medium about which he is nevertheless skeptical, given the popularity of two of his bogeymen, Rush Limbaugh and Howard Stern. "If you look at them in an objective way," he said in a 1994 interview, "they're really trashy people . . . But when you tune them in, you're drawn into their point of view. That's how Hitler came to power, you know." (Ah, the delicate brush for which Keillor is fabled.)

Along the way, Keillor managed to realize still another American Dream, taking as his second wife a woman he had met when she was a Danish exchange student. This facilitated his flight to Scandinavia, where he played brooding expat for a while before trekking back home to the limelight. He now seems resigned to America, dividing his time between the Upper West Side of Manhattan and a place in Wisconsin. He tells his New York audiences things like, "I'm a real midwestern kind of guy: I know what kind of leaves make the best toilet paper." Even when he seems to be talking fondly about "his people," he does so with a wink at those who are his actual people. He perhaps returns to the Midwest to collect his material, but his soul seems firmly on the Upper West Side, where the votes are Democratic, his books sell briskly, and all morning long black women push strollers containing tousle-haired white kids. (Where, I often wonder, are their mothers? Brokering deals on Wall Street or in bed consuming bonbons?)

Throughout his career, Keillor has been intensely political, a nasty polemicist—yet somehow, he is never given the credit, or blame, for this. He is a Gene McCarthy-style progressive, yes, but also curiously conservative, in the killjoy way of Ralph Nader, who once had fits of puritan apoplexy over something so frivolous on cars as tail fins. (Keillor, as it happens, frequently boasts of his Puritan ancestry, in the guise of deprecating it.) Similarly, Keillor decries cable television, e-mail, and other trappings of modern society. In fact, one of the things he liked about his adoptive country was that "planning makes Denmark look good. It's why there's no sprawl of junkyards and trailer parks and Mr. Donut drive-ins . . ." What's more, "Everybody ought to have a Dane to have lunch with: They will listen to you and they will not judge you." Keillor will, however, and when he wants to denounce American culture, he simply reaches for one of his swearwords—"Wal-Mart" or "Gap" will do—and there you have it.

For Bill Clinton, his affection is almost quaint. Shortly after the 1992 election, Keillor wrote, "These are good times to be alive in America. The tide of hogwash is receding a little and, with the Republicans in eclipse, pious humbug also is slightly reduced. The young president seems to have a tonic effect on everything," and—get this—"he isn't full of himself." Clinton, he would later write, is "full of soul," and, better yet, "he is a president who reads books"! He has "the dignity of someone who has always known who he is" (seriously). And why did he clean up in 1996? Because "you look at him at the lectern and you look at the sweaty young Republicans," and "it's not a hard choice." (As for Reagan, "he was a charming man who twinkled at people, and there's your explanation for the Conservative Revolution. It wasn't about his ideas.")

For Keillor, the Republican party isn't merely laughable or distasteful. Oh no. He declared in 1995, "This is a criminal party." Its policies are "evil." "Deeply evil." And "I am truly ashamed of religious people who have signed up" with the GOP, because "this is truly a betrayal of their own faith. This is not"—and here is the Reverend Keillor, raging from the pulpit—"what Jesus called us here to do." Newt Gingrich, for example, according to the Nonjudgmental One, "has no real grounding or base in the faith. He is not a man of faith."

When the Republicans swept Congress in 1994, Keillor perceived a new night fallen. "Out of the mists," he wrote, "dim figures emerged, and lo and behold, it is the same old gang of fraternity boys, geezers in golf pants, cheese merchants, cat stranglers, corporate shills, Bible beaters, swamp developers, amateur cops, and old gasbags that we have known since time immemorial." (Hang on a second: cheese merchants?) As Keillor saw it, we were "back in the Gilded Age, among portly men who regard great wealth as the surest sign of Divine Grace and who amuse themselves by railing against the poor and calling for more prisons. Thomas Nast, Mark Twain, H. L. Mencken, Sinclair Lewis—every satirist there ever was has watched this same parade go tooting past."

And this cuts to the heart of it: Here is Keillor's canon, here is the tradition in which he places himself, and he is not wrong—he does indeed resemble those men, not least in their intolerance for the beliefs and habits of ordinary people, especially those hooked on the Bible.

Throughout Clinton's impeachment ordeal, Keillor was by turns indignant, sarcastic, and despairing. No muckraker, he had written in 1994 that, "when I was 16, my parents were like the Washington press. They felt that they were entitled to know a great deal more about my life than they knew." And yet, a little earlier, he had been scandalized by the yawning corruption of the Bush administration, including the savings-and-loan debacle: "the hundreds of billions of tax dollars spent to pay off the bad debts of guys in loud sportcoats, the years of generous support of the Saddam Hussein regime during which American cities rotted and decayed," and so on. Clinton, by contrast, received Keillor's wholehearted and combative support. Wrote Keillor, "The America that the Thirteen Angry House Managers envision is a rather bleak place where most of us would be in prison or within view of it." If the Republicans could cramp a president "full of soul," what would they do to the rest of us sinners?

Lately, Keillor has been afforded some relief, not only by the defeat of the anti-Clinton SS but by the arrival of a juicy new target, Governor Ventura, whom he calls "Jesse Helms with pectorals and a stronger chin." Following the recent election, Keillor wrote, "We are a state of highly repressed Scandinavians"—this is just his shtick, mind you; he's not referring to himself—"and sometimes we like to surprise ourselves. Minnesota is a $12 billion-a-year operation, and we have taken the janitor and made him the CEO."

Keillor's new book is a smug little volume titled *Me*, which purports to be the memoir of a Ventura-like governor "as told to" the master himself, Keillor. The work is a compendium of every left-wing bias, crotchet, and shibboleth imaginable. From the phony dedication to the final sentence, it is an attack on Ventura and on right-oriented populism generally, but it is also—even primarily—a tribute to the intelligence, humanity, and wit of the "ghost," Keillor. In his author's note, Keillor states formulaically that the book "should not be construed in any way as an autobiography of an actual governor of Minnesota, God bless him"—but we are not to take that seriously. And he doesn't really mean, "God bless him," either. What he means is closer to, "Damn him to hell."

The book opens with, "The day of my conception was a pellucid June afternoon" (about which, more in a moment). Keillor waits until the second sentence to go racial, mentioning a table in a country club at which "no Jews or Negroes" have ever sat. Of course, the only people left in America who use the word "Negro" are Keillor types, who use it to convey their impression of what conservatives think of black people. In fact, *Me* is a perfect expression of what left-liberals think, when they are thinking most crudely, about what conservatives think. Keillor is ever on the alert for boobish anti-elitism, as when he has his protagonist say, "The votes of truckers count just as much as those of people who read the *New York Times*." Sometimes the protagonist breaks the narration to joust with the ghost. "You are not a writer," he says at one point, "only a ghost. This is my story. I don't want to find words like 'pellucid' in here."

You understand, don't you? The likes of Keillor know what "pellucid" means and the likes of Ventura do not. All right, then.

The protagonist grows up in a pathetic home, which includes, predictably, a kooky grandmother who passes out religious pamphlets. The young man takes up bodybuilding and eventually joins the Navy, becoming a "Walrus" (not a SEAL, as the real-life Ventura did). The Walruses are a bunch of savage louts who bark in code, have a secret handshake, and live to destroy. When they are ordered to Vietnam, the Ventura character mouths ideas that we are intended to accept as moronic: "This is a time for us all to make sacrifices. America's strategic interests are threatened by Communist-led wars of so-called national liberation [Keillor, of course, doesn't consider them wars of "so-called" national liberation at all], and if Vietnam falls, Cambodia is next, Laos, Malaysia . . . The Red Wave could spread . . ." (Odd how the domino theory is absurd to all but the Cambodians and Laotians, at least those who are still alive.)

The war in Keillor's conception is a fantasy, a Marxist cartoon, as though designed to confirm draft evaders and protesters in the choices they made. The U.S. troops are mindless and bloodthirsty rubes who exult in devastation and refer to the Vietcong as "atheist midgets." It's only satire, sure, but the author's evident disdain for the soldiers who served in Vietnam is nonetheless astonishing. When he writes the phrase "the American fighting man," he does so ironically, and his devotees are meant to snort, which no doubt they do.

In time, the protagonist returns from Southeast Asia and discovers the marvel of professional wrestling. Soon he is prancing in arenas that roar with "mouth-breathers and people who think Elvis is talking to them through the mail slot and women with many interesting tattoos and the Flat Earth people and men obsessed over the secret covenants of the world Zionist U.N." (But, come now, doesn't everyone know that it's the U.N. that despises Zionism?) He is enticed into politics, running for governor on Minnesota's Ethical Party ticket, and wins. In short order, he becomes a candidate in the 2000 presidential campaign (unlike the real Ventura), competing against the good and decent Al Gore—who, truth be told, is probably too good and decent to be elected by the Barnum-happy public.

That, essentially, is the book. Did I mention that it is droll, inventive, beautifully literate, and occasionally even brilliant? So is Keillor. And that's the tragedy of it. He is a man of impressive gifts, but he becomes so jittery with his anti-conservative tics that he can hardly see or write straight. So reflexively ideological is he in his politics that he winds up saying jarringly stupid things. He, like his models Twain, Mencken, and Lewis, is a hater, and on many days he fails to harness that rollicking hatred. He is like millions of other small-town kids who chafe at the Babbittry they see all around them. But most grow out of it. Keillor warns conservatives that they are "in danger of becoming the party of Uncle Harrys, the uncle with the big eyebrows who came over for a big Sunday dinner and grumped about the damned liberals," but it is he who is Uncle Harry, a leftist curmudgeon who is perpetually grumping about the conservatives and moralizing about the moralists.

Keillor is now in his mid-50s, prolific and versatile. He has many more writing years ahead of him. Perhaps he should aim a bit higher than Al Franken (author of the subtle tract *Rush Limbaugh Is a Big Fat Idiot*). He might consider ending his adolescent rebellion, getting morally and critically serious, and wowing one and all with a new maturity—before he drowns in a sea of his own crazy bile.

—April 19, 1999
National Review

Shrill Waters

The life and career of 'Big Bad Max'

Rep. Maxine Waters, the notorious Los Angeles Democrat, is a believer in the public outburst. During the Whitewater hearings five years ago, she screamed, "Shut up! Shut up!" at a Republican colleague, who had dared ask discomforting questions of Margaret Williams, the First Lady's chief of staff. Williams, it is necessary to note, is black, as is Waters—and the congresswoman proudly acts the part of Defender of the Race, as well as of Womanhood. On the House floor the next day, she declared that she was "pleased" to have run interference for Williams, as "the day is over when men can badger and intimidate women, marginalize them, and keep them from speaking." All the while, the (Democratic) Speaker tried to gavel her down, in vain.

Last month, on Impeachment Day, Waters again raised a ruckus, when Bob Livingston—then Speaker-to-be—urged the president to resign. That was far too much for Waters, the most excitable Clinton defender in Congress: Slamming her hand on a table and leading a chorus of Democratic booers and hissers, she yelled, "You resign! You resign!" And, lo, he did.

Waters, to say the least, is no violet. She may in fact be the foremost hater in American politics. She is known in her home state as "Maxine the Mouth," or "Mad Maxine," or "Big Bad Max." After she offered rationalizations for the L.A. riots in 1992, one of her antagonists, the radio personality Larry Elder, dubbed her "Kerosene Maxine." Now, her scowl and vituperation are known coast to coast, thanks to her prominence on the Judiciary Committee. She spent most of 1998 reviling Kenneth Starr and propping up Clinton, interpreting the effort to impeach him as (yes) an attack on black America. She is a political radical, a talented self-promoter, and more than a bit of a racial messianist (she is in the habit of referring to "my people," whom she protects from "the enemy"). To her admirers, she is a populist fighter, pleading the causes of the ignored and the dispossessed. To her opponents, she is (in Elder's words) a "dangerous, irresponsible, loudmouth, race-hustling victocrat" (Elder's term for a trader on victimization). Either way, Big Bad Max—whose personal motto is, "I don't have time to be polite"—is a new power in the Democratic party, a star of the clenched-fist Left.

Waters, scrappy at 60, grew up in St. Louis, one of 13 children in a family that relied, sporadically, on welfare. After moving to Los Angeles, she became an activist and campaign operator. She was elected to the state assembly in 1976, serving 14 years, and rising to chairman of the Democratic caucus. In 1991, her constituents in South Central L.A. sent her to Congress—just in time for the Gulf War. Waters was not only opposed to that war, she was one of a handful of House members who voted against a pro-forma resolution rallying behind it, well after it was under way. She had told a student audience, "Many African-American men and women, Latino Hispanics—they will not have any future. They're going to die." (The white soldiers, presumably, were impervious.) She wondered, "How can you tell the Crips and the Bloods [rival gangs] that you do not defend your territory by battling it out when we have our own leaders battling it out?" Later, at the war's conclusion, she sponsored a resolution praising black and Hispanic troops for their contributions and calling for special government programs to aid them back home. (Waters, incidentally, uttered not a peep of public protest when President Clinton throttled Iraq on Impeachment Eve.)

It was during the L.A. riots, in April 1992, that Waters first tasted serious national fame. She described those riots as a "rebellion" or "uprising," claiming that "the anger in my district is a righteous anger," to be appeased by a "sharing of resources." Why, "I'm just as angry as they are," she avowed. Her own office burned to the ground, but she dismissed her former digs as "just another victim of the rebellion." She took offense when Mayor Tom Bradley, her erstwhile political patron, characterized the rioters as "hoodlums and thugs." No, she insisted: "There were mothers who took this as an opportunity to take some milk, to take some bread, to take some shoes. . . . One lady said her children didn't have any shoes. She just saw those shoes there . . . G**d*** it! It was such a tearjerker. I might have gone in and taken them for her myself."

As to the suffering of Korean-American shopkeepers, the particular objects of murder, arson, and theft during the mayhem, Waters explained, "Blacks don't hate anybody. They just don't understand how [Asian entrepreneurs] can move in and have businesses and be the owner of things they can't have." And when she was chastised for appearing to fuel, rather than discourage, the violence, Waters had an answer, shared with a church congregation: "People want to know why I'm not saying exactly what they want me to say. They want me to walk out in Watts, like black people did in the Sixties, and say, 'Cool it, baby, cool it.' Well, I'm sorry: The fact of the matter is, whether we like it or not, riot is the voice of the unheard." Besides which, "it only makes them madder when you call them hoodlums and thugs."

For all this, Peter Jennings of ABC designated Waters "Person of the Week," a "woman who simply will not go unheard."

Waters has been heard repeatedly in the ensuing years, whether throwing fits, chaining herself to the White House gates (in protest of Haiti policy), or pushing conspiracy theories. Joel Kotkin, a Democratic policy analyst and professor at Pepperdine, remembers when he conducted a briefing for California Democrats in Congress, at the request of Rep. Howard Berman. Waters, irked at something he had written, marched in halfway through and heckled him, then marched back out. Other congressmen simply looked at the floor, embarrassed and uncomfortable. One explained to Kotkin, "Look, this is Maxine, and we just put up with it." Kotkin registers a common complaint when he says that Waters is a "bully," who "has the media completely cowed: She is beyond criticism, untouchable."

Indeed, few murmured when Waters championed the contention that the CIA, through the Nicaraguan contras, had spread crack cocaine through central Los Angeles, for the purpose of addicting and demoralizing the black population. She has recently supplied the foreword to *Dark Alliance*, by Gary Webb, the leading purveyor of this theory. (Webb first made his charges in the *San Jose Mercury-News*, which, after thorough debunking by other newspapers, was forced to apologize for the story.) Waters maintains in the current issue of *Essence* magazine that, as far as CIA drug-trafficking in inner cities is concerned, "They are still in it." She also wonders whether "there isn't some agreement with newspapers not to talk about the CIA based on national security." While "the black press has been wonderful," she says, "most of the major media would like me to shut up and go away." And drug czar Barry McCaffrey, with his focus on the suburbs, has "a soccer-mom mentality": He "doesn't show up in our communities or cooperate with the caucus" (meaning the Congressional Black Caucus, of which Waters has just finished a term as chairman).

So too, Waters has linked arms with the conspiratorial Right in suspecting that commerce secretary Ron Brown, who with 34 others died in a plane crash in 1996, was, in fact, murdered. Along with comedian-activist Dick Gregory and the NAACP's Kweisi Mfume, she has demanded an investigation.

On the international front, Waters wrote a highly unusual note last September to Fidel Castro—a note of apology and explanation. She had voted for a measure calling for the extradition from Cuba of one Joanne Chesimard, who, as a member of the "Black Liberation Army," murdered a policeman in 1973. Chesimard was imprisoned, but escaped in 1979, fleeing to Castro's island, where she was granted "political asylum." Waters wrote to Castro that, in casting her vote, she had not been aware that "Joanne Chesimard was the birth name of a political activist known to most Members of the Congressional Black Caucus as Assata Shakur." The "Republican leadership," she said, had "quietly slipped this bill onto the accelerated calendar," which, she helpfully explained, "is supposed to be reserved for non-controversial legislation like naming federal buildings and post offices." As "evidence of their deceptive intent," she continued, GOP leaders "did not mention Assata Shakur, but chose to only call her Joanne Chesimard." Hence, the erring vote. She confided to Castro that the Sixties and Seventies had been "a sad and shameful chapter of our history," when "vicious and reprehensible acts were taken against" black revolutionaries, resulting in the need to "flee political persecution." Concluded Waters, "I hope that my position is clear."

If any member of Congress had before written a dictator to lament the tactics of the other party, that missive is unknown.

It is her unceasing agitation for Clinton, however, that has made her a full-blown celebrity. She seconded Clinton's nomination at the '92 convention, but warned, "This is the last time I support an all-white anything." From 2000 on, there had to be "minorities or women" on the ticket, "or I will not be a Democrat supporting it." Meanwhile, "I am going to help [Clinton and Gore] get elected, and they better not mess with me once they get in." Needless to say, they have not. (Clinton promptly appointed Waters's husband, Sidney Williams, a former NFL player and Mercedes-Benz dealer, ambassador to the Bahamas.)

As soon as the president faced fire over Monica Lewinsky, Waters was at the ramparts, pronouncing herself the "fairness cop," who would not let the president be "railroaded." "More than anybody else," she told the press, black Americans "understand what it means to have fairness. We understand what it means to make sure there is not an abuse of power" (meaning, naturally, the independent counsel's). When Clinton appeared at a fundraiser for her in August, she declared, in a widely quoted comment, "We're not fair-weather friends. We will be with you to the end."

During the impeachment hearings, she glared disturbingly at Starr as he testified, and she jumped all over Republican colleagues who seemed to be scoring points, shouting, "Point of personal privilege!" Her identification of Clinton's predicament with race is near total. In her final statement before the committee, she said, "I am here in the name of my slave ancestors, to insist that the president be afforded" his constitutional rights. She recounted that she had awakened "in the middle of the night, with flashes of the struggles of my slave ancestors for justice." Before the full House, on Impeachment Day, she asserted that Republicans were the tools of "right-wing Christian Coalition extremists" seeking "to direct and control our culture." The president, she said, "is not guilty of the trumped-up charges" contained in the impeachment articles; rather, he "is guilty of being a populist leader who opened up government and access to the poor, to minorities, to women, and to the working class."

After reminding her audience that "I am an African-American woman" and judging Starr "guilty," she rose to her peroration, somewhat amazing, given the source: "I am greatly disappointed in the raw, unmasked, unbridled hatred and meanness that drives this impeachment coup d'état." If the House voted to impeach, she admonished, that action would be enshrined in history as "despicable."

One veteran Judiciary Committee staffer holds that Waters has actually mellowed over the years, and that the committee's true firebrand is the imperious Sheila Jackson Lee of Texas (crowned by the staff "Queen Sheila"). Raphael Sonenshein, a California political scientist who once worked for Waters, argues that she is not the "one-dimensional character," the scowling face, seen on television, but a "multifaceted" public servant who knows how to bargain, compromise, and effect sound policy. She enjoys one of the safest congressional seats in the country, and her national following grows apace. One black theater group, in a performance commissioned by Lincoln Center, offered a fantasy that had Waters inaugurated as president.

Shelby Steele, the social critic, has little patience for Waters and her brand of racialism. He regards her as a stalwart of "the grievance elite," bent on "extracting favors from the larger society." The curious thing, he says, is that "the militancy you see in her is a militancy for black dependence, the very opposite of black nationalism"—making her "a militant Uncle Tom." Waters "gets away with it," Steele observes, "because the larger society [as represented, for example, by white journalists] feels it doesn't have the moral authority to call her on it." For Waters, "there is no such thing as a loyal opposition. The other side is simply evil. The impulse behind this is a little fascistic, a little totalitarian. She never engages her opponents, but only demonizes them." (Waters declined to speak to *National Review*.)

Larry Elder, too, regrets that the congresswoman refuses to participate in a little give-and-take. She has shunned his radio program for years. But Big Bad Max is no doubt about the business—every hour, every day, every week—of protecting "my people" from "the enemy." And, as she will tell you, if you happen to catch her, "I don't have time to be polite."

—January 25, 1999
National Review

The Attack Man

Bob Shrum and the Democratic style

This piece was written in the summer of 2000, when Shrum was handling Vice President Gore. Four years later, he handled the next Democratic nominee, John Kerry. And in 2008?

Al Gore, as the country now realizes, is a rough campaigner—even a nasty one. His rhetoric is extreme, and his tactics are brutish. Naturally, he has formed a campaign team in his own image. There's general chairman Tony Coelho, who made his reputation smashing the face of Ronald Reagan in the 1980s. There's campaign manager Donna Brazile, who pops off wildly, sometimes shooting herself in the foot. And then there's Bob Shrum, the media strategist and all-purpose guru, who is the most aggressive, the most slashing, the most ruthless of them all. The campaign of George W. Bush knows to buckle its seat belt: It's going to be a very bumpy ride.

Shrum is probably the most important Democratic operative of the last 20 years. He has been at just about everyone's side, in the thick of nearly every fight. He is a legend in his own time: Everyone in politics, Democrat or Republican, has a fund of Shrum stories, and opinions. Most people like him; some are in awe of him; some—and not only Republicans—are repulsed by him; more than a few fear him. Bring up his name, and you'll get an earful of canine metaphors: Shrum is an "attack dog," a "pit bull," a "Rottweiler," a "junkyard dog." Some have used other images, however. Years ago, in thinking about Shrum's work, the New Jersey Republican Tom Kean said, "You hire an ax murderer, you're going to get an ax murder."

No one doubts that Shrum has a gift, or many gifts. As one rival says, "He does things seamlessly." He writes speeches, crafts ads, and plots strategy. He is also a fluent, if sometimes comically partisan, talking head on television. For his clients—particularly Ted Kennedy—he has written some of the most lapidary, most soaring Democratic oratory of our time. And yet no one is more adept at the low blow, at kicking Republican teeth in, especially in the last days of a campaign, when the target is too stunned, or too battered, to respond. Shrum is a curious type: the poet-goon.

On top of all this, he is a first-rate businessman—perhaps the most successful political consultant in Washington. Shrum, to put it mildly, is rich as Croesus. And he got that way, first by being capable, and second by connecting with politicians who are themselves rich. The deeper a candidate's pockets, the more likely Shrum is to be in them. As one observer puts it, Shrum is a master at "fleecing saps from the hinterland who don't know how to run a media campaign." Says another, "He goes for rich and stupid. They just don't know what has happened to them." Shrum's former firm, Doak & Shrum, was known by some as "Soak and Run." Quips one of Shrum's fellow operatives, "Bob has convinced political neophytes to play the game of 'Who Wants to Be a Former Millionaire?'"

Currently, Shrum is handling Jon Corzine, the Senate candidate and ex-Goldman Sachs partner in New Jersey. Other wealthy clients have included Al Checchi in California, Herb Kohl in Wisconsin, Howard Metzenbaum in Ohio, Metzenbaum's son-in-law, Joel Hyatt, in the same state, Charlie Owen in Kentucky, and John Edwards in North Carolina—all loaded, all free-spenders. Of course, every other consultant would like the rich clients, too, as Shrum's peers happily admit. It's just that the smooth and clever Shrum has shown a remarkable ability to land them.

In the course of his prodigious politicking, Shrum has become a fixture on the Washington social scene. Indeed, he is a pillar of it. He and his wife, the writer Marylouise Oates, are part of that cozy community that features Al and Judy, Jim and Kate, and (not least) Ben and Sally. Says an insider,

"Bob likes money, no doubt about that. He has an extravagant and expensive lifestyle." Shrum is a wide-ranging reader, a bon vivant, a lover of Italy. And he runs a starry Georgetown salon. Says one wistful Washington figure, no longer invited, "I always enjoyed him." The Shrum home "was the gathering place in Washington of all the thinkers on the Democratic side, with a few Republicans sprinkled in. I met everybody there. You go there for the amazing food and the incredible conversation. And when you leave, you feel like you just dined at the Smithsonian. Frankly, I miss it."

RISE OF A PRO

Shrum, now in his mid-fifties, grew up in Los Angeles. He won a scholarship to Georgetown University, where he was named the top college debater in the country (no less). Then he went to Harvard Law School, where he earned still more honors. He never practiced law, however, jumping into the political arena immediately. He wrote speeches for John Lindsay, then for Ed Muskie in the 1972 presidential campaign, and after that for the party's nominee, George McGovern. Four years later, he signed on with Jimmy Carter—whom he left after a grand total of ten days. In quitting the campaign, Shrum accused Carter of duplicity, of saying one thing in public and another in private. He also implied that Carter was something of a closet conservative. Jody Powell, the press secretary, said that Shrum had acted in a "childish and hurtful manner." As Carter himself told it, the young scribe had assumed "that he could just deliver me a speech and I would parrot it." Well, "I've never done that."

Next time around, in 1980, Shrum was a Kennedy man, trying to bump off President Carter in the primaries. Kennedy fell short, but Shrum wrote the famous "dream shall never die" speech that the senator delivered at the Democratic convention. Among political liberals, this is holy writ.

For the next four years, Shrum served as Kennedy's press secretary. He is probably responsible for the term "Star Wars" to describe missile defense—one of the most devastating political coinages of this age. After President Reagan gave his historic speech proposing missile defense in March 1983, Kennedy, on the floor of the Senate, denounced "the misleading Red Scare tactics and reckless 'Star Wars' schemes of the president." Ah, the tenor of the times! The term "Star Wars," associated as it was with a president who had been a movie actor, stuck. Who can know how much it has done to slow the progress of missile defense? Al Gore, when he is feeling especially sniffy, uses the term to this day.

Though he left Kennedy's office in 1984, Shrum has never stopped

writing for the senator. Apparently, he has drafted all of Kennedy's important utterances of the past two decades, including the quasi-apology in
1991 for lapses in personal behavior, and the eulogies for Jackie Onassis
and John Kennedy Jr. Shrum does some extra-political ghosting, too: He
provides material for such extravaganzas as the Emmy Awards and the
Kennedy Center Honors. Shrum is in constant demand, and his customers
are usually satisfied.

As a full-time political consultant, he quickly racked up an impressive
client list: Alan Cranston, Barbara Mikulski (with whom his wife has
written novels), Tom Bradley, Geraldine Ferraro, David Dinkins. In the
1988 presidential race, Shrum's horse was Dick Gephardt, who ran a relentlessly negative campaign, with a strong populist, and protectionist, bent.
You will perhaps recall the $48,000 Hyundai, set against a Chrysler K-car
that was supposed to cost the equivalent amount in Japan. So ferocious
were Gephardt's tactics against Michael Dukakis that a major Gephardt
supporter, Claude Pepper, complained, and apologized to the Dukakis campaign.

In 1990, Shrum had one of his most notorious years, busting heads in a
way that shocked even Democrats across the nation. In Florida, he handled
Rep. Bill Nelson in the primary for governor against Lawton Chiles, a
veteran, gentle, well-loved pol. Shrum blitzed Chiles with a series of ads
that portrayed him as old, out of touch, and maybe a bit nuts (Chiles had
admitted being treated for depression). The ads also accused Chiles of
securing sweetheart loans for himself and his son. The state of Florida
recoiled—and Chiles won handily.

Over in Texas, Shrum worked for state attorney general Jim Mattox
in the gubernatorial primary against Ann Richards, the state treasurer.
Richards had acknowledged a struggle with drink, but she had refused to
address whether she had indulged in other substances as well. So, Shrum
went on the air with an ad that said, "Did she use marijuana, or something
worse, like cocaine . . . not as a college kid, but as a 47-year-old elected
official sworn to uphold the law?" The reaction to this sally was furious.
The *Boston Globe*, a liberal and exceedingly Shrum-friendly paper, registered its disgust. Richards's adviser, Bob Squier (since deceased), declared
that Shrum's ad was "the most despicable spot I have ever seen in politics."
Roger Ailes, the Republican impresario who two years before had made
the Massachusetts murderer Willie Horton world-famous, was quoted as
saying, "Honest, whatever you think of me, I wouldn't do that."

When it was presidential time again—1992—Shrum hooked up with

Bob Kerrey, the war-hero senator from Nebraska. Seldom does a political adman have a juicier product to sell. But in the New Hampshire primary, Shrum chose to portray Kerrey as a Gephardtian, Japan-bashing protectionist. The strategy flopped. Later, out West, Shrum did an ad attacking the front-runner as an environmental menace: "Under Bill Clinton, Arkansas dumped more toxic waste into rivers and lakes per capita than any other industrial state."

When Clinton won the nomination, however, he did not turn his back on Shrum's talents. Shrum helped him write his convention speech, and would go on to draft President Clinton's State of the Union addresses. Moreover, he wrote the semi-famous Speech That Was Never Given, intended for Clinton to deliver in August 1998, after his grand-jury testimony in the Lewinsky affair. The brief address was contrite, measured, and graceful. Evidently, the president wanted no part of it, instead letting loose an angry, defiant blast at his enemies. Clinton paid the price in public opinion.

It was in 1998 that Shrum hit the jackpot with Al Checchi, the billionaire in California. Checchi spent about $40 million in a losing effort to grab the nomination for governor. Several of those million—no one is quite sure how many—went to Shrum. Somewhat awkwardly, you would think, Shrum went up against a former client of his, Rep. Jane Harman (also a billionaire, as it happens). His ads tagged her as an enemy of the poor and elderly for her votes to contain Social Security and health-care costs; as a partner in crime of the hated Newt Gingrich; as a "career politician." They were—even by Shrumian standards—"grossly misleading," in the words of a prominent Democrat in the state, Sen. Dianne Feinstein. Said Feinstein, "It's one thing to have a lot of money and use it to tell people what you're for. It's another thing to have a lot of money and use it to falsely depict, to mislead and destroy." In the end, a third candidate—Gray Davis—won the nomination, going on to Sacramento.

There's worse. A lot worse. The 1998 gubernatorial election in Maryland pitted the Republican Ellen Sauerbrey against the Democrat Parris Glendening. The race was neck and neck until the final days of the campaign, when Glendening and Shrum played the race card. Really, that is understating it: They lit that card and proceeded to torch the landscape. As a state legislator, Sauerbrey had voted against minority set-asides and a "hate crimes" bill. She had also opposed a measure—deviously labeled a "civil-rights act"—that had to do with sexual-harassment suits, and that was ultimately quashed by the Democratic state senate. Reaching his lowest, Shrum unleashed an ad that smeared Sauerbrey as a racist, with a "shameful record on civil rights." (Just to be sure, he also blanketed black communities with a flier that did the same.)

A good portion of the state was aghast. Several black Democrats, including Baltimore mayor Kurt Schmoke, rose to Sauerbrey's defense. Schmoke told the press pointedly that he knew the "difference between a political conservative and a racist." He made clear that he did not regard the Shrum spot as "truth-in-advertising." Schmoke refused to make an ad for Glendening that faulted Sauerbrey on civil-rights grounds. Even *The New Republic* balked, editorializing against the "dishonorable" practice of "race-baiting." It also noted that a "short-run gain to the governor may come at some cost to the racial atmosphere in his state."

The ad, however, worked its terrible magic. It apparently frightened black Marylanders, boosting their turnout and putting Glendening over the top. According to *Campaigns & Elections* magazine, this was the "Most Brutally Effective Attack Spot" of the year.

Today, Ellen Sauerbrey warns that the Bush campaign had better be prepared for more of the same. Shrum, she says, "has no scruples about distorting the record to try to scare African-American voters. This is a nasty man, without a conscience, who will drag someone through the mud and use the most divisive political issues he can think of." Look, she continues: "If you attack people on something like their environmental record, after the election, you haven't done any lasting harm. But when you divide and polarize communities on the basis of race, I think it has long-term and very nasty effects."

THE TONGUE THAT BURNS

The voice of Democratic politics is, in essence, the voice of Bob Shrum. It has his tone, his language, his thrust. Listen to him back in 1988, explaining how the Democratic presidential nominee ought to talk. Little has changed. "The candidate," he said, "should tie the Republicans to the far Right and paint them as anti-environmental. Both tactics have worked well for the Democrats in recent elections. The Republicans now have a party that is in thrall to the far Right. Theirs is no longer the party of Abraham Lincoln and Theodore Roosevelt. It has become the party of Jesse Helms, Pat Robertson, and James Watt." (That last, to be sure, is an anachronistic note. Today, Shrum would substitute . . . Bob Jones.)

Yet there is a part of Shrum's 1988 schtick that would not work well for the Democrats in 2000. Hard as it is to believe now, Democrats such as Shrum once pretended that the Reagan administration was a carnival of corruption. Twelve years ago, Shrum asked, "What has happened to public values? I envision an administration where no presidential appointee ever takes the Fifth Amendment, and no special prosecutor has to be appointed, because no special favors have been granted, and no secret, illegal plans have been concocted. . . . The standard this administration has set has infected everything. We now have a public ethic on Wall Street that says, Whatever you can get away with is right. There must be a higher standard than that—and that standard must be set in the highest councils of government."

We should hardly expect to hear this from Bill Clinton's vice president this year.

In assailing the Republicans, Shrum can be piercing, but also a little silly. He mentions Herbert Hoover a lot. Five years ago, he said, "One reason we have millions of hungry children is [that Republicans] sponsored a whole bunch of people and put them in power who thought ketchup was a vegetable." Most hilariously, he said last year that George W. Bush "threatens to reinstall the supply-side economics that brought his father's administration down." Shrum, who knows a thing or two, must be aware that President Bush was a determined foe of supply-side economics, whose devotees despised his administration.

Most of Shrum's circle swears that he is a true believer, a (Ted) Kennedyite to the core, a bleeding heart. A few describe him as a democratic socialist, and as a political Catholic in the mold of Dorothy Day. Indeed, Shrum pointed out in 1998 that "the Pope has constantly emphasized" that the "great duty of Western societies now, through the public sector, is to create a fairer society in terms of issues like health care, child care, and a whole range of services." Yet Shrum is vigorously pro-choice on abortion. He runs tough abortion ads against pro-lifers, and also against pro-choicers who are deemed less than rock-solid on the issue. He did this to Rudy Giuliani, for example, while working for David Dinkins.

There is a second school of thought about Shrum—one that holds that he is less of a bleeding heart than meets the eye, that says that, if his heart bleeds anything, it is not so much Kennedy red as high-dollar green. It is certainly true that there is an element of the pure professional in Shrum. In 1988, for instance, he made ads for California senatorial nominee Leo McCarthy, a committed foe of offshore drilling. At the same time, he also made ads for Occidental Petroleum, which was trying to retain the right to drill offshore. Or consider this: In late 1997, Shrum wrote a speech for Dick Gephardt decrying the course of the Democratic party as too pragmatic. Less than two weeks later, Ted Kennedy rebutted this criticism—in a speech also written by the flexible Shrum.

Says one Shrum critic, "His ideology? Come on: His ideology is to make money, go to Italy, have parties, and be a big deal."

Always, though—always, always—there is the toxic issue of race. Shrum, as the quintessential modern Democrat, rides it for all it is worth. Recently, his colleague Donna Brazile attacked Republicans as racists, who "would rather take pictures with black children than feed them." Said Shrum, "The fact of the matter is that what Donna said is true." And Shrum was there in California, in 1996, doing his worst to defeat Proposition 209, the ballot initiative that sought to ban race and gender preferences in that state's public institutions. When he finished an ad, the anti-209 camp rejoiced that he had "designed a nuclear bomb." The ad was classic Shrum: David Duke, burning crosses, the whole nine yards. The message, too, was classic Shrum: Preferences of this type could be opposed only by the Ku Klux Klan. The night riders were coming.

Ward Connerly, who spearheaded 209 (which eventually prevailed), writes of Shrum in his new book, *Creating Equal*. He met the Democratic maestro before a taping of *Firing Line*. "Sitting in the green room," remembers Connerly, "I asked him about the ad. 'We didn't have much money,' he shrugged, 'and had to get the biggest bang we could for the buck.' As he spoke, his voice and manner conveyed a quintessence of nihilism, and I had the image in my mind of Saddam Hussein mindlessly lobbing Scuds at Tel Aviv long after it was clear that he had lost the Gulf War."

We are told incessantly that "politics ain't beanbag"; that "if you can't stand the heat, stay out of the kitchen"; that the political racket is "not for the fainthearted," etc. Anyone who questions the Shrum way of conducting politics is apt to be dismissed as a romantic or a naïf. Surely, though, we should resist the notion that there can be no decency—no honesty, no fairness—in our politics. For many years now, Shrum has been a vial of poison in those politics. He is the undisputed master at, as the old cliché goes, "playing to people's fears." And how a liberal Democrat—considering what liberal Democrats once were—can make a living by rubbing racial tensions raw is a mystery.

Not a mystery is what Shrum and his partners will do to George W. Bush, especially if Al Gore is trailing as Election Day nears. There is only one consolation: Even as he scorches the earth, Bob Shrum doesn't always win.

—July 3, 2000
National Review

Rosie O'Donnell, Political Activist

A celebrity and her platform

They call her the "Queen of Nice," but she didn't ask for the title, and she refuses to wear the crown. "I am not the Queen of Nice," she says emphatically, indeed, angrily. She likes her TV talk show to be sweet and light, but "I have serious and strong views"—about Woody Allen, for example, who married his wife's daughter (or something like that), and O. J. Simpson, who . . . well, we all know what he did. And she is very, very tough on conservatives. In fact, Rosie O'Donnell has become the celebrity who most inflames the Right. She has surpassed Barbra Streisand, the Baldwin brothers, and even Jane Fonda, who has apparently found religion. Whether she's plumping for the Clintons, socking it to Rudy Giuliani, or leading the cry for gun control, Rosie is making conservatives choke. She is using the bully pulpit of her stardom with a vengeance. And, in some ways, she is the perfect expression of modern liberalism.

Of her fame, there is no doubt: It is dizzying. Walk into any supermarket, glance at the magazine rack, and there's Rosie. (Bill Buckley once noted the impossibility of "Mr. Carson"; it had to be "Johnny." So it is with Rosie.) She's a movie star, a television personality who rivals the almighty Oprah, a stand-up comic, a Broadway entertainer, an author, and an industry. She has a Barbie doll made in her likeness (yes), and that ultimate stamp of celebrity: a Christmas album. *Time* magazine listed her as one of the 25 most influential people in the country. About her activism, Rosie says, "I have a responsibility as well as an opportunity to speak to millions of people on a daily basis. It's sad that celebrities' opinions are given so much weight, but they are, in the culture we live in."

Politically speaking, she considers herself primarily a child-welfare advocate. "I always knew," she says, "that if I were ever in a position to have an effect on society, I would use it to benefit kids." Rosie herself had a rough upbringing, of the Frank McCourt variety. And she has certainly put her money where her mouth is, devoting millions of dollars to children's charities, mainly through a foundation of her own devising. Her political heroes? That's easy: Hillary Clinton and Marian Wright Edelman, stalwarts of the Children's Defense Fund. ("I'm a devout follower of hers," says Rosie of Edelman.) Her fondest dreams are thoroughly Hillaryesque: national health care and national day care—in addition, of course, to gun control.

ON A SOAPBOX

Shortly after her show began in 1996, Rosie revealed herself as a Democrat. She was a bit nervous at first. As she explained to *Entertainment Weekly*, "I thought, 'Uh-oh: I guess there's a reason Dave [Letterman] and Jay [Leno] never get into their political affiliations. I'm going to get letters from Republicans about this.' Then I realized: 'What Republicans are watching daytime television? They're too busy trying to make more money than anybody else.'" Rosie has a certain tic about Republicans and money. Recently, she opined that her neighbors in Greenwich, Conn., "have too much money." Rosie's liberalism—heavy with emotion—tends to be a cartoon liberalism: Every Republican is a sniffy man in a top hat and limo, instructing his driver to run down any urchin he can spot.

Since her unveiling as a Super Dem, Rosie has been relentless. She decried Republican welfare reform, signed into law by President Clinton, as "literally heinous" (she still thinks so). She raised money for the Clinton-Gore reelection, knocking Republican heads as she went. For Hillary, her affection is unbounded. She told her friend Nora Ephron, in an interview for *Redbook*, "I wish that she were running for Senate as a divorcee, but I will support her" in any case. The First Lady has been on the Rosie show at least five times. At last fall's "Broadway for Hillary" fundraiser, Rosie spilled acid on Mayor Giuliani, then the likely Republican nominee versus Hillary. She said that he looked like a Pez dispenser. She said that if he wrote a book, it would be called "It Takes a Village Idiot" (her material is usually not so worn). Worse, in a joke about a mainly black Broadway cast, she implied that Giuliani was a racist. Hillary expressed her thanks by calling Rosie "absolutely incomparable."

The talk-show host wasn't through with the mayor. In December, as the Senate race was getting hot, she used her show to attack Giuliani for his policies on the homeless (which Giuliani supporters would characterize as "tough love"). "He's out of control, this guy!" said Rosie. "Sure, just, you know—arrest all the homeless people." Then she flashed the mayor's phone and fax numbers on the screen, inviting her fans to register their outrage. She threatened to take to the streets herself, to be arrested. Giuliani, not surprisingly, had a response: "There's no question that she's a political operative."

But the crucial moment for Rosie had come earlier in the year, in April: Columbine. The lesson of the tragedy, she decided, was the evil of guns. In a fit of fury, she said, "Outlaw all guns, and put all gun owners in jail!" Prior to this awful event, she now explains, "I wasn't immersed in the gun issue. Child advocacy was my thing. I didn't know who Wayne LaPierre was [he's head of the National Rifle Association]. I felt spiritually called to the table." What Rosie means is this: "There's a part of the Mass—I don't attend now, but I used to, as a kid—that goes, 'This is the Lamb of God, who takes away the sins of the world. Happy are they who are called to His supper.' And I thought, 'Those kids are like the sacrificial lamb,' and it called me to the supper." Rosie vowed to take up gun control as a crusade. She also likes to cite a line from *Les Misérables*, being a Broadway maven: "If I speak, I am condemned; if I stay silent, I am damned."

Not long after Columbine, Tom Selleck was a guest on Rosie's show, and the two of them had a testy—indeed, bitter—exchange over the NRA and guns. It was a strange moment for daytime television, and it is now part of gun-debate lore. Here is a taste of what Rosie said that day: "I think the Second Amendment is in the Constitution so that we can have muskets when the British people come over in 1800. I don't think it's in the Constitution to have assault weapons in the year 2000." On the heels of the fracas, Rosie faced a problem: It was pointed out that Kmart, for whom she did commercials, was a major retailer of guns. Did that make her a hypocrite? She was reluctant to give up the gig, as all of her earnings from the spots went to charity, but she did so at the end of the year, realizing that her position was untenable.

Rosie's latest political performance was as "emcee" of the "Million Mom March," the rally for gun control held in Washington. In a sign of true political arrival, she was interviewed by Cokie Roberts on *This Week*. She was, as she usually is, fluent and impassioned as she trotted out every gun-control canard in the book: 4,000 "children" killed per year by guns, 20,000 gun laws riddled with "20,000 loopholes," the NRA "stranglehold over Congress," the rarity of gun deaths in other countries, and so on. At the rally itself, she charged, "The NRA is buying votes with blood money." Charlton Heston, for his part, had little recourse but to laugh her off as "Tokyo Rosie."

RUMBLES LEFT AND LEFTER

As Rosie herself implied with her comment about Letterman and Leno, it's unusual for a talk-show host—at least one of this sort—to wax political. Her predecessors, who are also her models and idols—Mike Douglas, Merv Griffin, Dinah Shore—never did so. Neither did Johnny. Jack Paar, who preceded Carson on *The Tonight Show*, could be a jerk about politics, and a lucky thing, too, for it led to one of Bill Buckley's most dazzling and popular essays: "An Evening with Jack Paar" (found in the Buckley collection *Rumbles Left and Right*). Buckley appeared on the show in 1962, and he so unnerved his host that the poor man went on a several-day tear against Buckley, grouping him with the Nazis and Communists, in that charming liberal way we've come to know so well. For his troubles, Paar received a congratulatory phone call from President Kennedy.

In more recent times, Oprah Winfrey—bigger than Paar ever was—has largely avoided politics, although she did clash with cattlemen over the safety of American beef. And we must not forget Phil Donahue—a total political beast who, himself, is a definer of today's liberalism.

Many TV insiders believe that Rosie runs a risk with her politicking: There are millions of Americans—customers—who are bound to take offense. Does she worry? "I never enter it into the equation," she says. Neither is she troubled by questions of equal time and balance. "I can understand the concern," but, in the case of Giuliani, for example, "I don't know that anyone from his campaign would have wanted to be on the show" (fat chance). "We did have the other side with Tom Selleck, as badly as that turned out. I don't think either of us was particularly proud of that, but I think he was brave to come on and discuss the issue with me—and that is the other side." Following Selleckgate, "three or four people [who were to be guests on the show] canceled, and one other person, a country-western singer, called me," seeking reassurance that all would be peaceful.

In the year since Columbine, Rosie's stance on guns has softened, and she has learned the language of pragmatism. "As a mother, my emotional response was, 'Let's get rid of all guns.' But that's not going to happen." Sure, "in a perfect world, I would love it if we didn't have any handguns, but that's not what I'm striving for, nor is it attainable. That's an extremist view." She now says, "I'm not against someone having a gun, as long as it's licensed, registered, and has a child-safety lock." Furthermore, "I don't think gun owners are the enemy. I don't think they're evil." Charlton Heston has pledged, bearing a rifle aloft, "From my cold, dead hands." Says

Rosie: "I don't want to take his gun from his cold, dead hands, or his warm, live ones. That's not what we're asking for."

She stresses that her push for gun control is part of her overall effort to aid children. So, does she believe that the NRA cares less about young ones than she does? She pauses for a second, then answers, "I would say, maybe they care about their own kids. But not kids in general. The only life that is important to them is white, Republican life." The gun industry, she continues, "has a vested interest in not being regulated," but "we don't have a financial interest, because we're mothers." She attributes no decent motivation whatever to the NRA. Its position, she asserts, "is based on financial gain, not on patriotism or love of children."

On the day of her talk with *National Review*—May 25—Rosie was all over the news: One of her bodyguards had applied for a gun permit in Greenwich. For conservatives, this was Christmas morning. Here was one of the nation's most visible gun haters, apparently seeing to it that she herself was protected by a gun while campaigning to leave everyone else defenseless. (Rosie and her family have been the targets of threats, stemming, she believes, from her anti-gun stance.) The hypocrisy seemed stinking, blatant. Yet Rosie pleads innocent: "The security people who work in my home do not have guns. The statistic is that you're three times more likely to be a victim of violence if you own a gun. That's why I choose not to have them in my home. But in public places, my security people, who are off-duty policemen, have guns"—which, she holds, is another matter.

In her politics, she remains a Clintonite to the core, but she does have misgivings about the president: "I have severe disappointments in his personal ethics. I lost a tremendous amount of respect for him during [the Lewinsky affair], and it has not been recovered. I haven't forgotten, nor will I. But that's a code of shame on him, not on Hillary." Did she lose any respect at all for Hillary, what with her wild charges of a "vast, right-wing conspiracy" and so on? No way. "I believe she believed her husband. I don't believe for one minute that she sat on the *Today* show [where the First Lady alleged the "conspiracy"] knowing the truth of that situation. I believe her husband lied to her, as he did to everyone else, and that she found out only later that he'd betrayed her."

About the ex-Senate candidate and still-mayor, Giuliani, Rosie is unyielding. She has no patience with the argument that he has made city life broadly tolerable again: "That's what a white conservative who's rich would say, but not someone in a poor neighborhood." But consider a more profound, more fundamental question: Rosie is a fervent defender of children and their rights. What about abortion? "I'm pro-choice," she says—then adds, with utter conviction, "but I personally would never have an abortion." This she relates to the gun issue, explaining that she recognizes the right to own a gun, but would never pick up one herself.

AN OLD PRO REFLECTS

In light of the ongoing controversies of Rosiedom, it's of more than passing interest to hear from one of her beloved forerunners: Mike Douglas, the smooth-voiced host who ruled the afternoon air for years. Now, Rosie loves Mike, and Mike loves Rosie. She always wanted to do a show just like his. And she is responsible for a bit of a Douglas revival, putting him back into the public eye and spurring him to pen his memoirs—for which she wrote the introduction. Douglas leaves no doubt that he is Rosie's number-one fan. He feels indebted to her. But he is skeptical, to put it mildly, about the course she has taken.

"I had plenty of political figures on the show," he recalls, including Malcolm X ("He was scary"), Martin Luther King, and Buckley (repeatedly). But "I myself was apolitical on the show. I always had the feeling that, if I said something about this person or that, I'd be alienating half of my audience—or maybe more than half. I didn't think that [voicing political opinions] was entertaining, and I still don't." When a guest made some political point or other, "I couldn't even say, 'I agree with you.' I felt I had to remain neutral. That's the difference. As a professional matter, I didn't think it was right."

Douglas is especially chagrined at Rosie's treatment of Giuliani: "I don't live in New York, but I get there every now and then, and I'm telling you, that man has done wonders for that city. There's a visible change when you come to New York now. Before, it was an absolute pigpen. So I think her comments were out of place, myself. I love Rosie, but I think that was wrong." As for Tom Selleck, "that poor guy: Rosie was really loaded for bear that day. I wouldn't call it sandbagging, but it was close." (Rosie says that Selleck had clearly understood that the two would discuss guns.) "If you have a platform," continues Douglas, "you have to use it responsibly." For instance, "if you have the one side on, you have to have the other side—absolutely. And if you have one candidate on, you should have them all on. Otherwise, it's not fair. You're showing a bias." Informed that Rosie has had Hillary Clinton on her show about five times, Douglas quips, "You think she likes her?" (Rosie maintains that Hillary has appeared strictly in her capacity as First Lady.)

Despite all their boosterism, celebrities, Douglas believes, have little influence on the public: "I don't think the people take their cues from entertainers. I really don't, never have. That's why I don't understand why Rosie's doing this." He is particularly perplexed at the enthusiasm of so many celebrities for the current president: "They're all on Bill Clinton's side. After what this man did—I can't understand that. I think he disgraced the office, and I don't know if we'll ever get that dignity back. At one time, you were so proud when the president and his wife went abroad. But not any longer. I know Bill Clinton is a very bright man and all, but—say, is it possible to be bright and stupid at the same time? Imagine a Rhodes Scholar going and doing what he did! They ought to hang a sign on his door: 'Discreet.'"

Douglas confides one more thing, of particular relevance to Rosie's situation. At the height of his career, "we had a kidnap threat on my youngest daughter. You never read anything about it, because I wouldn't let anything like that get out, but we were really uptight about it. I felt that her guard had to be armed. In fact, I was told by the mayor of Philadelphia [where the family was living] that I myself should carry a gun. I didn't want to do that, and the mayor said, 'Well, then your daughter should.' So we had her driver carry a gun. I felt that it was necessary."

THE QUEEN OF CANDID

Rosie O'Donnell is not your average show-biz bubblehead. Not only is she lavishly talented and generous, she is no worse a spokesman for left-liberal causes than full-timers like Al Hunt and Bill Press—or the typical Democratic congressman. She spits out the same talking points and statistics, drawn from such groups as Handgun Control, Inc., and the Children's Defense Fund. She exhibits the same disdain for the reasoning, motives, and experience of political adversaries. And if she, who got her start on Ed McMahon's *Star Search*, was "heinously" wrong about the effects of welfare reform, what about Professor-Senator Moynihan, who insisted that America would see "children on grates" and other "scenes of social trauma such as we haven't known since the cholera epidemics"? Neither one of them has had any comeuppance.

Also, Rosie is just about devoid of spin: Ask her a question, and you'll get a straight answer. She is dismayed by celebrities who, when pressed on something, "do the candidate's shuffle," as she says—"a little to the right, a little to the left." She says matter-of-factly, but with a measure of disgust, that "most public figures don't take risks." There is, indeed, something refreshing about a TV personality so forthright and undisguised. Better an in-your-face Rosie than an equally biased Katie Couric or Bryant Gumbel, who insults you with a charade of objectivity.

Last, there is a certain humility about Rosie, appealing to even the most hidebound conservative. She doesn't go in for such high-flown stuff as Barbra Streisand's "The Artist as Citizen" (the title of the singer's Kennedy School lecture). "I'm not a journalist," says Rosie, and "anyone who takes my word as *the* word is wrong. I happen to have a TV show, and I choose to use it." Her bottom line: "I do everything I can to use my celebrity for good. And whether you think that's right or not, you have to know that."

—June 19, 2000
National Review

Air Rummy

A conversation with the secretary of defense—and the missus

Out West

Donald Rumsfeld's up and at 'em, raring to go—as usual. Big grin, bounce in his step, shiny as a penny. We're at the Broadmoor Hotel in Colorado Springs, where the secretary has just hosted a conference of NATO defense ministers. The Broadmoor has a significant place in Republican history, and in American history: It's the resort where George W. Bush had his famous 40th-birthday bash, at which point he said, "*No más*—no more drinking," and began the ascent that culminated in the presidency.

But anyway, Rumsfeld is leaving the Broadmoor and flying to the Los Angeles area, where he's giving a speech at the Reagan Library. Our departure from the hotel is rather quiet, not to say ho-hum. Other defense ministers have roared out with sirens blaring, lights flashing —a lot of pomp. But the Rumsfeld motorcade emits no noise, flashes no lights, breaks no traffic laws—just proceeds to the base where the secretary will meet his plane for the two-hour flight to California.

Aboard the plane, Rumsfeld continues chipper. This is supposed to be a "bad week" for him because there's been a controversy in the press concerning authority over Iraq: Rumsfeld is alleged to have lost some to Condoleezza Rice. He waves off the controversy, however, saying that everything's proceeding normally, with a proper division of labor among the National Security Council staff, the State Department, and the Pentagon.

We talk about a range of things, beginning with NATO—as that has been the main business of the week. Do we still need NATO, more than ten years after the collapse of the Soviet Union? Yes, says Rumsfeld, and it has been freshened by new entries from the East. In fact, when Rumsfeld made that notorious remark, last January, about "Old Europe" and "New Europe," he was really thinking of NATO: old, established NATO, and the new, augmented NATO. "The center of gravity had shifted to the east," he says, "and I was being hit with all sorts of questions about, 'Europe's against you,' and I was thinking to myself that the overwhelming majority of the European countries were supporting us—it just happened that the ones that weren't were Germany and France." Rumsfeld likes to point out that the formerly Communist countries have been eager to aid the U.S. in Iraq, having a keen appreciation of freedom, and opportunities for a new beginning.

Discussion soon turns to the size of the military. A great many people argue that we need a bigger military: more people, more matériel, more of pretty much everything. How can we attend to our global responsibilities—or the ones we've assumed for ourselves—with (to be blunt) a Clinton-sized military? Mark Helprin made a powerful case for the "more" side in *National Review* ("Phony War," April 22, 2002).

Rumsfeld says, first off, "Mark's a smart fellow"—the understatement of the day. But he goes on to defend the current size of the military, stressing "flexibility" and "deconfliction" (i.e., the need to keep different parts of the military out of one another's way). He cautions against a "mindset that's still back in the 20th century," and claims that "the people who really get it are the ones who just went through" the Afghan and Iraq campaigns. "It's a cliché to say, 'Well, technology may be more sophisticated these days, but that doesn't change the need for boots on the ground,' and we know that." It should be recalled, however, that "the Soviets had 300,000 troops on the ground in Afghanistan, and they lost."

Moreover, he says, we must make sure, in Iraq, that we don't become a permanent presence, around which "everything grows." Foreign forces—including those from the United States—"ought to be there to help stabilize the situation" and then get out. It's encouraging, he says, that "we now have 56,000 Iraqis who are contributing to their own security, and I don't mean just standing around and observing." No, "they're contributing in non-trivial ways—fighting and *dying*." He adds that he'd be "the first one in the world" to recommend more of our own troops in Iraq, if he were told by those in charge over there that we needed them.

Likewise, would he ask for a bigger military, overall, if he thought it were necessary, no matter what the political or budgetary considerations? Hell, yes (in a word—or two). Rumsfeld says that, when he first went to Washington in 1957, the U.S. was spending a much bigger percentage of GDP on defense, and we could easily do so again—if necessary.

I read him a couple of quotes from the *New York Times*, having to do with the Rumsfeld-Rice-reshuffling story: An "administration official" (anonymous) has said, "This is about more than just how we handled Iraq. It's about getting the Rumsfeld crowd to understand the reality of what's happening, and what's not working." And a "senior American diplomat" has said, "Rumsfeld doesn't like this because he doesn't want to admit anything went wrong. So, what else is new? It's Rumsfeld."

Does he have anything to say about that? The SecDef practically leaps out of his chair: "He's talking about *me*! And this isn't about me! It's so far beyond individual personalities. It's about Iraq, and the future of that country, and the future of our own country!" Anything else, he contends, is insignificant, including intra-administration intrigue—the existence of which he downplays anyway.

Speaking of intra-administration politics: I bring up the secretary of state. "Colin Powell has a very good world press," I note. "Excellent," Rumsfeld interjects, gulping down coffee: an *excellent* press—"and in the U.S., too." "Yes, I meant to include that," I continue. "And you, on the other hand, have a rather less good press. Do you have a bit of a good cop/bad cop routine going on, and do you find Secretary Powell's excellent press just the slightest bit irksome?" No, he says, there is no good cop/bad cop, at least not consciously, and certainly not on his part. As for the press, "The only thing I worry about is what's best for the country, and what's best for the administration," and that entails doing your job, in fair press weather or foul.

I further point out that a lot of people believe that Rumsfeld enjoys war, that he's belligerent—that the War on Terror has been a high for him. He ponders for a while, then gives a two-part answer. First, anyone who believes this of him doesn't know him. He and his wife—who is traveling with him, incidentally—have visited many military hospitals, seen men with limbs blown off, without faces. And second, he is, it's true, very competitive—and if there's a fight, he seeks to win it.

We come back to the press. It has plenty to say about Rumsfeld; what does he have to say about *it*? In the main, he thinks that the press is a little lazy and a little gullible—unwilling to check things out, too ready to accept assertions at face value. "Washington has changed so much since I first [arrived]. Today it seems so organized around talking points." On a Sunday-morning talk show, you might hear a fellow saying the same thing "five, ten times in 28 minutes." And "you get the feeling, 'Fair enough: Either he believes what he's saying, or it's a talking point.'" And the talking point may be true: but doesn't the "journalistic community" have a responsibility to go find out?

He cites a few specifics: 1) "Go it alone"—the idea that, in Iraq, the United States was "going it alone." 2) "We need more troops" (in Iraq). 3) "No plan"—the U.S. was unprepared for after-Saddam. And 4) our old friend "imminence"—the Iraqi threat wasn't imminent, and the administration said it was. Rumsfeld knocks down all of these, in emphatic detail. About No. 4, he asks, "When, by the way, was 9/11 'imminent'? An hour before it happened? A week before? A month before? A year before?"

I ask whether Rumsfeld reads Maureen Dowd, the *New York Times* columnist who regularly makes sport of him. He allows that he reads the headline and the first paragraph or two. Then, having gotten the drift, he quits. "Do you know her?" he asks me. "No," I say, "but you've been good for her career." He responds: "I'm not so sure about that—that this has been good for her career." A highly interesting point, which there is too little time to pursue.

PARTNER FOR LIFE

Any subject may be pursued with Joyce Rumsfeld, the secretary's wife of nearly 50 years. This is a famous marriage in political circles, and Mrs. Rumsfeld is an impressive and admired figure in her own right: a reader and a thinker, a doer and an advocate, warm and open. She and the secretary both come from Chicago, as can be heard in their accents (hers even more than his). When did they meet? "In high school, when we were 14." Was he the most popular guy in school? "Yes." Was she the most popular girl? "No!" And what did she like about him? "He was fun, exciting. There was a little mystery there. I sort of followed him around." They were married right after college.

Mrs. Rumsfeld is happy to be back in Washington, after a 25-year hiatus.

(Following his stint as defense secretary in the Ford administration, Rumsfeld went into business, although he performed several tasks for the government during those years.) Mrs. Rumsfeld is obviously a patriot and an idealist. Besides, she says, "This is a good age, the age at which Don and I find ourselves"—perspective has been gained, and criticism is unstinging. What's more, she likes this president, George W. Bush: "He's my kind of person. He's straightforward, he knows his own mind, he *believes* things. He doesn't flop around."

And what's it like, if I may, to be married to a man widely considered a . . . sex symbol. "Odd," she says. "Very odd. And Don finds it bewildering. People just love him, just mob him, wherever we go." (A military aide nearby, and overhearing this conversation, chimes in, "Yeah, sometimes I feel like I'm a roadie with Pearl Jam"—a rock group.) Mrs. Rumsfeld talks of being in New York recently, and dropping by Bergdorf's, the department store, with her husband. "A clerk was helping some customers, and she just dropped them when Don came in. She was so flustered. She couldn't speak. Later she actually apologized. She said, 'I don't know what came over me. Movie stars pass through here all the time, and it doesn't faze me. But when your husband showed up, I thought I was going to pass out.'"

I ask Mrs. Rumsfeld whether her husband has occasioned this sort of excitement throughout his career (he was elected to Congress at 30). No, she says: It's a recent phenomenon. And how would she explain it? "C-SPAN"—that's her best guess. The public can see Rumsfeld for themselves, taking in whole press conferences, if they like, forming their own opinions, not having to rely on snippets or others' reports. This has made an astounding difference.

At this point, the secretary bounds back and says to his wife, "We're comin' up on the Grand Canyon"—and remembers the time when he and Mrs. Rumsfeld had to *walk* out, because he had a bad back and was unable to sit on his horse. Nine hours, it took them. "In what decade was this?" I inquire. "Oh, about eight or nine years ago," he answers. That, and whitewater rafting, and other such activities are the Rumsfelds' idea of fun.

Mrs. Rumsfeld is a bit of a media maven, and I ask whether she reads the *New York Times*. Yes, she says, "but faster than I used to." She likes the *Washington Post*'s editorials, because they're "thoughtful, worthwhile, and not knee-jerk." And does she read Maureen Dowd? "Yes, I do." And . . . ? "Well, she's clearly a bright and talented person," but her mission seems to be ridicule—artful ridicule, with little content or argument. The whole thing is soaked in cynicism. And "there is nothing I like less in a person than cynicism. I hope that [the columnist] is not cynical in the rest of her life. Because, to be cynical 100 percent of the time—that would be sad."

NO CHOICE BUT TO WIN

Donald Rumsfeld, like his wife, is plenty idealistic, but he's also very hard-headed (and so is she, for that matter). I ask him a question of the hour: Can the Middle East undergo a democratic transformation, or should the U.S. confine itself to eliminating terrorists and their state supporters, whenever possible? "Well," he says, "the global war on terror is about us"—our own security, our own defense (for there is no true and tight defense at our border). If we can get "another one or two or three countries to allow their people to be free," that would be "terrific"—it would also contribute handsomely to American security. But the central purpose of the war is self-defense.

And what about "preemption"? Has this overtaken deterrence and containment as the leading U.S. doctrine? Rumsfeld says, essentially, that all of the above are necessary—and that, "in history," we have always had all of the above. "I mean, if a duke saw a neighboring army forming on the border, he probably wouldn't wait around. There are certain things that are readily deterrable, and there are certain things that are not readily deterrable. The Afghan government was not deterred from harboring Osama bin Laden and his people"—even after 9/11, when the Taliban was given an ultimatum. And "Saddam Hussein was not deterred. We didn't want to go to war with Iraq. We went through all this pain at the U.N., went through all these efforts, gave them last chances"—but nothing.

A final question concerning the War on Terror: Will Americans stick with it, or will they get worn down? "They stuck with the Cold War," Rumsfeld quickly notes. "And I think Americans have a good sense of what's important. I have a lot of confidence in people."

As we land at the airport near the Reagan Library, the secretary spots an old plane on the ground and calls back to his wife, "Joyce, do you see that?" "Yes, Rummy," she answers. The secretary was a naval aviator in the '50s, and Mrs. Rumsfeld has already told me, "We lived at the end of every airstrip."

At the library, the event begins with the Pledge of Allegiance. This is not a public school, so there is no trouble. [N.B.: There recently had been a national controversy about whether the pledge could be recited in school.] Introducing the speaker, Frederick J. Ryan, chairman of the board here, says, "Americans are very fortunate that he is secretary of defense, and America's enemies are very unfortunate." Rumsfeld proceeds to wow 'em (which is easy, granted). And, hours later, at the end of a long day, he pulls away in an SUV—still chipper, still jaunty, still grinning, still bouncing, still shiny, evidently loving what he's doing, and having no doubts about the justice of it.

—November 10, 2003
National Review

Ashcroft with Horns

This is dedicated to the one they hate

Not just a piece on attorney general John Ashcroft, but sort of a snapshot in time—a year before the Iraq War began.

After September 11, everything changed, they say—and many things did. The dominant press took a new look at the administration. President Bush—formerly a clueless frat boy—was okay. Donald Rumsfeld—once a Ford-era caveman—was okay too. And Colin Powell, who'd never been not-okay, was even more okay than ever.

But John Ashcroft, the attorney general? Definitely not okay—in fact, something of a terror. Ashcroft bore the brunt of the liberals' fury, or confusion. Even some of the liberals themselves will admit that 9/11 was a disorienting event for them. Everything had been upset. "National security" was no longer a Republican buzz phrase, meant to bloat the defense budget. "The American way of life" was no longer a piece of cheap oratory, fed to simpletons. And the notion of "good and evil" was suddenly plausible.

It could be that the Left needed something to hold on to: something familiar and comforting; something "9/10." And that something was, to a degree, John Ashcroft as devil figure: Ashcroft as threat to the Constitution, as enemy of civil liberties, as representative of dark, religious impulses in the land—impulses liable to run wild under a genuine foreign attack. It was almost as if, after the planes got through destroying all those people, many said, "The terrorists must be stopped, I grant you. But John Ashcroft must be stopped too!" It would be Scoundrel Time all over again, this time led by a Christian conservative from Missouri.

Indeed, "McCarthy" and "Hoover" (as in J. Edgar) were heard frequently in reference to Ashcroft. The least that critics call him is "extremist." It's also widely alleged that Ashcroft is "scary"—"the scariest man in government," wrote the *Washington Post*'s Richard Cohen. Al Hunt, in the *Wall Street Journal*, said, "Sept. 11 has enabled John Ashcroft to be John Ashcroft. That's a scary spectacle."

It was Anthony Lewis of the *New York Times* who best summed up the deepest liberal opinion about Ashcroft. The columnist was retiring after 50 years with the *Times*, and the paper did a farewell interview with him, at the end of last year. What had he learned? First, said Lewis, "certainty is the enemy of decency and humanity in people who are sure they are right, like Osama bin Laden and John Ashcroft." It has come to that: There are circles in which easy comparisons can be made between bin Laden and Ashcroft, with no raised eyebrows.

John Ashcroft will never be a liberal darling, that's for sure. He is liked—even loved—by his own, but he doesn't go out of his way to make himself respectable to elite opinion. He has not "grown" in office—which is to say (sarcastically) that he hasn't moderated his positions. As a conservative Christian, he is easy to mock as an anti-dancing Elmer Gantry. Liberals go after Ashcroft in the same way they went after Kenneth Starr. Back in Lewinsky times, James Carville sneered, "[Starr] goes down by the Potomac and listens to hymns, as the cleansing water of the Potomac goes by . . ." Ashcroft's even worse: He sings hymns in public (about which, more later).

The attorney general has managed to enter the culture. Consider just a couple of offbeat items: *The New York Times Magazine* ran a spread on an eclectic gallery in L.A. It included a photo of an African coffin on which Ashcroft's face has been painted. The gallery owner explained to me that Ashcroft was to be the death of affirmative action, *Roe* vs. *Wade*, and so on. Item No. 2? At a major Washington, D.C., synagogue, Ashcroft figured in a "Purim spiel": He was equated with Haman, a figure of extreme danger—of mass murder—to Jews. Traditionally, Hitler, say, would be equated with Haman.

One veteran Washington reporter—not particularly partisan—shakes his head: "The depth of the hatred that certain liberals have for Ashcroft is hard to fathom. It doesn't seem logical, even given all of Ashcroft's conservative views. It's like a prejudice, it's visceral. There's some Ashcroft mooma-jooma—some mo-jo, some karma, some vibe—that drives liberals nuts. It makes otherwise sane people say crazy things."

It seems clear that Ashcroft serves, in part, as a proxy for Bush: that is, liberals and Democrats generally have had to lay off Bush, owing to his popularity and his standing as commander in chief. But they need *someone* on whom to vent their frustration: and that's Ashcroft. He may not like it, but he does Bush the favor of being the administration's lightning rod, its big fat target.

IN THE ARENA

For someone who's supposed to be scary and extreme, John Ashcroft has done awfully well with the public. In Missouri—one of America's great swing states—he was elected attorney general twice, governor twice, and U.S. senator once. When he was state AG, he was chosen by his peers to be chairman of the National Association of Attorneys General. When he was governor, he was again chosen by his peers, to be chairman of the National Governors Association. As one Ashcroft-watcher maintains, "That's a remarkable fact. These groups contain some of the most ambitious, most cut-throat people in the country. They're pits of vipers. And for those people—both Republicans and Democrats—to settle on Ashcroft as their leader is extraordinary."

In 2000, Ashcroft lost his Senate reelection campaign by a whisker—and in most unusual circumstances (a dead opponent; a looming widow; courtroom and polling-place shenanigans). George W. Bush, and others, were impressed by how graciously Ashcroft handled everything—and the president-elect tabbed him to be attorney general.

His confirmation hearings were a nasty affair, chaired by Sen. Patrick Leahy at his nastiest. Good ol' John—whom all the senators had known and, from all outward appearances, liked—was suddenly a racist, a segregationist, and a menace. Even Ashcroft's handlers (no babes in the wood) were shocked by the ferocity of the assault. Sen. Barbara Boxer said the Ashcroft nomination was "driving a stake into the heart of large numbers of Americans." Ted Kennedy screamed that it was *treason* to suggest, as Ashcroft had, that the Bill of Rights was meant, in part, as a check against tyranny. Rep. Maxine Waters said: "I know a racist when I see one. Senator Ashcroft acts like a racist, walks like a racist, talks like a racist."

The left-leaning press was no better. The mildest thing they said was that Ashcroft was a bone to the far Right—and not just any bone, Hendrik Hertzberg of *The New Yorker* would later write, but "the femur of a tyrannosaur" (get it?). An op-ed piece in *USA Today*—penned by the paper's former Supreme Court reporter—openly asked, "Can a deeply religious person be attorney general?"

Ashcroft was eventually confirmed by his ex-colleagues, 58–42. Permanent Washington—society Washington—was not amused. One mark against Ashcroft, it seemed, was that he lacked charm—that he wasn't at all right for cocktails. *Newsweek*'s Jonathan Alter has written that Ashcroft has "the charm of a walnut." Al Hunt, speaking on television, said that Gov. Frank Keating—whom Bush had considered for AG— at least "would have brought charm." It's hard to argue with Alex S. Jones, a former *New York Times*man, now at Harvard, who told the *Buffalo News*, "John Ashcroft will never be described as a sex toy."

Once ensconced at the Justice Department, Ashcroft made few waves, except to continue his Senate practice of holding a prayer meeting (voluntary and ecumenical) every morning. This was made out to be both kooky and un-American.

But then came the awful day in September: and Ashcroft was left with an enormous responsibility, especially considering that federal law enforcement was judged to have fallen down badly on the job. His policies—or rather, the administration's—quickly came under attack. Hundreds of foreigners who had violated U.S. law were detained, so that agencies could determine whether they had connections to terrorism. Of these detainees, Richard Cohen wrote, "They exist in an American gulag—a term I use with purposeful exaggeration." (Yes, but tell it to a Russian, or a Chinese, or a Cuban.) Garry Trudeau used his *Doonesbury* to compare American policy to Saddam Hussein's Iraq. The theme of an episode of *The Practice*, a show on ABC, was (as a character put it), "We're back to interning people. Sticking them in prison because of where they were born." The *New York Times* was moved to say—in an editorial titled "Disappearing in America"—"We trust the Bush administration is not seriously considering torture."

These reactions were unhinged from reality.

Then there was "eavesdropping": the government's listening in on conversations between inmates and their attorneys. According to Justice, this has been done with 16 foreigners being held under "special administration measures"—that is, they're suspected of conducting criminal activity from their jail cells. It's not "eavesdropping" either, insists Justice, because both parties—inmates and attorneys—are told what is happening. Furthermore, any evidence gathered may not be shared with prosecutors, except by consent of a federal judge. Reasonable analysts, in possession of the facts, tend to find all of this reasonable. Yet a coalition led by the ACLU condemned "an unprecedented frontal assault on the attorney-client privilege and the right to counsel guaranteed by the Constitution."

Then there were the military tribunals—an instrument of American wartime justice for many generations. President Bush, wanting to be more scrupulous than his predecessors, ordered the Defense Department to devise clear procedures for such tribunals: and Ashcroft got smacked for installing "kangaroo courts."

There was also a furor concerning guns: Many liberals, both in Congress and in the press, charged that Ashcroft had prevented the FBI from searching a database of gun records. His tender concern for the Second Amendment, they said, trumped any proper concern for anti-terrorism or the well-being of the country. But this was nonsense: When the FBI moved to undertake such a search, FBI lawyers said: No—the law doesn't permit it. Ashcroft concurred. Under fire in Congress, he said that he was simply enforcing the law; if legislators wanted to change their law (enacted in 1998), they were free to do so.

In early December, Ashcroft—fed up with false allegations, and evidently sick of being portrayed as Torquemada—came out blazing before the Senate Judiciary Committee. He called for "an honest, reasoned debate, and not fear-mongering," and went on to say, "To those who scare peace-loving people with phantoms of lost liberty, my message is this: Your tactics only aid terrorists, for they erode our national unity and diminish our resolve."

That did it: All hell—or much hell—broke loose. Lots of people cried "McCarthyism!" and worse, if there *is* worse. Ashcroft was talking about . . . well, brazen and groundless fear-mongering, as he said, not ordinary criticism or dissent; but his words were somewhat clumsy, and he left himself open to the Red Scare stuff. In an editorial, the *Washington Post* denounced "The Ashcroft Smear." Bob Herbert in the *New York Times* wrote, "I experienced the disturbing sense of a 21st century official morphing alternately into J. Edgar Hoover and Joe McCarthy." Hendrik Hertzberg, in that week's *New Yorker*, had already called on Bush to fire Ashcroft. His name was muddier than ever.

BREASTGATE . . . PLUS, CATS: NOW AND FOREVER
The war aside, this AG has been swimming in bad raps. Maybe the baddest of them all has been Breastgate. Surely you are familiar with the statues that live in the Great Hall of the Justice Department: the Spirit of

Justice (a lady) and the Majesty of Law (a gent). (Spirit has a nickname, by the way: Minnie Lou.) Because these statues are partially nude, they are noticed only during conservative Republican administrations. Minnie Lou and her one exposed breast became famous when photographers gleefully took their picture with Ed Meese, as he announced President Reagan's report on pornography back in the mid-1980s. The presence of the Breast was thought to have "stepped on" the administration's "message." Washington liberals are still yukking about that one today.

The Breast was pretty quiet during the eight years of Janet Reno. As one peeved administration official puts it, "No cameraman was ever at Reno's feet, trying to get a shot of her with that thing." But Minnie Lou's outstanding feature stormed back with Ashcroft. When President Bush visited the Justice Department to rededicate the building to Robert Kennedy, his advance men insisted on a nice blue backdrop: "TV blue," infinitely preferable to the usual dingy background of the Great Hall. Everyone thought the backdrop worked nicely—made for "good visuals," as they say. This was Deaverism, pure and simple. Ashcroft's people intended to keep using it.

An advance woman on his team had the bright idea of *buying* the backdrop: It would be cheaper than renting it repeatedly. So she did —without Ashcroft's knowledge, without his permission, without his caring, everyone in the department insists.

But ABC put out the story that Ashcroft, the old prude, had wanted the Breast covered up, so much did it offend his churchly sensibilities. *New York Times* columnist Maureen Dowd, ever clever, wrote that Ashcroft had forced a "blue burka" on Minnie Lou. Comedians had a field day (and are still having it). The *Washington Post* has devoted great space to the story, letting Cher, for example, tee off on it—as she went on to do on David Letterman's show.

And yet the story is complete and total bunk. First, Ashcroft had nothing to do with the purchase of the backdrop. Second, the backdrop had nothing to do with Breast aversion. But the story was just "too good to check," as we say, and it will probably live forever. Generations from now, if we're reading about John Ashcroft, we will read that he was the boob who draped the Boob. The story is ineffaceable.

Things get weirder: Andrew Tobias doubles as treasurer of the Democratic National Committee and a web columnist. He wrote that Ashcroft's advance team, scouting out the American embassy at The Hague, "saw cats in residence, and got nervous. They were worried there might be a calico cat. No, they were told, no calicos. Visible relief. Their boss, they explained, believes calico cats are signs of the devil. (The advance team also spied a statue of a naked woman in the courtyard, and discussed the possibility of its being covered for the visit, though that request was not ultimately made.)" Ashcroft's people sigh: Pure fabrication, an invention. Yet it entered the mainstream media—*New York Times*, no less—and added to the Legend of Ashcroft.

What else? It was objected that Ashcroft, even with *a war going on*, "found time" to "overturn" the law in Oregon permitting assisted suicide. Here again was the zealot pursuing his own fundamentalist ideology, and being a hypocrite too, for didn't he believe in "states' rights"? But Ashcroft was merely stating the obvious: that state law cannot nullify federal law, and that if supporters of assisted suicide wanted federal law to allow different state laws on the subject, they could go ahead and change the federal law—he would enforce it.

Then came the little Islamic contretemps. The conservative Christian journalist Cal Thomas reported that Ashcroft had made the following remark to him: "Islam is a religion in which God requires you to send your son to die for Him. Christianity is a faith in which God sends His son to die for you." Naturally, Arab groups and others pounced on Ashcroft for defaming Islam. Ashcroft, though—like other U.S. officials—has gone out of his way to show "sensitivity" to Muslims. Embarrassed, he explained that, in making that statement, he did not mean to refer to Islam itself, but to the radicals who kill in its name. According to an aide, Ashcroft had used this line—about radical Islam and sons and dying—many times before.

Certainly, Ashcroft could lie a little lower—could tend to his press image—but he doesn't seem willing to mute himself. He kicked up a fuss when he addressed the National Religious Broadcasters convention in Nashville. Speaking in rolling, religious tones, he contrasted "the way of God" and "the way of the terrorists." He said that "civilized people—Muslims [note that lead-off!], Christians, and Jews—all understand that the source of freedom and human dignity is the Creator." It was a stirring speech, belonging to a grand American tradition—and he was flayed for it, by the usual wall-of-separation zealots (who hold Ashcroft to be a religious zealot). One Ashcroft staffer grouses that, when Sen. Joe Lieberman, for example, quotes Scripture or otherwise waxes religious, the reaction tends to be "Ahhh." But when Ashcroft does: "Eeek!"

And, yes, it's true: Ashcroft may just break out in song on you. At the end of another recent speech, at a seminary in Charlotte, N.C., he launched into a song that he himself wrote, "Let the Eagle Soar," a sort of gospel/patriotic number that made the media hoot and howl. Footage of the AG in full vocal flight, so to speak, immediately became a running gag on the Letterman show. Ashcroft may have graduated from Yale College and the University of Chicago Law School—but he has his feet in an American earth that his fellow elites find alien, comical, or frightening.

Every day, John Ashcroft is hit for one thing or another, playing out his role as administration lightning rod. He is called a racist and a fanatic so often, it has almost become boring. Many liberals evidently want to be civil-liberties heroes, preventing, or at least wailing against, the fall of Ashcroftian night. They have not just a bogeyman but a straw man. The attorney general's backers are weary of seeing their man maligned, but they trust that the attacks are backfiring. Ashcroft's approval rating is high, around 75 percent. Even most Democratic voters tell pollsters they think Ashcroft is doing a good job—and it is an immense job, in new, peculiar, and daunting circumstances. So, if he needs it, he can take comfort in this: Not everyone is susceptible to the Ashcroft "mooma-jooma."

—March 25, 2002
National Review

Cap, a Life

Weinberger's journey from the Golden Gate onward

A review of In the Arena: A Memoir of the 20th Century, *by Caspar W. Weinberger, with Gretchen Roberts.*

O f all the men in the Reagan era, few made as deep an impression as Caspar Weinberger. And by "Reagan era," we mean, in this case, Sacramento, too, for "Cap" was there—working by the governor's side. He was also with Nixon and Ford, in Washington. And he has managed to be in several other interesting places as well. In 1990, Weinberger published a book called *Fighting for Peace: Seven Critical*

Years in the Pentagon. It was a solid book, but the Weinberger career—and life—deserved a better one. With *In the Arena*, it is here.

The phrase "in the arena" will be instantly familiar to any student of American politics, culled as it is from the famous Teddy Roosevelt passage about "the man who is actually in the arena, whose face is marred by dust and sweat and blood"—who is not a mere spectator, or critic. The title was used by Nixon, for one of his many post-presidential books, and also by Charlton Heston, for his 1995 autobiography. By the time Weinberger realized this, it was too late: The book had already gone too far in the publication process. But, worn as it may be, the title fits.

From the beginning, Weinberger identified with TR, for Cap, like that president, was a sickly boy, who aspired to be a man of strength and importance. He was born in San Francisco in the portentous year of 1917. Weinberger subtitles his book "a memoir of the 20th century"; the description is not overly grand. He attended a parade in honor of Lucky Lindy, who had just crossed the Atlantic. He went to see a defeated President Hoover cast his vote in November 1932. And he remembers the building of the Golden Gate Bridge: the "lines of desperate, out-of-work, able-bodied men who would wait, day after day, for one of the construction workers to fall or injure himself so they could take his place."

The boy was always smitten by politics and government. By 15, he was reading the Congressional Record "avidly and daily." He made endless scrapbooks filled with bits about the national conventions and the like. He was an incorrigible Republican, arguing to one and all about the "Soviet menace" and the beauty of small government. In his senior year of high school, he was elected student-body president, promising a new constitution. His graduation speech was entitled "The Honorable Profession of Politics."

With a scholarship to Harvard College, he was really on his way. He majored in government, though he found the classes "lifeless" and tinged with "liberal bias." He spent much of his time in journalism, contributing a column to a magazine back home, and becoming president of the *Crimson*, the student newspaper. He was intensely idealistic, then as now: The "street side" of Dexter Gate said, "Enter to Grow in Wisdom"; the "Yard side" said, "Depart to Serve Better Thy Country and Thy Kind." "It has been an inspiration to me ever since." There is no snickering in Weinberger.

He went on to Harvard Law School, but then the war came, although the U.S. was not yet in it. Weinberger wanted to get started nonetheless. He tried to join the RAF or the Canadian force, but poor eyesight kept him out.

He finished law school in June 1941, then signed up with the U.S. infantry in September, still eager, and restless: He idolized Churchill, and saw the conflict as one of pure good and evil. After Pearl Harbor, he was sent to Australia, and ended up a captain on General MacArthur's intelligence staff. One day, Eleanor Roosevelt came to visit—and Weinberger, ever the die-hard Republican, made himself scarce. "I took my politics rather too seriously then," he nicely notes.

After V-J Day, it was back to California and law practice—and politics. Weinberger always had a perfectly fine job at a law firm, but he was forever looking for ways into public life. "The trouble with Cap," said a friend, "is that he can't stand making money." His all-enduring wife, Jane, would sigh over her husband's "non-profit activities." He was elected to the state assembly, ran for attorney general—losing—and served as chairman of the California GOP. He also kept his hand in journalism, writing a column and hosting a public-TV show called *Profile: Bay Area.* Among his guests was "an extremely eloquent and persuasive Malcolm X."

When Reagan was elected governor, he called on Weinberger to be the state's finance director. Not long after, Nixon called, from Washington—to ask Cap to serve as chairman of the Federal Trade Commission. He did so. Then he became deputy director of the Office of Management and Budget (under George Shultz), then director. (It was in this period that Weinberger earned the nickname "Cap the Knife"—a William Safire coinage.) He ended his Nixon-Ford career as secretary of Health, Education, and Welfare. Weinberger is engrossing on the various Nixon weirdnesses, and on the major policy debates of the time, including the (pathetic) imposition of wage and price controls. Gerald Ford, he holds in suitably high esteem.

It was when Reagan called again—this time after being elected president—that Weinberger had his real rendezvous with destiny: serving as secretary of defense at a time when the military desperately needed rebuilding; only six years after the helicopters had lifted off from the embassy roof in Saigon; when the Soviet Union was enjoying unprecedented advantage. Weinberger may be seen as the very embodiment of Peace Through Strength, a meaningful slogan for once. He saw things with rare moral clarity, and talked that way, and acted that way. He and Reagan were intent on *rollback*—musty notion—not détente. In the present volume, Weinberger gives what is probably as good a short brief for Reagan's foreign and defense policies as can be found.

He also includes a chapter on the Iran-contra affair, a nightmare for him, as for many others. The harassment of Weinberger was clearly unjustified, and he was (preemptively) pardoned by the first President Bush on Christmas Eve Day 1992. Weinberger immediately wrote Bush a letter thanking him, and he has written a similar note of appreciation on December 24 every year since. About the president-between-the-Bushes, Weinberger is blistering, charging that "the Clinton administration inexcusably hollowed out our military capability"—and charging much more, too. He closes his book with reflections on his recent experiences as a top man at Forbes, Inc.

It is, in many ways, a formidable book. It comments incisively on the events, ideas, and political personalities of a very long and difficult stretch. There is a ton of detail here, and the reader will not want to wade through it all; but it is not frivolous detail. Weinberger is at least as absorbed by domestic affairs as he is by grand world affairs. He has written a deeply personal book, too. He expresses great love: for his parents, for his brother, for his wife, for his children—and that's not to mention other objects of love, such as California and country (and cooking—Weinberger is always critiquing the food, from the Army to the Bohemian Grove). The author, throughout, is modest, self-deprecating, amusing, candid, earnest, and naturally patriotic. There is in these pages an overarching sense of decency. Weinberger is a throwback (high compliment). He is a Frank Capra American, though never naïve. He reminds one a lot of Reagan: a more detail-oriented Reagan, without the Hollywood past.

The book is far from sugary, and not only with respect to Bill Clinton and other Democrats: Weinberger unquestionably has Nixon's number, and he jabs repeatedly at George Shultz, who was long a rival, and often in Cap's way (as Weinberger would see it). This is by no means a score-settling or resentful book, but neither is it docile.

In telling his story, Weinberger is keen not only to pronounce on major events, but to inform readers what it was like simply to be around: what the desks and telephones in the defense secretary's office were like; how a typical day went. Although he is "in the arena," he is also the wide-eyed spectator, delighting in the workings and pomp of government. He is wowed at inaugurations, and reverent in the presence of Congressional Medal of Honor winners. At one point, he writes, "Now I, a schoolboy from California, was making decisions that might affect the course of history." OMB was "particularly good fun for someone as fascinated by government as I am." OMB "particularly good fun"? Weinberger is a wonk with a song in his heart.

It is impossible—at least I found it so—not to read this book in the light

of September 11. It is also impossible—at least I found it so—not to conclude that this is exactly the kind of man we could use right now, many
times over. But then, he is the kind of man this country can always use.

One of his best anecdotes involves a college visit to the home of a
buddy's fiancée: The fiancée was a younger sister of Katharine Hepburn.
Mrs. Hepburn—the mother—"was a vigorous, earthy woman," and also a
staunch political liberal.

> At dinner one night, she listened to me defend, in a rather halting and shy
> way, some of my conservative beliefs, and finally she grabbed my hand
> and said, "Let me see your palm! Where *do* you get all this?!" She stud-
> ied it for quite a while, and then, with great irritation, pronounced, "My
> God, you're going to live forever!"

If only.

—December 3, 2001
National Review

Yes, He Has Lived

The invaluable Richard Pipes

A review of Vixi: Memoirs of a Non-Belonger, *by Richard Pipes.*

For half a century, Richard Pipes has been one of the world's foremost scholars of Russia, and a man of political and policy influence
as well: In the 1970s, he headed "Team B," the group directed to
challenge the CIA's assumptions about the Soviet Union (which were
wrong). And in the early 1980s, he served on the National Security Council
staff of President Reagan. From the time of his birth in Cieszyn, Poland, to
now, when he has assumed emeritus status at Harvard, Pipes has lived a
rich, meaningful life. Fortunately, he has the ability to recount it, richly and
meaningfully.

He calls his memoirs *Vixi*, which is Latin for "I have lived." In his preface, Pipes says, "It may sound strange coming from a professional historian, but I have always had trouble dealing with the past"—meaning his own past. It is of a piece with the author's character that he overcame any such trouble. When the Nazis and Soviets signed their pact, sealing Poland's doom, Pipes had just turned 16. He and his parents would get out—barely—but "much of my family and nearly all my school friends . . . perished without a trace in the Holocaust." One of the reasons for writing this book was that "their memory not be entirely lost."

Pipes's account of the weeks between September 1, when the Nazis began to bomb Warsaw, and late October, when the family escaped, is gripping. (The Pipeses had moved to the capital when the author was four.) These pages are even cinematic, if that is not too cheap or insulting a word. Pipes includes items large and small—the radio kept playing Chopin's "Military" Polonaise, "to keep our spirits up." He quotes from his own diary of the time (powerfully written, and perceived): "Houses collapsed, burying thousands of people or else spreading fire along the streets. Mobs of nearly crazed people, carrying children and bundles, ran along streets that were covered with rubble. German pilots, the worst beasts in the world, deliberately flew low to rake the streets with machine-gun fire."

On October 1, the Germans arrived by truck, and "I noticed with surprise that the soldiers were not the blond supermen of Nazi propaganda: many were short and swarthy and quite unheroic in appearance." Five days later, young Pipes watched Hitler—come to take a victory lap—from a fourth-floor window: "He rode in an open Mercedes, standing up in the familiar pose, giving the Nazi salute. I thought how easy it would be to assassinate him."

Pipes learned indelibly the lesson of appeasement, which he would apply over and over again, not least to the Soviet Union. His hatred of tyranny, lies, and accommodation is almost physical. He also saw, in those horrible weeks, "how quickly the everyday overwhelms the 'historic'"—Polish life returned to something like normal "with surprising rapidity." This experience left Pipes with "the abiding conviction that the population at large plays only a marginal role in history, or at any rate in political and military history, which is the preserve of small elites: people do not make history—they make a living."

In time, the family reached America, and Pipes began a life bursting with opportunity, for so talented and determined a person. In one of the most arresting passages of his book, he writes:

The main effect of the Holocaust on my psyche was to make me delight
in every day of life that has been granted to me, for I was saved from certain death. I felt and feel to this day that I have been spared not to waste
my life on self-indulgence or self-aggrandizement but to spread a moral
message by showing, using examples from history, how evil ideas lead to
evil consequences. Since scholars have written enough on the Holocaust,
I thought it my mission to demonstrate this truth using the example of
communism. Furthermore, I felt and feel that to defy Hitler, I have a duty
to lead a full and happy life . . .

In addition, "I admit to having little patience with the psychological
problems of free people, especially if they involve a 'search for identity' or
some other form of self-seeking." Pipes is a hard nut, but his hardness—if
it is that—is well earned.

An eager immigrant, Pipes went off to wholesome Muskingum College
in Ohio, and then into the Army—where he did a lot of reading (among
other things). From boyhood, Pipes read like a demon. In fact, one of the
pleasures of this book is that the author records his intellectual development, through books, chiefly, but also through art and music. In the Army,
he was assigned to learn Russian, and he learned it at Cornell—from which
he was eventually graduated. Then it was on to Harvard, where he earned
his doctoral degree, and where he would soon gain tenure. "When it was
granted to me," he writes, "I gained lasting happiness." This is the voice of
a natural-born scholar speaking.

Pipes tells any number of charming, or tart, academic anecdotes. He
also makes clear the extreme cowardice and vanity of the modern faculty
(and administration). Along the way, he draws sketch after sketch of famous
personages: Isaiah Berlin, George Kennan, Richard Nixon. The sketch of
Berlin is priceless, describing in a cinching way what I have sometimes
called Isaiah Berlin Syndrome (knowing what is right but refusing to stick
your neck out, or to open your mouth). Perhaps the saddest thing about
Pipes's book is one of the saddest things about his career: the enmity that
exists between him and Alexander Solzhenitsyn. They say jarringly harsh
things about each other. For years, they were about the only two anti-
Communists east of the Hudson River: and to be at war. It is like a cruel
joke of history. What divides them is the question of whether Soviet Communism has its roots in Russia generally. Pipes says yes; Solzhenitsyn says
it is an insult to Russians, and unsupported by facts or logic. Admirers of
them both can only wince.

In Washington, Pipes made waves, disturbing the CIA, the State Department, the détenteniks at large. We revisit the claims of Sovietology, and we remember just how bad they were, those Sovietologists. How can they stand to re-read what they wrote? Maybe they avoid it—Pipes does not.

Pipes made waves in the Reagan White House as well, up against what might be called the "peace camp," headed by Nancy Reagan and Michael Deaver. The author draws some more of his sketches—of Alexander Haig, Richard Allen, Henry Kissinger. Not all of these portraits are fond, to put it mildly. And he is especially interesting on the president himself: "[Reagan] possessed to a high degree the imponderable quality of political judgment. He instinctively understood, as all great statesmen do, what matters and what does not, what is right and what wrong for his country. This quality cannot be taught: like perfect pitch, one is born with it." Yet Reagan "was altogether incapable of thinking abstractly: his mind worked either emotionally or in reaction to individuals whom he could visualize." Even those who disagree with Pipes should have to ponder his arguments.

In whatever he has done, he has attracted controversy. Why? Pipes himself quotes Samuel Butler, who explained in a letter: "I never write on any subject unless I believe the opinion of those who have the ear of the public to be mistaken, and this involves, as a necessary consequence, that every book I write runs counter to the men who are in possession of the field; hence I am always in hot water . . ."

It is stirring to be in the company of this mind—Pipes's, not Butler's—for 250 pages. They are filled with immense learning and insight. They are leavened, too, by humor and idiosyncratic asides. The story of his marriage to Irene, a tall and warm beauty, is touching. And I happen to find touching Pipes's notorious stubbornness—often a kind of righteous stubbornness. He tells a funny tale about having to visit the Soviet Embassy after Brezhnev died, and being asked to sign the condolence book. Trapped, he thought fast: and did sign his name, but completely illegibly.

And I have a story from my own experience, and *National Review*'s. At the dawn of 2000, we published our "millennium issue," consisting of big-think pieces by big thinkers, including Pipes. In his essay, Pipes cited a book by Henri Frankfort, *Kingship and the Gods* (on ancient Near Eastern religion and society). He had the *g* in "gods" down—in the lower case—but, as it was in the title, I, of course, as editor, put it up. He insisted on its being put back down. "I am a Jew," he said, "and there is one God, and I will not have the plural word capitalized." "But Professor Pipes," I pleaded, "I am as monotheistic as anyone, but this is a matter of style, and to have the word up doesn't imply any idolatry: It's just a word in a title, like 'table' or 'chair.'" No, no, said Pipes, it could not be up, title or not.

So, that's how it appeared in the magazine: *Kings and gods*. It looked weird, and wrong (because it was weird, and wrong)—but, in the Pipesian world, it was really wonderful, and right.

—November 24, 2003
National Review

Rodney Rules

Dangerfield at 80

I n early May, Avery Fisher Hall, home of the New York Philharmonic, played host to another American cultural institution: Rodney Dangerfield. Said Rodney, midway through his act, as he sized up his surroundings, "I can take a classy place like this and turn it into a [not very pleasant place]."

Yes, he can. But he can also turn it into an exceptionally pleasant place, because Dangerfield is a gifted and endearing man. He is also the last of a line, pretty much; the last of a generation of comedians on whom several generations of Americans grew up. Traditional stand-up comedy is getting rarer. Our comedy today tends to be high-concept, slightly artsy, heavily ironical. Rodney Dangerfield still gets up on a stage and tells jokes—lots of 'em—and so leaves his audience warmly happy. When he goes, something priceless will go, too, and that is depressing.

Dangerfield is 80 this year. He was born in Long Island, with a typical comedian's name: Jacob Cohen. And then, also typically, he changed it to something snappy. As a young man, he did everything he could to break into show business, but came up short. He accepted the indignity of an office job, but never stopped trying. Eventually, in his forties, he caught on. Rodney was a late-bloomer, and that added to his legend. He suffered, and overcame, serious depression, and people admired him for that, too. Rodney traveled the club circuit from coast to coast, and he appeared on every TV show imaginable, from Ed Sullivan (on which he was a smash) to

Conan O'Brien (likewise). He has performed on *The Tonight Show* a cool 70 times, the record.

Along the way, he became a minor movie star, making—to name three of his biggest—*Caddyshack* (1980), *Easy Money* (1983), and *Back to School* (1986). It may surprise certain readers to know, but there is a cult of *Caddyshack*, populated in particular by those who have spent a good chunk of life around a golf course. Rodney's lines are stuck in our memories. It was no surprise that Gov. Jesse Ventura, when he met the Dalai Lama, wanted mainly to ask whether he had seen *Caddyshack*. (The Tibetan holy man is featured in the movie's signal monologue, though one uttered by Bill Murray, not Rodney.)

So, Dangerfield—outlasting everyone, outperforming everyone—became an institution. His trademark white shirt and red tie are on permanent display at another institution, the Smithsonian.

At Avery Fisher Hall, there was a typical Rodney crowd, which is to say, one that included every type: young and old, male and female, fancy and plain. The crowd was rowdy, hepped-up, not the usual symphonic audience, for sure. Dangerfield had as his warm-up act a youngish comedian named Harry Basil, who was loud, frenetic, and capable. He is the kind of entertainer who does Jerry Lewis singing "Lady" (a Kenny Rogers song). As a warm-up comedian, he is in a ticklish position: He ought to be good, but not too good, because the star has to shine. When some boors in the audience called, prematurely, for Rodney, Basil responded: "You know how when you order a hamburger you get a pickle, even though you didn't ask for a pickle? I'm the pickle. Enjoy the pickle!"

In due course, it was Rodney time. Much about the evening seemed elegiac, including the fact that the prop man was elderly and gimpy. The boys in Rodney's backup band were touchingly dated, too. As for the octogenarian Rodney, he looks essentially as he always has. It's hard to imagine a more distinctive-looking guy: those bulging, leering, chortling eyes; the generous, dancing nose; the *aliveness*. We saw him sweating, nervous, put-upon, tugging at his tie—being everything he was supposed to be. Dangerfield's presence is at once magnetic and reassuring.

His speech is a little slurred now, which is a problem, because he goes 100 miles an hour. But one slowly gets used to his speech, as one would a difficult foreign accent. Rodney tells a dizzying range of jokes, the bulk of them aimed at himself: "I went up with a prostitute. I dropped my pants. She dropped her fee." He does a lot of age jokes now, with relish: "I stopped biting my nails. My wife hid my teeth." Some of the jokes are extremely

familiar—"My doctor said, 'You're crazy.' I said, 'I want a second opinion.'
He said, 'You're ugly, too'"—but, in Rodney's delivery, they seem new. He
will utter something offhandedly, and cause the audience to double over:
"My kids are good-looking. Good thing my wife cheats on me."

The Dangerfield style is beyond presto. I estimated that he told between
seven and ten jokes a minute. In 50 minutes' work, he must have told over
400 jokes. His patter and timing are practiced and surefire. After he tells
a joke, he gauges the reaction perfectly, then begins the next one slightly
before the laughter from the previous one has subsided. At one point—probably needing a rest—he observed, simply, "I know a lot of jokes." (This is a
cleaned-up version.) These hundreds of jokes follow no apparent organization. Rodney might tell 15 about his wife's girth, 5 about his daughter's
sexual promiscuity, and 10 about drugs. But then he will tell 20 or 30 or
40 jokes in a row that have nothing to do with one another. There are no
segues; it's just a stream of consciousness, a disgorging of memory.
Astoundingly, he never forgot what he had told; he never repeated himself
once.

Every now and then, he sat down on a stool. He suspended his stream
a few times to mop his face and suck down some water (or whatever),
which allowed him to gather himself, and allowed the audience to catch its
breath. Then he was off again. Just once, the audience responded with (from
the comedian's perspective) insufficient laughter. He barked at them, "That
was a funny line, don't give me any of that [garbage]!" *That* was funny.

Rodney may be a throwback, but he is thoroughly modern, too. He
rarely offended the going sensibility. He said "Chinaman" once. He started
a series of gay jokes, but there were a few—just a few—titters, and he
seemed to notice those, and stopped at three. Throughout his act, he never
said anything political, nothing to irk a Democrat or a Republican, nothing
from the headlines, nothing from the popular culture, absolutely nothing
topical. These were timeless and (at least from Rodney's mouth) hilarious
jokes about daily living, the usual human concerns.

Even when the jokes might have offended—for their sheer raunchiness,
for one thing—they never did, for Dangerfield seems a genuinely agreeable
man. A lovable man. A good Joe, and an ordinary Joe, although one with an
extraordinary talent. When the evening wound down, Dangerfield seemed
not to know how to end it. He left the stage a few times, then came back for
what seemed like encores. But it was hard to tell. Finally, he held out his
hand and said something that sounded heartfelt: "My old man was in vaude-
ville, and he said, 'You can always count on a New York audience.'" With

that, he waved and tottered off, leaving in his wake only happiness, and a disturbing sense that—this was it.

—June 11, 2001
National Review

Brief Encounter

Ring Lardner Jr., at home

The below served as an obituary in the December 4, 2000, National Review.

The last surviving member of the Hollywood 10 died on October 31, aged 85. As it happened, I met him on a blustery day last spring—in his own apartment.

Coming back from my morning walk in Central Park, I encountered a lady who was struggling against the wind. I asked if I could help her. I could. I asked if she would like me to see her home. She would.

The woman was Frances Chaney Lardner, wife of the once-blacklisted writer. She was delighted to learn that I was a journalist. Would I please come up and meet her husband? I demurred, but she insisted. And so—in shabbiest clothes on Central Park West—I ascended in the elevator to the Lardner apartment.

Some would call this "Only in New York." I started out the morning ordinarily; I ended it in Ring Lardner's home looking at his Oscars. There were two of them: one for *Woman of the Year*, the other for *M*A*S*H*. I had never seen an Oscar before—they're big.

The walls were covered with memorabilia, including photographs of actors, and athletes, and writers. One item in particular drew my attention, so emblematic was it of this couple: It was a certificate showing that Mrs. Lardner had won the Roger Baldwin Award of the Massachusetts—not the American, mind you, but the Massachusetts: even better—Civil Liberties Union.

We had a nice chat, and Mr. Lardner—who was sharp as a tack, but deficient in hearing—treated his wife with charming and touching tenderness. After a while, a moment of truth came. Asked Mrs. Lardner, "Where do you work, Jay?"

Please consider the situation: I work for *National Review*. I was talking to a couple one of whom went to jail for refusing to testify before HUAC.

After an awkward pause, I cleared my throat and said, "Mrs. Lardner, I work for *National Review*. I'm afraid I'm a bit of a conservative." (I'm not sure why I threw that "a bit of" in there—must have felt the need to soften it.)

Mrs. Lardner's eyes danced, and she said, "Oh, Jay, don't be embarrassed! We won't judge you! We're very open-minded people!" I smiled, sort of relieved. Turning to her husband, she touched his knee and repeated herself: "Oh, Ring: Jay's embarrassed. But, really: We don't judge him. We're very open-minded people!"

Mr. Lardner just smiled, gently—seeming less sure, perhaps.

We continued our visit and after much expression of goodwill bade farewell.

This was a strange and memorable encounter, full of meaning, I suspect. Communism, to me, is monstrous. My anti-Communism, to them, must have been little less. Yet here we were, three friendly strangers, happy to get to know one another a little on a blustery spring morning.

"The human element" runs strong.

THE
WORLD

Change and Determination

After 9/11, a shaking up.

This was a speech to a conference at Salonika, Greece, on September 11, 2002—the first anniversary of the terrorist attacks. The conference was called "September 11: Media and Terrorism."

L adies and gentlemen: I thought I'd begin by telling you a little about my day last September 11th. I'm a New Yorker—at least by adoption. I come from the state of Michigan, but I've lived and worked in New York for the last several years.

September 11th, 2001, was an election day in New York—perhaps fittingly. The gulf between the U.S. and its enemies is great, not least in the freedoms that Americans enjoy. I went to vote in the New York mayoral primary. And then I walked to work, south toward the World Trade Center—or where the towers had been. The smoke in the sky was ghastly; the color of the sky was ghastly; but worst of all was that you could see sky—only sky, where these immense towers, full of human beings, had been.

It was strange to be in a city under attack. I thought I might experience this once in my life as a war correspondent (something I've never been). But in my own country, my own city? No. This does something to a journalist, as well as to any other citizen: to be in a city under attack, from an enemy committed to your ultimate destruction.

September 11th was a so-called "production day" at our magazine—we had to get the magazine out—so I wasn't able to follow the news as I would have wanted to. But I kept receiving the most extraordinary bulletins. Nothing less than war had begun. In time, a smell—a hideous, ungodly smell—came through my windows; it was blowing from the towers, a couple of miles away. That was unnerving. So was the news that an acquaintance of mine—a friend of many at the magazine—had been on the plane that was crashed into the Pentagon. Our friend had done everything in her power, via her cellphone, to avert that attack.

You will understand that, though I may be a journalist, I'm far from a neutralist. Our president has said, "You're either for us or against us." This has been denounced as simplistic; I would call it clear.

All of us—my colleagues and I—were a little shaken, of course. But we were also weirdly energized. We were filled with purpose. It's almost shameful to say, but rarely had one felt so alive. We felt that we were given something truly important to cover, something truly important to think about, to struggle with. Most journalism, as you know, is mundane: We cover the most recent election, the most recent policy initiative, the most recent diplomatic contretemps. But this was world-defining, and we wanted to get it right.

I've been asked to say something about professional obligations, ethical obligations. Immediately, it seemed to me that the obvious one was to tell the truth. To discover the truth to the extent possible, and to tell it unflinchingly. This was not a time for squirming or shading or equivocating. It wasn't a time for delicacy or fear or what is known, at least in America, as "political correctness." It was a time for hard, cold realism. Feelings—or somebody's notion of feelings—weren't to be spared. With so many dead around you, and that stench continuing to fill your office, other people's feelings weren't the most important thing in the world.

Above all, I think that covering and commenting on this war has meant an end to pretending—an end to pretending that everyone's a friend, or potential friend, that every grievance is just, that a certain kind of hatred can be appeased, that America is to be blamed for humanity's woes, that radical Islam is just another viewpoint, that there is never right and wrong, only personal subjectivity. When the prime minister of Italy said that a free, open, pluralistic society is better than a closed, stifled, lied-to one, everyone professed shock and indignation. This is the kind of pretending that gets harder to do.

It occurred to me on 9/11 and after that this was a time for true colors: Everyone was showing his true colors. I thought of the phrase "*in vino veritas*"—after a bit of the grape, people tend to reveal themselves. So it was after the attacks. The sadness and outrage were terribly real; and the gloating and jubilation were terribly real. I will never forget the sight of people dancing and ululating on the streets of the Middle East. I will never forget the reports of Arab Americans in Brooklyn cheering—that was heartbreaking. Less than a year before, I'd been in Egypt, for an extended stay.

Now I was seeing cabbies rejoicing in Cairo squares, some of them shout-ing, "Bull's-eye!" I had perhaps been in the cabs of some of those very drivers. That, too, left an impression.

But understand them, people say. And one does: But sometimes under-standing is not comforting, or flattering to the understood.

A further personal item: A friend of mine in Alexandria sent me an e-mail. She's as educated, as Westernized, as liberal a person as you're like-ly to find in that great city. Has traveled all over the world, speaks perfect English and French, lectures at the university—etc. She wrote and said, "Oh, I'm so sorry. I hope you're all right. I hope you know that Osama bin Laden and al-Qaeda couldn't possibly have done this. It must have been the Jews."

If this woman was in the grip of such delusion, what chance did the man in the street have? It was time for a reckoning with the Arab world.

True colors appeared in America as well. Nowhere were they more visi-ble than in New York. Just as there are no atheists in a foxhole, there were few pacifists and anti-patriots in New York. People who didn't think of them-selves as America-loving suddenly found that they were—that their society and way of life were worth preserving, worth defending. Hard-bitten leftists found themselves flying the flag. One famous leftist wouldn't, but her daugh-ter insisted on it. The mother said, "Okay, but only from your own room."

Many of us hoped that terrorism and radicalism would become less chic, and less excused. On the very day of the attacks—September the 11th—the *New York Times* published a glowing piece about Billy Ayers. Ayers is a famous domestic terrorist, a member of what was called the Weather Underground. Among their deeds, amazingly enough, was the bombing of the Pentagon. These people have been lionized by much of our elite press for many years. But now it was beginning to be embarrassing. (Incidentally, when Ayers was acquitted in our courts of law, he said, "Guilty as sin, free as a bird. What a country, America!")

It seemed to me that it was incumbent on us to reexamine a great many things: not just obvious things, like military preparedness, counter-terrorism, and intelligence; but some less obvious things, like immigration and assimilation, the character of alliances, and the state of our journalism.

It was impossible not to glance backward somewhat. Many people—many of *us*, I might say—had warned for years about Islamic extremism and mili-tancy. Also about state harborers and abettors of terrorists. In 1993, the World Trade Center itself was bombed, but only a few died. Everyone kind of shud-dered, and then promptly forgot about it. Our men were murdered in the Khobar Towers, on Saudi soil. Many more people were murdered at the U.S.

embassies in Africa. Then, the U.S.S. *Cole*, in Yemen, was attacked. And yet these incidents were far away, and, besides, weren't most of the dead soldiers? They were in a dangerous business anyway.

But this thinking itself was dangerous. Some people said, at the time of the *Cole*, that this was not an act of terror—there's a vague word, "terror"—but an act of war, and ought to be treated as such. And yet the U.S. did little; there was a collective shrug. And that undoubtedly emboldened America's enemies for more. A colleague of mine pointed out the old French expression, "*L'appétit vient en mangeant.*" Appetite comes with eating. So it proved.

We were forced to think about the costs of appeasement, and looking the other way. I couldn't help recalling Italy and the *Achille Lauro* affair. You remember: Terrorists hijacked a cruise liner, and threw Leon Klinghoffer, who was bound to a wheelchair, into the sea—for the sole reason that he was a Jew. The United States managed to capture these terrorists, but they were jailed in Italy—and rather quickly released, one by one, until there were no more. Mrs. Klinghoffer at least had the satisfaction of spitting in their faces—literally spitting in their faces—during their brief confinement.

I must warn you that Americans, at this hour, are in a spitting mood.

And then, there was that thorny question of immigration, or, more to the point, assimilation. What is a free society to do? How do you handle people who come to America, or Holland, not to be American or Dutch, but to pursue jihad? You handle them harshly, I would think. But then, you have to safeguard civil liberties. Everyone knows there's work to be done in the Middle East—but there's work to be done in Michigan, too, and in Hamburg. Journalists should help investigate this problem: but to do so is to invite charges of racism and xenophobia. These charges, at this juncture, should have no sting.

One great pressing need, after 9/11, was to understand the Muslim world. Strangely enough, the United States is often accused of being an arrogant and self-absorbed nation. I must say that I don't see it that way: It seems to me that we're the most self-questioning, self-critical, self-flagellating nation on earth. If there are other candidates, I'd love to hear about them. Americans rushed to read the Koran. Classes in Middle Eastern Studies filled up. Every expert and near-expert and would-be expert in the land got himself on television.

I, for one, found it necessary to reacquaint myself with those who had been the most unflinching about the Middle East—who'd been the most clear-eyed, the most honest, the bravest. There was my colleague David

Pryce-Jones, the British journalist, author of *The Closed Circle*. There was the great Bernard Lewis, dean of Middle East historians, but always out of favor with radicals. There was the late Elie Kedouri, a Jew from Iraq, whose very life told some of the story of the 20th-century Middle East. And then there was Fouad Ajami, and Daniel Pipes, and that incredibly brave Iraqi dissident, Kanan Makiya, who wrote *The Republic of Fear*. It did not seem a time to pay heed to the usual suspects, the ones whose constant and only song is West-blaming.

And it was absolutely critical to discover what Arabs were saying among themselves. What was in their newspapers, and school textbooks, and sermons? What was on their televisions? For too long, the Arab world had been dark to us. It was time to let in some light. Many Arab leaders—Yasser Arafat, for example—had for decades been playing a double game: saying one thing to the West, in English, and quite a different thing at home, in Arabic. Take just one example: After September 11th, Chairman Arafat made a great show of giving blood, for the injured, presumably, in New York and Washington. He called the cameras in, and they duly disseminated the pictures all over the West. He expressed his sympathy. But at the same time, his official organs were hailing the attacks as a great and noble act. How did we know this?

This is where the Middle East Media Research Institute came in. This is a group, found at www.MEMRI.org, dedicated to the translation of raw materials from the Middle East. So often has MEMRI been referred to as "the invaluable Middle East Media Research Institute," I have joked that "the invaluable" has become part of its name. Its presence means that the double game can't be played with such ease anymore. Many of us in the American media have been relying on the institute's translations: It's a way not to be ignorant.

May I cite another example? After the attacks, the leading imam in New York, an Egyptian named Muhammad al-Gamei'a, said all the right, soothing things; he participated in interreligious ceremonies; and he stood as an example of humane Islam. Then he went home to Egypt, to Al-Azhar University, and gave the most remarkable interview: The Jews had done this, and the media were covering it up; Arabs were being shot on the streets, with the police doing nothing; Arab Americans were afraid to take their children to hospitals, because the Jewish doctors there would poison them; Hitler, of blessed memory, hadn't gone far enough—the whole routine. This is the same man who had been all sweetness and light, in English, in New York.

He was found out—we were able to find out—only because of the MEMRI group. And this brought up another point: It was time to take a fanatical, murderous anti-Semitism in the Middle East seriously, at long last. No more closing our ears, as we had at Durban, only days before the attacks. A famous Middle East scholar once said to me, "You know, the Islamic world is full of *Mein Kampf*s—little *Mein Kampf*s. For example, the ayatollah Khomeini wrote one. But no one knows it." Come to think of it, the foreign minister of Syria has published a book articulating the ancient blood libel. This is something to come to grips with.

I stress over and over, in my work, the need to take Arabs and Muslims seriously: to hear what they're saying, to credit them with meaning what they say. To do otherwise is to be condescending, at best. I further believe that we should do all we can to promote democrats and reformers in the Islamic world. This, in fact, is part of the mission of the Middle East Media Research Institute. Recently, a lot of us have been writing about Saad Ibrahim, the Egyptian human-rights activist sentenced to seven years' hard labor. This is in one of the more benign countries, mind you—to which the United States contributes billions a year. Those who care about Arab people don't make excuses for the systems under which they live; they want them to be free of tyranny, corruption, illusions, and war.

I must say that I've become less patient in the last year—less patient with an unthinking anti-Americanism; less patient with an absurd moral equivalence, or abdication, in the mainstream media. Shortly after September 11th, the head of ABC News declared that it wasn't for him to say whether the attack on the Pentagon was justified. (After criticism, he backtracked.) The *New York Times* published an article about a homicide-bomber and one of her victims: "Two Young Lives," said the headline, "United in Tragedy." Famous intellectuals like Günter Grass declared that 9/11 represented the comeuppance of the rich.

This is the sort of thing for which all my patience is spent. I think a robust—even bristling—impatience is now the appropriate stance.

On this anniversary, I've been thinking, too, about complacency—about the lure of it, and the need to resist it. There have been no additional September 11ths in the last twelve months, true. But we've had some near-misses. Has it been a matter of luck, particularly lucky police work? An attack was foiled in Singapore. The police in Rome discovered a plot having to do with the Via Veneto, where the American Embassy is. What about Richard Reid, the so-called shoe-bomber? How many minutes away was he from slaughtering hundreds of people in mid-air? How about the so-called "dirty bomber," Padilla, captured in Chicago? What about this couple in Heidelberg? And so on. I think of that chilling maxim that terrorists have long recited: "*You* have to be lucky all the time; *we* have to be lucky only once."

Many, I know, view America as obsessed and misguided. I would say that America is obsessed, but not misguided. We're obsessed with our own defense, our own preservation—and our own awareness of the dangers that lurk in the world. Secretary Rumsfeld likes to say that this is not a war of retaliation, retribution, or revenge—they are the three wrong R's. No, it's a war of self-defense. Our enemies have already killed us in the thousands, and they have vowed to kill thousands more. As there is no real, traditional defense against this sort of thing, one's only option is to wage war—even in the face of criticism and ill wishes.

Of course, America's wars aren't for America's benefit only. Who can forget—or have people forgotten already—the images from Kabul, Afghanistan, where music was heard for the first time in years? Where men and boys played soccer on execution grounds? Where women could know the simple pleasure of putting one's face to the sun? I can't help thinking that Bernard Lewis is right: If America went on to liberate Iraq and Iran, the images in Baghdad and Teheran would make those in Kabul look funereal.

Back to the American scene for a brief moment. Not long after September 11th, I was moderating at a forum that included Vernon Walters, the American general and diplomat, since deceased. I asked a basic question: What do we owe the dead? What do we owe the murdered of 9/11? He answered, "That it never happen again." That is, that we take the steps necessary to ensure, insofar as possible, that it never happen again. This is what is heavy on my mind on this anniversary, and heavy on the minds of other Americans.

America is a much more popular nation worldwide than some elites suppose, or would wish. Not long ago, I heard V. S. Naipaul say that the Third World masses are united in one thing: the desire for a green card. While Americans are happy to be popular, they'd much rather be safe. And they accept the grim necessity of the war we are waging, even as they did in pivotal moments past.

I have spoken very bluntly today. As you can tell, I'm a journalist—an opinion journalist—not a diplomat! But I trust that you wouldn't have wanted it otherwise. There was no point in traveling thousands of miles merely to chat lightly.

Thank you.

European Communities

A report from Greece and Albania

This piece followed the trip that included the foregoing speech, "Change and Determination."

G reece is said to be the most anti-American country in Europe, and Albania the most pro-American. As it happened, my itinerary included both countries. I was to speak on 9/11 and the ongoing war, and to mix it up a little with local journalists and intellectuals. Anything learned? Many things, among them that there is really no such thing as a European: The continent is not a monolith, no matter what the grandees in Brussels might wish. Also, that anti-Americanism is something of a house of cards, ready to collapse with a breath of reason and explication. Of course, you can do nothing about the die-hards. But what can you do about die-hards anywhere, including on an American campus?

The first thing an American is told in Greece is, "Don't say anything about terrorism"—meaning, domestic terrorism, with which Greece has had a problem. The Greeks are very sensitive to criticism on this score, particularly coming from Americans. Recently, government authorities rounded up the terrorists of the November 17 group, which has wreaked havoc for the last 25 years. In the course of their work, they murdered five Americans, and the Greek political establishment did not seem especially sorrowful or alarmed. In light of the current American-led war, and the coming of the Olympic Games to Athens in 2004, the Greeks were feeling extra pressure to do something about terrorists in their midst. Good for them. I was certainly not going to mention it, even to laud it.

But a young journalist in Thessaloniki (or Salonika, as we once called it) was quick to spring it on me: Why are you Americans so sensitive about this terror group, since merely five of your people died at its hands? This attitude—rather bristling and callous, actually—reminded me of something that had just been reported in *The* (London) *Spectator*. The magazine's editor, Boris Johnson, interviewed the Saudi ambassador to London, one Ghazi Algosaibi, notorious for penning poetic homages to Palestinian suicide-bombers. The ambassador, in an obvious effort to flatter his interviewer, said, "The American psyche is unlike the British psyche. . . . You have two prime ministers almost killed, and you say, Oh, well, some things are fated, some are not. The Americans say, We are going to go and get them."

This is a typical criticism, certainly heard in Greece: American over-reaction (to go with American arrogance, bullying, ignorance, and all the rest). I, for one, found it helpful to cite Donald Rumsfeld's line, which is that the present war is not a war of revenge, retaliation, or retribution—those are the three wrong R's. No, it is a war of self-defense, because unless our enemies are subdued, they will kill many more, as they have vowed. Recite this argument, and heads are likely to nod; at least there is a willingness to consider.

After the 9/11 attacks, there was an unseemly amount of gloating in Greece, as well as outright celebration. "Serves them right" was a too-common sentiment. Greeks, and not all of them on the hard left, offer the usual complaints against the U.S., not forgetting to cite Kyoto, the International Criminal Court, and globalization (seen as an assault on the Third World rather than a boon to it). Terrorism has a "root cause," and that is "international poverty," which America does too little to address. The country is a glutton for oil, which is all Washington cares about in the Middle East, no matter what it says about security, stability, peace, and freedom.

An idea of how far the scales are tipped against America among the Greek elites may be seen in the comment of a journalist—the same one who badgered me about sensitivity to November 17: During the Kosovo war, his position was that Milosevic was a brutal dictator who deserved removal, but that the American action was contrary to international law. This, he explained, with a certain twinkle, made him a pro-American apologist in the eyes of many of his friends and colleagues—even to suggest that the goal of restraining the Serbs was just. If this is what passes for a pro-American toadyism in Greece . . .

But condolences for the dead of 9/11, expressed over the recent anniversary, were numerous and heartfelt. A moving ceremony was held at the U.S. consulate in Thessaloniki, involving both local and national officials, and including the chanted prayers of black-hatted Orthodox clerics. Indeed, moving ceremonies were held all over Europe. And this raised a point that is slightly awkward to make: Some in Europe, as elsewhere, are perfectly happy with America as a victim nation, brought low by mass murder. They may be slightly less happy with America as a self-defending nation—a people willing to do something about it. Jacques Chirac's eyes fill with tears when he remembers the dead of September 11; his expression turns harder when it comes to steps designed to prevent future September 11s.

Even so, a little talk—a little arguing, insisting, and cajoling—can go a long way. Take the U.N. (please, our conservative Henny Youngmans might say). At every turn, Greeks are quick to mention the U.N., and, more particularly, the insufficient American deference to that body. They seem unused to hearing a well-grounded skepticism about the U.N. You can make the old Solzhenitsyn point, that this body is not so much the united nations as the united governments, or regimes. It is only as good as the governments that compose it. Furthermore, the U.N. is an organization the head of whose human-rights commission is Syria; the next head is scheduled to be Libya. Can you forgive a person, or a country, for being less than reverential about a body like that? And really, when you get down to it, Kofi Annan and the U.N. are not responsible for the safety and security of the American people; the president and the American government are. No American would begrudge any other country—Greece, for example—the right to defend itself, however it could. And you say it is illegitimate to go it alone? Can any civilized nation or person be sorry that Menachem Begin went it alone, in 1981, when he took out the Iraqi (and French) nuclear reactor, much to the displeasure of the entire world, including the United States—the Reagan-led United States, at that?

Again, heads may nod, and a certain understanding dawn, even if persuasion is not complete. It seems a sad fact that many of the Americans whom Greeks and other Europeans encounter are on the left. They are a parade of professors, journalists, and others, who may share the very assumptions and prejudices of local anti-Americans. Susan Sontag seems widely read, and she is distressingly widely quoted. Before arriving in Greece, I was told that if I, as a *National Review* editor, showed up without horns and a tail, that itself would be a victory. It is surely salutary for a European audience to hear a forthright, Republican-leaning American voice every now and then—if only to understand how such as Reagan and George W. Bush can be elected in the Land of Sontag (and Chomsky).

It should be remembered, too, that, even in a robustly anti-American country like Greece, there are reservoirs of support (or even dissent, you may call it). A friend of mine pointed out that there is a "red-state" Europe just as

there is a "red-state" America—a population whose views withstand the contradiction and censure of the dominant classes. It was remarkable to see an
older Greek man rise at a forum to say, "I'd like to show you the greatest gift
I have ever received in my life." He then reached into a bag and jammed on
his head an "FDNY" cap (representing the Fire Department of New York). To
be rather Agnewesque about it, this might not have gone down well with the
professors and editorialists; but it brought at least one grin.

'THE ISRAEL OF THE BALKANS'

On the northwestern border of Greece is Albania, a country that experienced the worst that Communism had to offer. For 50 years, it was a
virtual dungeon, a kind of European North Korea, with no one coming in
and no one getting out. So pure a Communist was the dictator, Enver
Hoxha, that he broke from both Moscow (in 1961) and Peking (in 1978),
judging them dangerously liberal. In the last years, Albania suffered near-
famine.

Now, however, it is struggling to rejoin the world, and the country is as
good a friend as America has in Europe, if an unfortunately powerless one.
Albanian fondness for America is longstanding, going back to at least
1913, when Woodrow Wilson declared that the country should go its own
way, have its independence, instead of being carved up by its neighbors.
Albanians speak of Wilson as if he had been president yesterday.

Shortly after Communism fell in 1991, Secretary James Baker made
a visit, and he was thronged by cheering, weeping, practically delirious
Albanians in the main square of Tirana, the capital. Some even kissed his
car. Adding to the regard for America was the U.S. role in the Yugoslav war.
Whereas Greeks are likely to decry American intervention—anywhere—
Albanians are likely to plead against American withdrawal or disengagement of any kind, seeing U.S. forces as the only thing between humanity
and the beast. In the present war on terror, Albanians are so supportive of
America that other Europeans have sneered at them, "You're the Israel of
the Balkans!" I suggest, using a trite American political phrase, that the
country ought to wear this as a badge of honor.

Albania is often cited as a Muslim nation, and it is true that a majority
of its citizens profess Islam. But this is misleading. For one thing, Balkan
Islam is apt to be nominal, and if it is not, it is of a distinctly non-Saudi,
tolerant style. For another, the main "religion" of Albania is something
called "Albanianism," a national feeling or devotion intended to thwart
clashes among Muslims, Orthodox, and Catholics. The Saudis and other

Gulf Arabs, however, are doing their best to radicalize and thus destabilize the country. They spread money around, virtually bribing mothers to veil their daughters, and to send their sons to Islamic schools, often far away. If those sons do go, they come back changed, frighteningly. Throughout Albania, Gulf Arabs have refurbished madrassas long disused: The price for such physical refurbishment, of course, is an adherence to Wahhabist ideology.

Most local analysts do not believe that Albania will be sucked in: Their Islam is too different, and they wish desperately to be integrated into Europe. If all goes well, Albania will have its EU membership in 20 years. Right now, it is the poorest country in Europe, "except possibly for Moldova," one journalist notes. (This reminds me of the old saying in Arkansas: "If it weren't for Mississippi . . .") In truth, Albanians would rather deal with Americans than Europeans, on the grounds that Americans are more straightforward, more direct, less slippery. Certainly the Albanian intelligentsia—and, yes, there is one (as more people will realize once Ismail Kadare wins the Nobel Prize in literature, as he almost undoubtedly will)—is with America, and baffled at the anti-Americanism in other parts of the continent. One Albanian journalist recounts to me his experience on a panel with an editor for *Le Monde*. Wide-eyed, shaking his head, he remembers that this man was not only pro-Castro and pro-Chávez, but perilously close to pro-bin Laden.

It is becoming axiomatic that the U.S. should hunt where the ducks are —should seek its friends where they exist. In Europe, those friends are readily found in the formerly Communist countries, where an appreciation of America is keener. One Albanian suggests that the very concept of "the West" needs adjusting. Consult a map. To begin with, Prague is west of Vienna. (This is one of the great party questions having to do with geography. The favorite in America is: Which is farther west—Reno or L.A.? The answer, of course, is the unexpected.) Athens has always been considered a Western capital, a NATO capital: It is east of Sofia, Budapest, Warsaw, and all three Baltic capitals, just to name a few. There is every evidence that George W. Bush grasps this. This president is no fan of state dinners, which perhaps keep him up past his bedtime, and in an annoying tuxedo. He has held only two in his entire time as president: the first for the president of Mexico, and the second, last summer, for the president of Poland. That is "no accident," as the Marxists say.

This country has friends in Europe, even where those friends are out-numbered, or outshouted. They should be encouraged; others should be engaged. "Public diplomacy," to use the going euphemism for old Information Agency work, can do only so much. But it can do something. Anti-Americanism can be muted, and pro-Americanism can be emboldened. "Don't scuttle the Pacific," MacArthur liked to say. There is no need to scuttle Europe. Divide it, perhaps. Talk to it, coax it, bat it around a little —definitely. And whenever you are feeling low about our European cousins, remember the Double-Headed Eagle—the symbol of the Albanian nation. They remember you.

—October 14, 2002
National Review

A Case of Liberation

Think, for a moment, about
Iraq's Marsh Arabs

When the United States and its allies went into Afghanistan and Iraq, they liberated about 56 million people. Those people had suffered under two of the most brutal regimes imaginable. A lot of people choke on that word, "liberated"—for others of us, it is entirely appropriate.

The scope of this achievement—the liberation—is almost too great to comprehend. Too many lives, communities, and situations are involved. But can we focus on merely one case—that of the "Marsh Arabs," in southern Iraq? Saddam Hussein succeeded in destroying the environment in which they lived; he almost succeeded in destroying the people themselves. Now those marshes are coming back, and the people are coming back, too.

No matter whether we supported the Iraq War or opposed it, can't we all rejoice in these results of the war? The answer is, of course, no.

The Mesopotamian Marshlands—home of the Marsh Arabs—exist at the confluence of the Tigris and Euphrates rivers. Many have imagined this area the site of the Garden of Eden. Until the early 1990s, this "Eden" was the Middle East's largest wetland, covering about 7,500 square

miles. The Marsh Arabs—also known as the Madan—are among the oldest peoples on earth, dating back 5,000 years. They are a link to the
Sumerians. For all these millennia, they have lived in their marshes, glid-
ing in their skiffs, called "mashoofs," and dwelling in their reed huts.
They have subsisted on fish and water buffalo, chiefly. The British explor-
er Wilfred Thesiger made them famous in the 1960s, when he published
his book *The Marsh Arabs*.

The marshes were always a mysterious place, a haven and hideout for
rebels, bandits, dissenters. When the Shiites failed in their uprising against
Saddam after the Persian Gulf War, many of them sought refuge in these
marshes. And the local residents, hating the regime—like most Iraqis—
sympathized with them. Saddam decided that the area and the people had
to be eradicated.

What happened next is a picture of pure evil; it can scarcely be
absorbed. In a massive push called the Third River Project, the regime
created dams, dikes, and canals—and dried up the marshes. One new canal
was called the Mother of All Battles River; there was also the Fidelity to the
Leader Canal. With amazing speed, this vast wetland became a desert. The
plants died, the animals died, water was nowhere. One newspaper report
had residents saying that it was as though someone had pulled a plug.
Saddam destroyed a full 90 percent of the Mesopotamian Marshlands,
establishing a military zone in their place.

But there's much, much more. The elimination of the marshes caused
the people to starve, flee, or die—and Saddam did all he could to make sure
they died. He poisoned the lagoons; he shelled villages; he set reedbeds
ablaze; he imprisoned, tortured, and executed; and he attacked these Iraqis
with WMD—with chemical weapons. He left no technique untried. In
August 1993, a British writer and filmmaker, Michael Wood, said that the
dictator's "slow genocide of the Marsh Arabs is nearing its climax." Yet it
had not been so slow, really.

And the world knew. In March 1993, *Time* magazine wrote of a doomed
people. Some of the most moving reporting of this period was done by
Chris Hedges of the *New York Times*. (A decade later, he would become a
shockingly vicious opponent of the Iraq War, condemning the United States
as the real oppressor.) Officials of the Clinton State Department testified to
Congress about exactly what the regime was doing. Vice President Gore
was appalled by the ruin of the wetlands, and spoke out strongly about Iraq:
"In the interests of regional peace and for the sake of human decency,
[Saddam Hussein] must be removed from power. That is the policy of this

administration. It is the policy I support. It is the policy I am personally committed to." (That statement was made in 2000.) In 2001, the U.N. Environment Programme released satellite photos, showing brown where marshlands had been.

And then the war came. The second they could, what Marsh Arabs remained punctured dikes, knocked down sluice gates, and otherwise tried to undo Saddam's project. Speaking of moving reporting, here is some by the *New York Times*'s James Glanz:

> . . . when Mr. Hussein's government fell in April 2003, villagers went to [a particular dike] and gouged holes in it using shovels, their bare hands and at least one piece of heavy equipment, a floating backhoe. Since then, something miraculous has occurred: reeds and cattails have sprouted up again; fish, snails and shrimp have returned to the waters; egrets and storks perch on the jagged remains of the walls, coolly surveying the territory as if they had never left.

Those mashoofs glided once more, and reed huts were built again. Desert was disappearing; wetlands were returning. Journalists from around the world collected expressions of gratitude and joy, and I offer a sampling: "The water is our life; it is a gift from God to have it back." "Everyone is so happy; we are starting to live like we used to, not the way Saddam wanted us to live." "[I am] like a person detained in prison who is set free." "This war has brought two joys for us: the end of Saddam and the return of the water." "This is what we call rebirth." And here is a snippet from the *Washington Post* of April 14, 2003: "[Men of the Wafi tribe], Shiite Muslims, said they had been banned from observing their religion until last Friday, when their imam was free to preach for the first time in years, and gave a talk 'thanking God and the coalition forces for giving us freedom,' as the sheik put it."

As soon as they could, the United States and its allies moved in to regenerate the marshlands and assist the people. The U.S. Agency for International Development and others are training Iraqis, equipping them—helping them help themselves. One prominent group is called Eden Again, and two of its guiding lights are Azzam Alwash and his wife, Suzie Alwash. Both are Ph.D.-holding environmental scientists. He is an Iraqi who grew up in Nasiriyah, the son of an irrigation engineer; she is a Texan.

Suzie Alwash reports that about 40 percent of the marshlands have been re-flooded. And about half of that has been revegetated: "It's amazing, when you look at pictures of the place, from month to month, how fast this stuff is revived." Some areas will never be revived, but the Mesopotamian Marshlands will again have a life. Another scientist—Thomas L. Crisman, a wetlands specialist at the University of Florida—says that he doesn't like to use the word "restoration": "You're not God; you can't put it back." He prefers "rehabilitation," arguing that, with time and smarts, reasonable goals can be obtained.

As with Iraq at large, not all has been well in the marshlands since Liberation Day. Numbering about 500,000 mid-century, the Marsh Arabs were maybe half as many by the time of the 1991 war. After Saddam's depredations, those in the area dwindled to about 75,000; the others were dispersed or killed. According to Suzie Alwash, some 100,000 Marsh Arabs have returned since the liberation: from the towns, cities, and camps of their exile. (Some had gone to neighboring Iran.) Different Marsh Arabs want different things: Some want a more modern life, tired of the reeds; some want to farm, instead of coping with the fish and water buffalo. There are problems with the water: very salty, not as life-giving as it was. Turkey's dams affect southern Iraq, and water politics are always sticky.

Yet this is a story to celebrate, if we have celebration in us. Those calling themselves liberals might take a particular interest. For decades, they've expressed intense concerns about wetlands: Practically the worst thing you can do in America is fill in a swamp. Saddam Hussein destroyed one of the world's largest wetlands; the region has come back thanks to U.S.-led efforts. But George W. Bush as environmental hero is far too much to swallow. Last summer, the U.N. Environment Programme noted that the "fabled wetlands" are "home to rare and unique species like the Sacred Ibis, and a spawning ground for Gulf fisheries." Bush as savior of the Sacred Ibis? Again, impossible to choke down.

And what about the human aspect of the liberation—the lives of people, in addition to the life of nature? (Of course, the two are closely linked, in this case.) Forgetting the value of human lives simply because they are human, liberals have always been reverential about ancient ways of living. (This is regardless of whether the people themselves wish to modernize.) Yet another reason to rejoice over what has taken place, one would think.

If Hollywood could calm down about George W. Bush—and accept any good from the Iraq War—they could make a wondrous movie about the Marsh Arabs. Imagine Liberation Day: the scene in which gaunt, bedraggled people go out, bare-handed, to tear at dikes and such, causing the waters to rush back. I can just hear the surging music—perhaps the opening pages of Prokofiev's Piano Concerto No. 1.

But there will be no music, from the worst of Bush's critics. They sometimes claim that the invasion and occupation—what I have repeatedly called the liberation—has left Iraq worse off than before. They should look toward the Marsh Arabs. Indeed, they should look toward Iraq as a whole.

—January 30, 2006
National Review

Thanks for the MEMRI (.org)

An institute, and its website, bring the Arab world to light

After the 9/11 attacks, the West realized that it knew little about the Arab world—in fact, dangerously little. Why do they hate us so, and did this come out of the blue? It seemed imperative to learn more about the Arabs—to learn, for example, what they were saying to one another, in their media, in their schools, and in their mosques. The Arab world had always been dark this way; it needed to come into the light.

And this is where www.MEMRI.org proved "invaluable," as everyone has said. It is more than a website, of course; it is an institute, specifically the Middle East Media Research Institute, or MEMRI. What it does, mainly, is provide translations of Arab newspaper articles, television shows, political statements, sermons, textbooks, and so on. MEMRI invites one and all to "Explore the Middle East Through Its Own Media"—which is what many people, including journalists, began to do last fall. Plenty of journalists leaned heavily on MEMRI's translations, citing "the invaluable Middle East Media Research Institute." In fact, "invaluable" was written so often before MEMRI's name that one could have been forgiven for thinking the word was part of the name. MEMRI served as an antidote to darkness, as a way not to be ignorant.

Consider the case of Sheikh Muhammad al-Gamei'a, as "mainstream" a Muslim as one could have hoped for. He was head of the Islamic Cultural Center and Mosque on New York's Upper East Side, the very symbol of Muslim splendor in America. Al-Gamei'a was the kind who participated in interreligious services and offered soothing words about peace, healing, and brotherhood. This is the sort of role he played—speaking in English—immediately after September 11.

But then he went home to Egypt and, on October 4, gave an eye-opening interview to a prominent Islamic website. The sheikh told his audience that, after September 11, Arabs in America could not go to hospitals, because Jewish doctors were making them sick; that Americans were firing on mosques and murdering Arabs in the street, with impunity; that Americans knew that the Jews—not radical Arabs—were responsible for the attacks, but were afraid to speak up about it, for fear of being labeled anti-Semitic.

After expounding on secret Jewish control, al-Gamei'a turned to Hitler—as Arab opinion-makers tend to do (a fact documented sickeningly and undeniably by MEMRI). Said the sheikh: "Now [the Jews] are riding on the back of the world powers. These people always seek out the super-power of the generation and develop coexistence with it. Before this, they rode on the back of England and on the back of the French empire. After that, they rode on the back of Germany. But Hitler annihilated them because they betrayed him and violated their contract with him."

Al-Gamei'a then explained that "on the news in the U.S. it was said that four thousand Jews did not come to work at the World Trade Center on the day of the incident, and that the police arrested a group of Jews rejoicing in the streets at the time of the incident." But "this news item was hushed up imme-diately after it was broadcast," because "the Jews who control the media acted to hush it up so that the American people would not know. If it became known to the American people, they would have done to the Jews what Hitler did!"

Under ordinary circumstances, the sheikh's words—so unlike those he had uttered, in English, while Muslim leader in New York—would have gone unnoticed in the West. But circumstances had changed, and journalists were attuned to MEMRI, meaning that the usual double game—sweetness and reason in English, lies and hate in Arabic—could not be played, in the dark. The al-Gamei'a story made it all the way to the top, which is to say, into the *New York Times*. The newspaper duly had "two independent trans-lators" confirm the MEMRI translation—the institute's work has never been found to be anything but honest, accurate, and meticulous. And the sheikh was exposed.

Why do ordinary Arabs believe such awful things about us? rings the question. And the answer—or at least part of the answer—is that they hear them from their authorities, incessantly.

The stream of materials kept coming from MEMRI, many of them startling conventional U.S. journalists, in part because a great deal of them came from Egypt and Saudi Arabia, two nations always counted among the "moderates." Those acquainted with the Middle East were unsurprised, but everyone else—who took the question seriously—was somewhat awed. The anti-Israeli feeling could have been expected; but the anti-Americanism was, if anything, more breathtaking. Still more breathtaking was the anti-Semitism: not garden-variety anti-Semitism, and not present-day European anti-Semitism, but anti-Semitism on the Nazi level. A veteran Middle East scholar once confided to me that the Muslim world is full of *Mein Kampf*s, big and little. Some are full-length books, some are essays, editorials, pamphlets, all declaring intentions, all divulging convictions, all remarkably candid. They have only to be read.

MEMRI made clear that the people celebrating in the Middle East over September 11 were not only the radicalized masses, but the elites who had radicalized them. Well before that terrible day, the Arab media were full of exultation over the attacks that Osama bin Laden and al-Qaeda had already committed against America, and were anticipating and urging yet more spectacular ones. In July, Dr. Faisal al-Qassem, host of a talk show on al-Jazeera—sometimes described as the "Arab CNN"—said, "Has bin Laden not become a worthy opponent, feared by America—for whom [America] moves its fleets and puts its army and embassies on highest alert? . . . Who smashed one of its destroyers on the high seas? Who fought it in Somalia and caused its troops to run like rabbits? Who made its embassies through-out the world into fortresses [whose residents] fear even a light breeze? Who caused America to yelp in pain one hundred times?"

Yet the host did fault bin Laden on one score: "Where are bin Laden's attacks on Israel? True, according to opinion polls we conducted, America is Enemy No. 1 . . . but Israel is the spearhead. Where is his struggle, his jihad against Israel? Why are we not seeing it?"

After September 11, of course, bin Laden became an even greater figure, although some commentators—moderates, one might even call them—preferred to concentrate on the evil of the American war. Ibrahim Nafi' is editor-in-chief of *Al-Ahram*, the government daily in Cairo. In October, he wrote that U.S. forces were dropping their food for desperate Afghans in minefields. He further suggested that this food had been "genetically treated," with "the aim of affecting the health of the Afghan people" (for the worse, naturally). Therefore the Afghans would be unlucky either way: blown up by mines or poisoned by America's food gifts. We should bear in mind that Nafi' is not some "crazy" spouting off in a renegade organ, but the equivalent of the principal editor of the *New York Times*, although appointed by the head of state.

A VITAL SERVICE

The veil has been lifted by MEMRI. The institute is the brainchild of Yigal Carmon, who, with co-founder Meyrav Wurmser, began these efforts four years ago. (Wurmser is now at the Hudson Institute in Washington, while Carmon continues with MEMRI.) An Israeli, Carmon was born in Romania, to parents speaking Romanian, Hungarian, and German. Carmon would go on to speak several more languages. He is of a type more common in his country than in others: a military man—he is a retired military-intelligence colonel—and an intellectual, a scholar. He is a specialist in Arabic, Arab literature, and Arab politics. Carmon served as counter-terrorism adviser to two prime ministers, Shamir and Rabin, and participated in negotiations with the Syrians.

In establishing MEMRI, he wanted to bring the Arab world to Western governments, journalists, and publics at large, without filters and without distortions. Few outsiders learn Arabic, and Westerners—including Middle East correspondents—have always been at the mercy of what Arabs tell them in their own tongues. Carmon's idea was that political elites (in particular) should read editorials in *Al-Ahram* the same way they read editorials in the *Jerusalem Post* or the *New York Times*—with their morning coffee.

At first, he focused mainly on the Palestinian Authority and Egypt, with the most urgent attention being paid to the P.A. Yasser Arafat would speak to his people preaching jihad—on P.A. TV—and few on the outside knew it. Carmon simply translated these speeches and distributed them to all interested parties. Some in the Israeli government were profoundly irritated by this project, because to hear Arafat in the raw was to doubt that he could be a "partner for peace," as the Israeli leadership very much needed him to be. Foreign minister Shimon Peres once chided, "The point is not to expose them but to change them." MEMRI retorts that exposure—knowledge, openness, understanding—is a precondition to change.

From small beginnings, the institute branched out, literally. It is now headquartered in Washington, and has offices in Jerusalem, London, and Berlin. MEMRI translates into English, French, Spanish, German, Russian,

Hebrew, and Turkish; soon it will do Italian, and perhaps Japanese. The institute's staff number about 30, and they are of assorted nationalities and religions. The outfit runs on a shoestring, with Carmon constantly on a hunt for money. MEMRI exists entirely on private donations—there are about 250 donors, including some foundations—and will not accept any government money, as a matter of policy. Independence and objectivity are matters of pride here. Staffers work virtually around the clock, with an almost missionary spirit, feeling that their work is vital, that their moment is now.

Carmon and his team are most eager to stress that a major part of their mission is to highlight the "good guys" in the Middle East: the democrats, or near-democrats; the liberals, or near-liberals—anyone who evinces the slightest interest in reform. If a professor somewhere in the Gulf writes a letter-to-the-editor expressing reasonableness or the hope of change, MEMRI seizes on it, trumpeting it, holding it out as a flower amid the weeds. The institute is useful for "gotcha"—for a kind of ideological and rhetorical whistle-blowing; but it is most interested in encouraging democracy and reform. Carmon dreams of, to borrow language from another region and period, *perestroika* and *glasnost* in the Arab world.

For the time being, however, the "gotcha" elements will remain in the fore. When Arafat appears on *60 Minutes*—as he did—he can now be confronted with his Arabic statements—as he was. When Hanan Ashrawi, the PLO's smooth and earnest-seeming spokeswoman, is interviewed on Fox News, she is faced with the Friday sermons broadcast on Palestinian Authority TV. Egyptian officials are queried about the steady Hitlerism in their country's official media, and they huffily deny it—but then a columnist goes and reiterates, "Thanks [be] to Hitler, of blessed memory, who on behalf of the Palestinians revenged in advance against the most vile criminals on the face of the earth. Although we do have a complaint against him, for his revenge on them was not enough."

Just as many Arab officials and opinionists praise bin Laden for September 11 in one breath, and in the next breath insist that the Jews, rather than bin Laden, perpetrated it, they are apt to deny the Holocaust in one breath, and then hail it in the next. They seem not to be able to decide whether the Holocaust is a Jewish lie, meant to gain world sympathy, or a mighty act. They regularly peddle anti-Jewish fabrications, such as the infamous *Protocols of the Elders of Zion* and the Nazis' *Handbook on the Jewish Question* (1935). The foreign minister of Syria, Mustafa Tlass, is the author of *The Matza of Zion*, which perpetuates the blood libel.

And speaking of blood libel, America's ally, Saudi Arabia, was discomforted briefly by the exposure of an article in one of its official dailies. In *Al-Riyadh*, Dr. Umayma Ahmad al-Jalahma of King Faisal University had a column entitled "The Jewish Holiday of Purim," holding that "the Jew must prepare very special pastries" for this event: specifically, pastries filled with the blood of non-Jewish adolescents. MEMRI spread this news, and many Western outlets picked it up, awake to something rotten in the "desert kingdom."

And pity Yasser Arafat, who now has MEMRI listening in. His ministers in the P.A. frequently reassure the populace that any move toward peace and negotiation is a mere tactic. One of those ministers, the late Faisal al-Husseini, had been considered by the West a Great Moderate Hope. Shortly before he died last summer, al-Husseini gave an interview to an Egyptian newspaper in which he described the Oslo accords as a Trojan Horse, elaborating on the metaphor with specificity and relish. That shook the "peace camp" in Israel. And Arafat himself is "caught" when he, for example, gives an interview to Egyptian TV. While under siege from the Israeli military, he vowed to take Jerusalem and said—repeatedly, almost as an incantation—"martyrs by the millions. To Jerusalem we march—martyrs by the millions." When his interviewer closed with, "We are with you in our hearts and souls and we pray for your safety and the safety of the Palestinian people," Arafat responded, "Man, don't wish me safety! Pray for me to attain martyrdom! Is there anything better than being martyred on this holy land? We are all seekers of martyrdom." Speaking to Abu Dhabi TV, Arafat said of Ariel Sharon, "True, he uses all the weapons prohibited by international law. True, he uses depleted uranium. True, he uses toxic gases . . . but we are steadfast." Such lies are "unhelpful," to use a President Bush adjective.

Wading or clicking through MEMRI's materials can be a depressing act, but it is also illusion-dispelling, and therefore constructive. This one institute is worth a hundred reality-twisting Middle Eastern Studies departments in the U.S. Furthermore, listening to Arabs—reading what they say in their newspapers, hearing what they say on television—is a way of taking them seriously: a way of not condescending to them, of admitting that they have useful things to tell us, one way or the other. Years ago, Solzhenitsyn exhorted, "Live not by lies." We might say, in these new circumstances, "Live not by ignorance about lies, either." Anyone still has the right to avert his eyes, of course. But no one can say that that is not a choice.

—May 6, 2002
National Review

Terror on Trial

Thinking about Shining Path, and those like them

Every so often, the world relearns the difficulty of trying a certain kind of monster in court. Nuremberg stands as the eternal example; some people still think they should have been lined up and shot. In The Hague the other day, Milosevic dropped dead, frustrating his prosecutors, and others. Saddam Hussein, of course, continues his judicial theater. Although the judge in the case—currently Raouf Abdel-Rahman—sometimes gets the upper hand. On March 15, Saddam boasted, "I am the head of state." Judge Abdel-Rahman corrected, "You used to be a head of state. You are a defendant now."

A half a world away, Abimael Guzmán is also a defendant. In the roster of 20th-century monsters, he has a place. The difference between Guzmán and Saddam Hussein—and the Nazis and Milosevic and the Rwandan butchers and many others—is that Guzmán never gained power. But in his country, Peru, he managed to kill at least 40,000 people, depending on how you do the accounting. He also wreaked $30 billion in material damage, and left a legacy of fear. Not bad for twelve years' work, accomplished by a former philosophy professor at a provincial university.

You may have forgotten Guzmán and his movement, Shining Path, but I will inflict some reminding. Abimael Guzmán Reynoso was born in 1934, and his university was in Ayacucho, high up in the Andes. He was a leader in the China-favoring faction of the Peruvian Communist party. In 1970, he christened his movement the "Shining Path of José Carlos Mariátegui," after the founder of that party.

Guzmán thought of himself as the heir to Marx, Lenin, and Mao. He had no use for the contemporary Soviets, viewing them as soft. The Cubans and the Nicaraguans—the Castroites and the Sandinistas—were laughable pipsqueaks to him. He reviled Deng Xiaoping, for his departures from Mao. The Communists he really admired were the Khmer Rouge, and he shared their totalizing philosophy. Guzmán was openly genocidalist. At its peak, his movement had 10,000 fighters, and these included adolescents. They killed with particular ease and glee.

Guzmán's plan was to control the countryside and then strangle the cities, conquering all of Peru through "a river of blood." The plan was launched in earnest on May 17, 1980, when his forces attacked a polling place in tiny Chuschi. This was deeply significant. Peru was just emerging from more than ten years of dictatorship; democracy was in bud. At Chuschi, Shining Path burned the ballot boxes. They could not tolerate any democratic flowering, because that was not the future they had in mind for Peru.

If you discern a similarity to the current insurgency in Iraq, you are not undiscerning. Indeed, to review the campaign of Shining Path in the 1980s and '90s is to be struck by many similarities to today's Iraq.

Shining Path took care to kill all the politicians it could—and all the government officials, and all the voters, and anyone at all who dared participate in the democracy. People refused to run for office, for fear that they or their families would be killed. Sometimes, when they ran and won, they immediately resigned. In 1988 alone, Shining Path killed 17 provincial mayors.

And they did a great deal more. They kidnapped, they robbed banks, they bombed embassies. They bombed police academies, they bombed churches, they bombed businesses. They killed anyone, foreign or Peruvian, engaged in relief or development work. Europeans felt they had to withdraw from the country. Just about the only thing missing from Shining Path's repertoire was beheading—but they made up for it by hacking to death with machetes. The stories that come out of the Shining Path period are as gruesome as any you have heard.

Testifying before Congress in March 1992, the U.S. assistant secretary of state for inter-American affairs, Bernard Aronson, put it well: "In [Shining Path's] mind, any Peruvian or any foreigner who takes up the democratic cause, tries to ease human suffering, or resists terrorist threats is hampering the development of revolutionary consciousness . . . ." Abimael Guzmán put it even better. Talking to his Central Committee, he said, "Our policy is to raze to the ground, to leave nothing. . . . In a war, what you cannot use or carry off, you destroy, you burn."

He meant every word. In addition to attacking people, Shining Path attacked infrastructure, which is another way of attacking people. They blew up bridges, irrigation projects, and electrical towers. They caused many blackouts—including one in Lima while the Pope was visiting—and water shortages. Their goal was simply to make life intolerable, to bring Peru to its knees. And they came very close. Peruvians remember this—it was not so long ago—and they shudder.

The similarities to Iraq's insurgents are obvious. And we might consider one more: Shining Path spread lies, preying on the ignorant. For example, they would say, "The American government—in combination with local lackeys—is poisoning your children with herbicides." Iraq's tormentors do no less. But while the similarities are obvious, there are dissimilarities, too. Michael Radu, a Romanian-born scholar in Philadelphia who has studied Shining Path, notes a couple: Shining Path had a clear ideology, and they also had a clear plan. Guzmán was nicknamed "President Gonzalo"; his philosophy was "Gonzalo Thought." And his blueprint for taking the country was known to all. The Iraq terrorists are more ragtag and random, deadly as they are.

UPSTAIRS, WATCHING TELEVISION

Peru got its big break on September 12, 1992, when Guzmán was at last nabbed, after his dozen years of mayhem and murder. He was upstairs in a Lima safe house—a not-so-safe house—watching television. Then Peruvian forces moved in. It was a historic triumph for President Alberto Fujimori, who five months before had staged his "self-coup," dissolving Congress and other institutions of democracy. His rationale had been counterterror. After Guzmán's capture, Shining Path withered, for it had been highly dependent on its leader.

Guzmán was tried in a military court. He was made to wear prison stripes, and put in a cage; members of the judicial panel were hooded. Lest you judge Peruvian authorities too harshly, for their undemocratic ways, remember this: Prior to this time, it had been impossible to try Shining Path terrorists, because their confreres kept murdering judges, or their families, or their friends, or anyone they could touch. In a two-year period—1991–92—Shining Path killed 120 judges. Hundreds of others resigned, unwilling to sacrifice themselves (to no end). Of course, those participating in Saddam Hussein's trial live under constant threat as well.

There was some question whether Guzmán should have been killed—killed upon capture—and that question lingers today. This is almost always a question, when such a monster is apprehended. Do you do it the Ceausescu way, or the Saddam/Nuremberg way? In any event, Guzmán was given a life sentence. The court could not impose the death penalty on him, for that penalty was reserved for those committing treason in time of war (against another country). Guzmán was lucky for the leniency of even Fujimori's presidential dictatorship.

He would get luckier still, but more about that in a moment.

When Guzmán was first tried in 1992, he had some support on the international left, but not complete support. *The Nation* magazine ran an article on the debate: Should leftists rally to Guzmán or not? Some of the usual suspects said yes: Noam Chomsky, Ramsey Clark, a Berrigan brother (Philip). Clark, as you know, is a member of Saddam Hussein's legal-defense team today. Back at the time, he explained to *The Nation* that Guzmán required patience and understanding: "I met with Saddam Hussein, who is supposed to be the closest thing to the devil. If we want to have some peace in Peru, we have to recognize the humanity of all sides." He refused to utter any criticism whatsoever of Guzmán or Shining Path.

Guzmán sat in his cell until 2003, when something astonishing happened: His sentence was overturned; the verdict against him was rendered void; his trial was declared invalid. So it was with all Shining Path prisoners—about 2,000 of them. Put briefly, Peruvian democracy was embarrassed by the Fujimori period. And that period included the military tribunals that had locked away Shining Path. The entire lot of them would have to be re-tried, in civilian court. This threw the system into chaos, severely overloading it. Hundreds of prisoners—perhaps as many as a thousand—were outright released.

Not Guzmán, of course. He had another day in court, and this one was very different from the first one. No prison stripes, no cage. Instead, Guzmán was looking rather professorial, and he was surrounded by friends: his co-defendants, old comrades in arms, including his girlfriend and No. 2, the dread Elena Iparraguirre. They all embraced and chatted. Reporters on the scene said it looked like a family reunion. The group started chanting slogans—"Long live the Communist Party of Peru!" "Glory to Marxism, Leninism, and Maoism!"—and pumped their fists in the air. Circus time. They turned the courtroom into a political forum, attempting to prosecute the judicial system itself. (Saddam Hussein would do exactly the same.) A judge remarked to the press, "Once a trial has this kind of atmosphere, it is very hard to continue moving forward."

PLAYING A NUMBER OF CARDS

The Guzmán trial has moved forward, but in fits and starts. No one is sure when it will end. Álvaro Vargas Llosa is a prominent Peruvian intellectual. He says, "Peruvian justice is notably slow, corrupt, very unpredictable, and always very, very sensitive to the political climate." Fortunately, there is no support for Shining Path in Peru today—even the Left, the Communists, have no truck with it. But, as Alberto Bolívar—another Peruvian intellectual—points out, leftists in other parts of the world harbor a fondness for Shining Path, and they are waging the usual propaganda campaign.

Guzmán and other Shining Path prisoners spend a lot of time talking about justice, their rights, due process. This is rich: For years, they dedicated themselves to the destruction of "bourgeois institutions" such as courts. Radicals elsewhere behave this way, too, of course, including in the United States: Kathy Boudin, Susan Rosenberg, Linda Sue Evans, and the rest of the Weather Underground used to scorn everything about "the system," perhaps especially the courts. To avail oneself of them was "counterrevolutionary." But after some years in prison, they started singing about rights and citing the Constitution. (In the waning hours of his presidency, Bill Clinton granted clemency to Rosenberg and Evans. He has never explained that action. Boudin has since been paroled.)

In all likelihood, Guzmán's original sentence will be confirmed: life in prison. But it is also likely that he will appeal to the Inter-American Court of Human Rights in Costa Rica. Shining Path is now playing any number of political, legal, and public-relations cards. The old Guzmán, needless to say, would have roared against this.

And the Shining Path movement itself—is it dead? In Lima, there is a Terror Museum, designed to keep a record of those atrocious years, 1980–1992. The museum houses Shining Path soap carvings, music boxes that play Communist hymns. All of this kitsch has Guzmán's picture on it. But Shining Path is not yet merely a memory. They are still in the jungle, killing people. In March 2002, they exploded a car bomb in Lima, near the U.S. embassy. This was three days before President George W. Bush visited. They killed ten people. (Car bombing, you may recall, had been a Shining Path specialty, in the worst days.) Then, when all those verdicts were overturned, the movement got a shot in the arm. They felt rejuvenated. The sight of their President Gonzalo and his lieutenants, whooping it up, cheered them.

As David Scott Palmer, an expert on Shining Path at Boston University, observes, lots and lots of Guzmán's followers have been released from prison—so this has provided a reinforcement of a movement that had been moribund.

Some say that judges are again being intimidated, or bribed. Certain Peruvians are calling for the return of the hoods—to protect judges. And

Peruvian democracy in general seems in a fragile state. Alberto Bolívar is one who believes that Shining Path is biding its time, waiting to launch another, all-out campaign. And most agree that Guzmán's continued existence is a comfort and inspiration to the guerrillas now in operation, or waiting. This same kind of talk, of course, is heard in, and about, Iraq.

It might have been neater if Fujimori's men had simply snuffed Guzmán, on that glorious, saving day of September 12, 1992. But civilized people do not operate that way—do not operate as Guzmán does, and as Saddam does. Each of those is having his day in court, or many days. And even as they create their circuses, they are being tried for what they have done. And maybe people, all over, see that the way of the brute does not—with awful inevitability—triumph.

—April 10, 2006
National Review

Doses of Davos

Chronicles from on high

Every January, the World Economic Forum has its Annual Meeting in Davos, way up in the Swiss Alps. Here are reports from those meetings, 2003–2007. All were published in National Review. *I have done some cutting to avoid too much repetition, and this cutting is indicated with ellipses. The first report—2003—is reprinted in full, and so is the final one: which is all about global warming. "Fever in the Alps,"* NR *called that one.*

2003

I t's really true: Everyone is here. I mean, everyone and his brother. No wonder the resentful resent Davos so much. It's almost enough to make you believe in conspiracy! The World Economic Forum features heads of state, foreign ministers, finance ministers, CEOs, and many others who move and shake. There are about 2,500 participants in all. What was that Bill Buckley crack? That he'd rather be governed by the first 2,000 names in the Boston phonebook than by the Harvard faculty? Well, would he rather be governed by the poohbahs of Davos?

Our motto—I mean, the Forum's motto (see? I'm putting on airs already)—is "Committed to Improving the State of the World." It would be hard to improve on the state of this village itself. Davos looks like a Disney version of Switzerland, or, alternatively, it looks like a sno-globe. We are in *Magic Mountain* land. We are also in Heidi Land. That's what I see in an advertisement: "Get Your Mineral Water, Straight from Heidi Land!" You remember Heidi, don't you? She's the one who interrupted that football game.

The theme of this year's Forum—actually, it's called the Annual Meeting of the World Economic Forum—is trust. I mean, Trust. In its researches, the Forum has discovered that trust is waning around the world. Trust in . . .? In government, in companies, in leadership generally. The thought occurs to me that a little distrust—a little skepticism—is a healthy thing in a populace. And, in fact, a U.S. congressman—Republican Rob Portman of Ohio—gives voice to exactly this view, in the Meeting's opening session. There aren't many right-leaners here. The air in Davos—pristine and glorious and Alpine as it is—soon fills with an anti-Bush stench.

First, though, who are the poohbahs of the Annual Meeting? I say again: Who's not? It's a little like the pages of the *New York Times* come to life. You've got those heads of state: King Abdullah, Vicente Fox, "Lula!" You've got your business bigs: Bill Gates, Michael Dell, the Google guy. You've got some off-beaters, like Ravi Shankar, the sitar player and yoga guru, and the actress Julia Ormond, who seems to be the resident babe (not that there's not a lot of competition in Switzerland). And—ecumenical as the Meeting is—you've even got AFL-CIO boss John Sweeney, looking like . . . well, a Disney version of a labor boss.

There's also a contingent of religious leaders, an assortment of sheikhs, rabbis, and priests. Davos wouldn't be Davos without a grand mufti or two (especially now). Among the religious is a man with my favorite title of all time: I'm talking about His Beatitude Dr. Anastasios, Archbishop of Tirana and All Albania. *His Beatitude!* How'd you like to be known as His Beatitude Joe Smith or whatever?

Our seminars, "working dinners," coffees, and so on, are endless, and their variety is infinite, too. Sure, you've got your usual topics, like "Helping Japan Avoid Another Lost Decade" and "Globalization at a Crossroads." But you've also got "Love: A Matter of Trust" and "Why Do

We Age and Why Do We Hate It?" (Ravi Shankar holds forth in that one—in both, actually). You can even drop in on "Shakespeare and Leadership," hosted by Richard Olivier, son of you-know-who.

On the first day of the Meeting, we seem to have a star: Mahathir Mohamad, prime minister of Malaysia. He's known as a shining moderate in the Muslim world. Which is a little alarming. In his remarks to the throng, he posits a strict moral equivalence between the United States and its enemies. America calls them the "Axis of Evil"; they call America the "Great Satan." Both sides—*both* sides—are "convinced they are right," which is the source of all this trouble. September 11 was merely a question of "the weak" lashing out at "the strong." America must determine what is bugging these folks and "negotiate" with them. Etc.

The crowd laps it up like milk. As the Meeting wears on, the question seems not so much "the West and the rest" as "the world against the United States" (or certainly against a Republican United States, led by a wearer of cowboy boots). I hear repeatedly about capital punishment in Texas, brutality at Guantanamo Bay, and the notorious American swagger. If Davos has a favorite American, it's Jimmy Carter. After him, it's Bill Clinton, who is, in fact, here (daughter in tow). He is referred to as "the President" and treated like a great sage. Clinton is a symbol of an earlier American sanity now sadly lost in the reign of Bush the Stupid and Dangerous.

As I look on, it occurs to me that Clinton is pulling a Carter—that he is rising above mere Americanness to become a kind of Global Man. Absent from his constant outflow of talk is any mention of U.S. interests. He is all Global Interdependency. But then, when in Davos . . .

Listen, though: America will never be the most despised country as long as there's Israel. Many Davosers casually assume that Ariel Sharon is a monster and that the Palestinians are the most abused people on earth. (They are among them, to be sure—thanks, not least, to their own "leadership." In whom much lack of Trust is warranted.) Shimon Peres is here, and he is, of course, the world elite's favorite Israeli. Didn't Abba Eban used to play this role? Peres swans around, accepting compliments, almost surely more popular in Davos than in Israel.

Back to America for a sec. Whenever I'm at an international conclave like this—not that there's anything quite like the Davos forum—I'm struck by the near uniqueness of American self-criticism. I am conscious of the absence of self-criticism from elsewhere, hearing the dog that doesn't bark. I just about never hear a Saudi curse—or even question—his country or its role in the world. The same goes for Indonesians, Nigerians, and others.

The Americans are critical of America; the non-Americans are critical of America. I think of one of Reagan's favorite jokes: An American and a Russian are having an argument, back in Cold War days. The American says, "I live in a free country—I can march past the White House and yell, 'Down with Reagan!'" The Russian says, "Big deal. I can march past the Kremlin and yell, 'Down with Reagan!'"

I notice a trait in my fellow journalists, too—those from the U.S. We have many opportunities to question foreign leaders, about anything (e.g., problems in their own countries and in their own foreign policies). But the questions from Americans tend to be invitations to bash the Bush administration. They have almost a goading quality. The gist of these questions is, "Hello, I'm Betty Brown from the *Chicago Herald-Gazette*. Isn't it a shame that George W. Bush is such an idiot?" And the foreign minister—or whoever—says, "Why, yes, as a matter of fact, it *is* a shame that George W. Bush is an idiot."

Still, one of the points of Davos is to blow off a lot of steam. It's a bit of therapy, in a way. The gab sessions may constitute a kind of release—because, in the final analysis, these opinions and denunciations matter little: Power comes down to the little twanger in the Oval Office. And talk is essentially all that these others—including American Democrats—have.

It falls to some of us to meet with a high official of Communist China. As we chat, I can't help thinking of the Nancy Astor question. According to legend, when Lady Astor met Joseph Stalin in the Kremlin, she said, "Pleasure to meet you. When are you going to stop killing people?" But this Chinese official is affable and sincere, and all the questions are polite and encouraging. No official from Taiwan, it seems, has ever been invited to Davos. Too bad. They've got officials from the Iranian regime here! And from Saddam's!

In due course, we meet a bevy of Latin Americans, starting with Álvaro Uribe Vélez, the new president of Colombia. There can hardly be another head of state with greater challenges on his hands. The country has long teetered on a precipice, assaulted by guerrillas and drug lords. Uribe seems filled with a sense of mission. Twenty years ago, his own father was killed by terroristic thugs. To say that he has a feel for the overall world situation—post-9/11—is to put it mildly. As for Mexico's President Fox, he strikes me as Reaganesque—in his person, that is. He is tall, imposing, and handsome. He's quick with a wink or a grin (or a grimace). You can see him on a horse. And yet, politically, he's something other than Reaganesque. His complaints about the U.S. are surprisingly de rigueur for a leader known as independent and imaginative.

But the real star of this show—certainly in the days following Mahathir of Malaysia—is Luiz Inácio Lula da Silva, or simply "Lula." Sorry: "Lula!" Brazil's new chief is a one-named wonder, like Madonna, Cher, and—more to the point—"Fidel!" He is accorded a hero's welcome and rouses his audience with a zingingly socialist speech.

And on we go, with five-year plans, ten-year plans, and just plain plans. The best "plan" of all, of course, is to ensure freedom and the rule of law, letting people and peoples determine their own destinies. But, gosh, it's more fun to plan! At the opening session, the president of Switzerland called the Annual Meeting at Davos "the most important party in the world." When the hour comes to leave it, everyone's a little sad, truth to tell. But leave it we must, Committed to Improving the State of the World—or at least committed to returning next year!

2004

. . . [One star at this year's Annual Meeting] is Mohammad Khatami, president of Iran—or "the Islamic Republic of Iran," as we're evidently forced to say. He is our Moderate Mullah, the great hope for reform in Iran, however forlorn or misplaced that hope is. When he enters the main hall of the Congress Center—heart of the World Economic Forum—he is greeted rapturously. He floats across the stage in his black robes and headwear, smiling benignantly, executing little bows. In his speech, he quotes—get this—Hume, Weber, and Hegel. A neat trick, huh? He also inveighs against propaganda, although I'm slightly amused to see that his bio lists him as having been Chairman of War Propaganda for Iran—war propaganda, no less.

He also tries a definition of politics, something about a combination of the ideal and the possible. I think of Hubert Humphrey: "Politics is the art of the possible." Mullah Khatami and HHH, peas in a pod?

Give a cheer too—a genuine cheer—for Olusegun Obasanjo, president of Nigeria. This is a Great African Hope, legitimately. Obasanjo is one of those ex-military men trying to make their countries safe for democracy, in his case a country that happens to be half Muslim, half Christian. Obasanjo says that he has read the Koran and the Bible from cover to cover, and sees little to choose between them, so similar are they. (Good politician, Obasanjo—and he just may mean it.)

He is for streamlining, debureaucratizing, modernizing; for openness, transparency, accountability—all that good stuff. No wonder the Bush administration is so high on him. And when asked about the ongoing agony of his continent as a whole, he says that Africa must lift itself—note *itself*—out of poverty: "Africa has to progress so as not to be a permanent problem to the world, and to itself." He declares that the first requirement of progress is "political will," on the part of Africans. The matter of Western assistance is far down his list. He is not a blamer, Obasanjo. By the sound of him, he's a realist.

What seems less real, however, is talk of poverty by the usual suspects. You know them: those princes of international conferences, talking in international-conference-ese. "Social justice" is maybe their biggest shibboleth, and the biggest shibboleth on the planet. James Wolfensohn, president of the World Bank, speaks at length about poverty, and the obligation of the rich to help the poor. Generally absent is any consideration of what makes rich, and what makes poor: such matters as freedom, the rule of law, hard work. If the Third World desires the prosperity of the First, should it not emulate some of the practices that made the First rich to begin with?

Carly Fiorina, CEO of Hewlett-Packard—or HP, as it's now known—is here, and she assures the assembled that the "fundamental objective" of her company is "to do good," "to be a good international citizen," not "to make money." When she says "to make money," she makes it sound so *dirty*. I find myself wishing, not for the first time, that businessmen would be a little less defensive and a little more self-confident. Does HP want to do good? Fine. Then let it invent and manufacture products that people need—or want, or that make their lives better—and sell them at affordable prices. That's doing good, baby.

Not to be more pro-HP than the CEO of HP . . .

INDISPENSABLE?

The man of the hour—[Bill] Clinton and Khatami aside—is Pervez Musharraf, president of Pakistan, who has arrived in the Alps fresh from two attempts on his life. In his remarks, and bearing, he is the picture of sang-froid. Questioned about these assassination attempts, he says the following (and I paraphrase): "I fight al-Qaeda and the Taliban on our western border. I deal with Kashmir and extremism on our eastern border. And I'm fighting extremists and terrorists in the middle of the country. So I step on a lot of toes. As for the assassins, I consider them occupational hazards. Fortunately, I have nine lives and I haven't used them all up yet." I wonder how many of the rest of us would be so cool.

Musharraf's persistent theme at the Meeting is "enlightened moderation." His hope for the Islamic world is that it will "reject extremism in favor of social and economic development." He conveys that the current struggle is basically one within Islam. Who will win out? The moderates and the modernizers, or the nuts? Abdullah, King Hussein's kid, who now runs Jordan, says the same: that this is no clash of civilizations—the king is not a Huntingtonian, and neither is Musharraf—but a crisis of Islam. Musharraf says that the Muslims need essentially three things from the United States: that it "heal" the Palestinian–Israeli conflict, Iraq, and Kashmir. Oh, is that all? Why not throw in the common cold, just for kicks? . . .

Also here are Iraqis, who perhaps feel awkward among so many hundreds who opposed their liberation. They strike defiant notes, hopeful notes—defiant because hopeful, really. The most prominent Iraqis are Hoshyar Zebari, the foreign minister—the one who told off Kofi Annan and the United Nations so splendidly in December—and Adnan Pachachi, the octogenarian member of the Governing Council. Pachachi is a wise, learned, dignified man, a reminder of what the Arab world was (in part) before sadists and fanatics with guns took over. His exile was long, and he is lucky to see his country have a second chance. Hoshyar Zebari is a Kurd, a former militant in that movement. He speaks of an Iraq for all Iraqis, not just a brutal elite. The spring in the step of these men is unmistakable.

There are several Saudis here, including Prince Turki al-Faisal al-Saud, the Kingdom's ambassador to London. Everyone is extra-nice to him, asking him, for example, whether his country's work is made harder by the attempt of Big Bad Bush to impose "American-style democracy" everywhere. No one thinks to ask him something like this: "Mr. Prince/Ambassador, the penalty for the crime of possessing a Bible in your country is beheading. Do you think that could be reduced to, say, the amputation of three limbs, or the burning of half the body?" One bright moment comes when Lord Carey of Clifton, the former Archbishop of Canterbury, mentions that it would be nice if there could be a church in Saudi Arabia, one day. The ambassador-prince responds that, if only Christians would accept Muhammad as a prophet, they could go to mosques to pray. Oh, well.

THE YANKS WEIGH IN

Americans are represented by a slew of cabinet members, including John Ashcroft, who keeps coming to the Meetings, no matter how reviled he is. Introducing him, David Gergen calls him "the point of the spear" in the American anti-terror war. Getting to the microphone, Ashcroft quips, "I thought the spear was pointing at me." He goes on to give a thoughtful and eloquent speech about public corruption, and takes a variety of questions, including one on the prisoners at Guantanamo Bay. This is a big subject at this Meeting: those prisoners of the U.S. The feeling is that any one of us, at any time, could be plucked from the street and tossed into a cell at Gitmo. Yes, there is tremendous concern for prisoners in Cuba—only the prisoners are not Castro's innocent ones, but America's guilty ones. To say again: Oh, well.

The lead American is Vice President Dick Cheney, making only his second trip abroad since being sworn in. At a reception the night before his speech, he remarks that Davos is okay, but "not as good as my valley in the Grand Tetons"—a touching display of loyalty. In the Congress Center, his speech justifies America's present course, and notes and pays tribute to our many allies. In the last few days, I have met a lot of those allies: including Spain's dynamic foreign minister, Ana Palacio, and the president of Poland, Aleksandr Kwasniewski, and the extraordinary and outspoken Vaira Vike-Freiberga, president of Latvia. One morning, the *New York Times* publishes a Maureen Dowd column describing America's allies as "a gaggle of poodles and lackeys." They don't seem it. Not at all.

When Cheney is finished, he's asked several questions, including a de rigueur one about Guantanamo, and one about the Paul O'Neill book, in which the ex-Treasury secretary dumps mightily on the administration. Cheney says, "I guess I'm not the best personnel officer in the world"—for it was he who urged Bush to appoint O'Neill. Indeed, Bush "put me in charge of the search for vice president," and look how that turned out!

The Grand Mufti of Bosnia, no less, rises to thank Cheney "for what you have done in Bosnia and Herzegovina. Please, Mr. Vice President, convey to the American people that we will never forget that you came to Bosnia to help us survive as Muslims in the Balkan peninsula. We will never forget that. We didn't have oil [in this, he is addressing the Davos audience], you didn't have an interest to gain. You came to Bosnia-Herzegovina to show your credibility and your sense of morality."

Cheney thanks him, as well he might. Then he leaves Davos to go to Rome, where he'll meet with Silvio Berlusconi, another of Maureen Dowd's "poodles and lackeys." Would that there were more of them. But even at the Annual Meeting of the World Economic Forum, it's plain to see that there are enough.

2005

. . . [At this year's conclave], you have your heads of state, your foreign ministers, your titans of business, your intellectuals (pseudo and real)—but you also have Sharon Stone, Angelina Jolie, and Richard Gere. Davos is pretty swell as it is, but with movie stars: wowza.

You may wish to know how Sharon Stone looks. Answer: great. Really great. Oughta be in pictures. And Angelina Jolie? I don't see her, but someone who knows someone I know does, and his testimony is, "She's actually unphotogenic. She's so much more beautiful in person, it's not even funny."

Sharon and Richard (Gere) are the marquee attractions at an Opening Day luncheon, and the topic is AIDS. Before she begins to speak, Sharon—Miss Stone, I suppose I should say—gets a serious, actress-about-to-address-something-grave look on her face. She swallows a little. She begins, "I really don't belong here, with all you smarty-pants. I don't have your education, and probably not your world experience, although I have a certain experience. But . . ." It is the most masterly downplaying of expectations I have ever seen. Right out of the Speaker's Handbook, Chapter One.

The gist of her remarks is that AIDS is readily solvable, but that "greed and arrogance stop us." We—we richies—simply don't want to spend enough, simply don't care enough. We are stingy and callous. The actress concludes, "If we just stopped arrogantly killing people all over the world, and channeled the money into AIDS, we would have a solution."

I imagine that "arrogantly killing people" is an allusion to America's War on Terror. I think for a minute about that phrase, *arrogantly killing people*. What a perfect way to describe the work of the Taliban and Saddam Hussein's regime! But this sort of thinking doesn't fly in Hollywood, and it doesn't much fly in Davos. I have said it before: There are many people—I keep encountering them, and reading them—who would rather homosexuals be stoned to death than that they be liberated by George W. Bush and the U.S. military. The latter is the greater indignity.

The atmosphere in Davos is not quite Durban—I refer to that hate-America, hate-Israel jamboree in South Africa, days before September 11—but it slides that way. Bush's name is mud, the War on Terror's name is mud. It's sort of assumed that you—that we all—will consider Bush a moron, and his administration a tragedy (if not a crime). The Davosers seem to be waiting it out until Hillary—one of their darlings—wins in '08. The administration has not sent any high-level officials to the meeting this year. (My apologies to labor secretary Elaine Chao, who is present.) Last year, they sent Cheney, and the year before that, Powell. This year, they haven't bothered—and it's hard to blame them. Whether they could have much effect is doubtful. Then again, nothing ventured . . .

To observe the American abroad—especially the American journalist abroad—is always a hoot. Many need to prove themselves more anti-Bush than thou, as though to assure the Euros that they're not Fox News–watching Bible-thumpers. Speaking of Fox News, the very name is a kind of obscenity, like *neocon*. Al-Jazeera is quite accepted (and there are several representatives here); Fox is the network non grata. You should see a major liberal reporter (American) explain to a major Middle Eastern editor that "if you really want to understand the American mindset, you've got to watch Fox News"—because the hicks from the sticks drink it in all day long, ending up drunk on propaganda. Beautiful.

The Bush administration does have its defenders, however: Tony Blair and John Howard. Blair gives a speech concentrated on aid to Africa and global warming, but he spends the first part of it explicating and hailing Bush's [second] inaugural address. He doesn't have to: He could just go to the safe stuff (because everyone at Davos agrees about Africa and global warming). But, not for the first time, he shows spine. The inaugural address is cited as "evidence of the 'neoconservative' grip on Washington," Blair says. "I thought progressives were all in favor of freedom rather than tyranny." The room is silent, rebuked. As for Howard, he is loose, confident, Australian to the core—and he basically tells the anti-Americans to stick it.

One of the more peculiar panels is chaired by Graham Allison, former dean of the Kennedy School of Government. It is on nuclear nonproliferation, and one of its guests is the foreign minister of Iran. (Read that again, if you have to.) The foreign minister, Kamal Kharrazi, says that the United States created al-Qaeda for the purpose of destroying the Iranian government. I'm perhaps not the only one who thinks, "They've done a lousy job of it, if so." Also on this panel is Mohamed ElBaradei, chief of the International Atomic Energy Agency. At one point, the moderator, Mr. Allison, says he wishes to speak "as an American." You see, our government, before the Iraq War, said Saddam had nukes, and ElBaradei said no, and our invasion proved the U.S. wrong, and ElBaradei right. Funny, but that's not the way I remember this recent history—and what government in its right mind would invade a country armed with nukes? But preemption seems too difficult a doctrine to explain to learned people.

CARTER'S COMPETITION

The big American kahuna, of course, is not Graham Allison, and not even Sharon Stone, but Bill Clinton. He sits on a panel dealing with aid to Africa, along with Blair, Bono (the rock star), Bill Gates (Microsoft), and the presidents of South Africa and Nigeria: Mbeki and Obasanjo. The moderator of the session, French anchorwoman Christine Ockrent, wheels on Clinton, demanding to know why America is so stingy when it comes to foreign aid (did you know we were?). He answers, "Because no one will ever get beat running for Congress or president" by failing to espouse such aid. I have complimented Clinton's Davos performances before—in general, he's pretty good abroad—but he is a bit shameful here. Then it gets worse.

Clinton says, "The White House has just announced another $80 billion for the war in Iraq, and we could take half of that" and solve all of Africa's problems. The crowd whoops and cheers. This is a cheap political technique: to say, "Instead of spending money on X, we ought to spend it on Y." If Clinton thinks we should spend more on foreign aid, he should say so. And if he opposes our efforts in Iraq, he should say so. But to spite the war while calling for more aid to Africa—cheap.

I think of what may be my favorite political cartoon of all time. (I'm sorry I can't credit the cartoonist, because I can't remember who drew it.) In the first of two panels, Tip O'Neill has his arm around Reagan, and he says, "Do you know how many hot school lunches your $100 million in aid to the contras would buy?" In the second panel, Reagan has his arm around the Speaker, responding, "Yes, Tip—half as many as your $200 million in aid to Ireland." (Young people will have to be told that, when Reagan wanted to spend money on the military, or on any aspect of the Cold War, Democrats would say how many "hot school lunches" you could buy with the same money. It was a perpetual tic of the 1980s.)

But Clinton isn't through yet: He says that anyone who complains about corruption in African governments—who expresses caution about handing over money to these governments—"should be put in a closet, so no one has to listen to [him]." That, too, elicits whoops and cheers. And it is an odd thing for a democrat to say. Some of us believe that Carter is our worst ex-president ever (the opposite of the conventional wisdom). But the Arkansan is nipping at his heels.

Well, we can count on John McCain, right? Less than I would have thought. At a dinner for journalists—that's his best audience: journalists—McCain takes up the subject of the Guantanamo Bay prisoners. They are Davos's favorite prisoners, those other prisoners on Cuba—innocent, democratic guests of Fidel Castro—not rating a peep. McCain is a "try 'em or release 'em" man. (He actually puts it in exactly those terms.) How you try terrorists nabbed on the Afghan battlefield, he does not venture to say. He does say, "Even Eichmann got a trial." Wrap your mind around that, will you?

His worst moment comes, however, when an Arab journalist rises to ask him whether "the neocons are still controlling policy in Washington." This is a golden opportunity: a chance to dispel a pervasive, somewhat sinister myth. But instead of dispelling the myth—that Bush is a puppet of foreign-policy Fagins—McCain more like reinforces it. He says, "There are always power struggles in Washington." Sometimes you're up, sometimes you're down. But Bush is feeling "more secure" in this second term—which implies that an insecure Bush could have been manipulated by others in the first. "Have I done a good enough job ducking your question?" the senator asks. The questioner—a bold, flashing-eyed lady—looks vindicated in her suspicions.

What American have I come to praise? Any? Try Barney Frank, the Democratic congressman from Massachusetts. On a panel, he and I spar over Bush's inaugural address—he disdains, I like—but he is gung-ho on the protection of Taiwan, and on holding the Chinese Communists to account. He won't hear anything about "Asian values," or "different styles of democracy"—democracy is democracy, he says, certainly in its essence. As the discussion continues, a distinguished Englishwoman who heads a "peace-research institute" in Stockholm says that China and Iran are two countries that don't worry her. Oh? wonders Frank. Which do? The answer: "Saudi Arabia, Syria, Iraq, Israel." "*Really?*" replies Frank. "You're more worried about Israel than about Iran or China?" But of course! One must remember what continent one is on.

Later in the week, Frank is on a different panel, this one concerning the media. A co-panelist is Eason Jordan, chief news executive of CNN. I am not present for this session, but I hear about it, from journalists and others, and many people are abuzz. Jordan has either stated or implied—accounts vary—that U.S. forces in Iraq target journalists for murder. Yes, murder. Barney Frank won't let this glide by: *Whoa, whoa, whoa, he says. What did you say? This is a deliberate policy? Your network has reported this, right?* Well, no, actually. Jordan starts to backpedal—he has gone too far, despite the enthusiasm in the room for what he has said. An odd thing about attending Davos is that liberal Dems such as Frank, Sander Levin, and Ed Markey can come off as John Foster Dulles. The context is everything.

FACES IN THE CROWD

Numerous at the Annual Meeting are Arabs, but I don't see many democrats or reformers. Wouldn't it be thrilling if Saad Ibrahim—the sometime Egyptian political prisoner—attended? I see lots of officials, and, of course, those Jazeera reps. One of them explains that her network must refer to suicide-bombers as "martyrs," because the Arab public would stand for no less: You see, Palestine is under occupation, and these bombers have no choice; hence, they are martyrs. I wonder what language is left over for their victims.

A star of the show is Saif al-Islam al-Qaddafi, son of you-know-who. He is the heir apparent, and a Great Arab Moderate—at least, that is his reputation. Handsome and urbane, he is a figure to reckon with. Over coffee with journalists, he says that he considers terrorism in Iraq "legitimate"—because this terror is "resistance" to "occupation." After all, Kofi Annan has declared the U.S.-led war illegal. America, continues the young man, has robbed Iraq—and, by extension, all Arabs—of "dignity and honor." And these are "very important to us." Fascinatingly, he holds that Arabs have lost all their wars against Israel because Israel is a democracy, while the Arab states are not. It will take democracy to improve Arab prospects. Quips an Israeli at the table—though somewhat nervously—"May you never have democracy." For the Palestinians and the Israelis, Qaddafi envisions a single state, on the model of South Africa. This is the "final solution," he says. Oops.

Toward the end of the coffee, Qaddafi is asked about the Holocaust, and the widespread Arab denial of same. The room tenses. Qaddafi begins—very, very hesitantly—"I'm not a historian, and I don't know all the facts." Uh-oh. One can see where this is heading. But he sort of catches himself and allows that "it is incorrect to deny the Holocaust." Why? Because the Soviets liberated Auschwitz—"We didn't learn about [the Holocaust] from the Zionists or the *New York Times*," but from the Red Army. So, again, "to deny the Holocaust is incorrect." The Davos official with us says, "On that conciliatory note . . ." Extraordinary: that an admission that the Holocaust occurred—because the Red Army said so—should be "conciliatory." But there you go.

If there's a man of the hour—and there is—it is Victor Yushchenko, the new president of Ukraine. He wears his opposition on his face, disfigured by poisoning. By a murder attempt, to be plain. It is an unbelievably noble face, and Yushchenko is an immensely dignified presence. Speaking to a packed auditorium, he wears an orange tie—symbolizing the Orange

Revolution—and carries an orange folder. (The latter is perhaps overkill.) He begins by quoting a bit of what he calls ancient Ukrainian wisdom: "If you struggle, and God is with you—if the Holy Will is with you—you will win." Who knew that Yushchenko was a kooky theocrat?

His main point to the crowd is that Ukraine is a European nation, longing to come home to Europe. At a lunch the next day with journalists, he makes similar points. And he is wonderfully candid: "My country is a deeply corrupt country." He has a message for investors, and anyone else doing business in Ukraine: "Do not offer bribes to anyone." In fact, you can enter a new line, when you do your accounting: "Saved expenses on ungiven bribes to Ukrainian officials."

As the first course is served, Yushchenko offers a toast: "I wish you prosperity in all your endeavors. I wish you physical and moral health. [A striking phrase, that.] And may you have a white angel sitting on your left shoulder, taking care of you." Then he claims that the toast—the act of toasting—originated in Kiev, centuries ago. At the time, the most common means of eliminating one's opponents was poison (!). So you clinked your glasses hard, causing drops from both drinks to spill into the other.

Everyone chuckles, warmed and amazed. At Davos, there is a lot of what Clare Booth Luce called globaloney—but there is also inspiration, and we have just had a strong dose.

2006

. . . I have to mention Kofi Annan, because he swans around like an emperor. His entourage disrupts things wherever they go. This is notable, because it is unusual in Davos: This is a place where you bump into world leaders all the time—I mean, literally, in hallways, staircases, lobbies. But the secretary general of the U.N. moves amid a small army. At one point, I sort of get in the way of this army, and I'm pushed aside by an enormous bodyguard. It's like I'm made of Kleenex or something. To add insult to injury, the bodyguard is . . . a woman. Huge, hulking—maybe the largest woman I have ever seen. Not fat and not unattractive, but just . . . big.

In any case, Annan is a royal presence at the Annual Meeting (and there's plenty of real royalty here, too!). The endless corruption around him seems not to have made a dent—not in these parts.

I should probably say something about the businessmen, for the World Economic Forum—as its name may suggest—started out as a fairly modest business club, before it morphed into an all-encompassing behemoth. Bill

Gates is here, sort of the leader of the pack, and that Texas upstart, Michael Dell. Also George Soros—though it's tough to tell whether he's more a business-world figure or a political one. Probably more the latter, by this time. And then there's Richard Branson—Sir Richard Branson, actually: playboy, adventurer, genius entrepreneur. Evidently, he pals around with Clinton (Bill, not Hillary), and they strike me as a pair made in heaven.

CHINESE, INDIANS—A GERMAN

Every year, the Annual Meeting has a theme, and some subthemes as well. Among the subthemes for 2006 are the emergence of China and the emergence of India. There is a robust presence from each country. Pity there's no presence from Taiwan, a free China, a plucky, endangered democracy. But there are protesters on the fringes of Davos, and not the usual, anti-globalization protesters, either: These are anti-Communist Chinese, raising banners, and raising quiet, civilized hell. The sight of such protesters does a heart much good.

The theme—the main theme—of this meeting is "The Creative Imperative." And that is the subject of the keynote address, given by Angela Merkel, the new chancellor of Germany. Klaus Schwab—the founder and executive chairman of the World Economic Forum—introduces her. He notes that, in the early 1990s, Merkel was a "Young Global Leader of Tomorrow." That's a category here in Davos. And look at her today! Dr. Schwab's system has, manifestly, worked.

I doubt you've ever seen a more unassuming-looking leader than Merkel: plain, ordinary, a real hausfrau. But when she opens her mouth, she is nothing short of extraordinary. She hits repeated notes of freedom: freedom for business, freedom for the individual, freedom for all. Her speech is essentially Reaganite, or Thatcherite. This is surprising, or at least it is to me: I always thought she was what we on the American right would call a squish—you know, sort of a German Nancy Johnson (congresswoman from Connecticut). But no—not by the evidence of this speech. Merkel sounds like a woman who grew up in a Communist country. Which, of course, she did.

Early on, she quotes her great predecessor, Ludwig Erhard, who said, "I want to prove myself by my own efforts; I want to meet the risks of life myself; I want to be responsible for my own fate. You, the state, must see to it that I'm in a position to live this way." She laments that Germany, like much of Europe, has been hamstrung: by regulation, taxation, fear. She begs her listeners not to be afraid of positive, liberalizing change. "Freedom is an elementary good for mankind," she says.

Now, this may seem Simple Simon to you, my dear American reader. But it is astonishing—and super-refreshing—out of a European leader's mouth. (Not counting the Reaganite knights of the East.) At the end of her speech, Merkel quotes James Watt—no, not President Reagan's interior secretary. That would be asking too much. The father of the steam engine, who knew the value of invention, and of perseverance. That is the spirit that Merkel wishes for today.

She may not succeed in her aims, opposed as she is by the powerful forces of conservatism and reaction. But if anybody can get creaking European machinery moving, just a bit—it's this lady, I wager. We must watch her.

STAYIN' ALIVE

Always extraordinary at the Annual Meeting is President Musharraf. I've been with him on maybe four occasions now, and he is amazingly chipper—bright, eager, cheerful—for someone with such a miserable job (one that comes with regular assassination attempts). Musharraf talks about a variety of topics during a coffee with journalists: the recent earthquake in Pakistan; the perpetual problem of Kashmir; the War on Terror. He emphasizes that terrorism and extremism are two different things: Terrorism, you can meet by force; extremism, however, is a state of mind, "and you can't fight it militarily." But you can try to treat it, before it bursts into violence.

Someone asks why Pakistan—and India, for that matter—should have an A-bomb, and Iran, not. Musharraf responds that the only reason to have a nuclear weapon is to deter aggression. And "I don't see a threat to Iran." What about A. Q. Khan? someone else asks. Musharraf has much to say about his country's atomic salesman. But he begins with, "He has affected very adversely the name and reputation of Pakistan." And what about the Israeli–Palestinian conflict? Well, for one thing, "who would have thought that the whole Islamic world would be praying for the recovery of Ariel Sharon?"

In due course, the room grills him about the recent American raid on al-Qaeda—on Pakistani territory. Wasn't this a violation of Pakistani sovereignty? say the journalists. Doesn't this injure the pride of the nation? How can you let Imperial America run amok? Musharraf reflects and says, yes, Pakistan condemns the American raid. Yes, we are jealous of our sovereignty. But what about al-Qaeda and other foreign terrorists on Pakistani soil? Don't they count as violators? And the United States is helping us be rid of them! Pakistan has captured Sudanese, Chechens, Uzbeks,

Arabs . . . If you want to talk about precious Pakistani sovereignty—why don't you ever consider them?

It may be my imagination, but I think that Musharraf sort of shames the room.

He later appears on a panel with other leaders from the Muslim world. The subject is what you might call the general crisis. Musharraf maintains that there is no conflict whatever between Islam and modernization. What there's a conflict between is Islam and Westernization. According to Musharraf, the Islamists are above all obscurantists: They love to equate modernization with Westernization. It isn't so, he says—and don't let them get away with it.

President Karzai is on this panel, too, and he is elegant in his cape, as always. He argues that Islam and democracy are not only compatible: They are practically best friends. Islam embraces equality, individual participation, protection for the unprotected, "what we would today call human rights." He says that, for many years, Islam was "one of the most advanced forms of human existence." But then something happened, a horrible halting, even a reversal. And this reversal itself needs to be reversed. When Karzai goes on in this vein, he sounds exactly—exactly—like Bernard Lewis, dean of our Middle East scholars (and author of *What Went Wrong?*, along with other important and true books).

Adorning this panel is Queen Rania of Jordan, probably the most beautiful woman in Davos—and one of the most beautiful in the world. She is a queen out of fairy tales. She speaks beautifully too, and sensibly. When she inveighs against the Islamists, she notes that they combine a "Stone Age mentality" with "21st-century technology." And that combination is responsible for much of our sorrow. It needs to be combated, she says, by humane Muslims (such as herself)—that is a calling.

A subsequent panel deals with international security, and it includes Mike Chertoff, our homeland-security chief. The most delicious moment of this hour comes in the Q&A, when a lady stands up and goes on about "root causes." Why do you focus so much on the "symptoms," she says, at the expense of the all-important root causes? Chertoff answers, "We focus on the symptoms because the symptoms kill you. And our first obligation is to make sure people don't get killed." He then speaks eloquently about root causes, and how to address them. But his initial answer—"The symptoms kill you"—lingers in the mind.

Chiming in is the markedly intelligent and articulate Gijs de Vries, counterterrorism coordinator of the EU. He says, "I am uncomfortable with this notion of 'root causes,' because it suggests a nice, lineal relationship between a cause and terror. The more we explore, the more we find that no such simple relationship exists." But, to be sure, there are problems that feed terror: lack of good governance, for one. Lack of freedom, really. This sort of talk acts as a tonic in the Davos air.

THE IRAQIS

The last full day of the meeting features a panel on Iraq. There are several Iraqis here, and they are the pride of the conference, as far as I'm concerned: working to establish a country under maddeningly trying circumstances. And doing it for the region, and the world, more widely, too. One of those Iraqis is the deputy prime minister, Ahmad Chalabi. He is disarmingly serene, ever smiling. He seems unaware that the multitudes—certainly the foreign-policy and media elites—hate his guts. Or maybe he's smiling because he knows it's so. He parries all questions deftly and convincingly.

Another impressive Iraqi is Humam Hammoudi, the constitution-drafting sheik. In his black robes and turban, he expounds on the principles of government: It must not be "dirigiste"; it must be "pluralist," which Saddam's regime certainly was not. "There was no freedom of action, no freedom of speech." But the new Iraqi constitution "recognizes the rights of all." Hammoudi says that, in his conception of society, there is no law forcing women to wear a veil; then again, there is no law prohibiting them from doing so.

In sum, this Middle Eastern cleric sounds like an American civics teacher, circa 1965—before the New Left took over and everything went sour.

A third impressive Iraqi? He is Barham Salih, the minister for planning and development cooperation. He talks of the peculiar position of his country. "I regret that Iraq is in the heart of the Middle East—it would be better if we were on a remote island of the Pacific." Under Saddam Hussein, he says, "Iraq was the North Korea of the Middle East." And now "we have the chance to be the South Korea." Won't the world give Iraq some space, as it did Germany, Japan, Korea? Borrowing a strong American cliché, Salih says, "Failure is not an option." On the contrary, "failure would be a catastrophe, not only for Iraq, but for the entire region."

The last word on the panel—or one of them—belongs to Jack Straw. He is the British foreign secretary, smart and snappy. "Don't freak out," he tells the audience. "Don't freak out at the involvement of religious parties in

Iraq." In Europe, lots of countries have state religions. They have Christian Democratic parties and so on. France is a very rare secular state. When home secretary, Straw himself swore in bishops. Again: "Don't freak out." Yes, don't.

BILLY J.

Taking center stage on this last day is Bill Clinton, Davos's annual heart-throb. Many remark that, this year, he looks unwell: thin, haggard, with big bags under his eyes. That may be so—but I have no doubt he can still do some damage.

Sharing the stage, Klaus Schwab asks him what his three greatest concerns for the world are. Clinton says, first, "climate change." He has become a big, big global-warmingist. Did you know that? It doesn't appear to be lip service, either (though this is very much a global-warmingist crowd); he has the look and sound of a true believer. Global warming, says Clinton, "has the power to end the march of civilization as we know it." He seems to be out-Gore-ing Gore.

His other two concerns are inequality and cultural divides. As a friend of mine points out, no terrorism, no nuclear proliferation. These don't crack the top three. Strange.

Later, he chides President Bush for not engaging with Hamas or the Iranian mullahs. Clinton does this indirectly, but clearly. He says that we should not be "scared" to talk to anybody. Thing is, Bush isn't scared—he makes such decisions out of strategic calculation. He may be wrong (though I doubt it), but it has nothing to do with fear. Remember Arafat? (Short guy, bad skin, terrorist.) During the eight years of the Clinton presidency, he was the most frequent foreign visitor to the White House. After the *Karine A*, Bush cut him off—cold. That wasn't necessarily wrong.

Anyway . . .

At the end of their colloquy, Schwab asks the 42nd president what advice he'd have for the 44th (i.e., the next one). "It could be someone in this room," says Schwab (he appears to mean John McCain); "or it could be someone you're married to." Clinton quips, "I better make it clear," given recent events [the push for gay marriage in the United States], "that Senator McCain and I are not married." After the riotous laughter dies down, he says something about doing hard and necessary things—like Bush hasn't?—and "the passion for climate change" that Hillary and McCain share.

Whatever.

I duck into a men's room, and here a graffito has been scrawled: "F***
Bush." (Only there are no asterisks.) Yes, the theme this year is "The
Creative Imperative." But, in one sense, the theme every year—from 2001
to 2009—could be what is spelled out in this john. Although this year has
seemed notably reasonable, to me. Probably depends on what you cock
your ear to.

2007

Every year, the Annual Meeting of the World Economic Forum has
a theme, and this year it's "The Shifting Power Equation." But the
real theme here in Davos is global warming—it's on everyone's
lips, and everyone's brain. There are 17—17!—separate sessions on global
warming, or, as you're supposed to call it, "climate change" (because
"climate change" covers everything under the sun). You have "The Security
Implications of Climate Change," "The Economics of Climate Change,"
"The Legal Landscape Around Climate Change," etc., etc. And if you're
still feeling climate-changey after hours, you can attend the Climate Change
Nightcap, whose hosts include Shimon Peres, the Israeli elder statesman,
and Claudia Schiffer, the German supermodel.

Oh, yes, the great and the good attend the meeting, as always. We have
heads of government, like Tony Blair, Angela Merkel, and Lula (just one
name, please), and captains of industry, like Bill Gates, Michael Dell, and
Sergey Brin (the Google guy), and some wild cards, like Anatoly Karpov,
the chess master, and Maxim Vengerov, the violinist, and Robert Trent
Jones Jr., the golf-course architect.

But no matter who you are, you are deeply, deeply concerned about
climate change, or at least pretend to be. Early on the first day, I find myself
on a panel with Arianna Huffington, the Greek-born writer and doyenne of
the L.A. Left (which is to say, of L.A.). She says that debate about global
warming has now ended. Television no longer pits one person arguing for
global warming against another person who says no-sir. The question is
settled.

I'm afraid I agree with this, although I don't think the shutting off of
debate is to be welcomed. A little dissent here would be helpful. The global-
warming people have scored a great lexical and rhetorical coup in calling
skeptics, or dissenters, "deniers." This is parallel to "Holocaust deniers,"
and, speaking of them, they are reigning supreme in Tehran, openly planning the second holocaust, even as they dismiss the first. I am hardly the

first to make this point, but it should be made more often. And, in Davos, there is much more concern about climate change than there is about a nuclear Iran.

Indeed, you hear, from many lips, that Ahmadinejad is just a blowhard, that he has no real power, that the relevant mullahs are more reasonable, and the subtext is that Iran is being used as an excuse for Bushian-Zionist belligerence.

There is no doubt that conservatives and other misfits are on the defensive about global warming. I see a column in the *Financial Times* by Gideon Rachman, and the column is headed, "How Iraq and climate change threw the right into disarray." Here is its second paragraph:

> From 1979 [when Thatcher was elected] to 2004, the right won the battle of ideas in the western world. Conservatives triumphed because they got the two big issues of the era right: they were in favour of free markets and against communism. But now the right is in disarray because it has found itself on the wrong side of the two dominating issues in contemporary western politics: global warming and the Iraq war.

Is that so? Iraq aside, I wonder whether global warming will be the death of us, and I mean, in a political sense. Between panels, I talk to a World Economic Forum official, good-natured. I express some disbelief at all the attention to climate change. It seems to me a spectacular example of groupthink, not to say hysteria. He says—good-naturedly—"Oh, come on, Jay! Don't tell me you still don't believe in global warming!"

Well, "believe" is an interesting word. I relate to him a little personal history: I grew up during the coming ice age, when we were in for a terrible freeze—there would be cross-country skiing in Miami. We also had the population scare. Remember population? It was the global warming of its time. Our planet was being choked off, because there were too many people—too many mouths to feed, too many bodies to care for. Population was the enemy. And responsible people were having only one child, or, preferably, none. The phrase "population control" was on everyone's lips.

Then, sometime in the 1990s, I began hearing about a "birth dearth." And—come to think of it—I haven't heard the phrase "population control" in years.

My point is, I, and my contemporaries, came of age in a period of environmental alarums—various and successive ones. And, for the rest of one's life, that makes one a wee bit wary of jumping on bandwagons.

Besides which, you have to wonder about the motivations of some global-warmingists, who seem as eager to punish the "greedy" American economy as they do to nurse the earth. I suggest the following, when talking to my World Economic Forum friend: It could be that global warming is, in fact, an impending disaster, and that mankind must take radical steps to save itself—just as everyone here says. Or it could be that future generations will look back at us and say, "What in the world were they smoking?"

BLOVIATION AND DESERTIFICATION

But no such skepticism—"denial"—is heard in Davos's Congress Center, where a German conservative, Chancellor Merkel, has the floor. She cites the Club of Rome, approvingly—I had always thought of them as something of an embarrassment—and warns of encroaching "desertification." But she says that, to be green, you don't have to "limit growth"; you need only to grow responsibly. And I think this is one of Merkel's best characteristics: responsibleness.

A few hours later, I moderate a dinner panel, and the theme is storytelling—specifically, "Getting the Message Across with a Story." Several business moguls speak of advertising, and how to do it effectively, but many people want to talk about global warming. They can't help themselves; the subject is simply unstoppable. One participant says he knows of someone who fears he will never be a grandfather . . . because of global warming. Not because the Jihad will snuff us all—well, many of us—but because of global warming. I find it hard to keep still, marveling at the fever that has gripped this illustrious audience. It seems a millenarian fever.

And someone has forwarded me an article, via the Internet: It was published in *The Journal of Affective Disorders*, and it is titled, "Global warming possibly linked to an enhanced risk of suicide: Data from Italy, 1974–2003." Really.

As the dinner winds down, I am grateful to one mogul who says all the right things about global warming—meaning, the politically correct things: This is a terrible threat, we all must adjust our behavior, etc. But he adds, as a kind of coda, that, last year in Davos, the big topic was bird flu—and "I've heard no mention whatever of it this year." Quite so.

Behind the scenes, some of us doubters—skeptics, deniers—get together and compare notes. An official from the Bush administration says that she has been accosted on global warming wherever she has gone. The line is, "Why is the United States letting the rest of the planet burn?" She has not disguised her heterodoxy, or heresy. One fancy lady said to her, "But haven't you seen Al Gore's movie?" The Bushie said no. The fancy lady said to her, not with malice, but like she was a pathetic, ignorant child, "Oh, you must learn, dear. I'll send the movie to you."

A friend of mine says that he attended a crowded session on the meeting's (official) theme: "The Shifting Power Equation." Global warming was not among the topics to be discussed. And the participants revolted—forcing the moderator to include it. They then judged global warming to be the single most important issue facing the world. They did this by actual votes.

As my friend tells it, one brave woman, perhaps Indian, got up and expressed amazement that Davos should be so "enamored" with global warming. And that word "enamored" provoked gasps. I would like to find the woman and throw some kind of medal around her neck.

A third doubter—more like a realist—tries to find a comparison to the 1930s. Today, the obvious and global danger is militant Islam. The wolf is not only at the door, it is in some cases already in the house. And yet the world—certainly as represented by Davos (a pretty good representative)—is obsessed with global warming. In the 1930s, as the Axis built, were they perhaps worried about the quality of lakes?

In due course, we all receive a bulletin in our Davos e-mail: CLIMATE CHANGE: MAKE DAVOS GREENHOUSE GAS NEUTRAL. The notice goes on to say,

> Climate Change is at the centre of our discussions [no kidding], and you can act now. Please consider compensating your greenhouse gas emissions related to participating in the Annual Meeting in Davos.
>
> This is possible with 1 click at any kiosk or at the Davos Climate Alliance desk.
>
> Many thanks for your help.

In other words, you can contribute to an anti-global-warming fund in order to relieve your guilt at having used, for example, an airplane. I put this in Jacksonian terms (I mean Jesse, not Andrew): *Don't be emittin' without remittin'*. Later, Kevin Schmiesing of the Acton Institute will write that these remissions remind him of the indulgences of old, whereby you washed away your sins by your financial contributions. The notorious German friar Johann Tetzel (allegedly) said, "As soon a coin in coffer rings, the soul from purgatory springs." (*He* was a rhymer too, at least in English translation.) And more than a few of us have described a certain kind of environmentalism as a modern religion.

BRITISH ACCENTS

Have you heard, by the way, about Prince Charles? He canceled his trip to Klosters—the next town over from Davos—where he has long skied. The reason was, he wanted to reduce his "carbon footprint." The prince would be a natural Davos attendee, in that he has declared global warming "the biggest threat to mankind."

Speaking of Brits, David Cameron, MP for Witney, is here. He is the new leader of the Conservative party, and thus a successor, in this sense, to Winston Churchill. And he is a firm, firm global-warming man (Cameron, I mean, not Churchill). He tells a group of us journalists that the "big question" is, "Are we going to act before it's too late?" He believes that Americans are finally waking up to this threat, as evidenced by the reelection of Arnold Schwarzenegger in California. Obviously, Cameron is not a student of American politics, or at least of California. But Schwarzenegger is an American hero in Davos, because he has made all the right moves on global warming. Cameron further says that enlightened politicians are trekking to Norway, "to see the importance of climate change firsthand." He himself has, and so have Hillary Clinton and John McCain.

As he continues with us, Cameron speaks of "green growth" and "green outcomes" and "gas-guzzling cars." No one in this town—this pretty Swiss village up in the Alps—can out-climate-change him, and that's saying something.

But the British prime minister, Mr. Blair, does fairly well. Giving a speech in the Congress Center, he calls global warming "a moral cause." And he, too, praises Schwarzenegger, and also McCain, who is in attendance. McCain, says Blair, has "driven the agenda forward in the United States." Soon, McCain himself is onstage, driving the agenda forward. He says, "I bring you good news"—and that news is that Congress will probably act quickly on global warming, and that the administration is coming along, too. "I freely admit to you that it's very late and may not be enough, but I think that for the first time there may be some action on this very important issue."

My sense is that McCain's global-warming passion is almost enough to make Davos forgive him for the Iraq War. In this, he is not unlike Tony Blair.

Some days later, the lights go out all over Europe, but not in the way

Sir Edward Grey meant: Frenchmen make the Eiffel Tower go dark, Italians make the Colosseum go dark, and Greeks make their parliament go dark, all in protest of climate change. I can't help feeling we're witnessing some large, end-of-the-world cult. The splendid British journalist Charles Moore, writing in *The Spectator*, has the same feeling:

> Now and again, one reads little news stories about sects which, believing that the end of the world is nigh, gather on a hill in Montana or in a car park in Geneva to await the Last Day, and then, when nothing happens, rather sheepishly go home. The same embarrassment threatens those environmentalists who say that if we fail to reverse greenhouse gas emissions now, it will be too late (latest Sunday Times headline: 'Last warning: 10 years to save world'). What will they do when the planet stubbornly refuses to die?

They will go on to the next cause, with nary a backward glance. Another Davos, another theme.

Davos-in-the-Desert

Chronicles from the Middle East

Each May, the World Economic Forum has a "regional meeting" in an Arab coun-try—Jordan or Egypt. Here are two reports, published in National Review*: The first is from the Dead Sea, Jordan (2005); the second is from Sharm El Sheikh, Egypt (2006).*

The Dead Sea, Jordan

T he World Economic Forum usually meets in Davos, Switzerland, but they have left the Alps to meet in the lowest place on earth: the Dead Sea. They hold a three-day conference here, focused on the Middle East. They first held such a conference in 2003, shortly after the U.S. invasion of Iraq. They wanted to "seize the moment," and that is, in fact, the motto of Davos-in-Jordan: "Seizing the moment."

On the first day, there is a panel on Iraq, featuring three participants in the new democracy: the foreign minister, Hoshyar Zebari; the speaker of the parliament, Hajim al-Hassani; and the governor of the Central Bank, Sinan al-Shabibi. Zebari is a former Kurdish militant, and he has sometimes been electrifying on the world scene. At the U.N. a year and a half ago, he told off that body memorably: "The United Nations as an organization failed to help rescue the Iraqi people from a murderous tyranny that lasted over 35 years. Today we are unearthing thousands of victims in horrifying testament to that failure." Talk about speaking truth to power.

Zebari leads off the panel by giving a speech: He notes that it has been only eleven months since the U.S. transferred sovereignty to the Iraqis themselves, "and we are not an occupied nation, but an emerging democracy." On January 30, "millions of citizens defied death" to cast their ballots, and people are "hungry for democratic progress." Unfortunately—and outrageously—"the insurgency has persisted." What are "Saddamists and foreign fighters" doing? They are trying to "foment civil war, undermine the new government, and spread terror," for the purpose of "destroying our vision." But the Iraqi people "will not have their future dictated by the atrocities of an extreme few."

The foreign minister cautions that his country is "not yet ready to be self-reliant." But "the faster we can build our military and security capacity, the sooner the multinational forces can go home." A free, self-governed Iraq is realizable, and is, in fact, taking shape before our eyes: It is not "an intangible ideal."

We then hear from Hassani, the parliamentary speaker. He begins by saying that he agrees with Zebari on every point, except one: "And we can disagree. This is the new Iraq, a democracy!" (The disputed point is this: Zebari has said that Sunnis, regrettably, chose not to participate in the Iraqi elections; Hassani argues that they had no choice, given the violence in their areas.) Hassani, like other Iraqis, asks for patience, as national pioneers go about the hard work of "building a new republic."

As for Shabibi, the central banker, he speaks of "moving from a war economy to a peace economy, from a command economy to a market economy, from a highly centralized system to a federalized one." He comports himself with the sobriety you might expect from a central banker.

Then it is the turn of a non-Iraqi, Lakhdar Brahimi. An Algerian and longtime U.N. official, he may be said to represent the Old Guard of Arab politics, an elite whose world is now uncertain. Brahimi starts in on Iraq, elaborating its failings. He takes care to talk about "our Iraqi brothers," but his annoyance at them is obvious: They have upset the regional apple cart, making it tough for the Old Guard.

About the insurgency in Iraq, Brahimi says, "There is no doubt that there are foreign elements." And "there is no doubt that there are some acts of terrorism: What else do you call bombing a mosque, or targeting an imam?" But—and you knew there would be a "but"—"there are definitely very legitimate aspects of the resistance that exists there, and it is terribly important, even if some of the manifestations are unacceptable, that you find a political solution to the problem."

This is an extraordinary moment. Despite his provisos, a high official of the U.N. has called the insurgency "the resistance." And he has called "aspects" of it "very legitimate." Furthermore, he has described the bombing of mosques, and the targeting of imams, as terrorist—but what about attacks on policemen, parliamentarians, voters . . .?

As Brahimi speaks, the look on the Iraqi faces is priceless: Zebari, in particular, is appalled.

When all the panelists have spoken, the moderator announces that there is a short time for questions from the audience. The period is dominated by Amr Moussa, sitting in the middle of the first row. Even more than Brahimi, the secretary-general of the Arab League—and the former foreign minister of Egypt—is the personification of the Arab Old Guard. And this panel, with these Iraqis, has clearly rattled him.

Moussa makes a dramatic statement about "Palestine." (Big cheers from the audience.) He praises an American professor on the panel for his criticisms of the Bush administration. (The professor nods appreciatively.) And then he turns to the Iraqis, to hector them about Sunni participation in the new process.

One thing is clear at this conference: The Iraqi Sunnis are the most important minority in the world (and maybe the most important group of people). No other minority is given the time of day—during Saddam's decades, the Kurds, Christians, and others certainly were not. But the Old Guard has an almost desperate investment in the line that, as long as any Sunni unhappiness exists, the Iraqi democracy is illegitimate.

Hajim al-Hassani has a response to Moussa. He agrees that the Iraqi government must do more to "reach out" to Sunnis. (Zebari and other officials say the same.) But then Hassani allows that he himself, the speaker of the parliament, is Sunni. He does not like to identify himself this way, however: because "we should all be Iraqis, without adherence to sect or ethnicity." Here we have a declaration of true Arab liberalism.

One other thing is crystal-clear at this conference: Today's Iraqis are like the Israelis, held to a higher standard than anyone else in the region.

The whole Middle East may swim in tyranny, autocracy, and corruption—but democratic Iraq is scrutinized for perfection. They must dot every "i" and cross every "t." The Iraqis had better get used to it. And it seems they already are.

Shortly after this panel, I witness a scene that may be of interest. The room for a subsequent session is full to bursting, and many of us are unable to get in. "It is full," we are told. But along comes Amr Moussa, who brusquely and wordlessly pushes his way through, despite the (weak) protestations of staffers and guards. I hear a voice behind me quietly say, "They should tell Mr. Moussa it is full." It is Sinan al-Shabibi, governor of the Central Bank of Iraq. In this small episode, I think I see the arrogance and presumptuousness of the Old Guard, in contrast with a new, aspiring spirit. Which will prevail?

APPLAUSE LINES, NON-APPLAUSE LINES

A leading American is Robert Zoellick, the deputy secretary of state, who gives a big speech, in a big hall. He talks about the winds of change in the Arab world (the phrase is Macmillan's, about Africa, but it is frequently heard here)—and he has a tough crowd. After all, many of the attendees are the very elites whose death knell Zoellick, and others, are sounding. Who wants to listen to his own obituary—especially when it is unflattering?

Zoellick begins, "We are here in a time and spirit of transformation. For some, the metamorphosis is invigorating—a welcome 'Arab Spring.' For others, the changes are alive with possibilities, but also pose uncertainties. A number are confused. . . . There are doubters, too, and even those whose opposition has hardened into enmity." His speech is sensitive, nuanced, and determinedly humble, but it is also principled. He ends by saying that "America will reach out to the countries of the Mideast as a respectful partner—for peace, development, democracy, and hope. We will celebrate your success, because it will be our good fortune, too."

And the crowd? Its applause is the very definition of tepid. In fact, it is barely applause at all. The room is eerily quiet. I don't think I've ever heard a speech receive such an awkward response—and, in my view, it damns the multitude in the hall. Even Dick Cheney, two Davoses ago, in Switzerland, got more applause. (But not nearly as much as Iran's president Khatami.)

Laura Bush is another leading American. She, too, gives a stirring speech, and stirring in more senses than one: She rocks a boat. Like Zoellick's, hers is a "change" speech, which cites the experience of the ex-Soviet bloc. Mrs. Bush even quotes Vaclav Havel, who once told her,

"Laura, you know, democracy is hard because it requires the participation of all the people." Comments the First Lady, "All people—men and women—want to contribute to the success of their country. And all people—men and women—must have the opportunity to do so." Those are not words to curry favor with the traditional Arab political class.

When she has finished, the man beside me gives an insta-critique, to his companions: "Arrogance, ignorance, and parochialism." Wrong on all three counts, particularly the last: Whatever else it may have been, this speech was resoundingly universalist. The man goes on to sniff, "She's supposed to be not very intelligent." Wrong again. Laura Bush has delivered a boffo, nerve-touching performance.

Liz Cheney will do no worse. The vice president and Lynne's daughter is a State Department official, responsible for Near Eastern affairs. Like her parents, she speaks crisply, knowledgeably, and comfortably. She is certainly that way in a session with a small group of reporters—and she is that way on subsequent panels. The first, I cannot attend, but a fellow journalist does, and he reports something extraordinary. At one point, Ms. Cheney said (something like), "I think we should stop mentioning 'Palestine,' just to get a cheap round of applause, and start concentrating on relevant issues of reform." At this point, says my fellow journalist, a couple of men behind him piped up, "She's a lesbian, she's a lesbian."

As it happens, she is not. But she is an excellent spokesman for U.S. policy abroad, and an excellent spokesman for liberal democratic values, too.

THE BIG DEBATE

Liz Cheney next appears in a debate televised by al-Arabiya, one of the Middle East's big networks. The subject is, "What Will It Take to Unleash an Arab Renaissance?" Alongside Ms. Cheney are two spectacularly unbudgeable members of the Arab Old Guard: Amr Moussa and Prince Turki al-Faisal, Saudi Arabia's former intelligence chief, and now its ambassador to Great Britain. Hoshyar Zebari participates, too: He keeps jabbing Moussa by quoting the slogan of the Egyptian opposition, "Kifaya," or "Enough"—enough with your rigidities, enough with your "emergency laws" (which last indefinitely), enough with your stiflings. In turn, Moussa claims that the man in the street does not want wholesale change so much as he wants a lessening of "bureaucracy and red tape."

I have called Amr Moussa unbudgeable—spectacularly so—but it also occurs to me that he, Brahimi, and their like have the opportunity to be great men. They, the Old Guard, can usher in a new, better order, securing their places in history. When the call of the people came, they answered. Or, they can dig in, and be swept away—if, as Zebari has said, a "wave" has been launched that "cannot be stopped."

Prince Turki dominates the Arabiya debate simply by filibustering. (The moderator does not hush him.) He may be no democrat, but he might make a fine Democrat, in the U.S. Senate. Immediately, he plays the Palestinian card, declaring, "The Palestinians must be freed." Nothing can happen until then. For "this is a bleeding wound of 60 years' duration, and it is impacting us negatively." Why the Palestinian situation demands that Saudi Arabia—or any other country—be a police state, the prince doesn't say. They never do.

The most astonishing person on the panel, however, is Bassam I. Awadallah, the Jordanian finance minister. He is young, clear-minded, and bold. You might be listening to a scholar of the American Enterprise Institute. He attacks the "regression of the Arab world," and counsels free markets, democracy, transparency, rights, the rule of law, and opportunity—lots of it. He might as well be Jack Kemp, c. 1978. Awadallah says, "We see Arabs in the U.S. and Europe succeeding. Why can't they succeed here? The answer is that we're not giving liberty to people." If King Abdullah has such men in high places, then he is indeed the reforming monarch he claims to be.

I meet one of his subjects outside the conference. He is a Palestinian, a restless, stifled entrepreneur, and one of his many remarkable observations is this: "We don't have ex-presidents in this part of the world. You in the West have ex-presidents. It would be so nice to meet one! Here, you're president for life. If you're not president anymore, it's because you're dead." Let us hope that, ere long, the Middle East becomes a land of ex-presidents. (Will Abu Mazen be the first? My Palestinian contact is doubtful.) At least a place where so wondrous a species is possible.

Sharm El Sheikh, Egypt

. . . For the last three years, [the World Economic Forum's Middle East conference] has been held in Jordan, on the Dead Sea. But this year [2006], the conference has come to Sharm El Sheikh, the famous Egyptian resort on the Red Sea. There is much discussion here about which site is preferable. I can't help framing it this way: Better Dead than Red, or better Red than Dead?

Egypt is proud to have snatched the conference away from the

Jordanians (who, regardless, will get it again next year). And this is a critical period for Egypt. Almost every day, the country makes worldwide news, most of it bad: democrats jailed; judges threatened; protesters beaten up. And terror still strikes. In April, bombs went off in Dahab, just north of here. About 20 people were killed. And last summer, about 65 were killed in Sharm El Sheikh itself. In the last year and a half, some 120 people have lost their lives to terror in this Sinai region. But Klaus Schwab, founder and leader of the WEF, refused to cancel or move the conference. For him, he explained in a memo to participants, it was a matter of solidarity, defiance, and determination.

If anyone was deterred from coming here, it doesn't show: Attendance is robust and enthusiastic. And security is tight, not to say stifling. You can hardly turn around without being checked, whisked, or otherwise examined. Indeed, you can hardly turn around. We are in a mini-police state—but I imagine most people are reassured, even as they, as we, chafe.

Egypt may be having problems on the political front, but they are making big strides on the economic front. And they're happy to trumpet it. On the roads to Sharm El Sheikh's Congress Center—specially built for this conference, in under eight months—are signs: "Egypt: Open for Business"; "Egypt: Open for Competition"; "Egypt: Open for Growth"; "Egypt: Open for Change." These are not empty claims, for the facts back them up. Tariffs, taxes, and other barriers are falling; GDP is rising (by a projected 6 percent this year). Inflation has been subdued. Foreign investment is pouring in, and the Egyptians are asking for more.

This burst of liberalization has been overseen by what the country's publicists call a "dream team," a "handful of reformist ministers." They are led by the prime minister himself, Ahmed Nazif. He is the face of what you might call the New Egypt.

Old Egypt, of course, is represented by Hosni Mubarak, president and boss of this country for 25 years now. He officially opens the conference, with a speech in Plenary Hall. Though nearing 80, he seems in blooming health, full of vigor. He looks like he could go on and on, through elections fair and foul. He also looks like a thug—unkind to say, but true. It's not his fault if he looks like a thug; it's his fault only if he acts like one. His speech to us is nothing much: full of platitudes, banalities, and little jabs at the United States. But he concludes with some nice poetry about the Sinai, and its importance to history: Moses and the Ten Commandments; Joseph and Mary's flight with their baby; and so on.

Mubarak takes no questions—but Nazif certainly does, over breakfast with journalists. The prime minister is stubbornly optimistic about his country's future. "There's no turning back," he says—no turning back from the reformist course that Egypt has set. "Some people are scared of change. But I'm not." A full transformation will take time, to be sure. "But we have time. We're not in a hurry." For years, Egypt was "a closed environment," but now it's opening up. "We're not used to it." Habits of democracy will have to be developed. But they will be. Overall, Nazif's message to this inky assemblage seems to be, *Have a little patience, and a little perspective.*

And, like many another politician or government official, Nazif complains about the media, particularly the foreign media. They portray Egypt as a glass half empty, he says. They ignore the good that has been accomplished. And, in any case, "we're filling in the other half!" A reporter attending the breakfast asks about presidential succession: Will Gamal Mubarak, now a big in the ruling party, replace his father? Nazif bristles a little at this. "We are an institutional country," he says, with established processes for such matters. *This is not a banana republic,* he seems to be saying (or a fig-and-date republic). He goes on to say—if I may again interpret—*If Gamal becomes president, it will be in the manner of Bushes and Adamses, not in the manner of the Syrian Assads.*

COMPUTER SCIENCE AND POLITICAL SCIENCE

Later, I interview Prime Minister Nazif one on one. He's an impressive-looking man, in his mid-50s, tall and solid, with a full head of gray-white hair. And he speaks like the intellectual he is. His Ph.D. is in computer engineering, from McGill, and his research was in computer vision. "What's that?" I ask. "In the simplest possible terms, it's making computers understand pictures, images." And "it is a beautiful science." A mark of Nazif's interests and inclinations is his membership in the American Association for Artificial Intelligence.

He spent most of the 1970s in the West, returning to Egypt in the early 1980s. As he tells it, the country had experienced the '73 war, the peace accords with Israel, the assassination of Sadat, the rise of Mubarak—"and we were all thinking, 'Where do we go from here?'" The message from the government was clear: Rebuild the country. And Nazif was intrigued with the idea of using computers to lift the country up, or aid it in some way. He worked in academia, business, and government. He co-founded the Internet Society of Egypt, among other organizations. And he served as Egypt's first-ever minister of communications and information technology, from 1999 to 2004. Then he became prime minister.

When you listen to Nazif—and I have heard him on several occasions—you think that you're listening, not to an Egyptian official, much less the prime minister, but to an oppositionist, a dissident. With his talk of markets, democracy, and freedom in general, he sounds like a chair-holder at the American Enterprise Institute. I ask whether he considers himself a liberal democrat. He says he does. And "one thing I've always done is challenge what exists. I'm pro-change, and I'm a builder by nature. Some people criticize in order to find faults; I criticize in order to remove faults, and that's a big difference."

I ask what he thinks of socialism. "It depends on how you interpret it. Socialism in the sense of Egypt in the 1960s, I'm completely opposed to. Because the idea then was, everyone is equal irrespective of their efforts, irrespective of what they give in return. But if by socialism you mean that we have to have some sort of redistribution of wealth to help the poor—yes. Again, though, how do you help the poor? How do you make them change their status? If you give a subsidy with no expectation of return whatsoever, you're just encouraging the poor to stay poor. There's no incentive. But if you demand something in return—self-improvement—then you are getting somewhere."

Inevitably, our talk turns to Ayman Nour. He is the democrat who challenged Mubarak in last year's presidential election, and who now finds himself in jail. The charges are absurd, or so many of us find: They have to do with forging signatures on petitions. Nazif gives no quarter on the subject of Nour. Speaking at length, he insists that the judicial process has taken its course, with no interference from "the government" (meaning, Mubarak et al.). He further says that, though the Nour case is a cause célèbre in the West, it is no such thing in Egypt, because it is better understood here. (Indeed, I find evidence at the conference that Arab journalists are put out by attention to Nour. One woman sniffs that the case has been "taken out of proportion." Like others, she is most interested in why Americans aren't hollering about the Egyptian government's treatment of the Muslim Brotherhood, the Islamic fundamentalists.)

And how about Judges Mekki and Bastawisi, who were subjected to disciplinary hearings when they pointed out fraud in recent elections? Again, Nazif makes no apologies, saying that appropriate procedures have been followed in these cases, too, and that they have been badly misunderstood in the West. He maintains that the judiciary has long enjoyed independence in Egypt. "This is not something that must now materialize."

Nazif is not at his most encouraging on these highly sensitive matters. But, on a range of issues—such as Sudanese refugees, the Palestinians, and

America's role in the Middle East—he is thoughtful, if not entirely persuasive. I think of a phrase popular, or once popular, in American culture: "as good as it gets." Nazif and his allies are as good as it gets in the Arab world, at least among ruling elites. What can an outsider do but root for them?

As I'm parting from Nazif, I remind him of the breakfast discussion about presidential succession. Would he himself be interested in running for the post? Like most any other politician, he smiles and demurs: "I think it's too early even to think about something like that, but I don't see the presidency in my future." I think of another American expression, this one from politics, which I adapt: Egypt could do worse, and probably will.

SONS AND SAVIORS

Will it be Gamal Mubarak who succeeds the incumbent? He is head of the policy secretariat of the National Democratic Party, or NDP. He has just come back from meetings in Washington, including with President Bush and Vice President Cheney. At Sharm El Sheikh, he talks a very good game—a reformist and liberal game. Whether he is for real remains to be seen. I have observed Saif Qaddafi, the Libyan dictator's son, at Davos. Gamal seems the more promising character, I must say. And Robert Zoellick, the deputy secretary of state, weighs in interestingly. In a session with journalists, Zoellick says that Gamal seems intent on overhauling his party, while "what I will politely call the more traditional NDP leaders I have met" exhibit no interest in change whatsoever.

Zoellick notes that the Egyptian government has made a number of "mistakes" lately. Like what? "Like beatin' people up," when they have taken to the street to protest. But, he says, we should not overlook the changes that have already occurred in Egypt. Five years ago, citizens would not have demonstrated—it was too dangerous. It's still dangerous, manifestly, but less so. And a major Egyptian businessman, M. Shafik Gabr—chairman of the Arab Business Council—says something memorable, in a panel discussion. "When I talked about privatization 15 years ago, I was called a traitor to the Egyptian government." Not anymore. Privatization is the policy of the government. And Gabr may be the first person I have ever heard use the phrase "trickle down" underisively.

On this same panel is another apostle of change in the Arab world, or rather, the Muslim world: Shaukat Aziz, the prime minister of Pakistan. He is a smooth, smooth operator, a former executive with Citibank. He remembers being "an armchair critic, sitting in my office in Manhattan"—but he went home in the late 1990s, to participate in his country's hoped-for revival.

He lists the elements of a country's success: "liberalization, deregulation, privatization, transparency, improvement in governance." This is sweet music, and you could call it the World Economic Forum's theme song. Aziz spends some time on resistance to change—"a natural human trait." In his telling, the entrenched interests in Pakistan have resisted change fiercely. But they have not been successful. "Globalization is upon us," says Aziz, "it is not a cliché." Having said that, he cites a cliché, and a true one: "Globalization is a tidal wave: You can either ride it, and go far; or resist it, and be swept away."

He emphasizes the need to explain to people what you are doing, as you go. In many parts of the world—Reaganites will have a hard time believing this!—"deregulation" is a dirty word. People interpret it to mean an abdication of governmental responsibility, a laying bare to predators. This mindset must be amended. And the prime minister tells several illustrative, and amusing, tales from Pakistan. For example, do you know what it's like to inform the communications ministry that it is no longer running the phone company? *What? Not running the phone company? But that's why we exist!* That is why they used to exist.

Yet another reformer is Bassem Awadallah, formerly finance minister of Jordan, now director of King Abdullah's office. He makes the point that, "if reform were easy, it would have happened a long time ago." Governments don't reform on their own, out of some moral awakening; they do so when crisis is upon them. And that opens the way for "a culture of meritocracy, the rule of law, freedom of expression." Some countries are moving faster than others (and some are not moving at all). But the pace of change matters less than that "the train is moving in the right direction." Like many others at this conference, Awadallah stresses that governments must make room for legitimate parties, a legitimate opposition. People must have choices other than the status quo or radical Islam; otherwise stalemate or disaster is ensured.

BEHOLD AN ARAB BLOG NETWORK

One bright morning, I moderate a panel on new media in the Arab world, and it has a title: "The Revolution Will Be Televised." There is no doubt that new media are making a difference in this region. Cable television is prominent, yes. But the Internet is increasingly a factor, and so are cellphones: on which text messages are sent. These messages fly around the Middle East (for purposes abhorrent or wholesome). Young journalists are present at this discussion, and they are encouraging: moderate, enlightened, reform-minded. The best of them have no desire to work for state-run media, and no desire to be bosses in them. They want independence, and a multiplicity of views.

A Palestinian says that taboos are being broken down. For example, in the territories, it used to be impermissible to discuss sexual harassment; now it is possible. And it's a pleasure to be introduced to iToot.net. This is an Arab blog network, run by a young Jordanian, Ahmad Humeid. On this network, freedom of expression is not merely an abstraction; it's a fact. And this is something fairly new under the Middle Eastern sun. Governments can always crack down, and some of them already have. But people, in general, are getting bolder. Someone on the panel suggests that there is all too much information on the Internet. Someone else counters, "Too much information! The thought of it makes my heart glad!"

What there is no debate over, really, is whether Muslim countries can become democratic. Rightly or wrongly, it is taken for granted. One afternoon, I decide to put the question to the Turkish prime minister, Recep Tayyip Erdogan. "Some people say that Islam and democracy are incompatible. What do you say?" Erdogan answers that his response need not be verbal; he can simply point to his country, Turkey. "We are a country in which 98 percent of the people happen to be Muslim. And we are a democracy, in which the rule of law, secularism, and the fundamental rights of liberty are held dear." Erdogan makes the common observation that Turkey is "a bridge between the Arab world and the West." And since many eyes are on Turkey—if I'm interpreting the prime minister correctly—"we are condemned to success." An arresting phrase, that: "condemned to success." Turkey cannot afford to fail, he seems to be saying; it needs to set an example.

Bob Zoellick says that, when he comes to the Middle East, he can sense the old order breaking down. He had the same kind of feeling in the last years of the Cold War. Not that the two situations are identical. He paraphrases Mark Twain: History doesn't repeat itself, but sometimes it rhymes. And Zoellick has little patience for those who say that democracy has no chance here. He recalls being a teacher in Hong Kong, in 1980. And his Chinese students said, "Oh, democracy's not for us—not for us Asians. They have democracy in Japan, in some odd form. But that's an exception." And now, says Zoellick, we see democracy in South Korea and Taiwan. And, to varying degrees, in other East Asian countries as well. "I don't believe anyone is immune to democracy."

Depending on what you choose to emphasize, you can say that the Middle East is going brilliantly, or going abysmally. We are all under the influence of the last person we have met, or the last article we have read. The truth is, all the good news is true; and all the bad news is true. Which is more important, and which will win out in the end? In Egypt, there are bright faces, like Ahmed Nazif, and that "dream team." And then there is Muhammad Abd al-Fattah, a member of parliament, who recently said that "9/11 was carried out by American agents," so that "Bush would have a pretext to declare war on Islam." But I have a feeling that these people—the authoritarians and the nut jobs—are yesterday's men. And that the liberals, or relative liberals, I have met are tomorrow's men. That train that Bassem Awadallah mentioned? Whatever its pace, it seems to be moving, and not backward, either.

About Sudan

What has been done? What can be done?

President Bush saw the movie *Hotel Rwanda*, twice. This is the movie that depicts the genocide in that country, and in particular the refusal of the U.N.—which had troops there—to lift a finger. Deeply interested, Bush arranged to meet the man on whose personal story the movie is based: the hotel manager, Paul Rusesabagina. They talked in the Oval Office, mainly about Darfur, Sudan. Rusesabagina said that what had occurred in Rwanda was occurring in Darfur. Bush said that he would do all he could to stop it. It is too late for some—for up to 400,000—but not, of course, for all. We may say that it is never too late to stop genocide while there are people left standing.

It was last September 9 that the United States—in the person of then-secretary of state Colin Powell—declared that genocide was taking place in Darfur. There is now some debate across the government about whether genocide continues, although there is no doubt that extensive murder and other terror are ongoing. Is the U.S. doing everything it possibly can? The answer is no, if the possibilities include the dispatch of American troops to the region. But this is not counted as a possibility by anyone of influence. Short of troops, it may well be that the U.S. is doing all it can. The United Nations is another matter, as usual. It is hard to see how the Darfur genocide will stop anytime soon, absent much greater concerted action.

One genocide has already occurred in Sudan, of course—that is, it has already been completed. That is the genocide in the south, where Christians and animists live (or lived, we might note grimly). The Sudanese government wiped out 2.2 million, and displaced another 4.5 million. This regime, in Khartoum, is almost unfathomably evil. Led by President Field Marshal Umar Hassan Ahmad al-Bashir, it is a military dictatorship that is also Islamist and terrorist. According to Freedom House, "the government of Sudan is the only one in the world today engaged in chattel slavery." Khartoum waged a long "jihad"—Bashir's word—against the south, featuring a terror-famine of the kind seen in Stalin's Ukraine and Mengistu's Ethiopia. Bashir blocked the humanitarian relief that the West sought to give; the U.N., and the United States, under President Clinton, did not push very hard. Bestialities in the south included bombings, razings, concentration camps (called "peace villages"), and rape after rape after rape. That may be what is hardest about inquiring into Sudan: the constant rape, that great and ancient weapon of terror.

Sudan is so bad, it expresses an almost comic-book evil. In the southern genocide, one hospital was bombed five times; children were beheaded in front of their parents; the hungry were strafed as they gathered to await food drops. The government even ran a "death train," in an almost willful imitation of the Nazis.

The West paid scant attention to these events, although some agitated, especially in America, especially on "the Christian right," as it is known. Such Republicans as Sen. Jesse Helms, Sen. Bill Frist, Rep. Frank Wolf, and Rep. Chris Smith were aroused, along with some Democrats, too, such as Rep. Donald Payne and former representative Walter Fauntroy. But mainly the United States, including its media, was uninterested. Nina Shea of Freedom House says that what press coverage existed tended to proclaim "how bad it was for conservative Christian groups to redeem slaves" (which is to say, to buy their freedom). "And every time the famine got bad, there was reporting on that, but it was always in the nature of, 'Isn't starvation terrible?' when the issue was jihad waged against these people." In a white paper, the Clinton administration forthrightly labeled Sudan a "backburner" issue, and the U.S. did not pay serious attention until George W. Bush took office.

In a May 2001 speech before the American Jewish Committee, the new president referred to Sudan's crimes as "monstrous," and said, "My administration will continue to speak and act for as long as the persecution and atrocities in the Sudan last." On the same day, he appointed a "special humanitarian coordinator," to try to ensure that U.S. aid reached its intended beneficiaries. Four months later, on September 6, he appointed former senator John Danforth to be his envoy to Sudan. When Islamist terrorists struck America five days later, the picture changed, dramatically: Khartoum, as an Islamist regime, was nervous. (It had sheltered Osama bin Laden from 1991 to 1996.) When the U.S. invaded Afghanistan, it was more nervous yet. It began to show a certain flexibility.

Working doggedly for about three and a half years, the United States achieved a peace agreement between the government of Sudan and rebel forces in the south. The agreement was finalized this past January. On April 13, a celebration was held in the Longworth Building on Capitol Hill, attended by Sudan activists, activist congressmen, and some Sudanese themselves. All described the mood as "jubilant." In a column, Chuck Colson, the evangelical leader, wrote, "We don't always get to see the results of our work in this life. That's especially true for those who work for human rights around the world." By the terms of the peace agreement, the south will enjoy self-rule, no longer subject to sharia (Islamic law). After six years, it may vote to separate itself from Sudan, although Senator Danforth is one who thinks this unlikely: "If you were to look at [the south], you would not think it could be an independent country. People might vote for that, but this would be a landlocked African country, with no roads."

Danforth reports that President Bush is totally engaged by Sudan: "I can tell you that, not only did the president appoint me as special envoy, he repeatedly talked to me about Sudan afterward. Every single time I went to either Sudan or Kenya for peace talks, I talked to the president in advance, either in the Oval Office or by telephone—every time. He was intimately involved in it." So was Secretary Powell. Congressman Wolf—who has been to Sudan five times—is another who testifies to Bush's interest, knowledge, and involvement. In fact, "I think the president deserves the Nobel prize. And I wanted to nominate him—but with Darfur going on, you just couldn't. I may nominate him later. But with Darfur going on," it would be unseemly.

GENOCIDE II

Ah, yes: Darfur. The genocide in the south is now over, with people there going about the rebuilding of life. For them, it is late 1945. But not for those in Darfur, a western region—their crisis still burns. In the first months of 2003, some Darfur Sudanese rebelled against Khartoum, tired of what they called discrimination and abuse; the government attacked with full fury, unleashing the same jihadist, genocidal hell that it had visited on the south. Darfur constitutes a fifth of the country, containing a seventh of the national population (but—to be grim again—who knows how that fraction stands this week?). The genocide's victims are black-African Muslims, killed by other Muslims who consider themselves racially and culturally superior. Bashir's regime has acted in concert with the "Janjaweed," and here we have a word to enter the lexicon of fear, along with "Gestapo," "Ton Ton Macoutes," and others. The Janjaweed are militias, men on horses and camels, who raid and rape and murder. Government forces and the Janjaweed consider their victims natural slaves, and, when attacking, shout, "Kill the slaves!" When raping, they may crack about making lighter babies. One refugee said a militiaman had claimed, "We kill all blacks and even kill our cattle when they have black calves." As Congressman Wolf and Sen. Sam Brownback reported last summer, after a trip to Darfur, "No black African is safe in Darfur." And "the Janjaweed are employing a government-supported scorched-earth policy to drive [these Africans] out of the region—and perhaps to extinction."

(Please note that most white people could not tell the difference between the "Arab" Sudanese Muslims and the black-African Sudanese Muslims, racially. Such is the mystery of racism.)

Bombed and burned out of their farmlands and villages, the Darfur Sudanese are herded into refugee camps, where they number about 2 million. These places are as squalid and wretched as you can imagine. Observers on the scene speak of a horrible dilemma, faced by the camp-dwellers: If the men venture out, for food and wood, they are liable to be killed, by Janjaweed who ring the camps, waiting for easiest prey; if the women venture out—rape. And the longer the people stay in the camps, the farther out they have to roam (for the food and wood), making life more dangerous all the time.

Darfur has not escaped the attention of the West, as the south for many years had. Our media cover it generously. Secretary Powell visited Darfur, as has Kofi Annan, as has—in the last few weeks—the deputy secretary of state, Robert Zoellick. With justification, Senator Danforth says, "The interest of our government in Sudan is astonishing." He phoned the *Washington Post* to upbraid an editorialist who had argued the opposite. U.S. policy is essentially this: to provide massive food aid; to keep pressure on Khartoum, through sanctions and incentives; and to try to prod international action. Powell declared genocide in September, but administration officials are more reluctant to use the word now, whether in public or in private. On his recent trip, Zoellick was pressed on the question, and he said, "I really don't want to get into debates about terminology . . ." Many have remarked, with some bitterness, that murdered Sudanese hardly care whether they are victims of "genocide" or merely of "crimes against humanity," which is the United Nations' preferred term.

As of the end of April, the U.S. had given $628 million in aid to Darfur, which is more than 50 percent of the world's total. Are Khartoum and its Janjaweed proxies blocking this relief, as they had for months? Reports are indefinite, but the answer seems to be no. There are still truck drivers who may balk at delivering, for fear of their lives, and rebel groups are sometimes as problematic as the forces they oppose. But the bulk of the aid is reaching the hungry. We might ask, however, whether food is enough. One response comes from what may be a surprising source, Kofi Annan. Writing in the *New York Times* on April 13, he said plainly that aid without protection is folly. Annan cited Bosnians, who "watched the aid trucks continue to roll while their neighbors were gunned down in broad daylight. 'We will die with our stomachs full,' they used to say." But food aid is saving many lives, because starvation—whether government-provoked or not—is the primary killer. Nina Shea notes that "the big numbers in the south came from mass starvation, which the government had caused. In a vast rural area—where there are no cities or skyscrapers—you can only kill so many with bombs, guns," etc. (Stalin and Mao racked up their big numbers in this way: through starvation.)

We must now ask whether there is anyone standing between the innocent and the murderous—and the answer is, Precious few. Troops from the African Union are in Darfur, about 2,000 of them, to cover an area the size of Texas. Their number is to rise by autumn (which is a long way off, in the midst of genocide, or quasi-genocide). The United States has assisted this group with logistics—spending about $80 million—and there is now talk that NATO will offer such assistance as well. The United States is pushing for NATO's participation, but not every country is eager. As the Associated Press reported, "France has been wary about NATO involvement in Africa, concerned that Paris's traditional influence could be undermined." That sentence pretty well sums up the French attitude toward Sudan and its suffering.

A LAUGHABLE WORLD BODY

To enlist the help of the U.N. has been an uphill struggle—perhaps that is why internationalists have to turn to the North Atlantic Treaty Organization to address an East African problem. In March of this year, the U.N. imposed some sanctions on Khartoum, but these are light sanctions, nothing like an oil embargo, which would have serious consequences. For the U.N. to move, you need the Security Council, and on that council sit some unhelpful actors: China, which is a huge investor in Sudan, and a huge military supplier; Russia, also a big military supplier (including of Antonov planes and Hind helicopter gunships, spearheads of Sudanese genocide); and France, which has proven itself more interested in thwarting the Americans than in doing right by Sudan. The United States pressed for an African court, to try Sudanese war criminals, on the model of the courts handling Liberia's Charles Taylor, and the Rwandans, and the Sierra Leoneans. But the French, along with other Europeans, blocked this effort, insisting on the International Criminal Court, to which the U.S., of course, is not a signatory. When the ICC referral came to a vote, the U.S. abstained. The Security Council has given the ICC a sealed list of 51 Sudanese war criminals; it would be unwise to bet that anything will come of it.

Frank Wolf is typical of the activist-experts in having little respect for the U.N. in Sudan. He points out that the U.N. was useless in Srebrenica, in Rwanda, and elsewhere, and is merely repeating its performance in Darfur. Senator Danforth, however—recall that he was ambassador to the U.N., following his stint as Sudan envoy—is more respectful of the U.N.'s performance, citing the body's role in the north-south peace. (Whether the U.N. would have done half as much without Danforth's commitment, and Bush's, is another question.)

What is apparently impossible is a U.N. force in Sudan, to protect the innocent. Even a formal no-fly zone—of the sort that saved many Kurdish and other lives in Iraq—is too tough. As Danforth says, "When we were passing resolutions last summer on Darfur, we wanted to talk about at least the threat of sanctions, but we could not pass anything with the word 'sanctions' in it. We had to talk about 'measures.'" If the U.N. shrinks from calling sanctions sanctions, how will it feel about any military intervention? Some have grumbled that a new coalition of the willing should enter Darfur, in the face of U.N. paralysis and African haplessness. If we mean "never again," and are truly sorry for Rwanda (President Clinton apologized), why not such a move? But there is no significant appetite for it; and success, militarily, would not be automatic. Then too, the world's Muslims might do some good, by objecting to the extermination of hundreds of thousands of their co-religionists. But those listening for a peep will be disappointed.

A curious fact about this genocide is that it may be the best known in history. The State Department, the United Nations, and other organizations—official and private—have meticulously documented what has gone on in Darfur. Simply go to the State Department's website, and you will see maps, charts, everything. As many have pointed out, no one in the future will be entitled to claim ignorance. At their Holocaust museum, Yad Vashem, the Israelis display an aerial photo of Auschwitz, taken by Allied forces in 1944. Such photos were revealed by CIA analysts in 1978, and President Carter turned over some originals to the Israelis in 1980. No fundamental mystery is even suggested about Sudan. Various entities keep almost a running tally: In 1985, there were a million Nuba people (from central Sudan) ; today there are 300,000.

We are all perhaps too quick to say "Never again," when never again recurs, again and again. If it is too hard to stop genocide, then we should simply say so, bowing to futility. As Nina Shea says, "The problem with declaring genocide," as the U.S. did last September, "is that, unless you go invade the next day, you're not doing enough. It is almost a deterrent to ever declaring genocide." (The Clinton administration was careful not to use what is called "the G word" about Rwanda, as the U.N. has eschewed it regarding Sudan. There is a Genocide Convention, and uttering that word entails responsibilities.) Shea and many others who are hard-line and heroic about Sudan think that, absent unilateral action, the U.S. government is doing about all it can, and that criticism of President Bush on the Sudan score is political, and empty.

Still, Philip Gourevitch, editor of *The Paris Review*, makes a point. He wrote a book about Rwanda with the arresting title *We Wish to Inform You That Tomorrow We Will Be Killed with Our Families*. He says, "Why not make life miserable for the Khartoum regime? Why not rachet up the rhetoric? Why not mention Sudan every single place you go, stick it to them? Why not stick it to our European allies on this?" Tony Blair, for example, expresses a great interest in Africa. Well, is not Sudan the largest African country (in area)? "Make the issue hot." Make a huge stink at the U.N. "Put lots of pressure on Thabo Mbeki [in South Africa], and on Museveni [in Uganda], and how about the Egyptians? We write them some big checks every year, don't we?" (In fact, the Sudanese regime harbored three men who had tried to assassinate President Mubarak.) "Why not put pressure on our new friend Moammar Qaddafi? Tie up a little foreign aid," do anything and everything at your disposal. This is genocide, after all.

Nevertheless, I maintain that Americans can take satisfaction in the fact that their government is doing as much as it is—even apart from the fact that this is infinitely more than any other government would do. And a range of humanitarian groups have been astounding. Pity that the United Nations, which might be expected to stop genocide, if to do nothing else, is not more capable. But that is the nature of the beast. Recall that Sudan—the government of Field Marshal Bashir, which engages in slavery, which is responsible for maybe 2.6 million dead, and 6.5 million displaced—sits on the U.N. Human Rights Commission. Its term expires in 2007. How many more Sudanese will have expired by then?

—May 23, 2005
National Review

Albania Votes

An emerging democracy, emerges

Tirana, Albania

Years ago, the columnist Charles Krauthammer joked about what he called "the Tirana Index." This was a way of measuring how unfree a country was. For example, election returns out of this capital would tell us that the Communist dictator, Hoxha, had received 98.6 percent of the vote. (You had to wonder about the other 1.4 percent.) The greater a dictator's vote, the more unfree the country was. That was the Tirana Index. Of course, Saddam Hussein, in Iraq, improved on Hoxha by securing a full 100 percent of the vote.

They don't do things like that in Albania anymore. I am in this country with a group monitoring elections. It is headed by Congressman Eliot Engel, a New York Democrat, who is America's foremost politician on Albanian affairs. This is his fifth visit to the country; he will undoubtedly make more. He has long been concerned about Albanians wherever they live: be it in Kosovo, Montenegro, Macedonia, or Albania itself. This is of a piece with his general commitment to human rights. He observes that, if Bill Clinton can be "the first African-American president," he, Engel, ought to be the first Albanian-American congressman.

He has with him a delegation from the National Albanian-American Council, which includes men and women born throughout the Albanian diaspora. They have prospered in America, and wish to help less fortunate people in their ancestral lands. They lend political support, make business investments. They are proud, and in some cases amazed, to see Albania spring back to life.

This country endured just about the worst of Communism, for 45 years. The only situation that compares to Hoxha-ruled Albania is North Korea. Compared with Albania, such Communist states as Poland and Hungary were Gardens of Eden. Hoxha broke with the Soviets in 1961, and with the Chinese in 1978—they were dangerously liberal. No contact with the outside world was permitted. Private use of automobiles was forbidden. In the last five years, there was near famine. This was Stone Age stuff.

Albania is a famously pro-American country—some might say it is notoriously so—and when Secretary of State Baker visited Tirana, when the country first opened up, they kissed his car. Seven decades before, President Wilson had insisted on Albanian independence; many have never forgotten that. And then, in the '90s, President Clinton bombed Serbia, saving the lives of countless Kosovar Albanians. On my first visit to this country, three years ago, a writer said to me, "We are so pro-American, our neighbors sneer at us as 'the Israel of the Balkans.'" I replied—what else?—"Wear it proudly."

And Albanians are quick to point out that they are in Iraq, with the coalition. They may not be committing many troops, but the number is a significant percentage of Albania's forces, and they are "the cream of this country's youth." Not long ago, the prime minister made it clear that Albania will never imitate Spain, and reverse course.

Since the fall of Communism, Albania has struggled to become a democracy. It is succeeding, in fits and starts. For several years, we said that it was the poorest country in Europe, but now Albanians note that Moldova has passed it in poverty. This reminds me of what used to be said in America: Alabamians are grateful for Mississippians. Crime is a serious problem in Albania, and a new threat casts a shadow: that of Muslim extremism. This is a majority-Muslim country, and the Saudis have been throwing some money around. For now, however, Albania stands as an example of a predominantly Muslim country that is willing to fight terrorism and pursue democracy.

In the three years since my previous visit, conditions in Tirana have obviously improved. Decrepitude has been lessened, and enterprise is more apparent. It may be my imagination, but I think the people have a healthier aspect. Even the dogs in the street seem less skinny. Women in gay dresses walk down boulevards, carrying parasols. For a block or two, this could be Rome. Around every corner, construction is taking place. Greater Tirana

can appear one vast construction site. And the old, drab Soviet-style buildings? Albanians are painting them in bright colors, sometimes pastels—you
get a touch, I kid you not, of South Florida.

The main aim, politically, is to join first NATO and then the EU. All parties agree on this. There are lots of parties, too, some 50. The dominant ones
are the Socialists, now in power, and the Democrats. They are led by two
larger-than-life political bosses: Fatos Nano, the Socialist (and current prime
minister), and Sali Berisha, the Democrat (formerly in power). One Albanian
says to me, cynically, but perhaps not inaccurately, that the Socialists and the
Democrats are like two great mafia families. The Socialists are regarded as
center-left, the Democrats as center-right. The Socialists have campaigned on
Continuity and Progress. The Democrats have campaigned on Reform and
Clean Hands—also a 50 percent tax cut.

Tirana is decked out with billboards, posters, and banners, promoting
the various parties and coalitions. The press seems robust, too. Many papers
jostle against one another on the newsstands. An Albanian complains to me,
"You can't trust any of them, they're all biased." But this is true throughout
Europe. Some may even say it's true in the United States.

On Election Day, people turn out to vote, in pretty big numbers—esti-
mates will be around 50 percent. People have their thumbs marked, as in
Iraq, to show that they've voted. When they fill in their ballots, they fold
them, and put them in a large box. As Congressman Engel remarks, no
chads, hanging or otherwise. There are complaints throughout the day:
"Five of us in my family registered, but only three of us are on the rolls,
allowed to vote." "I registered twice, just to be sure, but still they're not
allowing me to vote." It's hard to tell what is unfair play and what is simple incompetence, or confusion. What is encouraging is that citizens care so
much: They want to participate in the new democracy.

The Democrats and their allies say that the Socialists control the electoral process, and tip everything their way. They also say that the Socialists,
who are post-Communists, are really Communists at heart. President Bush
used an interesting phrase in his second inaugural address: "habits of
control." The Socialists, according to their opponents, have yet to shed
those habits. They have not yet learned to deal and govern democratically.

An Albanian who has no use for either major party is King Leka, son
of the late king Zog and his beautiful, Hungarian wife. We visit the king, on
the outskirts of Tirana, and he is not in good shape. His own wife died a
year ago, a bad blow. He himself appears gravely ill: thin, gaunt, ghostly.
He wears hospital clothes, and chain-smokes (elegantly).

Behind his chair stands an Albanian flag. And this rented house is full of books about the royal family, and mementos of them. Leka has an air of tremendous sorrow, but also tremendous dignity. His life cannot have been easy: He was only days old when his family was forced into exile, Mussolini having invaded. He bounced from host country to host country. Now he is at last back in the land of his birth, and he runs his own party, or movement. Some people snort at this sick man who calls himself "king"—but he is probably as patriotic and disinterested as anybody.

When I ask whether he has voted (for this is Election Day), he says the most kingly thing I probably will ever hear: "I don't vote. I am above all political parties, even my own." When Congressman Engel asks what America can do to assist Albania, he answers, "Help us out of this ping-pong game," between Fatos Nano and Sali Berisha. Power has constantly shifted between the two. "Until that finishes, we will never advance."

As of this writing—the counting is slow, and contested—Berisha and the Democrats appear to have triumphed in the elections, meaning that, for now, Berisha, not Nano, will sit in the prime minister's seat. But all of us outsiders, and well-wishers, have a single concern: that procedures be democratic.

It should be remembered, in thinking about democracy across the world, that Albania is a very unlikely candidate—an unlikely candidate for democracy. In their millennia-long existence, they have hardly known self-rule, to say nothing of democracy. And they suffered the deepest, darkest Communism imaginable. In the wild north, blood feuds are still in operation, which confines certain families to their homes, unable to vote. Albania is a challenge. But they are making a go of democracy. Their elections have not been perfect, but they have not been disgraceful, either. The people, by and large, have had their say. And if Albanians can achieve democracy, should we be so quick to dismiss the chances of others, even unlikely others?

The Albanian Americans with me rub their eyes that this country can have even imperfect democracy. As recently as 15 years ago, it was only a mocking dream.

—August 8, 2005
National Review

Solzhenitsyn at Harvard

His words are 'more relevant than ever'

June 8, 2003, marked the 25th anniversary of "A World Split Apart," the commencement address delivered by Aleksandr I. Solzhenitsyn at Harvard University. Harvard staged a conference commemorating the event, to which the below remarks were contributed. (I have shortened them some, to avoid an excess of overlap with other pieces in this collection.) You will see references to "Stephan" and "Ignat"—these are two of Solzhenitsyn's sons, and they both participated in the conference. Also, I might mention that the last line of this speech echoes the last line of Solzhenitsyn's own speech—of "A World Split Apart."

I t's a pleasure to be here, among so many I admire. It's a further pleasure to be a representative of *National Review*. This is a magazine that was pro-Solzhenitsyn before pro-Solzhenitsyn was cool. Is it unquestionably cool now? I think so—cooler, at least.

National Review actually published "A World Split Apart," in its issue of July 7, 1978. When we laid out the title, we had the words "split" and "apart" spaced quite far apart. Aren't we clever?

Like many here, I'm sure, I had the experience not long ago of re-reading "A World Split Apart," for the first time in a very long time. I must say, I found it "more relevant than ever." That's a terrible cliché, but one I feel I can use unapologetically. The speech incorporates many of the things that make Solzhenitsyn great, such as his boldness and his devotion to the truth, certainly as he sees it.

He begins that way, doesn't he? "Truth seldom is pleasant; it is almost invariably bitter." He went on to play his role of truth-teller, no matter whom it discomforts. As Charles Kesler remarked in an essay later, "Solzhenitsyn was arresting because he spoke of the truth as if it were true." Lovely line, and insight, that. Kesler also quoted another great foreign friend of America, Tocqueville, who said, "Enemies never tell men the truth."

I have a little story about Solzhenitsyn and truth—or rather, Solzhenitsyns and truth, because the apples didn't fall very far from the tree. Stephan, you may not know, is a minor celebrity in New York. He made the press—even the tabloid press!—in some scandal a couple of years ago. Stephan took the wrong side in some environmental controversy. By "wrong," of course, I mean anti–"hard green," as Peter Huber might say. One of his opponents chided, "Didn't he learn anything from his father?" Stephan retorted, "Yes—mainly that the truth isn't always popular."

Let it not be said that Solzhenitsyns can't do soundbites.

"A World Split Apart," of course, is a religious speech. Barely into it, he was quoting Jesus: that a house divided against itself cannot stand. No, that wasn't Lincoln, originally. Nor was "a shining city on a hill" Reagan—or John Winthrop, for that matter.

A short while later, Solzhenitsyn cautions against assuming that all peoples strain for liberal democracy, as we know it. No End of History for him, quite. He speaks of terrorism, and whether a free people has the nerve and self-respect to fight it. He speaks of self-sacrifice, alertness to danger, the false ideal of stability (when stability means continued oppression, no boat-rocking from freedom-seekers). You see what I mean by relevance. There are echoes of September 11th—or let us say "pre-echoes"—all over this speech. I thought it was eerie, at times.

Of course, there are some things in Solzhenitsyn's address that are hard to swallow—even for his most dedicated admirers. But all of these things need to be pondered, hard. In the column he wrote shortly after the speech, Bill Buckley said, "Such is the debt of free spirits to Solzhenitsyn that we owe it to him at least to consider anything he asks us to consider."

Perhaps most important in "A World Split Apart" is this business of courage—and its decline. In reviewing the speech, we should remember where we are. Or rather, when we are. Nineteen seventy-eight was perhaps not the West's best year ever. Three years before, the helicopters had taken off from the embassy roof in Saigon—despite President Ford's plea with Congress not to abandon the country that 58,000 Americans had just finished dying to save. This same President Ford, however, had denied Solzhenitsyn admission to the White House. About a year after the speech, the current president—Carter—would be in Vienna, kissing General Secretary Brezhnev (literally). This is the sort of thing that once caused Mr. Buckley to write a column titled, "For Moderation in Osculation." Solzhenitsyn says, "The Western world has lost its civic courage, both as a whole and separately, in each country, each government, each political party, and of course in the United Nations." I love that "of course," before "in the United Nations." For me, it is one of the most priceless parts of the whole speech. I have been studying the U.N. with particular concentration lately, and I am incessantly quoting Solzhenitsyn. If he received royalties, he'd be even richer: *The United Nations is not so much the united nations as the united governments or regimes, no better and no worse than those regimes on the whole.*

I can't help thinking what Solzhenitsyn would have made—indeed, did make—of his comments on courage after the election of Ronald Reagan in 1980. That was a strange and unexpected presidency. And the United States has progressed a long way from the atmosphere of 1978. After the first Gulf War, President Bush the Elder proclaimed that we had "kicked the Vietnam syndrome." Now, we have . . . what? Kicked it senseless to make sure it was dead? [This speech was given shortly after the American military's quick toppling of Saddam Hussein.]

On re-reading this speech, I was struck—as I'm sure many others were—by the speaker's repeated use of the word "evil." It must have fallen strangely on ears at Harvard in 1978. I didn't count the uses in the speech, but there must be, what, eight of them? Ten? A dozen? When Ronald Reagan said "evil," in an important speech during his first term, the roof practically caved in on him. People in all parts of the world denounced him for his simplicity, crudeness, and primitivism. Henry Steele Commager said it was the most embarrassing utterance in presidential history. Today, of course, George W. Bush says "evil," "evildoers," and so on freely. It doesn't sit well with a lot of people, even post-9/11.

I confess that, as I went back over this speech, I was astonished at how true it was. Even obviously so. I kept writing in the margins, "True." "So true." "Still true." "Blindingly true," I wrote once. (I believe this had something to do with the press.) I knew that "A World Split Apart" was one of the most controversial and notorious speeches in modern history. And yet I found it fairly unremarkable. No doubt this says more about me than about Solzhenitsyn's speech.

I'm reminded of a story, which I hope you'll find relevant. It concerns how historical events grow into myth, and get distorted. Stephen Ambrose, when he was doing his biographical trilogy on Nixon, went back and watched The Last Press Conference—or listened to it, I forget which. You remember that this is the press conference that Nixon conducted after he lost the California gubernatorial race in 1962. It is remembered that this was a low point for Nixon, that he was out-of-control, surly—probably drunk.

Ambrose was shocked to discover that, in reality, he had been composed, gracious, "appropriate," as we would now say. The line "You won't have Nixon to kick around any longer" was delivered with a smile and a wink, to appreciative laughter.

Go figure. (And, by the way, those "[expletive deleted]"s in the Watergate transcripts were pretty tame, according to Ambrose.)

There are so many things worth commenting on—let me just make a few points. Side points, you might call them. Solzhenitsyn, of course, is very hard on materialism, as well he should be: Anything that retards or blocks spiritual growth is his enemy, and ours. But I'd like to share with you a rather cheeky anecdote starring V. S. Naipaul. It comes from my friend and colleague David Pryce-Jones, who was there. Not long after winning the Nobel Prize, Naipaul was speaking at a conference in India. During the Q&A, someone stood up and said, "Sir Vidia, we are in the home of the spirit. India has always been the home of the spirit. Don't you think that this materialism that encroaches from the West damages our home?" Naipaul thought for a second and replied—in his inimitable fashion—"I rather like materialism: The poor need it."

A point concerning this business of law, or rather legalism, which provoked so much controversy. It should have been less controversial. Solzhenitsyn says, "One almost never sees voluntary self-restraint. Everybody operates at the extreme limit of the legal frames." Can anyone awake in America for the last many years doubt that this is true—truer than when Solzhenitsyn spoke those words?

And I must say that I see the expression of mindless, soulless legalism in chatter about "international law"—one of the major shibboleths of our time. "International law," not English—or French—is the lingua franca at the United Nations. Kofi Annan provided a parody of international legalism several weeks ago when he was asked about suicide bombers, or homicide bombers, if you like. "Most people" in the world, he said, would regard their attacks as "illegal." Well, that was a relief.

And consider, for a moment, one of the most famous passages of the speech. Some people here may know it by heart: "The human soul longs for things higher, warmer, and purer than those offered by today's mass living habits, exemplified by the revolting invasion of publicity, by TV stupor, and by intolerable music." I pause over that phrase "the human soul longs for things higher . . .": It reminds me that Allan Bloom's surprise bestseller, *The Closing of the American Mind*, was originally entitled "Souls Without Longing"—at least that's what Bloom wanted to call it. And, aside from that marvelous phrase "TV stupor," how about "intolerable music"? This criticism was much remarked on after the speech. And the most remarked-on portion of Allan Bloom's book would be his excoriation of contemporary pop music. The subject touches a nerve, obviously.

Cognoscenti may expect a *National Review* hand to say this, but Solzhenitsyn, in his speech, sounds, to me, very much like Whittaker Chambers. At the core of Chambers's life and thought was the question, "God or man?" It was that stark: Would we have a God-centered world or a man-centered one? Solzhenitsyn puts the same question. For that matter, so does Paul—who, in the words of his King James translators, asks whether we will serve "the creature" or "the Creator."

I say again, more broadly this time: How must this speech have fallen on the ears of its hearers that day! Those 10,000 souls—souls without longing?—sitting in the rain. We were in the Me Decade, remember. And here Solzhenitsyn was talking about self-restraint, sacrifice, God, and all that stuff. As Harold J. Berman, a law professor here, put it, "Solzhenitsyn seemed like a man from Mars." News reports tell us that there was frequent applause, and some hissing, chiefly from the student section.

The First Lady, Rosalynn Carter, used the National Press Club to defend her country against Solzhenitsyn's blasts. No, she insisted, "the people of this country are not weak, not cowardly, and not spiritually exhausted." How's that for playing to the peanut gallery? This same Rosalynn Carter, however, did not feel so good about the American people after November 1980. Asked to explain Reagan's success, she said, "I think he makes us comfortable with our prejudices."

Mary McGrory, too, rose to the defense of America: Not the least of Solzhenitsyn's achievement at Harvard was to wring a flag-waving column out of Mary McGrory. Not sure she's written one since. Arthur Schlesinger Jr., for his part, posed the question, "Can Solzhenitsyn really believe that bombing the Vietnamese back to the Stone Age is a test of courage?" Somehow, I don't think bombing them back to the Stone Age was what Solzhenitsyn had in mind for the Vietnamese. I think he had in mind sparing them what they in fact got.

In 1980, the Ethics and Public Policy Center published its volume *Solzhenitsyn at Harvard: The Address, Twelve Early Responses, and Six Later Reflections*. It is to the speech's credit that it occasioned much excellent and probing writing. As Sidney Hook put it—in a typically powerful essay called "On Western Freedom"—"Rarely in modern times . . . has one man's voice provoked the Western world to an experience of profound soul-searching." The speech was scrutinized a thousand different ways, from a thousand different angles. One question I asked myself while reading the Ethics and Public Policy Center's volume was, "Can any single speech—general as it must be—survive such scrutiny? Or at least come out unbruised?"

Let it be remembered, however, that Solzhenitsyn never much cared what his critics said. Frankly, he never much cared what his admirers said. It was fine that he was immune to criticism, but it was probably finer that he was—to use Book of Common Prayer language—"immune to praise." For a piece I did two years ago, Ignat told me that his father never read a single word that his critics penned, except in one instance, when he answered them in one fell swoop. As Ignat put it, "He could have written *The Red Wheel* or kept up with his critics—but not both." He almost never did anything to defend himself, or explain himself, or elaborate a little. Maybe he should have. But he got a lot of work done, didn't he? . . .

Finally, I should say that I'm writing these remarks after a visit to the House of Terror in Budapest—I mean, a couple of hours afterward. This is the museum meant to commemorate the Communist brutality from which thousands suffered. To go through this museum, with its cells, instruments of torture, photographs, films, and documents, is a grueling experience. Best about the museum, for me, is that it includes a wall covered with photographs of victimizers—not just victims. Many of them are still alive. You see the birth year, then a dash—nothing else!

The authorities in Hungary have tried to shut down the House of Terror many times. They come from Left parties, and this past is embarrassing to them. They are supposed to represent the "post-Communist Left," but many people wonder how "post-" they really are. The director said she had to fend off a new attack every day. Witness is hard. Courage is hard. Man seems to bottom out, time after time.

But then, we hear that no one on earth has any way left but—upward.

CUBA AND CHINA

Who Cares About Cuba?

Ninety miles away, far from our minds

I t is a bald question, and one that pops up from time to time: Why are Americans so indifferent to the plight of Cubans? Why do Americans, particularly our elites, scorn the exile community in Florida? Why do our elites continually excuse, or defend, or outright champion the Communist regime in Cuba? Why do the media ignore the heroics of Cuban dissidents, which should be the stuff of page-one stories, and magazine covers, and Movies of the Week? Why?

This is a question that Cubans and Cuban Americans ask all the time, in anguished and bewildered tones. Jeane Kirkpatrick, the former U.N. ambassador, says that all this is "both a puzzling and a profoundly painful phenomenon of our times." What is "especially puzzling," she continues, "is the extreme selectivity of concern over terrible, terrible suffering, the deprivation of all rights." Americans followed the saga of South Africa with intense interest, and activism. The abuses of the Pinochet regime in Chile are the subject of film, song, and much else. The victims of right-wing dictatorship can usually count on the world's attention. But those who dare to resist and challenge the regime in Cuba work in near-total darkness.

Let us take a couple of cases out of the darkness. Here are two that have crossed my desk in recent days.

The first involves a man named René Montes de Oca Martija. He is a dissident, a human-rights campaigner, and a Christian. Thirty-seven years old, he has been jailed or detained repeatedly. Montes de Oca was born into a family of oppositionists; his uncle, for example, was a well-known political prisoner. For this reason, Montes de Oca himself was singled out at school, denied what privileges there were and marked as an enemy. His mother was a Jehovah's Witness, which meant additional persecution. Montes de Oca himself is a Pentecostalist, and an official with the Human

Rights Party (illegal, of course), which is affiliated with the Andrei
Sakharov Foundation, watched over by the late physicist's widow, Yelena
Bonner.

Montes de Oca was arrested and imprisoned in July of last year. He was
charged with "threatening the security of the state." His actual offense was
to have called for the release of political prisoners, free elections, a fair
penal code, and the possibility of Christian education in the schools. On
April 20, he escaped. There is a kind of Underground Railroad in Cuba, a
network of people who help oppositionists. Montes de Oca could not very
well avail himself of this system, however, as he was a fugitive, and the
penalties for aiding a fugitive are severe. But he managed to contact Cuban
Americans in Florida who do what they can to help oppositionists, mainly
by simply taking their statements and trying to disseminate them somehow.
These helpers then turned to me. They knew that I had written about Cuba,
they knew that *National Review* was anti-Communist ("pro-Cuban" would
be another way to put that), and they thought we would be interested.
Would I be willing to interview Montes de Oca, if it could be arranged? I
spoke to him by phone on May 5.

The dissident related his story in an agitated but resolute voice. He
expected to be arrested again soon; he was desperate for his story to be
heard. He knew that, once he was recaptured, he would face not only heavy
punishment for having escaped, but trumped-up charges of "common"
crimes, such as thievery. The mother of his child had already lost her job
because the authorities demanded that she testify that Montes de Oca had
beaten her. She refused, and suffered the consequences.

Primarily, Montes de Oca was worried about his son, twelve years old.
The boy had been badly beaten a number of times at school, by older
boys who are sons of "patriotic" military personnel. This occurred with the
apparent blessing of the authorities. Police were dogging the son to and
from school. Montes de Oca's highest hope was that the boy would be
allowed to leave the country to receive medical care: He suffers from a
hernia affecting his testicles, and also from a twisted spine. Both conditions
require surgery. The boy is being denied treatment, however, because he is
the son of an oppositionist.

Montes de Oca has endured persecution that can hardly be imagined.
"Why do you persist?" I asked him. "Why do you take these risks? How can
you be so brave?" He answered, "There are many brave people in Cuba,
both men and women. We have always been faithful: a faithful community,
a faithful people. We take our strength from the Bible. We believe in love,

justice, and peace. We take God's truth to the darkest and loneliest places of human existence, like the prisons." And what did he want from Americans, I asked, beyond specific help for his son? "I would like them to remember their principles: their sense of unity, justice, and liberty, maintained over so many years." Last, he wished to say, "Human rights cannot exist without God."

Three days later, on May 8, he was indeed rearrested. In the afternoon, he spoke with supporters in the United States, wanting to provide as much information as possible, and then he went to the home of a fellow oppositionist. In the night, state security broke in and hauled both men off. No one has heard from Montes de Oca again; his family, at this writing, has been denied any information about him, and they fear the worst.

The second case I wish to discuss involves another dissident and political prisoner, José Orlando González Bridón. He is an officer with the Cuban Democratic Workers' Confederation, a trade union (illegal). González Bridón stands accused of distributing "enemy propaganda" and "false information" for the purpose of "provoking public disorder." His chief crime seems to have been to place on an American website—that of the Cuba Free Press Project—a statement questioning the regime's role in the death of a fellow trade unionist, Joanna González Herrera. He also incensed the regime with a protest at his home on November 23, 2000. On that day, a large group of oppositionists gathered in the presence of a CNN camera and reporter. The protesters were greatly encouraged by this opportunity to be heard. They are willing to challenge the regime under any circumstances; but, naturally, they would like some reward for the risks they take.

For reasons unknown, CNN declined to broadcast the protest, or to report on the matter at all. This dismayed and outraged the oppositionists. Several of them contend that CNN's reporter promised that the protest would be reported. A spokeswoman for the network says that it is CNN policy never to make such a promise.

Later, many of the Cubans who participated in the event were rounded up while attending a religious ceremony. They were beaten and jailed. González Bridón's wife has told supporters in the U.S. that she does not hold CNN responsible for the arrests; but she does believe that the network behaved unethically and misleadingly. Other oppositionists feel grossly betrayed by the network. They complain that CNN is consistently pro-regime. They note that the network's founder, Ted Turner, is a friend and admirer of Fidel Castro. CNN's spokeswoman counters that the network has reported on "both pro-Castro and anti-Castro demonstrations." Such evenhandedness is apparently the most Cuban dissidents can hope for; but they do not believe they get even that.

CNN did run a story from Cuba on November 23: It was about the reentry of Elián González, the "raft boy," into Cuban society, where (said the network) "he is a typical, happy-go-lucky schoolboy." CNN's Havana correspondent, Lucia Newman, said toward the end of the report, "What is unquestionable is that Elián's return to Cuba was a resounding political victory for Cuba's president, and a devastating blow to his arch-enemies, the anti-Castro exile community in the United States." Note the language there, because Cubans certainly do: the dictator as "president"; his opposition, "arch-enemies, the anti-Castro exile community in the United States." First, what of the anti-Castro community in Cuba? Second, the Florida Cubans are seldom described, in the mainstream press, as anti-Communist or pro-freedom or pro-democracy or pro–human rights. They are, at best, anti-Castro, and more often "right-wing" and worse. Robert Conquest, the great historian of Communist terror, notes that Orwell liked to observe that anti-Communists were always described as "rabid": rabid anti-Communists. Almost never was there a "rabid anti-Nazi," for example.

A DICTATORSHIP AND DOUBLE STANDARDS

So, there are a couple of names named: René Montes de Oca Martija and José Orlándo González Bridón. There are thousands of others, belonging to thousands of other political prisoners. Hear (merely) three more: Vladimiro Roca, Maritza Lugo Fernández, and Jorge Luis García Pérez (better known as "Antúnez"). These names mean nothing in our country, except to Cuban Americans. Perhaps the most inspiring name of all is that of Dr. Oscár Elías Biscet González, a virtual saint of the resistance. Biscet is a practitioner of civil disobedience in the tradition of Gandhi and Martin Luther King, his avowed models. He has been imprisoned and tortured since 1998. We know, through his wife, that he has blessed and forgiven his torturers even as they have tortured him. Here is a man—Biscet—whose name should be on many lips. Cuban dissidents complain bitterly that if he were a prisoner of a right-wing regime he would be a worldwide cause. Yet he is anonymous; not even his dark skin seems able to help him. The stream of American celebrities who go to Havana to sup, smoke, and banter with "Fidel" are oblivious.

One man who has thought long and hard about all this is Armando Valladares. He is the most famed of the dissidents, the author of the memoir *Against All Hope*, one of the most powerful testaments of this age.

Valladares persevered through years of imprisonment and torture, showing almost unfathomable courage, of every kind: physical, political, spiritual. Eventually he came to the United States, where he has devoted his life to truth-telling. Valladares has earned the designation "the Cuban Solzhenitsyn." One of the most bracing things President Reagan ever did, of many, was name Valladares U.S. delegate to the U.N. Human Rights Commission in Geneva.

Valladares divides those Americans who are neutral or friendly toward the Communist regime into two groups: those who lack information (a majority, he says, perhaps generously), and those—politicians, intellectuals, journalists—who should know better, to put it mildly. "I look at this from a psychological point of view," says Valladares. "Many Americans hate their own society, for whatever reason. Perhaps they have failed to attain their goals. So they sympathize with anyone who attacks American society. The cliché 'The enemy of my enemy is my friend' applies here. And remember: The most envied, the most hated country in the world is the United States of America. I felt this clearly during my years as U.S. representative in Geneva."

Robert Conquest points out that Western defenders of the Soviet Union were "always more anti-American than they were pro-Soviet"; so it is in the case of Cuba. Jeane Kirkpatrick finds it astonishing that "some of our elites are actually proud of their indifference to Cuba's victims, or China's, or Burma's. It is in bad taste, intellectually, to give much thought to these victims." And "frankly, there is something perverse about the hostility to anti-Communists." We saw in the Elián affair, she says, that Cubans in the United States are close to a pariah community.

Paul Hollander is another great historian of Communism and its fellow-travelers. He finds it especially noteworthy that "American intellectuals haven't been much interested in the incredible repression of their fellow intellectuals in Cuba. The Cubans have had it much worse than intellectuals in the Soviet Union, after the death of Stalin." The American academy proves all the time that it is nearly hopeless on the subject. One of the most shocking things I ever saw occurred at Harvard in the mid-1980s. Valladares arrived to give a talk to students about his experience; and the school paired him with a pro-Castro professor. Evidently, Harvard felt that Valladares's witness should not be given without rebuttal. To most anti-Communists, this is rather like "balancing" an anti-Nazi with a pro-Nazi. The further sad truth is that the pro-Castro professors, in their classrooms, are paired with no one, least of all with a giant of conscience.

And what of journalists? They seem weirdly unconcerned with the fates of their counterparts in Cuba. Journalists are commonly thought to be obsessed with their profession and the freedom to practice it. If that is true, they might look into the case of Bernardo Arévalo Padrón, once the director of an independent press agency, Linea Sur Press, and a political prisoner since 1997. His crime was to "insult" the dictator and his regime. Arévalo is being held at a forced-labor camp in Cienfuegos province, where he is undergoing what Castro's regime, like all such regimes, calls "political reeducation."

Vernon Walters—a second ex-ambassador to the U.N.—says that the indifference of the American press is "absolutely normal": "They would go to the death searching out Franco's or Pinochet's prisoners. But the attitude toward Castro's is, 'They probably deserve to be there anyway.' Anti-Communist prisoners are of no interest to anybody. A prisoner of a left-wing government is highly suspect, probably a fascist." Conquest points out that Western elites have always scorned resisters to, and refugees from, Communism: Accounts from Soviet Russia were "rumors in Riga"; refugees from Mao's China, when they staggered into Hong Kong, were bandits, warlords; "and the Cubans! They escaped, went to Florida, and started voting Republican, so they were clearly no good." The anti-anti-Communist mindset, says Conquest, remains fierce, above all with regard to Cuba.

Valladares, for his part, says that "the hardest part of our struggle is to fight against a double standard: one standard for right-wing regimes, another for left-wing ones. Torture and denial of rights are the same, no matter who perpetrates them."

POWELL'S GIVEWAWAY

The dissident community suffered a special blow on April 26, when the American secretary of state, Colin Powell, gave testimony in the House. Badgered by Rep. Jose Serrano, a New York Democrat and one of Castro's most ardent champions, Powell said, "He's done some good things for his people." The "he" was Castro. And when Powell uttered those words, he gave away more than he must have known, for they are a standard propaganda phrase. Apologists have always said, "Well, Fidel might deny his people [creepy phrase, by the way: "his people"] political and civil rights, but he has done some good things." By "good things" they usually mean advances in education, health care, housing, and race relations. These claims are entirely bogus, demolished ad nauseam by objective analysts.

But they are undying. After Powell's testimony, Castro praised and thanked the secretary for his concession, another blow to the dissidents.

Valladares has a ready answer to this business of "good things," given with patience and weariness: Say these things have been accomplished (which is laughable, but leave that aside). Could they not have been accomplished without torturing people? Without imprisoning them? Without denying them all rights? Is material well-being incompatible with human freedom? Besides which, few people go out of their way to stress the material achievements of other dictators: autobahns and so forth. The likes of Jose Serrano do not pause to acknowledge Chile's economic explosion. And then there is the matter of Castro's sheer longevity as dictator. Says Valladares, "I was talking to an American, a Democrat, the other day. I said to him, 'How would you like it if Richard Nixon got to be president for over forty years?' The man almost shrieked in horror."

American celebrities who trot to Cuba almost never see the country in which Cubans have to live; they see a Potemkin Cuba, set up for visitors and off-limits to Cubans. Outright leftists from America have always journeyed to Havana, to use and be used: Robert Redford and Ed Asner, Maxine Waters and Barbara Lee (two congresswomen from California). Other pilgrims, however, are less malicious than they are trendy and naive: Leonardo DiCaprio, Woody Harrelson, an assortment of pop musicians. A few years ago, the fashion models Naomi Campbell and Kate Moss had an audience with Castro. Campbell hailed the dictator as "a source of inspiration to the world." Castro complimented the ladies on their "spirituality." Jack Nicholson, too, had a high time in Cuba. He drank choice rum, smoked choice cigars, and buddied for three hours with Castro, afterward pronouncing Cuba "a paradise."

Such behavior may seem merely ridiculous, but it is not without its effect on dissidents. Valladares confirms the obvious: that it demoralizes them terribly. "It demoralizes not only the resistance inside Cuba, but all of us who have struggled for many years while we wait for the solidarity of those who believe in democracy." He may wait for that solidarity a long time. The likes of Naomi Campbell and Jack Nicholson, sadly, have far more influence on Americans than Armando Valladares ever could.

AGAINST FORGETTING

Cubans and Cuban Americans feel a persistent hurt over the general American attitude toward them. One exile in Boca Raton reports that he can no longer talk with his Anglo neighbors about his homeland. "If I explain to them the reality of Cuban life, all I get is, 'Oh, you're a right-winger,' or, 'You're biased against President Castro.'" Can you imagine being biased against the tyrant who deprives you of rights, throws you in jail, and makes life so intolerable as to force you into the open sea on a homemade raft? Many Cubans especially resent this honorific "President" before Castro, as if the dictator were the equivalent of a democratic leader. Worse is the affectionate, pop-star-ish "Fidel." We would never hear, for Pinochet, "Augusto." Gus!

The oppositionists and their supporters are extraordinarily, even disturbingly, grateful for any sincere attention they receive. They are accustomed to being snubbed or defamed. Another exile writes, "Prisoners cling to newspaper articles about human rights in Cuba as their only hope against being abandoned and forgotten. The sense of helplessness, that no one is listening, that no one cares, is what kills their souls. I've known many such people, including within my own family."

Back in the Reagan years, Jeane Kirkpatrick became a heroine in the Soviet Union for the simple act of naming names on the floor of the U.N.: naming the names of prisoners, citing their cases, inquiring after their fates. Later, in Moscow, she met Andrei Sakharov, who exclaimed, "Kirkpatski, Kirkpatski! I have so wanted to meet you and thank you in person. Your name is known in all the Gulag." And why was that? Because she had named those names, giving men and women in the cells a measure of hope. Kirkpatrick says now, "This much I have learned: It is very, very important to say the names, to speak them. It's important to go on taking account as one becomes aware of the prisoners and the torture they undergo. It's terribly important to talk about it, write about it, go on TV about it." A tyrannical regime depends on silence, darkness. "One of their goals is to make their opponents vanish. They want not only to imprison them, they want no one to have heard of them, no one to know who or where they are. So to just that extent, it's tremendously important that we pay attention."

Indignation and concern are not inexhaustible, of course; no one, including Americans, can watch the fall of every sparrow (although, somehow, it seemed possible in South Africa). But American attention is a powerful thing; so is an American consensus. "Fidel will eventually die," some people say, with a shrug. But certain other people have waited long enough.

—June 11, 2001
National Review

Che Chic

It's *très* disgusting

I t sometimes seems that Che Guevara is pictured on more items than Mickey Mouse. I'm talking about shirts and the like (but mainly shirts). One artist had the inspiration to combine the two: He put Mickey's ears on Guevara. Guevara's fans must not like it much.

The world is awash in Che paraphernalia, and this is an ongoing offense to truth, reason, and justice (a fine trio). Cuban Americans tend to be flummoxed by this phenomenon, and so do others who are decent and aware. There is a backlash against Che glorification, but it is tiny compared with the phenomenon itself. To turn the tide against Guevara would take massive reeducation—a term the old Communist would very much appreciate.

You find his items in the most surprising places. Or maybe they are not so surprising. The New York Public Library has a gift shop, and until just the other day, it sold a Guevara watch. The article featured Che's face and the word "REVOLUTION." The ad copy went like this: "Revolution is a permanent state with this clever watch, featuring the classic romantic image of Che Guevara, around which the word 'revolution'—revolves." Clever, indeed.

That one of the world's most prestigious libraries should have peddled an item puffing a brutal henchman was not big news, but some Cuban Americans, and a few others, reacted. On learning of the watch, many sent letters to the library, imploring its officials to come to their senses. One Cuban American—trying to play on longstanding American sensibilities—wrote, "Would you sell watches with the images of the Grand Dragon of the KKK?" It was also pointed out that Communist Cuba, which Guevara did a great deal to found and shape, is especially hard on librarians. The independent-library movement has been brutally repressed, and some of the most inspiring political prisoners stem from that movement.

Yet there is virtually no solidarity between Free World librarians and Cuba's librarians, or would-be librarians. A year ago, the civil libertarian Nat Hentoff "renounced"—his word—the award given him by the American Library Association, because the ALA cold-shoulders the Cubans, preferring to stick with the loved "socialist" tyrant, Castro.

In any event, the New York Public Library withdrew the watch just before Christmas, offering no statement.

The fog of time and the strength of anti-anti-Communism have obscured the real Che. Who was he? He was an Argentinian revolutionary who served as Castro's primary thug. He was especially infamous for presiding over summary executions at La Cabaña, the fortress that was his abattoir. He liked to administer the coup de grâce, the bullet to the back of the neck. And he loved to parade people past *El Paredón*, the reddened wall against which so many innocents were killed. Furthermore, he established the labor-camp system in which countless citizens—dissidents, democrats, artists, homosexuals—would suffer and die. This is the Cuban gulag. A Cuban-American writer, Humberto Fontova, described Guevara as "a combination of Beria and Himmler." Anthony Daniels once quipped, "The difference between [Guevara] and Pol Pot was that [the former] never studied in Paris."

And yet, he is celebrated by "liberals," this most illiberal of men. As Paul Berman summed up recently in *Slate*, "Che was an enemy of freedom, and yet he has been erected into a symbol of freedom. He helped establish an unjust social system in Cuba and has been erected into a symbol of social justice. He stood for the ancient rigidities of Latin-American thought, in a Marxist-Leninist version, and he has been celebrated as a free-thinker and a rebel."

Those who know, or care about, the truth concerning Guevara are often tempted to despair. The website of our own National Institutes of Health describes him this way: an "Argentine physician and freedom fighter." Guevara was a physician roughly like Mrs. Ceausescu was a chemist. As for freedom fighter . . . again, the temptation to despair is great.

And yet, Cuban Americans and their friends do not succumb altogether, as we have seen in the New York Public Library episode. Here is another episode: Not long ago, Burlington Coat Factory—a giant clothing retailer—ran a television ad featuring a teenager in a Guevara shirt. The ad was called—get this—"Values." Anti-Communists organized boycotts, picketing, and letter-writing, and the company withdrew the shirt—but not before calling the activists "provocateurs," "fanatics," and "extremists." (The company should get with it: The preferred Castroite term for democrats and human-rights advocates is *gusanos*, or "worms.")

Meanwhile, in Los Angeles, a store called La La Ling sells a Guevara shirt for babies—actually, a "onesie." The ad text is as follows: "Featured in Time Magazine's holiday web shopping guide, 'Viva la revolution [sic]!' Now even the smallest rebel can express himself in these awesome baby onesies. This classic Che Guevara icon is also available on a long-sleeve tee in kids' sizes . . . Long live the rebel in all of us . . . there's no cooler iconic image than Che!"

Who could argue with that? Despite protests, the store has hung tough. Its owner told the South Florida *Sun-Sentinel*, "[The onesie] is one of our top sellers. The Che image is just trendy right now. . . . I don't think people are buying the shirt necessarily because of his exact politics. I have a baby store, and in my eyes it's just a T-shirt."

DEGREES OF GUILT

Some key questions are encapsulated right there. It seems obvious that some people know what they're celebrating and some do not. Growing up in Ann Arbor, Mich., I saw Che's face quite a bit, and, for the most part, those people knew what they were doing: They liked what he stood for. Other people are totally ignorant. Still others are perhaps semi-ignorant, wanting merely to express outrage or defiance, or to advertise their non-conformity. (Actually, in Ann Arbor, to wear Che was to conform.) The comedienne Margaret Cho pictured herself in a Guevara pose for a "Cho Revolution" tour. The boxer Mike Tyson, when he was feeling particularly aggrieved, had Guevara tattooed to his torso.

And last summer, you could find Che at the Minnesota State Fair: He was portrayed in seeds. (You mean, you've never heard of seed art?)

One of the most nauseating recent celebrations of Guevara took the form of a movie, *The Motorcycle Diaries*, whose executive producer was Robert Redford (one of the most dedicated Castro apologists in Hollywood, which is saying something). The movie received a standing ovation at the Sundance Festival. About this obnoxious hagiography and whitewash, I will confine myself to quoting Tony Daniels: "It is as if someone were to make a film about Adolf Hitler by portraying him as a vegetarian who loved animals and was against unemployment. This would be true, but rather beside the point." There is another movie coming out about Guevara, directed by Steven Soderbergh. We can guess at its contents by the publicity material: "He fought for the people." Sure he did. A prominent Cuban American recently lunched with a famous and powerful actor to discuss a movie that tells the truth about Guevara. The actor was entirely sympathetic, but said it simply could not be done—Hollywood would not permit it.

Beyond the occasional protest or boycott, there is some of that Guevara backlash: in the form of T-shirts, or counter-T-shirts, if you like. (Yes, anti-Communism is countercultural, in a sense.) One shirt shows Guevara with a diagonal line drawn through him and the words, "Commies Aren't Cool." Another has Guevara in crosshairs (violent—too Che-like). Still another has the statement—underneath the image—"I have no idea who this is"! A fourth shirt is an exercise in camp, festooning Guevara in rhinestones and calling him "Liberache" (linking him to the late, flamboyant pianist).

A far more serious shirt is purveyed by the Center for a Free Cuba, in Washington, D.C. It does many things, one of which is to put "Cuba Libre" in Guevara's hair, and another of which is to list Cuban political prisoners on the back, complete with the lengths of their sentences.

In France, the remarkable group Reporters Without Borders took an image well known in that country: that of a policeman wielding a truncheon and a shield. But it put Guevara's face in place of the policeman's and cried, "Welcome to Cuba, the world's biggest prison for journalists." A woman named Diane Díaz López objected: She is the daughter of "Korda," the late Cuban photographer who snapped the "iconic image" of Che. She seems to be a bitter-end Marxist. She took Reporters Without Borders to court, and won—they had to abandon that particular tactic.

SADDENING AND MADDENING

There are some who will always have romantic feelings about Guevara, and the Cuban revolution. For this type, Guevara was a true man, not a namby-pamby liberal, but hardcore—pure in his willingness to do the necessary. An anti-Communist of my acquaintance asked a friend of his why she admired Guevara. She answered, "He never sold out." Frank Calzón, executive director of the Center for a Free Cuba, says, "Yes, Guevara was 'courageous' and 'committed.' So are many bank robbers." In the run-up to the Iraq War, I asked Bernard Kouchner—the great French humanitarian and politician—why so many of his countrymen seemed enthusiastic about Saddam Hussein. He said their enthusiasm for Saddam was akin to their attachment to Che: It was a way of expressing anti-Americanism (in brief), the facts about the two men aside.

But facts are not unimportant to Cuban Americans. Imagine being one of them and seeing celebratory images of Guevara all around you. Imagine—even further—being the son or daughter of someone whom Guevara personally executed. There are such people in the United States. Or imagine—further yet—being a Cuban political prisoner, and knowing that masses in free countries were wearing Che on their chests.

If you talk to Cuban Americans about how they feel, they will first mention Hitler and the Nazis: No one would sell or sport items celebrating those beasts; what's the difference, other than scale? Otto Reich is a Cuban American who has thought keenly about all this. He has been an official under the last three Republican presidents, and he was a refugee from the island; his father had been a refugee from Nazi Austria. Says Reich, "The first reaction [on seeing a piece of Che-wear] is revulsion. The second is more like pity, because these people have no idea what they're doing."

Ronald Radosh has written about a democracy activist in Hong Kong. In his innocence, this fellow—Leung Kwok-hung, nicknamed "Long Hair"—goes around in a Guevara T-shirt. As Radosh points out, Guevara would be appalled at this use of his image, and would "favor [Long Hair's] immediate imprisonment as a counterrevolutionary, if not his quick execution by firing squad." And I heard from an acquaintance in Japan, who teaches at an American school: "Imagine my shock when I saw a four-year-old student of mine come to class last week wearing a brand-name sweatshirt with that image of Che superimposed on an American flag. He's a great kid, and he obviously had no idea what it was, but just being in the same room as that shirt made me uneasy. Heck, just knowing the fact that that shirt exists in a size that fits four-year-olds made me uneasy." Obviously, my acquaintance had never seen the onesie.

A final story: A few weeks ago, the *Hartford Courant* ran a photo of a Trinity College freshman who was protesting the execution of a serial killer. He carried a sign that said, "Why do we kill people who kill people to show that killing people is wrong?"—and he was wearing a Che Guevara hat! Talk about sending mixed messages.

Some people take comfort in the fact that Guevara, the Communist who wanted to destroy everything capitalist, has become a commodity. But that comfort is cold—because the unending glorification of this henchman is, yes, an offense to truth, reason, and justice. Think of those who might take his place on those shirts—for instance, Oscár Elías Biscet, one of Castro's longtime prisoners. He is a democrat, a physician—a true one—and an Afro-Cuban (for those who care). He has declared his heroes and models to be Mohandas Gandhi and Martin Luther King. Not only does he deserve celebration, he could use the publicity—but nothing.

Part of the Guevara cult, no doubt, has to do with pulchritude (although I suppose Biscet is good-looking enough, despite years of sadistic abuse). More than one anti-Communist has lamented that Che's cheekbones have caused millions of hearts to flutter, and millions of consciences to crater.

Tony Daniels quotes an awed British journalist who met Guevara at the Soviet embassy in Havana in 1963: "He was incredibly beautiful." Poor Stalin, so stumpy and pockmarked. He could have been a star.

Guevara has a little competition, however, in that some American celebrities have been seen with Subcomandante Marcos T-shirts. Who is Subcomandante Marcos? The Mexican Che, roughly, although it seems unlikely that he will ever overtake Guevara, whose perpetual exaltation is one of the most heartbreaking and infuriating phenomena of the modern age.

—December 31, 2004
National Review

'I Can't Just Do Nothing'

A heroine out of Cuba

I f she were any but an anti-Communist heroine, she might well be famous: the subject of documentaries, movies, songs. Her image might be on posters and T-shirts. The Nobel Committee would possibly murmur her name.

Actually, to call her an anti-Communist heroine is not quite right, because she is a pro-democracy, pro-freedom, pro-human-rights heroine: and the tyranny she is fighting just happens to be Red. But her fame is confined to Cubans, Cuban Americans, and the relative few who are interested in them.

Maritza Lugo Fernández left Cuba for American shores on January 11. Her reception at the airport in Miami was tumultuous. For many years, she has been one of the most stirring of Cuba's political prisoners and democratic oppositionists. Not yet 40 years old, she has been jailed more than 30 times. Her husband, Rafael Ibarra Roque, is president of one of the country's main opposition groups; he is in the eighth year of a 20-year sentence in one of Castro's prisons.

I interviewed Lugo at the home of supporters in New Jersey. Her face is serious, troubled, and absorbed; she looks as though she had a great weight on her shoulders. She did not want exile. She felt she had no choice, however, as her younger daughter, age eleven, had been increasingly miserable. The constant harassment by the regime and the ever-present danger had taken their toll. Sometimes both parents were in prison, which posed a particular hardship. Many Cubans dream of leaving for the United States—and die trying—but it was an excruciating sacrifice for Lugo to leave her husband, her cause, and her country. She did so for the girl. It seems certain, though, that Cuba has not seen the last of her.

The regime was only too happy to see Lugo go—they had been "encouraging" her to leave for many years. Her activities had gotten under their skin, of course. An effective, heroic, fearless oppositionist like Lugo "contaminates" others, which is to say, inspires them, and emboldens them. Lugo had also attracted a little international attention—so the regime felt it was better off without her.

Conditions in the prisons are wretched, as Lugo confirms: isolation, beatings, rats, druggings, spoiled food, strip searches, filth, disease, the withholding of medical care. The regime likes to boast that it does not execute people, and European diplomats are impressed. But there are many, many suicides—and if the suicide should happen to fail, further punishment is severe. A suicide attempt is a serious breach of discipline. Many go crazy, their minds taken from them as well as their physical freedom.

Maritza Lugo has noticed that the world has reacted with alarm to the treatment of terrorist prisoners by Americans at Guantanamo Bay. What does she think of this? A trace of a smile crosses her otherwise sad face: "We [Cubans] would love to be treated that way."

The group to which Lugo and her husband belong, and which they help lead, is the Frank País November 30 Democratic Party (a mouthful). Who was Frank País? A democratic fighter against the Batista dictatorship (which preceded the Castro dictatorship). He was gunned down by fascist forces in 1957 (two years before Castro's seizure of power). Why November 30? That was the date—in 1956—of País's celebrated uprising in Santiago de Cuba.

Lugo's activities have consisted mainly in spreading the word about Cuba's political prisoners and trying to support the families of those prisoners. She has organized public demonstrations, in churches and on the streets. All of their activities are peaceful—but the actions directed against them by the might of the state are anything but.

A hopeful event in the life of Cuba came in 1998, when Pope John Paul II visited the island. Maritza Lugo was under house arrest at the time, but she joined the throng to hand out photos of political prisoners, and fliers about them, to the international press. She says, "For the little time the Pope was there, we felt free. We yelled things like, 'Freedom for Political Prisoners!' and 'Freedom for Cuba!' The state security surrounded us, as usual, but did not touch us." This accommodation lasted only as long as the Pope's visit did.

The journalists took the activists' photos and fliers, but they did so, says Lugo, "with a lot of fear. They said, 'Thank you, thank you,' and hurried away. They wouldn't ask questions. They seemed scared of receiving the information." Lugo relates this with another hint of a smile, as though having a hard time believing that foreign journalists—who were free, and untouchable by the regime—could be more scared than the oppositionists, who were risking everything. One gets the impression that, polite though she is, Lugo is amazed at the lack of courage of people who are lucky enough to be free.

From prison, in March of last year, Lugo wrote a "J'accuse," denouncing the abuses of the Castro system and appealing to the world community. She dared anyone with a conscience to discover the "raw truth" about Cuba. She tore into Castro's propaganda—about medicine, about literacy, about the races—and said that, with the success of that propaganda, the dictator was "laughing at the whole world." She decried a regime that turns people "into phonies and hypocrites merely to survive."

Lugo is a powerful writer—with powerful truths to tell. Her writings, taken together, have something about them of Martin Luther King's famous missive from the Birmingham jail. But, of course, the U.S. "civil rights" leadership is firmly pro-Castro, in the person of Jesse Jackson, Charles Rangel, and noxious others.

One cannot help being curious about what makes Lugo different from the mass of people: Why is she so brave and straightforward? How has she kept her sanity and morality in that system, which beats down individuals and breaks up families? She seems a little perplexed by the question: "People should be free. They should have basic rights. I see Rafael [her husband] being a victim all the time, and many others like him. I can't just do nothing." In addition, "I am a Christian. I have a conscience."

Lately, there has been a steady parade of Americans down to Havana to see and embrace the dictator. Sen. Arlen Specter led one delegation. A member of his group gave Castro a New York Fire Department hat—a golden propaganda opportunity. Castro put it on, of course, and, according to a writer present, "Castro for at least one moment looked no different from Rudy Giuliani."

The kids in the "Semester at Sea" program stopped by. The dictator gave them a whole four hours, in which he lied and lied. Teachers and supervisors swooned. So did the students. One girl had a question for him: "Can I give you a hug?" Castro obliged.

Then, a clutch of congressmen from California brought along some of the state's wines for Castro to sip. They also had with them the singer Carole King, who serenaded the dictator with "You've Got a Friend."

Maritza Lugo and her fellow democrats, political prisoners, and sufferers have rather fewer friends, among American elites. I ask whether it is hard for her not to hate the likes of Carole King: "No. They just lack information. The regime fools them. They keep them away from ordinary people. They only come in contact with privileged people, carefully selected. It's all very controlled. I cannot hate them, because I know they are deceived."

I inform her that she is more generous than some of us. Lugo hopes to use her time in exile to open American eyes as to the horror that is the daily Cuban reality. I gently counter that Americans have had 43 years to learn. Perhaps those who have not learned . . . would rather not. She understands the challenge.

Of course, she would like to meet President Bush, whom she admires enormously, particularly for his leadership in the current war. She also notes that he seems more interested in Cuba than his predecessor. Above all, she would like to tell him—and other Americans—that the democratic opposition in Cuba is stronger than they may suppose, and that people are getting bolder, tasting that their day is coming. They are not content to wait for Castro to die in power; they want to see him forced from power, at last giving way to the democracy movement frustrated in the 1950s.

But they could use a little help—moral support, at a minimum.

Preparing a piece last year called "Who Cares About Cuba?" I asked Jeane Kirkpatrick about the general neglect of the Cuba democracy movement and Cuban political prisoners. After some reflection and sighing, she pronounced this "both a puzzling and a profoundly painful phenomenon of our times." I also talked to another former U.N. ambassador, the late Vernon Walters. He snapped, "The media would go to the death searching out

Franco's or Pinochet's prisoners. But the attitude towards Castro's is, 'They probably deserve to be there anyway.' Anti-Communist prisoners are of no interest to anybody. A prisoner of a left-wing government is highly suspect, probably a fascist."

Yes, the name of Maritza Lugo should be in lights. Hollywood should come calling—her life story, all who know her agree, would be an extraordinary movie. But it is good that at least some of us know her. She is a great woman, who has endured much, who has spat at evil, and who is a living example of the Golden Rule, obeyed.

—March 11, 2002
National Review

Youth with Unfathomable Courage

An independent news agency in Cuba

One day toward the end of last year, Liannis Meriño Aguilera took her mom to the hospital. And it seemed to State Security a good time to seize Liannis and threaten her. They took her to the psychiatric ward, telling her to cease her reports on the country's health-care system, or face awful consequences. A psychologist warned her that she could be labeled mentally ill—adding that people who tell the truth about the country simply have to be crazy.

Liannis will not quite concede this point. "No," she says, "those of us who denounce the government and tell the truth are very clear in our thoughts. We want human rights to be upheld, and we want democratic change."

As you may possibly have surmised, Liannis Meriño is an independent journalist in Cuba, making her one of the bravest people on earth. She is the director of Jóvenes sin Censura, or Youth Without Censorship, a news agency. Liannis has written a piece called "To Be an Independent Journalist Is to Flirt with Death." And that is what these people do every day.

According to Reporters Without Borders, Cuba is the fourth-worst place in the world for journalists—the worst are North Korea, Turkmenistan, and Eritrea (in that order). Cuba has an official press, and everything else is illegal. The regime greatly fears and persecutes any peep of independence. In the crackdown of March 2003—known as "Black Spring"—27 journalists were arrested. Some have been released, even as others have been put away. There are now about 25 journalists in prison. And anyone who remains on the outside is constantly harassed, constantly disrupted, doing that dance with death.

Also, they work without the basic tools of the trade: a computer, the Internet. Often they don't have phones, because State Security rips them away. In addition to being brave, independent journalists in Cuba have to be more resourceful than anyone else.

Raúl Rivero is a well-known poet and journalist, once a political prisoner; he is now in exile, in Spain. He talked to the *Miami Herald* about his days in Cuba: "Whenever a foreign journalist came to interview or visit me and said, 'What can I do for you?' I would answer, 'Leave me your pen.'"

Under Castro, independent journalists are called American stooges, enemies of the people, and so on. Besides being subject to constant surveillance, they are subject to *actos de repudio*, or "acts of repudiation." This is when the government has a mob surround your house and throw stones at it, or beat up you and your family. The intimidation is fierce. And this warns others to stay away from you. Liannis Meriño, while she was in that psychiatric ward, was threatened with *actos de repudio*.

And the government can do far worse, of course: They can abduct you, torture you, or "disappear" you.

Independent journalists have been brought up on a variety of charges, and they have been imprisoned on no charges at all. Formal charges include "spreading false news against international peace," "putting in danger the prestige or credit of the Cuban State," and (my favorite) being "a precriminal danger to society." This last means that the individual has committed no formal offense, but simply makes the regime nervous. As Reporters Without Borders says, "the charge is often used to detain dissidents."

And yet, in the face of all this, Cuban independent news agencies keep at it. There are many, most of them very small, all of them incredibly daring. It is often unclear why some journalists are arrested while others remain at large. And, when one journalist is arrested, or vanishes, another one tends to take over. For example, last November, Raymundo Perdigón Brito and his sister, Margarita, started an agency called Yayabo Press. Twelve days later, he was carted off, and Margarita carried on.

Here in America, or wherever access to the Internet is allowed, one can read the work of independent journalists on various websites—at CubaNet.org, for instance, or PayoLibre.com, or Directorio.org. The third of these is the site of the Directorio Democrático Cubano, in Miami. CubaNet takes as its motto a statement from José Martí, the Cuban independence hero: "Only oppression should fear the full exercise of freedom." As for Cubans themselves, they may hear independent reports over Radio Martí or Radio República, where they are read.

Liannis Meriño embodies the spirit of democratic resistance, and the desire for truth. She is both tough-minded and impossibly idealistic. I talk to her by phone one afternoon, through the good offices of supporters in the United States. It is her twenty-third birthday. The words gush out of Liannis, articulately, and there is an urgency to her voice.

She relates that Youth Without Censorship was founded in 2005, by human-rights activists—including the heroic Juan Carlos González Leiva, a blind lawyer. They now have reporters all over the island, 16 in all.

Liannis began this work because, as she says, "in a totalitarian system, the people don't have access to information, and the regime can do or say anything it wants. It doesn't want anything brought to light." She explains that, "between Cuba and the world, the regime has built a wall. And we have not been able to penetrate that wall to communicate with the world. The government wants people to think Cuba is a paradise. That is not the case."

The young woman has been detained or jailed many times, and I ask whether she is afraid of something worse. She says, "Yes, sometimes—but the desire to work for my country, and to inform people, is bigger than any oppression. I see what the civic movements are doing, and that inspires me to keep going. If I have to go to prison, it will be unjust, but not in vain."

She has never been a conformist, has never been submissive, and was expelled from her university for "collaborating" with unauthorized organizations—human-rights groups. In January, she was detained by State Security after reporting on the firing of two young men from a cigar factory for homosexuality. The agents said, "Why do you defend these people?" Liannis replied matter-of-factly, "We defend the rights of all people, no matter who they are." She would also report decent acts by the government, if she could find any. Liannis represents a rare journalistic integrity.

Her mom and dad are "extremely scared" for her, because "they know what the government is capable of doing." But she has much support in her family and community, and knows that people are grateful, whether they can say so or not. With González Leiva, she has started a magazine called *Amanecer* (meaning "dawn"). And she and her colleagues will start another one whose name is the same as their group's: *Jóvenes sin Censura*. The magazine will be clandestine, of course, and who knows what will happen to it? It will not be heavily political, either: It will have entertainment news, a crossword puzzle—it will be a place where "people can be free," says Liannis.

I ask whether she has heroes, and she says it is the Cuban people themselves who inspire her: "people who are suffering, who have to hide in their homes out of fear, who need a voice." Mainly, she says, "my trust is in God," whom she carries "deep in my heart."

All the journalists in prison have demonstrated huge courage, and their cases should be known—well-known. One of the most remarkable is that of Juan Carlos Herrera Acosta. He is in Kilo 8 Prison, in the province of Camagüey. Like many others, he is kept in the most vile of conditions: surrounded by violent criminals, denied medical care, perpetually abused. One day in December, he took the extreme step—this is hard to understand outside the context of a totalitarian society—of sewing his mouth shut. The news was reported by a member of Youth Without Censorship, Luis Esteban Espinosa.

Some days later, Luis Esteban himself was arrested. He was beaten up by State Security, but, luckily, not imprisoned. He was merely detained for a couple of hours—and warned to quit his independent activities, lest a worse fate befall him.

But Luis Esteban has not quit, and I talk to him the same day I talk with Liannis Meriño, and via the same means. Luis Esteban is all of 20. Over the phone, he sounds impossibly youthful, but, as with Liannis, his voice burns with conviction and determination. He began this work at 18. He feels a particular commitment to "keep an eye on what happens to political prisoners," so that the world does not forget them entirely. He has very few materials, but extremely supportive parents.

And, like everybody else in his business, he knows full well that he could be "incarcerated or 'disappeared,'" as he says—State Security has threatened this many times. They have also tried to turn him, which is to say, have tried to make him an informant on his colleagues. This is standard operating procedure for State Security.

Naturally, Luis Esteban is uncertain about the future. But he hopes one day to live in a "free and changed Cuba," where he can work as a journalist under conditions the rest of us enjoy. "A human being has the right to express himself," he says—even in Cuba. And what does he wish Americans could know? "They should be more informed about the government's repression. We have no freedom here. People should support the dissidents. It's very important to know that there are people who care, who are watching."

I always feel a bit strange, when I get off the phone with such people, and resume the comfortable life. I wonder what will become of them—and whether I would have the spine and heart to act as they do, in similar circumstances. In preparing this piece, I talked to a woman who was trying to say how much she admired Youth Without Censorship: "They're so brave, so amazing, so good . . ." After sputtering for a bit, she said, with some embarrassment, "I'm sorry, I don't have the words." I know exactly how she feels.

But I can say this—I can share an observation. When independent journalists, dissidents, and other such people talk, one theme keeps coming up: love. They talk about their love of country, love of their neighbors, love of God. An independent journalist named Aini Martín Valero recently gave an interview to an American journalist, Marc Masferrer. She said, "I write my articles, news, chronicles, etc., with much love, because with my reports, I help people understand the Cuban reality."

It may not be normal to link journalism and love, but such a link exists.

—March 19, 2007
National Review

Meet the Diaz-Balarts

A couple of Castro's 'nephews'—in Congress

They're called the "Cuban Kennedys," and the appellation is inevitable. The family is big, influential, and sort of glamorous. They were political leaders first in Cuba and then in Miami. The sons, in fact, are princes of Miami, although no scandals attach to them. In this sense they're not very Kennedyesque, which is just the way the family would want it. The Diaz-Balarts are strong Republicans.

Two of the boys are in Congress: Lincoln Diaz-Balart, elected in 1992, and Mario Diaz-Balart, elected just last November. Another son is José Diaz-Balart, a television anchorman. He used to work on the CBS morning show, and is now a star of Telemundo. The fourth son—although the first-born, actually—is Rafael Diaz-Balart, an investment banker in Miami.

I visit the boys in Congress, meeting the two in Lincoln's office. (It's only right that Mario, the freshman and little brother, be forced to trek to the bigger brother's office.) I ask an easy, warm-puppies question: Are their parents proud of them? "Sure," answers Lincoln, "but they never put any pressure on us to have a political career. They never told us what they expected. They guided us by their example. A lot of the things we deeply believe in, we picked up from them."

In talking to the brothers, it's obvious that they're passionately, even quintessentially, American. And they're equally passionately Cuban, never forgetting—never forgetting the terror, depravity, and desperation in the homeland 90 miles away. Their father has said of his sons, "They're 100 percent American and 100 percent Cuban." As exemplified by the Diaz-Balarts, this is a formula that adds up.

The Diaz-Balart story is well known in Miami, but little known outside that community. The brothers, and others, will tell you that that's typical of the Cuban story in general. An ancestor, Rafael Balart, fought and died in the Cuban war for independence. Since then, there have been a lot of Rafaels in the family. "Everybody's Rafael," says Mario Diaz-Balart. "We don't forget that history." The boys' grandfather was Rafael Diaz-Balart, who was a country lawyer, mayor of his town, and counsel to the United Fruit Company. Lincoln Diaz-Balart knows that everyone's supposed to gasp at the mention of United Fruit, "but they were very good in Cuba. I don't know about Central America, but, in Cuba, they paid their taxes, they built infrastructure—everyone wanted to work for United Fruit. They were an influence for good."

That grandfather named his first son Rafael Lincoln Diaz-Balart: This is the boys' father. The grandfather revered President Lincoln, and so bestowed that name on his son. The grandmother, as it happened, was a deep admirer of Ralph Waldo Emerson: so another boy in that family was Waldo. Rafael Lincoln Diaz-Balart rose to become an important politician in the Republic. He would be majority leader in the House of Representatives. But first he was a friend, comrade, and roommate of Fidel Castro. One fatal thing the boys' father did was introduce Castro to his sister Mirta, whom Castro married in 1948. They had one son, before divorcing in 1954. That boy, Fidelito, was sent to the Soviet Union to study and be communized.

According to Lincoln Diaz-Balart, his mother always hated Castro, even when the young rabble-rouser was best friends with her husband. She never trusted Castro, and she was appalled at the way he treated Mirta, her sister-in-law. When Castro seized power, the Diaz-Balart family—which then numbered four—happened to be out of the country. How important was that to their survival? "Put it this way," says Mario Diaz-Balart, when I ask him: "If they hadn't been out of the country, you and I and Lincoln wouldn't be having this conversation right now." The Castroites burned and looted their home. Last November, when Mario was elected, *National Journal* said that the new congressman's "views on Cuba policy are likely to be colored by his family's experience." *Colored*. You think?

In the past, Castro has liked to say to visiting U.S. congressmen, "Give my best to my nephew, would you? He's in Congress, you know." Now he has two "nephews" in Congress. Lincoln says, "Castro likes to toy with us in that way. It's totally cynical. It's just part of his game. His visitors say, 'You've got a nephew in Congress?!' They're so impressed." The boys have no contact with their cousin, Fidelito. He was once out of favor with the regime, but is now back in, apparently. Lincoln says, "I don't wish ill on anybody—except on those who are running that place." Mario chimes in, "Look, Fidelito is one of the oppressors, he's part of that machine." Blood relative or not, "that's how we feel."

The boys' father, Raphael Lincoln Diaz-Balart, gave an extraordinary speech in the Cuban House in May 1955. Lincoln hands me a translation.

The father wanted to explain his opposition to a law that amnestied Castro and his band. The law had just been passed and was apparently popular. The majority leader said, in part,

> Fidel Castro and his group have repeatedly declared, from their comfortable prison, that they will be leaving prison only in order to continue plotting new acts of violence and whatever it takes to achieve the total power they seek. They have refused to take part in any type of peaceful settlement, threatening both members of the government and members of the opposition who support electoral solutions to the country's problems.
>
> They do not want peace. They do not want a national solution. They do not want democracy, or elections, or fraternity. Fidel Castro and his group seek only one thing: power, and total power at that. And they want to achieve that power through violence, so that their total power will enable them to destroy every vestige of . . . law in Cuba, to institute the most cruel, most barbaric tyranny— . . . a totalitarian regime, a corrupt and murderous regime that would be difficult to overthrow for at least twenty years. This is because Fidel Castro is nothing more than a psychopathic fascist, who could choose to align himself with communism only because fascism was defeated in the Second World War.

He ended, "I believe that this amnesty—so imprudently adopted—will bring days, many days, of mourning, pain, bloodshed, and misery to the Cuban people, even though these very people do not see it that way now. I ask God that the majority of the people and the majority of my fellow representatives present here be the ones who are right. I ask God that I be the one who is mistaken—for Cuba's sake."

GO-GETTERS

In Lincoln Diaz-Balart's office are the tokens of his life and thought. There are photos of his illustrious family, of course, and of prominent political prisoners in Cuba. There are Lincoln memorabilia. There's an image of the Shroud of Turin. There are pictures of early Cuban heroes, such as José Martí. There are photos of Reagan, Nixon—and of Álvaro Uribe Vélez, the new president of Colombia, whose job is one of the hardest on earth. Lincoln arrived in Congress after a career as a legal-aid lawyer, assistant state attorney, and Florida legislator. He is, indeed, lawyerly, a nimble and forceful debater. He is a constant reader and inquirer. Mario Diaz-Balart is often described as more laid back—almost a surfer dude. (He scuba-dives, actually.) Mario gives an impression of

Miami Cool, though he is a dedicated pol. Lincoln says, "He has much better people skills than I do."

Lincoln was born there, in 1954, and Mario here, in 1961. The younger brother left college to work for the mayor of Miami—and never went back. At 27, he was elected to the state house of representatives. At 31, he was elected to the state senate. As chairman of the ways and means committee, he was a ferocious budget-cutter. His nickname? "The Slasher." Employing his legislative virtuosity, he had a hand in drawing the district that would elect Lincoln to Congress. Years later, he had a hand in drawing the district that would elect . . . him. Most seem to think that his future in Washington is very bright. Mario was chosen to give a kind of pep talk to GOP senators about the Miguel Estrada judicial nomination: If you're Hispanic, you're supposed to be a liberal Democrat. The Diaz-Balarts are fervent Reaganites. They have naked contempt for the notion of race-as-destiny.

With Ileana Ros-Lehtinen, the brothers compose the Big Three of Miami Cubans in Congress. A fourth Cuban American, Robert Menendez, comes from New Jersey. "He's a partisan Democrat," says Lincoln, "but on Cuba we think exactly alike." The brothers are keen to be all-purpose American congressmen, and they are that, but they know they have a burden to keep an eye on Cuba. It's not a burden they reject or resent. "How can you do otherwise," asks Lincoln, "if you know what's going on?" They know the history of Cuba chapter-and-verse, and they know the names and particulars of political prisoners. Lincoln describes Castro's island as "a mixture of medieval feudalism and Al Capone-ism"—"with a touch of *One Flew Over the Cuckoo's Nest* thrown in," adds Mario.

Like all Cuban Americans, the Diaz-Balarts are disturbed by the persistent pro-Castroism among American elites, particularly in academia, the media, and Hollywood. It would be one thing if these elites merely ignored Cuba; but they weigh in actively for the regime. Castro plays the American press like a violin, the brothers note, giving the "eight-hour treatment," as Lincoln calls it, to Barbara Walters, Andrea Mitchell, and the like. "He doesn't give this treatment to just anyone," says Lincoln. "He has to suspect that you'll fall for it." And yet, the brothers insist, Americans in general still recognize Castro for what he is. "They know he's a tyrant," says Lincoln, "even though they've heard nothing but positive things about him for forty years."

The policies Lincoln and Mario favor are those usually described in our press as "hard-line." (That's not meant as a compliment.) And the press is full of stories alleging that the South Florida community is changing—that a new generation favors a softer, more accommodating line toward Cuba. The brothers both guffaw. "This story has been written, repeatedly, for years," says Mario. "And yet Lincoln, Ileana, and I are elected with 95 percent of the Cuban-American vote." The local media billed Mario's race last fall as "a referendum on U.S. policy toward Cuba." (His Democratic opponent advocated a softer line.) "Then when I won, big, it wasn't a referendum anymore!"

The Diaz-Balart brothers also do well among non-Cuban Hispanics, even though these Hispanics are often said to be hostile to the Cubans. "The Democrats try to play a game of divide-and-conquer," says Mario. But it has not triumphed in Greater Miami. Lincoln says that non-Cuban Hispanics are now as much a part of his political base as the Cubans. And he scores heavily among "Anglos."

In Congress, the Cubans aren't entirely lacking in Democratic allies. Lincoln cites some Jewish congressmen, such as New York's Eliot Engel and Gary Ackerman. They "get it," he says—understand what the Cubans are up against. (The Diaz-Balarts, in turn, are passionate supporters of Israel.) And then there's Rep. Tom Lantos, the Democrat from California who came to this country as a Hungarian refugee. Says Lincoln, "Lantos is practically the only one who has gone down to Havana and grasped everything. Unfortunately, most people who go down there don't have totalitarianism as a reference point in their lives. Lantos came back and said repression there is worse than in Ceausescu's Romania."

FOLLOWING REAGAN—AND JEANE

Both Diaz-Balart congressmen started out as Democrats, but switched parties in the 1980s. Why? Lincoln speaks essentially for both brothers: "Well, it was Ronald Reagan. He made me a Republican, with his fight against Communism, particularly in this hemisphere. The more I learn about him, the more I admire him. And Chris Dodd made me a Republican, too." Senator Dodd was a Democrat who fought Reagan constantly on Latin America. "It's kind of ironic, but now I'm in Congress, battling Chris Dodd on some of these same issues. He doesn't know it, but he had a lot to do with my becoming a Republican." Lincoln cites another former Democrat, Jeane Kirkpatrick, as his "soulmate," a woman whose way of thinking and analyzing is exactly in line with his own.

The brothers are deeply admiring of the current president. Lincoln avers that he's practically as good as Reagan! They're also admirers of the president's brother, the governor of Florida. "Jeb Bush is beyond smart,"

Lincoln says. "He's one of the smartest people I've ever known. You can talk big picture with him, you can talk about budget details—it doesn't matter. Jeb's on top of everything." Besides which, his Spanish is "excellent—fluent." (The governor's wife is Mexican.)

As for George W., Lincoln says, "I like his instincts. When a problem reaches his desk, he decides it in the correct manner." Whether information reaches his desk, however, is another matter. Lincoln says that vital information about Cuba—including Castro's role in international terrorism—seems not to make its way up the chain. Nor is he happy with the administration's Latin America policy overall. "I don't think that Secretary Powell has been sufficiently in tune with what's going on" in the region, he says. The situation in Venezuela is deteriorating, with Hugo Chávez having discarded "his democratic legitimacy." Colombia "needs more help, more attention, more emphasis." Granted, there's a mammoth war on terrorism in progress, plus nuclear-armed North Korea. "But there's a strange inertia in our country that leads to the ignoring of our own hemisphere."

When all is said and done, what fires the Diaz-Balarts is freedom. They can get as exercised about China as they do about Cuba. "I feel almost embarrassed for the human race that we just sit here and accept regimes like that," says Lincoln. He decries the fact that the Cubans have so few supporters and defenders on the world scene—Vaclav Havel is often a lonely voice.

And what about the post-Castro period—Liberation Day and after? Will there be a Diaz-Balart migration in reverse? Lincoln allows that "I'm going to know things that are useful. I often think, 'Gosh, when there's finally a parliament again, there should be a rules committee.' I have a duty to be generous with what I know." But leadership should be taken by the dissidents, he says—as in the former Czechoslovakia, as in Poland. Take the imprisoned and unfathomably heroic Oscár Elías Biscet: "I know what it means for someone like Dr. Biscet, who could be in exile, who could have become a physician in Miami, to have voluntarily chosen to take a stand that would lead him to a dungeon. So, if there's any justice in the world, the dissidents, the oppositionists, the democrats—the ones who have suffered and bled and risked everything—will be the ones in the lead."

Meanwhile, the Cuban Kennedys will cut a swath through Miami. And Washington.

—March 10, 2003
National Review

In Castro's Corner

A story of red and black

E ven as Castro's rule lingers on in Cuba, so does the romance of the American Left with that rule. It has been rekindled by the case of Elián González, the plucky survivor of a tragic crossing who is now at the center of a custody battle with Cold War overtones. Among Castro's most ardent admirers, right from the beginning, forty years ago, have been black political elites. He has always stroked them; they have always stroked back. It is perhaps the least surprising aspect of the present controversy that they are playing a prominent role in it.

In January, Rep. Maxine Waters led another of her delegations to Havana, to attend a "U.S. Healthcare Exhibition." While there, she and Rep. Barbara Lee met with Elián's father, who, Waters later said, "has a wonderful reputation." She also expressed confidence that she had "heard firsthand how the people of Cuba feel about the case." Lee, for her part, made the following statement: "As a trained social worker, I can unequivocally say that Elián's father is totally fit and equipped to raise his son in a loving environment."

When the boy's grandmothers traveled to the U.S.—resulting in a spectacle that was less Grandma than *Granma*—it was Waters who hosted them on Capitol Hill. She said to the grandmothers, "If you do not fight for Elián, they win. You fight, and you win." The Cuban ladies then went to Florida, to be reunited with Elián at the home of Sister Jeanne O'Laughlin, an educator and longtime friend of attorney general Janet Reno. After the visit, O'Laughlin announced that she had come to believe that the boy should not be returned to Cuba. She cited, among other factors, an "atmosphere of fear" created by the grandmothers' KGB-style minder. Maxine Waters was not pleased. "I am bewildered," she said. "Never in my wildest imagination would I think that a nun who was supposed to be a neutral party would undermine that neutrality."

Rep. Sheila Jackson Lee—no relation to Barbara Lee—is another congresswoman in the Waters mold, and she, too, has been all over the case, making TV appearance after TV appearance to urge Elián's return to Cuba, and to cast aspersions on the motives of those who hold another view. On one program, she was asked, gently, why the boy's father did not come to the U.S., to speak freely and reclaim his son. The father, she answered, had a newborn child at home and, besides, was afraid that "he would be entangled in legal procedures and proceedings" in the United States. He was "fearful of not being able to return, and not being able to return with Elián"—no more than that.

And, if the subject is Cuba, never far away is Rep. Charles Rangel— good ol' "Chollie": so affable, so quippy, so beloved by the Washington media. And so stubborn in his fondness for the dictator in Cuba. One of the lowest moments in his career occurred in 1995, when he greeted Castro in Harlem with a bear hug. In January, after Republicans proposed legislation that would make Elián a "permanent resident" of the U.S., Rangel was quick to introduce a "sense of the Congress" resolution that Elián should be returned. He is unsparing in his criticism of anyone with reservations about sending the boy back. Why should he stay here, Rangel asks, just because "we have some Cuban-American congressmen from Miami who are up for reelection"? Of any other argument, he evinces no understanding: "It is hard for me to see how people can hate Communist Cubans so much that they will hold this kid hostage."

Needless to say, it is not only black congressmen who take this sort of line. Sen. Christopher Dodd, for example, attributes any hesitation about returning Elián to Cuba to "hatred of an old man." The black Left is merely a subset of a national Left that is, to varying degrees, Castro-mad. But black leaders defend Castro, and pummel his opponents, with particular ardor, hard not to notice. They often plead his case in the major media; he, in turn, enjoys glowing treatment in the black-oriented press. To Havana, there is a steady parade of black visitors: politicians, activists, musicians, writers, actors. Usually they are wined and dined by the dictator himself. He listens to their grievances and theories. He shows them his capital's Martin Luther King Jr. Center. He proclaims, to their delight, that Cuba is a "Latin-African country" (although, to be sure, he does not talk this way to Cubans themselves). And he uses them as a kind of club against his democratic critics, in the time-honored Communist tradition of, "What about the Negroes in the South?" Knowing that blacks are the moral arbiters of American society, Castro has worked hard to woo them—and they are good and wooed.

It all began in 1960, during Castro's triumphal visit to New York City. He decamped from a plush midtown hotel to the Hotel Theresa up in

Harlem. Roger Wilkins, the civil-rights veteran, remembers the "dramatic impact" that gesture made: "I don't think there was a politically alive black person who wasn't aware of what Castro had done." The critic Shelby Steele notes that many black Americans saw the Cuban revolution as a "liberation struggle, with the masses and the dark people rising up." Castro has always been "very savvy about playing that theme with American blacks, and it has given him a little wedge into American life. There has been this flirtation back and forth." Also, says Steele, black politicians, by associating with Castro, are able to present to their constituencies "the look of internationalism, the feeling of being part of something much larger than American racial protest. Blackness automatically makes you a member of a large, worldwide oppressed proletarian class. That is attractive in [for example] South Central Los Angeles, where Maxine Waters holds forth."

In 1995, Castro made a smash return to Harlem, basking in the adulation of black New Yorkers, and receiving that embrace from Charlie Rangel. He spoke at a Baptist church, where the throng screamed "Fidel! Fidel! Fidel!" and "Viva Cuba!" Said Castro to his flock, "As a revolutionary, I knew I would be welcome in this neighborhood." He used the occasion to denounce conservative attempts to scale back affirmative action—not that he himself would ever practice any.

The dictator was even cooler, more glamorous, of course, in 1974, when Radical Chic still hung heavy in the air. That was the year that Huey Newton, the killer and Panther, electrified his admirers by fleeing to Castro's island. Before long, Cuba became a sort of "Underground Railroad" for the black Left, as Peter Collier, chronicler of the era, puts it—an asylum from white oppression, and from U.S. law.

The most celebrated of Castro's current protectees is Assata Shakur. She is almost on a level with her fellow cop-killer Mumia Abu-Jamal as a darling of black radicals. In 1973, when she was Joanne Chesimard, she murdered a policeman in New Jersey, and was sentenced to life. In 1979, however, she escaped. ("I was like Houdini," she told *Essence* magazine a few years ago. "I plotted day and night.") She ran down to Cuba, where she is now a smirking rebuke to *yanqui* justice. In that *Essence* interview, she provided a flavor of her life in exile: "I'm invited to give lots of presentations to people who come here. I talk about human-rights violations and political prisoners in the United States." When her American supporters visit her, "I ask how things are in the States," and "they don't give me the okey-doke: They say, 'Honey, things are hard.' It reminds me I have to keep struggling."

In 1998, Shakur was the subject of an amazing note that Maxine Waters sent to Castro—a note of apology and explanation. The congresswoman had mistakenly voted for a measure calling for the extradition of "Joanne Chesimard," unaware that the woman was the beloved Shakur. The "Republican leadership," Waters wrote to Castro, had been guilty of "deceptive intent" in using the outmoded name. Hence, her error. She went on to explain that the Sixties and Seventies had been "a sad and shameful chapter of our history," when "vicious and reprehensible acts were taken against" black revolutionaries, resulting in their need to "flee political persecution."

This letter—to a dictator, noxious with complaints about the other political party, defensive of a murderer—is possibly unique in congressional history.

The prototype of the Castroite congressman was, of course, Ron Dellums, of Oakland, Calif. His seat is now held by Barbara Lee, who for many years served the old lion as his top aide. She gained a bit of notoriety in 1983, when the U.S. invaded Grenada. Shortly before, Dellums had taken a "fact-finding" trip to the island, whose purpose was to persuade Congress that the air base there was meant for entirely benign uses. The invading Americans seized many official documents, among them the minutes of a highly unusual meeting of the Grenadian Politburo. They read: "Barbara Lee is here presently and has brought with her a report on the international airport done by Ron Dellums. They have requested that we look at the document and suggest any changes we deem necessary. They will be willing to make changes." Unfortunately for Lee, Dellums, and the fiction they perpetrated, the invaders also uncovered the diary of the former Grenadian defense minister. An entry in it reads: "The Revo[lution] has been able to crush counter-revolution internationally. Airport will be used for Cuban and Soviet military."

A second Dellums aide, Carlottia Scott, had written several notorious notes to the Grenadian strongman, Maurice Bishop, the most infamous of them being the most telling: "Ron [Dellums], as a political thinker, is the best around, and Fidel will verify that in no uncertain terms. . . . Ron had a long talk with Barb and me when we got to Havana and cried when he realized that we had been shouldering Grenada alone all this time. Like I said, he's really hooked on you and Grenada and doesn't want anything to happen to building the Revo and making it strong. He really admires you as a person, and even more so as a leader with courage and foresight, principle and integrity. Believe me, he doesn't make that kind of statement often about anyone. The only other person that I know of that he expresses such admiration for is Fidel."

Last year, the Democratic National Committee appointed Carlottia Scott to its "senior political leadership team."

If black America has a secretary of state, it is Randall Robinson, the stylish and respected head of the Washington-based foreign-policy group TransAfrica. He is best known for his advocacy of intervention in Haiti, but he is also a full-fledged member of today's Venceremos Brigade. A year ago, he shuttled down to Havana with a party that included such luminaries as Danny Glover, the movie star. The trip was typical: All came back gushing. "I admire the relationship that Castro has with African Americans," said Camille Cosby, wife of the entertainer. "It's nice to know that an international leader has that much interest in African Americans." Johnnetta Cole, the constantly honored former president of Spelman College, said, "What impressed me most [about meeting Castro] was the way in which his grounding in the history and reality of Afro-Cubans informs his view of Cuba; the sense of personal outrage he has over racial discrimination."

Robinson, in a lengthy report on the visit, made clear that his view of Cuba—its history, its problems, its relations with the United States—is identical to that of the regime, right down to his condemnation of "anti-revolutionary" elements in South Florida. Robinson found Castro utterly compelling—"frank and thoughtful."

It is this sort of thing that drives Cuban Americans to near despair. Rep. Lincoln Diaz-Balart has said, "For the life of me, I just don't know how Castro can seem cute after forty years of torturing people."

So: How to account for the enduring affair between black elites in America and the tyrant on Cuba—immune, seemingly, to post-Solzhenitsyn, post-Valladares, post–Cold War awakenings? First, there is the simple pleasure of tweaking white, conservative sensibilities. As Latin America scholar Mark Falcoff observes, "Castro is anti-American; therefore he has to be good. Jesse Helms hates him; therefore he has to be good." Then there is the question of resentment felt by a slice of black America toward Cuban Americans as a successful, and politically conservative, immigrant group. Then, too, there is the oft-expressed appreciation of Castro's military adventures in Africa, a gratitude for—as an article in *Emerge* recently put it—the "thousands of Cubans [who] volunteered in liberation wars in Ethiopia, Mozambique, and Angola, helping to defeat South Africa's apartheid military." Also, the idea persists that Castro, with his Communism, has been a friend to the poor. (The novelist

Alice Walker: "Fidel Castro respects poor people, and I can see that when I go to Cuba.")

Above all, though, there is the belief—as fixed as it is false—that Castro has been good for black Cubans, that his takeover from Fulgencio Batista, the right-wing dictator who preceded him in power, meant a kind of emancipation for a previously shackled population. As Roger Wilkins puts it, with understatement, "Castro talks a better game on race than Batista." Batista, however, was himself partly black, and contemned by the Cuban upper crust because of it. He may have been no Harry Truman, but he opened up the army for people like himself. Castro, in contrast, has created a nomenklatura that is as pale as he is. Even Charlie Rangel, his eye ever on the prize of affirmative action, said recently, "I've been giving Cuba's officials hell because I don't see enough African-Cubans [in government]—but they've improved a great deal."

One final thing pervades the thinking of black elites about Cuba: fear of the end of Castro's rule, and of a freer, more capitalist Cuba, with hordes of white-skinned reactionaries streaming back from Miami. Assata Shakur, naturally, is worried: "If the U.S. succeeds in destroying the revolution, my status will be like that of most Cubans: I'll be up a creek without a paddle. It will be devastating for people worldwide who believe in justice." Jesse Jackson, though, trying to keep hope alive, has cautioned that "no one should suppose that when Fidel leaves the scene, all the revolution's handiwork will vanish with him . . . The decades have formed a generation of Cubans—through almost universal schooling, through universal health care, through doctors and teachers dispatched to desperate reaches of the world, through military missions against the likes of South Africa, through long moral purpose and conditionings—that will not easily be separated from that experience." Even so, "some rightist elements of the Cuban-American community [hope] to inherit the ruins after an apocalypse there. We simply cannot allow the policy of the United States to become captured by such ambitions."

If Castro ever does bid farewell, there will be rejoicing in many places, foremost in his prisons. But there will be mourning too—and none more heartfelt than in a segment of the American Left that has never stopped swooning over him, and that will fight with him till the last trump.

—March 6, 2000
National Review

An Eye on China

Remarks at an award ceremony

The Chan Foundation for Journalism and Culture gives an award, named for its founder, Zhu Xi Chan. He was a Hong Kong newspaper owner who used his pages to expose events in Mao's China, including the murder of journalists. The award is meant to honor and encourage journalists "who use their talents to work for freedom and democracy in China." In July 2001, a ceremony took place in Chinatown, New York. In the audience were Tiananmen Square leaders, Cultural Revolution survivors, journalists and scholars, and dissidents generally. The below remarks were prepared for that occasion.

F riends, thank you for this honor. I am deeply grateful. We should never write or work in the expectation of thanks and praise; but when recognition comes, it is undeniably sweet.

I feel there is no sense in being a journalist if I can't do things such as shine a light on China. You will not think me proud when I say that too few journalists are willing to shine a light.

We are accustomed to thinking of China as a normal country. This is one of the evils of a tyranny that lasts a long time: We begin to see it as normal, we get used to it. China's one billion people are condemned to live under a brutal Communist system—that's that. Russians and other peoples were under the rule of the Soviet Communists for over seventy years. That came to seem normal. But we should resist thinking of tyrannical, illegitimate rule as normal, because that can blur into acceptance.

When a country is first taken over by tyrants, that seems an emergency. But then, the tyranny settles in, and the sense of emergency inevitably passes. In a sense, however, a country under tyranny is always in a state of emergency. Think of the North Koreans who starve and are denied all rights—that seems the natural state of things. It has been that way in North Korea for a long time. But this condition is not natural: It should never cease to alarm and rouse us. God means for man to be free.

Not long ago, I was talking with a man—a great man—who bears a very great name. It is a name synonymous with freedom, and resistance to tyranny, and the indomitability of the human spirit: Solzhenitsyn. This was Ignat Solzhenitsyn, one of the writer's sons, and he is a pianist and conductor. We were talking about China, and he said, "Sometimes people ask me, 'Have you performed in China?' And I say, 'No. I will not perform in a Communist country, a country with a vast gulag system, one that denies its people basic rights. You've got to be kidding.'" And, continued Ignat, "They look at me as though I had just come from the moon. They really cannot comprehend what I am saying. They regard China as a perfectly normal, legitimate state. They travel there as they would to Canada or the Virgin Islands—they think nothing of it." But China, of course, is not normal.

I myself would be reluctant to enter a country whose own people are forbidden to leave. That seems to me fundamental. Perhaps the first right of an individual is to leave a country that is dangerous to him. A government that will not permit its citizens to leave—in part because it fears what these individuals might have to tell—is a government that should be opposed with all our strength.

All of us, over the last couple of decades, have appreciated and rejoiced over what loosening has occurred in China. Every gain is to be cherished. But we would not be responsible, we would certainly not be brotherly, if we forgot the political prisoners, and the immense suffering, and the denial of rights that most people I know take for granted. A couple of years ago, I was stirred by Harry Wu's photos from Laogai. I was glad to see them, for the reminding they did. Often, we see pictures of markets in Shanghai—and I am delighted that there are markets in Shanghai. But how goes it with our people in the camps?

I have written from time to time about China, and I have done very little. I have hardly lifted a finger. Yet Chinese people seem grateful to me—inordinately so. This disturbs me, because it means that most other people are doing even less than I. Cuban people, too, are grateful for the little I have written about their country. I have simply offered a few crumbs— and they have responded as though to a great feast. Again, this disturbs and depresses me. To point out that a government is brutalizing innocent people should not be remarkable. To cock an ear to the screams of the tortured should not be abnormal.

Right this second, U.S. citizens—leave aside Chinese citizens for a moment—U.S. citizens are being held in Chinese Communist jails. We know little of their conditions; we can only guess and fear. They are, of course, guilty of nothing. And yet Americans seem unconcerned. The mainstream media hardly breathe a word. It is almost beneath notice. The U.S. administration has just declared itself neutral about whether Beijing should be granted the 2008 Olympic Games—at a time when the regime is cracking heads, hard, and banishing our own citizens to the dungeon. [As you know, those Games were, indeed, awarded to Beijing.]

No, China is not a normal country, deserving of such plums as the Olympic Games. No one should be lulled into thinking that it is. This lulling is something I try to work against in the journalism I do. The journalism that rouses—even if people would prefer to sleep—is an important kind of journalism.

How asleep are we? I'm sure you noticed, the other day, that Luciano Pavarotti sang a duet with Jiang Zemin. Yes. This makes it hard for people like you and me to rouse. After all, how bad can a country be whose head of state Pavarotti joins in song? Now, Luciano Pavarotti is not a bad man; he is just a fool, in this area of life. And we should point this out.

More and more, I am aware that the press has great power. It has power to harm or help. It has power to tell the truth or lie. Lies in the press can sometimes seem more powerful than any peep of truth. But I have learned, too, that a little truth-telling can go a long way; it can be the lump that leavens the whole loaf. A whisper of truth can have a surprising resonance.

When I am at my most optimistic, I believe that Americans can be made to care about the victims of Communism. I am often asked, though, why this should be so difficult. The question comes from Chinese people, and Cuban people, and people from eastern Europe (although this happens less often now, with the fall of the Berlin Wall). I sometimes despair of giving a satisfying answer. I can only say, first, that it is a rare person who cares about other people's problems, and, second, that the pull of the Left is very strong in this country. Certainly the feeling against anti-Communism is intense, and almost violent. In some quarters—I know, because I have lived and moved in them—anti-Communism is regarded as a kind of disease, or a mental defect. When I was in school, an anti-Communist was the craziest thing you could be. There was hardly a word spoken against the government in Beijing. Pictures of the great murderer himself, Mao, were everywhere; so were pictures of the great idol, Che Guevara.

I hope that most people who defend or excuse Communism are merely ignorant. But make no mistake: Some simply *like* the oppression of human beings for the sake of Communist ideology, or for the sake of standing against the anti-Communists. That is a hard truth that I have only fairly recently swallowed.

Robert Conquest, the great historian of Communist terror, jarred me recently. He pointed out that human testimony—testimony coming out of the Communist countries—has always been disbelieved. Western elites have preferred to believe false propaganda produced by the regimes. This was true from the beginning: Reports of Soviet oppression were dismissed as "rumors in Riga." After Mao took over, refugees began to stagger into Hong Kong, having suffered the worst deprivations, having made a harrowing journey—and they were branded "warlords" and "bandits." The exiles from Cuba could not be trusted, either: For one thing, they were suspiciously pro-American, too grateful for their refuge, even as they longed to be back in their homeland, freed of Communism. They were—and are— damned as zealots and fanatics.

One great trick of the Cuban Communists and their supporters is to pretend that political prisoners in Cuba are bad characters from the old regime, the Batista regime. Recently, I interviewed and wrote about a Cuban dissident named René Montes de Oca. He is now somewhere in Castro's prisons, or at least he is presumed to be; his family has been allowed no contact with him, no information. After my articles appeared, Castroites and pro-Communist apologists in this country said that Montes de Oca must be a bad man from Batista days, deserving of whatever Castro gives him. Please understand that René Montes de Oca is 38 years old. He was born in 1963, four years after the Communists seized power. The Communists and their allies will never, ever give up this lie about Cuba's prisoners. But it is our privilege, of course, as well as our duty, to point out that they are, in fact, lying.

I have come to believe, very strongly, that the ignorance excuse can only go so far. Anyone can learn the truth about what takes place in countries like China—all it requires is a grain of curiosity and an accompanying grain of good will.

I did not, to put it mildly, grow up in an anti-Communist environment. But I noticed things. I remember, when I was very young, seeing a picture of a small mountain of skulls in the *Christian Science Monitor*. It turned out to be from the Communist genocide in Cambodia. That told me something. Later I learned about the Soviet Union, and knew there was a man named Solzhenitsyn: His testimony would seep into my consciousness. In due time, I found William F. Buckley Jr. and *National Review*, and Norman Podhoretz and *Commentary*. These two organs countered for me a crush of false or faulty material. I got hold of Simon Leys; I saw that Edgar Snow was not telling the whole story—far from it. I read books and articles by Conquest and David Pryce-Jones and Paul Johnson. I read journalists like A. M. Rosenthal. In relatively short order, I simply found out about Communism. You do not need to know the particulars of nations and situations if you know about Communism. Whether in China or Korea or Russia or Cuba or Yemen or Mozambique—it is all the same. The same stamping boot, the same war against the spirit, the same river or ocean of lies.

Speaking of lies, I must say that the Communists are lying brazenly about Falun Gong. It is very important that we pay attention to Falun Gong, and defend them. They are not separate from us; they are, at the moment, bearing the brunt of the evil that the Chinese Communists have to mete out. One might be tempted to say, "These Falun Gong have nothing to do with me. They are a strange sect, performing strange exercises in parks, reading strange books, believing strange concepts, making trouble." But we should swarm around Falun Gong, in protection of them, and also in protection of ourselves. Let me explain: To stand up for Falun Gong is not only the right thing to do, morally, it is the selfish, or self-interested, thing to do: The authorities may be attacking Falun Gong today, but, tomorrow, they could be attacking us. This is a cliché, but perfectly true.

There is no one—no one—I admire more than the person who will stand up to the bully. I am in awe of those who have displayed the necessary courage: political courage, moral courage, physical courage. I think of Solzhenitsyn and Armando Valladares. I think of Harry Wu and Wei Jingsheng. There are countless others, less famous, or not known at all. These men have risked everything, sacrificed everything—they have not cowered before evil.

And the journalists I admire? They are the ones who search out the dark places, who subdue their fear, and who do not yield to discouragement. I admire journalists like Justin Yu, who is untiring, truth-determined, and impossible to intimidate. I mourn with you all the recent loss of his mother, another one to admire, another model to follow.

As I have admitted—it is only the truth—I have done next to nothing. But you might say that at least I have not done nothing. I will do more. I am astonished and moved to receive an award named for Zhu Xi Chan. He who publishes the truth, as Mr. Chan did, is a priceless servant—especially when that truth is not readily accepted, and constantly and deviously opposed. I am told that the Chan award is meant to encourage journalists. Well, I can happily report to you: I am encouraged. Let me say further—and this is a delicate matter—that it is good that you provide such an award; the world, by and large, is not eager to bestow laurels on people who expose or publicize abuses in Communist countries. We are generally regarded as nuisances, or exaggerators, or even liars. We are generally accused of—and here I reach for a phrase from the Cold War—"poisoning the atmosphere of détente."

I myself am all for trade and war-avoidance and harmony among nations. I understand the requirements of diplomacy and geopolitics. But I will not, personally, accept a deceptive and treacherous peace, wherein human beings are persecuted by the state unseen and unheard. I will not forget Laogai or Tibet or even the simple truth that no one, including the Chinese people, should have to live under tyranny.

I will also remember another simple truth: that this tyranny cannot possibly survive. It stands no chance. It was doomed from the beginning. Truth is not obliterated, and God is not dethroned.

Friends, I love what you stand for, I love the work you do, and I am honored beyond my ability to tell you to be in your company.

—July 7, 2001

Bearing Witness

With Anne Frank and Aleksandr Solzhenitsyn at her back, Youqin Wang chronicles the Cultural Revolution

YOUQIN WANG is a remarkable woman, engaged in a remarkable life's project. She is a lecturer in Chinese at the University of Chicago, but her true work goes far beyond. She has set herself the task of uncovering and documenting the depravity and crimes of the Cultural Revolution, that outbreak of evil in China that lasted from 1966 to 1977.

To this end, Dr. Wang has interviewed close to a thousand people: survivors, victims, relatives of the murdered, those with memories who can bear to speak. She has also determined to gather every scrap of paper related to the Cultural Revolution, for the Communist authorities have tried to suppress or destroy every vestige of it. In this, they have been alarmingly successful. But Dr. Wang is surrounded, in her Chicago apartment, with boxes that contain newspaper clippings, Red Guard fliers and posters, notebooks, "self-criticisms," and photos. She is resolved that the truth of this period will not be lost.

Dr. Wang first felt her "calling"—no other word seems as appropriate—years ago, when she was a teenager. Even as the Cultural Revolution was in progress, she read *The Diary of Anne Frank*, a book that inspired her to record what was happening around her. It was impermissible to speak of the daily horrors; so she confided what she saw and heard to a diary, addressing it as "Kitty," as Anne had. But unlike Anne, she destroyed her pages shortly after she had written them. You could be killed for what you said in your diary; many were.

While a student at Beijing University, Youqin Wang found Solzhenitsyn, a discovery that set the course of her life. She read *Cancer Ward*, a book that seemed to be speaking directly to her, telling the story of her own country. Even the smallest details seemed right. She was so excited, she could not sleep. Then she managed to get a hold of *The Gulag Archipelago*, of which there were very few copies in China. Hers came from a contact in the English department. When she read it, she realized she was bound to do something similar. "I had the idea that I shouldn't waste my life," she says. "I had to make it useful."

Dr. Wang has read every word of Solzhenitsyn, up to the latest essays. Chinese dissidents and others have long complained that China has had no Solzhenitsyn—and no Robert Conquest, really—and that this has made a terrible difference. The West has little understanding, and the Chinese have no chronicler, or defender. The government, of course, has repudiated the Cultural Revolution, but it permits no study of it, no teaching of it, no remembrance of it. Indeed, it has arrested and imprisoned those who have dared to investigate.

Over the years, the authorities have published the names of about 70 victims of the Cultural Revolution: high-ranking cadres or other prominent figures. It has therefore acknowledged dozens, not the thousands or millions. This is what has spurred Dr. Wang. She burns to memorialize ordinary people.

She knows she may not be able to do the work of Solzhenitsyn, but figures she can do a slice. Chinese scholars must band together, she says, to approximate the work of Solzhenitsyn on the history of modern Russia. Dr. Wang came to the United States in 1988, and had been returning to China each summer to carry on her researches. Lately, however, it has been too dangerous, with the government rounding on scholars such as herself. Thus far, she has concentrated on one horrible aspect of the Cultural Revolution: the attacks of students on their teachers. Her findings—meticulous, unrelenting—are collected on her website, *www.Chinese-Memorial.org.* It bears the message, "We Will Never Forget You."

The anti-teachers campaign started in the "Red August" of 1966, when Mao gave the go-ahead to treat teachers as "class enemies." At first, the students' abuse was merely verbal: They began to address their teachers disrespectfully, and to denounce them in "big-letter posters." This was shocking and unnatural in China, where reverence for teachers had been the norm. With frightening speed—a matter of weeks—the abuse turned physical. Students began to torture and murder their teachers in a mad frenzy. It was as though someone had thrown a switch, unleashing all that savagery. In a sense, someone had: Mao Zedong.

To read Dr. Wang's documentation is to descend into hell. The sheer *invention* of torture boggles the imagination: nail-spiked clubs, boiling water, hot cinders, drownings in fountains, the forced swallowing of chemicals, and nails, and excrement, and the beatings, always the beatings—the students even beat the corpses, not wanting to stop. They painted slogans in their victims' blood. And all the while they were cheered on by their government, which held them up as revolutionary examples.

Red Guard students—"little suns," Mao's wife called them—were sent from Beijing into the countryside, to instruct their fellow students in the brutalization of their teachers. Initially, the Red Guards themselves had to do the beating and killing, but once the psychological barrier was broken, the local students were happy to commit the deeds themselves. The atmosphere was gleeful, giddy. Any teacher or administrator was liable to be "struggled against" (the party euphemism for this violence). Children of teachers were made to join in attacks on their own parents. More than a few went insane as a result. Eventually, individual students—particularly those from the "wrong" families—were turned on as well.

Before the campaign was over, thousands of teachers and others, in Beijing alone, were murdered. Many committed suicide, unable to bear either further torture or the humiliation. For the most part, none of them breathed a word. Some tried to defend themselves, to save their lives, but to no avail—the students killed not only their principal targets, but their families, too. The teachers could do nothing. As Dr. Wang says, the majority were not cowards; they simply had no recourse.

Many of the survivors of the period have been willing to talk to

Dr. Wang, obviously, but many others have not. The trauma lasts, and the fear can be choking. So strong is the party's hold on the minds of its subjects that some say, "I will not speak of it—I don't want to damage China's reputation." Even in America, some Chinese are afraid to speak over the phone, believing that someone will be listening, that there will be a price to pay. Dr. Wang bought an expensive video camera, hoping to tape some of the testimonies. Of the hundreds, only three consented; fear governed the rest.

The work of this memorialization takes a toll on the memorializer herself, needless to say. Dr. Wang spends every spare minute in the company of evil: drawing it out of people, thinking about it, writing it down. This often leaves her depressed, and like Solzhenitsyn, she says, "I would rather not—but I must." Many of her countrymen encourage her, aware that she is rendering a service to them all. Dr. Wang says it gives her a thrill simply to list the names of victims on her website. These names were intended for oblivion; but she has rescued them.

For now, Dr. Wang is interested only in fact-gathering, not theorizing. "The facts have to be established," she says, "and any conclusions must come later." Much of the theorizing that does go on about the Cultural Revolution disgusts her. Many scholars dismiss crimes such as the anti-teachers campaign as the work of a few "idealists and radicals." Some say, "It's just like parents who beat their children. The party is our parents, and sometimes our parents beat us children without reason, but still, they are our parents, and we must not oppose them."

Sooner or later, says Youqin Wang, the Chinese people will have to take possession of their history and their consciousness, deciding that they do not have to be ruled by lies and fear and a false obedience. In the meantime, she will continue her labors, learning such truth as she can, and telling it, in the hope that this truth may, in some way, prove freeing.

—August 20/August 27, 2001
The Weekly Standard

Look and See

Confronting the Chinese Gulag

H arry Wu is a glorious pain, forever reminding the world of an awful fact: the existence of the "Laogai" system in China, or the Chinese Gulag. Wu knows a little about this. He spent 19 years in that system, having voiced criticism of Communist practices. He got out in 1979, and six years later came to America, where he went to work as a geology professor. But he could not, of course, forget Laogai and the people in it. In time, he chucked the teaching and dedicated himself to the task of reminding, reminding, always reminding.

He is now doing it with a little exhibit in Washington, D.C. It is called "Images of Laogai," and it includes photos that Wu himself took, secretly, during visits back to China. (He was finally caught in 1995, and held for 66 days, before being released to the U.S. authorities.) You'll find the exhibit in the Russell Senate Office Building. No matter how steeped you are in Laogai, or in anti-PRC matters in general, there is something about pictures—hardly an original thought, to be sure, but true. It's one thing to read about Laogai (or about Armenia, or Dachau, or Cambodia), another to see it.

The first photos are of the outsides of prisons. They don't look particularly sinister—they're just big, ugly prisons, like prisons all over. But when you realize who is in them, and why, they couldn't be more sinister. Wu's pictures have a decidedly homemade feel, right down to the computerized date in the lower right-hand corner. They might have been developed down at the corner store—and are all the more potent for it.

Accompanying the pictures are signs (also affectingly homemade) that say things like, "50 million people have been enslaved, tortured, and murdered within the walls of Laogai." That's a little bracing. Another sign says, simply, "A Living Hell." This is not normal imprisonment, insists Wu in his signs, but slavery. No photo is without its nugget, or homily, or point. Consider, "The vastness of the Chinese Laogai system, its unparalleled place in the modern world, the monumental number of its living victims, and its cruelty meets and exceeds that of its original model—the Soviet Gulag."

There are many such references to the Soviet system, testimony to Wu's continuing frustration that, while everyone knows the word "Gulag," relatively few know "Laogai." (Wu has expressed exactly that frustration in the pages of *National Review*.) A "farm," one of the signs notes, was set up in 1950 (that early!) by "Soviet Gulag experts." Another sign informs us that Qinghai province is known (but not by enough) as "China's Siberia." "Gulag," as it happens, is defined in a typical English or American dictionary, "Laogai" not. We are confronted, once more, by the terrible fact that there aren't enough Solzhenitsyns to go around.

Before long, we see pictures with actual people in them. So there they are, the slaves, with their guards! That's what they look like, a few of them, at least, among the millions. In one photo, men are working in a field, without shirts. One of them looks at the camera. What could he be thinking? Certainly not that I'd be looking at him, here on Capitol Hill.

The next photo is probably the most harrowing of the bunch: "Workers are forced to work naked in the chemical processing room of the Qinghai Hide and Garment Factory," where they soften animal hides. And there they are, the naked workers and the hides, horrifying. A book like Nicholas Kristof and Sheryl WuDunn's *China Wakes* will horrify you; this photo, alone, does almost as good a job.

The prisons, we learn, have a "dual identity," as both prison and factory. The Jingzhau Prison, for example, is also the Jingjiang Xinsheng Dyeing and Weaving Factory. Its products, we realize, are probably bound for us. We see pictures of the items that come out of these camps—slave-labor products—such as "Diamond"-brand tools. I feel a pang of guilt (or conscience): It's easy to ignore those "Made in China" labels. There are so many of them; they're so hard to avoid.

Touring the exhibit, you get a clear sense of the tremendous, age-old thirst to document, to lay down, to put on record. You can all but hear Wu and his Laogai Research Foundation say, "See, see? Look, look! Here they are. This is what they look like. We told you so." The pictures are, quite simply, priceless, as precious to Wu, no doubt, as anything material could be.

We also see photos of public executions, carried out to "deter class enemies." We look at the first two Tiananmen Square demonstrators to be executed. They are not in any mass now, but alone, and about to die. We see "public-sentencing rallies," ghastly things, which may provoke a twinge of gratitude for the ACLU, not to mention the Constitution. Prisoners are being manhandled, strangled, by gleeful, zealous-eyed guards.

Then there are documents, yanked from the offices of Laogai, concerning its inmates. They bear the bold, red stamps of Communist officialdom, and because we know what they represent—inhuman judgments on innocent beings—they are chilling.

At last we come to a little gallery of people—photos of individuals who have survived Laogai. Each photo has a little bio underneath, of course unspeakable. There is a priest, confined for 33 years. (But we should name him, for the defeat of anonymity is a purpose of this effort: Cai Zhong Xian.) There is the Dalai Lama's personal physician, Tenzin Choedrak, long imprisoned, who would have been forced to break rock and so on indefinitely but for the "opportunity to treat and cure several high officials." There is a lovely, smiling lady named Ho Kailing, standing next to the Liberty Bell in Philadelphia. The contrast between that serene face and that bio (horrid) is staggering.

And there is also—permit me one more—Liu Xinghu, arrested when he was 13 years old, for belonging to a family of "class enemies." Twenty-five years later, "he was simply told one day that the authorities had determined that he was not guilty of anything, and he was released immediately." A cruel system, and capricious.

Liu's father, too, had been in Laogai. He served out his formal sentence, but was then confined further, as a "free laborer" (taunting designation). Despairing that he would ever get out, he committed suicide. His son was made to clean up the body and uniform.

As I looked into the faces of these people, I thought of a favorite story, involving Jeane Kirkpatrick. She was in Moscow, with other foreign-policy VIPs, and met with Andrei Sakharov, who had just returned from exile. He recognized the former U.N. ambassador immediately and said, "Kirkpatski, Kirkpatski! I have so wanted to meet you and thank you in person. Your name is known in all the Gulag." And why was it known? Because in her speeches she had cited the cases and fates of particular persons, had, so to speak, named names—which thrilled those in the cells and stirred those beyond them. We may not be moved by the plight of millions, but how about the plight of one, or two, or three? Speaking of this recently, Kirkpatrick recalled a saying of Arthur Koestler: "Statistics don't bleed; it is the detail which counts."

So Wu's humble display has an effect—as did the jarring and undeniable photos that emerged from the Holocaust; as did the pictures, shown two years ago at the Museum of Modern Art in New York, of the Cambodian genocide; as did the film *Harvest of Despair*, about the "terror-famine" (as Robert Conquest named it) in Ukraine. There is something about a picture, yes. Think of Anne Frank's face, on the cover of the diary—so fresh, so gay, as beautiful as any face that ever beamed! Six million died, true; but also . . . Anne.

Harry Wu and his allies have done a wonderful thing. In this era of "strategic partnership"—in certain respects shameful—they have thrown Laogai in our faces. They have reduced an overawing phenomenon to manageable size. They seem to say, "Here it is: Deal with it."

Can we?

—November 8, 1999
National Review

Prisoner of the PRC

The experience of a Falun Gong practitioner

C harles Lee has a story to tell, and I have come to hear it, in a New York conference room. Dr. Lee has recently been released from a Chinese prison, after three years' confinement. He is an American—a U.S. citizen since 2002—and he talks like one: His conversation is peppered with "like," as in, "If you tried to move, they would, like, hit you." Dr. Lee is a remarkably composed and assured man. But he has been through a ghastly ordeal, which is no surprise, given the People's Republic and its ways.

Dr. Lee was born in 1965, in the eastern province of Jiangsu. His parents worked in a cotton mill. He himself went to medical school in Guangzhou (Canton). In 1991, he came to the United States, for further study and research at the University of Illinois and Harvard. In 1997, he became a practitioner of Falun Gong, a system involving meditation and exercises.

When Falun Gong first became popular in the 1990s, the Chinese government supported it, as a means of promoting both health and traditional Chinese culture. But when they discovered just how popular it was—100 million were practicing Falun Gong, they found—they banned it. That was in 1999. Since then, they have been waging a merciless campaign against practitioners of Falun Gong, seizing, torturing, and killing them. Indeed, these people might be said to be bearing the brunt of PRC brutality at the moment.

Dr. Lee decided to return to China to try to assist his fellow Falun Gong practitioners. He was especially concerned with countering the government's propaganda against the movement; this propaganda is pervasive and constant. He first went in 2002, for three weeks. He was arrested, but managed to get out. He went again in January 2003, and this time he was not so lucky.

His intention was to execute a brazen plan: to tap into government television—the only kind of television there is in China—and broadcast a 45-minute tape about Falun Gong, detailing the government's persecution of practitioners.

On landing at the Guangzhou airport, he was arrested. Right away, he started a hunger strike, as political prisoners have long done. The police kept Dr. Lee awake for 92 consecutive hours, badgering him, denouncing Falun Gong. On March 21, 2003, he had his trial—which he describes as a "show trial," in which he was not permitted to defend himself. Like other such figures, he insists on his legal justification: The Chinese government has violated its own constitution, and so on. After this trial, he was sent to prison in Nanjing.

There, the ordeal began in earnest, but I will be light on the details—light on them without avoiding them.

He spent 130 straight hours handcuffed—painfully handcuffed—while trying to write a letter to an appeals court. He was subjected to constant anti–Falun Gong propaganda, which attacked his most deeply held beliefs. He endured "reeducation sessions," or "condemnation sessions." He was not allowed to perform his Falun Gong exercises, of course, and he was constantly surrounded by other prisoners, who served as enforcers.

As a foreigner, he says, he was supposed to be kept with other foreign prisoners. But he was kept with Chinese ones, most of them drug traffickers and the like. Some of them befriended him; but then they were replaced by "more vicious ones."

During his three-year confinement, he went on hunger strike nine times, for a total of 50 days. Prison authorities force-fed him four times. Once, they left the tube in his stomach for 33 hours, for the sole purpose of torturing him. "It was agonizing," Dr. Lee says. One is sure he is understating it.

He tells of another forced feeding: "The scene was so violent, the cameraman fainted, right on the spot." Excuse me, the cameraman? "Yeah, the guy who was filming it. He was just a kid, green from the police academy." They were filming it? "Oh, yes: They filmed everything. They do this so as to piece bits of video together later, for their own purposes."

In late 2004, they forced him to sit on a bench, staring straight ahead, into a wall, all day long. He was allowed to sleep at night, but otherwise he could not move, and had to keep staring straight ahead. They made him do this for 48 straight days. "Your body starts to rot," Dr. Lee notes. Eventually his heart began to fail, and he had trouble breathing. They then took him to a doctor.

At other times during the three years, he was made to work in prison sweatshops. He assembled Christmas lights. "The room was small, and it was crowded with about 60 people. The temperature was over 42 degrees centigrade" (108 degrees Fahrenheit). He also made bedroom slippers with Homer Simpson's image on them. (Homer is the father on the TV cartoon *The Simpsons*.) You put your foot where Homer's mouth is.

I ask, by the way, what he thinks of people in the Free West who buy those slippers. He says, "Oh, they just want the cheapest product. But I feel that, if they knew about my situation, it would bother them."

I ask another question: What was the worst part of those three years? "My mother," he says. Dr. Lee's mother was very sick, and the authorities used her against him. This is standard practice for the PRC, especially where Falun Gong prisoners are concerned: They pressure family members to urge their loved ones to repudiate Falun Gong.

When Dr. Lee's mother was dying, his brother called the prison, asking the authorities to let Charles see her, once more. They waited a day. Then they took him to his mother's home. She had died an hour before. Dr. Lee feels certain they knew exactly what they were doing. (His family's home was watched all the time, as all such homes are.)

Did Charles think that he himself would die? "Yes. There was constant pressure. Constant pressure." He says that his experience was like that of Prometheus, who had his liver eaten out, every day. "They said to me, 'We will make living worse for you than dying.' They were very good at mental torture," as well as physical. "Some people mention the concept of 'the genocide of souls'—they kill your soul. They let you become a nobody."

You may ask where the U.S. government was in all this—Dr. Lee was, and is, after all, a U.S. citizen. He says he had monthly visits from a consular official. The official, much of the time, would report back to Dr. Lee's fiancée, Yeong-Ching Foo, who was in the United States. Throughout the three years, she worked tirelessly in Dr. Lee's behalf, in the tradition of Avital Sharansky, and others. Miss Foo is with us, by the way, in this New York conference room.

Dr. Lee is grateful for the consulate's support, and so is Miss Foo. But her gratitude is tempered by aspects of the State Department's dealings with her. She says that they warned her not to make too much of a fuss over Dr. Lee's imprisonment, lest his situation become worse. And to this day, they both say, the U.S. government has never said a word—a public word—about what happened to him.

Dr. Lee notes that the PRC's leader, Hu Jintao, will visit President Bush in Washington on April 20. He says it would be nice if our president "raised the issue of Falun Gong."

As his prison term neared its end, Dr. Lee's treatment got better, as often happens with such prisoners: Regimes want them relatively fit and sane, when the world sees them. And Dr. Lee considers himself extremely lucky: He would have had it far worse if he had not been a U.S. citizen. Other Falun Gong prisoners have been hung from ceilings, their bodies brutalized by electric truncheons. And then there's the fingernail torture.

Charles and Yeong-Ching will be married soon. It has not been easy, reestablishing their relationship. He has been through a lot; so has she. And what will he do with the rest of his life? "That's a good question. I'm not sure." But whatever he does, he says, it will involve helping his fellow Falun Gong practitioners. "They are suffering so much, and they have such lies told about them constantly."

Would he consider going back to China, to face the state again? "Yes, I will go back, if I have the chance." But why? Given the past three years, why on earth? "If we Falun Gong practitioners don't help other Falun Gong practitioners, who will? We have to be the first ones who stand up."

He says it with a conviction that brooks no further questioning.

—April 24, 2006
National Review

GOLF

My Country, Ryder Wrong

Patriotism, nationalism, and golf

A
s the Ryder Cup unfolded on television a few weeks ago, my thoughts turned naturally to the differences between patriotism and nationalism. Whose didn't?

The Ryder Cup is now the most important event in golf, eclipsing even the Masters and the two Opens, U.S. and British. The Cup is a three-day competition held every other year between the cream of the U.S. players and the cream of the European players.

In intensity, it makes the Final Four, the NBA championship, and the NFC title game (the new Super Bowl) seem as nothing. At the conclusion of this year's play, the European captain, Bernard Gallacher, was moved to remark, "It is almost becoming too much, this Ryder Cup."

In the weeks preceding the Cup, it occurred to me that I was supposed to support the American team. Not only am I an American, I am (yikes!) a registered Republican. The problem was that most of my favorite players, in all the world, were on the European side. Worse, many of my least favorite players were on the American side. It hardly seemed natural to be all rah-rah for the homeboys.

I believe that William F. Buckley Jr. once wrote, "I am as patriotic as anyone from sea to shining sea, but there isn't a molecule of nationalism in me." I have always felt this way about nationalism, even as a child. (Was I expected to go for some American girl over the winsome Olga Korbut? Not a chance.)

"Nationalism" has an air of chauvinism about it, a thoughtless veneration of "my country, right or wrong"; "patriotism," contrariwise, connotes an enlightened love of country, a rightful appreciation for it. Burke famously said of patriotism that a country, to be loved, ought to be lovely (and a Ryder Cup squad, to be loved, ought to be lovely as well).

It would have taken a lot to induce me to root against Seve Ballesteros, "the swashbuckling Spaniard" (as it is obligatory to call him in golf writing). He captured me when I was young, and imparted to me a sense of the game's possibilities. (His book, *Natural Golf,* is a holy text.) And how could I have wished defeat on Ian Woosnam, the Wee Welshman, or Bernhard Langer, the "phlegmatic Teuton," or Nick Faldo, the English Colossus? How about Costantino Rocca, an Italian and perhaps the most endearing player in the game?

This latter case is particularly instructive. Rocca is, excuse me, a classic "American" success story, as Algeresque as anyone who ever breathed. Into his mid-twenties, he labored in a plastics factory (barely escaping the permanent deformation of his hands), practicing in the fields after the whistle blew. He is a heroic Everyman: fearless, unlikely, inspiring.

In an instance of perfect symmetry—a happy accident—he was paired in the final round against the American Davis Love III. There is nothing wrong with Love, but he is, in many respects, the anti-Rocca: cool, polished, to the country club born, graced with a textbook swing, the son of one of the most renowned teaching professionals in the world.

Is it not possible to regard Rocca as the more "American" of the two, in the spiritual sense? Is it reasonable, is it moral, to ask someone to pull for a golfer—for anyone—on the basis of birth within common borders?

As the Cup approached its climax, and the U.S. had its back to the wall, something strange occurred. I found myself, against all my protestation and ratiocination, aching, dying, for an American victory. And when the Americans were beaten, I felt aggrieved. I cursed the U.S. team, and felt not the least satisfaction for the jubilant Europeans, my personal favorites among them.

Herewith a little fantasy: I am playing in the Ryder Cup, spangled in stars and stripes, about to win it all for the "U.S.A.! U.S.A.!" (as the crowds chant). When I hole the clinching putt, my teammates sprint from the bank behind the 18th green (for Faldo has taken me to the wire), embrace me wildly, and bear me aloft. (In addition to being the leading money-winner on Tour, I weigh less. This is a fantasy, remember.)

At the closing ceremony, the American flag is raised, and the anthem played. American faces glisten with joyful tears; European ones contort in pain. Surveying this colorful scene, I say inwardly, "Remember, now: You—and your teammates, and the Europeans, and all the world—belong to God. Alone."

So I take care not to mourn the American loss (or is it the loss of those twelve golfers who happen to hold U.S. citizenship?). I strive always to see man as man, not as race, creed, or nationality, and, by the way, can Mrs. Thatcher come over and be president, please?

—October 23, 1995
The Weekly Standard

Tiger Time

The wonder of an American hero

This piece was written immediately after Tiger Woods won the Masters in 2001—his fourth straight major.

S ometime last season, I e-mailed a friend of mine, a former college golf champion and a keen student of the game. "Are we ready to concede that Tiger is the best ever?" I asked. His answer was slightly ambiguous; I couldn't tell whether he was being sincere or sarcastic. So I asked for a clarification. "Oh, let me be perfectly clear," he replied. "Nicklaus in his heyday couldn't carry Tiger's clubs. Really."

Now, my friend and I were Nicklaus worshipers from way back—we still are. When it comes to Nicklaus, we are dangerously close to violating the First Commandment. So acknowledging the truth about Tiger came hard. Jack Nicklaus—this is gospel in golf—dominated his sport as no other athlete ever dominated any sport. I once began a piece about Nicklaus roughly this way: Boxing folks can talk about Louis versus Ali; baseball people can talk about Cobb and Ruth and Mays (or whomever); tennis people can have a high time about Laver and Sampras; but in golf, there's nothing to discuss.

What's more, no one else was ever supposed to dominate the game. Nicklaus was supposed to be the last giant, the last player ever to make the others quake, the last to win predictably. You see, "parity" had arrived: That was the big buzzword on Tour. There were now thirty, forty—maybe sixty guys who could win in any given week. Golf instruction—swing science—had equalized things. Advances in equipment had equalized things. Conditioning, nutrition, etc., had equalized things. If a guy won, say, three tournaments in a season, that would be practically a freak, and the fellow would be Player of the Year, for sure. We would never see anything close to Nicklaus again.

Furthermore, his mark of 18 professional majors—twenty majors, if you counted his two U.S. Amateurs (and most of us did, because we loved that round, awesome number)—was an inviolable record. It would stand forever. It was the most unapproachable record in golf.

All of this needs to be remembered, because people forget. I've seen this in my own (not terribly long) lifetime. When I was young, the greatest record in baseball—the one that would live unto eternity—was Lou Gehrig's 2,130 consecutive games. That, all the experts said, was the one mark no one would ever reach. But then, when Cal Ripken closed in on it, they changed. They cheated. Now they said it was Joe D's 56-game hitting streak that was numero uno. Ah, but I remember: I won't forget. Ripken's achievement must not be slighted—everyone said it was impossible.

And now Tiger: The non-golfer will simply have to trust me that no one was supposed to be able to do what Tiger has, in fact, done. His achievements are—or were—unimaginable. The question arises, Has Woods won the Grand Slam? I, for one, don't care: He has won something like it—four consecutive majors—and no one else has (forgetting Bobby Jones, in the "premodern" Slam). I vow not to forget—no matter how fuzzy the past becomes—that Woods has accomplished what was proclaimed by one and all unaccomplishable.

How to talk about Tiger Woods? I don't know. Start with this (a cliché, but a useful cliché): When Nicklaus first showed up at the Masters, Bob Jones said, "He plays a game with which I am not familiar." The same has to be said of Woods. Another friend of mine—a pro golfer and a genuine philosophe—made the following, arresting statement: "It's not just that Woods is the best ever to play the game; it is that he is the *first* ever to play it." Think about that for more than a second or two, and you grow dizzy. What does it mean? It means, I think, that Tiger is the first truly to exploit the possibilities of the game. That he is the first to swing the club as it ought to be swung. That he—this gets a bit mystical—sees a game that others have been blind to, or have caught only glimpses of.

In the last years of his life, I had lessons—and many long conversations—with Bill Strausbaugh Jr., the most decorated teacher in the history of the PGA. "Coach" was one of the wisest men I ever hope to meet in golf, or to meet, period. Speaking of Tiger—this was in 1998, I believe—he said,

"That young man has the best golf motion ever." (Coach disdained the word "swing"—he thought it gave his students the wrong idea.) I replied, condescendingly, like an idiot, "Oh, Coach, you must mean that he has *one* of the best ever. You've seen Hogan, Snead—all of them." He fixed me with a look and said, "No, Jay, I meant what I said: Tiger has the best golf motion ever." I was tremendously impressed by this, because the old are usually afflicted with the vice of nostalgia: No one is ever as good now as then. Thus, in baseball, for example, you hear, "Yeah, Roger Clemens is okay, but Grover Alexander! There was a pitcher!" Right.

Bill Strausbaugh also said, "Tiger has three things: a great golf motion, a great golf mind, and a great golf body. [This last, Coach maintained, is grossly underrated.] He is ideal—I never thought I would see it."

Tiger Woods was a legend before he ever turned pro. He had, I would argue, the greatest amateur career ever. (Bobby Jones idolaters—of whom I am one, from the crib—should just sit still. There is an argument here. And Jones wasn't an "amateur" in our present sense.) In fact, it's unfortunate about Tiger's dazzling pro career that it has been allowed to overshadow, inevitably, his amateur career. Tiger Woods, starting when he was 15 years old, won three straight U.S. Junior Championships and three straight U.S. Amateur Championships. This achievement is positively stupefying. I could try to explain, but, again, I say: Trust me.

Tiger was the youngest ever to win the Junior (15). No one had ever won twice, and he would win three times. He was the youngest ever to win the U.S. Amateur (18). He would be the only player ever to win the Am three years in a row. This takes a discipline, a kind of genius, that is hard to fathom. I argued, quite seriously, that if, God forbid, Tiger died before he ever had a chance to tee it up as a pro, he would die as one of the finest players in history. And he would have.

(I should interject here that Tiger—it is almost an afterthought—won the NCAA championship. He attended college—Stanford—for two years. Condoleezza Rice once told me—she had been provost of Stanford—that it was a shame that Tiger left school, understandable as it was, because he "really enjoyed it.")

Then there is Tiger the pro. Once more, how to convey the uniqueness—the impossibility—of it all? Tiger is only 25—and he has won 27 tournaments, including six majors (nine, if you count the way we do for Nicklaus). To provide a little comparison, Curtis Strange, who was the best player in the world for several years, won 17 tournaments, and two majors. At one stage, Woods won six PGA events in a row: Farewell, parity. Indeed, before Woods, it was absurd to say, "I think so-and-so will win this golf tournament," or even, "So-and-so is the favorite." Golf is not a football game, in which one team or the other must win. Tiger has introduced a strange element: predictability.

Let's grapple with some victory margins: In 1997 (at age 21, but that's a different matter), Tiger won the Masters by twelve shots. I once heard the TV commentator Ken Venturi, in the pre-Tiger era, say of a guy who was leading some tournament by three shots—three shots—"He's lapping the field." And he was. When you win the Masters, you win it by one shot, two shots—three shots, maybe. Often, you're forced to win it in a sudden-death playoff. Tiger won the 1997 Masters by twelve shots: He could have made a 15 at the final par 4 and still won—could have made 16 to play off.

In 2000, he won the U.S. Open, at Pebble Beach, by fifteen shots. He won the British Open, at St. Andrews, by eight shots. (These are all records, but we can't possibly begin to go into the record book.) I argued—only half-jokingly, or a third jokingly—that Tiger should retire then and there, rather as Bobby Jones did, at age 28. What did he have left to prove? Sure, he had dreamed all his life of breaking Nicklaus's lifetime records, but that was just a matter of longevity, of hanging around, of staying uninjured, of keeping oneself interested. What is there left to do after winning the U.S. Open at Pebble (by fifteen) and the British at St. Andrews (by eight), and in the millennial year of 2000?

Well, you can go on to win a type of Slam, I guess. And Woods is still charging.

Of course, he is more than a golfer: He is an important American, not least because of the racial or ethnic question. There is probably no one in the country more refreshing, more resolute about race than Tiger Woods. He is a one-man army against cant and stupidity. One of the most thrilling television moments I have ever seen occurred at the Masters, when Tiger was playing as an amateur. Jim Nantz of CBS asked him one of those softball, standard, perfunctory questions: "Do you think you have an obligation to be a role model for minority kids?" Tiger answered, quick as a flash, "No." I almost fell out of my chair. He continued, "I have an obligation to be a role model for all kids."

After Tiger won the Masters in '97, President Clinton asked him, the morning after, to join him the following day, to participate in a Jackie Robinson ceremony at Shea Stadium. Tiger said . . . no, to the President of the United States. The invitation was last-minute, and Tiger was suspicious of its motives. He had long planned a vacation in Mexico with friends, and he wouldn't scrap or alter it. Many people criticized Tiger for this decision; but he told them, essentially, to get lost. Here was a firm, self-confident democratic citizen, not a serf, complying with the ruler's summons. The same mettle Woods shows on the golf course, he shows off it.

A good number of people don't like Tiger's attitude—don't like it at all. Larry King asked him, in 1998, "Do you feel that you're an influence on young blacks?" Tiger answered, calmly, unmovably, "Young children." An annoyed King shot back, "Just 'young children'? Don't you think you've attracted a lot more blacks to the game?" Replied Woods, "Yeah, I think I've attracted minorities to the game, but you know what? Why limit it to just that? I think you should be able to influence people in general, not just one race or socio-economic background. Everybody should be in the fold." Again, I almost fell out of my chair. Tiger may be the most pointed universalist in public life.

Even Colin Powell, the current secretary of state, has gotten snippy with Tiger, or about him. Woods coined a word to describe his racial make-up: "Cablinasian." This is meant to stand for a mixture of Caucasian, black, Indian (American Indian), and Asian. Tiger's dad, a tough, no-nonsense career military man, is (to be disgustingly racial, but this is to make a point) half black, a quarter Chinese, and a quarter Indian; Tiger's mom is half Thai, a quarter Chinese, and a quarter white. Tiger is, in other words, 100 percent, pure American. Back to General Powell. On *Meet the Press* one Sunday in 1997, Tim Russert asked him (rather in the manner of Orval Faubus, actually), "If you have an ounce of black blood, aren't you black?" Powell responded that, like Tiger, he was of varied background, but "in order to not come up with a very strange word such as Tiger did, I consider myself black American. I'm very proud of it."

Well, despite his distaste for racial baloney, so is Woods: He is neither unaware nor unappreciative of the struggles of black people in this country. After winning the Masters that first time, he paid due homage to black players before him, including Charlie Sifford and Lee Elder (the first black to be allowed to play in the Masters, in 1975).

Yet Woods refuses to spend his life in obeisance to the race gods. At one point, he felt obliged to put out a "Media Statement," the purpose of which was "to explain my heritage." It would be—this is typical Tiger—"the final and only comment I will make regarding the issue":

> My parents have taught me to always be proud of my ethnic back-
> ground. Please rest assured that is, and always will be, the case . . . On my

father's side, I am African-American. On my mother's side, I am Thai. Truthfully, I feel very fortunate, and EQUALLY PROUD, to be both African-American and Asian!

The critical and fundamental point is that ethnic background and/or composition should NOT make a difference. It does NOT make a difference to me. The bottom line is that I am an American . . . and proud of it! That is who I am and what I am. Now, with your cooperation, I hope I can just be a golfer and a human being.

We're told that we shouldn't need heroes. Well, too bad: We got one.

Not every touring pro has been gracious about Tiger and what he means; envy and resentment run deep. But the Scottish champion Colin Montgomerie said a lot when he commented recently, "We never thought this would happen [Tiger's explosion] or that there was even a chance it would happen. We're fortunate to have the world's best athlete playing our game. We're all not bad. He's just better. He is magnificent in every department."

Yes, in every department. A rare spirit shoots through Tiger. Consider a few, disparate things. Every year at Augusta, the Champions Dinner is held, for which the previous year's winner selects the menu. In 1998, Tiger—age 22—chose hamburgers and milkshakes: the all-American meal. After he won the '97 Masters (remember, by a historic twelve shots), he took a look at the film and announced, "My swing stinks" (he didn't say "stinks," but I've cleaned it up a little). So he worked to make it even better—and it may become better yet. Woods is a perfect combination of the cool, self-contained golfer, à la Ben Hogan (or Nicklaus, for that matter), and the hot, impassioned golfer, à la Arnold Palmer, or Seve Ballesteros. And, finally, there is no better interview in sports: He handles himself superbly, and is not above displaying a contempt (usually sly) for dumb questions.

My golf friends and I have made our peace with Tiger, to say the least. Initially, I think we all had a fear of his displacing Nicklaus, which seemed . . . sacrilegious. It helped, however, that Woods is the biggest Nicklaus worshiper of all: He venerates him as Nicklaus venerated Jones, and as Nicklaus pledged to follow in Jones's footsteps, Tiger has pledged to follow in Nicklaus's. Said Nicklaus five years ago, "There isn't a flaw in [Tiger's] golf or in his makeup. He will win more majors than Arnold Palmer and me [Arnie was standing next to him] combined. *Somebody* is going to dust my records. It might as well be Tiger, because he's such a great kid."

Oh, it's a thrill to be alive in the Time of Tiger. Whether you give a hoot about golf or not, I ask you—a final time—to trust me: Rejoice.

—April 30, 2001
National Review

Hunting Tiger

Everyone wants a piece of him

The preceding piece was mainly about sports, and this one is mainly about social-political life. But there is some overlap, which I trust you will forgive!

The pressure on Tiger Woods is mounting, and it has nothing to do with golf: It's the pressure to blacken up—to be a social activist, a racial spokesman. Throughout his young career, Woods has resisted this, standing on individualism, and universalism. But it would be hard for even the strongest person not to crack.

Right from the start, Woods was a breath of fresh air, in every respect. When he appeared at the Masters as an amateur, Jim Nantz of CBS asked him whether he had a special obligation to be a role model for "minority kids." The expected answer was, "Yes, of course." The actual answer was, "No—I have an obligation to be a role model for all kids."

Later on, Larry King went at him on CNN. "Do you feel that you're an influence on young blacks?" Woods answered, "Young children." This seemed to annoy "the King": "Just 'young children'? Don't you think you've attracted a lot more blacks to the game?" Replied Woods, "Yeah, I think I've attracted minorities to the game, but you know what? Why limit it to just that? . . . Everybody should be in the fold." Woods was resolute, never allowing himself to be bullied, never indulging in racial-political games.

Well, almost never. In 1996, Tiger submitted to a Nike commercial which had him saying, "There are still courses in the United States that I am not allowed to play because of the color of my skin." (Nike, like Benetton, likes its ads to show "social conscience." It perhaps eases the guilt of commerce.) The claim was false, of course, and a company spokesman explained that Tiger's statement was more a "metaphor."

But by and large, Tiger has displeased the racialist crowd, going his own way. He is a very independent-minded cuss. After he won the Masters for the first time in 1997, President Clinton asked him to appear with him at Shea Stadium for a ceremony commemorating Jackie Robinson. Woods said, sorry, but he had longstanding plans with friends in Mexico. Many people—including some conservatives—thought that this was hugely disrespectful to the president, and an insult to the memory of Robinson, the great pioneer. Woods was unmoved.

In 2000, the NAACP asked him to boycott a PGA Tour event in South Carolina, in protest of the Confederate flag. Woods wouldn't go along. He said, "I'm a golfer. That's their deal, not mine." Some people viewed this as grossly irresponsible, and maintained that this cocky young man would simply have to "mature"—would have to get hip to the American reality. And yet Woods remained almost eerily unfazed, secure in himself.

'A GOLFER AND A HUMAN BEING'

In a country where the question of identity is burning, everyone wants a piece of the world's greatest athlete. Shall we rehearse the racial recipe one more time? Woods's dad, Earl—a tough, no-nonsense military man—is half black, a quarter Chinese, and a quarter Indian; Woods's mom is half Thai, a quarter Chinese, and a quarter white. When he was growing up, he coined a word for his ancestral mix: "Cablinasian" (enfolding Caucasian, black, Indian, and Asian). When the world first learned about this coinage, it drew hoots and howls from many quarters, with even Colin Powell, on *Meet the Press*, giving a snort. Asked Tim Russert, "If you have an ounce of black blood, aren't you black?" Powell answered that he, like Tiger, was of mixed background, but "in order to not come up with a very strange word such as Tiger did, I consider myself black American. I'm very proud of it." (Thus did Powell come within an inch of calling Woods a Tom.)

Of course, there is much truth—social truth—to this "one drop" business in America. The old saying is, America's the only country in the world in which a white woman can give birth to a black baby but a black woman can't give birth to a white baby. André Watts is considered, everywhere, a black American pianist. Who cares that his mother was a Hungarian? (And there is a long, long line of Hungarian pianists.) Tiger is not unmindful of all of this. He gives credit where credit's due, hailing, for example, black golf pioneers before him, including the legendary Teddy Rhodes (who never got a chance to strut his stuff on the proper professional stage). But neither is he bound by race.

Early in the game, he put out a "Media Statement," which he declared would be "the final and only comment I will make regarding the issue" of race and identity (fat chance—but the sentiment was nice). He said, "My parents have taught me to always be proud of my ethnic background. Please rest assured that is, and always will be, the case. . . . Truthfully, I feel very fortunate, and EQUALLY PROUD, to be both African-American and Asian! The critical and fundamental point is that ethnic background and/or composition should NOT make a difference. It does NOT make a difference to me. The bottom line is that I am an American . . . and proud of it! That is who I am and what I am. Now, with your cooperation, I hope I can just be a golfer and a human being."

Again: Fat chance.

When, after that Masters victory in '97, he told Oprah Winfrey "I'm just who I am," and to hell with the "genetic code," the you-know-what hit the fan. Many people charged him with virtual race treason. Leonard Pitts Jr., a columnist for the *Miami Herald*, said candidly, "It's simple. I want to claim him. I want him for my side." Mary A. Mitchell in the *Chicago Sun-Times* all but accused Tiger of passing, and said, "It is as if he thumbed his nose at an entire race of people." *Ebony* magazine commissioned a full-fledged symposium on the subject. In his contribution, Jesse Jackson said, "Many black people felt that we had this great emotional investment in Tiger and there was an intent by some forces to take him away from us. [By "some forces," the Reverend must have meant Woods's own, universalist statements.] . . . We have a sense that he is ours, and we are his."

A fellow golfer, however, asked for a little break. Vijay Singh, an Indian champion from Fiji, told William C. Rhoden of the *New York Times*, "When I first came to the United States, they approached me about the subject of my race and color. I just said, 'Hey, listen, I'm here to play golf.'" As for Tiger, "he's the best thing that's happened to golf in [years]. Let's leave it at golf, not color." But another athlete—Charles Barkley, the ex-NBA star and a Woods friend—has taken a different line. He once said, "Tiger likes to be okay with everybody, to appeal to all people. . . . [But] I tell him that Thai people don't get hate mail—black people do." (Barkley has also remarked Woods's fondness for scuba diving: "I don't get it. Black people aren't supposed to scuba dive." The hoopster's views on "buoyancy" are unknown.)

This last May, ESPN.com ran an article with a rather exasperated title:

"Will Tiger Ever Show the Color of His Stripes?" The author, Greg Garber, noted that Woods could check a full five boxes on the U.S. Census: white, black, Native American, Chinese, and Other Asian-American. (In fact, a bill in Congress to allow multiple check-offs was dubbed "the Tiger Woods bill"—as if in acknowledgement of the New American.) Garber quoted officials from various racial-ethnic groups, all kind of vying. And there was this lovely anecdote: The old champion Curtis Strange once said to Woods, "You have a multi-ethnic background. Is there a group you wish you were part of?" Woods answered, "I guess Boyz II Men" (of R&B fame).

Some are determined to stay unamused. *Sports Illustrated* had an interview with Jim Brown, the football great and con. Tiger is "focused on golf," said Brown, and "that's it." His interviewer protested that Tiger had set up the Tiger Woods Foundation, geared to helping disadvantaged kids. Brown answered, "Can I tell you something? Everybody does good things, but I'm talking about making major changes in the educational system that would impact an entire race. I'm talking about stopping these young gang members from killing one another. I'm talking about keeping prisons from overflowing. I'm not talking about teaching black kids to golf and get into country clubs. Come on!"

Not many commentators would put it just like Brown, but the sentiment is widespread.

'DISGRACE'

And you could hear some of it last July, when the controversy over Augusta National erupted. A women's group pressured the club (which holds the Masters) to admit women members, something it has so far resisted. As it happened, Woods, like the rest of the professional golf world, was in Scotland, trying to win the British Open—and, in Woods's case, trying to win the Grand Slam, of which he'd already won the first two legs. Tiger was immediately asked what he thought about Augusta policy, and he said, off the cuff, "They're entitled to set up their own rules the way they want them. It would be nice to see everyone have an equal chance to participate, but there's nothing you can do about it. . . . It's their prerogative."

Tiger was in a delicate position, as a three-time Masters winner and someone who, it seemed, did not equate a men-only policy with a whites-only policy. (Incidentally, the club at which the British Open was being played, the storied Muirfield, admits only men as members as well.) But the media class didn't see it Tiger's way, and came down on him with a startling ferocity.

Sally Jenkins of the *Washington Post* sicced Martin Luther King on him: "Those who sit at rest buy their quiet with disgrace." C. Jemal Horton of the *Indianapolis* Star sicced Malcolm X on him: "A man who stands for nothing will fall for anything" (and Woods's performance was "sickening," Horton said). The *Chicago Tribune* columnist Clarence Page suggested that Woods failed to win the British Open because "his conscience was bothering him." He also recommended that Woods boycott the Masters and the British Open, becoming, in this way, like Eric Liddell, the *Chariots of Fire* runner who refused to compete on Sunday. In his concluding sentence, Page warned that Tiger had better get "on the right side of history."

Many pundits compared Woods unfavorably to Jackie Robinson, and Muhammad Ali, and Smith and Carlos, the two tracksters who thrust black-power salutes at the Mexico City Olympics. They even contrasted him with Gary Player, the white South African who opposed apartheid. Everyone and his brother was brought in to analyze and judge. The *Christian Science Monitor* published a story—"Should Woods Carry the Black Man's Burden?"—that quoted the head of the International Society for Sports Psychiatry.

Woods, for his part, backpedaled somewhat, declaring on his website, "Would I like to see women members? Yes, that would be great, but I am only one voice. I'm not even a regular member." (A Masters champion is an honorary member.) At the recent PGA Tournament, on the general subject of political involvement, Woods observed, "It seems like the more putts I've holed and the lower my scores have become, the more knowledgeable I'm supposed to have gotten! . . . I can't be the leader in all causes. I'm still 26, and obviously I can probably do more as I get older and understand what I can and cannot give my time to. Right now, I'm very focused on my foundation's development and urban youth."

That's what he clings to, when these questions come up: that foundation. That's what his defenders cling to, too. See, they say, he's doing his part! (Tiger has even used these words: "I've done my part. That's what my foundation is all about. I'm trying to do my share.") And yet, what Tiger is doing more broadly—setting golf records, conducting himself in classy fashion, rising above racial-political madness—will do more for the "causes" than anything else. But what causes? Those of American unity, reason, good will.

A SPECIAL ROLE

It's true that Tiger has awakened interest in golf in black Americans particularly. I saw evidence of this with my own eyes. In the 1990s, I lived in Washington, D.C., and nearly every weekend would go down to one of the city's few ranges to practice. Place called Hains Point. The weekend after Tiger won the Masters for that first time—April '97—I went down to the range as usual, and the place was absolutely crawling with black young people, whacking at it for the first time. You couldn't help grinning. And Tiger Woods hadn't brought this about by any statements, or speeches at rallies, or denunciations. He'd done it simply by being himself—by existing, by doing his job, by excelling.

Just the other week, Jack Nicklaus, Tiger's predecessor, in many ways, got it exactly right. After playing with Woods in an exhibition, he said, "Tiger really got put on the spot with a question about, 'Why aren't you doing more for women?' It was all I could do to bite my tongue. I say, 'What more can he do?' Tiger Woods, just by being Tiger Woods, is doing a lot. He is doing a lot by the example he sets every day, the role model he is, the foundation he runs" (ah, that foundation always has to sneak in there—a security blanket; the former was enough).

That was too much—way too much—for Michael Wilbon, columnist for the *Washington Post*. He said, "Jack Nicklaus doesn't get to frame this conversation because it isn't about golf or championship competition. It's about social conscience and obligation as a person of color in America, and in that area, Nicklaus is no expert; he's not even in the game." In other words, "It's a black thing—you wouldn't understand." You could put in on a T-shirt (but then, somebody already has).

Without question, Tiger will never be "black" enough for some—for the "blacker-than-thou" crowd, as Thomas Sowell once put it. A few days ago, I saw a headline out of the nation's capital: "D.C. mayor 'proud' of his term; [Anthony] Williams disputes he's not 'black enough' to lead city." There are some who hate colorblindness—they fairly spit out the word—more than they hate racism itself. At least racism is something they can understand, being a type of racial obsession. A wag once said, "Philo-Semitism is the higher anti-Semitism." We might contemplate something similar in the realm of race.

Tiger, much against his will, is the rope in a kind of tug-of-war. All of us, indeed, want a piece of him. The racialists want to claim him—want him to be sort of the Maxine Waters of the fairways—and we anti-racialists want to claim him too. A lot of conservatives view him as one of them: He's devoted to excellence, he works in near solitude, he is utterly disciplined, he has a snappish independence, he asserts the right to be free from politics, he's hard to push around, he's financially shrewd ("tight," his father says), he despises whining, and—perhaps not least—he has a barely disguised contempt for the media! (At the PGA, a reporter asked him what was the "worst aspect" of being Tiger Woods. With a smile, Tiger pointed to the journos assembled for the press conference and said, "Easy: This.")

Michael Wilbon writes, "Tiger so has our attention, he has no idea what an agent for change he can be." Oh? Perhaps Tiger, who has lived with teeming, demanding crowds since he was a tyke, knows a bit more about this than the rest of us do. And why can't he be an agent for change in a universalist, colorblind, anti-racialist direction? Why can't his change tend toward transcendence? Writes Wilbon, "There's every reason to believe, given his intelligence and who his father is, that Tiger will develop his own social conscience." How amazingly condescending. What do you think his protests for One America—"all children," "everybody should be in the fold"—are, if not a social conscience? Wilbon: "A lot of people in this world are waiting to hear his voice." You mean, you haven't heard it? "The bottom line is that I am an American. I'm just who I am. A golfer and a human being."

Wilbon: "I'm one of those who believe that, when it's time, Tiger's voice will be clear and unwavering." It has been. It's just that a lot of folks haven't liked it. And they will hound him and hound him until he says what they want to hear. They'll never leave him alone. Never, never. Can Tiger hold out, be true to himself and the ideals he has already articulated? That would be as amazing as his golf record.

—September 16, 2002
National Review

Hootie vs. Hootie

The morality play surrounding
Augusta National

It may seem like ancient history now, but the New York Times, *some years back, campaigned for weeks against the Augusta National Golf Club. And the name "Hootie" was in the air.*

I t's strange that Augusta National's membership rolls should be such a big news story. Then too, it was strange that the 1948 presidential campaign should have been a big story—in December 2002. [N.B.: This is an allusion to a controversy engulfing Trent Lott, the Republican Senate leader.] Who knows how these things come about?

Well, I do—certainly in the case of Augusta National. The campaign to force the storied club to accept women members is the handiwork of two persons, primarily: Martha Burk, "chair" (as she says) of a group called the National Council of Women's Organizations, and Howell Raines, executive editor of the *New York Times*. Both have found a calling of sorts.

Augusta National is revered by much of this country, not least because it was founded by Bobby Jones, one of the greatest sports figures in our history, and because it hosts a touchstone tournament, the Masters. But the club is a soft target for activists, lampooners, crabs, and other nuisances: It's a golf club, first of all—always an object of mockery; it is a unique and exclusive one, famously hard to get into; it adheres to all manner of traditions, some of them laudable, some of them sort of silly; and it's located in the South. What could be more puncturable?

Listen to a columnist riffing and chortling in the *Washington Post*: "When boys build a neat treehouse, 'Members Only' is the first sign that goes up. Though, at the age when such things matter, the 's' in 'members' may be printed backwards. You need a special handshake, maybe give a drop of blood. As for icky girls, they can't come in at all. The most famous treehouse in America for little boys of all ages is located in the Georgia pines of Augusta. It's 'Spanky and Our Gang' for millionaires."

And who are these privileged and comical clubmates? Why, "Spanky, Alfalfa, and Hootie."

Who's Hootie? Ah, there's the killer. Why did he have to be named "Hootie"? Why did the current chairman of the Augusta National Golf Club have to be William W. (Hootie) Johnson, known to one and all by that nickname? This is Christmas morning—and Kwanzaa and the Fourth of July and everything else—for Augusta-bashers, and -ridiculers. It seems to confirm everything they want to believe about this peculiar and proud club: *Of course* the chairman would be named Hootie (if not Rufus, or Jefferson—as in Davis, of course, not the third president, slaveholder that he was).

Funny thing is, Johnson, a banker, has always been known as a progressive in his home state of South Carolina. He was a mover in the desegregation of the state's colleges and universities. He was a board member of the National Urban League (for heaven's sake). He was a trustee of Benedict College (a "historically black" institution). He received the Outstanding Citizen Award from the national B'nai B'rith—the only South Carolinian besides Bernard Baruch to be so honored, says one account of him.

No matter: In the national press now, he's just Hootie the Hoot, an "old coot," a cracker—some Bilbo or Boss Hogg.

And Martha Burk? Her bio describes her as a "political psychologist and women's equity expert," who has served on the board of NOW. Here's how she got the idea of going after Augusta National: As she related to that same *Washington Post*, she was watching last year's Masters on television. "The tournament was over, Tiger Woods has won, and it's time for the green jacket. So this guy comes out on camera and he says . . . 'A'hm Hootie Johnson, prezzz-a-dint of thuh Uh-gust-a National Golf Club.'" And Ms. Burk thought to herself, " Hootie Johnson, Ah'm a-gonna wraaaht yew uh letter!"

All class, this lady. One quirk of this story is that Martha Burk's childhood nickname was . . . Hootie. But, she says, meaningfully, "at some point I outgrew it." As for the moniker's relation to Chairman Johnson, "It's kind of cute, but it's a little hard to take a Hootie as seriously as you would a William or a Bill."

Yes. Anyway, she did indeed write Johnson a letter, and it was a classic of the genre. While subtle in spots, it said, essentially, "Start admitting women as members, or else." It was signed, "Martha Burk, Ph.D., Chair."

After Johnson got the letter, something very weird happened: He didn't wring his hands or ask for mercy or seek a quick, quiet solution. He came out firing. He went on the offensive. Rather like President Bush, he embraced a policy of preemption. Unlike the president (so far), he implemented it. In a personal letter, he told Dr. Burk—again, essentially—to stuff it. Then, in an official "statement," he warned of an anti-Augusta campaign ahead, complete with pickets, boycotts, and even Internet websites. But, he vowed, "we will not be bullied, threatened, or intimidated." It was clear that "Dr. Burk and her colleagues view themselves as agents of change and feel any organization that has stood the test of time and has strong roots in tradition—and does not fit their profile—needs to be changed. We do not intend to become a trophy in their display case." The chairman concluded, "There may well come a day when women will be invited to join our membership, but that timetable will be ours, and not at the point of a bayonet."

Well. That is about as strong a conservative statement as we have heard in a long time. Johnson was "taking his stand," as surely as John Crowe Ransom and all those other signers of the Southern Manifesto were doing. But was this a reprehensible stand? Was this some version of standing in the schoolhouse door? No, Johnson has insisted—repeatedly and eloquently (if with rough eloquence). There's nothing immoral or shameful—not to mention illegal—about an all-male club, or an all-female club, for that matter. Don't talk to me about civil rights, he says. This is an entirely different cat.

Hootie Johnson finds himself standing athwart history yelling, Stop—or rather, Y'all go on without Augusta.

Martha Burk, of course, did not stop. She threatened the commercial sponsors of the Masters telecast—Johnson said, "Okay, we'll do without sponsors. Why should they have to suffer from what is really a campaign against us?" She demanded that CBS stop broadcasting the tournament. The network said no thanks. She pressured the players—particularly Tiger Woods (a "minority," you know). She pressured individual members and their employers. She called on the PGA Tour to cease to recognize the Masters as an official event. She secured and published the membership rolls—"outing" the old fools, as she said.

And through it all, Hootie Johnson fumed. But he stood his ground, reasoning that Augusta National and its tournament were a good thing, and that attempts to sully them, or "reform" them, should fail.

The chairman is undoubtedly a piece of work. He rarely gives interviews, but when he does, he's about the bluntest, most irascible, most straight-talkin' guy out there. He may also have a touch of mischief. He told Clifton Brown of the *New York Times*, "We hold dear our tradition and our constitutional right to choose." Constitutional right to choose? Doesn't Johnson know that those words are to apply only to abortion? He insists that "single-gender organizations are good, and part of the fabric of America"— are you gonna go after the Girl Scouts and their cookies, too? He's a little like George W. Bush (again) in that he favors the monosyllabic answer: "Is there any chance that you and Martha Burk will meet face to face?" "No."

As for the other Hootie, Martha Burk (Ph.D., Chair), she's obviously having a ball. Her Warhol-allotted 15 minutes has extended to several months now. The media adore her. She poses for mags in green jackets (get it?). She's getting ready for big protests at the Masters come April. There has been talk of women in "green burqas." Jesse Jackson has promised to show up and help yell. Burk has launched a website called AugustaDiscriminates.org, which features a "Hall of Hypocrisy," meant to shame members who are corporate CEOs, with their "contempt for women" (no less).

Dr. Burk knows that there will be women members at Augusta one day. Johnson and his brethren pretty much know it too. It's just that they hate the idea that this eventuality will be interpreted as a correction of a moral failing. And they know that much of the heat on Augusta comes from sheer envy and resentment —and from too much time on certain hands, with too much real civil-rights work already accomplished.

Bobby Jones's club is, in its way, a "little platoon"—a little Burkean (although not Martha Burkean) brigade—and it is even a "point of light," seeing as it has given away $15 million in charity over the last five years. Martha Burk and the *New York Times* fancy that they're draggin' ol' Hootie into the 21st century, or the 20th, or the 19th, or whatever. Johnson acknowledges that, "in many ways, [Augusta] may be timeless. But there's nothing wrong with that."

He has a point.

—January 27, 2003
National Review

The Immortal Hogan

One man's greatness

W hen Ben Hogan died on July 25, the golf world seemed slightly stunned. He was 84 and had been sick for several years, but he was always a hovering presence around the game, a necessary part of its self-image. Not that he ever talked to anyone. He kept to himself at Shady Oaks Country Club in Fort Worth, smoking his cigarettes, staring out the window of the men's grill. Rule No. 1 at Shady Oaks was "Don't bother Mr. Hogan." But everyone revered him, and the staff of the club, during his long, final absence, kept a sign on his table that said "Reserved for Mr. Hogan."

He had been the greatest golfer in the world, and the sport's most mysterious hero. The first American star was Bobby Jones—scion of Atlanta society, Harvard-educated, the epitome of the gentleman golfer. Then came Hogan, who could not have been more different: hardscrabble, maniacal, obsessive about everything he touched. Next there was Arnold Palmer, golf's first television idol, who melted the screen with his charisma and approachability. And after him came Jack Nicklaus, the finest player ever, as even Hogan partisans will admit. [N.B.: This piece was written pre-Tiger.]

But it was Hogan who did most to develop the modern game. Before him, golf had been a "feel" sport, all art and no science, dominated by grizzled Brits and talented good-time Charlies like Walter Hagen. Hogan determined to make golf systematic and knowable. He was the first pro to make a religion out of practice. Hour after hour he stood on the shag range, experimenting with his swing, "digging it out of the dirt," as he said. He was a man utterly controlled by golf, and eventually he learned to control it. He could place his shots wherever he wanted, producing a "fade," a gentle left-to-right motion conducive to accuracy. He won 63 tournaments, including nine "majors," the tournaments that really count. In his banner year of 1953, he won three of the four majors—the Masters, the U.S. Open, and the British Open (all but the PGA)—an achievement still unequaled.

[Again, this was pre-Tiger.] At the time, he was the most famous athlete in the country, along with Joe DiMaggio and Ted Williams. All in all, Hogan defined a new standard and invited his opponents and imitators to meet it.

Every student of golf is familiar with the details of Hogan's life. He was born in 1912 in Stephenville, Texas, the son of a blacksmith. Ben was nine when his father took a gun and killed himself, with Ben in the room. Soon, Ben found a job as a caddy at a local club called Glen Garden. There, he threw himself into the game with a desperate abandon. He "practiced until his hands bled" (as innumerable fathers have recounted to their sons). He had no friends to speak of, only an imaginary companion named "Hennie Bogan," who sat on his shoulder and admonished him to do better. When night came, Ben slept in the course's sand bunkers. He announced to his mother that he would make himself a champion golfer or die. His boyhood was almost completely devoid of comfort or joy, but he later said, "I feel sorry for rich kids, I really do. They're never going to have the opportunity I had."

At 17, he dropped out of school and turned pro. Yet he was far from a brilliant golfer. He was adequate, and burned with a desire, never quenched, to get better. He failed, repeatedly, for some 15 years. He was so poor that he stole fruit from orchards and vegetables from gardens. In one well-known instance, he was robbed of the tires on his car in Oakland, Calif. He pounded on a brick wall and sobbed to another golfer, "This is the end. I can't move another inch." But he made his way to the course, wrapped himself in a mental cocoon, and shot 67, earning him a $285 check, the largest he had ever seen. He could go on.

Sometime in 1946, according to lore, Hogan had a revelation. In one version of the story, it came in a dream; in another, it came during one of his incessant practice sessions. He had always been plagued with a "hook"—a right-to-left running shot that leaves a golfer feeling helpless—but now he figured out how to hit a soft, manageable fade. This was Hogan's "secret," a much-debated insight about which Hogan himself was endlessly coy. (Sam Snead once remarked, disgustedly, "Anybody can say he's got a secret when he won't tell what it is.") Whatever he glimpsed, Hogan began to win, and win consistently.

There emerged a mighty triumvirate of Snead, Hogan, and Hogan's boyhood acquaintance Byron Nelson. The three men were markedly dissimilar: Nelson a near saint; Hogan a bitter perfectionist; Snead a crude, extravagantly gifted country bumpkin. It seemed that one of them would win every tournament on tour. But in time, by some unfathomable force of will, Hogan pulled ahead. He was unstoppable. The rest of the field would look at him and, demoralized, simply know that he would not falter. At 5 feet, 8 inches, 140 pounds, "Bantam Ben" was the most feared competitor in golf. In January 1949, *Time* magazine put him on its cover, with the legend, "If you can't outplay them, outwork them."

One month later came "the Crash," as it is known in golf history. Hogan and his wife Valerie were returning home to Fort Worth from a tournament in Phoenix. The fog around El Paso was thick. A Greyhound bus, not seeing the Hogans' car, tried to pass a truck and barreled straight toward them. A second before impact, Hogan hurled himself across his wife in an effort to protect her. His action probably spared his own life, as the car's steering column was propelled through the driver's seat. Valerie was relatively unharmed, but Hogan was close to death. For two months, the nation's attention was riveted on the hospital. Word was that, even if he survived, he would be an invalid. On April 1, he was taken from his bed on a stretcher and placed on a train back home. There, slowly, in extraordinary pain, Hogan began to sit up and later to walk. Cards, letters, and telegrams poured in to him from every state. No longer was he viewed as a cold, distant golfing machine, but as a valiant, lionhearted battler. Everyone—for a change—was rooting for him. Hogan had never succumbed to anything, and he would not, in fact, succumb to the Crash.

He first swung a club again in the autumn. In December, he played 18 holes, with the help of a motor scooter. Two weeks later, he entered the Los Angeles Open. Amazingly, despite his aching and fatigued body, he played Snead to a tie. He lost in the playoff, but, as Grantland Rice famously wrote, he really "didn't lose—his legs simply weren't strong enough to carry his heart around." In June the next year, 16 months after the car crash, Hogan won the U.S. Open at Merion near Philadelphia, an event Dan Jenkins called "the most incredible comeback in the history of sports." On the 72nd hole—the final hole of the tournament—Hogan laced a 1-iron to the green to cinch the championship. The photograph taken of Hogan's follow-through on that shot—with Hogan ideally posed, wearing his trademark "Hogan cap"—is a totem of the game, displayed on nearly every golf-shop wall.

In 1951, Hollywood made a movie about Hogan: *Follow the Sun*, starring Glenn Ford. In 1953, he sailed to Carnoustie in Scotland to participate in the British Open, the only time he did so. The Scots, astonished at the precision and concentration of the peculiar Texan who captured their tournament with ease, dubbed him "The Wee Ice Man." When his ship docked in New York, the city gave him a ticker-tape parade down Broadway, the first since General MacArthur's. The next year, Hogan founded a club-manufacturing company, which bore his name and which he was to oversee until 1993. In 1957, he contributed a series of instructional articles to *Sports Illustrated*, which became the bestselling *Five Lessons: The Modern Fundamentals of Golf*—a book that, though effective, confused many with its barely comprehensible talk of "pronation" and "supination." Hogan played creditable golf into the late '60s, but his putting—the bane of any golfer's advancing years—gave out on him, rendering his always-superb ball-striking moot.

While an admirable man, Hogan was not a pleasant one. In fact, many would say—even in a time of eulogy—that he was intolerable. Once, when he was sitting alone at his table for eight at Shady Oaks, someone cracked, "There's Hogan, with all his friends." Gary Player supposedly called him up from South America one day, suffering from a slump and seeking help. "What clubs are you playing?" asked Hogan. "Dunlop," answered Player. "Then call Mr. Dunlop," Hogan replied, hanging up. Nick Faldo once asked him what it took to win the U.S. Open. Hogan answered, with impeccable logic, "Shoot the lowest score." Similarly, when someone complained, "I'm having trouble with my long putts," Hogan came back with, "Why don't you hit the ball closer to the hole?" He once teased a golfer who yearned to know how to play a particular shot by saying, ludicrously, "I try to hit it on the second groove." And then there was the time when President Eisenhower phoned, and Hogan barked to his secretary, "I'm not going to play with that g**d**** hack." Hogan acknowledged no power above the ability to hit a golf ball soundly and to prevail in important tournaments.

"The Hawk" (this was another of Hogan's nicknames) was not the kind of hero that we have come to expect: the hero of the *Donahue* age, telling interviewers of his joys and sorrows, his triumphs and defeats, wearing his emotions on his sleeve. He once said—explaining his refusal to make public appearances, even to inaugurate the minor-league circuit christened the Hogan Tour—"Not everyone wants publicity, you know." Shrewd man that he was, he probably recognized the dangers of overexposure and the benefits of silence. He gave only one significant interview in the last decades of his life, in 1987 to a golf magazine: "The Hawk Talks!" the cover blared. His biographer, Curt Sampson, writes, "Insular types such as Bennie Hogan have always been drawn to golf, a sport requiring an ability to concentrate for long periods of time but with no mandate for cooperation or closeness with a teammate. He also enjoyed the utter fairness of the game, the way it compelled him to accept all the credit or all the blame. He loved its solitude, the way it absorbed him."

Hogan was unwilling to play the Senior Tour—on which Snead, Palmer, and others love to entertain and soak up the applause—because he could not stand for the public to see him at less than his best. But he still hit balls, never stopped practicing, never allowed his hands to grow uncallused.

Hogan—almost unique among professionals—did not play for glory (though he achieved it) or for money (though he earned it). He played in order to conquer the game, to solve its riddles, to bring it, at long last, to its knees. Upon hearing of Hogan's death, Ben Crenshaw said, "He defined the inner will that lives within us." No, it manifestly does not live within all of us—even dormant—but it lived unappeasably within Hogan, and because of it he was a great player, and a great man.

—August 11, 1997
The Weekly Standard

Dream Beat

Reporting from a PGA Tour tournament

No one likes a braggart, but here's a fact: A golf tournament is a much nicer experience with a press pass. And you feel the difference immediately.

You arrive at the Kemper Open, outside Washington, D.C., with thousands of other fans. You get to the public parking lot, where you've always left your car before, but you don't stop. You keep going . . . and going. At checkpoint after checkpoint, you're waved through by smiling young people, all because of the magical pass that dangles from your rearview mirror. When you finally reach your designated lot, you're practically in the clubhouse. No wonder people resent the press.

Then you check in at the media center, where you're greeted by a platoon of eager-beaver volunteers who will ensure that you have everything you need. So what do you need? Everything: programs (expensive to the average Joe), newspapers, PGA Tour paraphernalia, phones, fax machines . . . and the food tent. Ah, the food tent, where you feast all day on sandwiches and pie, exchanging Tour gossip with the grizzled press, some of whom are famous.

When the spirit moves you, you wander over to the practice range, to see who's warming up. Fans have lined the rope two and three deep, but you don't have to stand with them: You head straight for the entrance, where a couple of semi-huffy guards try to stop you. But they can't, because you have that thing hanging from your neck, and, in a second, you're mingling with the titans of golf—questioning them, joking with them, spying (or, if you like, reporting) on them.

Much of the talk—no surprise here—is about women: "I think that deal might have been firmed up last night," says one of the players. "Oh?" says another. "Horizontal?" Another pro, who styles himself "Big Daddy from Cincinnati," is a well-known connoisseur of the nation's strip bars, and, sure enough, he has a blonde with him right there on the range—and she doesn't look like his wife, or anyone else's.

But there are other scenes, too, best appreciated from a reporter's privileged vantage: swing gurus trying to straighten out their anxious clients; players yakking on their cellphones, inquiring about endorsement contracts; Jesper Parnevik (son of "The Johnny Carson of Sweden") cracking up his friends; Dicky Pride (now there's a name) instructing a portly volunteer who has asked for swing advice; and Justin Leonard—one of *Cosmopolitan* magazine's "25 Most Eligible Bachelors"—being teased about the gaggle of giggling girls waiting for his autograph.

Then, it's on to the first tee, scene last year of a notorious episode. Greg Norman, the president's jerk pal, threw a screaming fit at the announcer, simply because the man had made a gentle reference to Clinton's injury at Norman's Florida estate. The man has since died, and the Kemper people have installed a plaque in his honor. Norman also flipped the bird to one of his fans in the gallery last year. Swell guy, and totally deserving of Clinton.

Out on the course, you hunt down some of the more interesting players, looking for stories. Sandy Lyle is there, a hulking Scotsman who was once the world's top golfer but has been languishing for a decade. His demeanor is admirably stoic, as he struggles to recoup his game. You notice, though, that he says, "Sh**," after poor shots: just as he did on television one year at the Masters (whereupon Ken Venturi, in the booth, said, "That describes it").

You also spot Esteban Toledo, a former lightweight boxing champion from Mexico who has cast his fate with golf. He still looks like he could go twelve rounds with anyone, and his headcovers are—what else?—boxing gloves. Just as Lyle is followed by British-accented fans, Toledo is surrounded by Spanish-speaking ones, who shout *Viva!* after even mediocre tee shots. Toledo may be an average Tour player, but he's a remarkable athlete, adored by his public.

As the parade passes by, you realize that you know these guys embarrassingly well—from golf magazines and books and interview shows. This one is recovering from a divorce; that one has been to a hypnotist. This one is a fervent Bible student; that one is losing his putting stroke to drink. The caddies, too, are part of the pageant, some of them as familiar as their bosses. They are perhaps the motliest crew on earth—the carnies of the fairways—and they don't shy away from your notepad, especially if you have cigarettes to give.

Back in the media center, your glorious Walter Mitty/Ferris Bueller day is coming to a close. The print men tap at their laptops; the TV men fool with their hair; the radio men tape their spots. You wonder whether you are spoiled for life—whether you will ever again be able to attend a tournament in the ordinary way. But you don't wonder for long. You are jubilantly, almost impossibly happy. And you have a story to file.

—June 22, 1998
The Weekly Standard

Golf at the Movies

Lamenting *Tin Cup*, etc.

I t's not every day that golfers are treated to a movie about their sport, so they rejoice at every crumb from Hollywood's table—or recoil from it. The latest such crumb is *Tin Cup*, a Kevin Costner vehicle about a no-account practice-range operator who gets it together and shines at the U.S. Open. So golfers at last have their *Rocky* (sort of). But unlike the original, this one won't win any prizes, and shouldn't.

Tin Cup was anxiously awaited in the golf world for over a year, and the golf press reported on every stage of its development: the hiring of the *Bull Durham* team of director Ron Shelton and leading man Costner; the tutoring of Costner by journeyman pro and TV announcer Gary McCord; the actor's progress; the effort to achieve an air of authenticity by giving cameos to a host of PGA Tour players. The Internet's most prominent golf site created a special sub-site just for the movie. *Golf* magazine put it this way in its August issue: "All right, this is the last you'll hear from us about the movie, due out this month."

Golfers were nervous about *Tin Cup* for good reason: The game has never been accurately or meaningfully portrayed on the big screen. So, perpetually insecure about their image in larger society, golfers fretted about the impact of a big-time movie with big-time names (the links equivalent of "Is it good for the Jews?"). Spike Lee says that when he was making *Malcolm X*, black people would come up to him and say, "You'd better not mess this up." Golfers were fairly sure that the *Tin Cup* folks, however well-intentioned, would mess it up.

It so happens that American golf and the movies were born at about the same time. In 1888, a band of Scotsmen, nostalgic for their national pastime, scratched out a course in Yonkers, N.Y. (dubbing it "St. Andrews"); eight years later, the first golf movie was made, a one-reeler called *Golfing Extraordinary* that consisted of a poor klutz's taking a swing and missing. It's been pretty much the same treatment ever since. The Little Rascals made a golf movie, as did the Three Stooges. Hope and Crosby—who were superb amateurs—incorporated the sport in several of their Road movies. Tracy and Hepburn made *Pat and Mike*, in which Kate (who had grown up with the game in New England) played a pro and Babe Didrickson Zaharias strutted her stuff.

Things picked up a little in the early '50s when Glenn Ford starred as Ben Hogan in *Follow the Sun*, about Hogan's stirring recovery from a near-fatal car accident. But many golfers, including Hogan, were disgusted by the movie because Ford, on the course, was unbelievable as a professional, and virtually nothing of the game's emotional power was realized.

Strangely, the truest and most enduring golf movie of all is not really a golf movie but a raunchy, *Animal House*-inspired comedy: *Caddyshack* (1981). To say that this movie has a cult following among golfers is too mild; it has seeped into the bloodstream of most every golfer under 45, its sensibility and language rendered permanent, like Scripture or Shakespeare.

When preparing a shot: "Be the ball, Danny." When admonishing a balker: " You're going to play golf and you're going to like it." When fudging a score: "Mark me down for five." When fantasizing about a Masters triumph: " Cinderella story . . ." In praise of another: "That's a peach, hon."

When refusing to leave the course in torrential rain: "Looks like the heavy stuff won't be coming down for quite some time." When engaging in the kind of hyperbole endemic to the game: "Big hitter, the Lama—long" (that's Lama as in Dalai). When Bill Murray, a *Caddyshack* star, hits the pro-am circuit, he is bombarded by fans who shout swatches of the movie's script to him in unison.

So what of *Tin Cup*? The movie starts out promisingly, showing a tumbledown range in west Texas ("Last Chance to Hit Balls Fore 520 Miles"). But we quickly ascertain that the movie will be a gentle piece of nonsense: A charming rogue (Costner) will try to steal a fetching girl (Rene Russo) from a snooty, dislikable Tour pro (Don Johnson). The movie is sluggish and trite. But worse, it does a disservice to golf—and this from a film that was to help erase a bagful of bad cinematic memories.

How golf-ignorant is it? When Russo shows up for her first lesson, Costner has her hit a driver (unthinkable), unteed (unheard of). He, the pro, hits obvious chunks that are meant to be perfect. She slices a shot right of right, and they both point down the middle, beaming.

A charity best-ball tournament is played as a cut-throat competition and is broadcast on television. Golfers have caddies hit shots in the middle of play. Peter Kostis, one of the smartest teaching pros in the country, is made to say ridiculous things. Frank Chirkinian, the longtime "ayatollah" of CBS golf production, is furious that an unknown is leading the Open, when in fact he'd be thrilled out of his gourd. The expression "chili-dip" is egregiously misused. At one point, the gallery appears to be standing on the green.

So golfers don't yet have the movie they long for, and they may never: The sport may be impossible to capture in this medium. It is different from football, basketball, and baseball in that it is solitary, mental, interior. A golfer's struggle takes place in his head, and the mask seldom betrays much. The rhythms of golf are ponderous, subtly discerned. There is no team, with its various characters, all coming together for victory (or not); there is no coach (except for some pricey gurus); there is no frenzied stadium or arena (in golf, the applause comes later and is of a different nature). How could a moviemaker convey the chaos in a golfer's stomach and throat when he's facing a slick double-breaker on the 18th hole of a Friday round when he absolutely must make the cut and earn a check? How could a movie demonstrate the stark terror a golfer feels when he wakes up in the morning to find that, whereas he had it yesterday, he has totally and inexplicably lost it today?

Golf has fared slightly better in literature: F. Scott Fitzgerald, Ring Lardner, and P. G. Wodehouse wrote excellent short stories, and Walker Percy was and John Updike is golf-haunted in the extreme. Dan Jenkins, the sportswriter-novelist, has translated some of the game's nobility and devilishness, as in his *Dogged Victims of Inexorable Fate* and *Dead Solid Perfect*. But ultimately, golf may be a little like a religion—difficult to articulate and impossible to persuade others of. They will have to encounter it for themselves.

As golf's popularity increases, its custodians and devotees are going to have to get used to seeing their pet in movies, for better or worse. Clint Eastwood has bought the rights to Michael Murphy's novel *Golf in the Kingdom*, a fable of New Age mysticism that has befogged countless golf minds. A slew of other golf movies are forthcoming, with titles like *Swingtime*, *Fast Greens*, and *Out of the Rough*. And most portentously, there will be *Stroke of Genius*, the Bobby Jones story starring heartthrob Brad Pitt. Jones is the icon of American golf, our spiritual guide, the father of us all. *Don't mess this up.*

—August 26, 1996
The Weekly Standard

MUSIC

Farewell, Fat Man

Luciano Pavarotti bows out

He was our Caruso, and now he's gone—or almost gone. In the first half of March, Luciano Pavarotti bade farewell to the Metropolitan Opera with three appearances in *Tosca*. He is scheduled to retire altogether sometime in 2005—on his 70th birthday, he has said, which will be in October of that year. Many people claim that he should have bowed out long before, but it was hard for him to go, and, frankly, it was hard for the public to let him go. Pavarotti was a performer. He was also a superb—a historically superb—tenor and musician.

His story is familiar to anyone who has poked around opera. Born in Modena, Italy. His father a baker, his mother a worker in a tobacco factory. Luciano shared a wet nurse with Mirella Freni (the famed soprano)—that is one of the great trivial facts in opera.

The baker father also happened to be a singer—an amateur one, and by all accounts a gifted one—and he passed this enthusiasm to his son. The son learned, quickly, under excellent teachers. He boasted one of the most extraordinary voices of the century: It was essentially a lyric voice—a bel canto voice—but it had power that came out of nowhere. He was both graceful and strong, a hart and a lion. His technique was astoundingly secure and capable. He was a master of Italian declamation, one of the last such exemplars around.

And his personality? Big and sunny and rich and happy as Italy (pardon the sentimentality).

He became a key part of the bel canto revival around the world, joining Joan Sutherland, her husband Richard Bonynge, and Marilyn Horne. For his feats in Donizetti's *Fille du Régiment*, he was dubbed "King of the High C's," a label that stuck. The king sold a lot of records. His company, Decca, is describing him as "the most beloved opera star in the history of the recording industry." They are not to be argued with.

Pavarotti was occasionally dismissed as a simpleton with a freak instrument. This was absurd. Pavarotti was a marvelous musician, though not a schooled one. He was a natural. Anyone can acquire the schooling; musicality is not for sale. It has always been said—whispered, snorted— that Pavarotti can't read music. I, for one, was always skeptical of this claim. First of all, millions of schoolchildren around the world can read music—it's no big deal. Second, how could Pavarotti function, in his career, without reading music? It's on the order of functioning in the literary world without being able to read words.

Not long ago, I had a chance to speak to someone close to Pavarotti, a colleague (who adores him). "Would you put a myth to rest for me?" I asked. "What about this ridiculous notion that Pavarotti can't read music?" "He can't," replied my source. "He really can't"—which, of course, makes Pavarotti's achievement all the more remarkable. He has a phenomenal memory, a phenomenal ability to absorb, repeat, intuit.

Over the years, Pavarotti became a celebrity, one of the most famous musicians in the world (classical division). He was the big smiley guy with the big handkerchief and the big voice (the big, lyrical voice). Some of us affectionately called him The Fat Man. Taking a page from opera stars past, he appeared in a movie, *Yes, Giorgio*, forgettable but not without charm. He lost some goodwill when he divorced his wife of almost 40 years to marry his assistant—but the world doesn't care much about that kind of thing anymore, if it ever did.

Sometime in the 1980s—different people would pick different dates— Pavarotti began a decline, vocally (and physically, too: They are of course related). I recall a distinguished critic telling me in 1985, I believe, that "they should put that cow out to pasture." As you know, he sang for 20 more years, and he often sang well—splendidly well. He loved a crowd, and not just an opera-house crowd: He pioneered "stadium concerts," schlocky events featuring pastiches of arias and songs. Infamously, he was caught lip-synching at one such event. It was the most unforgivable thing The Fat Man ever did, professionally. It was an utter violation, impermissible in the classical world. He pleaded that he could not sing that day but didn't want to disappoint his fans. Whatever.

I myself attended one stadium-style concert, when out-of-town friends asked me to take them. The year was 1995; the venue was a sports arena outside Washington, D.C. The event was a horror, of course, with Pavarotti crooning and barking and cracking, all into a microphone, with a lousy pickup orchestra. But there were moments when he was his pure vocal, operatic, and musical self, and you forgot the jumbo video screens, and the championship banners hanging from the rafters, and the stickiness of spilled

Coke under your feet: You might have been in a box at La Fenice. A talent and a mind—a musical mind—like Pavarotti's will out. It will out even when covered in goop.

His great rival, of course, was Plácido Domingo, the suave Spaniard. But the rivalry was mainly in Plácido's mind, and in the minds of the fans. The Fat Man never paid Domingo much heed. I asked someone important in Pavarotti's career—another source—why Domingo wasn't a spur to Pavarotti, why Luciano didn't take better care of himself, just to keep up with Plácido. The source answered, "You don't understand: Plácido has always cared about Luciano; but Luciano has never given a damn about Plácido or anyone else. As far as Luciano is concerned, he has no rivals." Besides, Pavarotti "is the laziest son-of-a-bitch God ever made."

He was supposed to have his swan song at the Met two seasons ago (this was *Tosca* as well). But he canceled, pleading the flu. This caused some upset, although a singer's life is precarious, and when you're sick, you're sick—even if the gig is monumental. But, for some weird reason, Pavarotti wouldn't even come to the house to explain, apologize, and wave. As a major agent in New York put it, "all he had to do was show up and croak out 'I can't sing,' and the people would have gone mad in adoration." Joseph Volpe, general manager of the Met, said to Pavarotti, over the phone, "That's a helluva way to end a beautiful career"—and he related this conversation to the Met audience. But Volpe gave The Fat Man one more chance, in the form of the three *Toscas* this March.

On the first night, he was weak, vocally and physically. He did some Pavarotti-like singing, but not much of it. In body, he was quite infirm, sitting whenever he could, and hanging on to his colleagues—literally hanging on—when he had to stand.

But on the last night, he was much better, certainly vocally. He delivered a brave performance, and a dignified one. He went out with his head high, not as a clownish figure who had stayed too long, but as the historic tenor he is: *primo tenore assoluto*. The final ovation was emotional and long. Pavarotti smiled as big as he could, and waved as big as he could. Has anyone ever loved the audience more? Has the audience ever loved anyone more?

Look: After the hype fades, the recordings will remain, and they will tell the tale. Beverly Sills once said (and I paraphrase), "When they ask what all the fuss was about, I can trot out the records and say, 'Here: *This* is what all the fuss was about.'" So it will be with The Fat Man. Caruso made his first record in 1902, and we are still talking about him, more

than 100 years later. They will talk about Pavarotti 100 years from now.
Maybe 500.

—April 5, 2004
National Review

The Comeback Kid

Leon Fleisher with two hands

A momentous event occurred at Carnegie Hall on October 31,
Halloween night: Leon Fleisher played a recital with two hands.
Why such a big deal? Fleisher has been one of the most celebrated
pianists in the world for as long as most people can remember. But he had
not played a recital in Carnegie Hall—not with ten fingers—since 1947.
The evening was packed not only with musical power, but with emotional
power as well.

The Fleisher story is famous, at least in music circles, but I will run
through it. The pianist was born in San Francisco, to a father from Odessa
and a mother from Chelm. As a boy, he came under the guidance of Pierre
Monteux, the great French conductor who was resident in San Francisco. At
nine, he began to study with Artur Schnabel, a historic pianist. In the summer of 1938, young Fleisher traveled to Tremezzo, Italy—on Lake Como—
to take lessons from master. Not long after, the master, of course, had to
leave Europe in a hurry—and he went to New York. The Fleisher family
moved from California so that Leon could study full time with him.

"Was he a good teacher?" I ask. "Could he communicate what he
knew?" "He was an unbelievably good teacher," answers Fleisher. "Not
only was he able to communicate what he knew, he did so at a level of inspiration that was just staggering." And, by the way, how was his English?
"Oh, his English was extraordinary, for someone whose mother tongue it
wasn't. He sounded like Richard Burton with a German accent. He relished
each syllable."

In 1952—now age 24—Fleisher won the Queen Elisabeth Competition
in Belgium. On the jury: Artur Rubinstein, Robert Casadesus, and Rudolf

Firkusny, among others. Among the other contestants: Maria Tipo, Theodore Lettvin, and Philippe Entremont (who finished *tenth*, oddly enough).

Fleisher went on to a blazing career, making soon-canonical recordings of Beethoven and Brahms with the conductor George Szell, in Cleveland. How did Szell—who could be severe—treat Fleisher? "Very well, believe it or not. He adored my teacher, and it was through him that I met Szell when I was twelve or thirteen. I think it was clear that he had some crypto-paternal feelings toward me."

In 1964, Leon Fleisher was 37, and at the top of his game. But then disaster struck. He contracted what came to be known as dystonia, a neuro-logical disorder making normal use of a hand (for example) impossible. In this case, it was the right hand. Fleisher's left hand would always remain unaffected.

"For two years," he says, "I was in a deep funk," which is to put it mildly. It was hard to do anything. He divorced. Then he slowly started coming back to life, helping to form a chamber-music group, taking up con-ducting (which his ailment did not prevent him from doing)—and teaching. I hazard to ask, "Did you ever resent your students, who could play, while they might have had much less to impart, musically?" "No," chuckles Fleisher, before adding, "There might have been a certain irony."

At first, Fleisher would not look at the left-hand-alone literature, which is sizable: "I denied my condition" by ignoring this music altogether. But eventually, he came to it, playing the Ravel D-major concerto, Britten's *Diversions*, and other works, many of them commissioned by Paul Wittgen-stein, the pianist (and brother of the philosopher) who lost his right arm in World War I. Says Fleisher, "There are over 1,000 pieces for the left hand alone, and most of them are crap—forgive me. But there is one recital's worth, maybe two recitals' worth, of really good stuff." Fleisher is respon-sible for a lot of that stuff, as many composers of our own day came to write music especially for him.

I ask Fleisher whether, while practicing with his left hand, he would ever sneak in some right hand, just to check. "All the time, every day," he says. Was it ever any different? "It was always the same"—"petrified flesh," is one of the ways he puts it.

In 1979, another celebrated pianist, Gary Graffman, unfortunately joined him. He, too, lost the use of his right hand. Says Fleisher, with typi-cal candor, "On one level, I was kind of grateful when it happened, because it proved that a) I wasn't crazy, and b) I wasn't a freak. And it gave me strength to cry out about this problem. A lot of people out there with dystonia don't want to talk about it, they want to hide it. You will see cancellations by pianists because they are 'indisposed.' Very often, that 'indisposition' is dystonia, to one degree or another." Needless to say, "I felt for Gary, and I knew what he was going through, but, together, we could bring attention to this problem."

Fleisher tried every kind of treatment, "from A to Z and beyond," he says. "You name it, I've done it: alternative, conventional . . ." In 1981, he attempted a comeback, having found some relief, but it proved a mirage.

Flash forward to 1995, however: The pianist found greater and more enduring relief in a process called "rolfing," and then Botox. Rolfing is a kind of massage therapy that restores flexibility and softness to muscles. After two years of this therapy, Fleisher was ready for Botox—the very thing that actresses (and others) now use to straighten out their wrinkles. It has a more serious function in treating dystonia, altering the neurological picture.

After 30 years of silence—two-handed silence—Leon Fleisher made a return. "Now that I look back over it, and consider the lessons I have learned, I'm not so sure that, if I could relive my life, I would have it any different. The only reason I was able to come out of that depression around '66, '67, was the knowledge, the awareness, that my relationship with music was more than just as a two-handed piano player. I became a better teacher—I couldn't push a student off the chair and say, 'This is what I need.' I had to start to use words, to convey what is essentially unconveyable in words, because of what music is. And I started to conduct, which has afforded me some of my most meaningful and satisfying moments, not only in musical life, but in life in general. The greatest joys are those that are shared."

In sum, "I have tried to put this whole experience to the best use possible."

I ask him a dumb question: "Did you ever fantasize about coming back, with both hands?" "For 30 years." I ask a less dumb question: "Did you ever doubt you would?" "No," Fleisher says. "No. I knew that there was some kind of answer, if not a total answer." People should understand that the agony did not lie in the denial of a glorious career—it lay in the inability to play, even for himself, "to realize what was in my head, to make manifest what was inside me." But Fleisher had teaching, conducting, and the left hand, and these were means of doing "what keeps me going, what keeps me alive, which is making music."

At the recital in Carnegie Hall, on Halloween night, Fleisher began with some Bach: Egon Petri's arrangement of *Sheep May Safely Graze*. He devoted the second half of the program to Schubert's Sonata in B flat, D. 960, one of the most profound works in the piano literature. Fleisher does not believe that one should play an encore after this sonata, but he had one planned: He was going to repeat *Sheep May Safely Graze*, but this time he would have the aid of some of his students, placed throughout the hall. With tape recorders in their laps, they were going to play gentle sheep bleatings—just for some levity. But Fleisher was "thwarted," as he says, because vigilant Carnegie ushers would not allow the tape recorders into the hall!

So instead, he brought out a Halloween basket—one that looked like a jack-o'-lantern—and offered candy to patrons in the first row. A light, lovely touch from a man who has been through hell, and whose greatness is far more than musical.

—December 31, 2003
National Review

Jackie, Oh!

A 'pops recital' from Marilyn Horne

An aging diva has to ask some hard questions: When to retire? How much decline to accept? When to quit opera? How long to hang on in song recitals? What to sing?

Of course, different divas come up with different answers. Beverly Sills determined not to sing a note past 50 (though she agreed to a "Jingle Bells" with President Reagan). Leontyne Price bowed out of opera in 1985, then gave song recitals until 1998, when she was 71. (She came out of retirement just the other week, to participate in a benefit concert at Carnegie Hall for a World Trade Center fund. Someone had said, "It would be good to get someone like Leontyne Price." Someone else had replied, "Why not Leontyne Price?") The Italian soprano Magda Olivero went on for something like forever, and never really embarrassed herself.

As for Marilyn Horne, she wrote in her 1984 autobiography, "I have a deal with Marty Katz [her longtime accompanist]. He's promised to let me know when I'm no longer singing the way he and I know I want to sing. If I go on too long, blame Marty."

Who knows what kinds of conversations she has had with Katz? Horne is now 67, and she seems to be "retired from classical music," as the press clips have it, but she occasionally gives a kind of pops recital (to coin a necessary phrase). She gave such a recital on October 13 at little Converse College in Spartanburg, S.C. The diva in twilight tends to like to appear in out-of-the-way places (although Converse has a distinguished music program): Leontyne Price gave her last recitals in smallish venues, often on college campuses. Her very last recital—full recital—was in Chapel Hill, N.C., and it was attended by none other than Marilyn Horne: one American treasure paying tribute to, and soaking up the last notes of, another.

Now, Horne is almost universally acknowledged to be one of the greatest singers not just of her own time, but of all time. In her decades as a performer, "Jackie" (to use her nickname) set standards that are nearly impossible for others to reach. So how she spends her last professional years is of some interest. Mainly she busies herself with the Marilyn Horne Foundation, which is devoted to the nurturing of young singers, and of the song recital. She gave a master class at the Juilliard School last January, when she had a nasty cold and had injured her leg or foot, forcing her to use a cane. She told the students, "I was worried that I would come looking like the dowager voice teacher. Then it hit me: I *am* the dowager voice teacher!" But she has some of that historic voice left, she has loads of wisdom and musicianship, and she has what just may be an undimmed yen to perform.

Fortunately for her, she has always had an affinity for American popular music (meaning, by and large, folk songs, patriotic songs, and show tunes). She did much of her growing up in southern California, and she is encyclopedic about the popular culture—certainly the musical aspect of it—of an earlier, better era. After all, here's someone who was the (dubbed) voice of Dorothy Dandridge in the movie *Carmen Jones*, the "black version" of Bizet's opera *Carmen*—not bad for a chubby-cheeked white girl born in Bradford, P-A.

At Converse College, Horne presented a program made up chiefly of Gershwin, Jerome Kern, Cole Porter, and Irving Berlin. In collaboration with her was the Broadway arranger and all-purpose music man Don Pippin (Katz's services are no longer required, apparently). Horne is still recognizable as herself: that is, she sounds like Marilyn Horne, and often does some Horne-like things in her singing. It's sort of like seeing a beautiful woman who is well on in years: The face is still recognizable, but it has wrinkled and otherwise changed. We may delight in seeing that face, but at the same time we may be a little sad (and even ashamed of being so).

Horne was miked—she, one of the greatest vocal projectors in history. That itself was a jolt. She kept up a patter with the audience, revealing that well-loved personality: witty, bright, engaging. She treats these show tunes essentially as art songs, according them a dignity, and, of course, keeping her own dignity. It's a bit hard to hear her sing flat—the Horne intonation was always unshakable—and she suffered some most un-Horne-like wobbles. But her breathing is still a marvel, and model, and she remains one of the great singers in English—enunciators of English—ever.

This time, too, she was fighting a cold, but she never mentioned it, and worked easily around it. She had on stage with her a glass of water, remarking that she had always envied cabaret and lounge singers for the water they had by them. And now she could indulge! Her "In the Still of the Night"—once a favorite encore of hers—was shimmering and thrilling. "Over the Rainbow" was slow, delicate, and exquisite, the best treatment I, for one, have ever heard accorded this song (sorry, Judy). "Georgia" was southern, soulful, and well-nigh definitive (sorry, Ray). A graceful "Smoke Gets in Your Eyes" showed the difference between Horne and Eileen Farrell, the great soprano who spent the last portion of her career as a jazz singer: Horne applies her classical knowledge and standards to these . . . well, standards; Farrell performed in a separate jazz style. Each is irreproachable.

From what Horne did in South Carolina, it was clear that she could still sing proper recitals—classical recitals—if she wanted to. She has plenty of voice, plenty of technique, plenty of range. She could begin with some not-so-taxing Baroque pieces, continue with some not-so-taxing lieder or other art songs, throw in a manageable opera aria or two, and then—in the last quarter or third of her program—go pops. But this is the life she has evidently chosen for herself at this stage. Eileen Farrell declared, through a song, "I Gotta Right to Sing the Blues." And Horne certainly has a right to do whatever she desires—and she does it beautifully. And yet, as you listen to her, you can't help thinking, with a cringe, *Marilyn Horne is doing a lounge act*.

As she talked to the audience, Horne made frequent mention of her age, and of age generally. These questions are plainly on her mind. Toward the end of the evening, she said, "As I've gotten older, I've realized, more than ever, that you never want to 'phone in' a performance, because it just may be your last." She thanked the audience—touchingly—for "accepting what we [meaning herself and Pippin] are doing up here." She acknowledged—again touchingly—"I may never appear here again." Then she sang

"Always" and a magnificent, utterly convinced "God Bless America." Then she waved goodbye.

The question of when and how to exit is a haunting one, and has no absolute answer. Some—to switch fields for a moment—have cringed over the last ten or fifteen years to see Arnold Palmer (another small-town Pennsylvanian) still trudging on the Senior Tour: this great champion, finishing last behind scores of relative hacks. And yet he loves it, and his fans (the bulk of them) love it, begging their man not to retire, simply to let them see him, and cheer him. Marilyn Horne has made her decisions, and will make more. As for myself, I feel some discomfort—as I have indicated—in seeing and hearing "Jackie" in this new incarnation. But really, honestly, I—and lots of others—would pay to hear her cough in a nursing home.

—November 5, 2001
National Review

The Underwear Festival

Here commence four straight reports from the Salzburg Festival, 2003–2006. The festival, as you know, is the world's most prestigious summer music deal. That's not to say that it can't be very wacky.

Salzburg, Austria

The most important music festival in the world, and what do people want to talk about? The weather, of course. It's hot. Really hot. Record-breaking hot. If we were back home, in the U.S.A., everyone would be saying, "Hot enough for you?" As it is, they simply roll their eyes and fan themselves.

A concert of the Camerata Salzburg takes place in the Mozarteum—in the Grosser Saal. The windows and doors are shut tight, and there is no air

conditioning (to speak of). I nickname the place "the Grosser Sauna." I'm
surprised that people aren't taken out on stretchers. The men in the orchestra
have their jackets off, an unusual sight. The women are in spaghetti straps
and such. Only the conductor—Leonidas Kavakos, a young Greek—has his
jacket on. He should be applauded for that alone. Or psychologically examined.

For years, people have talked about the need for air conditioning, and
not just in the Mozarteum: in all the halls. But somehow, nothing ever
changes. Some suspect that this is the way the Salzburg authorities like it:
sweaty and stifling. It's part of the experience. The room may be a furnace,
but men will wear their dinner jackets anyway—they need them for their
medals. At a public forum, Michael Schade—the great tenor who is singing
the title role of *La Clemenza di Tito*—says he wants to start a new party in
Austria: the Air Conditioning party. He gets huge applause.

The Salzburg Festival is known as a bastion of tradition, but it should
be known—at least where opera is concerned—as a bastion of the ultra-
modern, not to say the outré. When people complain about the productions,
as sometimes they do, they're apt to say, "And in Salzburg, of all places!"

Mozart is the local hero, of course, and three of his operas are on the
schedule: *Tito*, as well as *Don Giovanni* and *The Abduction from the
Seraglio*. All of these productions are "controversial"—which is often the
polite word for outrageous, which may, in turn, be the polite word for
abominable or disgraceful.

Begin with *La Clemenza di Tito*, an opera that tends to be overlooked
in the Mozart oeuvre. Its director is Martin Kušej, a hotshot on the Continent, and someone those Salzburg authorities obviously think a lot of: He
is set to take over the festival's drama department in 2005.

As his *Tito* begins, young boys come out in their underwear. What does
this mean? Many interpretations have been offered, but I will give you my
own. It means, "I'm the director, I can do what I want, to hell with you—
and with Mozart, for that matter." This opening shot is reminiscent of the
ads that got Calvin Klein in trouble all those years ago.

You want sex? Kušej provides a fair amount of that, because, at this
festival, if you don't get sex, you've been shortchanged. There are two
couples, composed of four women, because two of the roles are trouser
roles. The women—the women women—are in their underwear. The grap-
pling that takes place isn't subtle. You've got breast fondling, butt grabbing,
lip locking—the whole nine yards. This is not so much titillating as discomforting, rude. A more suggestive approach would be sexier. At one

point, Sesto—portrayed by the brilliant Vesselina Kasarova—grabs at his/her crotch, affecting to tug on something that, in fact, isn't there. Oh, well.

Does anyone dare protest? Well, now and then. But you don't want to protest too aggressively, because you don't want to be labeled a square, a prude, a fuddy-duddy—someone not cool enough for today's opera. What's wrong with you, anyway? Repressed?

At the end of the opera, Martin Kušej brings the boys back—only this time, they're wearing undershirts, as well as briefs. Not to worry: They are promptly stripped of their shirts and draped over tables, served as sacrifices (or something). A man and a woman are seated at each table, apparently about to dine on the boy. They synchronize their expressions, giving a frozen frown or smile. The effect is utterly creepy, distracting from the denouement that Mozart, and his librettist, Metastasio, have planned. But who cares about them? This is a director's show.

The *Don Giovanni*, too, is a Martin Kušej show—unveiled for the first time last season. It opens with a large photo across the stage. This features about six girls, lying on their stomachs, their bare behinds to the camera. Two of the girls are playing with each other. You will find this sort of thing in any glossy, New York-based magazine. Once upon a time, it would have been provocative—now it's rather yawny.

Before long, real girls walk onto the stage, wearing sunglasses and trench coats. (Sunglasses, too, have become a cliché.) These chicks all sport sullen looks, in the manner of models. They quickly remove their trench coats, to reveal their underwear—in which they will remain for most of the opera. The Donna Anna is in underwear, too; but since she is Anna Netrebko—the gorgeous Russian soprano—you might forgive the director.

The stage is dominated by a kind of giant lazy Susan, which spins around to reveal all sorts of strange things. During Leporello's Catalogue Aria, we see a topless lady shaving her legs, football players clashing at the line of scrimmage (I kid you not), and a little girl skipping rope. Is this last creature one of the Don's future conquests? Or a current one? It's a disgusting question, but one such a production makes you ask.

You will have noticed that, so far, I haven't really touched on music. There is a reason for that: We are in the age of "director-driven" opera, so we're told, and the directors have so taken over, with their conceits and stunts, that the singers have been virtually shoved aside, along with the composers. Even so, Thomas Hampson—the Don—is a marvel in this production. He is not only the great Don Giovanni of our time, but one of the greatest of all time. Every word, every note, every gesture is right—a stunning performance.

But back to underwear: As the Don unravels, the pretty girls in their underwear are replaced by old ladies . . . in their underwear. These are women of a certain size, most of them, and they are gotten up (or down) to look as cronish as possible. Happy hell, Don Giovanni!

The third Mozart? You will be relieved to know that *The Abduction from the Seraglio* does not begin with underwear. No, a couple walks out just as Nature made them. This is FULL FRONTAL NUDITY, as Monty Python used to say. Soon enough, however, they get into their . . . underwear, and then into wedding costumes (don't ask).

The director, this time, is not Martin Kušej, but Stefan Herheim—another hotshot/bad boy. As he rips through Mozart's great opera, he simulates oral sex, and then intercourse. When Osmin and Blonde appear together, he lets them have clothes. But not really. Osmin ties around the girl an apron that depicts . . . "full frontal nudity." Now she *appears* to be naked, ha, ha, ha. Then Osmin plays with what I believe is a kitchen mixer—an item with a rod—waving it just below his waist. Ha, ha, ha, *again*.

But wait: In due course, Osmin *himself* gets an apron that is "full frontal"—male variety. At this point, there are some boos and catcalls, and several people leave (voting with their feet). This, naturally, is countered by ostentatious applauding and bravo-ing—by people eager to show that they, unlike the dinosaurs, are with the program.

A blunt question: Have directors gone nuts? Maybe they're just bored. Maybe they sit around, with their big budgets and big opportunities, thinking about what they might get away with next. (The answer is depressing, as much for them, probably, as for us: Anything.) If they really wanted to shock, they would conceive a production in harmony with the piece. As they parade around in their underwear and sunglasses—or have others do so—you want to shout, "The Emperor has no clothes!" But it's not just the Emperor . . .

I think of something Bill Buckley once said about Norman Mailer: "If only he would lift his gaze from the world's genitals." Yes, if only. But when people like me—when "conservatives"—lodge a complaint, we're apt to be told that we are "hung up." In truth, it is the directors themselves who are hung up, and should get over it. As an acquaintance of mine says—thinking about Osmin and that kitchen mixer (or whatever)—"Shouldn't we have been through with that by age 14 or so?"

There are other productions on offer here: the late Herbert Wernicke's *Don Carlo*, for example. It contains no nudity, no underwear. Eboli *does* have an eyepatch, making Olga Borodina, the great Russian mezzo, look like Moshe Dayan. David McVicar compensates for this relative square-ness, however, by purveying—in his new *Tales of Hoffmann*—naked, bloody flagellation, in addition to a string of rapes. How 'bout that?

Don't get me wrong. Salzburg, as usual, is full of magnificent things, magnificent music-making. In a world chock-full of summer music festi-vals, it is still king, by a wide margin. But this has been an undeniably weird season: the weather, these productions, the dress and undress. A distin-guished lady in town informs me that one of the festival's sponsors is Palmers, Austria's leading underwear manufacturer. Isn't that perfect?

—September 15, 2003
National Review

Mozart & Co.

Salzburg, Austria

T his is Mozart's town—and don't you forget it. Of course, you can't: His portrait greets you at the airport, and it's stamped on all the candy. People dress up as him, on the streets (e.g., in woodwind ensembles). Every January, the local Mozarteum holds a " Mozart Week." Truth is, every week's a Mozart week—and not just in Salzburg, but throughout the musical world.

The American Friends of the Salzburg Festival offers a series of talks; your correspondent is their moderator. Our first speaker is Prof. Dr. Rudolph Angermüller, of the Mozarteum. He is a musicologist and a big authority on Mozart—anything and everything about him. His topic for us is " Mozart and Money." You have perhaps heard that Mozart died a pauper, buried without notice. This is bunk.

Mozart, in fact, earned a ton of money—he was both rich and famous. But he lost a lot of money, too, and he was always sponging. How did he lose it? Gambling, mainly. When he wasn't composing, he was gambling—and when he was in arrears, he composed with a special urgency. We have another Mozart scholar on hand, too: Prof. Dr. Günther G. Bauer. He has just completed a book on Mozart and gambling. "Did he have what today we would call an addiction?" I ask. "Exactly," comes the answer.

Speaking of bunk: That movie, *Amadeus*? Bunk—false from beginning to end. But an enjoyable flick, many say.

The Salzburg Festival, as usual, is filled with Mozart, and given prominent place is a production of *Così fan tutte*. This is notable for several reasons, one of which is the youth of its cast—and its conductor. This is Philippe Jordan, born in 1974, son of the venerable Swiss conductor Armin Jordan. Philippe made a big impression in New York last summer, at the Mostly Mozart Festival, and he has Salzburg abuzz, too. A major career awaits him. Indeed, he has already begun it.

Also at the beginning of a major career is Elina Garanca, the Latvian mezzo-soprano who is part of this youthful cast. She has everything: voice, technique, personality, stage sense, and looks—lots of it. If you don't think this counts in opera, I have coffee for you to smell. As Dorabella, Garanca fairly dominates this *Così*.

And I'd like to mention the tenor, Saimir Pirgu, who is an excellent singer, although that's not the reason I'd like to mention him: He is an Albanian, an unusual thing to be in opera (or anywhere else). But the beauty part? His character, Ferrando, is one of the two guys who, in the elaborate trick of this opera, disguise themselves as "Albanians"—and here we have a real-live Albanian, pretending to be an Albanian.

This may not sound like much to you, but, trust me, opera people find it hilarious.

Along with the youngsters, two veterans appear in this cast, Sir Thomas Allen (Don Alfonso) and Helen Donath (Despina). Helen Donath? Yes, she's still singing, in her mid-60s, and singing well. She has had mainly a European career, married to Klaus Donath, the German pianist and conductor. In fact, many suppose that she is European—Austro-German. But she is from Corpus Christi, Texas, a land she left many decades ago. Chances are, she is better known in Vienna and Berlin than in Corpus Christi.

The next speaker in the American Friends series is Tony Palmer, the British filmmaker. He has made 108 films—count 'em, 108—most of them on musical subjects (Wagner, Stravinsky, Callas, Menuhin). He has also ventured into the popular culture, treating such subjects as Liberace and Hugh Hefner (though not together, alas). In 1974, he made a movie called *The World of Miss World*, a must-see.

He is currently at work on a film about Korngold, featuring Benjamin Schmid. Who is Korngold? Erich Wolfgang Korngold, the Viennese composer who was hailed—rightly—as the greatest child prodigy since Mozart, and who spent a long exile in Hollywood, writing for the movies.

Who is Schmid? A young Austrian violin sensation, who is affiliated with the Mozarteum. The festival is emphasizing Korngold this year: Schmid played the violin concerto at the opening concert; later, he participated in—led, really—the Suite for Two Violins, Cello, and Piano Left Hand (commissioned by Paul Wittgenstein, the pianist who lost his right arm in World War I).

The biggest Korngold work on offer is the opera *Die tote Stadt*, based on the Rodenbach novel *Bruges-la-Morte*. We host a lecture on the subject—the opera and the novel—by another Professor Doktor, Jürgen Maehder, of the Free University in Berlin. He is a musicologist of extraordinarily wide learning. His wife, Kii-Ming Lo, is a second musicologist, at the Normal University in Taiwan. They divide their time between Taipei and Berlin—an amazing commute, so to speak. Present for the *Tote Stadt* lecture is Korngold's granddaughter and her family, residents of Portland, Ore. She looks uncannily like him. Or am I just willing that? I don't think so.

The festival's production—Willy Decker, director—is a big success, with Torsten Kerl and Angela Denoke making a splendid Paul and Marietta, and Donald Runnicles, the Scottish conductor, doing a competent job in the pit. He currently holds positions in San Francisco, New York, and Atlanta. He was recently quoted in the Austrian press as saying that, if Bush wins re-election, he may well quit those posts—because once would be a "mistake," whereas a second election would mean "they actually want him." If the president wins, I imagine music in America will struggle on. I have a list of others whom I might nominate to shun the country—some of them home-grown!

Speaking of homegrown: The next event in the Friends series is a talk with Chester Patton, a bass from Mississippi. He is appearing in Bellini's *Capuleti e i Montecchi*, a bel canto *Romeo and Juliet*. Mr. Patton is not the most famous singer from Mississippi: That would be Leontyne Price, of Laurel (though Elvis Presley, of Tupelo, really takes the cake). Patton is from Columbia, although, as he says, he's not from the town, but "the county"—way out. He grew up in a music-loving family of nine children. Asked which singers he admired back when, he names, somewhat sheepishly, Michael Jackson. He has been compared to Paul Robeson, but he says that that is ridiculous, because their voices are nothing alike: It's just a matter of skin color. This reminds me of the critic who said of a certain young soprano (black), "She's the next Leontyne Price." That girl was as likely to be the next Leontyne Price as I am. But such is the hold of race.

Our final guest is a native Salzburger, Angelika Kirchschlager, the mezzo-soprano. She is doing the title role of *Der Rosenkavalier*, wowing 'em. She first appeared at the Salzburg Festival at the age of ten—she was in the children's chorus for *Carmen*. Later, she sold Mozart candies at what many of us consider the best café in town—Fürst. She also sold records, to the likes of Thomas Hampson, who are now colleagues. This summer, she is nearly the toast of the festival, and her parents are "bursting with pride," she concedes. You *can* go home again (Kirchschlager fled Salzburg 20 years ago), perhaps especially when you're on top of the world.

The *Rosenkavalier* production is "controversial," to use the polite word for . . . well, words that are less polite. The Canadian director Robert Carsen has set the third act, not in a tavern, but in a whorehouse, and we have lots of nudity, which is par for the course in Salzburg—I mean, in the opera productions—and also simulated copulation, fellatio, and other Strauss-Hofmannsthal necessities. Someone says to me, "Did it distract you?" I answer, "I couldn't take my eyes off it." And he guffaws as if to say, "Shame on you—you have only yourself to blame," to which I retort, "But they [Carsen et al.] *wanted* me to look at it. That's why they put it there—certainly not to be ignored!"

Anyway, I have been pronouncing my Salzburg Rule: In the audience, they're overdressed; onstage, they're underdressed. But then, people like me say, "*Quel scandale*," and the festival powers-that-be just smile, having achieved their objective. Again.

—September 13, 2004
National Review

Mozart Minus One

Salzburg, Austria

In a way, this summer is the calm before the storm—because next year marks the 250th anniversary of Mozart's birth, and the Salzburg Festival will go all out. What will they do for the homegrown hero? Mainly, they'll present all 22 of his stage works. Some of them—juvenile efforts—are almost never seen. This will be the mother of all Mozart bashes.

Of course, they're not neglecting him this year, either, because Mozart is not neglected in any year—anywhere. And speaking of juvenile efforts:

One of the operas onstage this summer is *Mitridate*, which the composer wrote when he was 14. The kid was okay. But does Salzburg's production serve the piece as he wrote it? Don't be silly, my friend: At this festival, the director rules, and he—whoever he is—is about the only one who can make Mozart take a backseat.

I'm surprised they don't take Mozart off the chocolate wrappers and replace him with the porny-freaky director du jour.

The most unfamiliar opera being presented this year is *Die Gezeichneten*, by Franz Schreker. The Salzburg Festival has been honoring composers whose music was banned or otherwise suppressed by the Nazis; they've been doing this for the past several seasons. It is in part an act of penance. Last year, the focus was on Korngold, and this year it's on Schreker. He was wildly popular in the 1910s and 1920s, but when the Nazis came to power, they stripped him of his position—director of the Berlin Conservatory—and declared his music "degenerate." He died early in the Reich, in 1934.

Did I mention Schreker was Jewish? At least his father was, and that was enough.

Schreker is relatively unknown today, but that's not the fault of the Nazis: They were defeated 60 years ago. No, Schreker, Korngold, Zemlinsky, and the rest have been ignored or attacked by a music establishment that turned hard against tonality and beauty. Their music has been scorned as middle-class, retrograde—in fact, degenerate. I raise this matter with Michael Haas, one of the experts speaking before the International Festival Society. This is a group that hosts a series of seminars (which I moderate). Yes, says Haas: These composers had to face "a second dictatorship." That is a severe phrase, and exactly right.

Die Gezeichneten—or *The Branded Ones*—concerns a hunchback, Alviano, who detests his ugliness, and builds a shrine to beauty on a nearby island. But some local nobles use this place for orgies, and abduct young women to this end. They also murder them. This being Salzburg, the director has made Alviano not a hunchback but a crossdresser. And the unfortunate young women? They aren't young women, but little girls—naked, shivering, bloody. As if Schreker's original weren't shocking enough. But so it goes, in the modern opera house.

A very starry speaker in the seminar series is Thomas Hampson, the American baritone—"the pride of Spokane, Washington," I call him, apologizing to former House Speaker Tom Foley. Hampson points out that Tom Sneva, the race-car driver, is from Spokane, too. That makes three

Toms. Hampson has lived in Austria for many years, and he is a fixture at the festival. This year, he is singing with orchestra, giving two recitals, and appearing in an opera—*La Traviata*, with the Russian sensation Anna Netrebko in the title role. Hampson is Germont, and a good one.

In any case, Hampson arrives at the seminar with a head full of steam: The national press has aired charges of financial impropriety against him and his family. In denouncing these charges, he is eloquent, profane, and hilarious. Hampson is a master performer, no matter what the stage or the circumstances. We talk a little about music, of course—but Hampson really wants to talk about the press. And politics. He teases me about mine—my politics, that is—asking, "Are you still a Republican?" I say (in effect), "You betcha, baby." He then gives a little homily about the glory of democracy, and civil disagreement, and concludes: "You're just wrong."

I can only shrug to the laughing audience, "It's my cross to bear." Hampson suggests that the word "cross" is key. Ah, yes: They all have the heebie-jeebies about the "Religious Right," don't they? Hampson goes on to assess the world situation, and all I have to say is that, as a geopolitical thinker, he is a superb baritone. (He's also a wonderful spirit, and a damn good sport.)

Two days later, we are treated to a new film by Tony Palmer, The *Adventures of Benjamin Schmid*. The subject is a violinist, and, like Mozart, a Salzburg boy. The film is absorbing, and so is Schmid. The following week, he appears at a seminar with Werner Hink, the concertmaster of the Vienna Philharmonic. They relate many interesting things, of which I'll share one with you: I ask Hink, "When a violinist like Benjamin Schmid plays a concerto with an orchestra, are the violinists especially supportive of him? Or are they all thinking, 'It oughta be me'?" Hink answers: The latter. "You didn't know that, did you, Beni?" he asks. Schmid replies, "Actually, I did—during breaks in rehearsal, they're always playing bits of the concerto."

One sunny morning, we bus to Garmisch, Germany, where Richard Strauss made his home. The composer built his villa in 1906, with the proceeds from *Salome*, a smash hit—"The Villa That *Salome* Built," Strauss liked to call it. I don't know about you, but I have never been able to feel closer to a historical figure by visiting his home, walking in his garden, or whatever. I wish I could; it has never worked. In Salzburg, I stay roughly 40 seconds from Mozart's home—where he was born and raised. I have stayed at this hotel for a cumulative six weeks. I have never been to the Mozart place—I lack the yen. (Although Austria has switched to the euro.)

In Garmisch, we are shown the Strauss home by the composer's grandson, Christian, a doctor in his seventies. Would you like a fun fact, *NR* fans? Dr. Strauss delivered one of the children of our Washington editor, Kate O'Beirne, and her husband Jim. They were stationed in Garmisch, in the Army. Dr. Strauss tells me he has delivered about 30,000 children—a small city.

In the composer's study, there is a sculpture of Beethoven, copied from a major statue in Vienna. Dr. Strauss tells about how a soldier from Texas came right after the war. The very word "Texas" sends up gales of laughter and snickers—apparently, "Texas" connotes everything crude and risible. Anyway, this soldier sits in the composer's chair, puts his feet on a table, points to the sculpture, and says, "Who's that?" The Strausses answer, "The Gauleiter of Munich." From that point on, the family referred to the sculpted Beethoven as "the Gauleiter."

It's a charming story—but you know what I'm thinking: If it weren't for boys from Texas, Western Europe might not have been liberated. And I think we can all agree that the Allies were extraordinarily generous to Richard Strauss.

Even if you're not looking for politics in Salzburg—and, boy, am I not looking—politics may find you. Take the average American expatriate. He is not exactly . . . how should I put this? An Eagle-level contributor to the Republican party. At one reception, a lady asks me whether President Bush will be impeached. Come again? She says, "You know—the Downing Street Memo." For those of you in the dark, "Downing Street Memo" is Left-speak for, "I have swallowed the Moore/Chomsky Kool-Aid." I have to disappoint the lady: I don't have my finger on the American pulse at the moment, but I don't believe Bush will be impeached. But then she asks whether Hillary will be reelected in '06—and I can reassure her on that score.

If America is not popular in this part of Europe, it's a darling, compared with the Little Satan, Israel. A quick anecdote: A friend of mine sits next to a German lady at a gala dinner. The lady will not let go of Israel. "Why does there have to be an Israel?" she asks. My friend murmurs something about historical events. Persistent, the lady asks, "Why can't the Jews have gone to Madagascar?" My friend just stares at his schnitzel.

But let's end gloriously. An especially distinguished speaker in our series is George Sgalitzer, a doctor in Seattle. He was born in Vienna, and is surely the festival's senior patron: He was at the first performance, on August 22, 1920. Seven years old, he was brought by his grandparents. He has attended every summer since, with the exception of the war years. Two Augusts ago, we celebrated his 90th birthday. In that same month, he took in his 1,000th performance at Salzburg. He has attended almost 300 in Bayreuth—on those hard, hard seats!—and countless others elsewhere. He has heard them all, known many of them, and remembers everything. His stories sparkle, and his opinions are sound. A living treasure, George Sgalitzer, expressing true Salzburg grace.

—September 12, 2005
National Review

The Big One

Salzburg, Austria

W ell, this is the big one, Elizabeth (as Fred Sanford used to say). (Note to the very young or unschooled: He was a TV-sitcom character.) For many years, this city has been preparing for 2006, the 250th anniversary of Mozart's birth. And Salzburg, of course, is the little guy's hometown.

The city gained other worldwide fame last century, when Rodgers & Hammerstein penned *The Sound of Music*. (It is set here, as you know.) But Mozart is unquestionably the main deal. His bust greets you at the airport, which is, in fact, called the W. A. Mozart Airport. (I don't think his descendants get royalties.) And Mozart never stops looking at you, wherever you go in the city. You never stop looking at him, either.

At the Salzburg Festival, every year is a Mozart year, just as it is in the musical world at large. But 2006 is a stunner. Virtually every program at the Festival—orchestral, chamber, recital—includes at least some Mozart, and often a lot of Mozart. And the only operas staged are Mozart's—22 in all.

According to Festival officials, never before have all of the composer's operas, or semi-operas, been presented all at once. These works range from juvenilia (*Bastien und Bastienne*, *La finta semplice*) to the last, glorious gasp: *La clemenza di Tito*.

Of course, the Salzburg Festival being the Salzburg Festival, not all of these operas are Mozart's own. That is, avant-garde stage directors toy with them and warp them until they are barely recognizable. But Mozart usually finds a way to out. I have long inveighed against the completeness craze in music, and I was opposed, in the run-up to this summer, to the all-22 concept, which I considered an unnecessary stunt. But I was wrong, I'm happy to say. To have the operas complete is an educational and exciting experience.

There's this to consider, too: One of the founding spirits of the Festival, Richard Strauss, said that Mozart ought to be honored in his hometown. And honored—doubly and triply honored—he is.

Amid the concerts, operas, parties, and scandals, the Salzburg Festival Society is holding a series of seminars or talks, moderated by . . . an interloper from *National Review*. One of our guests is René Pape, the German bass and a huge star on the international scene. It is not entirely common for a bass to be such a star—a soprano, a mezzo, a tenor, and even a baritone, yes, but not the lowest guys. We can think of exceptions to the rule—Chaliapin, Pinza, maybe George London (who in any case was a bass-baritone)—but not many.

Pape grew up in Dresden, and he is now 41. That means he was in his mid-20s when the Wall came down. His mother was a hairdresser, his father a cook. ("So you were always well fed," I say. "Yes," he answers, "and my hair looked good, too.") He was a member of the famed Dresden boys' choir, called the Kreuzchor. I ask what Pape, as a little soprano, sounded like: chirpy and piping, or more like René Pape? "I have always sounded like René Pape," he says sternly, to the audience's laughter.

I further ask what his boyhood hopes and dreams were. And I'm quickly made to realize what a careless question this is. There weren't many hopes and dreams in a Communist state. Pape reminds me, and the rest of us, how grim it was, how deprived and bleak. When he first came to Salzburg, he says, it was "like coming to heaven": the color, the food, the freedom. Amazing that one can forget about Communism, even a short 15 years later.

Pape is famous as a King Mark (*Tristan und Isolde*), as a Sarastro (*The Magic Flute*), and in several other roles. One he will tackle shortly is Hans Sachs, from *Die Meistersinger*. It is a difficult role, he says. Why? Because, for one thing, it requires a lot of waiting around, offstage. "And what will you do during these periods?" I inquire. "Make out your grocery list?" Yeah, he says—"and smoke."

Pape is an enthusiastic and unapologetic smoker, following the tradition of Dietrich Fischer-Dieskau. I ask him who other great smokers among singers are; and he protectively declines to name any of his current colleagues. He settles for, "Fischer-Dieskau and me—we are the greatest."

Throughout our discussion, Pape is terse, somewhat sardonic, and even a bit surly. But something surprising happens when he talks about the role of Boris Godunov, and what an emotional toll it takes. His eyes fill with tears. This seems to confirm what you hear about him: that, despite a tough exterior, he is highly sensitive, a deep-feeler. (And you hear this in his singing as well.)

Toward the end of the hour, I toss this out: Ever thought about a concert or recording with (the soprano) Renée Fleming, to be titled "Renée and René"? Pape's response is opera-star perfect: But, given the different spellings, whose name would come first?

A couple of days later, we have a movie—yes, a movie in Salzburg, and not *The Sound of Music*. This is *The Salzburg Festival: A Brief History*, Tony Palmer's latest. Palmer, a Brit, has made over 100 films, most having to do with the performing arts. And he has been widely honored for them. His new film is chockful of interviews, angles, and that marvelous stuff known as "rare footage": We see Backhaus at the piano, Knappertsbusch on the podium—everything. Any critic would have his objections to this film, but Palmer has accomplished (another) tour de force.

It has not sat well with the Festival brass, however—and I'm not talking trumpeters and tubists. Speaking to an audience at the Kino Theater, Palmer jokes (or at least I take it as joking) that he arrived at Mozart Airport in a false mustache, hiding amid "American tourists." (Why the tourists have to be American, I don't know. There are millions of tourists here, from every corner of the earth—but "American tourists" is meant to be comical, isn't it? Lucky for pathetic European economies that such tourists exist.)

The complaints of the brass, in brief, are that Palmer dwells too long and harshly on the Nazi period, and that he spots his film with factual errors. As for the first complaint, I maintain that Palmer has bent over backward to be understanding of Salzburg and its principal figures (e.g., Karajan, who joined the Nazi party twice, the first time when it was illegal). As for the second, these are not necessarily clear-cut. Moreover, I believe that, when initial passions have died down, the Festival will count this film as a feather in its (traditional, forest-green) cap.

The morning after the movie, we welcome an old favorite, Thomas Hampson, the glamorous and brainy baritone from Spokane. He has a lot to say, as usual, particularly about music and advancing technology. Hampson is a techie, and in particular a Mac user—he seems as knowledgeable as the geekiest geek. I'm quite sure he would rather read *Wired* magazine (which he does) than *Opera News*. (Don't know whether he reads that.)

In due course, I draw him out on bizarre, self-indulgent, and destructive opera productions—as I see them, I mean. Hampson is typically thoughtful. He neither excuses the relevant stage directors nor condemns them. And he relates a story about Elisabeth Schwarzkopf, the great German soprano who died on August 3. Hampson knew her well, having studied with her. One season, he invited her to Salzburg's *Don Giovanni* (in which he sings the title role). Schwarzkopf left at intermission, telling Hampson later, "How can you lend your talent to such a production? How can you participate in it?"

Obviously, Hampson disagrees with Schwarzkopf, else he wouldn't be singing *Don Giovanni* here. (The same production is still in place.) As for me, I have always had the highest regard for Schwarzkopf, musically and artistically. (We might discuss her Nazism later.) And she has now climbed even higher in my estimation.

One more guest: He is Clemens Hellsberg, a violinist in the Vienna Philharmonic, and that orchestra's chairman. (The Vienna Phil. has an exceptional form of governance.) At the end of a wide-ranging, fascinating hour, he talks about his love of Mozart, which is supreme. No, he hasn't tired of him, in this year of Mozart mania. He says that, in the afterlife, his first question will be, "Where's Mozart?" He has much he wants to ask him.

I must say that I gritted my teeth for this Mozart year—Mozart at 250—which began in earnest on January 27, the Birthday. I feared oversaturation, even burnout, even disgust. In the past eight months, I have attended, and covered, endless Mozart concerts and festivals. And you know what? I love the little guy more than I ever have. My appreciation of him has actually deepened. I say, believe the hype: Mozart really was—is—that great.

—September 11, 2006
National Review

Mere Excellence

Farewell to Maestro Kurt Masur

I have to say, I was wrong about Lorin Maazel's tenure—it proved very good, overall (and much criticized, of course). And I might reconsider some other points in this article. But, in general, I'll stick with it.

L ast month, Kurt Masur finished his second-to-the-last season with the New York Philharmonic; by this time next year, he will be gone—and that's a shame. Since he became music director in 1991, Masur has made this orchestra one of the mightiest in the world, restoring a glory that had been lost. Yet he has been grossly underappreciated in New York, by his own administrators, his own players, and the city's critics. They are giving him the bum's rush—a situation that is little less than perverse.

One forgets how bad the Philharmonic really was when Masur came to town; this forgetting, moreover, is part of the general ingratitude where this conductor is concerned. Under Zubin Mehta, the orchestra was a shambles, not necessarily because of Mehta's own failings, but because the orchestra, a notoriously fickle and petulant lot, were unwilling to play for him. The Philharmonic was really something of a joke; other orchestras—and not just first-tier ones—were playing rings around them.

But then came the sturdy maestro from Leipzig. As Rudolph Giuliani led a renaissance in the city at large—over approximately these same years—Kurt Masur led a renaissance at Avery Fisher Hall. Gone were the sloppiness and apathy of former times; in were discipline, consistency, and vitality. The Philharmonic was now no joke, but a formidable band, able to hold its head high. This did not happen by accident; it happened because Masur made the group work like dogs, and insisted on proper standards—standards necessary for mere respectability, to say nothing of glory.

And yet Philharmonic folk had various complaints and quibbles, never fully explained but probably all trivial, when not outright invalid. That's when they went to give him the bum's rush: They wanted him to leave in

1998, but the conductor, duly appalled, balked, and worked out an extension of his contract through the 2001-02 season. Even with this grace period, his exit is hasty and shabby: Masur is not yet through with the orchestra, musically. Over the last couple of seasons, he and they have been better than ever, hitting a kind of stride, producing some truly memorable performances (to go with the more ordinary ones). Worse yet, the orchestra is not exactly trading up, to put it as mildly as I can: Next on the podium is Lorin Maazel. How this came about is a tale unto itself, to be left, perhaps, for another day.

The knocks against Masur? They are several, and all dumb. The first is that, at 73, he is too old. Yet age is far from a handicap in the conducting field, most maestros needing a ripening. Some of the greatest conductors of the past (and, for that matter, present) have done their best work in their seventies, or even beyond. White hair is usually a reassurance on the podium. Besides which, Lorin Maazel is 71—and his own problems have nothing to do with his date of birth.

Then it is claimed that the New York Philharmonic ought to have an *American* conductor. This wish, if anything, is dumber than that for youth. The notion that an American should conduct an American orchestra—or a German a German orchestra—is foreign to the ideals and reality of music. (And need I mention that most of the critics wanting, or demanding, an American would no doubt shudder at nativism, or even too conspicuous a patriotism, in any other context?) Orchestras such as the New York Philharmonic are not "American orchestras"; they are orchestras on American soil, but given over to the service of music, nationality quite aside. Sure, the New York Philharmonic may play more Copland than the French National Orchestra, and the French National Orchestra may play more Roussel than the New York Philharmonic—but this is a question of a little flavoring, nothing more serious. A conductor, anyway, should be able to conduct music of any sort, even if he has an affinity or two. Think, too, of the orchestral past in America: Szell in Cleveland, Reiner in Chicago, Stokowski and Ormandy in Philadelphia, Munch in Boston, Walter in New York—did all those foreigners do any harm? Was their leadership such an affront?

Well, the flag-wavers got their American in Lorin Maazel: yet no one would mistake him for, say, Huckleberry Finn. Not only was this conductor born in France, spending his first few years there, he has had as international a career and life as anyone in the business, or any business. Frankly, I myself had never really thought of Maazel as an American until Philharmonic brass (management, that is, not trombonists) started trumpeting him as a native son. Said the executive director, when announcing him, "He is an American, and this is the oldest American orchestra." Accurate, but utterly irrelevant. And he's not an *American*, for heaven's sake, he's Lorin Maazel!

The very greatest rap against Kurt Masur is that he has not programmed enough contemporary music, that he is wedded to the standard works of the Central European repertory. It simply cannot be overstated how much critics—particularly those of the *New York Times*—value the showcasing of contemporary music. At times, this seems their only concern, their highest criterion. It is practically a daily obsession. In ways both bald and subtle, they mark down those who program the old—the musical equivalent of Matthew Arnold's "best that has been thought and said"—and praise those who will roll out the new. The surest way for a conductor to curry favor with critics is to go modern; the surest way to irk them is to throw at them a Schumann symphony, no matter how well performed it is.

One passage may serve to illustrate the mentality. It comes from Allan Kozinn, a *Times* critic and a very sharp one. In May, he reviewed a Philharmonic concert that offered Schoenberg, Beethoven, Debussy, and Ravel. Wrote Kozinn, "Schoenberg was represented by his 'Accompaniment to a Film Scene' (Op. 34), a piece that lasts a mere eight minutes, or less than half the duration of the intermission. True, the orchestra opened its program with it; but there was a clear sense of getting it out of the way and getting on with the good stuff." You see here that it's hard for the Philharmonic to win. A conductor is damned if he does, damned if he doesn't—and this is quite apart from the fact that Schoenberg's music is now squarely mainstream (and not terribly "contemporary," some of it being a hundred years old).

To make matters worse, the charge against Masur—that he eschews contemporary music—is not even true. He programs plenty of contemporary music, more, it would seem to me, than is required for politics' sake. The season before last, he conducted works by—count 'em, now—Kernis, Adès, Corigliano, Saariaho, Lutoslawski, Satoh, Henze, Kancheli, Marsalis, Rihm, and Liebermann. Last season, he led works by Sheng, Henze (again), Paulus, Gubaidulina, Danielpour, Kalhor, and Matthus. Next season, he will give premieres of music by Botti, Dun, and Turrin. These are not exactly—how to put it?—canonical names. Masur is clearly doing his "duty."

But his critics are never satisfied, because impossible to satisfy. When Masur does give them something contemporary, they are churlish—exam-

ples abound. One has to pity the conductor: He goes to the trouble of offering a large portion of contemporary dreck, and he gets no credit for it. He
might as well stick to the masters if he's going to be tagged in any case as
a Teutonic fuddy-duddy.

Ah, yes, fuddy-duddyism. A further slam against Masur is that he is not
"hip" enough. I give you another *Times* critic, writing in January: "The
Philharmonic should consider younger, hipper, and preferably American
candidates for music director." Remember that we are talking about the
podium of the New York Philharmonic, not the manager's job of a trendy
nightclub. With a mind to marketing possibilities, the critic wrote, "Imagine
an enormous poster of [the long-haired Californian] Kent Nagano, outside
Avery Fisher Hall," radiating the conductor's "youthful charisma, lithe
physique and cool mane." Again, this is *music* we are talking about, and one
of the world's most important symphonic posts. The *Times*'s critic then
popped the name of Marin Alsop: "Her breaking of the gender barrier alone
would totally transform the image of classical music in America." Thinking
like this will sink the chances of a conductor such as Kurt Masur, who can
only offer ability, wisdom, and excellence.

The maestro's final concert of the recently concluded season was the
kind that drives his critics nuts: all Strauss, consisting of that composer's
three great tone poems and the *Four Last Songs*. The performances were
typical of Masur at his best: tasteful, intelligent, bracing. Although the
music was familiar, the playing was fresh and inspiring. My main thought
was: This tenure really should not end; it's foolish, even mean. And also:
What a bunch of ingrates. First-rate performances of the standard repertory
are not a dime a dozen; in fact, they are quite rare, and not to be taken for
granted. Masur has perhaps spoiled New York.

They will be sorry, I predict. As so often happens in human affairs, Masur
will probably be better appreciated after he has gone. An orchestra, like a city
after a rescuing mayor, can go backward. At the moment, the Philharmonic is
making up, falling all over itself in tribute to its hounded-out chief. They are
billing the next, the final season as one of "Thank you, Kurt Masur." They
invite the public to come "celebrate the Masur era"—an era they are cutting
short, to no good.

—July 23, 2001
National Review

Yankee Doodle Discs

Classical music from American pens

The New York Philharmonic has released another of its "special editions," this one a boxed set of ten compact discs devoted to American music. It is entitled, plainly enough, *An American Celebration*, and it includes 49 works by 39 composers, interpreted by 21 conductors. It is not only a survey of one nation's orchestral music, but a record of the life of an orchestra, and a treasury of some of the century's greatest conductors. It also comes with two fat booklets, stuffed with essays, biographies, and interviews, along with photos so unfamiliar and heartwarming that they alone are almost worth the price ($185) of the set.

All in all, one cannot imagine a finer "salute" (as the Philharmonic also calls it) to American music, or at least to American orchestral music. Sedgwick Clark, producer of the set, has acquitted himself with his usual excellence. But the key and barely utterable question is: Does American music deserve it?

We have now set off a powder keg. In music, as in other areas of life, there is affirmative action—in the case of music, most often national affirmative action. Americans, with their traditional insecurity vis-à-vis Europe, are worse than others in this regard. They tend nervously to favor their own; or rather, they feel an obligation to perform and champion those of their countrymen who happen to compose. This is accepted simply as a fact of life, and an unquestionable good. No one has ever objected when a conductor (it is usually a conductor, rather than a singer or instrumentalist) says, "I pledge to search out and advocate American music."

Thus, when Leonard Slatkin was appointed music director of the National Symphony Orchestra several years ago, it was very heavily emphasized that he was an American conductor who went out of his way—way out of it—to showcase American music. That this was a desirable practice and impulse—particularly for an orchestra that bills itself as "National"—went, of course, entirely unquestioned. The merits of the music (or, for that matter, of the conductor) were, at best, secondary. What mattered was nationality, and a peculiar form of nationalism. Even the present director of the New York Philharmonic, the German Kurt Masur, takes care to note, in a letter written for *An American Celebration*, that the Philharmonic has always felt a "strong responsibility" to the homegrown composer. Masur, inevitably—this was a little insurance—placed contemporary American works on his inaugural program with the Philharmonic, in 1991. (One of them was John Adams's *Short Ride in a Fast Machine*, a fun piece, included in the just-issued set.)

The tug of national pride—or of a sense of national duty, or entitlement—is, of course, far from new. In one of his sprightly essays for the set's booklets, the critic Alan Rich cites the case of one George Frederick Bristow, a "violinist, composer, and new-music activist." In 1854 (that early), Bristow fired off an angry letter to the New York Philharmonic Society, which at the time was dominated by Germans. He accused the Society of "a systematized effort for the extinction of American music"! (This despite the fact that the orchestra had by then programmed a concert overture of Bristow's, a piece now lost to time, probably without great injury to our souls.) "Is there a Philharmonic in Germany," he thundered, "for the encouragement of American music?"

Elsewhere in the booklets, however, we learn of a contrary case, that of Edward MacDowell, who understood full well the affirmative-action mentality of some in organized music, and resented it. He once refused to allow a work of his to be included in an all-American program. He wanted his music to be judged solely for itself, performed because it was worthy, or not at all. (This tidbit comes from that stalwart critic of yesteryear, Irving Kolodin. Another of the delights of this package is that it offers a parade of critics and annotators, down through the decades. One suspects, though, that a little Bowdlerizing has gone on: Chances are that Irving Kolodin did not employ the term "African-American.")

Composers, needless to say, have always groused that performers ignore the new and nearby (which is to say, them). In truth, however, to be new and nearby is to have a leg up—is to be able to play on the guilt and ethical presumptions of performers. Some portion of what our orchestras program today is programmed only because it is a) American and b) new. This is a way, goes the thinking, of tending and extending the national heritage. But what is that heritage, exactly? Is it a heritage of greatness, or is it one of mediocrity, propped up by the patriotic, moral, and professional notions of a large segment of the musical establishment? This is a question that the Philharmonic's ten discs can help to answer.

FANFARES, OVERTURES, SUITES, AND MORE

Disc 1 opens with Aaron Copland's *Fanfare for the Common Man*, regarded as one of our national anthems. It does not, frankly, wear well. It is a little pompous, a little overblown, with its crashing cymbals and blustering drums. Then there is George Chadwick's *Melpomene*, a *Dramatic Overture*. It is dramatic indeed, not to say melodramatic, mostly a series of Romantic outpourings, held together by their dull sameness. The work is included here, one may guess, only because it is a handy example of late-19th-century American music. Then there is MacDowell's *Indian Suite* (spiritedly conducted by Leonard Bernstein, who gets the lion's share of the baton time in this set). It is a dated and hokey piece, though not without a certain charm and ingenuity. Then we have a classic—*the* classic, really—of American Impressionism, *The White Peacock* by Charles Tomlinson Griffes, in a lovely performance by another composer, Howard Hanson. Following that is Ernest Schelling's *Victory Ball*, a *Fantasy for Orchestra*, once a rather big deal in American music, now no more than an historical oddity.

Along with Charles Ives's *Three Places in New England*, those pieces constitute the first of the discs. As we can see here, there is a lot of "program music"—which is to say, music meant to depict a story, or event, or thing—in this collection, as against "absolute" or "pure" music (such as any Beethoven symphony, except the "Pastoral," which is an example, if an exceptionally high one, of program music). Many of the compositions are decidedly second-rate, even student-like, hardly cause for much patriotic chest-thumping (or even, perhaps, a *Celebration*).

More Copland comes with his *Music for the Theatre*, an engaging work. (When Copland's fellow composer Roy Harris first heard it, we learn from a note by Phillip Ramey, he "jumped up excitedly, threw out his hands, and exclaimed with delight: 'But that's *whorehouse* music!'" This was 1925, and Europe was seeming farther and farther away.) There is a great deal of Copland in this set, arguably too much, given the ground to be covered and the space available. His *Lincoln Portrait*—here conducted by Bernstein and narrated by William Warfield—is an amazingly shallow, bombastic, and stupid work, incapable of impressing anyone over the age of, say, twelve. His *Salón México*, on the other hand, manages to survive—though barely—the ethnomusicological earnestness that prompted it.

The French-born Edgard Varèse is represented by his *Intégrales*, performed in his memory not long after his death. Indeed, many of these performances took place for ceremonial reasons, rather than for what might be considered normal, or everyday, ones: It was this one's 75th birthday; it was the 50th anniversary of that one's death. It is possible that this says something not entirely reassuring or flattering about the quality of the music. Ned Rorem (represented in the set by his superb Third Symphony) once said that the highest compliment that had ever been paid him was when Leopold Stokowski programmed a piece of his without telling him about it. Stoki simply went ahead and scheduled it, as though Rorem were a regular composer, not needing to be present, not needing to stand and acknowledge applause, and so on. He was just a composer, a grown-up, like, oh . . . Haydn.

A few of the pieces assembled here are so poor as to be laughable. Consider *Old California* by William Grant Still (conducted by the august Frenchman Pierre Monteux, who was something of an old Californian himself, given his association with the San Francisco Symphony). It is shot through with hokum, attempting to recreate tribal chants, Spanish yelps, and the like, all for the glory of the City of Los Angeles's 160th anniversary (for which the piece was commissioned). It could serve as the accompaniment to a particularly campy film: Where are Bing, Bob, and Dorothy Lamour? William Grant Still was a better composer than revealed in this piece, an oddity that he, if he could, would probably be glad to bury.

Other works in the set, however, deserve to be more widely known than they are. Ernest Bloch's *Concerto Grosso No. 1* is an intelligent piece, bowing to a form of the past while incorporating the modern. Henry Cowell's *Hymn and Fuguing Tune No. 2* displays a similar keenness, here beautifully rendered by another French conductor, Paul Paray. Carl Ruggles's *Sun-treader* is a complicated work, brilliant in a way, not one to clutch to the heart, but featuring an uncanny orchestral architecture, not unreminiscent of Bruckner. George Crumb's *Star-Child* is a similarly strange and wonderful creation. And Peter Mennin's *Concertato* is no less than a rediscovery, taut and driving.

THE QUESTION OF HERITAGE

When all is said and done—and listened to—this anthology is both hugely rewarding and hugely irritating. We may draw from it a few broad lessons. If there is any doubt, for example, that there is an American school—a distinctive style of American classical music—it is dispelled by these discs. To begin with, many of these composers were educated by the same teachers. They also borrowed from one another like mad. They socialized together, performed together, and, in some cases, slept together. The gang's all here, almost. Every listener will note certain omissions about which he will be tempted to sniff—I, for instance, might cry, "What, no Gian Carlo Menotti? No Vincent Persichetti? No John Corigliano? No Walter Piston!"—but Sedgwick Clark has done a skillful job of mining what has come to be a vast musical heritage.

Still, the question nags: What about that heritage? Is it . . . worth it? Most striking about *An American Celebration* is its relative paucity of great music: music that will endure, that can stand on its own, without the ministrations of special tenders. Musical folk, curiously enough, are not known for being especially patriotic, but they get all blood-and-soil crazy when it comes to the concert life. These discs are, in part, the product of sheer will, of an eat-your-peas sense of what is good for us. The missionary and proselytizing spirit abounds ("Are you listening, conductors around the world?" demands Clark in one of the booklets).

This is our heritage, yes, in a way; and orchestral music in America has been as good as that in most countries during this century. Furthermore, not every piece of music that is performed and "celebrated" need be great; otherwise, the repertory available to concerts and recordings would shrink intolerably. But Americanness is not nearly enough; it is a woefully insufficient credential.

All the more reason, then, to rejoice that our musical heritage, like our larger national one, flows from every nation, and certainly from Europe. Those Germans who so agitated George Frederick Bristow—Beethoven, Schubert, and Brahms—are our kin, just as much as Elliott Carter, Jacob Druckman, and Ellen Taaffe Zwilich. Music, as has long been observed, is a nation unto itself. And if there is pride to be taken, why not take it in that?

—November 22, 1999
National Review

One Vote for Willson

On the creator of *The Music Man*

I s there a Great American Novel? That is a silly conversation. Is there a Great American Musical? That is a less silly one. Obvious candidates include *Oklahoma!*, *Guys and Dolls*, and *Carousel*. But perhaps the strongest contender is *The Music Man*, now in revival on Broadway.

The creator of *The Music Man* was Meredith Willson, a versatile, happy, much-loved figure who died in 1984. His life story is just as American as his show. Born in 1902—"aught two," his characters would say—he grew up in Mason City, Iowa, inspiration for the theatrical "River City, I-o-way." His father was a baker; his great-grandfather had been one of the town's settlers. Of his magnum opus, Willson would say, "I didn't have to make up anything. I simply remembered Mason City as closely as I could."

He was a kid who soaked up everything musical. Any instrument he could get his hands on, he would play. He had the first mail-order flute in town (shades of the Wells Fargo wagon). One of his memoirs—Willson was a marvelously graceful prose writer—is entitled *And There I Stood with My Piccolo*. It is the book on which *The Music Man* is based. When he was 17, Willson struck out for the big city, New York, where he enrolled in the Institute of Musical Art, the forerunner to the Juilliard School (and, as it happens, the alma mater of Richard Rodgers). Meeting up with two of the musical titans of the age, he became flutist for the John Philip Sousa Band and Arturo Toscanini's New York Philharmonic.

He then went to California, to conduct orchestras and work in radio. He composed, arranged, played, conducted—the classic jack-of-all-musical-trades. He worked as music director of Tallulah Bankhead's *Big Show*, for which he wrote the most un-Bankheadian song "May the Good Lord Bless and Keep You." ("Take a bow, Meredith," the rapacious old siren would say.) He composed scores for such films as *The Great Dictator* and *The Little Foxes*. He wrote a good deal of classical music, including two symphonies. And he was responsible for countless trifles, among them one that made it sort of big—"It's Beginning to Look a Lot like Christmas."

After *The Music Man*, which appeared in 1957, Willson wrote two more musicals: *The Unsinkable Molly Brown* (based on the life of the famed *Titanic* survivor) and *Here's Love* (an adaptation of *Miracle on 34th Street*). After he was rich and famous, he retained the common touch, often returning to Mason City, where he presided over the North Iowa Band Festival. When he died, his widow chose an obvious inscription for his tombstone: "The Music Man." President Reagan conferred on him the Medal of Freedom, posthumously. About 25 years before, President Kennedy had presented him with an award for civic activism (the word had a better connotation then). In 1999, the government issued a stamp in his honor. Willson was not only a talented fellow, but, by every account, an exceptionally good Joe—and this is reflected in his music.

His two symphonies are almost as obscure as his hit show is familiar, but they can be heard on a disc from the Naxos label. The first is subtitled "A Symphony of San Francisco," and it was written in 1936 to commemorate the thirtieth anniversary of that city's earthquake. This is an impressive work, of a kind—as good as several of the pieces included in the New York Philharmonic's recent collection of American music. It is a frank example of "program music," telling a story of disaster and subsequent rebirth. It is haunting, imaginative, tuneful, and intelligently structured. As befits the product of a bandmaster, it makes particularly effective use of the brass and woodwinds. The work has an American robustness, an openness about it. It is also proudly celebratory, if a shade bombastic. And, like most everything that came from Willson's pen, it expresses a striking love of country.

Here is a taste of the explanatory notes that Willson wrote to accompany the piece: "Generally speaking, the first movement is intended to convey pioneer courage, loyalty, strength of purpose and freedom." The trumpet motive in the closing Allegro "is a call of defiance to the very elements themselves that had the temerity to dispute the spiritual strength and courage of the golden city of the West." A little Rotarian, yes—but so what?

The Symphony No. 2, composed immediately after the first, bears the subtitle "The Missions of California," and it is a tribute to Father Junípero Serra, the "padre-pioneer." This work, like its predecessor, is a little bombastic and hokey, but it shows undeniable skill. The slow movement is gorgeously lyrical, a sort of sustained hymn. The scherzo is a pleasant depiction of the return of the swallows to San Juan Capistrano. From beginning to end, there is that distinctive love, and optimism, and gratitude, and joy—strange qualities for the 20th century. The pops conductor Arthur

Fiedler used to speak of "first-rate second-rate music." The Willson symphonies may be described this way.

Furthermore, Willson shows both a knack and an affection for all types of music and musical devices. Thus, in the Serra symphony, he throws in elements of Gregorian chant. At the end of "Gary, Indiana," there is a little jig, for the Irish Mrs. Paroo to dance to. This is charming, sure—but it is also fine craftsmanship.

Willson had one masterpiece in him, and it will live as long as there is anything like musical theater. *The Music Man* (for which Willson also wrote the lyrics) is an astonishing creation. It came in a spurt of brilliance. It is shot through with originality, verve, and—why not go all the way?—genius. People love it, can't get enough of it, can't stop performing it—and they are not wrong. For closing in on a half-century now, *The Music Man* has been performed continually, in every American city, town, and village, and in other parts of the world as well, not excluding Peking.

How American is it? Totally, almost lustily. The show is set in 1912, five years before America's entry into the world war, a relatively innocent time. The place is Iowa, a very American state in a very American region. The show expresses not only love of country, but, more particularly, love of American music, as epitomized by the marching band. Carl King, who along with Sousa is the very idea of a band composer, was an Iowan. And Willson's "Seventy-six Trombones" is probably the last march to enter the permanent repertory.

The show begins with "Rock Island"—"Whaddya talk! Whaddya talk!"—which is a proto-rap. It is pure joy in rhythm and words, dazzlingly brought off. We continue with "Iowa Stubborn," sung by the people of River City. In the current Broadway production, two of them are made to look like the pair in Grant Wood's *American Gothic*. (Wood, of course, was another Iowan.) *The Music Man* is sometimes charged with being corny, but it is in reality anti-corny. Willson ribs his home folks, but gently, lovingly. Here is "Professor Harold Hill," the con man from back East, trying to frighten the community about the well-being of its children: "Are certain words creeping into [their] vocabulary? Words like . . . like 'swell'? Aha! And, 'So's your old man'!" The show has a broad liberality, as in its anti-censorship theme ("Chaucer, Rab-eh-laze, *Bal*-zac!"). It is warmly patriotic, and yet it has a little fun with the dumber sort of patriotism: "Remember the *Maine*, Plymouth Rock, and the Golden Rule!" It also has a dose of raciness, as when Professor Hill, in "The Sadder but Wiser Girl," confesses, "I hope and I pray for Hester to win just one more A!"

At every turn, music is exalted—in the piano teacher, the little girl taking lessons, the barbershop quartet, the evocation of the great composers, and, at the center of it all, the excitement over the coming boys' band. Professor Hill even issues the old (but false) bromide that singing is nothing more than "sustained speech." Willson sprinkles his score with jazz, ragtime, burlesque—the whole of our musical grab bag.

And there is hardly a shallow or pedestrian note. Willson puts on a clinic of melody, harmony, modulation, and rhythm (including "elegant syncopation"). "Pick a Little, Talk a Little" is a novelty number, but a novelty number of very high quality, especially as it merges with the barbershop quartet's "Good Night, Ladies." The slinky "Marian the Librarian" has that little chromatic motive that is one of the glories of the literature, instantly recognizable to just about all sentient Americans. "Shipoopi" is a ridiculous song—but then, it is meant to be.

By the final curtain—this would kill Sinclair Lewis—the big-city slickster is won over by the homely River Citians (but primarily, to be sure, by the fair Marian). He wants to become one of them, live among them, be absorbed in their goodness. Babbitt has a pretty fine life, and we know it. In the current revival, as if to drive home the Americanness of it all, the performance ends with the dropping of an enormous, *Patton*-sized flag. There will always be those who sniff that the show is "feel-good"—but, oh, it feels good to feel good. And the main reason *The Music Man* feels so good is that it *is* good—a great American musical.

So, is it *the*? This is just a parlor game—no need for a ruckus. But here is one vote for Willson.

—June 5, 2000
National Review

The Color of Music

Racial politics spreads its poison everywhere

T he Baltimore Symphony Orchestra has announced its 1996-1997 season, and in most respects it is an unremarkable one, offering the usual subscription series dedicated to "Pops," "Celebrity," "Favorites," and so on. But there is also a revolutionary series called "Classically Black." This is a group of concerts with nothing in common except that the soloists or guest conductors happen to be black. They are concerts that have been plucked from the rest and set aside. They have been—in a word—ghettoized.

The formula is uncomplicated: If a concert features a black musician— no matter what the salient characteristics of that concert—it is eligible for "Classically Black." For example, the orchestra will perform an all-Tchaikovsky program. Because the music is familiar and well-loved—the polonaise from *Eugene Onegin*, the first piano concerto, etc.—the concert is part of the "Favorites" series. But because the soloist in the concerto, Terrence Wilson, is black, the concert is part of "Classically Black" as well.

Or consider a gala concert titled "Great Opera Choruses," a "special event" and therefore not ordinarily part of any subscription series. But a singer has been booked to perform a couple of arias from *Carmen* between choruses. And because that singer is black—she is the mezzo-soprano Marietta Simpson—the evening is designated "Classically Black."

The pianist André Watts will come to town, for a Rachmaninoff concerto. Watts is one of the most famous musicians in the world, so he is on the "Celebrity" series. But he is also the son of a Hungarian woman and a black American GI, so he beefs up "Classically Black," too. Watts is—in the crude lingo of a crude game—a "two-fer."

The St. Louis Symphony Orchestra has its own "Classically Black" series, borrowed from the Baltimoreans, who pioneered it in 1990. Leading this series next season is a performance of Beethoven's Ninth Symphony. How did it get there? The symphony's last movement includes a large chorus and a vocal quartet, and in that quartet the mezzo-soprano (again,

Marietta Simpson) and the tenor (Curtis Rayam) are black. The series brochure makes no mention of the soprano or bass, or of the conductor, who is the key performer in the work. This is possibly without precedent. Typically, members of the quartet are afterthoughts, certainly compared with the conductor. Here, though, it is color that counts. Terrence Wilson will make a St. Louis appearance, too, this time with the Grieg concerto. It need hardly be stated where that concert may be found.

If it seems simple, it is: You go by color. In days gone by, a program of Tchaikovsky war-horses would have been just that; it was the music that gave such a concert its distinctiveness. So too with an evening of opera excerpts. But today, race has wormed its way into the concert hall, as it has so many other domains, and a musician's color is widely regarded as a significant fact, capable of rendering a piece of music either "relevant" or "irrelevant." This is a startling departure for an art that is chiefly aural and spiritual—an art so divorced from the considerations of body that orchestras have long placed applicants for permanent positions behind screens, in "blind auditions."

'AMAZING. AMAZING.'

Marietta Simpson reacts with astonishment when told that she is part of the two "Classically Black" series. For several moments, she is silent. "Amazing," she finally says. "Amazing. I was totally unaware of it. That's totally unbelievable. When my agent called, I was thinking that this was a series devoted to the music of African-American composers or something. . . . I think that's in pretty poor taste. I mean, I can't imagine that anybody would have to divide the concerts like that. I can understand the need to bring in a varied audience, but there are other ways to do it. To make it appear that Beethoven's Ninth Symphony . . ."

She continues, "I don't understand why it has to be categorized like that. If there were a Russian vocalist or pianist, would that concert qualify in an all-Russian series? If Russian singers were in the quartet for the Ninth, would Beethoven then be stuck in a Classically Russian series?"

She would, she says, prefer to be known as a singer, plain and simple. Yet "for me, it's not a matter of being known as anything. It's a matter of, I'm black, I'm proud of being black, and there's nothing I could do about it even if I weren't proud. It's going to be a way of distinguishing me. But I don't get where that becomes my calling card. If I'm doing the Brahms Alto Rhapsody, I'm not sure how that gets on something called 'Classically Black.'"

She agrees that the successes of black musicians ought to be publicized, "but there are more subtle ways to do it. I don't think you have to put us on a billboard and say, 'These are the black people who are appearing, so I hope all you black people out there will come on out.' I find it offensive to say, 'These are the black ones, so this is "Classically Black."' I would like to think that all of us in this series are known as good musicians first and that this is why we were engaged."

About racial hiring in general, Simpson says, "It's a double-edged kind of thing. Racism has been so rampant, the idea has been to correct what has been wrong. I think that in the process you can go to the other extreme, but I think it needs to be dealt with."

She takes strong exception to the notion that the look of a musician on stage makes the music either "relevant" or not: "Who stands in front of the orchestra has nothing to do with it. On a personal level, I find [this division] really offensive. I am very happy about who I am, but to design a concert series after my race is offensive to me, because what happens when it's no longer PC to have a 'Classically Black' series? Does that mean you no longer have to hire black singers or instrumentalists? If you label us now because it's convenient, it might be convenient to remove the label—and the musicians with it—later on."

Terrence Wilson, for his part, is not so disapproving of the series, finding it to be, on balance, a "valid effort to reach out." "But I *am* cautious," he says. "I'm careful as to how many of these events I'm hired to participate in, because it labels me in a way that I don't want to be labeled as a musician. I don't want to get pigeonholed. I don't want to be 'Terrence Wilson, the African-American pianist'; I want to be 'Terrence Wilson, the pianist.'"

"See," he explains, "the elements that can help are the same elements that can be detrimental." If "Classically Black" is "just the first step to try to reach a vaster audience," Wilson is willing to tolerate it as a temporary measure. Nonetheless, "there is a failure to recognize that a performer is just a performer. . . . It all goes back to the misconception of classical music as being something European and the question of, 'Whose music is it?' It's not anybody's music; it's just music."

Wilson is well aware that his color is a desirable commodity in a society smitten by race: "I've realized all along that, given these conditions, in some cases race would be an important factor in getting hired. My way of dealing with that is to be cautious and recognize when that is the case." But how do you know? "You don't always know," he allows. "But the only thing you can do is . . . When presenters approach my manager with me in mind for some special event that has African-American this or that or the other on it, he will require that it be followed up by something that has nothing to do with it. When an orchestra keeps asking for Martin Luther King tribute concerts over and over, with no invitations for regular subscription series, then it becomes obvious." Wilson's first appearance with the Baltimore Symphony was, indeed, for a Martin Luther King concert. He accepted on the condition that the orchestra provide him with three other dates in the bargain.

The pianist looks forward to a time when skin color no longer touches the musical realm. He recalls, "People would say to me when I was growing up, 'You're going to be the next André Watts.' This came from both African Americans and Caucasians. They never said, 'You're going to be the next Richard Goode or Radu Lupu or Vladimir Horowitz or Artur Rubinstein or Martha Argerich'—those were my musical heroes."

A BUZZY CONCEPT: 'RELEVANCY'

The orchestras' intentions are several: corrective, expiatory, commercial, and psychological. Most would contend that they are also benign. Miryam Yardumian, the music administrator in Baltimore, chooses her words carefully: "We are always looking for African-American artists at the highest level and we are always trying to attract African Americans to our concert audience." Demography is of prime concern: "If we had a large Asian or Russian population, we would want to do things to attract that audience, too."

Lee Anna Good, director of public relations for the St. Louis Symphony, reports that some St. Louisians had qualms about "Classically Black" but were reassured by the lack of backlash in Baltimore. "Relevancy to your life," she says, "is a good way to enter the concert-going experience. We've been told numerous times by the black community, 'Why should I go to a concert when the people on stage have nothing to do with me, when they don't have my life experience?'"

Is the premise, then, that black people would rather hear music performed by black musicians than by others? That music cannot be "relevant" to black hearers unless the music-makers share their pigmentation? Yardumian answers, "It makes it perhaps more interesting, more of an inducement." Good says much the same: "It probably shouldn't matter, but if it's a way to get them in in the beginning, then it can make the music more relevant to them."

Prickly and unavoidable is the question of hiring: Did the Baltimore Symphony set out to hire black soloists and guest conductors for "Classically Black," or did it book the season in an undiscriminating fashion and then simply deposit concerts involving black musicians into the series? "There was probably some of both," Yardumian responds. Asked to confirm that race is a factor in the engagement of musicians in Baltimore, she pauses: "It is not a factor," she says; "it is a consideration."

And has St. Louis made special efforts to feature black musicians? "Yeah," says Lee Anna Good, "probably. I guess you could classify it that way. It's something we're conscious of, in the backs of our minds."

They, like other orchestra officials, seem torn about whether race should play a role in musical life. In one breath, Yardumian lauds the meritocratic imperative: "Music is the most important thing. If you have other goals, unfortunately things go awry." But in the next, she cannot keep from insisting, in acknowledgment of a remedial purpose, "It's going to take generations to undo all of the wrongs that have been done. It's going to take generations."

Thus do today's orchestra officials sound much like their counterparts in the universities. The buzzwords that trip most frequently from their lips are "relevance," "outreach," and, that pet, "diversity." An orchestra is now likely to have an "outreach committee," part of whose function seems to be to exert pressure on music administrators to make race-conscious, rather than strictly musical, choices. (It was from such a committee that the idea of "Classically Black" came in Baltimore.) The administrators seem not to mind—either because race-consciousness comes naturally to them or because they perceive a financial advantage in it.

The new spirit was nicely expressed in 1993 by James Wolfensohn, then the chairman of the Kennedy Center for the Performing Arts in Washington, D.C., and now the president of the World Bank: "You've got to make orchestras more relevant to the broad level of the community. A wholly white middle-class orchestra doesn't appeal to a large segment of the country. We don't want to watch white players and white audiences— it's a matter of morality and economics."

AN EMERGENCY HIRE

The issue of race intruded on the music world in a big way in 1989. The venue, appropriately, was Detroit, than which no city is more race-obsessed and race-driven. Two state legislators threatened to block $2.5 million in funds for the Detroit Symphony Orchestra unless it breached its policy of blind auditions and hired a black musician. They also threatened a boycott.

The orchestra's management convened an emergency meeting and quickly capitulated. Within days, it hired a black bassist without benefit of competition, blind or otherwise. The executive director at the time braved it out in a press release: "We took this unique initiative to demonstrate our strong commitment to our affrmative action goals." She subsequently told the press, "The Detroit Symphony was in a weakened financial situation. If we had not hired a black musician, it would have meant immediate bankruptcy." Said the bassist, in a telling instance of post-affirmative-action *tristesse*, "I would rather have auditioned like everybody else." But he accepted anyway.

From that moment, the Detroit Symphony moved vigorously on the racial front. It began by changing its audition policy. The screen is still up, but auditions may not be held unless there are black musicians in the pool. The orchestra also established what it calls "African-American fellowships." Says executive director Mark Volpe, "The rationale is to identify young African-American musicians right out of school [and] hire them to play a number of weeks. They're paid union wages, the same compensation as the permanent members, and the weeks they're not playing, they have coaching, including mock auditions." The orchestra also pays for the fellows to travel to other cities to audition for other orchestras. Volpe avows that there is no discomfort among symphony offcials that these ministrations aid only a certain group of musicians, based on race, and no one else.

The zero-sum aspect of such practices is unlamented. On the contrary: Volpe is forthright and confident in defense of race-conscious policy. "We want to be sensitive to the community," he says. "A positive irony is that [one of the threatening legislators] has become one of our greatest supporters." How so? "With appropriations and things like that." Moreover, "some of the earlier criticism was legitimate. The orchestra was paying lip service to the need for more diversity, in terms of people on stage, and really hadn't created the programs to do anything other than talk the game."

But should an orchestra have a social mission? Is it not sufficient to offer great music performed by the finest musicians available? This notion is treated as quaint, a luxury from a former day, no longer applicable in an age of racial hardball and scrambling for arts funding. "It's not enough to play Mozart and Brahms," Volpe says. "With the kind of money we expect, we have to be an educational institution. We have to be proactive in terms of educational programming and, again, serve a mission that's broader than just playing Brahms."

The fact remains that the Detroit Symphony was bullied, and the Atlanta Symphony has been, too: In 1991, it lost $70,000 from the city's Bureau of Cultural Affairs because it was judged "weak" in the "cultural diversity" of its programming, personnel, and audiences. One blinks to remember that a symphony's "outreach" once consisted of tacking a poster to a wall, or placing a notice in the newspaper, informing people that a concert was in the offing and inviting them to attend.

It may be naive to maintain that music should be immune to the race-fever that afflicts contemporary America. But if affirmative action is allowed to gain further ground in music, the following disaster might result: If one noticed a black soloist (for example) on a program—especially if that soloist were young and unknown—one might assume that the soloist had been hired for race, and not ability. One might be wrong, of course. But it would not be an unreasonable assumption, nor would it be hateful. (Indeed, the reverse used to be true: If a black soloist appeared on a program, one could assume that the soloist was especially meritorious, given the racial barriers that had to be overcome.) As a black trombonist in the Atlanta Symphony put it at the time of the Detroit controversy, "It doesn't do any good for players' self-esteem if they feel the rules were bent for them."

That racial separatism should come to music is tragic. The only black and white of it ought to be the notes on the page, or the keys of a piano. The choral movement of that Beethoven symphony—the one on St. Louis's "Classically Black" series—uses a famous ode by Schiller, regarded as a kind of anthem for music. Its universal message does not expire: "Let thy magic bring together / All whom earth-born laws divide; / All mankind shall be as brothers / 'neath thy tender wings and wide." And later: "Love toward countless millions swelling / Wafts one kiss to all the world."

—May 20, 1996
The Weekly Standard

The *Shine* Man

Critics are wrongly enraged at the David Helfgott 'circus'

L
ast year, David Helfgott was a former music student who had fallen victim to a crippling mental illness. This year, he is the most famous pianist in the world. All because of a movie.

Shine tells the story of Helfgott's unusual life, depicting him as a prodigy raised in Australia by a cruel and twisted father. David endures years of abuse, attracts regional renown, and finally breaks with his father to study in London. But he is unable to cope with estrangement from the man who shaped him and, after winning a competition with his playing of Rachmaninoff's Third Concerto, goes mad. He is then returned to Australia, where he is confined to a series of institutions. In time, he finds a wine bar in which to entertain customers and meets an astrologer named Gillian, who marries him, improves his health, and steers him back to the stage.

The facts of the movie are in dispute—Helfgott's siblings, for example, say that the portrayal of their father is a travesty, and many contend that Helfgott is as sick as ever—but the 50-year-old pianist is now an internationally beloved example of triumph over adversity.

As the movie became a hit, the *Shine* team—led by Gillian Helfgott and the filmmakers—organized a North American tour for Helfgott encompassing ten cities. Every one of the concerts sold out immediately. In the same period, Helfgott's recording of the Rachmaninoff concerto shot to number one on the classical charts, and even made an appearance on the popular charts, too. It is one of the bestselling albums in the history of RCA—a label whose catalogue boasts the likes of Toscanini, Artur Rubinstein, and Leontyne Price. But not everyone has rejoiced in Helfgott's success. Music critics, in particular, have been unsporting. They have been angry, crabbed, and confused.

When Helfgott played his first concert, in Boston, the critical reaction was fierce. Helfgott was not an ordinary professional pianist, and he was far from "cured." Instead, he was a babbling, tic-filled sufferer from what physicians term a "schizoaffective disorder," and his playing reflected that condition. Richard Dyer of the *Boston Globe* decried "a sad spectacle" and "a morally bankrupt atmosphere," concluding that "Helfgott should not have been in Symphony Hall last night, and neither should the rest of us." Tim Page of the *Washington Post* wrote that "the whole event seemed profoundly exploitative" and that the pianist "was excruciating to watch" (an interesting word, that last, in a review of a piano recital).

As the *Shine* Tour continued, virtually the entire American critical establishment heaved with indignation. They were frustrated by Helfgott's appeal, annoyed at the thousands who flocked to him, and suspicious of the handlers and packagers who shared in his profits. Many were protectively pitying, like Mark Swed of the *Los Angeles Times*, who wrote that " guileless as Helfgott surely is, guile surrounds him." The Associated Press found a Juilliard teacher who said, "He's not a man who should be making money playing the piano," but one who "should be playing at home for therapeutic reasons." The *New York Times*—which ran several Helfgott pieces—took the rare step of publishing an editorial, which remarked that Helfgott's "tour is more about the powers of celebrity and empathy than about great musicianship," and that he "seems to be the captive of an entrepreneurial enterprise being manipulated for maximum profit." The *Post*'s Page, invited on National Public Radio, said, "I really wondered why he was being exhibited when he could be being helped," and then demonstrated exactly what has stuck in so many craws: "We have reached the point in . . . the history of classical music in this country that the hottest person in classical music is a disturbed man who can hardly play the piano."

Page and the *Post* were close to obsessed with *Shine*-dom. The paper printed not only a feature piece and a review by Page (both of them longish, and excellent), but also a weird little item titled "On Tour, Helfgott Hits Many a C-Note," in which Page tried to figure out how much money the tour was making. Moreover, the *Post* ran an extraordinary review—this one in addition to Page's—by the harpsichordist Igor Kipnis. It was odd that Kipnis would have agreed to write such a piece. For one thing, it opened him to charges of envy and pique, for Kipnis, a superb musician on an unglamorous instrument, will never achieve anything like the recognition and riches that have come Helfgott's way. Kipnis wrote that Helfgott's playing "was so uniformly devoid of poetry and rhetorical thrust, and so full of unwanted and unmarked accents, as to cause one to wonder what in the world musically sophisticated listeners might make of it all." Kipnis himself should have been caused to wonder why he, who has his faculties and a fine life, was writing public criticism of a man who is not his peer but a symbol of perseverance and hope. The review, in a sense, was more embarrassing than Helfgott could be at his feeblest.

The *Shine* phenomenon reached a high pitch on Oscar night, when Geoffrey Rush, who plays the older Helfgott in the movie, picked up the Best Actor award and defended the tour against accusations that it was a "circus." Helfgott himself was on hand to play *The Flight of the Bumble Bee*. He was obviously nervous—as performers of all kinds tend to be on such an occasion—and he played poorly, but he got through it and warmly accepted the audience's lusty cheers. Two days later, David Daniel in the *Wall Street Journal* was witty and merciless: "Bumble bees had a right to picket," though "the audience seemed to love it anyway, as no doubt did several gazillion TV viewers," in a "mass demonstration of tin ears and false sentiment."

One thing about *Shine* that the tin-eared and falsely sentimental masses are in love with is the Rachmaninoff concerto, which is a star of the movie. This magnificent work has always lived in the shadow of its predecessor, the Rachmaninoff Second, whose concluding theme was transformed into the song "Full Moon and Empty Arms." A moviegoer encountering the concerto for the first time will naturally march to the record store, if he is interested, and buy . . . which recording? The Helfgott, of course, and why not? There are better recordings (meaning all of the others), but the movie-goer doesn't know that, and, if he did, he wouldn't care.

Nor should he: The point of his purchase is not the performance but the music. Yet the critics begrudge even this. Eliot Morgan, also in the *Wall Street Journal*, said that the Helfgott recording's success "shows that people can be fooled at least some of the time," and Scott Cantrell of the *Kansas City Star* wrote, "What's sad is that hundreds of thousands of people buying this disc . . . will think the piece really sounds like this." Well, it does—the assertion that the concerto is unrecognizable in Helfgott's trembling hands is simply false, something that no one with a grip on himself could say.

Funny thing about the Helfgott recording: It doesn't sound like the playing of a crazy person. It isn't maniacal or uncontrolled (like some performances). Rather, it is reserved and mousy. Indeed, it is far and away the tamest, most tepid recording ever made of this mercurial and majestic work. But there is magic in it, magic put there by Rachmaninoff, and the fans who are buying it and loving it are not wrong to do so.

It is perhaps normal for elites to balk at the introduction of high art into popular culture, where distortion and degradation lie in wait. Musicians surely winced when Rush strode to the stage to accept his Oscar: He was accompanied by a soupy Hollywood-orchestra arrangement of the opening theme of the Rachmaninoff. Pianists stubbornly refuse to refer to Mozart's Piano Concerto No. 21 as the "*Elvira Madigan* Concerto," as it has been widely known since the appearance of that movie, which used it. *Ordinary People* and *Platoon* made lollipops out of Pachelbel's Canon in D and Barber's *Adagio for Strings*, and *Apocalypse Now* turned a Valkyrie ride into a clownish cliché. But the marriage of music and the movies can be beautiful, as in the recent *Romeo and Juliet*, which closed with Leontyne Price's recording of the "Liebestod" from Wagner's *Tristan und Isolde*. To employ music untraditionally is not necessarily to sully it.

David Helfgott should never have been judged as an ordinary pianist. He, manifestly, is not. And if people go to hear him "more for the madness than the music," as the *New York Times* editorialized, so what? Concertgoers have innumerable motivations, and Helfgott is an exceptional experience amid hundreds and hundreds of everyday ones. I, for one, would rather hear Helfgott play once than a long-established banal pianist play banally yet again.

And Helfgott, though unwell, is not a victim; neither are those around him his victimizers. He is better off on stage, where he both delights and is delighted, than drooling unnoticed on a couch in Perth. Gillian Helfgott, astrologer or not, analyzes keenly when she says, "I think there are people who are coming to see a man who has fought his way through the wilderness [rather than for pianism]. But if they come for that reason, I think they leave deeply touched. Critics have a right to express their views, but people have a right to express *their* views, too."

For his part, David Helfgott seems not so damaged as to be unable to speak for himself, and what he says, in his flighty patter, will ring true to anyone who has been fortunate enough to touch a musical instrument: "It's a miracle. I'm very lucky. One mustn't be so serioso. It's all a game. Must be grateful." Yes, must be.

—April 14, 1997
The Weekly Standard

Singing His Own Song

The nonconforming, and
wonderful, Lee Hoiby

Not long before Christmas, an important operatic event took place in New York. It was not at the Metropolitan Opera, or even City Opera. It was at the Manhattan School of Music—and the opera was Lee Hoiby's *A Month in the Country.* Hoiby is an unsung American composer, and here he was: sung. Few nights at the opera will be so satisfying this season. And many more people will hear Hoiby on February 5, when another of his operas—*Summer and Smoke*—is broadcast over National Public Radio. If we are not in a Hoiby hour, we may be in a Hoiby minute. Which is better than no time at all.

The composer will turn 80 next year, and he continues to work diligently, at his home in Long Eddy, N.Y., about 130 miles from Manhattan. If he is known for anything, he is known for his songs, of which he has written close to a hundred. They were championed by the soprano Leontyne Price, who sang them in recital after recital. When she retired in 1997, a great Hoiby voice was stilled. But there will be others, because these songs are too good to die.

There are five Dickinson songs—American composers always set Dickinson—including "Wild Nights" and "There Came a Wind Like a Bugle." There is "Always It's Spring" (on a Cummings poem), and the wonderfully comic song "The Serpent" (Theodore Roethke). In 1986—the centennial year for the Statue of Liberty—the composer took Emma Lazarus's words ("Give me your tired, your poor . . .") to write "Lady of the Harbor." Hoiby's assessment of the song is my own: "It's just a minute long, but it's a kick-ass piece."

And then there is "Goodby, Goodby, World," which uses Thornton Wilder's lines from *Our Town.* Hoiby says, "It is my best song." Whether that is true or not (I would count it tied with others), it is one of the great art songs in the American repertory.

A peculiar thing happened when Lee Hoiby was coming of age. (It would be hard to put a date on it; it simply happened, like an illness that becomes set.) Music took a sharp turn, toward the atonal and cerebral, and away from the tonal and heartfelt. (I oversimplify, but it is unavoidable.) Music that smelled of the Romantic was not only frowned on, it was reviled, and virtually outlawed. The music establishment could be Leninist in its severity. And Hoiby wanted to write music that was now considered backward—although "wanted" is the wrong word. He had no choice but to write such music, for that was the music that was in him.

First, however, Hoiby wanted to be a pianist, and he was a very good one. He remains one today. This Madison, Wis., native studied with, among others, Egon Petri, one of the great pianists and teachers of the first half of the 20th century. "I have never known anyone so capable of putting into words how a passage in music should go," says Hoiby. "He had a way with analogy and simile that was astounding." Hoiby keeps a picture of Petri on his wall.

But the young man could not keep away from his manuscript paper, and he gave in to composing. He studied with Darius Milhaud at Mills College, and then moved to Philadelphia, to work with Gian Carlo Menotti. His great influences were Mahler, Richard Strauss, and Samuel Barber. And Schubert—"It was Schubert who taught me how to write songs."

In 1952, Hoiby won a Fulbright scholarship to study at the Santa Cecilia Academy in Rome. But—wouldn't you know—they would not let him in. They rejected him on grounds that he was too old-fashioned, too conservative, a square. But, recalls Hoiby, "that was wonderful, because I didn't have to go to classes. I was contemptuous of this crowd. I knew something they didn't, namely that I was a good composer, or that I might become one." One day, Hoiby played some piano preludes for Goffredo Petrassi, a big figure at Santa Cecilia. Petrassi praised Hoiby's talent, but said, "Why don't you try some newer language?" Recounts Hoiby, "I smiled and said thank you—and went on my way."

He has a favorite metaphor: "I wanted to grow heirloom roses, but you were allowed nothing but cactuses."

Hoiby recognizes what some of the rest of us do: that he is the real radical, the real artistic rebel. "I am a nonconformist," he says. "I always refused to conform, and I paid a heavy price for it. But"—and this is an important but for Hoiby—"let me not whine about it: It was all a blessing in disguise. It left me with my whole life open, to do what I pleased, because there were always enough people around—mostly singers—who would commission something, and I could earn some money, to stay alive. I always kept my head above water."

For a while, Erich Leinsdorf, the conductor, programmed some of his music. But then, remembers Hoiby, a critic in San Francisco was savage (*How could Leinsdorf be playing this retrograde stuff?*)—and Leinsdorf never touched him again. I call this cowardice. Hoiby, characteristically, is forgiving, saying that even major conductors respond to pressures, to orthodoxy.

In recent times, this orthodoxy has relaxed somewhat; tonality has made a minor comeback. Ned Rorem—another American nonconformist—said to me in a 2002 interview that he feels like the Prodigal Son's brother: "I never went astray," never succumbed to fashion, always followed his musical conscience. And yet Modernism—often preceded by the adjective "thorny"—is still regnant. Night after night, as a critic, I sit in halls, hearing the same few pieces, though written by many different composers. Elliott Carter and the serialists—"the serial killers," Rorem calls them—can get a hearing any day; Hoiby and his brethren are still marginal.

And what of Hoiby should be central, or at least familiar? Well, begin with the operas. *A Month in the Country* is based on the Turgenev play, of course, and *Summer and Smoke* is based on the Tennessee Williams. In 1964, Williams heard *A Month in the Country*, and asked whether the composer would like to set one of his own plays. "Which one?" inquired Hoiby. "Take your pick, sweetheart," came the reply. Hoiby passed over *A Streetcar Named Desire*, judging it untreatable. For one thing, how could you give music to Stanley Kowalski's shouting of "Stella!" at the top of his lungs?

About 35 years later, André Previn set *Streetcar*, and what did he do with the shouting? He just let Stanley shout. "That's a perfect solution," says Hoiby. "It never occurred to me." Still, for him, *Summer and Smoke* was the much smarter bet, musically.

Others of Hoiby's operas include *The Tempest*, from which we sometimes hear a tenor aria, "Be not afeard." He also composed two monodramas, *The Italian Lesson* and *Bon Appétit!* (text by Julia Child, adapted by Mark Shulgasser). Jean Stapleton has performed them both.

Amidst all the vocal writing—not just the songs and the operas, but oratorios and anthems—the composer has not neglected his own instrument. A disc on the MMC label contains the Piano Concerto No. 2, a piece called *Narrative*, and the *Schubert Variations*. This last, in particular, is a work that pianists would be wise to exploit.

Also on that CD is Hoiby's Sonata for Violin and Piano, which—here I go again—ought to be a staple in that repertory. It is very American, nicely crafted, beautiful in its simplicity. (Says Hoiby, "It was Strauss, in the last scene of *Capriccio*, who gave me the courage to write simple lyricism.") The second movement has some bite—a quality that the very tuneful and humane Hoiby is sometimes said to be lacking. But even this movement has a melody: a simple, American melody. The final movement is jagged and jazzy—but, naturally, Hoiby manages to insert a song.

He has written a piano quartet, a recording of which will soon be available from Albany Records (purveyor of other Hoiby material as well). This is *Dark Rosaleen*, a "Rhapsody on an Air by James Joyce." It came about in an unusual way. At Mills College, Hoiby had a roommate whose father had been a friend of James Joyce ("Jim," to him). One day, the father came to Hoiby and said, "Would you write something down?" Joyce had sung to him a melody, to accompany James Clarence Mangan's poem "Dark Rosaleen." Hoiby saved it on some scrap found decades later—and incorporated it into this extraordinary piano quartet.

In our recent conversation, I asked Hoiby which works of his, currently unrecorded, he would like to see recorded. His initial response was, in essence, *Recorded, hell—how about performed?* He has many manuscripts on the shelf, "gathering dust." There is a flute concerto, a cello sonata. His latest opera is another Shakespeare work, *Romeo and Juliet*. Is he pleased with it? "Oh, I'm ecstatic about it. As with *The Tempest*, I dreaded to see the last line coming into view, because I loved the material so much."

It is well to remember that reputation is a funny thing: You never know when a composer will emerge, in history. Modest and serene as he is, Hoiby wouldn't mind tasting some wide acclaim—and he may just yet. "My family is very long-lived, you know." He stresses again that he is not a whiner, is not discontent, does not think of himself as a victim. "If I never hear certain pieces performed, I have written them, which is something wonderful. I have had the thrill of writing music. It is a great privilege, this musical life."

At times, he has thought of himself as lazy, but "when I see lists of my works, and the variety of them, I realize that I have done something. I have a body of work. And I'm feeling pretty good about that." So he should. And so should we.

—February 14, 2005
National Review

Wild About Earl

A virtuoso pianist at 90

L ast month, Earl Wild celebrated his 90th birthday, with a recital in Carnegie Hall. Who's Earl Wild? He is one of the outstanding piano virtuosos of the 20th century. A lanky Pittsburgher, with huge hands, Wild has a monster technique, capable of anything. He has always played the hardest music, the showiest music—but he is more than a technician. Wild has an interesting musical head. He is a throwback to an earlier time of unabashed Romanticism, and barnstorming pianism.

Born two years before America entered the First War, Wild studied with one of the great piano pedagogues of the age, Egon Petri, who in turn had been a student of Busoni. To review Wild's biography is to touch history. He played with Mischa Elman, a violinist who now seems almost as distant as Paganini. He played in the NBC Orchestra under Toscanini. He pioneered Gershwin, that whippersnapper from Tin Pan Alley. He worked on television with Sid Caesar. Some people, with a wrong idea of sophistication, have sniffed at Wild, for this varied background (not to mention his old-fashioned repertoire). Wild has let them sniff: He has had a fun and fulfilling career.

That career has included composing, because, when Wild was young, there was no great division between composer and performer: They were often the same person. He has specialized in transcriptions—in arrangements for the piano—like so many other virtuosos of his kind. Among those transcriptions is an album of Gershwin songs. A friend of mine recently remarked to Wild, "I'm going to learn your 'Liza.'" He responded, "It's hard, you know." Indeed.

Five years ago, I attended, and reviewed, Wild's 85th-birthday recital, also in Carnegie Hall. One had to make few allowances, if any. I reviewed him essentially straight, as I would a pianist of 45, say. A reader—a woman from Ohio, I think—wrote me an angry letter, saying, "How can you say those critical things about this great and venerable musician?" I replied that I was paying him the compliment of regarding him as I always had: He was himself.

And he has continued to be himself. Forget the recordings—there have been several recent ones—because they can be deceptive. (Recording engineers have more tricks than fashion photographers.) What about live performances? Two years ago, Wild traveled to Carnegie Hall to play in the memorial service for Harold C. Schonberg, the longtime critic of the *New York Times*. Schonberg loved pianists—particularly Romantic virtuosos like Wild—and, in fact, wrote a classic book called *The Great Pianists*. At the memorial service, Wild played a Liszt ballade, and played it well, as always.

Music history is replete with masterly older pianists. Artur Rubinstein played inspiringly in his 80s and 90s, enjoying what someone dubbed his "Indian summer." Shura Cherkassky had a kind of renaissance in his 80s, or at least a new fame. Mieczyslaw Horszowski was concertizing—and well—at almost 100. And among non-pianists, we could cite the cellist Pablo Casals, a force in his 90s, and the guitarist Andrés Segovia (ditto). Leopold Stokowski, the conductor, is an outstanding case: He conducted compellingly right up to his death at 95.

And Earl Wild is not the only musician to have celebrated his 90th birthday at Carnegie Hall recently. A week after Wild appeared, the hall staged a 90th-birthday concert for the composer George Perle. And he is practically a pup compared with Elliott Carter, born in 1908, who has been seen in Carnegie Hall and elsewhere a lot this season. Taking the cake, however, is Leo Ornstein, the visionary composer who lived from 1892 to 2002. (Digest those numbers for a minute.) At the Wild recital, the music scholar David Dubal remarked to me that Ornstein is the only composer to have worked in three different centuries.

Tuck that into your cocktail-party repertoire.

Arriving at Carnegie Hall last month, Wild was not in his best shape physically. He had had a heart operation, among others, and his vision was poor. But he looked essentially as he always has, so tall, so erect, so elegant, with that shock of white hair. I asked a member of his management team something embarrassingly gossipy: "Is that a toupée?" No, that's Wild's hair, every follicle, and there are tons of them.

He does not play old man's recitals, this pianist: not gentle Schumann pieces, or Chopin mazurkas, or the Ravel *Pavane*. His recitals are still Wildean. He began with something relatively calm, however, a recent transcription of his: an Adagio by Marcello (of the Italian Baroque). In this piece, Wild was beautifully in balance, demonstrating a singing tone and bringing out all voices. He played freely—with ample pedal, for example—but not without taste. He suffered a slight memory lapse—he had had some in his 85th-birthday recital, too—but quickly recovered from it. A relaxed, almost nonchalant man, he has never been one to sweat the small stuff.

After Marcello came Beethoven: his Sonata in D major, Op. 10, No. 3. This is a difficult work, sometimes fiendishly so. Wild was not a model of Beethoven playing here, but he exhibited a certain command, and he gave the final movement—the Rondo—notable character.

Then—you must have this in a Wild recital—Liszt. And not introspective, technically undemanding Liszt, either, but the *Jeux d'eau à la Villa d'Este*. With those relaxed arms, sweeping over the keyboard, Wild produced sparkling effects. I had the thought that, not long before, I'd heard the Hungarian pianist Zoltán Kocsis—now in his prime—play this same work. Was he better than Wild? Sure, but not by much, I tell you, not by much.

The recitalist then turned to Chopin, his G-minor Ballade, and as he played, I had another thought: The objections I had to this performance were those I had always had to Wild's playing. (Briefly, I find him a little blunt.) My objections had nothing to do with age, with a decline either technical or interpretive.

And there was a lot to admire in Wild's playing of the Ballade, as there was in his playing of subsequent Chopin works. One of them was the Scherzo in B-flat minor. Wild does not play with the same fire or force he once did, but he compensates for it in what you might call poetry. The Scherzo didn't sound much like a scherzo, frankly—it sounded more like a nocturne. But you have never heard it so beautiful! You perhaps never knew there was such beauty in it. An autumnal, ruminative Scherzo in B-flat minor? Turns out it's possible.

Wild also played Chopin's Fantaisie-Impromptu (from which we get the pop song "I'm Always Chasing Rainbows"). In these hands, it was amazingly nimble, gossamer.

To end the printed program we had another recent Wild transcription—this one a flashy one (none of this stately Baroque stuff). The piece? The *Mexican Hat Dance*. I kid you not. Wild put on a circus act, dazzling, irresistible. Toward the beginning, he had a little lapse, didn't care, and started over again—finishing superbly.

As the audience stood and applauded, something a bit strange occurred: The soprano Aprile Millo—another old-fashioned musician, as it happens—appeared on the stage, with the composer Ned Rorem (spry and randy at 82). Millo gave a little talk, in her grand-diva way, commenting that Wild has "the ocean in his hands" (which is true). It seemed that she would sing "Happy Birthday"—but, sadly, she merely started the audience in it, while Rorem played the piano.

And then Wild gave a single encore: not another dazzler, but a piece dazzling in a different way: Respighi's *Notturno*. This was dreamy, beguiling, almost impossibly lovely. Who would ever have thought that Earl Wild—thunderer of the piano, heir to the Liszt tradition, to the Busoni tradition—would end his career as an exquisite colorist?

But I should not be so quick to say he is ending his career. I wouldn't be surprised to cover his 95th-birthday recital, in November 2010. Many people have said that he's the last of a line, the last of a breed—"the last Romantic." But people are always saying that, about this one or that one. If you counted up the Last Romantics in recent decades, you might reach 20. There was even a Horowitz documentary of that title: *The Last Romantic*. Right now, I could name you ten young pianists who are virtuoso Romantics (most of them from Russia, to be sure—mother of that breed). But Wild is something special, an American original, and when he is gone, why . . .

But there will be many, many recordings. He made his first recording in 1934. He made his most recent last year—i.e., 70 years later.

Pretty good.

—December 31, 2005
National Review

Daughter of the Vikings

Birgit Nilsson, 1918–2005

Opera is a field of legends—and opera lost a legend when Birgit Nilsson died, apparently on Christmas Day. (The news is imprecise about this.) The Swedish soprano was 87. She'd had a long career, too, singing from her debut with Stockholm's Royal Opera in 1946 until the mid-'80s. The world simply loved her—and it still does.

She's often called the leading Wagnerian soprano of her generation, and that is probably true. For many, she is the definitive Brünnhilde, and one of the great Isoldes. And then there are her Strauss roles: Salome and Elektra, in which she crackled. She also sang Turandot (Puccini)—and many another role requiring indomitable strength.

Nilsson was the very embodiment of a certain kind of opera star. She was almost a Warner Brothers cartoon of the Wagnerian soprano: a Nordic block of granite—or maybe of ice—with a battleship voice. About that voice, there was debate: Some thought it was a bit harsh, metallic, unbending. Others thought this was nuts. All could agree that the voice was positively extraordinary.

What Nilsson had, beyond a doubt, was volume—as much volume as anyone has ever heard. I myself never had the privilege of hearing Nilsson in the flesh; those who did get kind of mystical when talking about that sound—particularly its volume. When they reflect on it, they can hardly believe that they heard it—that it was real.

A few years ago, I was talking to a famous opera singer about Nilsson, and this lady was waxing rhapsodic about that incredible sound. "It was so loud, it blew your hair back! It rattled your bones!" I asked, "But did you find her musical?" The singer thought for a second and replied, "She could be cold. But that sound! Jay, it was so *loud*! You had to have heard it—it was electrifying."

One of the funniest things I have ever witnessed was the baritone Thomas Hampson imitating Nilsson in a master class. (That is, in a master class of his own.) Years before, he had attended a Nilsson master class, in which the soprano attempted to demonstrate high, soft singing. And in Mr. Hampson's imitation, that sound was fabulously loud. She simply couldn't help it.

I also treasure a remark made by Benita Valente, a soprano with a pure, lightish, lyric voice. She once said, "If I were Birgit Nilsson, just for a weekend, I'd sing for 48 straight hours, and peel the paint off the walls."

The world at large last saw her ten years ago, when she participated in the Metropolitan Opera gala honoring James Levine. (The conductor had completed 25 years with the company.) Nilsson—aged 77—practically stole the show. She came on, gave a little talk, and said that, "since I'm a daughter of the Vikings," she had to give a certain salute: whereupon she sang Brünnhilde's cries of "Hojotoho." The place went absolutely mad.

Opera people love to tell stories, and Birgit Nilsson provided plenty of them. I'll relate a few. The most famous one, of course, is her response to the question, "What does it take to sing Isolde?" "A comfortable pair of shoes." (That opera—being by Wagner—is a marathon.) And, do you know this one? At tax time, Nilsson is asked whether she has any dependents. "Only Rudolph Bing" (the general manager of the Met). And this? Nilsson, in her retirement, is participating in a joint interview with another great soprano, also retired: Eileen Farrell. The latter is asked whether she ever heard Nilsson perform. She answers no. Says Birgit, "You really missed something!" It was merely true.

Over the decades, Nilsson made many, many recordings, and I will mention just one—not a particularly famous one, either. Actually, it's a radio broadcast. I'm referring to the *Fidelio* (Beethoven) of January 1956, conducted by Erich Kleiber. Nilsson is Leonore, of course, and the voice was never more beautiful: It is refulgent, pliant, all-capable. Musically and dramatically, Nilsson is just about all you could want in this magnificent role.

But I must mention a second recording—this one, maybe the weirdest I own, or have ever heard. It's Nilsson singing "I Could Have Danced All Night," from *My Fair Lady*. And with whom does she sing it? With that famous Broadway maestro, Herbert von Karajan, and that famous Broadway band, the Vienna Philharmonic. The sheer incongruity of this recording—Nilsson! Karajan! Lerner! Loewe!—is breathtaking. And so is the performance.

Nilsson revels in this song, toying with it, delighting in it. You can't understand a word—English was not her language—but that's okay. It is as though she is combining Eliza Doolittle and Brünnhilde.

The last line, as you recall, is, "I could have danced, danced, danced all night." Nilsson is singing the song in C major. On the penultimate note—"all"—she goes up to a G. *Uh-oh. She's not going to do it. She just can't*—but she does. On that final word "night," she nails a high C: a big, huge, heavens-filling C. Bizarro, but totally thrilling.

We often say of singers—and people generally—"She's irreplaceable. There's no one else like her." Most of the time, this isn't true. We may be unique to God, but we're not necessarily unique in the opera house or on the concert stage, or in life. But it's true of Birgit Nilsson: She was original, singular; there's no one else like her; and who knows when we will see her like again?

But we have those recordings. And those who heard her without the aid of vinyl—or newer material—have their memories.

—January 13, 2006
The New York Sun

American Sounds

The music of our presidential campaigns

T he big question on everyone's mind at our political conventions is: What music are they going to play?

Well, this may not be the biggest question, but it is an interesting one nonetheless. Music has been part of our politics since the beginning—fifes and drums and all that. At the conventions, aficionados like to speculate about what music the organizers will play for certain speakers. (Sometimes—in fact, usually—this speculation is mischievous.) They also like to divine hidden meaning in the music that those organizers have, in fact, chosen.

This choice, though minor, is not inconsequential: Get it just right, and the speaker has a lift; get it wrong somehow, and you weigh him down.

Gerald Ford provides an interesting case (really). For him, they have always played "Hail to the Victors," the University of Michigan fight song. Problem is, the song features the word "hail," sung over and over, always accompanied by the thrusting out of an arm. When a stadium, or an arena, gets rockin', it looks unnervingly like the rally at Nuremberg.

For Jimmy Carter, they often played "Marching Through Georgia," until the candidate complained that this was, after all, a northern song, celebrating the South's—particularly Georgia's—most ignominious hour.

When Ronald Reagan entered a hall, they usually used "California, Here I Come," which was a little awkward, because—at least in 1976, 1980, and 1984—he was trying to get to, or return to, Washington, D.C., not wanting to be sent "right back where I started from."

This year, too, contained its share of musical fun. At the Republican convention, John McCain strode out to the theme from *Star Wars*, reminding people that he had used imagery from this movie during the primaries ("I'm Luke Skywalker, trying to get out of the Death Star"). For the Texans, there was a lot of "Deep in the Heart of Texas," along with "The Yellow Rose of Texas"; they both make for rousing convention numbers.

The Republicans' cutest moment, however, came when Congressman

Vito Fossella walked out to talk about Social Security reform. The music? "When I'm Sixty-four."

And the GOP, bless its flag-waving heart, has found a bona fide anthem: Lee Greenwood's "God Bless the U.S.A." They have used it for the past five presidential campaigns, and it holds up surprisingly well, especially in emotion-charged settings. This must be the most successful marriage of song and party since "Happy Days Are Here Again" and the Democrats. If the Republicans play their cards right, they will be firing up "God Bless . . ." for another generation at least.

At the Democratic convention, Hillary Clinton was greeted with "New York, New York," a somewhat dicey choice: It emphasized that she is a newcomer to the state, hoping to "make it." For her husband, the president, they played terrible, electronic, fascist-sounding music, to accompany his terrible, fascist-seeming entrance through the unseen (except on gigantic video screens) corridors of the arena. Talk about Nuremberg; some of us wondered whether Leni Riefenstahl had died (she has not).

Clinton ended his speech with the admonition "Don't stop thinking about tomorrow," whereupon, with sure timing, the convention-meisters blared the Clinton theme from 1992 and 1996 (Fleetwood Mac's "Don't Stop . . ."). This has been an effective song for the president, as every politician wants to be thought of as forward-looking. ("Coming to America" seemed not to work for Michael Dukakis in 1988, but then, to be fair to the song, Michael Dukakis seemed not to work as a candidate.)

Caroline Kennedy got, naturally, "Camelot," which was not really appropriate to a political convention. The song is simply too fruity, too light, too nothing. Her uncle, Senator Ted, however, was accorded the perfect song for his entrance: "You're Still the One." It is a terrific pop number anyway, and it delivered exactly the message the Democrats sought for their liberal lion, forever a convention favorite.

For Joe Lieberman? Not "Hava Nagila," as one Lieberman-weary wag had speculated, but the theme from *Chariots of Fire*. This music, easy to swallow at first, soon turns treacly and cloying—not unlike the candidate. But millions love the *Chariots* theme, and the movie happens (well, probably not happens) to feature a Jewish athlete who overcomes discrimination.

Finally, the Big Kahuna, Al Gore: He enthused his way through the crowd to the strains of syrupy, stringy, vaguely patriotic-sounding music that evidently was composed specially for this event. If his fall campaign is not better than this music, the Republicans have little to worry about.

Speaking of politics and music, there has recently been released an album that should belong to political junkies everywhere: *Presidential Campaign Songs, 1789-1996*, available from Smithsonian Folkways Recordings. The songs are performed by the veteran folk artist Oscar Brand, and they are not only instructive, but a sheer delight.

Given the confines of a single compact disc, there is no room for the losers; only winning candidates are represented here (with the exception of Henry Wallace; folkies—being lefties—cannot help themselves). The songs are rich and varied. They are uplifting, obnoxious, tender, wicked, hilarious, and probably libelous. Many of them use popular tunes (such as "Yankee Doodle"); some were written by noted composers (such as Stephen Foster—for James Buchanan). So numerous were the ditties composed for political campaigns that parties would publish whole books of them, for a single political year (as in, *The Republican Songster for the Campaign of 1860*).

We begin at the beginning: with George Washington, who had no opponent but who had songs nonetheless, including one that goes, "The day is broke, my lads! March on, and follow, follow Washington." John Adams's entry stresses his friendship with the great man, the first president. Jefferson's is in a minor key—it is a typical Scottish reel—and its words dramatically oppose the Alien and Sedition Acts, promising that "the reign of terror now is o'er," and continuing, "Rejoice, sons of Columbia! To tyrants never bend the knee. Join with heart, with soul and voice, for Jefferson and liberty."

These first presidential songs, unsurprisingly, remembered the Revolution—the patriots dying, and so on. They were also pointedly anti-faction. Monroe's anthem includes the line, "Oh, say, sovereign people, whose voice is the law; whose will is supreme and keeps faction in awe!"

Care for some negative campaigning? Try John Quincy Adams's "Little Know Ye"—another Scottish reel, menacing and relentless—which warns of all the bad things that will happen "if John Quincy not be comin'": "Slavery's comin', knavery's comin', plunder's comin', wonder's comin', hatin''s comin', Satan's comin' [yes, you read that right]—if John Quincy not be comin'."

One of the most entertaining and derogatory of all these songs is that for Martin Van Buren in 1836. Using a beloved lullaby, it mocks the candidate's opponents, William Henry Harrison (Tippecanoe) and John Tyler, drawing particular attention to the old general's . . . thirst: "Rockabye, Baby, Daddy's a Whig; when he comes home, hard cider he'll swig. When he has swug, he'll fall in a stew; and down will come Tyler and Tippecanoe." (It gets worse—and more uproarious.)

Harrison, though, fired back with a song of his own, of which the killer stanza is, "Who rules us with an iron rod? Who moves at Satan's beck and nod? Who heeds not man, who heeds not God? Van Buren!"

Millard Fillmore's entry begins, "There's right and wrong in parties, and right is on our side." Our thirteenth president was a divider, not a uniter.

"Lincoln and Liberty, Too" states that "Our David's good sling is unerring, the slave-o-crat giant he slew. So shout if you're freedom-preferring, for Lincoln and liberty, too." "Grant, Grant, Grant" (set to the tune of "Tramp, Tramp, Tramp") lambastes Andrew Johnson for being too soft on the South, taunting, "Goodbye, Andy, you must go. For to Grant, a traitor is ever a foe." (Furthermore, "We all will cheer the happy news, and the Ku Klux Klan will shiver in their shoes.")

Twelve years later, Garfield, too, played on fears of southern ascension. His "If the Johnnies Get into Power," sung to the tune of "When Johnny Comes Marching Home," warns, "Our laws they'll jeer, our flag they'll flout; they'll try to turn our officers out. And we'll all wear gray if the Johnnies get into power."

Grover Cleveland's song, "Democrats, Good Democrats," stokes resentment over the Stolen Election of 1876 ("Eight years ago, we won the prize, and then were robbed by tricks and lies"). Benjamin Harrison's ditty makes vicious sport of Cleveland's conduct in the Civil War (he arranged for a substitute); no Republican even *thought* to say anything so harsh about Bill Clinton in 1992.

And so the collection progresses into the 20th century, finishing with "Don't Stop (Thinking About Tomorrow)." The entry for 1924, "Keep Cool and Keep Coolidge," celebrates that president's humility and simplicity. The message of Herbert Hoover's song is fixed right in the title: "If He's Good Enough for Lindy [the aviator Charles Lindbergh], He's Good Enough for Me." (A rule in politics: If you have the nation's foremost endorsement, flaunt it.) Jimmy Carter's ballad for 1976 asks the governor's none-too-modest question, "Why Not the Best?"

At the end of his second inaugural address, Ronald Reagan spoke of the "American sound." Well, these are American sounds, in all their strange and cantankerous glory. They are not as lofty as the abstraction that Reagan described; but they make our politics sweeter—and more lovable—all the same.

—September 11, 2000
National Review

Stagedoor Jay

The confessions of a Price-head

I must've been twelve when I first heard Leontyne Price. I didn't like vocal music much—young people seldom do. But she was on the concert series, sandwiched between the likes of Horowitz and Milstein, so I went.

It was a revelation, to bow to the cliché. Price was not only a singer, but a real musician. Then, as now, she sang Handel and Strauss and Poulenc and Barber—all with total authority.

Ever since, I haven't been able to shake her. Oh, hang on a second: She hasn't been able to shake me. I wanted to hear her again and again, and she wasn't getting any younger, so I kept a close eye on her schedule. Would this be her last year? Better get to Boston. How about *this* year? Better drive to Columbus.

I craved the high of a Price recital the way a heroin addict does his needle. (Was I a heroine addict? Sorry.) My friends started to refer to me as a "Price-head." One of them warned, as I headed off to New Haven, "Remember, Jay, there's a fine line between a fan and a stalker." Yeah, but rarely has a pastime been so joyous, so pure, so justifiable.

Funny thing is, I never wanted to meet the woman. Her public always thronged the greenroom after a recital, proffering flowers and hugs and tears. I spat on that. Personality is usually a gross intrusion into music. And I hadn't been in a greenroom since I was a boy.

The first time I went backstage, it was to meet Eugene Ormandy. People were lined up for miles, waiting for their programs to be auto-graphed. Ormandy was sitting at a table, signing, barely looking up. No one was talking to him, which I thought was strange.

When I got there, I said, "Mr. Ormandy, I just wanted to tell you I thought you did a very good job." The maestro was startled. I had nothing for him to write on. "Huh?" he said. I repeated myself. He then stood up (all four-foot-ten of him), embraced me, and thanked me as though he'd never been complimented in his life.

The next time, I guess, was for Horowitz, who sat on a couch, sphinx-like. The boy ahead of me was Asian. Horowitz said, "Japanese?" The boy nodded. Horowitz beamed as though he had just formulated the theory of relativity. To me he said nothing.

Then there was Mstislav Rostropovich, perhaps the most ebullient spirit in music, a man who kisses everyone he encounters without restraint. His nickname, in the Russian fashion, is "Slava." Some call him "Saliva."

But mainly I remember Alicia de Larrocha, my pianist hero, who turned out to be not-so-warm. I adored her. She came to town one year with another Spaniard, the soprano Victoria de los Angeles, for a duo recital. About the singer—and her art—I cared nothing. In fact, I resented her very participation in the evening.

After the final encore, I hurried back, excited to greet de Larrocha. She was standing between two men—management, probably—with a highball in her hand. I stood before her for what seemed an eternity. It took a tremendous act of will for her to ignore me.

As I made for the door, stung and angry, I heard an *Eh!* from the other end of the room. It was, of course, de los Angeles, who had witnessed the entire scene. This enchanting woman—redolent of sweet sweat and make-up and perfume—beckoned me, murmured something tender, and stroked my face. I floated out (still ticked, though).

It was in Newark—which, don't laugh, has a superb hall and a lively musical life—that I first met Leontyne Price. I had been sitting down in the front left, and, as I was exiting, I found that I was practically at the greenroom door. Why not?

The room, as always, was presided over by Price's manager, her brother, the retired Army general George Price. General Price is a remarkable man: a rough-talking, rigid-backed soldier with a golden heart and an ample knowledge of music. He once commanded divisions; now he commands—with equal dignity—his sister's Kleenex, bottled water, and lipstick.

My brief conversation with the diva was . . . well, sublime. Since then, I have accosted her whenever possible. Particularly nice was Chapel Hill, where Price performed shortly after I'd gotten married. When I introduced her to my wife, her eyes widened, and she said—with Mississippi heavy in her voice—"Why, hello, pumpkin!" I've been saying, "Hello, pumpkin" to my wife ever since (which, needless to say, is making her homicidal).

Price is in her seventies now—fulfilled, laureled, triumphant. She can't go on forever (as I've been saying for at least 15 years). Last week, she gave a master class at Howard University. She was, simply, everything she is: smart, haughty, sly, grand, impossibly musical.

And she also received the single most elegant introduction I've ever heard: "The greater the person, the less you have to say about him. Ladies and gentlemen, Miss Leontyne Price."

So I'll stop now. But, gosh, I'm nuts about her. You'd be, too.

—November 23, 1998
The Weekly Standard

PERSONAL

Love on the Arno

Studying abroad, becoming
an American

Sometimes you write a piece that has a lot of people saying, "Me too, me too!" This is one of them.

I 've been thinking about Florence, and I've been thinking about patriotism. Let me tell you why.

I've just returned from a visit to Florence (Italy, not South Carolina), where I was once a student; and, while there, I read Norman Podhoretz's beautiful and muscular new memoir about his "love affair with America." The memoir—I should blush to say—reminded me a lot of myself; of my own experiences, my own growth.

Norman P. sailed off to Cambridge University in 1950. He was always a patriotic kid, but he came back more patriotic—more America-appreciating—than ever. A dose of European anti-Americanism will do that to you. Some of those he encountered were even "more horrified by the prospect of being drowned by Coca-Cola and poisoned by hamburgers" than they were by Washington's foreign and defense policies.

My own school was not exactly Cambridge: It was the humble (but lovable) Istituto Michelangelo, an Italian-language school for foreigners. The year was 1984, a dark year for Orwell but a bright and pivotal one for me. I set off from Detroit on Icelandair, then the cheapest way to get to Europe. You stopped briefly in Reykjavik (where you were supposed to buy one of those grayish sweaters), then proceeded to either Luxembourg or Frankfurt. I chose Luxembourg.

On the train down to Florence, I had one of those encounters—small-seeming—that stay with you forever. I sat across from a young American woman who was a fellow student. (I believe she was from Berkeley, but that would be almost too perfect.) She had a broad face, sandy hair, and a splash of freckles. And she was deeply ashamed of her country. Reagan was president, you see, and he had planted missiles in Western Europe, and everything was grim. She confided to me that she could hardly bear to be associated with America.

Then she uttered the (to me) immortal words, "I'm hoping I can pass for German."

Please pause a second to consider that statement. Here we were in Europe—in France, actually, traveling through—only 39 years after V-E Day; only 39 years (less than two generations) after the ovens at Buchenwald and Bergen-Belsen had stopped belching. And this creepy, but, sadly, typical, girl—from *the United States*—was saying, "I'm hoping I can pass for German."

I was not yet fully formed, politically. I was certainly no flag-waver. But I wasn't like that, not like her. That I knew.

And so this process continued once I was ensconced at the Istituto Michelangelo. It wasn't so much the anti-Americanism of the Europeans that had an effect on me; that was par for the course. It was the self-hating Americanism of many of my compatriots around me. It is hard to recount now—in this happily different age—how they despised their country; how they hung their heads in shame about it. They bitterly mocked the American tourists on the Florentine streets: See how crude they were! So loud, so monolingual, so *fat*—the type that would ask for ketchup or piss in the bidet.

Also that year—this was a summer semester—were the Los Angeles Olympics. An American housemate of mine was beside herself about these—all that red, white, and blue, and, worst, Reagan, smiling that idiot smile of his, as if he didn't know how contemptible he and his "U.S.A.! U.S.A.!" were. She was especially appalled by Mary Lou Retton, the little ball of fire and joy from West Virginia (perhaps the self-hating American's least favorite state). The ebullient gymnast was becoming America's sweetheart, but she was a demon in that house at 20 Giovanni Bovio Street. My housemate recoiled at the girl's country twang and her equally country first name: "Mary Lou!" the housemate would sing out in mockery, trying to sound like a demented Minnie Pearl. "Mary Lou!"

All the while, I was becoming more and more repulsed by this attitude, and more and more . . . patriotic (though this was considered a horribly anti-intellectual thing to be—the disorder of boobs and know-nothings and losers). I went out of my way to be friendly and helpful to American tourists, whom I found easy to like. Did they want to know where the Ponte Vecchio or Vivoli's was? Did they need help with the menu? It would be my pleasure. To irk my irksome American classmates, I would have donned a pair of Bermuda shorts and a garish floral-print shirt, and thrown a camera around my neck—even chomped on a cigar.

I simply refused to cringe at my countrymen. I sort of willed it. I didn't want to be that kind of traveler, age-old, who fancies himself superior and admirably sophisticated. Listen to Miss Lavish, in Florence, at the beginning of E. M. Forster's *Room with a View*: "Stop a minute [she says to her companion, Lucy]. Let these two people go on, or I shall have to speak to them. I do detest conventional intercourse. Nasty! They are going into the church, too. Oh, the Britisher abroad! . . . Look at their figures! They walk through my [my!] Italy like a pair of cows. It's very naughty of me, but I would like to set an examination paper at Dover, and turn back every tourist who couldn't pass it."

One day, a teacher at the Istituto decided to conduct a little political session. After the usual denunciations of the U.S. and its cowboy president, the teacher turned to me (I must by now have acquired a reputation) and said, "And now, Jay will defend America." I stood up and said, "America, given all that it has done for the world, particularly on this continent, has no need of a defense." Then I sat down. Everyone went "ooh."

I had discovered something wonderful: the World War II card (which can—and should, I believe—double as a World War I card; for that matter, it should triple as a Cold War card). To play it may be a little underhanded, but it can be hard to resist. Don't get me wrong: I didn't expect, or want, anyone in the Old World to throw flowers at my feet, the way they did Woodrow Wilson. (For one thing, I had had nothing whatsoever to do with the achievements of the American army.) But, you know: *un po' di rispetto, eh?* When I need cheering up, I like to think of that glorious moment when Charles de Gaulle told Dean Rusk that he wanted all American troops out of France, pronto. Replied Rusk, "Would that include the ones buried in the military cemeteries, General?" This must be the greatest riposte in American history.

In the fall of '84, after I had gotten home, Vice President Bush debated Geraldine Ferraro—and he said something that sounded strange to many ears, but that was sweet music to mine. He said (speaking of Reagan, of course), "It's a joy to serve with a president who does not apologize for the United States of America." I knew just what he meant. Exactly.

Travel, they say, is broadening. So it is. You are apt to learn as much about your home country, or yourself, as you are about the places of your journey. When I got back from Florence, I was hopelessly in love with that city, and with Italy, longing to return. But, like Norman Pod., I also had a

new (or renewed) feeling about America. Burke said that a country, to be
loved, ought to be lovely. Okay. There is plenty to love about America and
Americans. Even—no, especially—the Mary Lous.

—August 14, 2000
National Review

A Name of My Own

Me and Reagan

In the summer of 2004, the fortieth president passed away, and National Review
published a memorial issue. This was my contribution to it.

O f all the things Ronald Reagan did for me, maybe the best was
that he gave me something to call myself. I am a Reaganite. It can
be difficult to answer when someone says, "What are you,
politically?" The word "conservative" is subject to a thousand interpretations. You don't want to launch into a lecture about the Scottish
Enlightenment, the strange journey of the word "liberal," the advent of
Frank Meyer, etc. So, instead you can say—if it's true—"I'm a Reaganite."

Everyone has an idea of what Reagan was: Some think of him as
a mainstream conservative, others think of him as a right-winger, or as a
genuine liberal, or as a Neanderthal—whatever. The point is, people know
what you mean.

He had a view of America's place in the world, and of the place of
government in America, and of what this republic should be. I share that
view, wholly.

Although I wasn't destined to. I was born into a quite left-wing
environment—Ann Arbor, Mich.—and Reagan's name was mud. Actually,
it was sometimes "Ray-gun," ha, ha, a popular epithet in the early '80s.
We're all supposed to love, or at least respect, Reagan now, so it's hard to
convey just how hated he was when his career was live. The Left hates
W. now, to be sure. They hated Reagan no less, trust me.

In my world, "conservative" meant bigot, warmonger, plutocrat, ignoramus . . . shall I go on? And Reagan was the worst of the conservatives. He was a "nuclear cowboy"—that was the phrase—and his superficial charm would hoodwink the American public into electing him. How could the voters throw out Jimmy Carter, pure, sweet Jimmy Carter, who read the Bible in Spanish and cared so much about human rights?

Rosalynn Carter said, about Reagan, "He makes us comfortable with our prejudices." Yeah, that was it.

Reagan's election was considered a national disaster in Ann Arbor. I was a sophomore in high school. After being sworn in, Reagan set about doing many shocking things, like cutting taxes ("for the rich") and challenging the Soviet Union. Why, he was the kind of guy who might even fire air-traffic controllers! (Reagan would say, "I didn't fire them—they quit." The union had vowed not to strike, you see.)

A pivotal day came on March 30, 1981, when Reagan—along with those three others—was shot. It was pivotal for me, that is. I was amazed by the grace and courage he showed in that situation. From then on, you couldn't tell me that he was an empty B-movie actor, with no substance whatsoever. I wouldn't believe it; he'd given the lie to it. I wasn't necessarily ready to agree with him—but I would listen to him.

And I did. I was a natural anti-Communist. That was caring about human rights too, wasn't it? Didn't the millions who lived under Communism have the same right to liberty and decency as Filipinos, South Africans, and Chileans? And, even at my leftest (which wasn't very left), I couldn't hate America. I knew that, as Donald Rumsfeld would later put it, "America is not what's wrong with the world."

But, oh, at my university, Reagan was what was wrong with the world. On the last day of one class, a history professor told us that he doubted we'd live into real adulthood, because Reagan, through his rejection of détente, would incinerate the world. And in the reelection year of 1984, the kids around me chanted, "Reagan, Bush, you can't hide, we charge you with genocide!" What they meant was that the administration had slowed the rate of growth of social-welfare spending.

Brick by brick, my entire edifice—never all that solid—fell. I opened my mind to free-market economics. And I could no longer believe—I don't think I ever believed—that abortion was merely a matter of a woman's sovereignty over her own body. The feminists had a slogan: "A fetus in a woman's womb has no more standing than a hamburger in her stomach." That slogan was repulsive to me.

If I hadn't liked Reagan so much, as a man, would I have swung around to his views? Probably—but it would have taken longer. There was his humor, his "security in his own skin," as everyone said. People wanted him to be embarrassed by his acting career, especially his role in *Bedtime for Bonzo*, in which he played alongside a chimp. But Reagan wasn't the least embarrassed. Someone gave him a still from that picture to sign—Reagan with Bonzo. He wrote, "I'm the one with the watch."

And I remember that a TV reporter, hugely frustrated with Reagan, yelled at him, as he was walking back into the White House, after some outdoor event, "Mr. President, do you think you have no responsibility whatsoever for the federal budget deficit?" (I am paraphrasing.) Reagan turned back, cocked his head, and said, "Well, I was once a Democrat."

And it was extremely important to me that Reagan had been a Democrat. I'd been one, too (in a way). Reagan would say, "I didn't leave the Democratic party; the Democratic party left me"—that wasn't quite true, for Reagan had moved significantly rightward, but it was partly true.

By the end of my college days, at least one classmate teasingly called me "Gip," short for "Gipper" (itself the nickname of George Gipp, whom Reagan had played). It will sound trite, but Reagan made me what I am today, politically (along with WFB and *National Review*, and Norman Podhoretz and *Commentary*). I will never forget him. He will always be my president. He shaped me, stamped me.

Later in life, when I got to know a lot of people who'd been around Reagan, I pumped them endlessly for stories, and they happily obliged. These stories are now mine, weirdly enough, as though I'd been there.

And I was, in a way—there in Reagan's America, when politics was hot, and when I was being forged. Reagan's greatness is as clear to me as Beethoven's. Even many who were his enemies concede that he was the right man at the right time. Frankly, friends, George W. Bush isn't so bad, either.

—June 28, 2004

A Man and His Primer

On (not) learning Greek

I f you received a poor education, there are a couple of things you can do: You can gripe about it for years afterward; or you can set out to rectify the situation. I had the misfortune to go to school just as the New Left was solidifying its grip on American education—primary, secondary, and collegiate. This was fine for knowing that Crispus Attucks won the Revolutionary War single-handedly and that Ida Tarbell saved the country from Standard Oil. And it was terrific for knowing all about Japanese internment and McCarthyism, the two central facts of the 20th century.

But it was lousy for most everything else, which is why, in adulthood, I occasionally try to make up for it. I like to haunt used bookstores now and then, to see whether I can acquaint myself with some of the knowledge that grimy farm children were granted as a matter of course a hundred years ago. Have you ever looked at a McGuffey Reader? These volumes fairly shimmer with high learning, and they don't make you wait for doctoral studies in Italian to show you a Petrarch sonnet.

Of the gaps in my education, the one that bothers me most acutely is that concerning antiquity. This inadequacy I feel with great force when in the company of my polymath grandmother, the once-and-forever valedictorian. To her, not knowing Greek and Latin is akin to not knowing how to tie your shoes. Not long ago, I was perusing her bookshelves when I lit on a small, worn volume titled *The Elements of Greek*. I figured I should give it a whirl, because, you know . . . better late than never.

The book was published in 1902 and authored by one Francis Kingsley Ball, Ph.D., "instructor in Greek and German in the Phillips Exeter Academy." Gracing the frontispiece is a serene picture of the Acropolis. Dr. Ball begins his preface with the lament that "Greek is not studied as much as it ought to be" and asks, "Are not the treasures of Greek literature richly worth the finding? May not these treasures be brought within the reach of the average boy or girl?"

That's about all of the preface I understand, however, because it quickly moves to a discussion of declension, oxytones, penults, mute verbs, liquid verbs, aorist systems, and the Anabasis. I look again at the picture of the Acropolis. Next I flip to the introduction, which opens with the reassuringly cornball sentence, "Hellas, the sunny home of the Greeks . . . ," and ends with the truism that "the study of language is the study of life, and the study of life is the learning of truth."

Thus ennobled, I proceed to Lesson One: the alphabet. The first letter is just like our A, so I'm cruising. The second letter is B—no sweat. Now the letters get a little funky, so that when I reach Omega, I'm dizzy. But I copy them out, much as Laura Ingalls and her schoolmates might have done on their slates. I'm not yet ready for Euripides in the original (which falsely implies that I'm ready for Euripides in modern English translation), but it's a start.

After a briefing on vowels (short, long, and—get this—"doubtful") and a dance with diphthongs (involving "smooth breathing" and "rough breathing"), it's time for my First Declension, which I celebrate as a kind of rite. I don't celebrate for long, though, because I can't understand the words. Not the Greek, the English ones, like "nominative," "genitive," "dative," "accusative," and "vocative," to say nothing of "proparoxytone feminine nouns." I've barely learned to gurgle in this tongue, and already I'm being asked to recognize Greek sentences meaning "There was a rout of the Persian guards" and "Cowardly was the flight of the garrison." Remember: All of this is intended for "the average boy or girl," which prompts the question, Just how capable were they in 1902? Because these lessons are stupefyingly difficult, requiring enormous discipline, will, and perseverance. If Dr. Ball's little primer were placed before typical college students of today, they would either laugh or rebel. Attic Greek is the province of the brainy and strange, not of the multitudes, who seem content with their gruel.

So, I've suspended my latest foray into self-education (and "suspended" is to be polite). I admit that I'm hazy on the subjects that preoccupied Gibbon, Jefferson, and a billion less famous others. But if you'd like to know about Joe McCarthy and that slithery Roy Cohn, just ask.

—June 3, 1996
The Weekly Standard

Brother of the Bride

Weddings, receptions, and glory

J ust as there are cat people and dog people, there are wedding people and reception people. Most people, I imagine, belong to the latter category—impatient for the ceremony to be done with, eager for the party to begin. Because that's all a "reception" is, really: a big fat party, only one where certain people are unusually dressed and there is this pestilent clinking of glasses.

I'm a wedding person, in part because there is no end of interesting things to look for: Will the mothers cry, and what will the nature of those tears be? How will the father comport himself as he walks his daughter down the aisle? Will the bridesmaids be fetching, and will there be obvious flirting between them and the groomsmen? The clergyman: Will he be blandly ecumenical or pointedly parochial? In reciting the vows, will the couple be clear and strong, or quavering and uncertain? And the kiss? Will it be brief and chaste, or one of those save-it-for-the-dark numbers?

Then there's the music. You will inevitably hear, as the guests gather, Bach's *Jesu, Joy of Man's Desiring*, whose angelic triplets will be carelessly broken. Rarely now is the bridal march from Wagner's *Lohengrin* used as the processional—it has been hopelessly lampooned as "Here Comes the Bride" ("all fat and wide"). Instead, you will likely hear one of three trumpet voluntaries: Purcell, Clarke, or Stanley. If there is singing, it will be a friend of one of the principals, and she will be bad. The recessional presents no end of exciting possibilities: Mendelssohn's march has never ceased to thrill, and, if the organist can handle it, Widor's toccata, taken like the wind, is a knockout.

I had always harbored a touch of a desire—just a touch—to plan a wedding. To actually script and run the thing. But I figured, reasonably enough, that I would never get the chance. Then a strange and wonderful thing happened: My sister—whom I had always taken for a reception person—decided that she would get married. In New Orleans. At a hotel.

On July 19. She and her fiancé had but a single question for me: Would I organize and conduct the wedding?

At first, my plans were grand and glorious. I was a kid let loose in the nuptial candy shop. I was going to produce a wedding to end all weddings, a model to the world (or at least to those few attending): impressive yet tasteful, thought-provoking yet blithe, religious yet unobjectionable, informal yet purposeful.

My study was intense. I reflected on the ceremonies of several denominations. I reviewed Scripture. I read poetry. I thought about the wedding at night before drifting off to sleep, and in the morning before rising.

I was going to begin with a little address, to give the "service" a dash of what *The Book of Common Prayer* calls "solemnization." Then there would be copious readings, both secular and not. In due course, a judge—right and proper—would step in and administer the vows.

And the music! It would be done through recordings. That way, you could have whatever you wanted, performed by whomever you wanted. Jessye Norman would be free to sing. And the organ would be played by a great virtuoso, not by Mrs. Brown, the little old lady whom the church can't get rid of because she's a member and has been there forever.

Finally, I got it all together and e-mailed an outline to my sister. When she called back, rather than e-mailing, I suspected there might be a problem. "Uh, Jay?" she said. "Isn't this a little over the top? I mean, we'd like something short and sweet out on the veranda. It's going to be a million degrees. And don't you think that running back and forth from a CD player would be a little . . . well, tacky?"

I had gotten slightly carried away, yes. My sister argued that the word "solemnization"—as in, "We are here to witness the solemnization of a union"—sounded perilously like "sodomization." A half-dozen e-mails ensued between us, but we still couldn't achieve the desired medium: less than a papal ordination, more than wham-bam-thank-you-Pastor.

On the appointed day, we all arrived at the Columns Hotel (where *Pretty Baby*, the soft-kiddie-porn movie, was filmed). The wedding was to begin at 4:00. At 3:50, my sister and I were still negotiating the language of the opening and trying to settle on a Psalm. At about 3:57, she decided what shoes to wear, and I lighted on Psalm 100. The opening, I would more or less wing. We trooped downstairs.

It was hot. Very hot. The bridal party emerged and formed a perfect tableau. The guests, though fanning themselves, seemed rapt. The trolley clanged in the background. The singer, a friend of the bride's, was excellent (spoiling tradition). The white-maned southern judge—straight from Central Casting—played his part to a tee. After months of deliberation, of debate and delight, the wedding went beautifully.

And the reception, oddly, was nice, too.

—August 11, 1997
The Weekly Standard

Miracle of the Mundane

A change of tire, a change of self

At this remove, I find the below pretty pretentious, but it's all true, and I include it in this collection—hesitantly.

Something strange happened to me the other day: I got a flat tire. And even stranger, I changed it. I am still dizzy with amazement.

I had always feared I would get a flat tire, but had never gotten one. That particular misfortune happened to other people. I would see them on the side of the road, doing their thing, and think, "That hasn't happened to me. It might. I should rehearse, because I haven't the foggiest idea what to do. I should really address it someday." But I never did.

So there I was, driving from Washington to Williamsburg to play golf, when I heard something. I was listening to a Bach cello suite. I turned up the volume. But I still heard something. I looked at the cars on either side of me and figured the noise had to be emanating from one of them. My car was relatively new and in fine shape. But the noise persisted, louder. It was me. I pulled over and slowed the car to a jog.

I didn't know much about cars, but I knew I had a flat tire. There was an exit—the "West Point" exit, 20 miles from Williamsburg—and I took it. The sign said an Exxon was near. I determined to get to it, even if it meant totally ruining the tire, because I wanted, needed, people nearby when I stopped. If I couldn't get there, I would hitchhike, then call a friend, already in Williamsburg, to tell him that I'd miss that afternoon's round and that I required his help.

Understand, now, that up until then you could sooner have asked me to assemble a spaceship than change a tire. That had been the rap against me— humanist, you know, without an ounce of practical sense. A co-worker at a golf course once said, "That boy may read a lot, but he doesn't know to come out of the rain." Another friend said, describing a certain appreciation of comfort, "Jay's idea of roughing it is going a day without *MacNeil-Lehrer* and Nestle's Chocolate Quik." The stigma was not undeserved.

I limped into the Exxon and came to a halt. This wasn't a "service station"—those seem to be extinct—but a convenience store with some pumps outside. I approached the woman at the counter: "I have a flat: Can someone here help me?" No. "Well, is there any place around that could help?" Not on Sunday. She asked whether I had a spare tire. I blushed to answer, "I don't know, really. I don't think so. But if I do, do you have a jack?" No.

I then remembered the car salesman's giving me a tour of the vehicle. I thought he had shown me a spare. I looked. Do you know that there is a compartment underneath your golf clubs that contains a spare tire? Of course you do, because now that I do, everyone does. And not only that, there was a jack—brand new, apparently standard issue.

Great. Now that I had the necessary parts, all I had to do was find someone to change the tire and pay him. Only there was no obvious candidate. And self-reliance called. A spooky determination settled over me: I was going to change that tire—me, no one else—and furthermore I was going to do it well.

There were instructions on the compartment cover, and I was actually excited, grateful for the chance to prove something. The wrench unfolded as it should have, and I got the hubcap off. Step One, finished. Loosening the bolts came next, and then it was time to raise the car. The instructions here were murky—the illustrations as poor as the text—but I got daylight between the tire and the asphalt. The flat came off, and I rolled it to the side. Merit badges were due. I was cocky, greasy, and fired with mission. With time, I slid the spare on, tightened the bolts, and lowered the car to the ground, pulsing with accomplishment.

I strode into the store, smiled at the lady ("Yes, turned out I had a spare and a jack, ma'am—no problem"), bought a root beer, and went on my way—unflummoxed, undeterred, and unhelped, except by God, and a desire to be rid of a hindering suggestion of inability. I was close to smug, having undergone a rite of passage that conferred a new virility and a new confidence.

It's nice to translate a Petrarch sonnet, sure, but it's nicer to master the elementary and not to have to depend on the kindness of friends or access to professionals. Truly, I could not have felt more satisfied—not if I had been invited to join the French Academy, not if I had won the Masters (well, attended the Masters). I had gotten a flat, taken care of it, and proceeded. I want to do it again.

—April 7, 1997
The Weekly Standard

'Travel Is Broadening'

An extraordinary seatmate

T he plane, overbooked, was crawling with irritable travelers. After some seat reshuffling, I squeezed by a burly, hostile-looking man and settled in. I figured on an unpleasant flight. The man and I wrestled over our shared armrest for about five minutes, until I gave up.

When the drinks cart came around, I heard him say, "Gin and tonic," in an accent I couldn't place. Curious, I decided to attempt conversation: "Kind of cold in here, isn't it?" I said. "Indeed," he answered, and there ensued seven of the most interesting hours I have ever spent.

He had come from Bucharest, and that led to topics Romanian. I would start safe, cultural: Dinu Lipatti (a pianist, who died young in 1950)? Yes, he knew of him, cherished him, and had at that moment a set of recordings by Lipatti in his duffel bag.

I mentioned Clinton's recent trip to Bucharest. My, how the crowds had cheered, even though the United States had refused to admit Romania to NATO. "Yes," the man said, "but we know we'll get in, and we were over-joyed to see the American president—not the individual, understand, but the idea."

In time, the dark name of Ceausescu came up, and he began—slowly at first, then with gusto—to speak of life under Communism: its brutality, its abnormality, its terrors large and small. I had forgotten, sort of, how bad it was. The Iron Curtain crumbled not ten years ago, yet the Soviet bloc can seem as distant as the Ottoman Empire. My seatmate brought back to me the horror of it all, how the dictator and his miserable, murderous wife had suffocated Romanian citizens day and night, in quest of a perfect totalitarianism.

And where had he been, when news came of the regime's collapse? "In the strangest of all places: the middle of the ocean." He had served—and still served—as an electrical engineer aboard ships. His big plan, years ago, was to join the merchant marine and escape to America. But two days before he set sail, he met a woman—Monica, an English teacher—and "suddenly, the prison house was bearable. With her, I could live anywhere."

So he was in his bunk, fiddling with a shortwave radio, when he heard that the Ceausescus had fled. He could not believe his ears—thought it was a hoax, or a mistake, or his own hallucination. He was afraid to speak to anyone about it, because "even at sea, they watched you, through their agents." Eventually, he informed his captain, who informed the rest of the men. They murmured and grinned, then laughed and shouted, then wept and sank to their knees. "It was," the man told me, "the happiest day of my life."

After an hour or so, an astounding fact came clear: He knew everything. That is, he had read everything, thought about everything, seen (through his voyages) everything. He had devoted his life to teaching himself languages and traversing the world's great literature. At sea, he was permitted to have 40 kilograms of personal material, and 30 of those he reserved for books. He worked "for my bread" until 5 o'clock, after which he fed himself fiction, history, and art until he could stay awake no longer.

He was a particularly keen student of Latin American literature and had translated four or five of the more important novels into Romanian. "How about that buddy of Castro," I asked, "the *Hundred Years of Solitude* guy?" "A bad character, but an enormous literary talent." "Isabel Allende? Don't people read her because of her political associations?" "Perhaps, but they ought to anyway." He went on at engrossing length about Julio Cortázar, scribbling the names of his books for me on a napkin.

I began to pepper him with questions—about Bosnia, Homer, Catholicism and Orthodoxy, American letters (Cheever, he admired), the quirks of Communist rule ("You will be disappointed," he confided, sorrowfully, "that Lipatti's brother was for 20 years ambassador to France, a pet of the regime"). He made me think of certain qualities that I had let slip away:

a love of discovery, a reverence for the masters, an unprofessionalized dedication to knowledge.

As the plane descended—my friend was, amusingly, a nervous flyer, though he had traveled to the far corners of the globe by ship—I thought of the chestnut "Travel is broadening." And so it is—for the British Museum, the Acropolis, and Victoria Falls, sure, but also for encounters with strangers, like Radu Niciporuc, who, for my money, is one of the most extraordinary people alive.

—October 27, 1997
The Weekly Standard

Showdown on
WEIR-AM

Rockin' and rollin' on West Virginia radio

I f you don't know Dr. Ray Greco, you don't live in the northern tip of West Virginia, and a shame, too. Norman Rockwell couldn't have drawn a more appealing physician—kindly, wise, all-capable. Dr. Greco is also a bit of a radio star, hosting a Saturday-morning call-in show called "Let's Talk Health." The show is a casual, meandering affair, broadcast from a tiny studio near Weirton. It doesn't have a great many listeners, but those it does have are eager and devoted.

About a month ago, I found myself a guest on this program: Dr. Greco is my wife's grandfather. He is also a Democrat, and when I say Democrat, I mean a Democrat like none you've ever met—Tip O'Neill, by comparison, never gave a thought to party. Dr. Greco is not exactly thrilled to have a Republican granddaughter, and, worse, he's got me.

Early on, I took Dr. Greco for a typical Democrat of his generation—something like a present-day Republican. But no. He didn't cross over to vote for Ronald Reagan, and his party identification is more than a habit. He actually believes the stuff, and so do his friends. For them, it's always

1930, with a Hooverville in every park. So I have a little fun with Dr. Greco, as he does with me. The week before I was to join him on the radio, he announced to his audience, "Hang on to your hats, folks, but we're going to have a Republican in here next time. Hate to do it to you."

As we arrived at the studio, I figured we were in for an hour of pleasant banter. I would say provocative things about the local hero, Sen. Bob Byrd, and Dr. Greco would chide me for Republican selfishness and greed. After a time, his friends would call up and say, "We're with you, Ray, but go easy on the boy, would you? He doesn't know any better."

Instead, "Let's Talk Health," on that Saturday, was a cauldron of political bile. It started out mildly enough. Dr. Greco welcomed me to the show, and I said that I was happy to integrate the place—the community had been without philosophical diversity for long enough. "Will you tell your listeners that I don't have horns and a tail?" I asked. Dr. Greco didn't seem so sure. (You may wonder what all this has to do with health, but, as Dr. Greco says, his show is about health "broadly defined," as in, "To vote Republican, you must be mentally ill.")

I might have sparked things just a tad when I said, "How can a decent, patriotic American like you be a Democrat in the Age of Clinton? If Harry Truman were alive today, he'd be a Republican, and so should you." The lone technician in the studio rolled his eyes and shot me a look (not for the last time). The switchboard, normally calm, lit up like a Christmas tree. On a sleepy, wintry morning, I had struck a nerve.

The first call turned out to be the friendliest: "Oh, we like Republicans here in West Virginia," the man said. "We like 'em few and far between." The next caller delivered a wide-ranging diatribe: Dan Quayle was a dunce (still?); Paula Jones was a lying skunk; and Ken Starr was a Republican operative, bankrolled by the hard Right, out to destroy the president (and this was pre-Monica).

As the calls streamed in, I had a mini-revelation: These were political nuts—C-SPAN junkies, probably—who seldom had anybody to talk back to. I was an unexpected opportunity for them, and they were letting me have it with both barrels. Dr. Greco was amused, and a little surprised. Most of his listeners, he had told me, were elderly, interested mainly in pills and twinges. But these screechers were young and combative. Not that Dr. Greco didn't hit hard, too. I tried to keep the conversation light—"Hey, every building I see around here is named for Senator Byrd and his wife. How about one for the dog?"—but he insisted on inveighing about the haves and have-nots.

On the ride home, as Dr. Greco dialed up his buddies on the car phone, cackling about our performance, I realized that I was exhausted, and a little taken aback. This was an exotic breed of Democrat—unsmitten by race and gender, but convinced of the saving power of big government, and absolutely besotted with Bill and Hillary Clinton. I was glad to get back to Washington that night. The political atmosphere around Weirton had been awfully hot.

And how do Dr. Greco and his gang feel now, in the throes of Monica fever? Rallied and defiant. Dr. Greco told me the other day, "I love the guy, and I love his wife even more." He also mentioned the subject of his next show—"On a Healthy Character Structure." Wish I could tune in.

—February 16, 1998
The Weekly Standard

The Conservative on Campus

Some memories, some points

The below is a speech given in May 2002, to the twentieth-anniversary dinner of The Harvard Salient, *the conservative publication on that campus.*

T hank you for inviting me. It's a great honor to be here. I know that every speaker says that, as a matter of course—but, in this case, it couldn't be more true. There are few people I admire more than conservatives on campus. Really, they're some of the best and bravest people I know. The smartest, the toughest, the most spiritually resilient. Sometimes in life, I have simply marveled at the existence and grit of conservatives on campus.

I remember one kid at Harvard. He was an undergrad while I was a graduate student. We were in at least one class together. I can't remember his name—not sure I ever knew it—but I can see his face, clearly. I'm fairly certain he worked on the *Salient*—this would have been 1986, '87, in there. I thought maybe I would see him tonight. Anyway, he wore on his lapel— or on his shirt or whatever—this little pin of tiny feet. I looked closely at it; I guess I asked what it was. And he said it was meant to represent the unborn, to express an anti-abortion position. I remember thinking this was maybe the bravest, studliest kid I ever knew. I could no more imagine myself doing it than walking on the moon. This guy was outspoken in class, too: not obnoxious, but bold, sure-footed, and unflinching. He seemed indifferent to any barbs or scorn that could be directed at him.

Really, I was kind of in awe. I've never forgotten him.

I myself wasn't all that brave. I guess I wasn't all that "conservative" either, when I started out. But, by the time I got through with college, I was ragingly conservative—the Left had seen to that. I have sometimes wondered, "If the Left weren't so awful—so mean, so dishonest, so hateful—would I still be a liberal?" I remember the aftermath of the first debate in the presidential election of 2000, Gore versus Bush. My impression was that Gore had cleaned his clock. But the public thought that the vice president had been rude and boorish—terribly off-putting. I said something like, "Good thing Gore's such a jerk—he saved our bacon." (I have cleaned up that quote.)

But I apply this idea to my own experience: I would like to think that I would have arrived at my present positions through sheer reason and inquiry. Maybe I would have. But there's a bit of backlash in me—or rather, a response to the Left as I found it.

That was in Ann Arbor, Michigan, my hometown—one of the perfect villages of the Left in this country. This is the atmosphere in which I grew up. I'm not talking strictly of the university, though I would attend it, as an undergraduate. I'm talking about the elementary schools, the secondary schools, the arts scene, the press, the physical environment—everything.

Round my way, "conservative" was something of a dirty word. It was an obscenity, really. It meant bigot, racist, ignoramus, exploiter, and other unpleasant things. There was always the vague—or sometimes not so vague—association with Nazism. The Left was the party of enlightenment, compassion, reason, and so on.

I will simplify, grossly: American history was a story of barely relieved oppression, hypocrisy, and destruction. What mattered was slavery, McCarthyism, Jim Crow, and Japanese internment—everything else was superfluous. Pictures of Che and Mao were everywhere. Ronald Reagan was a villain, intent on re-enslaving blacks and degrading women, and on incinerating the world. Why had he been elected? Rosalynn Carter spoke for many: "He makes us comfortable with our prejudices."

I had many turning-points—a great many (if it's possible to have more than one)—but one of those was the assassination attempt on Reagan. I saw the bravery, the grace, the humanity. I could never again accept the cartoon of Reagan as an empty-headed, soulless nuclear cowboy. I saw that all those drawing that cartoon were either dumb or lying. Besides, my grandparents liked him, and they were the best people I knew—so how bad could he be?

'I REMEMBER. I WAS THERE.'

I attended the University of Michigan—began in 1982. To say the place was soaked in political correctness is to say too little. (And, by the way, some people now maintain that "political correctness" was a term invented by conservatives to mock the Left. Not so. As Bob Dole once said, I remember. I was there. "Political correctness" was used utterly unironically by the Left, to denote behavior and thought that was acceptable, and behavior and thought that was not.)

People weary, I guess, of conservatives' war stories from campus. I guess we sometimes look whiny and self-pitying. I certainly don't want to be whiny and self-pitying—we should leave "victimhood" to others. But I do want to be realistic, and I tell you that there was a whiff of violence in the air, on that campus of mine. There really was. Of course, you have to be careful whom you talk to this way, because you could be marked off as an exaggerator or paranoid or worse. But, again, I remember, I was there. You got the clear sense that, if you weren't careful in what you said or did, things could turn out very badly for you.

Ideology—not scholarship, not learning—was king on that campus. ("Dictator" would be a better word.) I knew a kid who took chemistry, physics, and the other hard sciences—I did not. He came back to the dorm one day to say that one of his instructors had spent the whole session talking up the FMLN in El Salvador—this was in math or something. Professors and, even more, the teaching assistants were using their lecterns as political podiums. They were proselytizing, indoctrinating. I thought this was wrong—I mean, quite apart from my own political beliefs, which were forming. I thought: "You know, I wouldn't do this, if I had this power, this responsibility—the academic lectern." And that wasn't just self-flattery: It was true. I wouldn't. I still wouldn't. And that knowledge had an influence on me.

It sounds ridiculous to say now, but it took something like an act of courage to buy a conservative magazine, in certain shops. I had seen Buckley on television—I was interested in *National Review*. I couldn't believe that such views could be expressed, and so self-confidently, even cheekily! I took to buying *National Review*, *Commentary*, *The American Spectator*. But one had to screw up one's courage. The clerk, if he knew about the magazines—and, amazingly, he often did—would glare or scoff or make some remark. I have a colleague who remembers buying the conservative magazines out in Berkeley, at a shop called Moe's. He'd feel the need to say something like, "Well, have to see what the opposition's up to." I'd say the same thing: plead diversity, curiosity, you know. William Safire once quipped, "I have to go down to the corner newsstand to buy a *Hustler* magazine, so as to have something respectable to hide my *National Review* in."

In Ann Arbor, I worked at a bookshop called The Little Professor. The manager there wouldn't put out right-of-center magazines, or gun magazines. A friend of mine nicknamed it The Little Suppressor.

As a student, I kept my head down, mostly—although I was too mouthy, then as now, to do so entirely. I once took a class in classical rhetoric—it was in the classics department. Had a wonderful professor, and a highly ideological, radicalized T.A. As an exercise, I wrote a rebuttal—to be delivered by Reagan—to Mario Cuomo's celebrated keynote address at the Democratic convention in San Francisco. The T.A. said something like, "He [Reagan] doesn't deserve such eloquent words, and I can't imagine him delivering them"—this, about the finest political speechmaker of our times! But she could not help giving me a grade of A, much as it might have rankled.

I then wrote a little speech responding to some of Bishop Tutu's criticisms of the United States. Tutu had just won the Nobel Peace Prize, I believe, and was regarded as a saint. That tore it. The T.A. was aghast, writing a nasty note on my speech—and giving me a bad grade (must have been an A minus). (Just kidding—I'm sure it was worse than that.) Somehow I had the gumption to take it to the professor, suggesting that I had been ideologically graded. He agreed immediately and graciously, and plunked an A on that speech. Such a man keeps the flame burning, however low, on campuses.

And I'm sure, incidentally, that he'd never voted Republican, and never would—he was just a real teacher.

THE SCURRIERS

At Harvard, I found the atmosphere much less stifling: more open, more pluralistic, more in line with what a university should be. Ideology and politics weren't the only point, and maybe not even the main point. But still: This is a modern Western university. If Ann Arbor was owned by the Left, the Left had at least the majority share in Harvard.

Here I go again, with my war stories, but I'll never forget something that happened to me after class one day. It was dark outside. Must have been dead wintertime—6 o'clock or so, when it can be very dark. (I fancy that this adds a little drama to the story.) A young man from the class scurried up to me, sort of looking around, making sure that no one was looking. He said to me, "I just wanted to tell you that I like what you say in class, and think that you get short shrift, which isn't right." Then he scurried off.

I'm sure this has happened to a lot of us here in this room. Funny thing is, I hadn't thought of myself as getting short shrift—one is simply used to it. It's normal. Also, I really hadn't said very much—I mean, I was hardly Braveheart. I had probably offered some tentative suggestions that perhaps the reigning orthodoxy should be questioned—and this must have made me seem like Yeltsin on the tank, or something. I certainly did a lot less than, for example, those who wrote for *The Salient*. But—in those days, at least—even some cautious peeps seemed thrilling, to some: and could get the peeper marked as a heretic. Here's a simple lesson I've learned, in my time as a journalist, as a public writer. You all know it: When *you* speak, you speak for lots and lots of people who either can't speak or won't. You are not speaking merely for yourself. You are giving lots of others comfort and encouragement, whether you find out about it or not. Most of the time, you won't find out about it. But more often than you might suppose, you do. I hear from people all the time. And when you hear from one, you can figure that that person stands for ten, a hundred, a thousand—who knows?

It can be rather annoying to have "private support." That's what Tom Sowell calls it: "private support." People scurry up to him all the time, too, particularly black people: "Nice going, Tom, tell it like it is"—then they scurry off. As I once heard Sowell put it, "I'm right behind you, Tom—*way* behind you."

But that's okay. Part of being a public conservative is to be on the front line, absorbing shots, and firing them off, for the sake of non-fighting others, not least. I can't tell you how grateful I was for *National Review*, *Commentary*, and the other conservative publications when I was in school. I'm grateful for them now, of course. But it will never be the same. Never again, I'm sure, will I seize those magazines with the same desperate hunger—the hunger for something different from what I was being fed, and for a validation that, no, I wasn't crazy: These were legitimate, even correct, views. Anti-Communism wasn't a sickness, wasn't an element of the paranoid style; it was, at a minimum, human decency, a modicum of compassion for one's fellow man.

I had a class here on the history of post-war foreign policy, taught by a nice ADA liberal—a Kennedy-Johnson liberal, a solid academic citizen, a good guy. We had in that class a German—a West German, no doubt—who was more or less a Communist. I once heard him speak of the "Katyn accident," referring to the massacre committed by Soviet troops in Poland. One day—after we'd written some papers, I guess—the professor called both of us up to the front of the class to speak, in opposition to each other. We were to debate the origins of the Cold War: Who was responsible? Uncle Sam or Uncle Joe? I realized we were being posited as extremes. One fellow was speaking for—and here I am only being honest—the Communist lie; the other fellow, me, was speaking for what was only the clear truth of the matter, nothing fancy. I've never forgotten that.

I also remember—this'll be my last story, from Harvard—an appearance by Armando Valladares at the Kennedy School. Valladares, of course, is the great Cuban dissident, the author of *Against All Hope*. He is sometimes called "the Cuban Solzhenitsyn," and not without reason. Valladares had come out of long imprisonment and torture, and he wanted to tell an elite audience about it. Of course, he faced hostile questioning: How dare you say that you were abused in Fidel Castro's country! If you were, you must have deserved it, *gusano*. That was the tone of the questioning.

But the truly remarkable thing was that the school put someone on the platform *in opposition* to Valladares: some professor, from the faculty here. He pointed out the alleged great strides that Cuba had made in health care and literacy—the usual propaganda. Valladares responded, Maybe so, but other countries have those things without torturing people, without the denial of basic rights—why can't we?

I guess I keep talking about never forgetting, but I will never forget that Harvard felt the need to "pair" Valladares with someone who was on, more or less, the other side. It was as though a survivor had been paired with a professor ready to provide a more "nuanced" view of the Nazis. That seems a horribly harsh thing to say, but I have for the last couple of years been immersed in the story of totalitarian persecution in Cuba. It's pretty bad.

In time, I became what we call a "conservative"—though I still sort of choke on the term. This has to be a hangover from my youth. I like to consider myself a genuine liberal, believing in limited government, equality of opportunity, equality under the law, pluralism, toleration, constitutionalism, colorblindness, a robust, internationalist foreign policy, sound and equal education, a common culture, etc. Nowadays, that makes you a flaming right-winger. But it shouldn't be so.

It sure doesn't take much to be a "conservative" now, does it? It takes, really, not being a leftist. One of the things I do, when talking to young conservatives—interviewing them for internships and so on—is ask, "Why are you a conservative?" or, "What kind of 'conservative' are you?" or, "How did you happen to become what we call a 'conservative'?" One day I put this to a young man in my office. He said, "Well, my parents are survivors, and . . ."—then he sort of fumbled around, at a loss for words. And I interjected, "Oh, you mean you're anti-evil." And he broke out into a broad smile and said, "Yes, I'm anti-evil."

PROFESSORS TO CELEBRATE

Ladies and gentlemen, I'm so grateful for the courage and persistence of conservative students and professors. You have meant a great deal to me, and to countless others. You may think my gratitude somewhat weird. Conservative students now, I have noticed, are amazingly self-confident. They have kind of a swagger, a breeziness. That, I never had. Maybe times have changed. The Cold War is certainly over, and that was important. It could be, too, that all that good conservative work in the vineyard has borne fruit. It may be that there is now no great penalty to being an "out" conservative on campus: a penalty administered in grades, social discomfort, and so on. But in my time and place, I assure you, to be known as a conservative was to be labeled an untouchable, practically. And when you found someone who thought like you—or who was at least willing to tolerate you—you felt a delight, a relief, and a gratitude that was almost unbelievable.

I was saying how grateful I was for conservative students and conservative professors. Faculty members who are willing to associate themselves with conservative students and their activities are greatly to be prized. I'm sure it's not always easy for them; they don't want to be "conservative" professors; they just want to be professors. And we should stand, I believe, for the depoliticization of the campus. But I bless those right-leaning professors who are willing to be "involved"—there's a great Left word: "involved." I bless those willing to stand up to ideological bullies, or to show independent-minded students how.

And when a Stephan Thernstrom is attacked—threatened by the bullies—we must rally around him, protecting him, and showing him who his friends are: who are the people on campus willing to defend the old principles of liberalism, or, I should say, the principles of the old liberalism.

In addition, we should do everything we can to thank and encourage and praise the liberal professor—even the leftist professor—who is fair to us, who understands and abides by the spirit of scholarship. Those professors, too, are a breed greatly to be prized. I remember a professor I had at Michigan, a woman named Emily Cloyd, who taught Johnson and Boswell. She was in love with books and ideas and history. Had studied at Columbia, I believe. I talked to her once—I sensed I could—about the oppressiveness I was finding on campus. She said that, in her day, it had been a problem to be too left—openly left—so she understood. I didn't quite trust that there had ever been such a day; it seemed impossible! But I appreciated her kindness and understanding.

And then there was my beloved Barbara Fields, the historian of the South. For the last many years, she's been at Columbia. A leftist in her political beliefs, she was still a shining example of a teacher, determined to give her students the tools to investigate and think for themselves. Her standards were daringly high: and they were academic standards, never ideological ones. She valued fine writing, because she thought it ought to go with fine thinking. She was patient and generous with me, jousting with me during office hours, teasing me, listening to me summarize some article in the recent *National Review*, letting my beliefs develop, not trying to steer them but demanding that they have reason and grounding.

Professor Fields is now, down in New York, my friend. When clucking over something wrong in our economy, she'll say—invariably—"your beloved free market." And she remains my model of what a university professor should be. She has no use—none whatsoever—for political nonsense on campus, and she is duly embarrassed and disgusted when "her side" acts up, as it can't help doing. You may have heard about a class at U-Cal, Berkeley, on "The Politics and Poetics of Palestinian Resistance." The course description advises, "Conservative thinkers are encouraged to seek other sections." On the one hand, I appreciate this little caveat. At some schools, the entire course catalogue should have stamped on it, "Conservatives are encouraged to seek other curricula." Entire schools should be stamped, "Conservatives are encouraged to seek other schools—here's a map to Hillsdale, Michigan." On the other hand, of course, this is an outrage to be fought against. I don't want a conservative counter-culture and counter-establishment, necessarily (although these things arise out of necessity); I'd rather have integration and openness and political disinterestedness, certainly on campuses.

At many schools—including Berkeley—our student publications are being stolen. Stolen in bulk. Thrown out, burned, whatever. And the administrations, as usual, aren't defending us, or are doing so weakly. I wonder whether it's possible to shame these alleged liberals: to utter the words "free speech" and "First Amendment" and "diversity" and "tolerance," and see them hang their heads. Maybe it's not possible: These are some awfully illiberal liberals we're dealing with. But let's at least flush them out, as leftist enforcers, hypocrites, or cowards (an unlovely line-up).

THE GHETTO AND WITHOUT

I must tell you, I've always been of two minds about conservative papers on campus. I guess I wish they didn't have to exist; I wish we could be simply part of the mainstream, accepted, unremarkable; I also wish I pitched for the Detroit Tigers. But I see that progress is being made. Your Ross Douthat, who was an intern of ours at *National Review* last summer, is a columnist for *The Crimson*—the big time (sorry). An intern coming to us this summer is Jason Steorts, also a Harvard student. He doesn't write for *The Salient* at all; he, too, is a columnist for *The Crimson*. And I say, Great. Hats off. But thank God for *The Salient*: a place to go home to, a refuge when others have shut you out—our Israel.

Let me confess something to you, speaking of the Jews. When I was young—quite young—I was appalled at the notion of Jewish country clubs. I thought that was a disgusting notion: a country club only for Jews? It was unfriendly, separatist, un-American. But when I got a little older, I learned something about the origin of those Jewish country clubs: It's not that Jews wanted to build them; it's that they were barred from the other clubs. If they wanted to belong to a club—if they wanted to play—they had to build their own. So they did.

I feel that the same is true with us. We have had to build our own, because we haven't been let in by others, or weren't. As I indicated, I'm all for going mainstream, if possible. By all means, avoid the conservative ghetto, or get out of it, if you're in it—but let us tend that ghetto, for as long as we need it. And, of course, we do need it. I work in conservative opinion journalism, always have—no one else has asked me! Although I may bridle now and then, I'm deeply grateful for our conservative homes: *National Review* and all the rest. If I were rich, I'd donate like crazy to them—these journals have always existed on the kindness of strangers, but strangers who are friends.

Permit me to say that we conservatives have an advantage, in a way. You may view this as a species of ridiculous bright-side-ism, or silver-lining-ism: but we should be pretty tough, pretty battle-hardened. We have not been lulled by popularity, and we have seldom known the comfort of the herd. We know what it's like to have "Nazi" yelled at us—this has happened to children of survivors, to survivors themselves, to everyone. We know what it's like to have swastikas daubed on our newspaper boxes, our doors. Not to be trite on you or anything, but sweet are the uses of adversity, my friends. I sometimes think that, being a conservative in an iron-fisted left-wing environment, you almost have to be like a black man in the pre-civil-rights South: You have to do everything better. You have to be smarter, more tenacious, less reproachable. Your paper has to be so good that there's no way some teaching assistant can screw with it. Your articles have to be five times better to get published. You have to be five times better to be hired. And so on.

Again, I don't want to go in for victimhood. But neither am I unmindful of realities as I have witnessed them with my own eyes.

About a week ago, I received a letter from a high-school senior in Chicago. He says, "I am president of our Conservative Club at school. Including me, there are four members. Our school has 2,300 students. Our district has two schools of approximately equal size. The other school doesn't even have a conservative organization. On the other hand, in my time here, I have seen the likes of the SDS (yes, *that* SDS) and various other clubs enjoy not only great attendance, but also great cooperation from our school's administrators. I was told by one of my administrators that the only reason I started my club was to promote the hatred of homosexuals. He said this to my face. The fact that he himself, like many of my teachers, is homosexual is irrelevant. The fact that a teacher can tell a student what his morals are without even knowing or questioning the student is appalling, especially in a school that has spent over $100,000 on a 'Respect Initiative,' designed to foster respect throughout the school."

I imagine this kid is going to do just fine—in college, and after. Life doesn't allow him to be a baby.

Once again: There are few people I admire more than the conservative on campus. I have learned from them, been inspired by them, and been emboldened by them. They have sort of set my path in life. Happy anniversary, and give 'em hell.

Alexandria the Great

Egypt's 'second,' fabulous city

This piece was written during that strange Florida "post-election"; and, of course, many months before 9/11.

'W here are you meeting Amr?" my mother said. "Alexandria," I replied. "Virginia?" she said. She must have thought we were flying together out of Dulles. "No," I said: "Egypt."

It ain't suburban Washington. And nothing can prepare you for the sensual shock of it.

Well, that's not quite true. I had prepped by reading André Aciman's memoir of his upbringing in "Alex," *Out of Egypt*. If ever a book could transport you to a time and place, it is this one.

Aciman's time is long past—Nasser brought it to a close in the 1960s. But, in many ways, his place remains. The alert visitor sees touches everywhere of the mottled, polyglot, wildly international city of pre-nationalist days. The Greeks, the Arabs, the Turks, the Italians, the Jews, the French, the English—everyone and his brother contributed to the local bouillabaisse. Together, they created a spot nearly unique.

No wonder the "foreigners" cried so when they were kicked out.

The Americans have been here lately—at least in the form of their eateries. The city is dotted with Hardee's, Arby's, Chili's, Pizza Hut, Baskin Robbins, Kentucky Fried Chicken—heck, the Colonel's face is almost as ubiquitous as Mubarak's.

And then there's Tweety. Oh, is there. I mean Tweety Bird, as in "I tawt I taw a puddy tat." He (she?) may be more prominent than either the Colonel or Mubarak. The sweet, puzzled look of this creature is seen in cars, on signs, in shops, on shirts. Tweety is enjoying a considerable rage, all over the country.

My friends and I—soaked for days in Egyptology—joke that, if the present civilization were somehow obscured, archeologists of the future might conclude that Tweety was a god. Are we so sure about Ptah?

We stay in the Palestine Hotel on the grounds of the Montazah Palace, the kings' old summer pad. Farouk hightailed it from here in 1952. Nasser was in favor of exile; Sadat, of murder. Interesting, in light of their later courses.

The entire Montazah complex is enough to make the senses groan and ache and swoon. There's the palace itself—out of a fairy tale—and the long, dreamy gardens, and the former guesthouse (now a luxurious, intimate inn), and the palm trees, heavy with dates, and the Greek-style theater, and the snaky stone peninsula that ends in an old lighthouse. A more appealing scene is hard to imagine. How the revolutionaries must have gaped at it when they crashed the gates! Mubarak—no dummy—has built nearby.

But mainly there is the sea. Somehow it looks different, better from this side (with due apologies to St-Tropez). I arrived at night, and couldn't really see anything till morning. When I stepped out on the balcony, I, too, gasped and gaped. And I thought—immediately, involuntarily, and less preciously than you might think—of *Antony and Cleopatra*, and those heart-swelling lines about the queen having a sail upon the sea. Shakespeare, you old wizard! How did you know? You must have been here! How did you get the setting so right?

A word about the weather, that most tiresome of subjects: Alexandria's, in November, is perfect. It makes San Diego's look foul. Of course, because it's 76 and there's a breeze, Alexandrians think it's winter, and bundle up. They consider a visit to the beach preposterous—but you must go nonetheless.

And too bad the food's no good (a bit of exuberant sarcasm, mind you). The fish and meat and rice and fruit are the stuff of Eden. Feel like something to drink? How about mangos, guavas, or pomegranates, squeezed directly into your glass?

Too bad the women are so ugly, too (more exuberant sarcasm, needless to say). *Les alexandriennes* are exquisite—a guy could break his neck in this town. In all, Alexandria must be one of the great people-watching capitals of the world.

The old and the new blend here in what seems an endless series of *National Geographic* photos. Sports cars whip annoyedly around donkey carts. Certain ladies are draped in haute couture, and others are cloaked in the orthodox Muslim fashion. Cellphones are as common as water pipes—go into any café and you will see patrons talking and sucking at the same time. I saw a woman fully wrapped and veiled—all covered up except for the slit for her eyes—gab on her cell. Now *there* was a picture.

And too bad the people are so unfriendly. All over town—in the ritziest clubs and the rankest alleys—they strain to make visitors feel welcome. It's as though the entire population were engaged in some worldwide Most Hospitable People contest. Schoolchildren call out their "hello"s, and most everyone offers, "Welcome in Egypt " (few seem to have gotten the hang of that "to").

To be invited into a home is to be engulfed in affection and solicitude. Be careful not to praise some object, or you may have to take it with you. If you eat enough food for only five people, you won't be judged to have carried your load—and you'll want to.

One afternoon, I had the pleasure of meeting a four-year-old girl named Ola, who sang for me (just a few days before Ramadan) "Jingle Bells," in her soft Oriental accent. You could have died from melting. She also threw in—as bonuses—"Head, Shoulders, Knees, and Toes" and some song with the words "boogie woogie" in it, sung to the shake of four-year-old hips. "Priceless," as those commercials say.

So, what do people—everyone: professors, security guards, pensioners—want to talk to an American about? The election, of course (or the post-election, or non-election, or whatever it is). Egypt, to put it mildly, is Bush country. He must have greater support here than in Utah. People say, "We are for Bush," as if speaking authoritatively for every Egyptian—and they probably are.

One conversation went as follows:

"We are for Bush."

Great.

"Bush seems honest and trustworthy. Gore seems mean and corrupt."

Yes.

"We hate Gore."

Uh-huh.

"And we hate Lieberman even more."

Uh-oh.

The Connecticut senator, I come to learn, has alarmingly high name recognition in Egypt. And this, naturally, gnaws at the gut.

Truth is, any political conversation here is apt to be dicey—and deeply depressing. At war are two utterly different sets of facts, or perceived facts. I talk with a young woman who is fancily educated, worldly, widely traveled—a doctor and university lecturer. To hear her tell it, the Middle East conflict is essentially a matter of the Israeli passion for mowing down Arab kids bearing stones. The notion that Israel might be prepared for peace, if only its enemies felt likewise, is too fantastic even to consider.

With thinking like this—and from the cream of society—how can we ever get anywhere?

But politics you quickly put aside, as though you've touched something very, very hot. Nice weather we're having, huh? Or maybe we can discuss the traffic—a topic that could fill hours, and volumes.

Alexandria is a riot of cars, knocking about in a free-for-all: There are no rules; only a semi-metaphysical sense of maintaining the flow. Pedestrians simply wade into traffic—I mean, simply wade in, at any point, no matter how thick and furious the cars. How do you get across the street? My friend Yasser—all-knowing, all-explaining—says, "Don't think—that is the key. If you think, you're in trouble." Professor Harold Hill had his Think Method; Yasser has his Don't Think Method. Yasser's works.

It can be a little overwhelming, inner-city Alex: the congestion, the noise, the exhaust. But you can always work your way out to the sea—the saving sea, with its restoring breezes, as you breeze along the Corniche, soaking it all up, grateful to be in this dazzling, raucous place, if only for a few days.

Really, can any city be more stimulating? Does any pack a greater punch? Is any more able to make you feel that you've truly *traveled* some-where—somewhere foreign, and memorable, and rare?

Ah, let's talk for a second about Cairo!

—December 18, 2000
National Review

Index

Aaron, Henry, 80
ABC News, 198, 220
Abdel-Rahman, Raouf, 237
Abdullah, King of Jordan, 243, 248, 271, 276
Abraham Lincoln Brigade, 111
Abrams, Robert, 155
Abu Mazen (Mahmoud Abbas), 271
Abu-Jamal, Mumia, 81, 84, 327
Achille Lauro, 218
Aciman, André, 475
Ackerman, Gary, 323
Acropolis, 455, 456, 463
Adams, John (composer), 410
Adams, John (president), 441
Adams, John Quincy, 441
Adès, Thomas, 407
African Union, 282
Ahmadinejad, Mahmoud, 262
Ahram, al-, 131, 233, 234
Ailes, Roger, 175
Ajami, Fouad, 219
Albania, 222, 225–27, 285–88
Albright, Madeleine, 6, 137, 143–51
Alexander, Grover, 353
Alexander, Lamar, 46
Alexandria (Egypt), 475–78
Algosaibi, Ghazi, 223
Ali, Muhammad, 351, 361
Allen, Richard V., 207
Allen, Sir Thomas, 395

Allen, Woody, 98, 180
Allende, Isabel, 462
Allison, Graham, 251, 252
Alsop, Marin, 408
Alter, Jonathan, 196
Alwash, Azzam, 229
Alwash, Suzie, 229, 230
Amadeus, 395
Amalrik, Andrei, 115
Amanecer, 317
Ambrose, Stephen, 291, 292
American Association for Artificial Intelligence, 273
American Enterprise Institute, 271, 274
American Home, 161
American Library Association, 305
American Spectator, The, 468
AmeriCorps, 96
Amin, Idi, 112
Amis, Kingsley, 110
Amis, Martin, 109, 110, 112
American Celebration, An, 409–17
Anarchist Cookbook, The, 83
Anderson, Annelise, 120
Anderson, Martin, 120
Andrei Sakharov Foundation, 298
Angeles, Victoria de los, 444
Angermüller, Rudolph, 394
Animal House, 375
Ann Arbor, Mich., 55, 56, 73, 98, 307, 452, 453, 466, 468, 469

Annan, Kofi, 224, 248, 254, 255,
   281, 282, 292
Antony and Cleopatra, 476
Apple, R. W. "Johnny," 92
Arafat, Yasser, 153, 219, 234–36,
   260
Arévalo Padrón, Bernardo, 302
Argerich, Martha, 421
Arias, Oscar, 149
Arnold, Matthew, 407
Aronson, Bernard, 238
Ashcroft, John, 62, 193–200, 248,
   249
Ashrawi, Hanan, 235
Asner, Ed, 303
Astor, Lady Nancy, 245
Atlanta Symphony, 423, 424
Attucks, Crispus, 455
Augusta National Golf Club, 91,
   360, 364–67
Auschwitz, 254, 284
Avery Fisher Hall, 208, 209
Awadallah, Bassem I., 271, 276,
   278
Ayers, Billy, 217
Azhar University, al-, 219
Aziz, Shaukat, 275, 276

B'nai B'rith, 365
Bacall, Lauren, 19, 21
Bach, Johann Sebastian, 38, 41,
   386, 457, 459
Back to School, 209
Backhaus, Wilhelm, 403
Baker, James A., III, 225, 286
Baldwin brothers, 180
Ballesteros, Seve, 350, 356
Baltimore Symphony, 418, 421
Balzac, Honoré de, 131

Bankhead, Tallulah, 414
Barber, Samuel, 428, 430, 443
Barkley, Charles, 359
Barnes & Noble, 56, 57
Barone, Michael, 91
Barr, Bob, 80
Barrow, Jamal "Shyne," 42–44
Barry, Marion, 8, 9
Baruch, Bernard, 365
Bashir, Umar Hassan Ahmad al-,
   279, 281, 285
Basil, Harry, 209
Batista, Fulgencio, 311, 330, 334
Bauer, Güther G., 394
BBC, 99
Beatty, Warren, 150
Bedtime for Bonzo, 454
Beethoven, Ludwig van, 385, 400,
   407, 411, 413, 418, 419, 424,
   435, 438, 454
Begala, Paul, 130
Begin, Menachem, 224
Bellini, Vincenzo, 396
Benedict College, 365
Benetton, 357
Bennett, William J., 5, 45, 46
Berger, Sandy, 150, 151
Berisha, Sali, 287, 288
Berkeley, University of California
   at, 138, 449, 468, 472, 473
Berlin, Irving, 388
Berlin, Isaiah, 206
Berlin Conservatory, 398
Berlusconi, Silvio, 250
Berman, Harold J., 293
Berman, Howard, 169
Berman, Paul, 306
Bernstein, Leonard, 13, 411
Berrigan, Daniel, 83

Berrigan, Philip, 240

Bin Laden, Osama, 104, 192, 194, 217, 226, 233, 235, 280

Bing, Rudolph, 438

Biscet, Oscár Elías, 300, 309, 324

Bishop, Maurice, 328

Bizet, Georges, 388

Black Liberation Army, 82

Black Spring (Cuba), 315

Blackman, Ann, 150

Blair, Jayson, 91

Blair, Tony, 251, 252, 261, 265, 284

Bloch, Ernest, 412

Bloom, Allan, 292, 293

Bob Jones University, 29–35, 152

Bogart, Humphrey, 19, 21

Bohemian Grove, 203

Bolívar, Alberto, 241, 242

Bonilla, Henry, 86

Bonior, David, 149

Bonner, Yelena, 298

Bono, 252

Bonynge, Richard, 381

Book of Common Prayer, The, 458

Borders Books, 56, 57

Bork, Robert H., 5, 75

Borodina, Olga, 394

Botti, Susan, 407

Boudin, Kathy, 81, 241

Boxer, Barbara, 195

Boyz II Men, 360

Bradley, Bill, 152, 153

Bradley, Tom, 168, 175

Brahimi, Lakhdar, 267, 268, 270

Brahms, Johannes, 385, 413, 419, 423

Brand, Oscar, 441

Branson, Sir Richard, 256

Brawley, Tawana, 155, 156, 159

Brazile, Donna, 71, 75, 172, 179

Breastgate (phony scandal involving John Ashcroft), 197

Brezhnev, Leonid, 207, 290

Brin, Sergey, 261

Bristow, George Frederick, 410, 413

British Empire, 113

British Museum, 463

British Open, 349, 354, 360, 361, 368, 370

Britten, Benjamin, 385

Broadmoor Hotel, 187

Brookhiser, Richard, 7, 60

Brown, Clifton, 367

Brown, James, 154

Brown, Jim, 360

Brown, Ron, 169

Brown, Tina, 162

Brownback, Sam, 281

Bruckner, Anton, 412

Brzezinski, Zbigniew, 6, 145, 146

Buchanan, James, 441

Buchanan, Patrick J., 23, 28, 161

Buck, Marilyn Jean, 82, 83

Buckley, William F., Jr., 7, 90, 96, 180, 183, 185, 243, 290, 334, 349, 393, 454

Budapest, 226, 294

Buddha, 49

Bukovsky, Vladimir, 122

Bull Durham, 374

Burk, Martha, 364–67

Burke, Edmund, 112

Burlington Coat Factory, 306

Burnham, James, 122

Burns, John F., 93

Burt, Richard, 114

Burton, Richard, 19, 384

Burton, Sybil, 19, 22
Bush, George H. W., 29, 70, 87,
    111, 136, 140, 143, 144, 147–50,
    164, 178, 203, 291, 451, 453
Bush, George W., 29–33, 57,
    59–61, 65, 66, 69–77, 85, 88–90,
    92, 97–99, 103–108, 115, 117,
    127, 132, 135, 136, 138, 140,
    143, 152, 172, 177–79, 187, 191,
    193, 195–98, 224, 226, 230, 231,
    236, 241, 243–45, 247–51, 253,
    260, 261, 264, 268, 275, 278–80,
    283, 284, 287, 291, 313, 346,
    366, 367, 396, 400, 454, 466, 477
Bush, Jeb, 76, 323, 324
Bush, Laura, 269, 270
Busoni, Ferruccio, 433, 436
Butler, Samuel, 207
Byrd, Sen. Robert, 464

Caddyshack, 209, 375, 376
Caesar, Sid, 433
Cage, John, 38
Cairo, 478
Callas, Maria, 395
Calzón, Frank, 308
Cambridge University, 449
Camerata Salzburg, 390
Cameron, David, 265
Campaigns & Elections magazine,
    177
Campbell, Earl, 76
Campbell, Naomi, 303
Cannon, Lou, 93
Cantrell, Scott, 427
Capra, Frank, 203
Carey, Lord, of Clifton, 248
Carlos, John, 361
Carmen Jones, 388

Carmon, Yigal, 234, 235
Carnegie Hall, 384, 386, 387, 433,
    434
Carnoustie (golf course), 370
Carousel, 414,
Carsen, Robert, 397
Carson, Johnny, 180, 183
Carter, Elliott, 413, 431, 434
Carter, Frank, 78
Carter, Jimmy, 146, 174, 244, 252,
    284, 290, 439, 442, 453
Carter, Rosalynn, 293, 453, 467
Caruso, Enrico, 381, 383
Carville, James, 194
Casadesus, Robert, 384
Casals, Pablo, 434
Castellucci, John, 82
Castro, Fidel, 5, 113, 159, 170, 226,
    249, 253, 299–304, 306, 307,
    309, 311–15, 319–22, 324–30,
    334, 462, 470
Castro, Fidelito, 320
CBS, 319, 354, 357, 366, 376
Ceausescu, Elena, 6, 239, 306, 462
Ceausescu, Nicolae, 239, 323, 461,
    462
Center for a Free Cuba, 308
Center for National Policy, 150
Chadwick, George, 411
Chalabi, Ahmad, 259
Chaliapin, Feodor, 402
Chambers, Whittaker, 293
Champions Dinner (Augusta
    National), 356
Chan, Zhu Xi, 331, 335
Chao, Elaine, 250
Chapel Hill, N.C., 388, 444
Chaplin, Charlie, 19, 21
Chariots of Fire, 361

Charles (Prince), 265

Charles, Ray, 389

Chávez, Hugo, 226, 324

Checchi, Al, 173, 176

Cheever, John, 462

Cheney, Liz, 270

Cheney, Lynne, 270

Cheney, Richard B., 89, 117, 249, 251, 269, 270, 275

Cher, 198, 246

Cherkassky, Shura, 434

Chertoff, Michael, 258

Chesimard, Joanne (Assata Shakur), 170, 327, 328, 330

Chicago Daily Tribune, 70

Chicago Times, 99

Child, Julia, 431

Children's Defense Fund, 181, 186

Chiles, Lawton, 175

Chirac, Jacques, 224

Chirkinian, Frank, 376

Cho, Margaret, 307

Chomsky, Noam, 57, 83, 224, 240, 400

Chopin, Frédéric François, 205, 434, 435

Christian Science Monitor, 334, 361

Christmas (as word), 62–66

Christopher, Warren, 150

Churchill, Winston, 11, 13, 149, 202, 265

Chuschi (Peru), 238

Cisneros, Henry, 22

Clapp, Stephen, 36

Clark, Ramsey, 240

Clark, Sedgwick, 409, 413

Clarke, Jeremiah, 457

Clemens, Roger, 353

Cleveland, Grover, 442

Clift, Eleanor, 77

Clinton, Bill, 22–24, 27, 70, 74–81, 85, 89, 97, 111, 117, 128, 130, 143, 144, 150, 151, 160, 161, 163, 164, 167, 168, 170, 171, 176, 178, 180, 181, 184, 186, 188, 203, 228, 241, 244, 247, 252, 256, 260, 279, 283–86, 354, 358, 373, 440, 442, 461, 464, 465

Clinton, Hillary Rodham, 6, 72, 85, 97, 129, 152, 153, 160, 161, 180, 181, 184, 185, 250, 256, 260, 265, 400, 440, 465

Clinton, Chelsea, 78, 244

Cloyd, Emily, 472

CNN, 299, 300

Cobb, Ty, 351

Cochran, Johnnie, 42, 43

Coelho, Tony, 172

Cohen, Jacob (Rodney Dangerfield), 208

Cohen, Richard, 194, 196

Cohn, Roy, 456

Cole, Johnnetta, 329

Cole, U.S.S., 218

Collier, Peter, 81, 85, 327

Colson, Chuck, 280

Combs, Sean "Puffy," 41–43

Commager, Henry Steele, 49

Commentary, 334, 454, 468, 469

Confucius, 50

Congressional Medal of Honor, 203

Congressional Record, 201

Connerly, Ward, 15, 17, 179

Connor, Bull, 137

Conquest, Elizabeth, 112

Conquest, Robert, 109–113, 300–02, 334, 337, 342

Converse College, 388
Coolidge, Calvin, 442
Copland, Aaron, 406, 411
Corigliano, John, 407, 413
Cornell University, 16, 206
Cortázar, Julio, 462
Corzine, Jon, 173
Cosby, Bill, 155, 329
Cosby, Camille, 329
Costner, Kevin, 374–76
Coulter, Ann, 59
Couric, Katie, 11, 12, 187
Cowell, Henry, 412
Cranston, Alan, 175
Crapo, Mike, 130
Crenshaw, Ben, 372
Crisman, Thomas L., 230
Crosby, Bing, 375, 412
Crosby, John, 93
Crumb, George, 412
Cuba Free Press Project, 299
CubaNet.org, 316
Cultural Revolution, 331, 336–39
Cummings, E. E., 429
Cuomo, Mario, 468
Currie, Betty, 78, 80

Dachau, 340
Dalai Lama, 209, 342, 376
Daley, Richard J., 74
Daley, William M., 74
Dalton School, 61,
Dandridge, Dorothy, 388
Danforth, John C., 280, 281, 283
Dangerfield, Rodney, 208–11
Daniel, David, 427
Danielpour, Richard, 407
Daniels, Anthony, 306, 307, 310
Davies, Marion, 21

Davis, Angela, 49
Davis, Gray, 176
Davos (World Economic Forum), 242–78
Day, Dorothy, 178
Dayan, Moshe, 394
De Gaulle, Charles, 451
Dead Sea (Jordan), 266, 271
Deaver, Michael, 207
Debussy, Claude, 13, 407
Decker, Willy, 396
DeLay, Tom, 99
Dell, Michael, 243, 256, 261
Dellums, Ron, 328
Democratic National Committee, 93, 329
Dempsey, Jack, 122
Deng, Xiaoping, 237
Denoke, Angela, 396
Des Moines Dispatch, 121
Detroit Symphony Orchestra, 422, 423
Detroit Tigers, 473
Diallo, Amadou, 159
Díaz López, Diane, 308
Diaz-Balart, Lincoln, 159, 319–324, 329
Diaz-Balart family, 319–324
Diaz-Balart, Mario, 319–324
DiCaprio, Leonardo, 303
Dickens, Charles, 131
Dickinson, Emily, 429
DiMaggio, Joe, 352, 369
Dinkins, David, 153, 157, 175, 178
Directorio Democrático Cubano, 316
Dixie Printing Company, 104
Dobbs, Michael, 150
Dodd, Christopher, 149, 323, 326

Dohrn, Bernardine, 81
Dolan, Tony, 125
Dole, Bob, 29, 467
Domingo, Plácido, 383
Don Giovanni, 40
Don Quixote, 51
Donahue, Phil, 183
Donaldson, Sam, 161
Donath, Helen, 395
Donizetti, Gaetano, 381
Dorsett, Tony, 13
Dostoevsky, Feodor, 44, 131, 138
Douglas, Mike, 183, 185, 186
Douthat, Ross, 473
Dowd, Maureen, 88, 92, 190, 191,
   198, 249
Downing Street Memo, 400
Dr. Dre, 43
Druckman, Jacob, 413
Dubal, David, 434
Dukakis, Michael, 146–50, 175, 440
Duke, David, 179, 192
Dulles, John Foster, 138, 139, 143,
   253
Dun, Tan, 407
Dunn, Jennifer, 86
Durban (conference in South
   Africa), 220, 250
Dyer, Richard, 426

Eagleton, Tom, 71
Eastwood, Clint, 377
Easy Money, 209,
Eban, Abba, 244
Ebony magazine, 359
Edelman, Marian Wright, 181
Eden Again, 229
Edward VIII (British king who
   abdicated), 20

Edwards, John, 173
Economist, The, 90
Einstein, Albert, 5
Eisenhower, Dwight D., 22, 371
ElBaradei, Mohamed, 251
Elder, Larry, 167, 172
Elder, Lee, 355
Election Night 2000, 69–77
Electoral College, 123
Elliott, Bentley, 125
Elman, Mischa, 433
Emerge, 329
Emerson, Ralph Waldo, 320
Emmy Awards, 175
Engel, Eliot, 285, 287, 288, 323
Entremont, Philippe, 385
Ephron, Nora, 181
Erdogan, Recep Tayyip, 277
Erhard, Ludwig, 256
Erickson, John, 138
Espinosa, Luis Esteban, 317, 318
Estrada, Miguel, 322
Ethics and Public Policy Center,
   293, 294
Eureka College, 124
European Union, 112, 226, 287
Evans, Don, 74
Evans, Linda Sue, 81–83, 85, 241

Falcoff, Mark, 329
Faldo, Nick, 350, 371
Falun Gong, 335, 343–46
Family, The, 82, 83
Farrakhan, Louis, 88
Farrell, Eileen, 389, 438
Farris, Michael, 46, 47
Fattah, Muhammad Abd al-, 278
Faubus, Orval, 78, 96
Fauntroy, Walter, 279

Feinstein, Dianne, 176
Fenice, La, 383
Ferraro, Geraldine, 146, 147, 175, 451
Fettmann, Eric, 159
Fidelity to the Leader Canal (Iraq), 228
Fiedler, Arthur, 416
Fields, Barbara J., 472
Fifth Amendment, 178
Fillmore, Millard, 442
Finch, Atticus, 80
Fiorina, Carly, 247
Firing Line, 179
Firkusny, Rudolf, 385
First Amendment, 45, 130, 473
Fischer-Dieskau, Dietrich, 402
Fishawi's (Cairo), 133
Fisher, Eddie, 19
Fitzgerald, F. Scott, 161, 377
Flatt, Dicky, 128
Fleetwood Mac, 440
Fleisher, Leon, 384–77
Fleming, Renée, 403
Florence, Italy, 449, 451
FMLN (El Salvador), 467
Foda, Farag, 134
Foley, Tom, 398
Follow the Sun, 370, 375
Fonda, Jane, 180
Foner, Eric, 49
Fontova, Humberto, 306
Forbes, Inc., 203
Ford, Gerald R., 83, 121, 191, 193, 200, 202, 290, 439
Ford, Glenn, 370, 375
Forster, E. M., 451
Fossella, Vito, 440
Foster, Stephen, 441

Fox News, 235, 251
Fox, Vicente, 226, 243, 245
Franco, Francisco, 302, 314
Frank, Anne, 336, 337, 343
Frank, Barney, 253
Frank País November 30 Democratic Party, 311
Frankel, Max, 93
Franken, Al, 56, 57, 166
Frankfort, Henri, 207
Franklin, Aretha, 4
Freddy's Fashion Mart, 158
French Academy, 461
Freni, Mirella, 381
Friedman, Milton, 9, 122
Frist, Bill, 279
Fromme, Lynette "Squeaky," 83
Front, The, 98
Frum, David, 90, 104, 108
Fujimori, Alberto, 239, 240, 242

Gable, Clark, 19, 20, 22
Gabr, M. Shafik, 275
Gallacher, Bernard, 349
Gamei'a, Muhammad al-, 219, 232
Gandhi, Mohandas, 79, 300, 309
Garanca, Elina, 395
Garber, Greg, 360
García Pérez, Jorge Luis, 300
Gardner, Ava, 20
Garfield, James, 442
Garland, Judy, 389
Gates, Bill, 243, 252, 256, 261
Gates, Henry Louis, 3, 4
Gehrig, Lou, 352
Genocide Convention, 284
Georgetown University, 146, 174
Gephardt, Richard A., 175, 178
Gere, Richard, 250

Gergen, David, 248
Germond, Jack, 70
Gershwin, George, 388, 433
Gershwin, Ira, 14
Gerson, Michael, 108
Gestapo, 281
Gettysburg Address, 49, 99
Gibbon, Edward, 456
Gibson, Charlie, 153
Gier, Delta David, 37
Gingrich, Newt, 94, 129, 163, 176
Gipp, George, 454
Girl Scouts, 367
Giuliani, Rudolph, 85, 152, 157,
    158, 178, 180–85, 313, 405
Glanz, James, 229
glasnost, 113, 235
Glassman, James K. 28
Glen Garden (golf club where
    Nelson and Hogan caddied), 369
Glendening, Parris, 176, 177
global warming, 242, 251, 260–66
Glover, Danny, 329
Goetz, Bernhard, 154
Gogh, Vincent van, 13
Golden Gate Bridge, 200, 201
Goldwater, Barry, 121
Golf magazine, 371, 375
Golfing Extraordinary, 375
González, Elián, 76, 300, 301, 325,
    326
González Bridón, José Orlando,
    299, 300
González Herrera, Joanna, 299
González Leiva, Juan Carlos, 316,
    317
Goode, Richard, 421
Gorbachev, Mikhail, 115, 139, 140
Gordimer, Nadine, 133

Gore, Al, 24, 26, 34, 42, 69–71,
    73–77, 89, 127, 132, 152, 153,
    166, 170, 172, 174, 179, 181,
    228, 260, 264, 440, 466, 477
Gore, Tipper, 42
Gourevitch, Philip, 284
Graffman, Gary, 385
Graham, Rev. Billy, 19
Graham, Ruth, 19
Gramm, Phil, 126–30
Grand Mufti of Bosnia, 249
Granma, 325
Grant, Ulysses S., 442
Grass, Günter, 220
Great Depression, 103, 124
Great Dictator, The, 414
Greco, Dr. Ray S., 463–465
Greece, 215, 222–25
Greek, 455, 456
Greenwood, Lee, 440
Gregory, Dick, 169
Grenada, 147
Grey, Sir Edward, 266
Griffes, Charles Tomlinson, 411
Griffin, Merv, 183
Gromyko, Andrei, 123
Ground Zero, 104
Gubaidulina, Sofia, 407
Guerrilla Warfare, 83
Guevara, Che, 305–310, 333, 466
Gulag(s), 114, 118, 196, 304,
    340–42
Gulag Archipelago, The, 115, 337
Gulf War, 140, 145, 150, 168, 179,
    228, 291
Gumbel, Bryant, 187
Guys and Dolls, 414
Guzmán, Abimael ("President
    Gonzalo"), 237–42

Haas, Michael, 398

Hagen, Walter, 368

Haig, Alexander, 207

Haiti, 150, 169

Haman, 194

Hamas, 117

Hammett, Dashiell, 20

Hammoudi, Humam, 259

Hampson, Thomas, 392, 397–99, 403, 404, 437

Handbook on the Jewish Question, 235

Handel, G. F., 443

Hanson, Howard, 411

Harding, Warren G., 8

Harman, Jane, 176

Harrelson, Woody, 303

Harris, Roy, 411

Harrison, Benjamin, 442

Harrison, William Henry, 441, 442

Hart, Jeffrey, 7

Hartford Courant, 309

Harvard, 3–7, 61, 64, 196, 201, 204, 206, 243, 289, 291, 293, 301, 343, 368, 465, 469, 470, 473

Harvard Crimson, 201, 473

Harvard Law School, 60, 174, 201

Harvard Law School Republicans, 60

Harvard Salient, 465, 466, 469, 473

Harvey, Paul, 122

Hassani, Hajim al-, 267, 268

Havel, Vaclav, 269, 324

Hayakawa, S. I., 54

Haydn, Franz Joseph, 412

Haynes, John Earl, 111

Hearst, William Randolph, 21

Hedges, Chris, 228

Hefner, Hugh, 395

Hegel, G. W. F., 246

Helfgott, David, 425–28

Hellman, Lillian, 20

Hellsberg, Clemens, 404

Helms, Jesse, 92, 126, 164, 177, 279, 329

Helprin, Mark, 90, 188

Hentoff, Nat, 155, 305

Henze, Hans Werner, 407

Hepburn, Katharine, 20, 21, 204, 375

Herbert, Bob, 79, 88, 197

Here's Love, 415,

Herheim, Stefan, 393

Herrera Acosta, Juan Carlos, 317

Hertzberg, Hendrik, 195, 197

Heston, Charlton, 42, 44, 182, 183, 201

Hewlett-Packard, 247

Hillsdale, 472

Hink, Werner, 399

Hitchens, Christopher, 109–12

Hitler, Adolf, 155, 162, 194, 205, 206, 219, 232, 235, 307, 309

Hitlerism, 103, 235

Hogan, Ben, 353, 356, 368–72, 375

Hogan, Valerie, 370

Hoiby, Lee, 429–32,

Hollander, Paul, 98, 301

Holly, Buddy, 162

Holocaust, 110, 205, 206, 235, 254, 261, 284

Holtzman, Elizabeth, 157

Home Depot, 51

Homer, 462

Hook, Sidney, 293

Hoover, Herbert, 178, 201, 442

Hoover, J. Edgar, 78, 194, 197

Hoover Institution, 112, 120

Hope, Bob, 375
Horne, Marilyn, 381, 387–90
Horowitz, David, 81, 85
Horowitz, Vladimir, 421, 436, 443, 444
Horszowski, Mieczyslaw, 434
Horton, C. Jemal, 361
Horton, Willie, 175
Hotel Rwanda, 278
Hotel Theresa, 326
House of Terror (Budapest), 294
Howard, John, 251
Howard University, 445
Hoxha, Enver, 225, 285, 286
Hu, Jintao, 346
Huber, Peter, 290
Hudson Institute, 234
Huffington, Arianna, 261
Hume, Brit, 90
Hume, David, 246
Humeid, Ahmad, 277
Humphrey, Hubert, 246
Hundred Years of Solitude, 462
Hunt, Al, 4, 186, 194, 196
Hussein, King of Jordan, 248
Hussein, Saddam, 106, 107, 150, 164, 179, 192, 196, 227–31, 237, 239, 240, 242, 245, 250, 251, 259, 268, 285, 291, 308
Husseini, Faisal al-, 236
Hyatt, Joel, 173

Ibarra Roque, Rafael, 310
Ibrahim, Saad, 220, 254
Imus, Don, 160, 161
Ingalls, Laura, 456
Institute of Musical Art, 414
Inter-American Court of Human Rights, 241

International Criminal Court, 223, 283
International Society for Sports Psychiatry, 361
Internet Society of Egypt, 273
Iparraguirre, Elena, 240
Iran-contra affair, 202
Israel, 225, 233, 236, 244, 248, 250, 253, 254, 257, 273, 286
Ives, Charles, 411

Jackson, Andrew, 264
Jackson, Henry M. "Scoop," 111, 115
Jackson, Jesse, 7, 76, 78, 80, 154, 156, 264, 312, 330, 359, 367
Jackson, Jesse, Jr., 79
Jackson, Michael, 396
Jalahma, Umayma Ahmad al-, 236
Janjaweed, 281, 282
Japanese internment, 455, 466
Jazeera, al-, 233, 251, 254
Jefferson, Thomas, 441, 456
Jenkins, Dan, 370, 377
Jenkins, Sally, 361
Jennings, Peter, 12, 100, 169
Jerusalem Post, 234
Jiang, Zemin, 333
Jim Crow, 466
John Paul II, 312
John Philip Sousa Band, 414
Johnson, Andrew, 442
Johnson, Boris, 223
Johnson, Don, 376
Johnson, Lyndon B., 22
Johnson, Nancy, 256
Johnson, Paul, 334
Johnson, William W. "Hootie," 364–67

Jolie, Angelina, 250
Jones, Alex S., 196
Jones, Bob, Jr., 33
Jones, Bob, III, 30, 33, 34, 177
Jones, Bobby, 30, 352–54, 356,
    364, 367, 368, 377
Jones, Paula, 464
Jones, Robert Trent, Jr., 261
Jordan, Armin, 395
Jordan, Eason, 253
Jordan, Philippe, 395
Jordan, Vernon, 78, 150
Journal of Affective Disorders, 263
Jóvenes sin Censura (Youth Without
    Censorship), 314–318
Joyce, James, 432
Joyner, Tom, 78

Kadare, Ismail, 226
Kael, Pauline, 94
Kahlo, Frida, 20
Kalhor, Kayhan, 407
Kancheli, Giya, 407
Karajan, Herbert von, 403, 438
Karine A, 260
Karpov, Anatoly, 261
Karzai, Hamid, 258
Kasarova, Vesselina, 392
Katyn Forest, 122, 470
Katz, Martin, 387, 388
Kavakos, Leonidas, 391
Kavanaugh, Patrick, 37–41
Kean, Tom, 173
Keating, Frank, 196
Kedouri, Elie, 219
Keillor, Garrison, 160–66
Kemp, Jack, 271
Kemper Open, 372–74
Kennan, George, 206

Kennedy, Caroline, 440
Kennedy, Edward M. "Ted," 75,
    173–75, 178, 195, 440
Kennedy, John F., 22–24, 148, 162,
    183, 415
Kennedy, John F., Jr., 175
Kennedy, Robert F., 198
Kennedy Center for the Performing
    Arts, 422
Kennedy Center Honors, 175
Kerik, Bernard, 85
Kerl, Torsten, 396
Kern, Jerome, 388
Kernis, Aaron Jay, 407
Kerrey, Bob, 176
Kerry, John, 172
Kerry-Edwards buttons, 59–62
Kesler, Charles, 289
Khan, A. Q., 257
Kharrazi, Kamal, 251
Khatami, Mohammad, 246, 247, 270
Khmer Rouge, 237
Khobar Towers, 217
Khomeini, Ayatollah Ruhollah, 134,
    220
Kimball, Roger, 3
King, Carl, 416
King, Carole, 313
King, Larry, 34, 355, 357
King, Martin Luther, 5, 6, 22, 78,
    79, 158, 185, 300, 309, 312, 326,
    361, 421
Kipnis, Igor, 426
Kirchschlager, Angelika, 396, 397
Kirkpatrick, Jeane J., 297, 301, 304,
    313, 323, 342
Kirsanow, Peter, 92
Kissinger, Henry A., 6, 86, 96, 139,
    207

Kitt, Eartha, 44
Klehr, Harvey, 111
Kleiber, Erich, 438
Klein, Calvin, 391
Klinghoffer, Leon, 218
Knappertsbusch, Hans, 403
Koch, Edward I., 158
Kocsis, Zoltán, 435
Koestler, Arthur, 342
Kohl, Herb, 173
Kolodin, Irving, 410
Kondracke, Morton, 149
Korbel, Josef, 137
Korbut, Olga, 349
Korda (Cuban photographer), 308
Korngold, Erich Wolfgang, 395,
    396, 398
Kosovo, 223, 285
Kostis, Peter, 376
Kotkin, Joel, 169
Kouchner, Bernard, 308
Kozinn, Allan, 407
Kramer, Hilton, 93, 98
Krause, Eddie, 55
Krauthammer, Charles, 12, 149,
    285
Kreuzchor (Dresden), 402
Kristof, Nicholas, 341
Kunstler, William, 83
Kušej, Martin, 391–93
Kwasniewski, Aleksandr, 249
Kyoto, 223

La La Ling (L.A. store), 306
Lader, Linda, 97, 100
Lader, Phil, 97, 100
Langer, Bernhard, 350
Lantos, Tom, 323
Laogai, 332, 336, 340–43

Laogai Research Foundation, 341
LaPierre, Wayne, 182
Lardner, Frances Chaney, 211, 212
Lardner, Ring, Jr., 211, 212
Lardner, Ring, Sr., 377
Larrocha, Alicia de, 444
Laver, Rod, 351
Lazarus, Emma, 429
Le Monde, 106, 226
Leahy, Patrick, 195
Lear (Shakespeare king), 75
Ledeen, Michael, 93
Lee, Barbara, 303, 325, 328
Lee, Charles, 343–46
Lee, Sheila Jackson, 171, 325
Lee, Spike, 375
Lehane, Chris, 76
Leinsdorf, Erich, 431
Leka (King, Albania), 287, 288
Lenin, V. I., 237
Leno, Jay, 181, 183
Leonard, Justin, 373
Lerner, Alan Jay, 438
Letterman, David, 181, 183, 198,
    200
Lettvin, Theodore, 385
Leung, Kwok-hung, 309
Levin, Sander, 253
Levine, James, 437
Lewinsky, Monica, 75, 77, 170,
    176, 184, 194, 464, 465
Lewis, Anthony, 194
Lewis, Bernard, 219, 221, 258
Lewis, Jerry, 209
Lewis, John, 79
Lewis, Sinclair, 164, 166, 417
Leys, Simon, 334
Liberace, 395
Liddell, Eric, 361

Lieberman, Joe, 89, 199, 440, 477
Limbaugh, Rush, 57, 73, 92, 100,
    122, 162, 166
Lincoln, Abraham, 99, 100, 103,
    177, 290, 320, 321, 442
Lindbergh, Charles, 201, 442
Lindsay, John B., 174
Lindsey, Brink, 28
Lindsey, Lawrence, 6
Linea Sur Press, 302
Ling, Jahja, 36
Lipatti, Dinu, 461, 462
Liszt, Franz, 434–436
Little Foxes, The, 414
Little Professor (bookstore), 55,
    468
Little Rascals, 375
Livingston, Bob, 167
Lo, Kii-Ming, 396
Locke, John, 112
Loewe, Frederick, 438
Lombard, Carole, 19, 20
London, George, 402
Long, Earl, 9
Lopez, Jennifer, 42
Los Angeles, Calif., 226, 261, 412
Los Angeles Open, 370
Los Angeles riots, 167, 168
Lott, Trent, 80, 94, 364
Louis, Joe, 351,
Love, Davis, III, 350
Lowe's, 51
Lowery, Joseph, 78
Lowry, Rich, 73
Luce, Clare Booth, 255
Lugo, Maritza, 300, 310–314
Lupu, Radu, 421
Lutoslawski, Witold, 407
Lyle, Sandy, 373, 374

*M*A*S*H*, 211
Maazel, Lorin, 405–407
MacArthur, Douglas, 202, 227, 371
MacDowell, Edward, 410, 411
Macedonia, 285
Macmillan, Harold, 269
MacNeil-Lehrer, 460
Maddox, Lester, 96
Madonna, 246
Maehder, Jürgen, 396
Magic Mountain, The, 243
Magna Carta, 49
Mahathir, Mohamad, 244, 246
Maher, Bill, 97
Mahfouz, Naguib, 131–35
Mahler, Gustav, 430
Mailer, Norman, 393
Makiya, Kenan, 219
Malcolm X, 185, 202, 361, 375
Mandela, Nelson, 78
Mangan, James Clarence, 432
Manson, Marilyn, 44
Manhattan School of Music, 429
Mao, Tse-tung, 237, 282, 302, 331,
    333, 334, 338, 466
Marcello, Benedetto, 434, 435
Marcos, Subcomandante, 310
Marilyn Horne Foundation, 388
Markey, Ed, 253
Marsalis, Wynton, 407
Marsh Arabs, 227–31
Martí, José, 316, 321
Martín Valero, Aini, 318
Marx, Karl, 237
Masferrer, Marc, 318
Masta Ace, 45
Masters (golf tournament), 349,
    351, 352, 354–62, 364–68, 373,
    375, 461

MasterWorks Festival, 36–41
Masur, Kurt, 405–408, 410
Matthews, Chris, 153
Matthus, Siegfried, 407
Mattox, Lester, 175
May 19th Communist Organization, 82
Mays, Willie, 351
Mbeki, Thabo, 252, 284
McCaffrey, Barry, 169
McCain, John, 29, 31, 33, 252, 253, 260, 265, 439
McCarthy, Eugene, 163
McCarthy, Joe, 194, 197, 456
McCarthy, Leo, 178
McCarthyism, 455, 466
McConnell, John, 108
McConnell, Mitch, 130
McCord, Gary, 375
McCourt, Frank, 181
McGill University, 273
McGovern, George, 94, 95, 143, 145, 174
McGrory, Mary, 293
McLaughlin Group, The, 70
McMahon, Ed, 186
McVicar, David, 394
Medicare, 96
Meese, Edwin, 198
Mehta, Zubin, 405
MEMRI (Middle East Media Research Institute), 219, 220, 231–36
Mencken, H. L., 160, 164, 166
Mendelssohn, Felix, 457
Menendez, Robert, 322
Mengistu, Haile, 279
Mennin, Peter, 412
Menotti, Gian Carlo, 413, 430

Menuhin, Yehudi, 395
Meriño Aguilera, Liannis, 314–17
Merion Golf Club, 370
Merkel, Angela, 256, 257, 261, 263
Messinger, Ruth, 157
Metastasio, Pietro, 392
Metropolitan Opera, 40, 381, 429, 437
Metropolitan Opera House, 59
Metzenbaum, Howard, 173
Meyer, Frank, 452
Mfume, Kweisi, 169
Mickey Mouse, 305
Middle East Media Research Institute (MEMRI), 219, 220, 231–36
Midori, 36
Mikulski, Barbara, 175
Milhaud, Darius, 430
Million Mom March, 182
Millo, Aprile, 435
Mills, Cheryl, 78, 80
Milosevic, Slobodan, 140, 223, 237
Milstein, Nathan, 443
Minnesota State Fair, 307
Miracle on 34th Street, 415
Misérables, Les, 182
missile defense, 71, 89
Mitchell, Andrea, 322
Mitchell, Mary A., 359
Mohammed, 50
Moldova, 226, 286
Mondale, Walter F., 75, 123, 146, 147
Monroe, James, 441
Montazah Palace (Alexandria), 476
Montenegro, 285
Montes de Oca Martija, René, 297–300, 334

Monteux, Pierre, 384, 412
Montgomerie, Colin, 356
Month in the Country, A (opera by Hoiby), 429, 431
Monty Python, 393
Moore, Charles, 266
Moore, Michael, 56, 58, 400
Morgan, Eliot, 427
Morgan, Joy Elmer, 47
Morris, Dick, 75
Morrison, Toni, 78
Morton, Bruce, 89
Moseley-Braun, Carol, 138
Moss, Kate, 303
Mostly Mozart Festival, 395
Mother of All Battles River (Iraq), 228
Motorcycle Diaries, The, 307
Moussa, Amr, 268–70
Moynihan, Daniel Patrick, 153, 157, 186
Mozart, Wolfgang Amadeus, 131, 391–95, 397–99, 401–04, 423, 428
Mozarteum (Salzburg), 390, 391, 394, 396
Mubarak, Gamal, 273, 275
Mubarak, Hosni, 272–75, 284, 475, 476
Muhammad, Khalid, 88, 152, 158
Muirfield (golf course), 360
Munch, Charles, 406
Murphy, Michael, 377
Murray, Bill, 209
Museum of Modern Art, 342
Museveni, Yoweri, 284
Musharraf, Pervez, 247, 248, 257, 258
Music Man, The, 414–17

Muskie, Edmund S., 145, 146, 174
Muskingum College, 206
Muslim Brotherhood, 274
Mussolini, Benito, 11

NAACP, 358
Nachman, Jerry, 97
Nader, Ralph, 163
Nadler, Jerrold, 85
Nafi', Ibrahim, 233
Nagano, Kent, 408
Naipaul, V. S., 221, 292
Nano, Fatos, 287, 288
Nantz, Jim, 354, 357
Nasser, Gamal Abdel, 133, 475, 476
Nast, Thomas, 164
Nation, The, 240
National Albanian-American Council, 285
National Association of Attorneys General, 195
National Council of Women's Organizations, 364
National Democratic Party (Egypt), 275
National Education Association, 46–50
National Endowment for the Humanities, 89
National Football League, 141, 147
National Governors Association, 195
National Institutes of Health, 306
National Journal, 320
National Organization for Women (NOW), 365
National Public Radio, 100, 160, 426, 429
National Religious Broadcasters, 199

National Review, 69, 73, 97, 100,
   104, 108, 135, 188, 207, 212,
   224, 289, 293, 298, 334, 341,
   402, 454, 468, 469, 472, 473
National Review Online, 113
National Rifle Association (NRA),
   182, 184
National Symphony Orchestra, 409
National Urban League, 365
National Youth Movement, 154
NATO, 140, 187, 188, 226, 282,
   287
Nazif, Ahmed, 272–75, 278
NBC Orchestra, 433
Nelson, Bill, 175
Nelson, Byron, 369
Nelson, John, 36
Nelson, Ozzie, 38
Netrebko, Anna, 392, 399
New Criterion, The, 111
New Republic, The, 177
New York City Opera, 429
New York Philharmonic, 36, 37, 63,
   208, 405–15
New York Post, 154, 159
New York Public Library, 305, 306
New York Times, 3, 4, 79, 88,
   90–93, 100, 125, 165, 189–91,
   194, 196–99, 217, 220, 228, 229,
   232, 234, 243, 249, 254, 282,
   359, 364, 367, 407, 426, 428, 434
New York Times Magazine, The,
   125, 194
New York Yankees, 152
New Yorker, The, 162, 195, 197
Newfield, Jack, 154
Newman, Lucia, 300
Newton, Huey, 327
Ney, Bob, 25

Nicaragua, 144, 149
Nicholson, Jack, 303
Nicklaus, Jack, 351–54, 356, 362,
   368
Nickles, Don, 130
Nike, 357
Nilsson, Birgit, 436–38
Nitze, Paul, 122
Nixon, Richard M., 7, 94, 109, 143,
   200–03, 206, 291, 292, 303, 321
Nobel Peace Prize, 468
Noonan, Peggy, 125
Norman, Greg, 373
Norman, Jessye, 458
North Iowa Band Festival, 415
Notorious B.I.G., 4
Notre Dame, 138
Nour, Ayman, 274
Nuba, 284
Nudel, Ida, 122
Nuremberg, 237, 239, 439, 440

O'Beirne, Jim, 400
O'Beirne, Kate, 72, 400
O'Brien, Conan, 209
O'Donnell, Rosie, 180–87
O'Laughlin, Sister Jeanne, 325
O'Neill, Eugene, 19
O'Neill, John, 55
O'Neill, Paul, 249
O'Neill, Tip, 95, 128, 252, 463
Oates, Marylouise, 173
Obasanjo, Olusegun, 246, 247, 252
Occidental Petroleum, 178
Ockrent, Christine, 252
Ogletree, Charles, 5
Oklahoma City (terror bombing),
   85
Olivero, Magda, 387

Olivier, Sir Laurence, 244
Olivier, Richard, 244
Olson, Barbara, 57
Olympic Games, Athens, 222
Olympic Games, Beijing, 333
Olympic Games, Mexico City, 361
Onassis, Jacqueline, 175
One Flew Over the Cuckoo's Nest, 322
Opera News, 403
Orange Revolution (Ukraine), 254
Ordinary People, 428
Ormandy, Eugene, 406, 443
Ormond, Julia, 243
Ornstein, Leo, 434
Orwell, George, 109, 111, 112, 115, 300, 449
Osbourne, Ozzy, 104
Oslo accords, 236
Owen, Charlie, 173
Oxford, 112

Paar, Jack, 183
Pachachi, Adnan, 248
Pachelbel, Johann, 428
Padilla, Jose, 221
Paganini, Niccolò, 433
Page, Clarence, 361
Page, Tim, 426
Pagones, Steven, 155, 156
País, Frank, 311
Palacio, Ana, 249
Palestine Hotel, 476
Palestinian Authority TV, 234, 235
Palmer, Arnold, 356, 368, 372, 390
Palmer, David Scott, 241
Palmer, Tony, 395, 399, 403
Palmers (Austrian underwear manufacturer), 394

Pape, René, 402, 403
Paray, Paul, 412
Parkening, Christopher, 36, 41
Parks, Rosa, 80
Parnevik, Jesper, 373
Pasternak, Boris, 21
Pat and Mike, 375
Patterson, Orlando, 88
Patton, Chester, 396
Patton, 417
Pavarotti, Luciano, 333, 381–84
Payne, Donald, 279
PayoLibre.com, 316
PBS, 100
Pearl, Minnie, 450
Pearl Jam, 191
Pebble Beach Golf Links, 354
Peck, Gregory, 75
Peltier, Leonard, 81
People magazine, 19–22
Pepper, Claude, 175
Percy, Walker, 377
Perdigón Brito, Margarita, 316
Perdigón Brito, Raymundo, 316
Peres, Shimon, 234, 244, 261
perestroika, 235
Perkins, Bill, 152
Perle, George, 434
Persichetti, Vincent, 413
Petrarch, 455, 461
Petrassi, Goffredo, 430
Petri, Egon, 386, 430, 433
PGA of America, 352
PGA Tour, 353, 358, 366, 372, 375
PGA Tournament, 361, 363, 368
Pinochet, Augusto, 297, 302, 304, 314
Pinza, Ezio, 402
Pipes, Daniel, 219

Pipes, Richard, 204–08
Pippin, Don, 388, 389
Pirgu, Saimir, 395
Piston, Walter, 413
Pitt, Brad, 377
Pitts, Leonard, Jr., 359
Platoon, 428
Player, Gary, 361, 371
Podhoretz, John, 125
Podhoretz, Norman, 334, 449, 451,
    454
Porter, Cole, 388
Portman, Rob, 243
Poulenc, Francis, 443
Poussaint, Alvin, 79
Powell, Adam Clayton, 154, 158
Powell, Colin, 10, 11, 87, 88, 150,
    189, 193, 251, 278, 280, 281,
    302, 303, 324, 355, 358
Powell, Jody, 174
Powell, Morris, 158
Practice, The, 196
Prague, 226
preemption, 192
Presley, Elvis, 42–44, 396
Press, Bill, 186
Pretty Baby, 458
Previn, André, 431
Price, Gen. George, 444
Price, Leontyne, 387, 388, 396,
    425, 428, 429, 443–45
Pride, Dicky, 373
Prokofiev, Sergei, 230
Proposition 209, 179
Protocols of the Elders of Zion,
    235
Pryce-Jones, David, 219, 292, 334
Psalms, 118, 119
Purcell, Henry, 457

Qaddafi, Moammar, 6, 284
Qaddafi, Saif al-Islam al-, 254, 275
Qassem, Faisal al-, 233
Quayle, Dan, 464
Queen Elisabeth Competition, 384

Rabin, Yitzhak, 234
Rachman, Gideon, 262
Rachmaninoff, Sergei, 418, 425,
    427, 428
Radio and Television
    Correspondents Dinner (D.C.),
    160
Radio Martí, 316
Radio República, 316
Radosh, Ronald, 309
Radu, Michael, 239
Rahman, Omar Abdel, 134
Raines, Howell, 91, 364
Ramey, Samuel, 411
Rangel, Charlie, 78, 312, 326, 327,
    330
Rania, Queen of Jordan, 258
Ransom, John Crowe, 366
Ravel, Maurice, 385, 407, 434
Rayam, Curtis, 419
Reader's Digest, 161
Reagan, Maureen, 87
Reagan, Nancy, 63, 87, 207
Reagan, Ronald, 29, 63, 72, 75, 88,
    95, 108, 115, 117, 119, 120–25,
    128, 139, 140, 143–49, 151, 160,
    163, 172, 174, 177, 198, 200,
    202–04, 207, 224, 245, 252, 257,
    290, 291, 293, 301, 304, 321,
    323, 387, 415, 439, 442, 449,
    450–54, 463, 466, 467, 468
Reagan Library, 187, 192
Red Guerrilla Resistance, 82

Redford, Robert, 303, 307
Rehnquist, William H., 79
Reich, Otto, 309
Reid, Richard, 220
Reiner, Fritz, 406
Renaissance Weekend, 96–100
Reno, Janet, 71, 198, 325
Reno, Nev., 226
Reporters Without Borders, 308, 315
Republic of New Afrika, 82
Respighi, Ottorino, 436
Retton, Mary Lou, 450
Reynolds, Debbie, 19
Rhoden, William C., 359
Rhodes, Teddy, 358
Rice, Condoleezza, 6, 10, 88, 136–42, 188, 189, 353
Rice, Grantland, 370
Rich, Alan, 410
Rich, Marc, 81
Richards, Ann, 175
Riefenstahl, Leni, 440
Rihm, Wolfgang, 407
Ripken, Cal, 352
Rivera, Diego, 20
Rivero, Raúl, 315
Roberts, Cokie, 182
Roberts, Gretchen, 200
Robertson, Pat, 177
Robeson, Paul, 396
Robinson, Jackie, 354, 358, 361
Robinson, Peter, 125
Robinson, Randall, 329
Roca, Vladimiro, 300
Rocca, Costantino, 350
Rockwell, Norman, 463
Rocky, 374
Rodenbach, Georges, 396

Rodgers & Hammerstein, 401
Rodgers, Richard, 414
Roethke, Theodore, 429
Rogers, Kenny, 209
Rogers, Will, 122, 160
Romeo and Juliet (1996 movie), 428
Romeo and Juliet (Hoiby opera), 432
Romeo and Juliet (play), 396
Roosevelt, Eleanor, 202
Roosevelt, Franklin D., 22, 103
Roosevelt, Theodore, 177, 201
Rorem, Ned, 412, 431, 435, 436
Rosenberg, Susan, 81–85, 241
Rosenthal, A. M., 335
Ros-Lehtinen, Ileana, 322, 323
Rostow, Eugene, 122
Rostropovich, Mstislav, 444
Roussel, Albert, 406
Royal Opera (Stockholm), 436
Rubin, Jamie, 144
Rubin, Robert, 24, 28
Rubinstein, Artur, 384, 421, 425, 434
Rudenstine, Neil, 3
Ruff, Charles, 80
Ruggles, Carl, 412
Rumsfeld, Donald, 10, 187–93, 221, 223, 453
Rumsfeld, Joyce, 190–92
Runnicles, Donald, 396
Rusesabagina, Paul, 278
Rush, Geoffrey, 427, 428
Rushdie, Salman, 134
Rusk, Dean, 451
Russert, Tim, 355, 358
Russo, Rene, 376
Ruth, Babe, 80, 351

Rwanda, 278, 283, 284
Ryder Cup, 349–51

Saariaho, Kaija, 407
Sadat, Anwar, 133, 273, 476
Safire, William, 202, 468
Said, Edward, 111, 133
Sakharov, Andrei, 115, 116, 304, 342
Salih, Barham, 259
Salonika (Thessaloniki), Greece, 215, 222, 223
Salzburg Festival (Austria), 390–404
Sampras, Pete, 351
Sampson, Curt, 371
San Diego, Calif., 476
San Francisco Symphony, 412
Santa Cecilia Academy, 430
Satoh, Somei, 407
Sauerbrey, Ellen, 176, 177
Schade, Michael, 391
Schelling, Ernest, 411
Schiff, Karenna Gore, 153
Schiffer, Claudia, 261
Schiller, Friedrich, 424
Schlesinger, Arthur, Jr., 4, 95, 293
Schmid, Benjamin, 395, 396, 399
Schmiesing, Kevin, 264
Schmoke, Kurt, 177
Schnabel, Artur, 384
Schoenberg, Arnold, 407
Schonberg, Harold, C., 434
Schreker, Franz, 398
Schubert, Franz, 387, 413, 430
Schumann, Robert, 407, 434
Schumer, Charles, 85
Schwab, Klaus, 256, 260, 272
Schwarzenegger, Arnold, 265

Schwarzkopf, Elisabeth, 404
Scott, Carlottia, 328, 329
Scowcroft, Brent, 136, 138
Scully, Matthew, 108
Second Amendment, 44, 45, 182, 197
Segovia, Andrés, 434
Seldes, George, 91
Selleck, Tom, 182, 183, 185
Semester at Sea, 313
Sendero Luminoso (Shining Path), 237–42
Serrano, Jose, 80, 302, 303
Sessions, Jeff, 130
Sgalitzer, George, 400, 401
Shabibi, Sinan al-, 267, 269
Shakespeare, William, 375, 476
Shakur, Assata (Joanne Chesimard), 170, 327, 328, 330
Shalem Center, 114
Shamir, Yitzhak, 234
Shankar, Ravi, 243, 244
Sharansky, Avital, 118, 119
Sharansky, Natan (formerly Anatoly), 114–119
Sharm El Sheikh, Egypt, 266, 271, 272, 275
Sharon, Ariel, 114, 116, 117, 236, 244, 257
Sharpton, Al, 7, 88, 151–59
Shawn, William, 162
Shea, Nina, 279, 282, 284
Shea Stadium, 354, 358
Shelton, Ron, 374
Shiflett, Dave, 92
Shine, 425–28
Shining Path (Sendero Luminoso), 237–42
Shore, Dinah, 183

Shroud of Turin, 321
Shrum, Bob, 71, 172–79
Shulgasser, Mark, 431
Shultz, George P., 125, 202, 203
Sills, Beverly, 383, 387
Silva, Lula da, 243, 246, 261
Simpson, Marietta, 418–20
Simpson, O. J., 78, 79, 180
Simpson, Wallis, 19
Simpsons, The, 345
Sinai, 272
Sinatra, Frank, 20, 22
Singh, Vijay, 359
60 Minutes, 235
Skinner, Kiron K., 120
Slatkin, Leonard, 409
Smiley, Tavis, 79
Smith, Adam, 28
Smith, Chris, 279
Smith, Philip, 36
Smith, Tommie, 361
Smithsonian, 174, 209
Snead, Sam, 353, 369, 370, 372
Sneva, Tom, 398
Snow, Edgar, 334
Social Security, 69, 72, 89, 129
Soderbergh, Steven, 307
Sofia, Bulgaria, 226
Solzhenitsyn, Aleksandr, 109, 110,
    115, 131, 138, 206, 224, 236,
    289–94, 301, 329, 332, 334–37,
    339, 470
Solzhenitsyn, Ignat, 289, 294, 332
Solzhenitsyn, Stephan, 289, 290
Somalia, 233
Sontag, Susan, 111, 224
Sorenstam, Annika, 16
Soros, George, 256
Sound of Music, The, 401, 403

Sousa, John Philip, 416
Southern Manifesto, 366
Sowell, Thomas, 362, 469
Spanish, 12, 51–54
Spectator, The, 223, 266
Specter, Arlen, 313
Spice 1 (rapper), 43
Spielberg, Steven, 113
Sports Illustrated, 360, 371
Squier, Bob, 175
Srebrenica, 283
St. Andrews (Scotland), 354
St. Andrews (Yonkers, N.Y.), 375
St. Louis Symphony Orchestra, 418,
    421
Stalin, Josef, 109, 113, 245, 279,
    282, 470
Stanford University, 136–38, 141,
    353
Stanley, John, 457
Starr, Kenneth, 167, 170, 171, 194,
    464
Starr report, 79
Steele, Shelby, 171, 327
Steinem, Gloria, 6
Steorts, Jason Lee, 473
Stern, Howard, 162
Still, William Grant, 412
Stillman College, 137
Stokowski, Leopold, 406, 412, 434
Stone, Sharon, 250, 252
Strange, Curtis, 353, 360
Strausbaugh, Bill, Jr., 352, 353
Strauss, Christian, 400
Strauss, Richard, 397, 399, 400,
    402, 408, 430, 432, 437, 443
Stravinsky, Igor, 395
Straw, Jack, 259, 260
Streisand, Barbra, 180, 187

Sudan, 278–85
Sullivan, Andrew, 111
Sullivan, Ed, 208
Summers, Lawrence, 3, 4
Sundance Festival, 307
Sunday, Billy, 38, 39
Sutherland, Joan, 381
Swed, Mark, 426
Sweeney, John, 243
Swift Boat Vets, 55
Szell, George, 385, 406

Taft, Robert, 9
Tagliabue, Paul, 141
Taiwan, 245, 253, 256, 277
Talbott, Strobe, 150, 151
Taliban, 104, 106, 135, 192
Tarbell, Ida, 455
Taylor, Charles, 283
Taylor, Elizabeth, 19
Tchaikovsky, Piotr I., 418, 419
"Team B" (concerning the CIA),
  204
Telemundo, 319
Temple, Shirley, 47
Tetzel, Johann, 264
Texas A&M, 127
Thatcher, Margaret, 144, 145, 262,
  351
Thernstrom, Stephan, 472
Thesiger, Wilfred, 228
Thessaloniki (Salonika), Greece,
  215, 222, 223
Third River Project (Iraq), 228
Thomas, Cal, 199
Thomas, Clarence, 142
Three Stooges, 375
Thurmond, Strom, 79
Tiananmen Square, 331, 341

"Tiger Woods bill," 360
Tiger Woods Foundation, 360–62
Time magazine, 228, 307, 370
Tin Cup, 374–77
Tipo, Maria, 385
Tlass, Mustafa, 235
Tobias, Andrew, 198
Tocqueville, Alexis de, 289
Tojoism, 103
Toledo, Esteban, 373, 374
Tolstoy, Leo, 131, 138
Ton Ton Macoutes, 281
Tonight Show, The, 183, 209
Torquemada, 197
Torricelli, Bob, 29
Tosca, 381, 383
Toscanini, Arturo, 414, 425, 433
Tracy, Louise, 21, 22
Tracy, Spencer, 20, 21, 375
TransAfrica, 329
Trinity College, 309
Tripp, Linda, 78
Trudeau, Garry, 160, 196
Truman, Harry, 138, 148, 330, 464
Turkey, 230, 277
Turki, Prince, al-Faisal al-Saud,
  248, 270, 271
Turner, Ted, 299
Turrin, Joseph, 407
Tutu, Desmond, 468
Twain, Mark, 160, 162, 164, 166,
  277
Tyler, John, 441
Tyson, Mike, 307

U.N. Environment Programme,
  229, 230
U.N. Human Rights Commission,
  285, 301

U.S. Agency for International Development, 229
U.S. Amateur (golf tournament), 352, 353
U.S.-embassy bombings, Africa, 218
U.S. Junior Amateur (golf tournament), 353
U.S. Open (golf), 354, 368, 370, 371, 374
United Fruit Company, 320
United Nations, 106, 122, 123, 136, 224, 248, 267, 278, 279, 282–4, 291, 292
University of Chicago, 336
University of Chicago Law School, 200
University of Denver, 137, 138
University of Georgia, 127
University of Illinois, 343
University of Michigan, 467
University of Minnesota, 162
Unsinkable Molly Brown, The, 415
Updike, John, 377
Uribe, Álvaro, 245, 321

Valente, Benita, 437
Valladares, Armando, 300–03, 329, 335, 470
Van Buren, Martin, 441, 442
Vance, Cyrus, 150
Varèse, Edgar, 411
Vargas Llosa, Álvaro, 240
Vengerov, Maxim, 261
Ventura, Jesse, 140, 161, 164–66, 209
Venturi, Ken, 354, 373
Victoria Falls, 463
Vidal, Gore, 111

Vienna, 226
Vienna Philharmonic, 399, 404, 438
Vietcong, 166
Vietnam War, 144
Vike-Freiberga, Vaira, 249
Voigt, Deborah, 63
Volpe, Joseph, 383
Volpe, Mark, 423
Vries, Gijs de, 258

Wagner, Richard, 13, 395, 428, 438, 457
Walker, Alice, 330
Wall Street Journal, 4, 5
Wallace, George, 96
Wallace, Henry, 441
Walter, Bruno, 406
Walters, Barbara, 322
Walters, Vernon, 14, 221, 302, 313
Wang, Youqin, 336–39
Warfield, William, 411
Warsaw, 226
Washington, George, 441
Washington Post, 191, 197, 198
Watergate, 292
Waters, Maxine, 79, 142, 167–72, 195, 303, 325, 327, 328, 362
Watt, James (father of the steam engine), 257
Watt, James (former U.S. interior secretary), 86, 177
Watts, André, 358, 418, 421
Watts, J. C., 86
Weather Underground, 81, 217, 241
Webb, Gary, 169
Weber, Max, 246
Wei, Jingsheng, 335
Weinberger, Caspar, 144, 151, 200–04

Weinberger, Jane, 202
Weirton Steel, 23–28
Wernicke, Herbert, 393
West, Cornel, 3–5
West Point, 104, 105
West Virginia, 23–28, 450, 463–65
White, E. B., 162
White, Mary Jo, 84
Widor, Charles Marie, 457
Wilbon, Michael, 362, 363
Wild, Earl, 433–36
Wilder, Thornton, 429
Wilkins, Roger, 80, 327, 330
Williams, Anthony, 362
Williams, Margaret, 167
Williams, Sidney, 170
Williams, Ted, 369
Williams, Tennessee, 431
Willson, Meredith, 414–17
Wilson, Pete, 138
Wilson, Terrence, 418–21
Wilson, Woodrow, 103, 105, 225, 286, 451
Winfrey, Oprah, 127, 180, 183, 359
Winthrop, John, 290
Wired, 403
Wittgenstein, Ludwig, 385
Wittgenstein, Paul, 385, 396
Wodehouse, P. G., 377
Wolf, Frank, 279, 280, 281, 283
Wolfensohn, James, 247, 422
Woman of the Year, 211
Wood, Grant, 416

Wood, Michael, 228,
Woods, Earl, 355, 358
Woods, Tida, 355, 358
Woods, Tiger, 80, 141, 351–63, 365, 366, 368, 369
Woosnam, Ian, 350
World Economic Forum (Davos), 242–78
"World Split Apart," "A" (speech by Solzhenitsyn), 289–94
Wright, Jim, 149
Wu, Harry, 332, 335, 340–43
WuDunn, Sheryl, 341
Wurmser, Meyrav, 234

Yad Vashem, 284
Yale, 200
Yayabo Press, 316
Yeltsin, Boris, 469
Yes, Giorgio, 382
Youth Without Censorship (Jóvenes sin Censura), 314–18
Yu, Justin, 335
Yushchenko, Victor, 254, 255

Zaharias, Babe Didrickson, 375
Zebari, Hoshyar, 248, 266–68, 270, 271
Zemlinsky, Alexander von, 398
Zoellick, Robert, 269, 275, 277, 281
Zog (King, Albania), 287
Zola, Emile, 131
Zwilich, Ellen Taaffe, 413

About the Author

Jay Nordlinger is a senior editor of *National Review*. He contributes pieces on politics, foreign affairs, the arts, and many other subjects. He is music critic for *The New Criterion* and the *New York Sun*, as well as for *National Review*. For *National Review Online*, he writes a column called "Impromptus." He has won awards for his work on human rights, in particular. A native Michigander, he lives in New York.